Program Evaluation

Program Evaluation

Alternative Approaches
and Practical Guidelines

THIRD EDITION

Jody L. Fitzpatrick

University of Colorado, Denver

James R. Sanders

Western Michigan University

Blaine R. Worthen

Utah State University

Boston • New York • San Francisco
Mexico City • Montreal • Toronto • London • Madrid • Munich • Paris
Hong Kong • Singapore • Tokyo • Cape Town • Sydney

Senior Editor: *Arnis Burvikovs*
Editorial Assistant: *Christine Lyons*
Marketing Manager: *Elizabeth Fogarty*
Production Editor: *Paul Mihailidis*
Manufacturing Buyer: *Andrew Turso*
Cover Administrator: *Kristina Mose-Libon*
Electronic Composition: *Omegatype Typography, Inc.*
Editing/Production Services: *Chestnut Hill Enterprises, Inc.*

For related support materials, visit our online catalog at www.ablongman.com.

Library of Congress Cataloging-in-Publication Data

Fitzpatrick, Jody L.
    Program evaluation : alternative approaches and practical guidelines / Fitzpatrick, Jody L., James R. Sanders, Blaine R. Worthen. — 3rd ed.
        p.   cm.
    Includes bibliographical references and index.
    ISBN 0-321-07706-7
    1. Educational evaluation—United States.   2. Evaluation research (Social action programs)—United States.   3. Evaluation—Study and teaching—United States.   I. Sanders, James R.   II. Fitzpatrick, Jody L.   III. Title.
LB2822.75.W67 2004
379.1'54—dc21

                                                                                2003051860

Printed in the United States of America

10   9   8   7   6   07   06   05

Contents

11 *Setting Boundaries and Analyzing the Evaluation Context*   **199**

12 *Identifying and Selecting the Evaluation Questions and Criteria*   **232**

13 *Planning How to Conduct the Evaluation*   **260**

PART FOUR • *Practical Guidelines
for Conducting and Using Evaluations*   **301**

Preface

The beginning of the twenty-first century is an exciting time for evaluation. The field is growing. People—schools, organizations, policy makers, the public at large—are interested in learning more about how programs work—how they succeed and how they fail. Many people are interested in accountability from schools, government agencies, nonprofit organizations, and corporations. They want to know whether these organizations are doing what they claim to do. Performance measurement and outcome assessments are expanding around the globe. People who work in organizations are also interested in evaluation. They want to know how well they're doing, how to tackle the tough problems, and how to improve their performance.

Evaluation, today, is changing in a variety of ways to help stakeholders obtain this information. Many different methods are being developed and used—a wide array of qualitative and quantitative approaches to design and data collection, increasing involvement of new and different stakeholders in the evaluation process, expanded considerations of the uses of evaluation, and more effective and diverse ways to communicate findings. Evaluation is expanding around the world and the experiences of adapting evaluation to different settings and different cultures is enriching the field.

We hope to convey the dynamism and creativity involved in conducting evaluation to you in this new edition. Each of us has many years' experience in conducting evaluations in a variety of different settings, in schools, public welfare agencies, mental health organizations, criminal justice settings, environmental programs, nonprofit organizations, and corporations. We also have years of experience teaching students how to use evaluation in their own organizations or communities. Our goal is, and has always been, to present information that readers can use either to conduct or be a participant in evaluations that make a difference to their workplace, their clients, and their community. Let us tell you a bit about how we hope to do that in this new edition.

As in the past, the book is organized in five parts. Part One introduces the reader to key concepts in evaluation, as well as its history, and some of the current and emerging trends in the field. (These include high-stakes testing in schools; performance monitoring in cities, states, and the federal government; and technologically sophisticated means of collecting evaluation information and reporting results.) Part Two gives the reader a foundation in the different approaches used to conduct evaluation. (Determining whether objectives have been achieved isn't the only way to approach evaluation!) In Parts Three and Four, the core of the book, we describe how to plan and carry out an evaluation study. Extensive graphics, lists, and examples are used to help students learn the craft. An ongoing case study concludes each chapter, illustrating some of the concepts described therein. Finally, in Part Five we describe some special current issues in evaluation (evaluating training programs, personnel, and multiple-site programs; planning and organizational renewal) and the future of the field.

Although we present different approaches to evaluation in Part Two, our goal is to introduce the reader to many different methods and approaches so that you can select those most appropriate for collecting valid, reliable, and useful information that meets the needs of stakeholders, the organization, and society. We are eclectic in our approach to evaluation. We believe the methods and measures one chooses should match the context, program, and questions to be answered. Thus, we present both qualitative and quantitative methods, management-oriented and participant-oriented approaches. We hope you will do the same.

To facilitate learning, we have continued the consistent pedagogical structure we have used in past editions. Each chapter presents information on current and foundational issues in a practical, accessible manner. Tables and figures are used frequently to summarize or illustrate key points. A case study is introduced in Part Three and continued at the end of each chapter in Parts Three and Four. All chapters conclude with an Application Exercises and a list of Suggested References for readers to consult on that topic. In addition, we have added two new pieces to the end of each chapter: (1) "Major Concepts and Theories" summarizes the key issues in the chapter, and (2) "Discussion Questions" presents issues for consideration in class discussions.

What have we changed? Each chapter has been revised by considering the most current books, articles, and reports. Many new references and contemporary examples have been added. The case study has been updated to reflect some trends in current practices. We also did some reorganizing of the book to reflect changes in the field and a structure better fitting the organization of an evaluation study. Specifically, in the previous edition, we included one chapter on qualitative methods and one on quantitative methods. Today, the debate over qualitative and quantitative methods is over. Most evaluators recognize that a mix of methods is necessary to answer the vast majority of important questions in an evaluation. Therefore, these chapters were updated and reorganized to form two new chapters: one on issues concerning the design of the study and sampling, and another on data collection, analysis, and interpretation. Each chapter presents an array of qualitative and quantitative methods and approaches.

In Part Two, we largely retained our previous organization of chapters, which continue to reflect major theoretical differences in approaches to evaluation. (A chapter on adversary-oriented evaluations was eliminated, but its methods of presentation were described in Chapter 16 on reporting.) Within each chapter, however, we discuss the current status of long-established approaches and review new approaches that have evolved from the original approaches. For example, in Chapter 4, concerning objectives-oriented evaluation approaches, we describe new approaches that make use of logic models and program theory to understand programs and direct the evaluation. Perhaps the most change has occurred in participant-oriented evaluation approaches in the last few years. We review and comment on those approaches, including participatory and empowerment evaluation, in Chapter 8. Further, applications of different approaches and their influence on the field are discussed throughout the book. In Chapter 2, performance measurement is reviewed. Methods for developing program theory and logic models are discussed in Chapters 11 and 12 as ways to clarify the evaluation request and set boundaries for the evaluation.

Finally, ways to use technology to improve evaluation are discussed throughout the text. Software packages for storing, organizing, and analyzing qualitative data are reviewed. Web-based surveys are described. Ways to use technology to distribute evaluation findings are discussed. A new appendix has been added that lists Web sites with evaluation-related information. These sites link readers to evaluation organizations, reports, texts, software, and listserves to communicate with others interested in evaluation issues.

We hope this book will inspire you to think in a new way about issues—in a questioning, exploring, evaluative way—about programs, policy, and organizational change. For those readers who are already evaluators, this book should provide you with new perspectives and tools for your practice. For those who are new to evaluation, this book will make you a more informed consumer of or participant in evaluation studies or, perhaps, even inspire you to undertake your own. Welcome to the new world of evaluation in the twenty-first century!

Acknowledgments

We are grateful for the insightful comments of the following reviewers:

Weldon Beckner, Baylor University
Marcie Boberg, San Diego State University
Jim Connors, The Ohio State University
Traci Webb Dempsey, West Virginia University
Ken Hancock, University of Tulsa
Beverly Irby, Sam Houston State University
Kristen Renn, Southern Illinois University-Carbondale
Susan Twombley, University of Kansas
Wendon Waite, Boise State University

Program Evaluation

Part I

Introduction
to Evaluation

This initial section of our text provides the background necessary for the beginning student to understand the chapters that follow. In it, we attempt to accomplish three things: to explore the concept of evaluation and its various meanings, to review the history of program evaluation and its development as a discipline, and to acquaint the reader with some of the current controversies and trends in the field.

In Chapter 1, we discuss the basic purposes of evaluation and the varying roles evaluators play. We define evaluation specifically, and we introduce the reader to several different concepts and distinctions important to evaluation. In Chapter 2, we summarize the origins of today's evaluation tenets and practices and the historical evolution of evaluation as a growing force in improving our society's public, nonprofit, and corporate programs. We then review some recent developments and trends in evaluation that have marked the past decade. These movements were either not apparent or still too embryonic to deserve attention when our 1997 text was written. Today, no discussion of evaluation should overlook movements such as the expanding uses of technology in evaluation, the emergence of performance measurement and standards-based education and the widespread attention these indicators receive, current controversies over the role and meaning of advocacy in evaluation, and the burgeoning growth and practice of evaluation in other countries.

Our intent in Part One is to provide the reader with information essential to understanding not only the content of the sections that follow but also the wealth of material that exists in the literature on program evaluation. Although the content in the remainder of this book is intended to apply to the evaluation of *programs*, most of it applies as well to *projects, products,* and *processes* used in those areas, indeed, to any object of an evaluation. In Part Two we will introduce you to different approaches to evaluation to enlarge your understanding of the diversity of choices that evaluators and stakeholders make in undertaking evaluation.

1

Evaluation's Basic Purpose, Uses, and Conceptual Distinctions

Orienting Questions _____

1. How does evaluation serve society? Why is it important?
2. What is the difference between formal and informal evaluation?
3. What are some purposes of evaluation? What roles can the evaluator play? Give some examples from your experience with evaluation.
4. What are the major differences between formative and summative evaluations?
5. What is an example of an issue an evaluator might address in a needs assessment, a process evaluation, and an outcome evaluation?
6. Under what circumstances might an external evaluator be preferable to an internal evaluator?

The challenges confronting our society in the twenty-first century are enormous. Few of them are really new. In the United States and many other countries, the public and nonprofit sectors are grappling with complex issues: educating children for the new century; reducing functional illiteracy; strengthening families; training versatile employees; combating disease and mental illness; fighting discrimination; reducing crime, drug abuse, and child and spouse abuse. More recently, pursuing and balancing environmental and economic goals and working to insure peace and economic growth in developing countries have become prominent concerns. Each new decade seems to add to the list of challenges as society and the problems it confronts become increasingly complex.

As society's concern over these pervasive and perplexing problems has intensified, so have its efforts to resolve them. Collectively, local, regional, and national agencies have launched a veritable flotilla of programs aimed at identifying and eliminating the underlying causes of these problems. Specific programs judged to have been ineffective have been "mothballed" or sunk outright, usually to be replaced by a new program designed to attack the problem in a different—and, hopefully, more effective—manner.

In more recent years, scarce resources and budget deficits have posed still more challenges as administrators and program managers have had to struggle to keep their most promising programs afloat. Increasingly, policy makers and managers have been faced with tough choices, being forced to cancel some programs or program components to provide sufficient funds to launch new ones or continue others.

To make such choices intelligently, policy makers need good information about the relative effectiveness of each program. Which programs are working well? Which poorly? What are the programs' relative costs and benefits? Similarly, each program manager needs to know how well different parts of the program are working. Are some parts contributing more than others? What can be done to improve those parts of the program that are not contributing what they should? Have all aspects of the program been thought through carefully at the planning stage, or is more planning needed? What is the theory or logic model for the program's effectiveness? What adaptations would make the program more effective?

Answering such questions is the major task of **program evaluation.** The major task of this book is to introduce you to evaluation and the vital role it plays in virtually every sector of modern society. However, before we can hope to convince you that good evaluation is an essential part of good programs, we must help you understand at least the basic concepts in each of the following areas:

- How we—and others—define evaluation
- How formal and informal evaluation differ
- The basic purposes—and various uses—of formal evaluation
- The distinction between basic types of evaluation
- The distinction between internal and external evaluators
- Evaluation's importance and its limitations

Covering all of those areas thoroughly could fill a whole book, not just one chapter of an introductory text. In this chapter, we provide only brief coverage of each of these topics to orient you to concepts and distinctions necessary to understand the content of later chapters.

A Brief Definition of Evaluation

In the previous section, the perceptive reader will have noticed that the term **evaluation** has been used rather broadly without definition beyond what was implicit in context. But the rest of this chapter could be rather confusing if we did not stop briefly to define the term more precisely. Intuitively, it may not seem difficult to define evaluation. For example, one typical dictionary definition of evaluation is "to determine or fix the value of: to examine and judge." Seems quite straightforward, doesn't it? Yet among professional evaluators, there is no uniformly agreed-upon definition of precisely what the term *evaluation* means. In fact, in considering the role of language in evaluation, Michael Scriven, one of the founders of evaluation, recently noted there are nearly sixty different terms for evaluation that apply to one context or another. These include *adjudge, appraise, analyze, assess, critique, examine, grade, inspect, judge, rate, rank, review, score, study, test* and so on (cited in Patton, 2000, p. 7). While all these terms may appear confusing, Scriven (cited in Patton, 2000) notes that the variety of uses of the term *evaluation* "reflects not only the immense importance of the process of evaluation in practical life, but the explosion of a new area of study" (p. 7). This chapter will introduce the reader to the array of variations in application, but, at this point, we would like to focus on one definition that encompasses many others.

Early in the development of the field, Scriven (1967) defined *evaluation* as judging the worth or merit of something. Many recent definitions encompass this original definition of the term (Mark, Henry, & Julnes, 1999; Stake, 2000a; Stufflebeam, 2001b). We concur that evaluation is determining the worth or merit of an evaluation object (whatever is evaluated). More broadly, we define *evaluation* as the identification, clarification, and application of defensible criteria to determine an evaluation object's value (worth or merit) in relation to those criteria. Note that this definition requires identifying and clarifying defensible criteria. Often, in practice, our judgments of evaluation objects differ because we have failed to identify and clarify the means we, as individuals, use to judge an object. One educator may value a reading curriculum because of the love it instills for reading; another may disparage the program because it does not move the child along as rapidly as other curricula in helping the student to recognize and interpret letters, words, or meaning. These educators differ in the value they assign to the curricula because their criteria differ. One important role of an evaluator is to help stakeholders articulate their criteria and to stimulate dialogue about them. Our definition, then, emphasizes using those criteria to judge the merit or worth of the product.

Evaluation uses inquiry and judgment methods, including: (1) determining **standards** for judging quality and deciding whether those standards should be relative or absolute, (2) collecting relevant information, and (3) applying the standards to determine value, quality, utility, effectiveness, or significance. It leads to recommendations intended to optimize the evaluation object in relation to its intended purpose(s) or to help stakeholders determine whether the evaluation object is worthy of adoption, continuation, or expansion.

Differences in Evaluation and Research

It may be important here to distinguish between evaluation and research. While some methods of evaluation emerged from social science research traditions, there are important distinctions between evaluation and research.[1] One of those distinctions is *purpose*. Research and evaluation seek different ends. The primary purpose of research is to add to knowledge in a field, to contribute to the growth of theory. While the results of an evaluation study may contribute to knowledge development (Mark, Henry, Julnes, 1999), that is a secondary concern in evaluation. Evaluation's primary purpose is to help those who hold a stake in whatever is being evaluated (stakeholders), often consisting of many different groups, make a judgment or decision. Research seeks *conclusions;* evaluation leads to *judgments.* Valuing is the *sine qua non* of evaluation. A touchstone for discriminating between an evaluator and a researcher is to ask whether the inquiry he is conducting would be regarded as a failure if it produced no data on the usefulness of the thing being studied. A researcher answering strictly as a researcher will probably say no.

These differing purposes have implications for the approaches one takes. Research is the quest for laws—statements of relationships among two or more variables. Thus, the purpose of research is typically to explore and establish causal relationships. Evaluation, instead, seeks to describe a particular thing. Sometimes, describing that thing involves examining causal relationships; often, it does not. Whether the evaluation focuses on a causal issue depends on the needs of the stakeholders.

This highlights another difference in evaluation and research—*who sets the agenda.* In research, the hypotheses to be investigated are chosen by the researcher and his assessment of the appropriate next steps in developing theory in the discipline or field of knowledge. In evaluation, the questions to be answered are not those of the evaluator, but rather, come from many sources, including those of significant stakeholders. An evaluator might suggest questions, but would never determine the focus of the study without consultation with stakeholders. Such actions, in fact, would be unethical in evaluation.

Another difference concerns *generalizability of results.* Given evaluation's purpose of describing a particular thing, good evaluation is quite specific to the context in which the evaluation object rests. Stakeholders are making judgments about a particular evaluation object and have less desire to generalize to other settings than a researcher would. (Note that the setting or context may be large, national programs with many sites, or small, a program in one school.) In contrast, because the purpose of research is to add to general knowledge, the methods are designed to maximize generalizability to many different settings. If one's findings are to add to knowledge in a field, ideally, the results should transcend the particulars of time and setting.

Research and evaluation differ further in the *criteria* or standards used to judge their adequacy. Two important criteria for judging the adequacy of research are internal validity, or causality, and external validity, or generalizability to other

---

[1]Research itself varies across a wide spectrum, from basic research (which we use here to highlight the distinction of research and evaluation) to applied research, which sometimes resembles evaluation in being applied to solve educational, social, and private sector problems or issues. For a more extended discussion of the differences and similarities of research and evaluation, see Worthen and Sanders, 1973.

settings and other times. These criteria, however, are not sufficient, or appropriate, for judging the quality of an evaluation. Instead, evaluations are typically judged by their *accuracy* (the extent to which the information obtained is an accurate reflection—a one-to-one correspondence—with reality), *utility* (the extent to which the results serve practical information needs of intended users), *feasibility* (the extent to which the evaluation is realistic, prudent, diplomatic, and frugal), and *propriety* (the extent to which the evaluation is done legally and ethically, protecting the rights of those involved). These standards were developed by the Joint Committee on Standards for Evaluation to help both users of evaluation and evaluators themselves understand what evaluations should do. (See Chapter 18 for more on the Standards.)

Finally, the *preparation* of researchers and evaluators differs significantly. Researchers are trained in depth in a single discipline, their field of inquiry. This approach is appropriate because the researcher's work, in almost all cases, will remain within a single discipline or field. Evaluators, by contrast, are responding to the needs of clients and stakeholders with many different information needs and operating in many different settings. As such, evaluators' education must be interdisciplinary. Only through interdisciplinary training can evaluators become sensitive to the wide range of phenomena to which they must attend if they are to properly assess the worth of a program or policy. Evaluators must be broadly familiar with a wide variety of methods and techniques so that they can choose those most appropriate for the particular program and needs of stakeholders. Finally, evaluators differ from researchers in that they must establish personal working relationships with clients. As a result, they require preparation in interpersonal and communication skills (Fitzpatrick, 1994).

Sanders (1979) identified several general areas of competence important for evaluators. These included the ability to describe the object and context of an evaluation; to conceptualize appropriate purposes and frameworks for the evaluation; to identify and select appropriate evaluation questions, information needs, and sources of information; to select means for collecting and analyzing information; to determine the value of the object of an evaluation; to communicate plans and results effectively to audiences; to manage the evaluation; to maintain ethical standards; to adjust for external factors influencing the evaluation; and to evaluate the evaluation (metaevaluation).

In summary, research and evaluation differ in their purposes and, as a result, in the roles of the evaluator and researcher in their work, their preparation, the generalizability of their results, and the criteria used to judge their work. These distinctions lead to many differences in the manner in which research and evaluation are conducted.

Of course, evaluation and research sometimes overlap. An evaluation study may add to our knowledge of laws or theories in a discipline. Research can inform our judgments and decisions regarding a program or policy. Yet, fundamental distinctions remain. Our discussion above highlights these differences to help those new to evaluation to see the ways in which evaluators behave differently than researchers. Evaluations may add to knowledge in a field, contribute to theory development, establish causal relationships, and provide explanations for the relationship between phenomena, but that is not its primary purpose. Its primary purpose is to assist stakeholders in making value judgments and decisions about whatever is being evaluated.

We will discuss shortly the matter of how one's definition of *evaluation* is the product of what one believes the purpose of evaluation to be. First, however, we need to distinguish between systematic, formal evaluation studies—the focus of this book—and the much more informal, even casual evaluation that is a part of our everyday life.

Informal versus Formal Evaluation

Evaluation is not a new concept. If one focuses on the aspect of "examining and judging, to determine value," then the practice of evaluation doubtlessly long preceded its definition, tracing its roots back to the beginning of human history. Neanderthals practiced it when determining which types of saplings made the best spears, as did Persian patriarchs in selecting the most suitable suitors for their daughters, or English yeomen who abandoned their own crossbows in favor of the Welsh longbow. They had observed that the longbow could send an arrow through the stoutest armor and was capable of launching three arrows while the crossbow sent only one. Although no formal evaluation reports on "bow comparisons" have been unearthed in English archives, it is clear that the English evaluated the longbow's value for their purposes, deciding that its use would strengthen them in their struggles with the French. So they relinquished their crossbows, perfected and improved on the Welsh longbow, and the English armies proved invincible during most of the Hundred Years' War.

By contrast, French archers experimented briefly with the longbow, then went back to the crossbow—and continued to lose battles. Such are the perils of poor evaluation! Unfortunately, the faulty judgment that led the French to persist in using an inferior weapon represents an informal evaluation pattern that has been repeated too often throughout history.

As human beings we evaluate everyday. Practitioners, managers, and policy makers make judgments about students, clients, personnel, programs, and policies. These judgments lead to choices and decisions. They are a natural part of life. A school principal observes a teacher working in the classroom and forms some judgments about that teacher's effectiveness. A program officer of a foundation visits a substance abuse program and forms a judgment about the program's quality and effectiveness. A policy maker hears a speech about a new method for delivering health care to uninsured children and draws some conclusions about whether that method would work in his state. Such judgments are made every day in our work. These judgments, however, are based on informal, or unsystematic, evaluations.

Informal evaluations can result in faulty or wise judgments. But, they are characterized by an absence of breadth and depth because they lack systematic procedures and formally collected evidence. As humans, we are limited in making judgments by both the lack of opportunity to observe many different settings, clients, or students and by our own past experience, which both informs and biases our judgments. Informal evaluation does not occur in a vacuum. Experience, instinct, generalization, and reasoning can all influence the outcome of informal evaluations, and any or all of these may be the basis for sound, or faulty, judgments. Did we see the teacher on a good day or a bad one? How did our past experience with similar students, course content, and methods influence our judgment? When we conduct informal evaluations, we are less cognizant of these limitations. However, when formal evaluations are not possible, informal evaluation carried out by knowledgeable, experienced, and fair people can be very useful indeed. It would be unrealistic to think any individual, group, or organization could evaluate formally everything it does. Often informal evaluation is the only practical approach. (In choosing an entrée from a dinner menu, only the most compulsive individual would conduct exit interviews with restaurant patrons to gather data to guide that choice.)

Informal and formal evaluation, however, form a continuum. Schwandt (2001) acknowledges the importance and value of everyday judgments and argues that evaluation is not simply about methods and rules. He sees the evaluator as helping practitioners to "cultivate critical intelligence." Evaluation, he notes, forms a middle ground "between overreliance on and overapplication of method, general principles, and rules to making sense of ordinary life on one hand, and advocating trust in personal inspiration and sheer intuition on the other" (p. 86). Mark, Henry, and Julnes (1999) echo this concept when they describe evaluation as a form of assisted sensemaking. Evaluation, they observe, "has been developed to assist and extend natural human abilities to observe, understand, and make judgments about policies, programs, and other objects in evaluation" (p. 179).

Evaluation, then, is a basic form of human behavior. Sometimes it is thorough, structured, and formal. More often it is impressionistic and private. Our focus is on the more formal, structured, and public evaluation. We want to inform readers of various approaches and methods for developing criteria and collecting information about alternatives. For those readers who aspire to become professional evaluators, we will be introducing you to the approaches and methods used in these formal studies. For all readers, practitioners and evaluators, we hope to cultivate that critical intelligence, to make you cognizant of the factors influencing your more informal judgments and decisions.

Distinguishing between Evaluation's Purposes and Evaluators' Roles and Activities

We mentioned earlier that how one defines evaluation stems from what one perceives evaluation's basic purpose to be. We treat that topic in more depth in this section as we attempt to separate the basic *purpose* of evaluation from the *roles* a professional evaluator can play in different evaluations and the *activities* under-taken to complete an evaluation successfully.

Purposes of Evaluation

Just as evaluators are not all agreed on one final, authoritative definition of evaluation, they are by no means unanimous in what they believe evaluation's purpose to be. Consistent with our earlier definition of evaluation, we believe that the basic purpose of evaluation is to render judgments about the value of whatever is being evaluated. Many different uses may be made of those value judgments, as we shall discuss shortly, but in every instance the central purpose of the evaluative act is the same: to determine the merit or worth of some thing (in program evaluation, of the program or some part of it).

This view parallels that of Scriven (1967), who was one of the earliest to outline the purpose of formal evaluation. In his seminal paper, "The Methodology of Evaluation," he noted that evaluation plays many roles but argued that it has a single goal: to determine the worth or merit of whatever is evaluated. He distinguished between the goal of evaluation, providing answers to significant evaluative questions that are posed, and evaluation roles, the ways in which those answers are used. According to Scriven, evaluation's goal usually relates to value questions, requires judgments of worth or merit, and is conceptually distinct from its roles. Scriven made the distinction this way:

> In terms of goals, we may say that evaluation attempts to answer certain *types of questions* about certain *entities*. The entities are the various . . . instruments (processes, personnel, procedures, programs, etc.). The types of question include questions of the form: *How well* does this instrument perform (with respect to such-and-such criteria)? Does it perform *better* than this other instrument? What *merits,* or drawbacks does this instrument have . . . ? Is the use of this instrument *worth* what it's costing?
> . . . But the roles which evaluation has in a particular . . . context may be enormously various; it may form part of a . . . training activity, of the process of curriculum development, of a field experiment, . . . of . . . an executive training program, a prison, or a classroom (pp. 40–41).

In the decades since this original distinction between evaluation's basic purpose (goal) and its diverse uses (roles), Scriven (1980, 1991a, 1991c) has greatly elaborated his view without abandoning it. While he has more recently added that "evaluation is concerned with significance, not just merit and worth" (1994, p. 380), he continues to present powerful philosophical arguments that evaluation of any object (e.g., a marketing plan, a school curriculum, or a residential treatment facility for drug abusers) is undertaken to identify and apply defensible criteria to determine its worth, merit, or quality.

This view of evaluation's basic purpose has been most widely adopted by prominent evaluators working in the field of education, ultimately being incorporated into the Program Evaluation Standards developed by the Joint Committee on Standards for Educational Evaluation (1994). Yet, while this view is broadly held, other articulate colleagues have argued that evaluation has several purposes. For example, Talmage (1982) notes that "three purposes appear most frequently in definitions of evaluation: (1) to render judgments on the worth of a program; (2) to assist decision makers responsible for deciding policy; and (3) to serve a political function" (p. 594). Talmage also notes that, while these purposes are not mutually exclusive, they are clearly different. Rallis and Rossman (2000) have argued that the fundamental purpose of evaluation is learning, helping practitioners and others better understand and interpret their observations.

Some recent discussions of the purposes of evaluation move beyond these more immediate purposes to evaluation's ultimate impact on society. Weiss (1998b) and Henry (2000) have argued that the purpose of evaluation is to bring about social betterment. Mark, Henry, and Julnes (1999) define achieving social betterment as "the alleviation of social problems, meeting of human needs" (p. 190). Chelimsky (1997) takes a global perspective, extending evaluation's context in the new century to worldwide challenges rather than domestic ones: new technologies, demographic imbalances across nations, environmental protection, sustainable development, terrorism, human rights, and other issues that extend beyond one program or even one country. House and Howe (1999) argue that the goal of evaluation is to foster deliberative democracy. This goal, which they recognize as idealistic, calls on the evaluator to work to help less powerful stakeholders gain a voice and to stimulate dialogue among stakeholders in a democratic fashion.

Mark, Henry, and Julnes (1999) have articulated four different purposes for evaluation: assessment of merit and worth, oversight and compliance, program and organizational improvement, and knowledge development. They note that oversight and compliance is often viewed as achieving the purpose of assessing merit and worth, but because such activities generally focus only on whether the designated services are delivered to the appropriate clients, Mark and his co-authors do not see them as effectively contributing to decisions about overall merit and worth. Similarly, they separate program and organizational improvement from merit and worth because, while such activities can focus on the merit and worth of subsets of programs, such evaluations do not lead to overall judgments of merit and worth. They note, as do we, that knowledge development can be a useful outcome or corollary to evaluation. We would emphasize, however, that it is not the primary purpose.

We will expand on these differing views of evaluation later in the book. At this point, we want to present them to introduce the reader to differing views on purposes. These views are useful in shedding light for the reader new to evaluation on the types of things evaluation might do and what evaluation means. Determining merit and worth is a quite abstract concept. The views of these different authors, we would argue, help illustrate what determining merit and worth means and what it can involve. For this text, we will continue to define the primary purpose of evaluation as determining merit and worth because it emphasizes the valuing component of evaluation that we see as critical and because we believe many, if not most, of these distinctions can be subsumed within determining merit and worth.

Roles and Activities of Professional Evaluators

Scriven (1967) discusses the roles of evaluation in terms of how evaluation is used, but evaluators as practitioners play numerous roles and conduct multiple activities in performing evaluation. Just as discussions on the purposes of evaluation help us to better understand what we mean by determining merit and worth, a brief discussion of the roles and activities pursued by evaluators will acquaint the reader with the full scope of activities that professionals in the field pursue.

A major role of the evaluator that many in the field emphasize and discuss is that of encouraging use (Patton, 1996; Shadish, 1994). While the means for encouraging use and the anticipated type of use may differ, considering use of results is a major role of the evaluator. In Chapter 16, we will elaborate the types of uses of evaluation and ways to maximize use. Henry (2000), however, has cautioned that focusing primarily on use can lead to evaluations focused solely on program and organizational improvement and, ultimately, avoiding final decisions about merit and worth. His concern is appropriate; however, if the audience for the evaluation is one that is making decisions about the program's merit and worth, this problem may be avoided. (See discussion of formative and summative evaluation in this chapter.) Use is certainly central to evaluation, as demonstrated by the prominent role it plays in the professional standards and codes of evaluation (see Chapter 16).

Others' discussions of the role of the evaluator illuminate the ways in which evaluators might interact with stakeholders and other users. Rallis and Rossman (2000) see the role of the evaluator as a critical friend. As noted, they view the primary purpose of evaluation as learning. They then argue that, for learning to occur, the evaluator has to be a trusted person, "someone the emperor knows and can listen to. She is more friend than judge, although she is not afraid to offer judgments" (p. 83). Schwandt (2001) describes the evaluator in the role of a teacher, helping practitioners develop critical judgment. Patton (1996) envisions evaluators in many different roles including facilitator, collaborator, teacher, management consultant, OD specialist, and social-change agent. These roles reflect his approach to working with organizations to bring about developmental change. Preskill & Torres (1999) stress the role of the evaluator in bringing about organizational learning and instilling a learning environment. Mertens (1999), Chelimsky (1998), and Greene (1997) emphasize the important role of including stakeholders, who often have been ignored by evaluation (see Chapter 2 on recent trends). House and Howe (1999) argue that a critical role of the evaluator is stimulating dialogue among various groups. The evaluator does not merely report information, or provide it to a limited or designated key stakeholder who may be most likely to use the information, but instead stimulates dialogue, often bringing in disenfranchised groups to encourage democratic decision making.

Evaluators also have a role in program planning. Bickman (2001) and Chen (1990) emphasize the important role evaluators play in helping articulate program theories or logic models. Wholey (1996) argues that a critical role for evaluators in performance measurement is helping policymakers and managers select the performance dimensions to be measured as well as the tools to use in measuring those dimensions.

Certainly, too, evaluators can play the role of the scientific expert. As Lipsey (2000) notes, practitioners want and often need evaluators with the "expertise to track things down, systematically observe and measure them, and compare, analyze, and interpret with a good faith attempt at objectivity" (p. 222). Evaluation emerged from social science research. While we will describe the growth and emergency of new approaches and paradigms, and the role of evaluators in educating users to our purposes, stakeholders typically contract with evaluators to provide technical or "scientific" expertise and/or an outside "objective" opinion.

Thus, the evaluator takes on many roles. In noting the tension between advocacy and neutrality, Weiss (1998b) writes that the role(s) evaluators play will depend heavily on the context of the evaluation. The evaluator may serve as a teacher or critical friend in an evaluation designed to improve the early stages of a new reading program. The evaluator may act as a facilitator or collaborator with a community group appointed to explore solutions to problems of underemployment in the region. In conducting an evaluation on the employability of new immigrant groups to a state, the evaluator may act to stimulate dialogue among immigrants, policy makers, and non-immigrant groups competing for employment. Finally, the evaluator may serve as an outside expert in designing and conducting a study for Congress on the effectiveness of annual testing in improving student learning.

In carrying out these roles, evaluators undertake many activities. These include negotiating with stakeholder groups to define the purpose of evaluation, developing contracts, hiring and overseeing staff, managing budgets, identifying disenfranchised or underrepresented groups, working with advisory panels, collecting and analyzing and interpreting qualitative and quantitative information, communicating frequently with various stakeholders to seek input into the evaluation and to report results, writing reports, considering effective ways to disseminate information, meeting with the press and other representatives to report on progress and results, and recruiting others to evaluate the evaluation (metaevaluation). These, and many other activities, constitute the work of evaluators. Today, in many organizations, that work may be conducted by people who are formally trained and educated as evaluators, attend professional conferences and read widely in the field, and identify their professional role as an evaluator or by staff who have many other responsibilities, some managerial, some direct work with students or clients, and some evaluation tasks thrown into the mix. Each of these will assume some of the roles described above and will conduct many of the tasks listed.

Uses and Objects of Evaluation

At this point, it might be useful to describe some of the ways in which evaluation can potentially be used. An exhaustive list would be prohibitive, filling the rest of this book and more. Here we provide only a few representative examples of uses made of evaluation in selected sectors of society.

Examples of Evaluation Use in Education

1. To empower teachers to have more say about how school budgets are allocated
2. To judge the quality of school curricula in specific content areas
3. To accredit schools that meet minimum accreditation standards
4. To determine the value of a middle school's block scheduling
5. To satisfy an external funding agency's demands for reports on effectiveness of school programs it supports
6. To assist parents and students in selecting schools in a district with school choice
7. To help teachers improve their reading program to encourage more voluntary reading

Examples of Evaluation Use in Other Public and Nonprofit Sectors

1. To decide whether to implement an urban development program
2. To establish the value of a job-training program
3. To decide whether to modify a low-cost housing project's rental policies
4. To improve a recruitment program for blood donors
5. To determine the impact of a prison's early-release program on recidivism
6. To gauge community reaction to proposed fire-burning restrictions to improve air quality
7. To determine the cost–benefit contribution of a new sports stadium for a metropolitan area

Examples of Evaluation Use in Business and Industry

1. To improve a commercial product
2. To judge the effectiveness of a corporate training program on teamwork
3. To determine the effect of a new flextime policy on productivity, recruitment, and retention
4. To identify the contributions of specific programs to corporate profits
5. To determine the public's perception of a corporation's environmental image
6. To recommend ways to improve retention among younger employees
7. To study the quality of performance-appraisal feedback

One additional comment about the use of evaluation in business and industry may be warranted. Evaluators unfamiliar with the private sector are sometimes unaware that personnel evaluation is not the only use made of evaluation in business and industry settings. Perhaps that is because the term *evaluation* has been absent from the descriptors for many corporate activities and programs that, when examined, are decidedly evaluative. Activities labeled as quality assurance, quality control, Total Quality Management (TQM), or Continuous Quality Improvement (CQI) turn out, on closer inspection, to possess many characteristics of program evaluation. In Chapter 20 we treat this topic more fully. Suffice it to say here that many uses are made of evaluation concepts in business and industry.

Uses of Evaluation Are Generally Applicable.   As should be obvious by now, uses of evaluation are clearly portable, if one wishes to use evaluation in the same way in another arena. The use of evaluation may remain constant, but the entity it is applied to—that is, the object of the evaluation—may vary widely. Thus, evaluation may be used to improve a commercial product, a community training program, or a school district's student assessment system. It could be used to build organizational capacity in the Xerox Corporation, the E. F. Lilly Foundation, the Minnesota Department of Education, or the Utah Division of Family Services. Evaluation can be used to empower parents in the San Juan County Migrant Education Program, workers in the U.S. Postal Service, employees of Barclays Bank of England, or residents in east Los Angeles. Evaluation can be used to provide information for decisions about programs in vocational education centers, community mental health clinics, university medical schools, or county cooperative extension offices. Such examples could be multiplied ad infinitum, but these should suffice to make our point.

A Word about the Objects of Formal Evaluation Studies.   As is evident from the previous discussion, formal evaluation studies have been conducted to answer questions about a wide variety of entities, which we have referred to as evaluation objects. The evaluation object is whatever is being evaluated. Like many disciplines, evaluation has developed its own technical terminology. For example, the word *evaluand* is sometimes used to refer to the evaluation object, unless it is a person, who is then an *evaluee* (Scriven, 1991a).

While we do not mind precise language, we see no need to use new terminology when familiar terms will do. Thus, except as they may appear in quoted material, we will not use *evaluand* or *evaluee* further, preferring to refer to both as *objects* of the evaluation.

In some instances, so many evaluations are conducted of the same type of evaluation object that it prompts suggestions for evaluation techniques found to be particularly helpful in evaluating something of that particular type. An example would be Kirkpatrick's (1983) model for evaluating training efforts. In several areas, concern about how to evaluate broad categories of objects effectively has led to the development of various subareas within the field of evaluation, such as product evaluation, personnel evaluation, program evaluation, policy evaluation, and performance evaluation.

Some Basic Types of Evaluation

Formative and Summative Evaluation

Scriven (1967) first distinguished between the formative and summative roles of evaluation. Since then, the terms have become almost universally accepted in the field. In practice, distinctions between these two types of evaluation may blur somewhat, but the terms serve an important function in highlighting the types of judgments, decisions, or choices that evaluation can serve. The terms, in fact, contrast two different types of actions that stakeholders might take as a result of evaluation.

An evaluation is considered to be **formative** if the primary purpose is to provide information for program improvement. Often, such evaluations provide information to judge the merit or worth of *a part* of a program. Three examples follow:

1. Planning personnel in the central office of Perrymount School District have been asked by the school board to plan a new, and later, school day for the local high schools based on research showing adolescents' biological clocks cause them to be more groggy in the early morning hours and parental concerns about teenagers being released from school as early as 2:30 P.M. A formative evaluation will collect information (surveys, interviews, focus groups) from parents, teachers and school staff, and students regarding their views on the calendar and visit other schools using similar calendars to provide information for planning the schedule. The planning staff will give the information to the Late Schedule Advisory Group, which will make final recommendations for the new schedule.

2. Staff with supervisory responsibilities at the Akron County Human Resources Department have been trained in a new method for conducting performance appraisals. One of the purposes of the training is to improve the performance appraisal interview so that employees receiving the appraisal feel motivated to improve their performance. The trainers would like to know if the information they are providing on conducting interviews is useful. They plan to use the results to revise this portion of the training program. A formative evaluation might observe supervisors conducting actual, or mock, interviews, as well as interviewing or conducting focus groups with both supervisors who have been trained and employees who have been receiving feedback. Feedback for the formative evaluation might also be collected from participants in the training through a reaction survey delivered either at the conclusion of the training or a few weeks after the training ends, when trainees have had a chance to practice the interview.

3. A mentoring program has been developed and implemented to help new teachers in the classroom. New teachers are assigned a mentor, a senior teacher who will provide them with individualized assistance on issues ranging from discipline to time management. The focus of the program is on helping mentors learn more about the problems new teachers are encountering and helping them

find solutions. Because the program is so individualized, the assistant principal responsible for overseeing the program is concerned with learning whether it is being implemented as planned. Are mentors developing a trusting relationship with the new teachers and learning about the problems they encounter? What are the typical problems encountered? The array of problems? For what types of problems are mentors less likely to be able to provide effective assistance? Interviews, logs or diaries, and observations will be used to collect data to address these issues. The assistant principal will use the results to consider how to better train and lead the mentors.

In contrast to formative evaluations, which focus on program improvement, **summative** evaluations are concerned with providing information to serve decisions or assist in making judgments about program adoption, continuation, or expansion. They assist with judgments about a program's overall worth or merit in relation to important criteria. More recently, Scriven (1991a) has defined *summative evaluation* as "evaluation done for, or by, any observers or decision makers (by contrast with developers) who need valuative conclusions for any other reasons besides development" (p. 20). Robert Stake has memorably described the distinction between the two in this way: "When the cook tastes the soup, that's formative evaluation; when the guest tastes it, that's summative evaluation" (cited by Scriven, 1991, p. 19). In the examples below we extend the earlier formative evaluations into summative evaluations.

1. After the new schedule is developed and implemented, a summative evaluation might be conducted to determine whether the schedule should be continued and expanded to other high schools in the district. The school board might be the primary audience for this information because it is typically in a position to make the judgments concerning continuation and expansion or termination, but others—central office administrators, principals, parents, students, and the public at large—might be interested stakeholders as well. The study might collect information on attendance, grades, and participation in after-school activities. Other unintended side effects might be examined, such as the impact of the schedule on delinquency, opportunities for students to work after school, and other afternoon activities.

2. To determine whether the performance appraisal program should be continued, the director of the Human Resource Department and his staff might ask for an evaluation of the impact of the new performance appraisal on job satisfaction and performance. Surveys of employees and existing records on performance might serve as key methods of data collection.

3. Now that the mentoring program for new teachers has been "tinkered with" for a couple of years using the results of the formative evaluation, the principal wants to know whether the program should be continued. The summative evaluation will focus on teacher turnover, satisfaction, and performance.

Note that the **audiences** for formative and summative evaluation are very different. In formative evaluation, the audience is generally the people delivering the program or those close to it, in our examples, those responsible for developing the new schedule, delivering the training program, or managing the mentoring program. Because formative evaluations are designed to improve programs, it is critical that the primary audience be people who are in a position to make changes in the program and its day-to-day operations. Summative evaluation audiences include potential consumers (students, teachers, employees, managers, or health officials in agencies that could adopt the program), funding sources (taxpayers or a funding agency), and supervisors and other officials, as well as program personnel. The audiences for summative evaluations are often policy makers or administrators, but can, in fact, be any audience with the ability to make a "go–no go" decision. Teachers make such decisions with curricula. Consumers (clients, parents, students) make decisions about whether to participate in a program based on summative information or their judgments about the overall merit or worth of a program.

A Balance between Formative and Summative.   It should be apparent that both formative and summative evaluation are essential because decisions are needed during the developmental stages of a program to improve and strengthen it, and again, when it has stabilized, to judge its final worth or determine its future. Unfortunately, some organizations focus too much of their work on summative evaluations. This trend is noted in the emphases of many state departments of education on whether schools achieve certain standards. An undue emphasis on summative evaluation can be unfortunate because the development process, without formative evaluation, is incomplete and inefficient. Consider the foolishness of developing a new aircraft design and submitting it to a "summative" test flight without first testing it in the "formative" wind tunnel. Program "test flights" can be expensive, too, especially when we haven't a clue about the probability of success.

Failure to use formative evaluation is myopic, for formative data collected early can help rechannel time, money, and all types of human and material resources into more productive directions. Evaluation conducted only when a project nears completion may simply come too late to be of much help. Apparently, many instructional designers and trainers understand this point. Zemke (1985) surveyed readers of *Training* magazine and found that over 60 percent reported that they used formative evaluation in their training activities. In a later survey of corporate training officials, Tessmer and Wedman (1992) found that nearly half of their respondents reported that they use formative evaluation.

Conversely, some organizations may avoid summative evaluations. Evaluating for improvement is critical, but, ultimately, many products and programs should be judged for their overall merit and worth. Henry (2000) has noted that evaluation's emphasis on encouraging use of results can lead us to serving incremental, often formative, decisions and may steer us away from the overall purpose of evaluation, determining merit and worth. While organizations may engage in more summative evaluations, Scriven (1996) has noted that professional evaluators are more frequently involved in the formative role and often obtain more satisfaction from it. As a result, he has often come to the defense of summative evaluations for purposes of balance.

Although formative evaluations more often occur in early stages of a program's development and summative evaluations more often occur in their later stages, as these two terms imply, it would be an error to think they are limited to those time frames. Well-established programs can benefit from formative evaluations. Some new programs are so problematic that summative decisions are made to discontinue. However, the relative emphasis on formative and summative evaluation changes throughout the life of a program, as suggested in Figure 1.1, although this generalized concept obviously may not precisely fit the evolution of any particular program.

Two important factors that influence the usefulness of formative evaluation are control and timing. If suggestions for improvement are to be implemented, then it is important that the formative study collect data on variables over which program administrators have some control. Also, information that reaches those administrators too late for use in improving the program is patently useless. Summative evaluations must attend to the timing of budgetary and legislative decisions that may affect program adoption, continuation, and expansion.

An effort to distinguish between formative and summative evaluation on several dimensions appears in Figure 1.2. As with most conceptual distinctions, formative and summative evaluation are often not as easy to distinguish in the real world as they seem in these pages. Scriven (1991a) has acknowledged that the two are often profoundly intertwined. For example, if a program continues beyond a summative evaluation study, the results of that study may be used for both summative and, later, formative evaluation purposes. In practice, the line between formative and summative is often rather fuzzy. Scriven (1986) himself

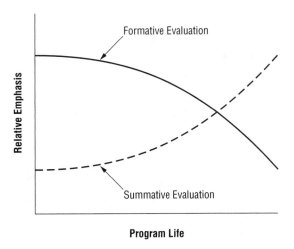

FIGURE 1.1 *Relationship between Formative and Summative Evaluation across Life of a Program*

FIGURE 1.2 *Differences between Formative and Summative Evaluation*

	Formative Evaluation	Summative Evaluation
Purpose	To determine value or quality	To determine value or quality
Use	To improve the program	To make decisions about the program's future or adoption
Audience	Program managers and staff	Administrators, policy makers, and/or potential consumer or funding agency
By Whom	Primarily internal evaluators supported by external evaluators	Generally external evaluators, supported by internal evaluators in unique cases
Major Characteristics	Provides feedback so program personnel can improve it	Provides information to enable decision makers to decide whether to continue it, or consumers to adopt it
Design Constraints	What information is needed? When?	What evidence is needed for major decisions?
Purpose of Data Collection	Diagnostic	Judgmental
Frequency of Data Collection	Frequent	Infrequent
Sample Size	Often small	Usually large
Questions Asked	What is working? What needs to be improved? How can it be improved?	What results occur? With whom? Under what conditions? With what training? At what cost?

suggested one reason why they sometimes blur, noting that, when programs have many components, summative evaluations that result in replacing weak components have played a formative role in improving the program in its entirety.

Needs Assessment, Process, and Outcome Evaluations

The distinctions between formative and summative evaluation are concerned primarily with the kinds of decisions or judgments to be made with the evaluation results. The distinction between the relative emphasis on formative or summative evaluation is an important one to make at the beginning of a study because it informs the evaluator about the context, intention, and potential use of the study and has implications for the most appropriate audiences for the study. However, the terms do not dictate the nature of the questions the study will address. Chen

(1996) has proposed a typology to permit consideration of process and outcome along with the formative and summative dimension. We will elaborate that typology here, adding needs assessment to the mix.

Some evaluators make use of the terms *needs assessment, process,* and *outcome* to refer to the types of questions the evaluation study will address or the focus of the evaluation. These terms also help make the reader aware of the full array of issues evaluators examine. **Needs assessment** questions are concerned with establishing (a) whether a problem or need exists and describing that problem, and (b) making recommendations for ways to reduce the problem, i.e., the potential effectiveness of various interventions. **Process,** or **monitoring** studies, typically describe how the program is delivered. Such studies may focus on whether the program is being delivered according to some delineated plan or model or may be more open-ended, simply describing the nature of delivery and the successes and problems encountered. Process studies can examine a variety of different issues including characteristics of the clients or students served, qualifications of the deliverers of the program, characteristics of the delivery environment (equipment, printed materials, physical plant, and other elements of the context of delivery), and the actual nature of the activities themselves. **Outcome** studies are concerned with describing, exploring, or determining changes that occur in program recipients, secondary audiences (families of recipients, coworkers, etc.), or communities as a result of a program. These outcomes can range from immediate impacts (for example, satisfaction of learners) to final goals and unintended outcomes.

Note these terms do *not* have implications for how the information will be used. The terms *formative* and *summative* help us distinguish the purposes of the evaluation. Needs assessment, process, and outcome evaluations refer to the nature of the issues or questions that will be examined. In the past, people have occasionally misused the terms *"formative"* to be synonymous with *"process evaluation"* and *"summative"* to be synonymous with *"outcome evaluation."* However, Scriven (1996) himself notes that "formative evaluations are not a species of process evaluation. . . . Conversely, summative evaluation may be largely or entirely process evaluation" (p. 152).

Figure 1.3 illustrates a typology of evaluation terms building on the typology proposed by Chen (1996); we add needs assessment to Chen's typology and label this dimension "evaluation focus." (Chen views this dimension as reflecting the stage of the program, but, while process studies typically precede outcome studies, the choice of focus depends, not on the stage of the program, but on the information needs of the stakeholders.) As Figure 1.3 illustrates, an evaluation can be characterized by the action the evaluation will serve (improvement or otherwise) as well as by the nature of the issues it will address. To illustrate, a needs assessment study can be summative (Should we adopt this new program or not?) or formative (How should we modify this program to deliver it in our school or agency?). A process study often serves formative purposes, providing information to program providers or managers about how to change activities to improve the quality of the program, but a process study may serve summative purposes when we find that the program is too complex or expensive to deliver or that program

FIGURE 1.3   *A Typology of Evaluation Studies*

	Judgment	
	What to revise/change *Formative*	*What to begin, continue, expand* *Summative*
Needs Assessment	How should we adapt the model we are considering?	Should we begin a program? Is there sufficient need?
Process	Is more training of staff needed to deliver the program appropriately?	Are sufficient numbers of the target audience participating in the program to merit continuation?
Outcome	How can we revise our curricula to better achieve desired outcomes?	Is this program achieving its goals to a sufficient degree that its funding should be continued?

Focus of Questions

recipients (students, trainees, clients) do not enroll as expected. In such cases, a process study that began as a formative evaluation for program improvement may lead to a summative decision to discontinue the program. Accountability studies often make use of process data to make summative decisions. An outcome study can, and often does, serve formative or summative purposes. Formative purposes may be best served by examining more immediate outcomes because program deliverers have greater control over the actions leading to these outcomes. For example, describing whether students are achieving immediate learning objectives is more useful to teachers in deciding how to revise their curricula than examining students' subsequent employment records or post-secondary performance. Policy makers making summative decisions, however, are often more concerned with the program's success at achieving "final" outcomes, e.g., employment, health, safety, because their responsibility is with these outcomes. Their decisions regarding funding concern whether programs achieve these ultimate outcomes. The fact that a study examines program outcomes, or effects, however, tells us nothing about whether the study serves formative or summative purposes.

The formative and summative distinction comes first, then, to help focus our attention on the judgment to be made or the action to be taken. In beginning an evaluation, evaluators are first concerned with determining this focus and, then, determining the extent to which the stakeholder can assist in making such judgments. (For example, a school board or state legislator is generally an inappropriate audience for a formative evaluation because they are typically too removed from immediate program activity. If the intention of the evaluation is formative and these are the primary audience, the evaluator should suggest that he work more closely with those involved in the day-to-day delivery of the program.) Only after the focus is determined will the evaluator proceed to examining whether the focus of the evaluation is needs assessment, process, or outcome and to developing the particular evaluation questions the study will address.

Internal and External Evaluations

The adjectives *internal* and *external* distinguish between evaluations conducted by program employees and those conducted by outsiders. An experimental year-round education program in the San Francisco public schools might be evaluated by a member of the school district staff (internal) or by a site-visit team appointed by the California State Board of Education (external). A large health maintenance organization (HMO) with facilities in six cities may have a member of each facility's staff evaluate the utility of their training of local residents to serve in paraprofessional roles (internal), or the HMO may hire a consulting firm or university research group to look at that paraprofessional training program (external).

Seems pretty simple, right? Often it is, but assume that the HMO sends a team out from their headquarters to evaluate the program in the six separate facilities. Is that an internal or external evaluation? Actually, the correct answer is "both," for such an evaluation is clearly external from the perspective of those in the individual facility, yet it clearly is an internal evaluation from the perspective of the headquarters administrators who assigned their staff to evaluate those parts of the parent HMO operation.

There are obvious advantages and disadvantages connected with both internal and external evaluation roles. Figure 1.4 summarizes some of these. Internal evaluators are likely to know more about the program, its history, its staff, its clients, and its struggles than any outsider. They also know more about the organization and its culture and styles of decision-making. They are familiar with the kinds of information and arguments that are persuasive, and know who is likely to take action and who is likely to be persuasive to others. These very advantages, however, are also disadvantages. They may be so close to the program that they cannot see it clearly. (Note, though, that each evaluator, internal and external, will bring his or her own history and "biases" to the evaluation, but the internal evaluators' closeness may prevent them from seeing solutions or changes that those newer to the situation might see more readily.) While successful internal

FIGURE 1.4 *Advantages of Internal and External Evaluators*

Internal	External
More familiar with organization & program history	Can bring greater credibility, perceived objectivity
Knows decision-making style of organization	Typically brings more breadth and depth of technical expertise
Is present to remind others of results now and in future	Has knowledge of how other similar organizations and programs work
Can communicate technical results more frequently and clearly	

evaluators may overcome the hurdle of perspective, it can be much more difficult for them to overcome the barrier of position. If internal evaluators are not provided with sufficient decision-making power, autonomy, and protection, their evaluation will be hindered.

The strengths of external evaluators lie in their distance from the program and, if the right evaluators are hired, their expertise. External evaluators are perceived as more credible by the public and, often, by policy makers. In fact, external evaluators typically do have greater administrative and financial independence. Nevertheless, the "objectivity" of the external evaluator can be overdone. (Note the role of the external Arthur Andersen firm in the 2002 Enron bankruptcy and scandal. The lure of obtaining or keeping a large contract can prompt external parties to "bend the rules" to keep the contract.) For programs with high visibility or cost or those surrounded by much controversy, an external evaluator can provide a needed degree of autonomy. External evaluators, if the search and hiring process are conducted appropriately, can also bring the specialized skills needed for a particular project. In all but very large organizations, internal evaluators must be "jacks-of-all-trades" to permit them to address the ongoing evaluation needs of the organization. When seeking an external evaluator, however, an organization can pinpoint and seek the types of skills and expertise needed for that time-limited project.

Possible Role Combinations

The dimensions of formative and summative evaluation can be combined with the dimensions of internal and external evaluation to form the two-by-two matrix shown in Figure 1.5. The most common roles in evaluation might be indicated by cells 1 and 4 in the matrix. Formative evaluations are often conducted by internal evaluators, and there are clear merits in such an approach. Their knowledge of the program, its history, staff, and clients is of great value, and credibility is not nearly the problem it would be in a summative evaluation. Program personnel are often the primary audience, and the evaluator's ongoing relationship with them can enhance the use of results in a good learning organization. Summative evaluations are probably most often (and probably best) conducted

	Internal	External
Formative	1 Internal Formative	2 External Formative
Summative	3 Internal Summative	4 External Summative

FIGURE 1.5   *Combination of Evaluation Roles*

by external evaluators. It is difficult, for example, to know how much credibility to accord a Ford Motor Company evaluation that concludes that a particular Ford automobile is far better than its competitors in the same price range. The credibility accorded to an internal summative program evaluation (cell 3) may be no better. In most organizations, summative evaluation is generally best conducted by an external evaluator or agency, but there are two circumstances in which we would alter that statement quite dramatically. First, in some instances, there is simply no possibility of the program's obtaining such external help because of financial constraints or absence of competent personnel willing to do the job. In these cases, the summative evaluation is weakened by the lack of outside perspective, but it might be possible to retain a semblance of objectivity and credibility by choosing the internal summative evaluator from among those who are some distance removed from the actual development of the program or product being evaluated.

For example, assume that an elementary school in a large (in geography, not budget) rural district in Saskatchewan needs to have a summative evaluation of an innovative French language and culture program they have been running. No funds are available to bring an evaluator in from outside the district, and, because much of the program is oral, it would be hard to bundle it up and send it off for review. Everyone in the school is either a zealous enthusiast or a bitter opponent of the program, so there is no way to get an unbiased internal evaluation. In this context, it is far better to obtain a "quasi-external" summative evaluation than do none at all. By "quasi-external," we mean that one should conduct the evaluation so as to maximize its "externality." Why not ask a qualified staff member of another school in the district to evaluate the program in return for helping with a later task in that school? While still internal to the district, this evaluator would be external to the school, hence quasi-external. If the evaluation were commissioned with a strong request for the quasi-outsider to "tell-it-like-it-is," with no punches pulled and no weaknesses overlooked, there is good reason to suspect that many of the advantages of a true external summative evaluation would occur. If one still worried that being in the same district tainted the outcomes, perhaps someone from an adjacent district, or a school not too far beyond the province's boundary, would make it a true external evaluation. Whatever definitional cutoffs one chooses to use, it is important to remember that there is a continuum from external to internal; it is a matter of degree, not black or white.

The second circumstance when we might soften our cautions about the biases that can occur in internal evaluations is when organizations have structured their internal evaluation unit (and its evaluators) to enhance their ability to be forthright about their findings. Such structuring can take many forms, but the key is that the internal evaluators are insulated and shielded from the consequences of displeasure of those whose program is evaluated.

Fortunately, a number of large agencies have structured their internal evaluation function to give it maximum independence (and avoid evaluators being placed in the untenable posture of evaluating programs developed by the boss or close associates). The larger the organization, the more insulated its evaluation staff can be and the fewer problems or pressures one might expect to be caused by hierarchical or close social relationships. Indeed, the unit (and its function) may even lose much of its internal flavor and appear more like a built-in external evaluation unit (if that non sequitur is permitted), free to pursue evaluations throughout the organization as need demands. Sonnichsen (2000) writes of the high impact that internal evaluation can have if the organization has established the conditions that permit the internal evaluator to operate effectively. The factors that he cites as being associated with evaluation offices that have a strong impact on the organization include operating as an independent entity, reporting to a top official, giving high rank to the head of the office, having the authority to self-initiate evaluations, making recommendations and monitoring their implementation, and disseminating results widely throughout the organization. He envisions the promise of internal evaluation, writing, "The practice of internal evaluation can serve as the basis for organizational learning, detecting and solving problems, acting as a self-correcting mechanism by stimulating debate and reflection among organizational actors, and seeking alternative solutions to persistent problems" (Sonnichsen, 2000, p. 78).

Evaluation's Importance—and Its Limitations

Given its many formative and summative uses, it may seem almost axiomatic to assert that evaluation is not only valuable but essential in any effective system or society. Scriven (1991b) has said it well:

> The process of disciplined evaluation permeates all areas of thought and practice. . . . It is found in scholarly book reviews, in engineering's quality control procedures, in the Socratic dialogues, in serious social and moral criticism, in mathematics, and in the opinions handed down by appellate courts. . . . It is the process whose duty is the systematic and objective determination of merit, worth, or value. Without such a process, there is no way to distinguish the worthwhile from the worthless (p. 4).

Scriven also argues the importance of evaluation in *pragmatic* terms ("bad products and services cost lives and health, destroy the quality of life, and waste the resources of those who cannot afford waste"), *ethical* terms ("evaluation is a key tool in the service of justice"), *social* and *business* terms ("evaluation directs effort where it is most needed, and endorses the 'new and better way' when it is better than the traditional way—and the traditional way where it's better than the new high-tech way"), *intellectual* terms ("it refines the tools of thought"), and *personal* terms ("it provides the only basis for justifiable self-esteem") (p. 43). Perhaps for these reasons, evaluation has increasingly been used as an instrument to pursue goals of organizations and agencies at local, regional, national, and international levels.

Potential Limitations of Evaluation

The usefulness of evaluation has led some people to look to it as a panacea for all the ills of society, but evaluation alone cannot solve all the problems of society. One of the biggest mistakes of evaluators is to promise results that cannot possibly be attained. Even ardent supporters of evaluation are forced to admit that many evaluation studies fail to lead to significant improvements in the programs they evaluate. Why? Partly it's a question of grave inadequacies in the conceptualization and conduct of many evaluations. It's also a question of understanding too little about other factors that affect the use of evaluation information, even from studies that are well conceptualized and well conducted. In addition, both evaluators and their clients may have been limited by an unfortunate tendency to view evaluation as a series of discrete studies rather than a continuing system of self-renewal. A few poorly planned, badly executed, or inappropriately ignored evaluations should not surprise us; such failings occur in every field of human endeavor. This book is intended to help evaluators, and those who use their results, to improve the practice and utility of evaluation.

A parallel problem exists when those served by evaluation naively assume that its magic wand need only be waved over an enterprise to correct all its malfunctions and inadequacies. For example, developing and measuring standards in education or in nonprofit agencies, as is the current trend, can certainly provide useful information for judging the quality of programs, but these performance monitoring programs are only the first step. Formative evaluations, specific to the context of the program, are then needed to bring about improvement. Though evaluation can be enormously useful, it is generally counterproductive for evaluators or those who depend on their work to propose evaluation as the ultimate solution to every problem or, indeed, as any sort of solution, because evaluation, in and of itself, won't effect a solution, though it might suggest one. Evaluation serves to identify strengths and weaknesses, highlight the good, and expose the faulty, but it cannot singlehandedly correct problems, for that is the role of management and other stakeholders, using evaluation findings as one tool that will help them in that process. Evaluation has a role to play in enlightening its consumers, and it may be used for many other roles, but it is only one of many influences on improving the policies, practices, and decisions in the institutions that are important to us.

Major Concepts and Theories

1. Evaluation is the identification, clarification, and application of defensible criteria to determine an evaluation object's value, its merit or worth, in regard to those criteria. The specification and use of explicit criteria distinguish formal evaluation from the informal evaluations most of us make daily.

2. Evaluation differs from research in its purpose, its concern with generalizability, its involvement of stakeholders, and the breadth of training those practicing it require.

(handwritten margin note: purpose)

3. The basic purpose of evaluation is to render judgments about the value of the object under evaluation. Other purposes include providing information for program improvement, working to better society, encouraging meaningful dialogue among many diverse stakeholders, and providing oversight and compliance for programs.

(handwritten margin note: roles)

4. Evaluators play many roles including scientific expert, facilitator, planner, collaborator, aid to decision makers and critical friend.

(handwritten margin note: formative / summative)

5. Evaluations can be formative or summative. Formative evaluations are designed for program improvement and the audience is, most typically, stakeholders close to the program. Summative evaluations serve decisions about program adoption, continuation, or expansion. Audiences for these evaluations must have the ability to make such "go–no go" decisions.

6. Evaluators may be internal or external to the organization. Internal evaluators know the organizational environment and can facilitate communication and use of results. External evaluators can provide more credibility in high-profile evaluations and bring a fresh perspective and different skills to the evaluation.

Discussion Questions

1. Consider a program in your organization. If it were to be evaluated, what might be the purpose of the evaluation? The goal? The role of evaluators in conducting the evaluation?

2. What kind of evaluation do you think is most useful, formative or summative? What kind of evaluation would be most useful to you in your work? To your school board or elected officials?

3. Which do you prefer, an external or internal evaluator? Why?

4. Describe a situation in which an internal evaluator would be more appropriate than an external evaluator. What is the rationale for your choice? Now describe a situation in which an external evaluator would be more appropriate.

Application Exercises

1. List the types of evaluation studies that have been conducted in an institution or agency of your acquaintance, noting in each instance whether the evaluator was internal or external to that institution. Determine whether each study was formative or summative and focused on needs assessment, process, or outcome questions. Finally, consider whether the study would have been strengthened by having someone with the opposite (internal/external) relationship to the institution conduct the study.

2. Think back to any formal evaluation study you have seen conducted (or if you have never seen one conducted, find a written evaluation report of one). Identify

three things that make it different from informal evaluations. Then list ten informal evaluations you have performed so far today. (Oh, yes you have!)

3. Discuss the potential and limitations of program evaluation. Identify some things evaluation can and cannot do for programs in your field.

4. Within your own organization (if you are a university student, you might choose your university), identify several evaluation objects that you believe would be appropriate for study. For each, identify (a) the use the evaluation study would serve, and (b) the basic focus of the evaluation.

Suggested Readings

Mark, M. M., Henry, G. T., & Julnes, G. (1999). Toward an integrative framework for evaluation practice. *American Journal of Evaluation, 20,* 177–198.

Rallis, S. F., & Rossman, G. B. (2000). Dialogue for learning: Evaluator as critical friend. In R. K. Hopson (Ed.), *How and why language matters in evaluation.* New Directions for Evaluation, No. 86, 81–92. San Francisco: Jossey-Bass.

Sonnichsen, R. C. (2000). *High impact internal evaluation.* Thousand Oaks, CA: Sage.

Stake, R. E. (2000). A modest commitment to the promotion of democracy. In K. E. Ryan & L. DeStefano (Eds.), *Evaluation as a democratic process: Promoting inclusion, dialogue, and deliberation.* New Directions for Evaluation, No. 85, 97–106. San Francisco: Jossey-Bass.

Stufflebeam, D. L. (2001). *Evaluation models.* New Directions for Evaluation, No. 89. San Francisco: Jossey-Bass.

2

Origins and Current Trends in Modern Program Evaluation

Orienting Questions

1. How did the early stages of evaluation influence practice today?
2. What major political events occurred in the late 1950s and early 1960s that greatly accelerated the growth of evaluation thought?
3. What significant events precipitated the emergence of modern program evaluation?
4. Are the current trends in performance measurement and standards-based education similar to earlier stages of evaluation? If so, how?
5. How has advocacy emerged as a controversial issue in evaluation?

Formal evaluation of educational, social, and private-sector programs is still maturing as a field, with its most rapid development occurring during the past four decades. Compared to professions such as law, education, or accounting or disciplines such as sociology, political science, and psychology, evaluation is still quite new. In this chapter we will review the history of evaluation and its progress toward becoming a full-fledged profession and **transdiscipline.** We will also introduce the reader to some of the new issues or debates that are central to evaluation practice and theory as we enter the twenty-first century.

The History and Influence of Evaluation in Society

Early Forms of Formal Evaluation

Some evaluator-humorists have mused that formal evaluation was probably at work in determining which evasion skills taught in Sabertooth Avoidance 101 had the greatest survival value. Scriven (1991c) apparently was not tongue-in-cheek in suggesting that formal evaluation of crafts may reach back to evaluation of early stone-chippers' products, and he was obviously serious in asserting that it can be traced back to samurai sword evaluation.

In the public sector, formal evaluation was evident as early as 2000 B.C., when Chinese officials conducted civil service examinations to measure the proficiency of applicants for government positions. And, in education, Socrates used verbally mediated evaluations as part of the learning process. But centuries passed before formal evaluations began to compete with religious and political beliefs as the driving force behind social and educational decisions.

Some commentators (e.g., Cronbach, et al., 1980) see the ascendancy of natural science in the seventeenth century as a necessary precursor to the premium that later came to be placed on direct observation. Occasional tabulations of mortality, health, and populations grew into a fledgling tradition of empirical social research that grew until "In 1797, *Encyclopedia Britannica* could speak of statistics—'state-istics,' as it were—as a 'word lately introduced to express a view or survey of any kingdom, county, or parish' " (p. 24).

But quantitative surveys were not the only precursor to modern social research in the 1700s. Rossi and Freeman (1985) give an example of an early British sea captain who halved his crew into a "treatment group" forced to consume limes, while their control counterparts consumed the sailors' normal diet. Not only did the experiment show that "consuming limes could avert scurvy," but "British seamen eventually were forced to consume citrus fruits—this is the derivation of the label 'limeys,' which is still sometimes applied to the English" (pp. 20–21).

Program Evaluation: 1800–1940

During the 1800s, dissatisfaction with educational and social programs in Great Britain generated reform movements in which government-appointed royal commissions heard testimony and used other less formal methods to "evaluate" the respective institutions. This led to still existing systems of external inspectorates for schools in England and Ireland and parallels the activities of presidential commissions in the United States today. President George W. Bush's Commission to Strengthen Social Security, exploring the economic benefits and risks to permitting people to invest their own social security funds, is a recent example. These commissions review existing research and hear testimony as a primary means of collecting information before making judgments and recommendations.

In the United States, educational evaluation in the 1800s took a slightly different bent, being influenced by Horace Mann's comprehensive annual, empirical reports on Massachusetts's education in the 1840s and the Boston School Committee's 1845 and 1846 use of printed tests in several subjects (the first instance of wide-scale assessment of student achievement serving as the basis for school comparisons). These two developments in Massachusetts were the first attempts at objectively measuring student achievement to assess the quality of a large school system. They set a precedent seen today in the standards-based education movement's use of test scores from students as the primary means for judging the effectiveness of schools.

Later, during the late 1800s, liberal reformer Joseph Rice conducted one of the first comparative studies in education designed to provide information on the quality of instructional methods. His goal was to "document" his claims that schooltime was inefficiently used. To do so, he compared a large number of schools that varied in the amount of time spent on spelling drills and then examined the students' spelling ability. He found negligble differences in students' spelling performance between schools, where one had students spend as much as 100 minutes a week on spelling instruction while another had students spend as little as 10 minutes per week. He used these data to flog educators into seeing the need to scrutinize their practices empirically.

The late 1800s also saw the beginning of efforts to accredit U.S. universities and secondary schools, although that movement did not really become a potent force for evaluating educational institutions until several strong regional accrediting associations were established in the 1930s. The early 1900s saw another example of **accreditation** (broadly defined) in Flexner's (1910) evaluation (backed by the American Medical Association and the Carnegie Foundation) of the 155 medical schools then operating in the United States and Canada. Although based only on one-day site visits to each school by himself and one colleague, Flexner argued that inferior training was immediately obvious: "A stroll through the laboratories disclosed the presence or absence of apparatus, museum specimens, library and students; and a whiff told the inside story regarding the manner in which anatomy was cultivated" (Flexner, 1960, p. 79). Flexner was not deterred by lawsuits or death threats from what the medical schools viewed as his "pitiless exposure" of their medical training practices. He delivered his evaluation findings in scathing terms (labeling, for example, Chicago's fifteen medical schools as "the plague spot of the country in respect to medical education" [p. 84]), and soon "Schools collapsed to the right and left, usually without a murmur" (p. 87). No one was ever left to wonder whether Flexner's reports were evaluative.

Other areas of public interest were also subjected to evaluation in the early 1900s; Cronbach and his colleagues (1980) cite surveys of slum conditions, management and efficiency studies in the schools, and investigations of local government corruption as examples. Rossi, Freeman, and Lipsey (1998) note that evaluation first emerged in the field of public health, which was concerned with infectious diseases in urban areas, and in education, where the focus was on literacy and occupational training.

Also in the early 1900s, the educational testing movement began to gain momentum as measurement technology made rapid advances under E. L. Thorndike and his students, and by 1918 objective testing was flourishing, pervading the military and private industry as well as all levels of education. The 1920s saw the rapid emergence of norm-referenced tests developed for use in measuring individual performance levels. By the mid-1930s, more than half of the United States had some form of statewide testing, and standardized, norm-referenced testing, including achievement tests and personality and interest profiles, became a huge commercial enterprise.

During this period, educators regarded measurement and evaluation as nearly synonymous, with the latter usually thought of as summarizing student test performance and assigning grades. Although the broader concept of evaluation, as we know it today, was still embryonic, useful measurement tools for the evaluator were proliferating rapidly, even though very few meaningful, formally published evaluations of school programs or curricula would appear for another twenty years. One notable exception was the ambitious landmark Eight Year Study (Smith & Tyler, 1942) that set a new standard for educational evaluation with its sophisticated methodology and its linkage of outcome measures to desired learning outcomes. Tyler's work, in this and subsequent studies (e.g., Tyler, 1950), also planted the seeds of **criterion-referenced testing** as a viable alternative to **norm-referenced testing.** (We will return in Chapter 4 to the profound impact that Tyler and those who followed in his tradition have had on program evaluation, especially in education.)

Meanwhile, foundations for evaluation were being laid in fields beyond education, including human services and the private sector. In the early decades of the 1900s, Fredrick Taylor's scientific management movement influenced many. His focus was on systemization and efficiency, discovering the most efficient way to perform a task and then training all staff to perform it in that way. The emergence of "efficiency experts" in industry soon permeated the business community and, as Cronbach et al. (1980) noted, "business executives sitting on the governing boards of social services pressed for greater efficiency in those services" (p. 27). Some cities and social agencies began to develop internal research units, and social scientists began to trickle into government service, where they began to conduct applied social research in specific areas of public health, housing needs, and work productivity. However, these ancestral, social-research "precursors to evaluation" were small, isolated activities that exerted little overall impact on the daily lives of the citizenry or the decisions of the government agencies that served them.

Then came the Great Depression and the sudden proliferation of government services and agencies as President Roosevelt's New Deal programs were implemented to salvage the U.S. economy. This was the first major growth in the federal government in the 1900s and its impact was profound. Federal agencies were established to oversee new national programs in welfare, public works, labor management, urban development, health, education, and numerous other human service areas, and increasing numbers of social scientists went to work in these agencies. Applied social research opportunities abounded, and soon social science academics began to join with their agency-based colleagues to study a wide variety of variables relating to these programs. While some scientists called for explicit evaluation of these new social programs (e.g., Stephan, 1935), most pursued applied research at the intersection of their agency's needs and their personal interests. Thus, sociologists pursued questions of interest to the discipline of sociology and the agency, but the questions of interest often emerged from sociology. The same trend occurred with economists, political scientists, and other academics who came to conduct research on federal programs. Their projects were considered "field research," providing opportunities to address important questions in their discipline in the field.

Program Evaluation: 1940–1964

Applied social research expanded during World War II as researchers investigated government programs intended to help military personnel in areas such as reducing their vulnerability to propaganda, increasing morale, and improving the training and job placement of soldiers. In the following decade, studies were directed at new programs in job training, housing, family planning, and community development. As in the past, such studies often focused on particular facets of the program in which the researchers happened to be most interested. As these programs increased in scope and scale, however, social scientists began to focus their studies more directly on entire programs rather than on the parts of them they found personally intriguing.

With this broader focus came more frequent references to their work as "evaluation research" (social research methods applied to improve a particular program).[1] If we are liberal in stretching the definition of evaluation to cover most types of data collection in health and human service programs, we can safely say evaluation flourished in those areas in the 1950s and early 1960s. Rossi et al. (1998) state that it was commonplace in that period to see social scientists "engaged in evaluations of delinquency-prevention programs, felon-rehabilitation projects, psychotherapeutic and psychopharmacological treatments, public housing programs, and community organization activities" (p. 23). Such work also spread to other countries and continents. Many countries in Central America and Africa were the sites of evaluations examining health and nutrition, family planning, and rural community development. Most such studies drew on existing social research methods and did not extend the conceptual or methodological boundaries of evaluation beyond those already established for behavioral and social research. Such efforts would come later.

Developments in educational program evaluation between 1940 and 1965 were unfolding in a somewhat different pattern. The 1940s generally saw a period of consolidation of earlier evaluation developments. School personnel devoted their energies to improving standardized testing, quasi-experimental design, accreditation, and school surveys. The 1950s and early 1960s also saw considerable efforts to enhance the Tylerian approach by teaching educators how to state objectives in explicit, measurable terms and providing taxonomies of possible educational objectives in the cognitive domain (Bloom, Engelhart, Furst, Hill, & Krathwohl, 1956) and the affective domain (Krathwohl, Bloom, & Masia, 1964).

In 1957, the Soviets' successful launch of *Sputnik I* sent tremors through the U.S. establishment that were quickly amplified into calls for more effective teach-

---

[1]We do not use this term in the remainder of this book because we think it blurs the useful distinctions between research and evaluation that we outlined in the previous chapter.

ing of math and science to American students. The reaction was immediate. Passage of the National Defense Education Act (NDEA) of 1958 poured millions of dollars into massive, new curriculum development projects, especially in mathematics and science. Only a few projects were funded, but their size and perceived importance led policy makers to fund evaluations of most of them.

The resulting studies revealed the conceptual and methodological impoverishment of evaluation in that era. Inadequate designs and irrelevant reports were only some of the problems. Most of the studies depended on imported behavioral and social science research concepts and techniques that were fine for research but not very suitable for evaluation of school programs.

Theoretical work related directly to evaluation (as opposed to research) did not exist, and it quickly became apparent that the best theoretical and methodological thinking from social and behavioral research failed to provide guidance on how to carry out many aspects of evaluation. Thus, educational scientists and practitioners were left to glean what they could from applied social, behavioral, and educational research. Their gleanings were so meager that Cronbach (1963) penned a seminal article criticizing past evaluations and calling for new directions. Although his recommendations had little immediate impact, they did catch the attention of other educational scholars, helping to spark a greatly expanded conception of evaluation that would emerge in the next decade.

The Emergence of Modern Program Evaluation: 1964–1972

Although the developments discussed so far were not sufficient in themselves to create a strong and enduring evaluation movement, each helped create a context that would give birth to such a movement. Conditions were right for accelerated conceptual and methodological development in evaluation, and the catalyst was found in the War on Poverty and the Great Society, the legislative centerpieces of the administration of U.S. President Lyndon Johnson. The underlying social agenda of his administration was an effort to equalize and enhance opportunities for all citizens in virtually every sector of society. Millions of dollars were poured into programs in education, health, housing, criminal justice, unemployment, urban renewal, and many other areas.

Unlike the private sector, where accountants, management consultants, and R & D departments provided constant feedback on corporate programs' productivity and profitability, these huge, new social investments had no similar mechanism in place to chart their success. There were government employees with some relevant competence—social scientists and technical specialists in the various federal departments, particularly in the General Accounting Office (GAO)—but they were too few and not sufficiently well organized to deal even marginally with determining the effectiveness of these vast government innovations. (A decade would pass before program evaluation became a formal charge in many of the agencies.) To complicate matters, many inquiry methodologies and management techniques that worked on smaller programs proved inadequate or unwieldy with programs of the size and scope of these sweeping social reforms.

For a time it appeared that another concept developed and practiced successfully in business and industry might be successfully adapted for evaluating these federal programs. This was an application of the systems approach used in the Ford Motor Company, the Planning, Programming, and Budgeting System (PPBS), brought to the U.S. Department of Defense (DOD) by Robert McNamara when he became Kennedy's secretary of defense. The PPBS was a variant of the systems approaches that were being used by many large aerospace, communications, and automotive industries. Aimed at improving system efficiency, effectiveness, and budget allocation decisions by defining organizational objectives and linking them to system outputs and budgets, many thought the PPBS would be ideally suited for the federal agencies charged with administering the War on Poverty programs. Few of the bureaucrats heading those agencies, however, were eager to embrace the PPBS. It is noteworthy here, however, for it was a precursor to the objectives-oriented and management-oriented evaluation approaches we discuss at length in Chapters 4 and 5.

However, the stage for serious evaluation was set by several factors. Administrators and managers in the federal government were new to managing such large programs and felt they needed help. Congress was concerned with holding state and local recipients of program grants accountable for expending funds as prescribed. Media reports of government waste, abuse, and mismanagement fueled public concerns about the costs and benefits of Great Society programs.

The first efforts to add an evaluative element to any of these programs were small, consisting of congressionally mandated evaluations of a federal juvenile delinquency program in 1962 (Weiss, 1987) and a federal manpower development and training program enacted that same year (Wholey, 1986). It matters little which was first, however, because neither had any lasting impact on the development of evaluation. Three more years would pass before Robert F. Kennedy would trigger the event that would send a shock wave through the U.S. education system, awakening both policy makers and practitioners to the importance of systematic evaluation.

The Elementary and Secondary Education Act.   The one event that is most responsible for the emergence of contemporary program evaluation is the passage of the Elementary and Secondary Education Act (ESEA) of 1965. This bill proposed a huge increase in federal funding for education, with tens of thousands of federal grants to local schools, state and regional agencies, and universities. The largest single component of the bill was Title I (later renamed Chapter 1), destined to be the most costly federal education program in U.S. history. Wholey and White (1973) called Title I the "grand-daddy of them all" among the array of legislation that influenced evaluation at the time.

When Congress began its deliberations on the proposed ESEA, concerns began to be expressed, especially on the Senate floor, that no convincing evidence existed that any federal funding for education had ever resulted in any real educational improvements. Indeed, there were some in Congress who believed federal funds allocated to education prior to ESEA had sunk like stones into the morass of educational programs with scarcely an observable ripple to mark their passage. Robert F. Kennedy was the most persuasive voice insisting that the ESEA require each grant recipient to file an evaluation report showing what had resulted from the expenditure of the federal funds. This congressional evaluation mandate was ultimately approved for Title I (compensatory education) and Title III (innovative educational projects). The requirements, while dated today, "reflected the state-of-the-art in program evaluation at that time" (Stufflebeam, Madaus, & Kellaghan, 2000, p. 13). These requirements, reflecting an astonishing amount of micro-management at the Congressional level, but also the serious Congressional concerns regarding accountability, included using standardized tests to demonstrate student learning and linking outcomes to learning objectives.

Although the passage of the 1965 ESEA deserves its historical designation as the birth of contemporary program evaluation, it was a beginning marked by great travail. Educators and other social scientists lacked the expertise to evaluate the programs effectively as the evaluation field was in its infancy. As the evaluation field was in its infancy, few training programs existed and methodologies were largely borrowed from field studies in the social and behavioral sciences.

Growth of Evaluation in Other Areas. Similar trends can be observed in other areas as the Great Society developed programs in job training, urban development, housing, and other anti-poverty programs. Federal government spending on anti-poverty and other social programs increased by 600% after inflation from 1950 to 1979 (Bell, 1983). As in education, the increased spending prompted concerns in Congress, the media, and the public about accountability. Increasingly, evaluations were mandated. In 1969, federal spending on grants and contracts for evaluation was $17 million. By 1972, it had expanded to $100 million (Shadish, Cook, & Leviton, 1991). The federal government expanded greatly to oversee the new social programs but, as in education, managers, political scientists, economists, and sociologists working with them were new to managing and evaluating such programs. Clearly, new evaluation approaches, methods, and strategies were needed, and also, perhaps, professionals with a somewhat different training and orientation to apply them.

Theoretical and methodological work related directly to evaluation did not exist, and evaluators were left to draw what they could from theories in cognate disciplines and to glean what they could from better-developed methodologies, such as experimental design, psychometrics, survey research, and ethnography. In response to the need for more specific writing on evaluation, important books and articles emerged. Suchman (1967) published a text reviewing different evaluation methods and Campbell (1969) argued for more social experimentation to examine program effectiveness. Campbell and Stanley's book (1966) on experimental and quasi-experimental designs was quite influential. Scriven (1967), Stake (1967), and Stufflebeam (1968) began to write about evaluation practice and theories. At the Urban Institute, Wholey and his colleagues (Wholey, et al.,

1970) recognized the political aspects of evaluation being conducted within organizations. Carol Weiss's influential text (1972) was published and books of evaluation readings emerged (Caro, 1971; Worthen & Sanders, 1973). Articles about evaluation began to appear with increasing frequency in professional journals. Together, these publications resulted in a number of new evaluation "models" to respond to the needs of specific types of evaluation (e.g., ESEA Title III evaluations or evaluations of mental health programs).

Some milestone evaluation studies that have received significant attention occurred at this time. These included not only the evaluations of Title I, but evaluations of Head Start and the television series *Sesame Street*. The evaluations of *Sesame Street* demonstrated some of the first use of formative evaluation as portions of the program were examined to provide feedback to program developers for improvement. The evaluations of Great Society programs and other programs of this era were characterized by an emphasis on innovation (Rossi, et al., 1998). The federal government, and some state and local governments, funded many "demonstrations" to test new programs. Evaluators viewed their work as part of this social experimentation (Campbell, 1969).

Graduate Programs in Evaluation Emerge. The need for specialists to conduct useful evaluations was sudden and acute and the market responded. Congress provided funding for universities to launch new graduate training programs in educational research and evaluation, including fellowship stipends for graduate study in those specializations. Several universities began graduate programs aimed at training educational or social science evaluators. In related fields, schools of public administration grew from political science to train administrators to manage and oversee government programs, and policy analysis emerged as a growing new area. Graduate education in the social sciences ballooned. The number of people completing doctorate degrees in economics, education, political science, psychology, and sociology grew from 2,845 to 9,463, an increase of 333% from 1960 to 1970 (Shadish, et al., 1991). Many of these graduates pursued careers evaluating programs in the public and nonprofit sectors. The stage for modern program evaluation was set by the three factors we have described: a burgeoning economy in the United States after World War II, dramatic growth in the role of the federal government in education and other policy areas during the 1960s, and, finally, an increase in the numbers of social science graduates with interests in evaluation and policy analysis (Shadish, et al., 1991).

Evaluation Becomes a Profession: 1973–1984

This period can be characterized as one of increasing development of a distinct field of evaluation through development of approaches, programs to train students to become evaluators, and professional associations. At the same time, the sites of evaluation began to diversify dramatically, with the federal government playing a less dominant role.

Several prominent writers in evaluation proposed new and differing models. Evaluation moved beyond simply measuring whether objectives were attained, as evaluators began to consider information needs of managers and unintended outcomes. Values and standards were emphasized, and the importance of making judgments about merit and worth became apparent. These new and controversial ideas spawned dialogue and debate that fed a developing evaluation vocabulary and literature. Scriven (1972), working to move evaluators beyond the rote application of objectives-based evaluation, proposed *goal-free evaluation*, urging evaluators to examine the processes and context of the program in order to find unintended outcomes. Stufflebeam (1971), responding to the need for evaluations that were more informative to decision makers, developed the *CIPP model*. Stake (1975b) proposed *responsive evaluation*, moving evaluators away from the dominance of the experimental, social science paradigms. Guba and Lincoln (1981), building on Stake's qualitative work, proposed *naturalistic evaluation*, leading to much debate over the relative merits of qualitative and quantitative methods. Collectively, these new conceptualizations of evaluation provided new ways of thinking about evaluation that greatly broadened earlier views, making it clear that good program evaluation encompasses much more than simple application of the skills of the empirical scientists. (These models and others will be reviewed in Part Two.)

This burgeoning body of evaluation literature revealed sharp differences in the authors' philosophical and methodological preferences. It also underscored a fact about which there was much agreement: Evaluation is a multidimensional technical and political enterprise that requires both new conceptualizations and new insights into when and how existing methodologies from other fields might be used appropriately. Shadish and his colleagues (1991) said it well when, in recognizing the need for unique theories for evaluation, they noted that "as evaluation matured, its theory took on its own special character that resulted from the interplay among problems uncovered by practitioners, the solutions they tried, and traditions of the academic discipline of each evaluator, winnowed by 20 years of experience" (p. 31).

Publications focused exclusively on evaluation grew dramatically in the 1970s and 1980s, including journals and series such as *Evaluation and Program Planning, Evaluation Practice, Evaluation Review, Evaluation Quarterly, Educational Evaluation and Policy Analysis, Studies in Educational Evaluation, Canadian Journal of Program Evaluation, New Directions for Program Evaluation, Evaluation and the Health Professions, ITEA Journal of Test and Evaluation, Performance Improvement Quarterly,* and the *Evaluation Studies Review Annual.* Others that omit evaluation from the title but highlight it in their contents include *Performance Improvement Quarterly, Policy Studies Review,* and the *Journal of Policy Analysis and Management.* In the latter half of the 1970s and throughout the 1980s, the publication of evaluation books, including textbooks, reference books, and even compendia and encyclopedias of evaluation, increased markedly. In response to the demands and experience gained from practicing evaluation in the field, a unique evaluation content developed and grew.

Simultaneously, professional associations and related organizations were formed. The American Educational Research Association's Division H was an initial focus for professional activity in evaluation. During this same period, two professional associations that focused exclusively on evaluation were founded: the Evaluation Research Society and Evaluation Network. In 1976, the Joint Committee on Standards for Educational Evaluation, a coalition of 12 professional associations concerned with evaluation in education and psychology, was formed to develop standards that both evaluators and consumers could use to judge the quality of evaluations. In 1981, they published *Standards for Evaluations of Educational Programs, Projects, and Materials.* In 1982, the Evaluation Research Society developed a set of standards, or ethical guidelines, for evaluators to use in practicing evaluation (Evaluation Research Society Standards Committee, 1982). (These Standards and the 1995 Guiding Principles, a code of ethics developed by the American Evaluation Association to update the earlier ERS standards, will be reviewed in Chapter 20.) These activities contributed greatly to the formalization of evaluation as a profession with standards for judging the results of evaluation, ethical codes for guiding practice, and professional associations for training and the exchange of ideas and learning.

While the professional structures for evaluation were being formed, the markets for evaluation were changing dramatically. During the 1970s, evaluators were vigorously sought after by a variety of U.S. federal agencies, including the National Institute of Education; the U.S. Office of Planning, Budgeting, and Evaluation; the Congressional Research Service; the Office of Technology Assessment; and the General Accounting Office. The need for evaluators was not limited to these federal agencies, however, for many of the social and educational programs that provided large sums of money to state and local agencies were accompanied by evaluation mandates. Consequently, many evaluators were employed on local or state projects supported by federal funds. Thus, federal funding of evaluation, coupled with evaluation requirements, had created a three-tiered employment (or consulting) base for evaluators working on local, state, or national projects in a wide variety of programmatic areas. Evaluation was a booming business that appeared likely to provide career stability for those choosing to pursue it.

The late 1970s saw a dip in the level of federal funding for evaluation, however, and it appeared likely that the U.S. job market for evaluators would decline dramatically. By the early 1980s, that possibility became a near certainty as Ronald Reagan's shadow fell over the evaluation scene. Much of the categorical funding to states and local institutions that had carried evaluation mandates was replaced by block grants that had no evaluation requirements at all. Many evaluators and political commentators predicted that evaluation, which had only been conducted because of federal insistence, would dwindle, if not die outright, as soon as the federal evaluation requirements were abolished. Those who calculated the impact during the 1980s reported evaluation staff and budget cuts at around 50 percent (Levitan, 1992) and a 90 percent reduction in the number of evaluation studies conducted by some federal agencies (Cordray & Lipsey, 1987). Evaluators who had depended on federal funding (and the accompanying evaluation mandates) began to see their livelihood slipping away. To many it appeared that evaluators were a vanishing breed.

Before long, however, it became apparent that many evaluators and evaluation agencies were not greatly affected by the decline in federally mandated and supported evaluations. Indeed, in many areas evaluation business continued to increase. Despite the fact that most state and local agencies first became involved with evaluation when it was thrust on them by federal mandates, many of these agencies apparently had come to value evaluation in its own right. Indeed, there were numerous instances of such agencies, along with foundations, corporations, and even churches, that were routinely building evaluation into their programs, even programs that had never had a dollar of federal support and were under absolutely no obligation to evaluate their efforts. So, while many state and local agencies did abandon or reduce evaluation when federal mandates were eliminated, many did not. Indeed, the function of evaluation appears to have been institutionalized in enough agencies that the career opportunities for evaluators once again looked promising.

The decline in evaluation at the federal level actually resulted in a diversification of evaluation, not only in settings, but in approaches (Shadish, et al., 1991). As noted, evaluations of Great Society programs had focused on "demonstrations" and experimentation concerning the effectiveness of what were perceived as innovative new programs. The focus was on studying outcomes and summarizing achievements. As the funders of evaluation diversified, the nature and methods of evaluation adapted and changed. Formative evaluations, examining programs to provide feedback for incremental change and improvement and to find the links between program actions and outcomes, became more prominent. Michael Patton began writing about utilization-focused evaluation, emphasizing the need to identify a likely user of evaluation and adapt questions and methods to that user's needs (Patton, 1975, 1986). Guba and Lincoln (1981) urged evaluators to make greater use of qualitative methods to develop "thick descriptions" of programs, providing more authentic portrayals of the nature of programs in action. Evaluators who had previously focused on policy makers (e.g., Congress, Cabinet-level departments, legislators) as their primary audience began to consider multiple stakeholders as different sources funded evaluation and voiced different needs. Thus, the decline in federal funding, while dramatic and frightening for evaluation at the time, lead to the development of a richer and fuller approach to determining merit and worth.

1985–the Present

Today, evaluations are conducted in many different settings using many different approaches and methods. Though there are fewer graduate programs training students in evaluation than there were in the heyday of the Great Society, the programs that continue in the United States, Canada, and Australia have matured into programs offering unique training opportunities—training tailored to fit the reconceptualized views of evaluation that had emerged (Altschuld, Engle, Cullen,

Kim, & Macee, 1994). The American Evaluation Association (AEA) was formed in 1985, merging Evaluation Research Society and Evaluation Network. The association serves a relatively stable 3000 members and holds annual conferences where members share their diverse practices and views of evaluation. The Association has developed a code of conduct, the Guiding Principles, and has engaged in a lively debate concerning certification or licensure of evaluators (Altschuld, 1999; Jones & Worthen, 1999; Smith, 1999). In 1995, AEA and the Canadian Evaluation Association (CEA) combined their annual conferences to meet in Vancouver, Canada, and invited evaluators from around the world to present and attend. This international conference has led to a growth in American's knowledge of evaluation approaches around the world, to a continuing interest in international issues, and to an institutionalization of evaluation in other countries. Today, more than fifty evaluation associations are active in countries around the world (Mertens, 2001).

In recent years, training of evaluators has expanded in nonacademic settings. Mandates for program improvement and accountability are directed not only to governing boards but also to practitioners, who are often expected to perform in evaluation roles without the benefit of evaluation training. Many schools, state agencies, businesses, and several national professional associations have sponsored in-service evaluation training for practitioners to allow them to get evaluation training in their home settings.

The need for evaluation specialists is generally recognized, but evaluators play many roles. Empowerment evaluation and participative evaluation work to help managers, program providers, clients, and other stakeholders in developing evaluation skills. Total Quality Management (TQM) and books on evaluation in learning organizations (Preskill & Torres, 1999) have prompted managers to take a more questioning attitude toward their organization's activities and to use data to examine effectiveness and to guide change. So, in some cases, evaluation specialists work as facilitators to help school and program personnel to improve their evaluation skills. In other cases, where summative decisions require careful and costly examinations of outcomes, evaluators' expertise in qualitative and quantitative methodology, as well as their skills in facilitating use and decisions regarding merit and worth, are essential in leading the project.

In the last fifteen years, evaluators have struggled to better define and institutionalize the field. Noting the current diversity in settings in which evaluation takes place and the methods evaluators use, Shadish et al. (1991) write: "Evaluation may be the broadest methodological specialty" (p. 31), but, they note, evaluation is much more than a method. However, few see evaluation as a discipline, like sociology or anthropology. Scriven has argued that, because of its versatility in providing services to all disciplines, evaluation is one of the most powerful of the transdisciplines. *Transdisciplines,* he writes, are "tool disciplines such as logic, design, and statistics—that apply across broad ranges of the human investigative and creative effort while maintaining the autonomy of a discipline in their own right" (p. 1). Others see evaluation as a profession or developing profession because of evaluators' relationships with clients (Fitzpatrick, 1999; Chelimsky, 1992). Whatever it is called, evaluation has become a vital social force, an area of professional practice and specialization that has its own literature, preparation programs, standards of practice, and professional associations.

Which brings us to the present. In the next section we will address in greater depth some of the issues and controversies that characterize evaluation writing and practice today. Meanwhile, Table 2.1 summarizes some of the historical trends we have discussed here.

TABLE 2.1 *Stages in the Development of Evaluation*

Period	Studies/References	Characteristics
Pre–1800	Sailors eating limes	Most judgments based on religious, political beliefs
1800–1940	Commissions Mass. reports on schools Thorndike and Tyler in ed. Taylor & efficiency Accrediation (Flexner)	Measurement and use of experts begins Focus on public health, education Formal testing begins in schools Social scientists move into government Studies explore social science issues
1940–1963	WW II research on military National Defense Ed. Act Cronbach (1963)	Social science methods increase Evaluations in schools increase to compete with Russia Evaluation expands to many areas Methods continue to rely on social science
1964–1973	ESEA of 1965 Head Start Evaluation Great Society Programs *Sesame St.* evaluation	Texts and articles in evaluation emerge Theorists develop first models Program administrators need help Graduate programs in evaluation begin Growth in Ph.D.s in ed. & social sciences
1974–1984	Joint Committee Standards ERS Standards Utilization-Focused Eval. Naturalistic Eval.	Professional associations, standards & ethical codes developed Federal support for evaluation declines Evaluation approaches and settings diversify
1985–present	Evaluation for the 21st Cent. 2nd Edition—Joint Committee Performance Monitoring Standards AEA Guiding Principles	Evaluation spreads around the globe Values in Evaluation & Advocacy, Deliberative Democracy, Social Research Ethical Issues, Technological Advances

Recent Trends Influencing Program Evaluation

There are many emerging trends that we believe are—or soon will be—influencing the practice of program evaluation. Rather than discuss them all in this section, we have preferred to treat most of these trends in whichever chapter we see as being most relevant. Those we discuss elsewhere are only listed in this section to serve as "advance organizers" for the student. The last four trends are discussed very briefly in this final section of Chapter 2.

Twelve emerging trends or issues we believe likely to influence the future of program evaluation significantly are:

1. Increasing priority and legitimacy of internal evaluation
2. Expanded use of qualitative methods
3. A strong shift toward using multiple and diverse methods (qualitative and quantitative) in program evaluations to address evaluation questions more fully and appropriately
4. Expansion of theory-based (or theory-driven) evaluation
5. Increasing concern over ethical issues in conducting program evaluations
6. Increased use of program evaluation in foundations and other agencies in the nonprofit sector
7. Increased education and involvement of stakeholders in the conduct of evaluation, often to empower stakeholders to conduct their own evaluations and/or to bring a new sense of learning to the organization
8. Increasing discussion of the appropriate role of evaluators in advocacy, often expressed as evaluating for less powerful stakeholders
9. Advances in technology available to evaluators, and communication and ethical issues such advances will raise
10. Performance measurement in the federal government and nonprofit organizations and standards-based assessment in education as means for tracking performance
11. Growth of evaluation internationally

The Role of the Evaluator in Advocacy

Historically, evaluators have been perceived as "neutral" or "value free." For many who contract with evaluators, that perceived neutrality or "objectivity" is, in fact, one of the major reasons for soliciting the work of the evaluator. Yet, evaluators are aware of the fallacies of this perception. Everyone has "baggage." Our own experiences and beliefs color our approach to evaluation and to the programs we study. No one is truly a blank slate, but the evaluator does bring a new and different perspective to the evaluation. Further, the evaluator's methods, while not necessarily replicable, are there for everyone to see. In other words, the means by which the evaluator forms her judgments or draws her conclusions are more visible and, hence, open to challenge and discussion. This is quite different from the informal means by which most people make judgments and decisions. (See Chapter 1 on the distinctions between formal and informal evaluations.)

Noting this history of evaluation, Greene (1997) acknowledges that "the very notion of *evaluation as advocacy* invokes shudders of distaste and horror among most members of today's evaluation community, theorists and practitioners alike" (p. 26). However, she argues "advocacy is an inevitable part of evaluation inquiry" (p. 26). For example, she notes, we take sides by choosing whose questions and criteria we address in a study. During the years of evaluating Great Society programs, policymakers' questions were paramount. Today, many models that seek to maximize the use of evaluation results focus on the questions of onsite program administrators. Responsive evaluations often address the evaluation questions and concerns of those closest to the program, generally onsite directors and staff. Similarly, evaluation theorists who espouse various models of evaluation are advocating for central tenets of their models. For example, House and Howe argue that evaluators should stimulate democratic dialogue and, hence, empower stakeholders who are often left out of the discussions regarding evaluation and program effectiveness. Henry (2000) advocates using evaluation for social betterment. Lipsey (2000) contends that evaluators should pay more attention to previous evaluations of similar programs, using meta-analysis to synthesize research findings and incorporate them in our thinking regarding program planning and evaluation. In other words, every evaluator is advocating for something. Greene herself argues that evaluation should be "a force for democratizing public conversations about important public issues" (p. 28), but her primary argument is that evaluators should recognize their role as advocates, to be explicit about those values, and to acknowledge the implications of those values.

Others in the evaluation field have argued that evaluators must be free from the shadow that any type of advocacy might cast. Chelimsky (1998), citing her experience in advising Congress as the director of the Program Evaluation and Methodology Division of the General Accounting Office (GAO), writes, "The need in a political environment is not for still another voice to be raised in advocacy, but rather for information to be offered for public use that's sound, honest, and without bias toward any cause. Policy makers in the Congress *expect* evaluators to play precisely such a role and provide precisely this kind of information" (p. 39). We agree that evaluators must be conscious of the unique role they play in providing information and that this role is, in fact, what provides evaluators with credibility. However, we also agree with House and Howe's (1999) useful assessment of Chelimsky's own work in evaluating chemical weapons programs for Congress. Chelimsky observed that most of the information that Congress received on this issue was from the Defense Department and favorable to chemical weapons. For her evaluation, Chelimsky chose to provide Congress with a more complete picture of the research on chemical warfare. As such, House and Howe argue, she was acting as an advocate to provide a full picture and include all sides in the debate. Like Greene, House and Howe maintain we should *not* advocate for programs or positions, but definitely should act as advocates to stimulate democracy and the public interest. This view was foreshadowed by Guiding Principle E of the American Evaluation Association, which states that evaluators have "Responsibilities for General and Public Welfare" (American Evaluation Association, 1995, p. 25).

It is important for evaluators to recognize that, in any evaluation, they are making choices—choices about stakeholders to include, evaluation questions to address, methodologies to employ, and methods for reporting information—and to be aware that such choices have implications for various groups. In making those choices, evaluators might be viewed as advocates, but we hope this issue will not become as divisive as the debate over qualitative and quantitative methods became in the 1980s. Instead, the discussion can make us aware of our multiple roles— roles that include being perceived as objective by various stakeholders—and yet, within the profession, continue a dialogue concerning how our actions affect the public interest and various stakeholder groups. Increasing our sensitivity to these issues can only be healthy, improving evaluation practice and the results of our work. Meanwhile, we can be conscious of the fact that the word *advocacy* is loaded and, because we often don't have time to give our users an entire course in the theories and philosophies about evaluation, we can, nevertheless, work to inform our users about our own goals in conducting an evaluation and how these goals coincide, or depart from, those of each stakeholder group in the context of that particular program.

For example, how would an evaluator act as an advocate in evaluating a program on standards-based education for a state? She certainly would include a review of work from evaluations of similar programs from many different perspectives. She would include students, teachers, parents, educational administrators, members of the state department of education, legislators and others in forming questions, considering methods, and disseminating results. She would work to insure that groups who might be overlooked, children and parents who speak different languages or have special needs, are included and empowered in the discussion. She would *not* advocate a particular point of view or program, but, as Chelimsky did with chemical weapons, she would attempt to present a full picture of the issue and, as such, stimulate effective dialogue among groups who often don't communicate with each other. As such, evaluation can be a powerful tool for facilitating a better society. Note that evaluation doesn't dictate what that "better society" is, but provides leadership in stimulating discussion so that parties can more equally arrive at their own conclusions about what that "better society" is in the context of the particular program they are considering.

Evaluators' Use of Technological Advances and Resulting Communication and Ethical Issues

The impact of electronic and other technological advances on the lives of today's citizens, in almost every country and society, has been enormous, perhaps incalculable. Its impact on evaluators is no less. The power and efficiency of today's personal computers, statistical and text/theme processing software, optical scanners, computerized laser visuals, E-mail, and the Internet will likely be eclipsed by newer, faster, and more flexible technological advances even before the printer's ink on these pages is dry. Space does not permit much speculation about such future developments here, but they seem sure to alter the practice of evaluation, if not our basic conception of its nature. Imagine pocket-size instruments that can scan a classroom or a city council chamber, record individual and group attitudes, and monitor each student's or citizen's level of intellectual readiness or grasp of specific content. Perhaps that day may never come, but it does suggest the sorts of ethical dilemmas evaluators may encounter in balancing technological capabilities with individual rights. It seems certain that technological advances will permit data collection to be much more rapid, reliable, and valid than is now the case. Today, we can conduct surveys over the Internet and rapidly download and analyze data and distribute findings to many different stakeholders. Individual interviews and group discussions can be conducted over long distances using improved computer or telecommunications technology. Photographs conveying real classroom experiences can be quickly disseminated to many stakeholders. Whom do such strategies empower? Whom do they disenfranchise? Evaluators should keep informed of new technological advances that can enhance their work and take full advantage of these to make their work more effective and efficient. Meanwhile, we should always be cognizant of the possibility that our use of technology—for data collection, dissemination, communications among stakeholders and staff, or other ends—may achieve unintended and undesirable outcomes, e.g., loss of privacy, leaving out those without access to technology, and so on.

The Internet is, of course, a vital source of information for evaluators. The Appendix provides addresses and descriptions of evaluation-related Web sites that can be very useful for the reader. We also encourage readers to sign on to American Evaluation Association's listserv, EvalTalk, which provides a forum for the exchange of ideas and requests for help among evaluators. (See links to join Eval-Talk in the Appendix.)

Performance Measurement and Standards-Based Education

The major movement at the beginning of the twenty-first century in assessing the performance of public and nonprofit organizations is performance measurement. Wholey (1996), one of the founders of performance measurement, defines it as "the periodic measurement of program performance . . . typically done annually to provide public accountability and assist budget decision making" (p. 146). Typically, it includes comparing performance (which may include any number of inputs, processes, or outcomes) with either past performance or some predetermined goal or standard. Measuring students' learning through standards-based tests is perhaps the best-known example of performance measurement. In 2002, forty-nine states have developed, or are developing, standards-based programs. Increasing numbers of states are using tests to determine promotion and/or graduation (Merrow, 2001). President George W. Bush has proposed legislation to mandate national testing of students to make public schools accountable.

Though assessing schools' progress on educational standards may be the most prominent example of performance monitoring, other examples abound. In 1993, Congress passed the Government Performance and Results Act (GPRA) requiring all federal agencies to establish goals and monitor their progress toward those goals. Other forms of performance monitoring have been adopted by the Canadian and Australian governments (Perrin, 1998; Winston, 1999). Performance monitoring is not new. It's been around in the U.S. Federal government since Robert McNamara introduced Program Planning and Budget Systems (PPBS) to the Defense Department during the Kennedy administration. Management by Objectives (MBO), another form of performance monitoring, was popular in the private sector in the 1970s. GPRA, the current federal initiative in the United States, attempts to improve over the past initiatives by encouraging stakeholder involvement in developing indicators, using multiple measures, and making use of pilot tests and several years of formative evaluations before full implementation (Bernstein, 1999).

While the founders of performance monitoring note that any performance can be monitored, most performance monitoring programs are characterized by a focus on outcomes. And, in fact, most performance monitoring programs were created in an environment characterized by public discontent with government, shrinking budgets, funders' frustration with a focus on process evaluation, and a general concern for greater accountability for the outcomes that programs hope to achieve. Thus, in K–12 education, standards-based initiatives focus on student learning. In higher education, states are examining graduation rates and success of students in jobs and on certification and licensure tests. In the nonprofit sector, United Way, which provides funding to many nonprofit agencies, mandated an outcomes-oriented evaluation approach in order for nonprofit agencies to be considered for funding.

While some commentators are skeptical regarding both the validity and utility of performance monitoring, even critics note the promise of performance measures as "one component of a broader, more comprehensive evaluation strategy" (Perrin, 1998, p. 375). In K–12 education, many see the standards movement as having great promise. Doesn't everyone work better if they know the direction in which they're headed? Writers in organizational development have long touted the advantages of clear goals in stimulating motivation and productivity. Schmoker and Marzano (1999), commenting on the promise of standards-based education, note: "The success of any organization is contingent upon clear, commonly defined goals. A well-articulated focus unleashes individual and collective energy. And a common focus clarifies understanding, accelerates communication, and promotes persistence and collective purpose. This is the stuff of improvement" (p. 137). As with many such promising initiatives, the devil is in the details!

There is much for evaluators to do in response to these initiatives. Wholey (1996) and Perrin (1998) see evaluators playing a major role in helping organizations define standards or identify the performance indicators they will assess. Evaluators can play critical roles in ensuring that standards are feasible, clear, and inspiring and that teachers and other staff are partners in their development. Good organizations involve employees; schools should too. Individual schools may benefit most from performance monitoring by developing standards appropriate to their school. Evaluators can make use of their skills in involving multiple stakeholders and facilitating discussions of goals and outcomes.

Of course, evaluators should play an important role in determining means for assessing performance. GPRA has at least encouraged multiple measures and diverse means (qualitative and quantitative) for assessing outcomes. Most states' means for assessing standards are sorely lacking. In fact, the sorry state of assessing educational standards in states within the United States prompted Thompson (2001) to regale "the authentic standards movement" and assail "its evil twin—high-stakes, standardized test-based reform." Problems include overreliance on a single outcome measure, lack of validation of tests, an undue emphasis on quantitative measures, and failure to educate the public concerning the meaning of labels such as "proficient" (which in Colorado corresponds to the 95th percentile on the high school standards math test).

Advocates see performance measurement as replacing "one-shot" evaluation studies and serving as the foundation for formative and summative evaluations. Wholey (1996) encourages evaluators to collect data more frequently and to examine subgroups further when the purposes are formative. We tend to believe that many one-shot studies, in fact, meet important, though temporary, information needs of diverse stakeholders. Performance monitoring systems, by their very nature, tend to address the needs of managers or policy makers and to measure permanent, or at least long-standing, outcomes. As such, they sometimes do not meet formative information needs of program staff or summative needs of clients and other interested stakeholder groups. However, we believe performance monitoring systems, having been around in some form or another for at least thirty-five years, are here to stay. Because performance monitoring has the potential to inform stakeholders and because evaluators have expertise in this area, we encourage evaluators to become more actively involved in performance monitoring. In education, evaluation expertise is greatly needed to help advise on and improve standards and systems of testing to insure that these strategies contribute to children's learning.

Growth of Evaluation Internationally

As previously noted, the Canadian Evaluation Association and the American Evaluation Association joined to hold their annual conferences together in Vancouver, Canada, and to invite other evaluators from around the world to participate. A second joint conference is being planned for Toronto, Canada, in 2005.

The theme of the 1995 conference was "Evaluation for a New Century—A Global Perspective," and evaluators from fifty different countries participated. This first step led to increased communication, writing, and organizational efforts across different countries and cultures concerning evaluation.

Chelimsky and Shadish (1997) edited a book of readings, *Evaluation for the 21st Century,* based on a selection of papers presented at the conference in Vancouver. This book demonstrates the rich array of practice in countries around the globe. The Topical Interest Group on International Evaluation at the American Evaluation Association has grown dramatically and attendees from many different countries now participate actively at each annual conference. Further, Mertens and others have secured funding from the W. K. Kellogg Foundation to organize meetings of officers of evaluation associations around the world to discuss how cross-fertilization of ideas and professional development activities can occur. As a result of their work, several meetings of officials of evaluation organizations around the world were conducted and the International Organization for Cooperation in Evaluation (IOCE) was formed. Its inaugural meeting was held in Peru in 2003. Today, there are more than fifty evaluation associations around the world, many in developing countries. Participants in the meetings of the IOEC have included representatives from evaluation associations in Africa, Central America, Europe, Israel, France, Malaysia, Kenya, Sri Lanka, the United Kingdom, Australasia, Italy, Canada, and the United States (Mertens & Russon, 2000).

The World Bank began training people working in international development in evaluation methods in 2001 and created an association, International Development Evaluation Association (IDEAS), to support evaluation in developing countries. This organization held its inaugural meeting in Beijing in 2002. In the past, evaluations of international development efforts have often been done by outside contractors who may be unfamiliar with the culture of the developing country. This training and the organization are designed to improve evaluation capacity in these developing countries.

Evaluation in different cultures and other countries is an exciting venture, not only because evaluation can be beneficial in helping address policy questions and issues in those countries, but because North American evaluators can learn new methods and organizational approaches from the efforts of other countries (Mertens, 1999). As any traveler knows, seeing and experiencing a culture different from one's own is an eye-opener to the peculiarities—both strengths and constraints—of one's own culture. Practices or mores that had not been previously questioned are brought to our attention as we observe people or institutions in other cultures behaving differently. This holds true in evaluation as well. We believe the twenty-first century will be a time for evaluators in the Western world to learn from the practices of their colleagues in other countries and that these efforts will both strengthen our own work and spread the culture of evaluation—collecting data to judge programs and form decisions—around the world.

Major Concepts and Theories

1. Commissions to report on specific problems, objective tests, and accreditations were among the early forms of evaluation. During the Depression, social scientists began working for the federal government to advise on means for curing social ills and improving the economy.

2. The Russians' launch of *Sputnik I* created unease in the United States about the effectiveness of techniques used to teach math and science to American students. Congress passed the National Defense Education Act (NDEA) of 1958, which began much evaluation in the educational arena.

3. During the 1960s and 1970s, with the Great Society legislation of the Johnson administration, the federal government began mandating evaluation in many education and social settings. This represented the first major phase in the growth of evaluation.

4. The growth of evaluation spurred the first efforts to train and educate professionals specifically to conduct evaluations. Different evaluation theories, models, and concepts to characterize and guide evaluation work began to emerge.

5. The profession becomes more fully established with the creation of professional associations such as the American Evaluation Association, standards for evaluation, and codes of conduct.

6. The field expanded its methods to include more qualitative approaches and discussions of how evaluators can ensure that evaluation is used by many diverse groups.

7. Evaluation has spread to many other countries and grown to include many different approaches. Contemporary issues include performance monitoring and standards and the role of evaluators in improving the society and including diverse stakeholders.

Discussion Questions

1. How did World Wars I and II help to pave the way for evaluation? What were the major questions war officials hoped to answer in WWI? WWII?

2. The Elementary and Secondary Act of 1965 (ESEA) and many Great Society programs required that agencies receiving funding submit evaluation reports documenting program results. Discuss the effect of requiring evaluation reports, the impact this mandate had on modern program evaluation, and the problems with both evaluations and evaluators this mandate brought to the surface.

3. Does your organization use performance monitoring or standards? What are the historical roots of these methods? How do they differ from other current evaluation trends? What beneficial and undesired outcomes have, or can, occur with such strategies?

4. What are the advantages and disadvantages of evaluators acting as advocates? In what ways or circumstances might it be appropriate for an evaluator to act as an advocate? Under what circumstances would it not?

Application Exercises

1. What do you see as the critical points in the history of evaluation? How did they shape how people in your field view evaluation? How they approach an evaluation study?

2. What is your view on the role of advocacy in evaluation? Should an evaluator "advocate" for something? If so, what?

3. How has performance measurement or standards-based education influenced work in your school or organization? Are these "evaluation measures" useful for your organization? For consumers? Why or why not?

4. How has technology influenced the collection and storage of data in your organization?

Suggested Readings

Chelimsky, E., & Shadish, W. R. (Eds.). (1997). *Evaluation for the 21st century: A resource book.* Thousand Oaks, CA: Sage.

Madaus, G. F., & Stufflebeam, D. L. (2000). Program evaluation: A historical overview. In D. L. Stufflebeam, G. F. Madaus, & T. Kellaghan (Eds.), *Evaluation models: Viewpoints on educational and human services evaluation.* Boston: Kluwer-Nijhoff.

Mark, M. (Ed.). (2002). *American Journal of Evaluation, 22* (3). This issue contains twenty-three articles by leaders in the evaluation field on the past, present, and future of evaluation. It is a follow-up to the 1994 issue of *Evaluation Practice, 15*(3), edited by M. Smith, in which different contributors considered the past, present, and future of evaluation.

Part II

Alternative Approaches to Program Evaluation

In Part One we referred to varying roles evaluation studies can play in education, government, business, nonprofit agencies, and many related areas, and readers were introduced to some distinctions related to the concept of evaluation. We hinted at differences that exist among some major schools of evaluation thought, but we have not yet exposed the reader to the range and variety of alternative conceptions of what evaluation is and how it should be carried out. Doing so is the purpose of the next seven chapters.

In Part Two we introduce the reader to the wealth of thought and writing that has taken place in evaluation in recent decades. In Chapter 3 we address the diversity of evaluation approaches and examine factors that have contributed to such differing views. Prior efforts to classify the many evaluation approaches into fewer categories are also discussed, along with presentation of the categories that we use throughout the remainder of this book.

In Chapters 4 through 8 we briefly summarize five general approaches to evaluation, one per chapter. These general approaches include those we see as most prevalent in the literature and most popular in use. Within each chapter, we briefly summarize previous thinking and writing pertaining to that approach, discuss how that approach has been used, and examine its strengths and weaknesses. Space does not permit exhaustive coverage of any particular evaluation model or conception; the chapters are necessarily too brief to provide the detail about any particular author's view of evaluation that would have been possible had we been willing to limit coverage to the thoughts of only a few evaluation theorists. We have preferred to cover a broader array of evaluation approaches in less depth, providing in each chapter references to which interested individuals may turn for a more in-depth discussion of any particular evaluation model.

We have attempted to include both the "old" and "new" approaches proposed for use in conducting program evaluation studies. Some readers will not find their preferred approach featured in our treatment of alternatives, and others may be distressed that we have included approaches they think we should have omitted. We have tried to concentrate on the most commonly used approaches to program evaluation.

In Chapter 9 the characteristics and contributions of the five general alternative approaches we have described are compared, along with cautions concerning strict adherence to any one approach and a plea for thoughtful, eclectic use of alternatives, especially when such an approach would strengthen evaluations more than adherence to a single view would.

Before examining the various alternative approaches to program evaluation, we need to define two terms. We have so far referred to *program* and *stakeholders* in contexts that we trust have given readers a general sense of what they mean. These terms are so pivotal to the remaining content in this book, however, that we need to define and comment on both here.

Stakeholders are various individuals and groups who have a direct interest in and may be affected by the program being evaluated or the evaluation's results. They hold a stake in the future direction of that program and deserve to play a role in determining that direction by (1) identifying concerns and issues to be addressed in evaluating the program, and (2) selecting the criteria that will be used in judging its value. As Reineke (1991) has wisely reminded us, evaluators need to identify stakeholders for an evaluation and involve them early, actively, and continuously.

Program is a term that can be defined in many ways. In its simplest sense, a program is a "standing arrangement that provides for a . . . service" (Cronbach, et al., 1980, p. 14). The Joint Committee on Standards for Educational Evaluation (1994) has defined *program* simply as "activities that are provided on a continuing basis" (p. 3). More broadly, it is a complex of people, organization, management, and resources that collectively make up a continuing endeavor to reach some particular educational, social, or commercial goal. Alternately, it might be defined as an ongoing, planned intervention that seeks to achieve some particular outcome(s), in response to some perceived educational, social, or commercial problem.

In their discussion of social programming theory, Shadish, Cook, and Leviton (1991) identified three components: (1) internal program structure, (2) external forces that shape programs, and (3) understanding how programs change to enhance societal goals. They see the internal structure of a program as the pattern in which "staff, clients, resources, outcomes, administration, internal budget allocations, social norms, facilities, and internal organization" are combined so as to relate "inputs to activities to outputs" (pp. 37–38). External forces could be local economic capacity, external funding agencies, prevailing political sentiments, pressures from powerful stakeholder groups, social mores, logistic or geographical constraints, and the like. Evaluators must understand how programs change—with or without evaluation—and how evaluation information can make those changes more functional and effective. "Programs can change by introducing incremental improvements in small practices, by adopting or adapting demonstration projects that are more effective than existing ones, and by radical shifts in values and priorities" (Shadish, et al., 1991, pp. 38–39).

Examples of educational programs would include Junior Achievement, Inc.'s elementary school economics program, a state's adult education program, a school district's year-round education program, or an elementary school's staggered reading schedule program.

Examples of programs in other sectors might include the U.S. Federal Aviation Association's program for certifying air traffic controllers, a state program for licensing and training local day-care centers, a community program aimed at reducing vandalism, or a county health center program to increase immunization of children against communicable diseases.

Examples of programs in business and industry would include Price-Waterhouse's national orientation and training program for first-year auditors; Texaco's Environmental Protection Program, aimed at preventing oil spills; Utah Power and Light Company's energy conservation program; or Jostens Learning Corporation's Vanguard program (an integrated, computer-based learning program for elementary schools). Any business or industry might run smaller, non-titled programs such as an employee orientation program, a training program for supervisors on performance appraisal, a new purchasing strategy, an in-house child care center, flextime, or job sharing.

In the nonprofit sector, examples of programs would include the W. K. Kellogg Foundation's national initiative to support land-grant universities in reconceptualizing the training of food systems professionals, the Knight Foundation's Fellowships and Training for Future Journalists of the Pacific Islands, or the Warren Buffett Foundation's program to prevent nuclear proliferation. Other foundations may have an interest in operating a program for preventing alcohol and drug abuse, or a program for increasing employee use of alternative means of transportation. However, nonprofits include many types of organizations other than foundations. Today, many services that were once delivered by public organizations are contracted out to nonprofit organizations. Such programs include shelters for homeless adolescents, parent training programs, substance abuse treatment programs, or health education programs such as those delivered by the American Cancer Society. They also include programs provided by United Way funded agencies.

These examples of programs are relatively easy to define and describe for they are relatively self-contained and have identifiable boundaries, goals, administrators and staff, and budgets. But programs are not always quite that simple. Some are complex, interrelated, and multilevel, and it is decidedly more difficult to evaluate those not-so-simple programs. For example, an evaluation of a specific program often must probe beyond the boundaries of that program to examine the broader context of neighboring programs or antecedent and concurrent conditions that may affect it. Consider the evaluation of a local Early Head Start program. That program may have multiple components within it (e.g., advertising and awareness campaigns to enroll parents and their children; parent education; activities for youngsters; referrals to other services; and literacy or English programs for parents). If so, the evaluator already may be evaluating more than one "miniprogram" as he pulls the evaluation findings for these components together into one integrated evaluation report. But the evaluation of the entire effort of Early Head Start to prepare infants and toddlers for learning is nested within the broader context of dozens of other programs offered in the community for families with children at risk.

3

Alternative Views
of Evaluation

Orienting Questions

1. Why are there so many different approaches to evaluation?
2. How would objectivists and subjectivists differ in their approach to evaluation?
3. Why is evaluation theory, as reflected in different approaches to evaluation, important to learn?
4. Do you believe it is useful to champion quantitative evaluation methods over qualitative evaluation methods or vice versa? Why or why not?
5. What practical issues contribute to the diversity of evaluation approaches?

In the early days, when evaluation was emerging as a field, it was troubled by definitional and ideological disputes. Those who wrote about evaluation differed widely in their views of what evaluation was, and those who conducted evaluation studies brought to the task diverse conceptions of how one should go about doing it. During the 1960–1990 era, nearly sixty different proposals for how evaluations should be conducted were developed and circulated. These proposals have been chronicled from the early days of thinking about evaluation approaches (Gephart, 1978) to more recent reviews of the development of evaluation models (Stufflebeam, 2001b). These different prescriptions have been implemented with varying degrees of fidelity. To complicate the picture further, some evaluations were designed without conscious reference to any existing conceptual framework, thereby resulting, if successful, in yet another evaluation approach.

This proliferation of evaluation models posed a perplexing dilemma for practitioners who were puzzled about which is best for their purposes. Each proposed approach came with its built-in assumptions about evaluation—what it is, and how it should be done. Each emphasized different aspects of evaluation, depending on the priorities and preferences of its author. Few came with careful step-by-step instructions that practitioners could follow, and even fewer were useful in settings and circumstances beyond those in which they were created. In short, few of evaluation's proposed prescriptions were easy for practitioners to follow.

The various approaches proposed by evaluators are the content of the field of evaluation. Today, although no singular description of evaluation can be drawn from that content, there is much more agreement than before.

Certain approaches to evaluation have emerged as the most commonly used and they are described in Chapters 4 through 9 herein. These approaches provide the conceptual tools for the evaluator to use in designing an evaluation that fits particular circumstances.

Diverse Conceptions of Program Evaluation

The many evaluation approaches that have emerged since 1965 range from comprehensive prescriptions to checklists of suggestions. These approaches have greatly influenced present practices. Some authors opt for a systems approach, while others view evaluation as a process of identifying and collecting information to assist decision makers. Others view evaluation as synonymous with professional judgment, where judgments about a program's quality are based on opinions of experts (whether or not the data and criteria used in reaching those judgments are clear). In one school of thought, evaluation is viewed as the process of comparing performance data with clearly specified objectives, while in another, evaluation is seen as synonymous with carefully controlled experimental research on programs. Others focus on the importance of naturalistic inquiry or urge that value pluralism be recognized, accommodated, and preserved and that those individuals involved with the entity being evaluated play the prime role in determining what direction the evaluation study takes. Some writers propose that evaluations be structured in keeping with legal or forensic paradigms so that planned opposition—both pro and con—is built in. And this barely dents the list of current alternatives.

The various models are built on differing—often conflicting—conceptions and definitions of evaluation, with the result that practitioners are led in very different directions, depending on which model they follow. Let us consider an example from education.

- If one viewed evaluation as essentially synonymous with professional judgment, the worth of a curriculum would be assessed by experts (as judged by the evaluation client) who observed the curriculum in action, examined the curriculum materials, or in some other way gleaned sufficient information to record their considered judgments.

- If evaluation is viewed as a comparison between student performance indicators and objectives, standards would be established for the curriculum and relevant student behaviors would be measured against this yardstick, using either standardized or evaluator-constructed instruments. (Note that, in this conception, there is no built-in assessment of the worth of the objectives themselves.)

- Using a decision-oriented approach, the evaluator, working closely with the decision maker, would collect sufficient information about the relative advantages and disadvantages of each decision alternative to judge which was best. However, although the decision maker would judge the worth of each alternative, evaluation per se would be a shared role.

- If one accepted our earlier definition of evaluation (see Chapter 1), the curriculum evaluator would first identify the curriculum goals and then, using input from appropriate reference groups, determine whether the goals were good for the students, parents, and community being served. He would then collect evaluative information relevant to those goals as well as to identifiable side effects resulting from the curriculum. When the data were analyzed and interpreted, the evaluator would judge the worth of the curriculum and (usually) make a recommendation to the individual or group responsible for final decisions.

Obviously, the way in which one views evaluation has a direct impact on the type of evaluation activities conducted, whether the evaluation is of a curriculum, a corporate training program, or a state program for aiding displaced homemakers.

Origins of Alternative Views of Evaluation

The diversity of evaluation approaches described in this section has arisen from the varied backgrounds and worldviews of their authors, which have resulted in diverse philosophical orientations, methodological predilections, and practical preferences. These different predispositions have led the authors of the various evaluation approaches—and their adherents—to propose widely different designs, data-collection and analysis methods, and interpretive techniques. Thus, the differences in evaluation approaches can be traced directly to their proponents' rather different views of the nature of evaluation.

Baker and Niemi (1996) proposed four disparate sources from which much of the thinking about evaluation has been drawn: (1) experimentation, (2) measurement, (3) systems analysis, and (4) interpretative approaches. These authors see experimentation as the use in evaluation of the social science experimental research tradition, complete with randomization, careful attention to units of analysis, and statistical tests. Measurement is described as the style of evaluation that presumes that use of a behavioral measurement device will yield numerical scores that provide evidence of a program's effectiveness. Systems analysis is proposed as examination of the interrelationships between broad sets of variables in complex processes or organizations, conducted to help managers make more defensible decisions. Interpretative approaches are uses of hermeneutic philosophy and interpretive theories of knowledge in generating holistic descriptive interpretations and judgments of complex programs.

While we concur that each of these four sources has influenced the evaluation literature, they obviously are not all on the same dimension. Experimentation and "interpretative approaches" are really alternate methodologies for collecting and interpreting empirical data. Measurement is simply one process of recording observations of some entity and translating them into simple descriptions of that entity. Systems analysis is an organizational strategy for collecting and using empirical information to improve decision making in the organization. We believe that a more fruitful way to understand the origins of alternative conceptualizations of evaluation is to examine differences in their authors' (and adherents') philosophical and ideological beliefs, methodological preferences, and practical choices stemming from prior experience. Collectively, these three dimensions encompass most of what we see as the important factors that have contributed to the different schools of evaluation thought.

Philosophical and Ideological Differences

There is no univocal philosophy of evaluation, any more than there is a single, universally accepted philosophy of science. Perhaps that lack has not hurt us too much; after all, evaluation seems to be doing reasonably well without one. The lack of a guiding philosophy has not prevented extensive discourse and debate concerning philosophical assumptions about epistemology and value. Indeed, different approaches to establishing worth or merit are largely responsible for the diversity of views about program evaluation.

Objectivist and Subjectivist Epistemology.

House (1980, 1983a, 1983b) has written thoughtfully about different philosophies of knowing (**epistemology**) and how they affect one's choosing an approach to evaluation. He has grouped evaluation approaches into two categories: *objectivism* and *subjectivism*.

Objectivism requires that evaluation information be "scientifically objective," that is, that it use data-collection and analysis techniques that yield results reproducible and verifiable by other reasonable and competent persons using the same techniques. In this sense, the evaluation procedures are "externalized," existing outside of the evaluator in a clearly explicated form that is replicable by others and that will produce similar results from one evaluation to the next. Objectivism is derived largely from the social science tradition of empiricism.

Subjectivism bases its validity claims on "an appeal to experience rather than to scientific method. Knowledge is conceived as being largely tacit rather than explicit" (House, 1980, p. 252). The validity of a subjectivist evaluation depends on the relevance of the evaluator's background and qualifications and the keenness of his perceptions. In this sense, the evaluation procedures are "internalized," existing largely within the evaluator in ways that are not explicitly understood or reproducible by others.

Objectivism held sway in the social sciences and in educational inquiry for decades, at least until the 1980s. There have been, however, many criticisms of objectivist epistemology, as well as the dominance of **logical positivism** in social and educational science. Campbell (1984) noted that "twenty years ago logical positivism dominated the philosophy of science. . . . Today the tide has completely turned among the theorists of science in philosophy, sociology, and elsewhere. Logical positivism is almost universally rejected" (p. 27). Scriven (1984) argued that any lingering positivist bias in evaluation should be eliminated. Bailey (1992) argued that traditional positivist methods should not be the preferred approach to studying public-sector programs. Guba and Lincoln (1981) challenged the "infallibility" of the hypothetico-deductive inquiry paradigm because of its limitations in dealing with complex, interactive phenomena in dynamic, septic, real-world settings. Although less sweeping and conclusive in his critique, House (1980) portrayed objectivism as inattentive to its own credibility, presuming validity because of its methodology, and therefore credible only to those who value such a methodology. He also noted that objectivism conceals hidden values and biases of which its adherents are unaware, because even the choice of data-collection techniques and instruments is not value-neutral, an assumption seemingly taken for granted by objectivist evaluators.

To counter the objectivist hold on the methodologies of evaluation, criticisms of objectivism have been extreme. Yet subjectivism has been no less soundly criticized, especially by those who see its procedures as "unscientific" and therefore of dubious worth. Critics (e.g., Boruch & Cordray, 1980) point out that subjectivist evaluation often leads to varying, sometimes contradictory, conclusions that defy reconciliation because that which led to the conclusions is largely obscured within the nonreplicable procedures of the evaluator. Similarly, as House (1980) put it,

> Critics of the phenomenologist epistemology note that there is often confusion over whose common sense perceptions are to be taken as the basis for understanding. Furthermore, if one takes everyday understanding as the foundation of inquiry, does one not merely reconstruct whatever ideologies, biases, and false beliefs already exist? How can one distinguish causal determinants and regularities, the strength of the positivist epistemology, from perceived beliefs? How can one evaluate conflicting interpretations? Phenomenology provides no way of doing so (p. 254).

And so the dialogue continues. The objectivists depend upon replicable facts as their touchstone of truth, whereas subjectivists depend upon accumulated experience as their way to understanding. Although both epistemologies carry within them "tests" that must be met if their application is to be viewed as trustworthy, they lead to very different evaluation designs and methods, giving rise to much of today's diversity in evaluation approaches.

Utilitarian versus Intuitionist–Pluralist Evaluation.   House (1976, 1983a) has also made a distinction closely related to that of objectivism and subjectivism, namely, **utilitarian** versus **intuitionist–pluralist evaluation.** Although this is a distinction concerning principles for assigning values, not epistemology, utilitarian and intuitionist–pluralist evaluation approaches parallel the objectivist and subjectivist epistemologies outlined above.

Utilitarian approaches determine value by assessing the *overall* impact of a program on those affected. These approaches have tended to follow objectivist epistemology. In his classic treatise on "justice in evaluation," House (1976) suggested that utilitarian evaluation accepts the value premise that the greatest good is that which will benefit the greatest number of individuals. Thus, "properly speaking, utilitarianism refers to the idea of maximizing happiness in society" (House, 1983a, p. 49). A single, explicitly defined ethical principle is operative. As a result, the evaluator will focus on total group gains by using average outcome scores (e.g., test scores, number of days absent from work) or some other common index of "good" to identify the "greatest good for the greatest number." The best programs are those that produce the greatest gains on the criterion or criteria selected to determine worth. Group averages on statewide assessment programs and large-scale comparative evaluations of welfare systems are utilitarian in nature. Most utilitarian evaluation approaches lend themselves to use by governments or others who mandate and/or sponsor evaluation studies for which managers and public program administrators are the major audiences.

At the opposite end of the continuum are **intuitionist–pluralist** approaches to evaluation, which are based on the idea that value depends on the impact of the program on *each* individual. These approaches have tended to follow subjectivist epistemology. Here the value position is that the greatest good requires attention to each individual's benefit. Thus,

> The ethical principles are [neither] single in number nor explicitly defined as in utilitarian ethics. There are several principles derived from intuition and experience, but no set rules for weighting them. This captures another meaning of ethical subjectivism—that the ultimate criterion of what is good and right are individual feelings or apprehensions (House, 1983a, p. 50).

This leads to a focus on the distribution of gains by individuals and subgroups (e.g., ethnic groupings). There can be no common index of "good" but rather a plurality of criteria and judges, and the evaluator is no longer an impartial "averager" but a portrayer of different values and needs. Data may include test scores, hours of training received, changes in income, or recidivism levels, but intuitionist–pluralist evaluators often prefer data from personal interviews and testimonials of program participants. Weighing and balancing the many judgments and criteria inherent in this approach is largely intuitive, and there are no algorithms to help reduce complex evaluative information to any unequivocal recommendation. The perceived merit or worth of the program depends largely on the values and perspectives of whoever is judging, and each individual or constituent group is a legitimate judge. "Likewise, the subjective utility of something is based on personal judgment and personal desires. Each person is the best judge of events for himself" (House, 1983a, p. 56). Within limits of feasibility, most intuitionist–pluralist evaluations try to involve as "judges" all individuals and groups who are affected by the program being evaluated rather than leave decisions and judgments to governmental sponsors and high-level administrators.

The Impact of Philosophical Differences.   Historically, evaluators tended to line up along the several continua described above or, worse, become polarized in "either–or" dichotomies. This debate over epistemology was, in prior decades, a major cause of rifts that permeated the field of evaluation. What one considered acceptable program evaluation often depended on the position one took along one of these philosophical dimensions. Yet, although differences in philosophy have led to alternative views of evaluation, the philosophical differences are not incompatible; for thoughtful contemporary evaluators polarization has given way to integration of perspectives. Multiple approaches to describing objects of study, drawn from both objectivist and subjectivist traditions, have been used in the same evaluations to achieve important goals (e.g., Chelimsky, 1994).

We recognize the right, if not the wisdom, of any evaluator to subscribe totally to the assumptions and premises of one particular ideology. Yet few evaluators who succeed in a wide range of evaluation settings can afford to consider philosophical ideologies as "either–or" decisions. The purist view that looks noble in print yields to practical pressures demanding that the evaluator use appropriate methods based on an epistemology that is right *for that evaluation,* or even multiple methods based on alternative epistemologies within the same evaluations.[1] There are few philosophical purists among today's evaluation practitioners. It is important to know, however, the assumptions and limitations of methods that are drawn from different worldviews about evaluation.

Methodological Backgrounds and Preferences

Different philosophical assumptions about knowledge and value give rise naturally to different evaluation methods. Indeed, evaluation philosophy and methodology are so closely intertwined that we might well have discussed both together in the previous section. But we believe it is useful to examine separately two methodological topics associated with the conduct of evaluation studies: (1) the use of **quantitative** and **qualitative** data, and (2) the need for evaluators to work across disciplinary and methodological boundaries.

Quantitative and Qualitative Evaluation.   Much has been said in recent years about the use of quantitative and qualitative data in evaluation as evaluators have learned to sort out the relative utility of both in their evaluations. Before we can

---

[1]More will be said about such multiple methods in later chapters of this book.

address this topic adequately, we must delineate (as clearly as we can in a short space) the differences between qualitative and quantitative data collection methods. Several authors have provided useful distinctions between the two (e.g., Hedrick, 1994; House, 1994b; Schofield & Anderson, 1984).

We reject references to qualitative or quantitative *paradigms,* reserving those adjectives to differentiate between two types of data (and the methods used to collect them). Qualitative data are nonnumerical. They take the form of narrative, verbal descriptions; quantitative data are numerical, and statistics are often used to summarize such data. Both are important in most evaluations.

The past two decades have seen a spectacular increase in the use and acceptability of qualitative techniques in program evaluation. The rapidity with which qualitative techniques have gained favor is apparent in the fact that, by 1992, the American Evaluation Association's topical interest group on qualitative methods had burgeoned to about 550 members, while its quantitative topical interest group remained at about 150 members (Sechrest, 1992). Where the evaluator's preferred tools were once quasi-experimental designs, operational definitions of key variables, objective measurement techniques, and statistical analyses, most contemporary evaluators would feel poorly armed if their toolboxes lacked the means for them to provide careful, thorough, narrative description, portray process, glean people's perceptions through interviews, and construct meaning from those individual or collective perceptions.

Disciplinary Boundaries and Evaluation Methodology.   It is ironic that in a field with such a rich array of alternative evaluation approaches, there still exists a tendency to fall prey to the "law of the instrument" fallacy[2] rather than adapt or develop evaluation methods to meet our needs. Our grasp of evaluation still seems partial and parochial, as may be expected in a young field. But it is unfortunate that we seem to carry with us into a new field the disciplinary allegiances we developed through earlier studies. Too often we fail to encourage methodological flexibility, unthinkingly adopting a single-minded perspective that can answer only questions stemming from that perspective discipline. Today's typical evaluation studies depend largely on methodology adapted from agronomy and anthropology, some facets of psychology, sociology, philosophy, and mathematics, and, to a limited extent, economics and history. These are disciplines with methodologies well suited to the pursuit of evaluative questions. Evaluation is not a traditional discipline but a transdicipline that necessarily cuts across disciplines (Scriven, 1991c), and evaluators must avoid the luxury of remaining within any single discipline-based inquiry paradigm.

Evaluators' predispositions and preferences on both philosophical and methodological dimensions lead to differing designs, data collection and analysis

---

[2]Kaplan (1964) described this fallacy by noting that, if you give a small boy a hammer, suddenly everything he encounters needs hammering. The same tendency is true, he asserts, for scientists who gain familiarity and comfort in using a particular method or technique; suddenly all problems will be wrested into a form so that they can be addressed in that fashion, whether or not it is appropriate.

methods, and interpretive techniques. Thus, the increasing variety of methodological perspectives gaining legitimacy in program evaluation is not only increasing the variety of ways evaluations are designed and conducted but also adding richness of perspective to a field that is still developing.

Different Metaphors of Evaluation

The importance of metaphors in evaluation has become increasingly clear during the past few decades.[3] Worthen (1978) described an early federally supported research effort to identify metaphors from various disciplines that might be adapted into useful new evaluation methodologies:

> If I may use a metaphor, we have proposed a planned expedition into other fields to find and capture those methods and techniques that might have relevance for evaluation and domesticate them so they will become tractable for our use. Again, limited resources will allow us to explore only so far, so we need to identify early those areas which appear most likely to contain good methodological candidates for domestication (p. 3).

Continued under the direction of Smith (1981), this research effort examined the possibility of using a variety of metaphors, such as investigative journalism, photography, storytelling, philosophical analysis, and literary criticism, to mention only a few. Although several of these metaphors have proven of limited use for evaluation, others have yielded many useful new methods and techniques for program evaluators.

One need not consciously seek metaphors; they already underlie and influence much of our thinking. Indeed, one reason for differing evaluation approaches is the different evaluation metaphors held by writers and practitioners. House (1983b) has demonstrated that much of our everyday thinking is metaphorical in nature and extends that point to argue that evaluation thought is also largely metaphorical. Further, he suggests that conflicts between existing evaluation schemes stem from differences in the underlying metaphors held by proponents of those schemes. For example, metaphoric conceptions of many social programs equate those programs with industrial production (leading to metaphors based on machines, assembly lines, or pipelines) or with sports contests or games (leading to metaphors of targets and goals).

The influence of such metaphors on evaluation is obvious. For example, one who perceives evaluation as retrospective backtracking of a program to discover the causes of its outcomes is likely to use an approach that resembles forensic pathology, whereas one who holds a connoisseurial metaphor of evaluation will

---

[3]A metaphor is a figure of speech in which the meaning of a term or phrase is transferred from the object it ordinarily designates to another object so as to provide new insight or perspective on the latter. For example, a researcher interested in how rumors spread might use epidemiology, the theory of how diseases spread, as a metaphor. This theory would suggest that the researcher look for carriers of rumor, that rumors spread from epicenters in regional clusters, and so on.

use an approach more akin to literary criticism. Those who see evaluation's role as helping public agencies respond to the constantly changing needs of its constituents and the broader citizenry will likely invoke metaphors of the opinion pollster in their approach. Those who see evaluation as the instrument for bureaucratic program monitoring will likely depend primarily on auditing as their operative metaphor. Yes, different metaphors account for much of the variation in evaluation approaches.

Responding to Different Needs

In proposing new evaluation approaches, evaluation theorists have not only been influenced by their different methodological and metaphorical preferences or their different ways of looking at knowledge and how it is achieved. They have also been responding to different needs that they perceived, needs such as corporate executives wanting better information for decision making in a profit-making environment, educators wanting a systematic way to determine which charter schools to establish, United Way personnel struggling for a better way to identify the top priority health and human service needs in their county, federal and state legislators monitoring resource allocations, and local stakeholders hoping to identify ways to make their towns and cities more livable. Each of these audiences works in a different environmental context, struggling with different types of economic and budgetary concerns, client needs, stakeholder interests, employee and management expectations, and so on. The evaluator must learn about each context and adapt the evaluation to it to be successful in meeting the needs of each audience.

Various evaluation approaches were developed to address different needs. In the aggregate, these different approaches help us comprehend the wide range of needs for program evaluation. We must learn to identify what is useful in each approach when faced with a specific evaluation need, to use it wisely, and not to be distracted by irrelevant evaluation approaches constructed to deal with a different need.

Practical Considerations

We have traced how epistemological issues, methodological preferences, metaphoric views of evaluation, and different needs all contribute to the diversity of alternative evaluation approaches. Several practical issues also contribute to this diversity.

First, evaluators disagree about whether the intent of evaluation is to render a value judgment. Some are concerned only with the usefulness of the evaluation to decision makers and believe that they, not the evaluator, should render the value judgment. Others believe the evaluator's report to the decision maker is complete only if it contains a value judgment. Such differences in views have obvious practical implications.

Second, evaluators differ in their general view of the political roles of evaluation. We discuss political aspects of evaluation in greater detail in Chapter 17.

Who has the authority and responsibility in evaluation? If the role of the evaluator is seen as tutor, mentor, and facilitator, the evaluation plan will be very different from studies in which the evaluator is seen as the evaluation director, manager, and CEO. Suffice it here to say that evaluators' views of their role affects greatly the style of evaluation conducted.

Third, evaluators are influenced by their prior experience. Each evaluator draws from certain strengths, from experience with certain types of problems and processes, and from a way of looking at things that grew out of his professional education and career. Each view is limited in perspective by the evaluator's prior experience.

Fourth, evaluators differ in their views about who should conduct the evaluation and the nature of the expertise that the evaluator must possess. Although this topic is too complex to be treated adequately in this chapter, an illustration might help. Considering one dimension of expertise—substantive knowledge about the content of that which is evaluated (e.g., knowledge of mathematics in evaluating a mathematics education program)—some evaluators (e.g., Eisner, 1975) see such expertise as the sine qua non of evaluation. Indeed, without such expertise, their evaluation approach would be futile. Other evaluators (e.g., Worthen & Sanders, 1984) not only question the need for the evaluator to possess such expertise but also suggest that there are advantages in selecting evaluators who are not specialists in the content of that which they evaluate. Such differences in perspective lead to different approaches to both the program and the evaluation.

Finally, evaluators differ even in their perception of whether it is desirable to have a wide variety of approaches to evaluation. Earlier, Gephart (1978) lamented the proliferation of evaluation models and urged that an effort be made to synthesize existing models. Conversely, Raizen and Rossi (1981) argued that the goal of attaining uniformity in evaluation methods and measures cannot be attained without prematurely inhibiting needed development in the field of evaluation. We agree with this latter view, believing that efforts to synthesize existing evaluation models would be dysfunctional (an argument that will be discussed later in Chapter 9). Regardless of which view you subscribe to, it is clear that either the inability to generate an idealistic evaluation model (after all, none has been forthcoming since the call for synthesis two decades ago) or resistance to trading the diversity of models for a unified view accounts, at least in part, for the continued variety of approaches that confronts the evaluation practitioner.

Themes among the Variations

Those who have published classification schemata are too numerous to list here, but examples include Guba and Lincoln (1981); House (1983a); Madaus, Scriven, and Stufflebeam (1983); Popham (1975); Scriven (1993); Shadish et al. (1991); Stake (1975b); Stufflebeam (2001b); Stufflebeam, Madaus, and Kellaghan (2000); and Worthen and Sanders (1973, 1987). All have influenced our thinking about the categorization of evaluation approaches, but we have drawn especially on our own work and that of House in developing the schema proposed below.

A Classification Schema for Evaluation Approaches

We have chosen to classify many different approaches to evaluation into the five categories described below.

1. *Objectives-oriented approaches,* in which the focus is on specifying goals and objectives and determining the extent to which they have been attained
2. *Management-oriented approaches,* in which the central concern is on identifying and meeting the informational needs of managerial decision makers
3. *Consumer-oriented approaches,* in which the central issue is developing evaluative information on "products," broadly defined, and accountability, for use by consumers in choosing among competing products, services, and the like
4. *Expertise-oriented approaches,* which depend primarily on the direct application of professional expertise to judge the quality of whatever endeavor is evaluated
5. *Participant-oriented approaches,* in which involvement of participants (stakeholders in that which is evaluated) are central in determining the values, criteria, needs, data, and conclusions for the evaluation

These five categories seem to us to fall (though not evenly) along House's (1983a) dimension of utilitarian to intuitionist–pluralist evaluation, as shown in Figure 3.1.

Placement of individual evaluation approaches within these five categories is to some degree arbitrary. Several approaches are multifaceted and include characteristics that would allow them to be placed in more than one category; for clarity we have decided to place such approaches in one category and only reference in other chapters, where appropriate, their other features. Our classification is based on what we see as the driving force behind doing the evaluation: the major questions to be addressed and/or the major organizer(s) that underlie each ap-

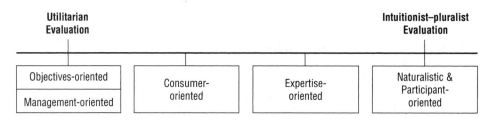

FIGURE 3.1 *Distribution of Five Evaluation Approaches on the Dimension of Utilitarian to Intuitionist-Pluralist Evaluation*

proach (e.g., objectives or management decisions, increasing the participation or power of stakeholders). Within each category, the approaches vary by level of formality and structure, some being relatively well developed philosophically and procedurally, others less developed. It should be noted that these frameworks deal with conceptual approaches to evaluation, not techniques; discussion of the many techniques that might be used in program evaluations is reserved for Parts Three and Four of this book. Also, we have not attempted to include, in any chapter, all of the proposed evaluation models that could fit there, for doing so would balloon this book by hundreds of more pages. Rather, we have selected for each chapter only an example or two of what we see as the most typical or influential example of that evaluation approach.

Major Concepts and Theories

1. The definition of program evaluation takes many forms depending on how one views evaluation, which in turn influences the types of evaluation activities conducted.

2. The methodologies and models an evaluator might employ in an evaluation depend in large part on the metaphors the evaluator uses to understand the program under evaluation and the needs of the program stakeholders.

Discussion Questions _____

1. Why is it important to understand the philosophical differences of evaluation team members? How could these differences impact an evaluation positively? Negatively?

2. How can the way in which one defines program evaluation impact an evaluation study? What would you do if all your evaluation team members had different definitions of program evaluation?

3. What implications does the statement "evaluation is not a traditional discipline but a transdiscipline" have for the methodologies an evaluator may decide to use in an evaluation?

Application Exercises _____

1. Think about how you could approach evaluation. Describe the steps you think you would follow. Then, analyze your approach according to your philosophical and methodological preferences. Explain how your background and what you would be evaluating could have affected your approach. Describe other things that might have affected your approach to evaluation.

2. Identify a program in your area that you would like to see evaluated. List some qualitative evaluation methods that could be used. Now list some quantitative methods that you see as appropriate. Discuss whether it would be appropriate to combine both methods within the same study, including reasons for your conclusion.

3. The Xerox Corporation has recently begun a new employee training program in which employees must undergo three consecutive weeks of instruction on the company mission statement, policies and procedures, political and cultural systems, and use of new technology. From the intuitionist–pluralist position, what questions would you ask if you were to conduct an evaluation of this training program? What types of data would you collect? How might this evaluation be conducted differently if you held a utilitarian perspective?

4. Think for a moment about your own educational and professional background and your philosophical and methodological preferences. Imagine you have been asked to conduct an evaluation of a confidence-building program for elementary students. This program begins with students identifying what their strengths and weaknesses are from their perspective and the perspectives of friends, teachers, and parents. Then, students are asked to describe activities they like and dislike and set immediate and long-term goals for themselves. Given your background and preferences and the information provided on this program, provide a brief synopsis on each of the following questions: Which evaluation model would you employ? What specific questions would you be interested in asking? Would you focus more on the individual or on the group?

5. Evaluate an evaluation you are currently working on, developing, or have worked on in the past on the types of data collected or to be collected for the evaluation. Were strictly quantitative methods, qualitative methods, or a combination of quantitative and qualitative methods used in the evaluation? Why were the specific methods selected?

Suggested Readings _____

House, E. R. (1983). Assumptions underlying evaluation models. In G. F. Madaus, M. Scriven, & D. L. Stufflebeam (Eds.), *Evaluation models: Viewpoints on educational and human services evaluation.* Boston: Kluwer.

Lincoln, Y. S. (1994). Tracks toward a postmodern politics of evaluation. *Evaluation Practice, 15*(3), 299–309.

Mark, M. M., & Shotland, R. L. (Eds.) (1987). *Multiple methods in program evaluation.* New Directions for Program Evaluation, No. 35. San Francisco: Jossey-Bass.

Reichardt, C. S., & Rallis, S. F. (Eds.). (1994). *The qualitative-quantitative debate: New perspectives.* New Directions for Program Evaluation, No. 61. San Francisco: Jossey-Bass.

Sechrest, L., & Figueredo, A. J. (1993). Program evaluation. *Annual Review of Psychology, 44,* 645–674.

Stufflebeam, D. L. (2001). *Evaluation models.* New Directions for Evaluation, No. 89. San Francisco: Jossey-Bass.

Stufflebeam, D. L., Madaus, G. F., & Kellaghan, T. (Eds.). (2000). *Evaluation models: Viewpoints on educational and human services evaluation* (2nd ed.). Boston: Kluwer.

4

Objectives-Oriented Evaluation Approaches

Orienting Questions

1. What aspects of Tyler's approach to evaluation have permeated all later objectives-oriented evaluation approaches?

2. In what forms has the objectives-oriented evaluation approach been used in education? In health and human services? In business settings?

3. What are some major strengths and limitations of objectives-oriented evaluation approaches?

4. What is "goal-free evaluation"? Does it have a useful role to play in program evaluation?

The distinguishing feature of an objectives-oriented evaluation approach is that the purposes of some activity are specified, and then evaluation focuses on the extent to which those purposes are achieved. In education the activity could be as short as a one-day classroom lesson or as complex as the whole schooling enterprise. In health and human services it is often a service or intervention. In business, it again could be as simple as a one-day meeting or as complex as a corporation's five-year strategic plan. The information gained from an objectives-oriented evaluation could be used to reformulate the purposes of the activity, the activity itself, or the assessment procedures and devices used to determine the achievement of purposes.

Developers of the Objectives-Oriented Evaluation Approach and Their Contributions

Many people have contributed to the evolution and refinement of the objectives-oriented approach to evaluation since its inception in the 1930s, but the individual credited with conceptualizing and popularizing it in education is Ralph W. Tyler (1942, 1950), for whom this approach has been named.

The Tylerian Evaluation Approach

Tyler's approach to evaluation was developed and used during the Eight Year Study of the late 1930s (Smith & Tyler, 1942). Travers (1983) did note, however, that an earlier work, Waples and Tyler's *Research Methods and Teacher Problems* (1930), set the stage for Tyler's later achievements in evaluation.

Tyler conceived of evaluation as the process of determining the extent to which the objectives of a program are actually being attained. His approach to evaluation followed these steps:

1. Establish broad goals or objectives.
2. Classify the goals or objectives.
3. Define objectives in behavioral terms.
4. Find situations in which achievement of objectives can be shown.
5. Develop or select measurement techniques.
6. Collect performance data.
7. Compare performance data with behaviorally stated objectives.

Discrepancies between performance and objectives would lead to modifications intended to correct the deficiency, and the evaluation cycle would be repeated.

Tyler's rationale was logical, scientifically acceptable, readily adoptable by evaluators (most of whose methodological upbringing was very compatible with the pretest-posttest measurement of behaviors stressed by Tyler), and had great influence on subsequent evaluation theorists.

Goodlad (1979) pointed out that Tyler advocated the use of general goals to establish purposes rather than premature preoccupation with formulating behavioral objectives. Of course, the broad goals for any activity eventually require operational definitions so that appropriate measurement devices and settings can be selected. Tyler's belief was that service providers primarily needed to discuss the importance and meaning of general goals of their service. Otherwise, in Goodlad's words, the premature specification of behavioral objectives results in objectives that, "could only be arbitrary, restrictive, and ultimately dysfunctional" (p. 43). The service Tyler was interested in improving was education, but his thinking applies to services in other sectors as well.

Tyler described six categories of purpose for American schools (Goodlad, 1979): (1) acquisition of information; (2) development of work habits and study skills; (3) development of effective ways of thinking; (4) internalization of social attitudes, interests, appreciations, and sensitivities; (5) maintenance of physical health; and (6) development of a philosophy of life.

Over the years, educators have refined and reformulated the purposes of schooling into various forms. One publication that reflects the thinking of the past sixty years on purposes of education is *A Handbook of Educational Variables* (Nowakowski, Bunda, Working, Bernacki, & Harrington, 1985). The *Handbook* divided elementary and secondary student development into these seven categories:

1. Intellectual
2. Emotional
3. Physical and Recreational
4. Aesthetic and Cultural
5. Moral
6. Vocational
7. Social

Each one of these categories was analyzed in detail too extensive to reproduce here. Such a resource exemplifies the extent to which Tyler's approach to evaluation has been refined.

Goodlad (1979) stressed that evaluation and improvement of American schools cannot make much headway until these purposes have been discussed, accepted, operationally defined, and monitored. It should be clear that a single standardized test of achievement of basic skills, or standards-based test, provides insufficient data to evaluate our schools. Yet the use of test results is still the most common form of school evaluation discussed in the popular media today. This oversimplification is a real danger of using only the objectives-oriented approach by itself to evaluate programs. The American Evaluation Association (AEA) has an excellent statement on the use of high-stakes testing on its Web site, www.eval.org.

Tyler stressed the importance of screening broad goals before accepting them as the basis for evaluating an activity. In education, the screen through which potential goals should be filtered includes value questions derived from three sources: philosophical (the nature of knowledge); social (the nature of society); and pedagogical (the nature of the learner and the learning process). Scriven (1967) reiterated the need to evaluate the purposes of any activity as a part of evaluating the activity and its consequences.

The question of how specifically to evaluate goals and objectives was addressed by Sanders and Cunningham (1973, 1974). Their approach was to consider both logical and empirical methods for evaluating goals. *Logical* methods included:

1. Examining the cogency of the argument or rationale behind each objective: If there are no justifiable reasons for a goal or objective, it cannot have much value. The *need* for accomplishing the goal or objective is a critical consideration.

2. Examining the consequences of accomplishing the goal or objective: By projecting logically the consequences of achieving a goal, both strengths and weaknesses

in competing goals may be revealed. Criteria such as utility and feasibility (cost, acceptability, political palatability, training, or other requirements) of the goal or objective could be used here. A search of literature may reveal the results of past attempts to achieve certain goals or objectives.

3. Considering higher-order values, such as laws, policies, fit with existing practices, moral principles, or the ideals of a free society, to see whether a goal or purpose is required or whether it will conflict with such values: If a goal or objective conflicts with higher-order values, achieving it may create more problems than it resolves.

Empirical methods for evaluating goals or objectives included:

1. Collecting group data to describe judgments about the value of a goal or objective. Surveys are the most common form of gathering information about a group's value position.

2. Arranging for experts, hearings, or panels to review and evaluate potential goals or objectives. Specialists can draw from knowledge or experience that may not be otherwise available. Their informed judgment may be very different from the group value data that surveys would produce.

3. Conducting content studies of archival records, such as speeches, minutes, editorials, or newsletters. Such content analyses may reveal value positions that conflict with, or are in support of, a particular goal or objective.

4. Conducting a pilot study to see whether the goal is attainable and in what form it may be attained. If no prior experience is available when evaluating a purpose or goal, it may be advisable to suspend judgment until some experience has been gained. Once a broad goal has been made operational or activities directed toward attaining the goal have been tried, it may take on a different meaning from that which it had in earlier discussions. This is one place where demonstration projects serve an important function in program evaluation.

Several evaluation approaches have used goals or objectives as a central focus in the evaluation procedure. These approaches may be seen, therefore, as further refinements of Tyler's approach. Noteworthy objectives-referenced evaluation approaches were those developed by Metfessel and Michael (1967), and Provus (1971). The use of logic models (United Way of America, 1996), and program theory (Rogers, 2000; Rogers, Hacsi, Petrosino, and Heubner, 2000) also add new insights into how programs may be studied within the Tylerian tradition.

Metfessel and Michael's Evaluation Paradigm

An early approach to evaluation suggested by Metfessel and Michael (1967) was heavily influenced by the Tylerian tradition. Eight steps in the evaluation process were proposed:

1. Involve stakeholders as facilitators of program evaluation.
2. Formulate a cohesive model of goals and specific objectives.
3. Translate specific objectives into a communicable form.
4. Select or construct instruments to furnish measures allowing inferences about program effectiveness.
5. Carry out periodic observations using content-valid tests, scales, and other behavioral measures.
6. Analyze data using appropriate methods.
7. Interpret the data using standards of desired levels of performance over all measures.
8. Develop recommendations for the further implementation, modification, and revision of broad goals and specific objectives.

One of the primary contributions of Metfessel and Michael was in enlarging the educational evaluator's vision of alternative instruments that might be used to collect evaluation data. Interested readers will find their lists of alternative instruments for data collection (Metfessel & Michael, 1967; Worthen & Sanders, 1973, pp. 276–279) to be a valuable resource.

Provus's Discrepancy Evaluation Model

Another approach to evaluation in the Tylerian tradition was developed by Malcolm Provus, who based his approach on his evaluation assignments in the Pittsburgh, Pennsylvania, public schools. Provus viewed evaluation as a continuous information-management process designed to serve as "the watchdog of program management" and the "handmaiden of administration in the management of program development through sound decision making" (Provus, 1973, p. 186). Although his was, in some ways, a management-oriented evaluation approach, the key characteristic of Provus's proposals stemmed from the Tylerian tradition. Provus viewed evaluation as a process of (1) agreeing on standards (another term used in place of *objectives*),[1] (2) determining whether a discrepancy exists between the performance of some aspect of a program and the standards set for performance, and (3) using information about discrepancies to decide whether to improve, maintain, or terminate the program or some aspect of it. Provus called his approach, not surprisingly, the Discrepancy Evaluation Model (DEM).

Provus determined that, as a program is being developed, it goes through four developmental stages, to which he added a fifth, optional stage:

1. Definition
2. Installation

[1]Although *standards* and *objectives* are not synonymous, they were used by Provus interchangeably. Stake (1970) also stated that "standards are another form of objective: those seen by outside authority-figures who know little or nothing about the specific program being evaluated but whose advice is relevant to programs in many places" (p. 185). Provus's use of the term is generally consistent with such accepted usage.

3. Process (interim products)
4. Product
5. Cost–benefit analysis (optional)

During the *definition,* or design, stage, the focus of work is on defining goals, processes, or activities, and delineating necessary resources and participants to carry out the activities and accomplish the goals. Provus considered programs to be dynamic systems involving inputs (antecedents), processes, and outputs (outcomes). Standards or expectations were established for each. These standards were the objectives on which all further evaluation work depends. The evaluator's job at the design stage is to see that a complete set of design specifications is produced and that they meet certain criteria: theoretical and structural soundness.

At the *installation* stage, the program design or definition is used as the standard against which to judge program operation. The evaluator performs a series of congruency tests to identify any discrepancies between expected and actual implementation of the program or activity. The intent is to make certain that the program has been installed as it had been designed. This is important because studies have found that staff vary as much in implementing a single program as they do in implementing several different ones. The degree to which program specifications are followed is best determined through firsthand observation. If discrepancies are found at this stage, Provus proposed either changing the program definition, making adjustments in the installation (such as preparing a special in-service workshop), or terminating the activity if it appears that further development would be futile.

During the *process* stage, evaluation focuses on gathering data on the progress of participants to determine whether their behaviors changed as expected. Provus used the term *enabling objective* to refer to those gains that participants should be making if longer-term program goals are to be reached. If certain enabling objectives are not achieved, the activities leading to those objectives are revised or redefined. The validity of the evaluation data would also be questioned. If the evaluator finds that enabling objectives are not being achieved, another option is to terminate the program if it appears that the discrepancy cannot be eliminated.

At the *product* stage, evaluation is to determine whether the *terminal objectives* for the program have been achieved. Provus distinguished between immediate outcomes, or *terminal objectives,* and long-term outcomes, or *ultimate objectives.* He encouraged the evaluator to go beyond the traditional emphasis on end-of-program performance and to make follow-up studies based on ultimate objectives a part of all program evaluations.

Provus also suggested an optional fifth stage that called for cost–benefit analysis and comparison of results with similar cost analyses of comparable programs. In recent times, with funds for human services becoming scarcer, cost–benefit analyses have become an essential part of almost all program evaluations.

The Discrepancy Evaluation Model was designed to facilitate development of programs in a large public school system, and later it was applied to statewide evaluations by a federal bureau. A complex approach that works best in larger systems with adequate staff resources, its central focus is on use of discrepancies to help managers determine the extent to which program development is proceeding toward attainment of stated objectives. It attempts to assure effective program development by preventing the activity from proceeding to the next stage until all identified discrepancies have been removed. Whenever a discrepancy is found, Provus suggested a cooperative problem-solving process for program staff and evaluators. The process involved asking: (1) Why is there a discrepancy? (2) What corrective actions are possible? and (3) Which corrective action is best? This process usually required that additional information be gathered and criteria developed to allow rational, justifiable decisions about corrective actions (or terminations). This particular problem-solving activity was a new addition to the traditional objectives-oriented evaluation approach.

Though this was one of the earliest approaches to evaluation, elements of the discrepancy model can still be found in many evaluations (Fitzpatrick & Fetterman, 2000). The fact that it can still be found to be influencing evaluation studies thirty years later is evidence of how these seminal approaches continue to be useful to evaluators long after their original authors have ceased to espouse them.

A Schema for Generating and Analyzing Objectives: The Evaluation Cube

Building on a concept developed by Hammond (1973), The Evaluation Center at Western Michigan University developed a three-dimensional framework for analyzing the objects of community-based youth programs. This approach can easily be modified to incorporate relevant dimensions for any objectives-oriented program. The cube (Dodson, 1994, p. 61) is reproduced as Figure 4.1.

The three dimensions of the cube are:

1. *Needs of youth* (the client): categories developed by Stufflebeam (1977) and expanded by Nowakowski et al. (1985) are:
   - intellectual
   - physical recreation
   - vocational
   - social
   - moral
   - aesthetic/cultural
   - emotional
2. *Age of youth* (this dimension could be any relevant characteristic of the client): prenatal through young adult
3. *Source of service to youth,* such as
   - housing
   - social services
   - health services
   - economic/business

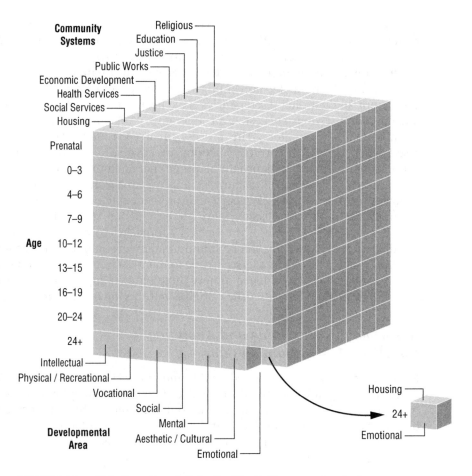

FIGURE 4.1   *Objectives-Based Cube for Youth Program Analysis*

Source: From *Interim summative evaluation: Assessing the value of a long-term or ongoing program, during its operations* (p. 58) by S. C. Dodson, 1994. Unpublished doctoral dissertation, Western Michigan University, Kalamazoo. Reproduced by permission.

- public works
- justice
- education
- religious

In any category along any of the three dimensions, those planning a community-based youth program may choose to establish relevant objectives. Few if any stakeholders in community-based programs will be interested in every cell of the cube, but the categories contained in each of the three dimensions will provide a good checklist for making certain that important areas or categories of objectives are not overlooked. Obviously, use of the cube is not limited to community-based programs but could extend to other types of programs as well.

Logic Models

Practitioner guides to evaluation have built on the concepts underlying Provus's Discrepancy Evaluation Model by recommending that program staff develop *logic models* for their programs. A logic model starts with the long-term vision of how program participants will be better off (changed) because of the program. This is seen as the ultimate program outcome (goal/objective). This outcome is then placed on a time line, say five years, and the question is asked, "If we are going to be there in five years, where should participants be developmentally in four years, three years, two years, and at the end of this year?" Also, "What do we have to do to reach these annual goals?"

This requires specification of:

Inputs—annual budgets, staffing facilities, equipment, materials, and so forth needed to run the program

Activities—weekly sessions, curriculum, workshops, conferences, recruitment, clinical services, newsletters, staff training, and so on that make up the program

Outputs—numbers of participants each week by demographic category, number of class meetings, hours of direct service to each participant, number of newsletters, and so forth that account for program expenditures

Immediate, intermediate, long-term, and ultimate outcomes—the longitudinal goals for participant change (development)

The program staff develops a logic for the program that can be used for program evaluation, i.e., are we where we expected to be each year? If not, what changes are needed in the program to get us there?

The United Way of America has published a useful guide for program evaluation based on the logic model concept (1996). Logic models are now used by many nonprofit organizations who receive funding from United Way. As a result, these models have come to play a central role in such organizations.

Program Theory

There are some evaluators who have taken the concept of logic models even further by seeking the specification of the mechanisms that mediate between delivery of a program and the appearance of outcomes of interest. What are the specific causes of observed outcomes, and what evidence do we have that supports causal conclusions?

Does this sound more like research than program evaluation? It is research if the primary goal is to generate generalizable knowledge about interventions. It is evaluation if the merit and worth of the activities of a specific program are being judged. Examining research literature and theory can help in generating evaluation questions. Considering the linkages between program activities and outcomes, and whether to assess these, can help avoid "black box" studies that describe outcomes but fail to explore the reasons the outcomes are achieved or not achieved. The selection of evaluation questions, however, should be based on the needs of the evaluation, not adding to knowledge in the research discipline. Those motives move program theory out of the universe of program evaluation.

Logic models and program theory are useful to evaluators in helping them learn more about how the program is intended to work and in identifying aspects of a program (specific inputs, activities, outputs, and outcomes) that bear scrutiny. This helps to focus the evaluation questions on how well each aspect is done, how adequate each aspect is, the strengths and weaknesses of each aspect, and changes in each aspect that might improve the program in some way.

For more on program theory see Bickman (1987, 1990), Chen (1990), Rogers (2000), Rogers, Hacsi, Petrosino, and Huebner (2000), and Weiss (1972, 1997).

How the Objectives-Oriented Evaluation Approach Has Been Used

The objectives-oriented approach has dominated the thinking and development of evaluation since the 1930s, both here in the United States and elsewhere (Madaus & Stufflebeam, 1989). Its straightforward procedure of letting the achievement of objectives determine success or failure and justify improvements, maintenance, or termination of program activities has proved an attractive prototype.

The technology of objectives-oriented evaluation can be taken to extremes as can be seen in the literature on behavioral objectives (Mager, 1962) and on program theory (Rogers, Hacsi, Petrosino, & Huebner, 2000). In these cases programs were analyzed down to the most minute detail. Done in moderation, however, the objectives-oriented evaluation approach is very workable and defensible.

Bloom and Krathwohl were influential in refining the objectives-oriented approach to evaluation with their work on the previously discussed taxonomies of educational objectives in both the cognitive domain (Bloom, Engelhart, Furst, Hill, & Krathwohl, 1956) and affective domains (Krathwohl, Bloom, & Masia, 1964). With the development of these taxonomies of objectives, educators had powerful tools to aid them in using Tyler's approach. Bloom, Hastings, and Madaus (1971) also prepared a handbook for educators to use in identifying appropriate objectives for instruction in the subject matter taught in school and in developing and using measurement instruments to determine students' levels of performance in each subject. Cronbach (1963), who also worked with Tyler on the Eight Year Study, developed an approach to using objectives and associated measurement techniques for purposes of course and curriculum improvement.

But the blockbuster in education, in terms of expenditure, has been the standards-based, objectives-referenced, or criterion-referenced testing movement originated in the 1960s and 1970s by federal and state governments. The National Assessment of Educational Progress (NAEP) was originated in the mid-1960s under the leadership of Tyler. This federal program was designed to collect performance data periodically on samples of students and young adults in the essential subjects of U.S. education. Great care was taken to select objectives generally accepted in this country as desirable achievements at the different stages of development measured (ages 9, 13, 17, and adult). Public reports have, since the mid-1960s, described the ability of Americans in these age groups to answer questions in subjects considered important.

Like those of the Eight Year Study, the instruments and objectives of NAEP have been made available to educators, but they have received limited use. Virtually every state has developed its own form of annual statewide testing, however, and many have generally followed the NAEP approach. The standards-based curriculum and testing movement in U.S. education is clearly an objectives-oriented approach to evaluating educational programs.

Derivative "objectives-oriented" movements appeared in the late 1960s in the form of school accountability (Lessinger & Tyler, 1971), competency or minimum competency testing (Berk, 1986; Jaeger, 1989; Madaus, 1983), objectives- and criterion-referenced test collections and exchanges, and federal project monitoring (Tallmadge & Wood, 1976), and several of these movements continue to be influential. A useful objectives-oriented guide to outcomes measurement in drug and alcohol prevention programs has been developed and is available from the U.S. Department of Health and Human Services, Office for Substance Abuse Prevention (1991). Management techniques that were not evaluative but were still based on the objectives-oriented tradition included goal attainment scaling (Kiresuk, Smith, & Cardillo, 1994), Management by Objectives (MBO), Planning, Programming, and Budgeting Systems (PPBS), outcome monitoring (Affholter, 1994), and the Government Performance and Results Act (GPRA) (National Performance Review, 1996). The tradition begun by Tyler over seventy years ago has had remarkable staying power.

Tyler's (1991) own statement on program evaluation has remained consistent for over a half century.

> To summarize, a comprehensive evaluation of the outcomes of an educational program requires clear definitions of the desired patterns of behavior and of other possible outcomes both positive and negative. It then requires the selection or development of test situations that evoke such behavior from the students, and it necessitates the use of relevant and important criteria for appraising the students' reactions in these test situations. Finally, the reporting of these appraisals should be done in terms that can be understood by those who can use the results constructively.
>
> For social programs other than those in education, the rationale is similar. For example, for a program seeking to reduce the number of persons without jobs, there needs to be a definition of "having a job." Does a person have a job if he or she is employed temporarily and is soon back on the street? Is it a job to have dead-end work with no opportunity for advancement or a "career"? Many job training programs place participants in jobs that are temporary or dead-end. The participants

fail to attain employment in work that permits continued learning and achievement. Developing test situations in job training and placement are experiments with samples of trainees, and the results should be appraised in terms of the definition of desirable jobs (p. 14).

Strengths and Limitations of the Objectives-Oriented Evaluation Approach

Probably the greatest strength and appeal of the objectives-oriented approach to evaluation lies in its simplicity. It is easily understood, easy to follow and implement, and produces information that program directors generally agree is relevant to their mission. This approach has stimulated so much technological development over the years that the processes of specifying objectives and developing or finding appropriate measurement procedures and instruments have been finely honed. The literature on objectives-oriented evaluation is extensive, filled with creative ideas for applying the approach (e.g., Bloom, et al., 1971; Cronbach, 1963; Metfessel & Michael, 1967; Morris & Fitzgibbon, 1978; Popham, Eisner, Sullivan, & Tyler, 1969; Stufflebeam, Madaus, & Kellaghan, Section II, 2000).

The objectives-oriented evaluation approach has caused program directors to reflect about their intentions and to clarify formerly ambiguous generalities about intended outcomes. Discussions of appropriate objectives with the community being served have given objectives-oriented evaluation the appeal of face validity—the program is, after all, merely being held accountable for what its designers said it was going to accomplish, and that is obviously legitimate. The objectives-oriented evaluation approach is one that directly addresses Standard U4, Values Identification, in *The Program Evaluation Standards* (Joint Committee, 1994). Its emphasis on clearly defining outcomes as the basis for judging the program helps evaluators and others to see the value basis for judging the program.

As a result of the attention placed on this approach, technically sound measurement practices have broadened to include unobtrusive measures (Webb, Campbell, Schwartz, & Sechrest, 1966) and non-paper-and-pencil evidence (Herman, Aschbacher, & Winters, 1992; Sanders & Sachse, 1977). These and other advances in the measurement of *outcomes* may be tied to the outcome orientation of Tyler. These advances, added to the many instruments, objectives pools, and step-by-step guides that have been placed in the hands of practitioners by various projects, have greatly expanded the available resources for evaluation.

Useful as this approach to evaluation seems to its many adherents, critics have asserted that it (1) lacks a real evaluative component (facilitating measurement and assessment of objectives rather than resulting in explicit judgments of merit or worth), (2) lacks standards to judge the importance of observed discrepancies between objectives and performance levels, (3) neglects the value of the objectives themselves, (4) ignores important alternatives that should be considered in planning a program, (5) neglects the context in which the evaluation takes place, (6) ignores important outcomes other than those covered by the objectives (the unintended outcomes of the activity), (7) omits evidence of program value not reflected in its own objectives, and (8) promotes a linear, inflexible approach to evaluation. Collectively, these criticisms suggest that objectives-oriented evaluation can result in tunnel vision, which tends to limit evaluation's effectiveness and potential.

To some extent, the rather elaborate technology developed to support this evaluation approach makes its use appear seductively simple to novice evaluators only partially familiar with its philosophical and practical difficulties. The assumption that human service is a technology—a body of techniques leading to prespecified means—has been criticized as the factory model of human services delivery. Many outcomes of human services programs are still highly variable and difficult to predict because of the many influences of human behavior.

Although it is often important to know whether an agency is attaining its stated objectives, such is not always the case, especially in a changing environment. It depends largely on whether the goals were worth attaining in the first place. Some goals that are attainable are hardly worth the effort. Some goals are attained because they were set too low or had already been attained, not because the program was effective. The situation is almost analogous to that in which one needs to identify which children are in good health and which are suffering from malnutrition, and height is considered a relevant indicator. There would be at least a measure of foolishness in asking the children to make their own tape measures, use them to measure their height, and then report how well they have attained the height they desired to reach at that point or whether they are too tall or too short for their age.

A related difficulty lies in the frequent challenge of trying to ascertain the goals or objectives of many human service endeavors. Evaluators have found that the objectives listed on paper do not always match those in the minds of program staff. As a result, their activities may conflict with or deviate from publicly stated objectives, sometimes for good reasons. Professionals will not become slaves to stated objectives if they believe alternative courses of action or goals are desirable. Such individuals tend to argue against strident and unthinking application of an objectives-oriented approach.

Many evaluators, lamentably, are not equipped by disposition or training to assist agencies in developing meaningful objectives. Thus, the objectives-oriented approach to evaluation frequently results in the verdict that a program cannot be evaluated, when the problem lies more with a narrow understanding of the approach and/or the insistence that all must become experts in behavioral specification before this method can be used.

Who really determines the goals and objectives? Do they include all important outcomes? Have all those affected by the program agreed on these particular goals or objectives? Who has determined that a particular criterion level is more defensible than alternatives? On what evidence? These and other questions must be addressed if an objectives-oriented approach is to be defensible.

Overemphasizing the testing components of this evaluation approach can prove dangerous. "Teaching for the test" may be only human when a teacher's performance is evaluated by how well students do on standardized or statewide assessment tests, but the misinformation that is introduced by such test score pollution (see Haladyna, Nolen, & Haas, 1991) can be very detrimental. Madaus (1983) describes how competency testing invariably turns into *minimum* competency testing when expectations for achievement become bounded by test content. Such narrowing of purposes is a negative, albeit unintentional, consequence this approach may have had. The American Evaluation Association (2002) has described how measurements based on a single outcome or standard can negatively affect the validity of a program evaluation. This statement on high-stakes testing is available at www.eval.org.

We should not leave our discussion of limitations of objectives-oriented evaluation without noting that Scriven's perception of its limitations led him to develop his now widely known proposals for goal-free evaluation (1972). Although intentionally the opposite of objectives-oriented approaches, it seems logical to discuss this proposal here.

Goal-Free Evaluation

The rationale for **goal-free evaluation** can be summarized as follows: First, goals should not be taken as given; like anything else, they should be evaluated. Further, goals are generally little more than rhetoric and seldom reveal the real objectives of the project or changes in intent. In addition, many important program outcomes are not included in the list of original program goals or objectives. Scriven (1972) believes the most important function of goal-free evaluation, however, is to reduce bias and increase objectivity. In objectives-oriented evaluation, an evaluator is told the goals of the program and is therefore immediately limited in her perceptions—the goals act like blinders, causing her to miss important outcomes not directly related to those goals.

For example, suppose an evaluator is told that the goals of a dropout rehabilitation program are to (1) bring school dropouts into a vocational training program, (2) train them in productive vocations, and (3) place them in stable jobs. She may spend all her time designing and applying measures to look at such things as how many dropouts have been recruited into the program, how many have been placed and remain placed in paying jobs, and so forth. These are worthwhile goals, and the program may be successful on all these counts. But what about the fact that the crime rate of others (nondropouts) who are receiving employment training has tripled since the dropouts were brought in? Indeed, a hidden curriculum seems to have sprung up: stripping cars. This negative side effect is much more likely to be picked up by the goal-free evaluator than by the objectives-oriented evaluator working behind her built-in blinders.

The following are major characteristics of goal-free evaluation:

- The evaluator purposefully avoids becoming aware of the program goals.
- Predetermined goals are not permitted to narrow the focus of the evaluation study.
- Goal-free evaluation focuses on *actual* outcomes rather than intended program outcomes.

- The goal-free evaluator has minimal contact with the program manager and staff.
- Goal-free evaluation increases the likelihood that unanticipated side effects will be noted.

It might be helpful to point out that objectives-oriented and goal-free evaluation are not mutually exclusive. Indeed, they supplement one another. The internal staff evaluator of necessity conducts a goal-directed evaluation. She can hardly hope to avoid knowing the goals of the program, and it would be unwise to ignore them even if she could. Program managers obviously need to know how well the program is meeting its goals, and the internal evaluator uses goal-directed evaluation to provide such administrators with that information. At the same time, it is important to know how others judge the program, not only on the basis of how well it does what it is *supposed* to do but also on the basis of what it *does* in all areas, on *all* its outcomes, intended or not. This is the task for the external goal-free evaluator who knows nothing of the program goals. Thus, goal-directed evaluation and goal-free evaluation can work well together. And, while the major share of a program's evaluation resources should not go to goal-free evaluation, it is tragic when all resources go to goal-directed evaluation on a program when the stated goals do not even begin to include all of the important outcomes.

Major Concepts and Theories

1. The objectives-oriented evaluation approach used by Ralph Tyler was designed to determine the extent to which program objectives were attained. Tyler used discrepancies between what was expected and what was observed to provide suggestions for any program deficiencies.

2. Before a program can be evaluated using the objectives-oriented approach, it may be necessary to fully evaluate the goals or objectives of the program under consideration, using either logical or empirical methods or a combination of the two. A logical evaluation would focus more on the justification for program goals, the feasibility and utility of goals, and whether goals conflict with other societal or organizational values. An empirical evaluation of the attainability of program goals before the evaluation commences may include collecting archival, group, and expert data as well as conducting pilot studies.

3. Provus postulated that program development and, thus, evaluation, goes through five stages: (1) definition, (2) installation, (3) process, (4) product, and (5) cost–benefit analysis. Evaluators then determine the discrepancies between expected outcomes or activities at each stage and actual, or observed, outcomes.

4. Goal-free evaluations were proposed primarily to identify any unanticipated side effects of a program that a goal-directed or objectives-oriented evaluation might miss because of the focus on the intended program outcomes rather than on the actual program outcomes.

Discussion Questions

1. What is the main reason for using an objectives-oriented evaluation approach?

2. From the vantage point of Goodlad and Tyler, discuss the importance of operationally defining the goals, purpose, or objectives of the program to be evaluated. Also, discuss how and why one would evaluate program goals before or during the evaluation.

3. What are the major strengths of the objectives-oriented approach?

4. What are the major weaknesses of the objectives-oriented approach?

5. Discuss what a goal-free evaluation approach is, the reasons it was developed, and the types of questions and data collection methods a goal-free evaluation may include.

Application Exercises

1. Cheryl Brown is a program administrator for a state department of social services. She has been responsible for implementing a parenting program in which the goal is to reduce the incidence of child abuse and child neglect. To evaluate the program she decides that she will depend on one performance measure—the number of cases of reported abuse and neglect.

   Use what you have just learned about Tyler's approach to evaluation, Provus's Discrepancy Evaluation Model, logic models, and goal-free evaluation to expand the evaluation design for this program. What would be wrong with basing the evaluation on just the one measure?

2. Jane Jackson is a member of the faculty of Greenlawn Middle School. Although students are still grouped by grades, within each grade a team of teachers cooperates to develop lessons that are interdisciplinary. Individual members of the team have been assigned responsibility for the areas of English, mathematics, science, and social studies. Mrs. Jackson has decided to evaluate her area of responsibility, the seventh-grade English section of the instructional program. Her evaluation tentatively includes the following:

   a. Administration of a standardized English achievement test in September and June (She plans to compare the means of the pre- and posttest groups with national norms for the tests.)

   b. Monthly interviews of a 10 percent sample of her class to assess student reaction to the English portion of the instructional program

   c. Complete record keeping of students' progress so their eighth-grade performance can be assessed

   d. Observation by an outside observer twice a month, using a scale she has devised to record pupil interaction during class discussions

   e. Comparison of the performance of Mrs. Jackson's seventh-grade class on the standardized tests with the performance of the seventh grade at Martindale Junior High School, a traditional junior high

   Using what you have just learned about Tyler's approach to evaluation, logic models, how the cube can be used in evaluation, and how Provus's Discrepancy Evaluation Model works, advise Mrs. Jackson on her evaluation design. What questions should she be addressing? How could she organize her evaluation? How might she change her design to make it better?

3. The state health department has funded a community-development program in your city to decrease alcohol and drug abuse, crime and delinquency, and graffiti. The project is located in a high crime neighborhood with moderate mobility among residents. The project funds a community neighborhood center to identify and direct neighborhood activities that will help residents band together to protect their neighborhood. Activities include neighborhood watch programs, tutoring and sports activities, a strengthened neighborhood association with bimonthly meetings, a speakers' program, and dances and games. As with most agencies, funds are limited and the project directors want to make sure they develop the best possible program the first time around, so they have asked you to assist them with both developing and evaluating their program.

    Given this information, apply both Metfessel and Michael's and Provus's evaluation models. Focus on what steps need to be taken with each evaluation model, what evaluation questions will be answered by each model, what data collection methodologies are needed, and the usefulness of each model to the police and fire departments both in developing the program and in determining its effectiveness.

Suggested Readings

Affholter, D. P. (1994). Outcome monitoring. In J. S. Wholey, H. P. Hatry, & K. E. Newcomer (Eds.), *Handbook of practical program evaluation.* San Francisco: Jossey-Bass.

Bloom, B. S., Hastings, J. T., & Madaus, G. F. (1971). *Handbook on formative and summative evaluation of student learning.* New York: McGraw-Hill.

Madaus, G. F. and Stufflebeam, D. L. (Eds.). (1989). *Educational evaluation: Classic works of Ralph W. Tyler.* Boston: Kluwer.

Metfessel, N. S., & Michael, W. B. (1967). A paradigm involving multiple criterion measures for the evaluation of the effectiveness of school programs. *Educational and Psychological Measurement, 27,* 931–943. Also in B. R. Worthen & J. R. Sanders (Eds.), (1973), *Educational evaluation: Theory and practice.* Belmont, CA: Wadsworth.

Nowakowski, J., Bunda, M. A., Working, R., Bernacki, G., & Harrington, P. (1985). *A hand-book of educational variables.* Boston: Kluwer-Nijhoff.

Provus, M. M. (1971). *Discrepancy evaluation.* Berkeley, CA: McCutchan.

Smith, E. R., & Tyler, R. W. (1942). *Appraising and recording student progress.* New York: Harper & Row.

Stufflebeam, D. L., Madaus, G. F., & Kellaghan, T. (Eds.). (2000). *Evaluation models: Viewpoints on educational and human services evaluation* (2nd ed.). Boston: Kluwer. (Section II)

Tyler, R. W. (1991). General statement on program evaluation. In M. W. McLaughlin & D. C. Phillips (Eds.), *Evaluation and education: At quarter century.* Ninetieth yearbook of the National Society for the Study of Education, Part II. Chicago: University of Chicago Press.

United Way of America. (1996). *Measuring program outcomes.* Alexandria, VA: United Way of America.

5

Management-Oriented
Evaluation Approaches

Orienting Questions

1. Why has the management-oriented approach to evaluation been so popular among local administrators, state, and federal government managers?

2. What are the developmental stages of a program and how can management-oriented evaluation help in program development?

3. What techniques are most useful for context evaluation? Input evaluation? Process evaluation? Product evaluation?

4. What are major strengths and limitations of the management-oriented evaluation approach?

The management-oriented evaluation approach is meant to serve decision makers. Its rationale is that evaluative information is an essential part of good decision making and that the evaluator can be most effective by serving administrators, managers, policy makers, boards, practitioners, and others who need good evaluative information. Developers of this method have relied on a systems approach to evaluation in which decisions are made about inputs, processes, and outputs much like the logic models and program theory that were described in Chapter 4. However, by highlighting different levels of decisions and decision makers, this approach clarifies who will use the evaluation results, how he will use them, and what aspect(s) of the system he is making decisions about. The decision maker is the audience to whom a management-oriented evaluation is directed, and the decision maker's concerns, informational needs, and criteria for effectiveness guide the direction of the study.

Developers of the Management-Oriented Evaluation Approach and Their Contributions

Important contributions to a management-oriented approach to evaluation have been made by many evaluators. In the mid-1960s, Stufflebeam (1968) recognized the shortcomings of available evaluation approaches. Working to expand and systematize thinking about administrative studies and educational decision making, he and others built on concepts only hinted at in the much earlier work of educational leaders such as Henry Bernard, Horace Mann, William Torey Harris, and Carleton Washburne (Travers, 1983). During the 1960s and 1970s, they also drew from management theory (e.g., Braybrooke & Lindblom, 1963). Stufflebeam (1968) made the decision(s) of program managers the pivotal organizer for the evaluation rather than program objectives. In the models proposed by him and other theorists (e.g., Alkin, 1969), the evaluator, working closely with the administrator(s), identifies the decisions the administrator must make and then collects sufficient information about the relative advantages and disadvantages of each decision alternative to allow a fair judgment based on specified criteria. The success of the evaluation rests on the quality of teamwork between evaluators and decision makers.

The CIPP Evaluation Model

Stufflebeam (1971, 2000; Stufflebeam & Shinkfield, 1985) has been an influential proponent of a decision-oriented evaluation approach structured to help administrators make good decisions. He views evaluation as "the process of delineating, obtaining, and providing useful information for judging decision alternatives" (Stufflebeam, 1973b, p. 129). He developed an evaluation framework to serve managers and administrators facing four different kinds of decisions:

1. **Context evaluation** to serve *planning decisions:* Determining what needs are to be addressed by a program and what programs already exist helps in defining objectives for the program.

2. **Input evaluation,** to serve *structuring decisions:* Determining what resources are available, what alternative strategies for the program should be considered, and what plan seems to have the best potential for meeting needs facilitates design of program procedures.

3. **Process evaluation,** to serve *implementing decisions:* How well is the plan being implemented? What barriers threaten its success? What revisions are needed? Once these questions are answered, procedures can be monitored, controlled, and refined.

4. **Product evaluation,** to serve *recycling decisions.* What results were obtained? How well were needs reduced? What should be done with the program after it has run its course? These questions are important in judging program attainments.

The first letters of the four types of evaluation—*c*ontext, *i*nput, *p*rocess, and *p*roduct—have been used to form the acronym CIPP, by which Stufflebeam's evaluation model is best known. Table 5.1 summarizes the main features of the four types of evaluation, as proposed by Stufflebeam and Shinkfield (1985, pp. 170–171).

As a logical structure for designing each type of evaluation, Stufflebeam (1973a) proposed that evaluators follow these general steps:

A. *Focusing the Evaluation*
   1. Identify the major level(s) of decision making to be served, for example, local, state, or national.
   2. For each level of decision making, project the decision situations to be served and describe each one in terms of its locus, focus, criticality, timing, and composition of alternatives.
   3. Define criteria for each decision situation by specifying variables for measurement and standards for use in the judgment of alternatives.
   4. Define policies within which the evaluator must operate.
B. *Collection of Information*
   1. Specify the source of the information to be collected.
   2. Specify the instruments and methods for collecting the needed information.
   3. Specify the sampling procedure to be employed.
   4. Specify the conditions and schedule for information collection.
C. *Organization of Information*
   1. Provide a format for the information that is to be collected.
   2. Designate a means for performing the analysis.
D. *Analysis of Information*
   1. Select the analytical procedures to be employed.
   2. Designate a means for performing the analysis.
E. *Reporting of Information*
   1. Define the audiences for the evaluation reports.
   2. Specify means for providing information to the audiences.
   3. Specify the format for evaluation reports and/or reporting sessions.
   4. Schedule the reporting of information.
F. *Administration of the Evaluation*
   1. Summarize the evaluation schedule.
   2. Define staff and resource requirements and plans for meeting these requirements.
   3. Specify means for meeting policy requirements for conduct of the evaluation.
   4. Evaluate the potential of the evaluation design for providing information that is valid, reliable, credible, timely, and pervasive (i.e., will reach all relevant stakeholders).
   5. Specify and schedule means for periodic updating of the evaluation design.
   6. Provide a budget for the total evaluation program (p. 144).

TABLE 5.1 *Four Types of Evaluation*

	Context Evaluation	Input Evaluation	Process Evaluation	Product Evaluation
Objective	To define the institutional context, to identify the target population and assess its needs, to identify opportunities for addressing the needs, to diagnose problems underlying the needs, and to judge whether proposed objectives are sufficiently responsive to the assessed needs	To identify and assess system capabilities, alternative program strategies, procedural designs for implementing the strategies, budgets, and schedules	To identify or predict in process defects in the procedural design or its implementation, to provide information for the preprogrammed decision, and to record and judge procedural events and activities	To collect descriptions and judgments of outcomes and to relate them to objectives and to context, input, and process information, and to interpret their worth and merit
Method	By using such methods as system analysis, survey, document review, hearings, interviews, diagnostic tests, and the Delphi technique	By inventorying and analyzing available human and material resources, solution strategies, and procedural designs for relevance, feasibility and economy, and by using such methods as a literature search, visits to exemplary programs, advocate teams, and pilot trials	By monitoring the activity's potential procedural barriers and remaining alert to unanticipated ones, by obtaining specified information for programmed decisions, by describing the actual process, and by continually interacting with, and observing, the activities of project staff	By defining operationally and measuring outcome criteria, by collecting judgments of outcomes from stakeholders, and by performing both qualitative and quantitative analyses
Relation to decision making in the change process	For deciding on the setting to be served, the goals associated with meeting needs or using opportunities, and the objectives associated with solving problems—that is, for planning needed changes—and to provide a basis for judging outcomes	For selecting sources of support, solution strategies, and procedural designs—that is, for structuring change activities—and to provide a basis for judging implementation	For implementing and refining the program design and procedure—that is, for effecting process control—and to provide a log of the actual process for later use in interpreting outcomes	For deciding to continue, terminate, modify, or refocus a change activity, and to present a clear record of effects (intended and unintended, positive and negative)

Source: From *Systematic Evaluation* (pp. 170–171) by D. L. Stufflebeam and A. J. Shinkfield, 1985, Boston: Kluwer-Nijhoff.

A guide for school program evaluation following these general steps has been published by Sanders (2000).

The UCLA Evaluation Model

While he was director of the Center for the Study of Evaluation at UCLA, Alkin (1969) developed an evaluation framework that paralleled closely some aspects of the CIPP model. Alkin defined evaluation as "the process of ascertaining the decision areas of concern, selecting appropriate information, and collecting and analyzing information in order to report summary data useful to decision-makers in selecting among alternatives" (p. 2). Alkin's model included the following five types of evaluation:

1. *Systems assessment,* to provide information about the state of the system (similar to context evaluation in the CIPP model)
2. *Program planning,* to assist in the selection of particular programs likely to be effective in meeting specific educational needs (similar to input evaluation)
3. *Program implementation,* to provide information about whether a program was introduced to the appropriate group in the manner intended
4. *Program improvement,* to provide information about how a program is functioning, whether interim objectives are being achieved, and whether unanticipated outcomes are appearing (similar to process evaluation)
5. *Program certification,* to provide information about the value of the program and its potential for use elsewhere (similar to product evaluation)

As Alkin (1991) has pointed out, his evaluation model made four assumptions about evaluation:

1. Evaluation is a process of gathering information.
2. The information collected in an evaluation will be used mainly to make decisions about alternative courses of action.
3. Evaluation information should be presented to the decision maker in a form that he can use effectively and that is designed to help rather than confuse or mislead him.
4. Different kinds of decisions require different kinds of evaluation procedures (p. 94).

Growth and Development of the Early Models

Both the CIPP and UCLA frameworks for evaluation appear to be linear and sequential, but the developers have stressed that such is not the case. For example, the evaluator would not have to complete an input evaluation or a systems assessment in order to undertake one of the other types of evaluation listed in the framework. Often evaluators may undertake "retrospective" evaluations (such as a context evaluation or a systems assessment) in preparation for a process or program improvement evaluation study, believing this evaluation approach is cumulative, linear, and sequential; however, such steps are not always necessary. A process evaluation can be done without having completed context or input evaluation studies. At other times, the evaluator may cycle into another type of evaluation if some decisions suggest that earlier decisions should be reviewed. Such is the nature of management-oriented evaluation.

Work using the CIPP model has produced guides for types of evaluation included in that framework. For example, Stufflebeam (1977) advanced the procedure for conducting a *context* evaluation with his guidelines for designing a needs assessment for an educational program or activity.

A guide for use in *input* evaluation was developed by Reinhard (1972). The input evaluation approach that she developed is called the *advocate team technique.* It is used when acceptable alternatives for designing a new program are not available or obvious. The technique creates alternative new designs that are then evaluated and selected, adapted, or combined to create the most viable alternative design for a new program. This technique has been used successfully by the federal government (Reinhard, 1972) and by school districts (Sanders, 1982) to generate options and guide the final design of educational programs. Procedures proposed by Cronbach (1963) provided useful suggestions for the conduct of *process* evaluation.

Techniques discussed in Chapter 6 of this book provide information useful in conducting *product* evaluations.

A good summary of the CIPP model and techniques that fit within the CIPP framework can be found in Chapter 16 of Stufflebeam, Madaus, and Kellaghan (2000).

Other Management-Oriented Evaluation Approaches

In Chapter 4, Provus's Discrepancy Evaluation Model was described as an objectives-oriented evaluation model. Some aspects of that model are also directed toward serving the information needs of educational program managers. It is systems-oriented, focusing on input, process, and output at each of five stages of evaluation: program definition, program installation, program process, program products, and cost–benefit analysis. Even cursory scrutiny of these five types of evaluation reveal close parallels to the CIPP and UCLA evaluation models with respect to their sensitivity to the various decisions managers need to make at each stage of program development. Likewise, the systems approaches of logic models and program theory focus on inputs, processes, and outcomes, as do the management-oriented evaluation approaches. They do not, however, stress the decision-maker orientation found in the management approaches.

The utilization-focused evaluation approach of Patton (1986, 1996) could also be viewed as a decision-making approach in one respect. He stressed that the process of identifying and organizing relevant decision makers and information users is the first step in evaluation. In his view, the use of evaluation findings requires that decision makers determine what information is needed by various people and arrange for that information to be collected and provided to them.

Wholey (1983, 1994) could also be considered a proponent of management-oriented evaluation, given his focus on working with management. His writings have concentrated on the practical uses of evaluation in public administration settings.

How the Management-Oriented Evaluation Approach Has Been Used

The CIPP model has been used in school districts and state and federal government agencies. The Dallas (Texas) Independent School District, for example, established an evaluation office organized around the four types of evaluation in the model. All evaluation activities in that district fell into one or more of these categories.

The management-oriented approach to evaluation has guided program managers through program planning, operation, and review. Program staff have found this approach a useful guide to program improvement.

This evaluation approach has also been used for accountability purposes. It provides a record-keeping framework that facilitates public review of client needs, objectives, plans, activities, and outcomes. Administrators and boards have found this approach useful in meeting public demands for information. Stufflebeam and Shinkfield (1985) described these two uses of the CIPP model as shown in Figure 5.1.

FIGURE 5.1   *The Relevance of Four Evaluation Types to Decision Making and Accountability*

	Decision Making (Formative Orientation)	Accountability (Summative Orientation)
Context	Guidance for choice of objectives and assignment of priorities	Record of objectives and bases for their choice along with a record of needs, opportunities, and problems
Input	Guidance for choice of program strategy; input for specification of procedural design	Record of chosen strategy and design and reason for their choice over other alternatives
Process	Guidance for implementation	Record of the actual process
Product	Guidance for termination, continuation, modification, or installation	Record of attainments and recycling decisions

Source: From *Systematic Evaluation* (p. 164) by D. L. Stufflebeam and A. J. Shinkfield, 1985, Boston: Kluwer-Nijhoff.

Strengths and Limitations of the Management-Oriented Evaluation Approach

This approach has proved appealing to many evaluators and program managers, particularly those at home with the rational and orderly systems approach, to which it is clearly related. Perhaps its greatest strength is that it gives focus to the evaluation. Experienced evaluators know how tempting it is simply to cast a wide net, collecting an enormous amount of information, only later to discard much of it because it is not directly relevant to the key issues or questions the evaluation must address. Deciding precisely what information to collect is essential. Focusing on informational needs and pending decisions of managers limits the range of relevant data and brings the evaluation into sharp focus. This evaluation approach also stresses the importance of the utility of information. Connecting decision making and evaluation underscores the very purpose of evaluation. Also, focusing an evaluation on the decisions managers must make prevents the evaluator from pursuing unfruitful lines of inquiry that are not of interest to the decision makers.

The management-oriented approach to evaluation was instrumental in showing evaluators and program managers that they need not wait until an activity or program has run its course before evaluating it. In fact, educators can begin evaluating even when ideas for programs are first discussed. Because of lost opportunities and heavy resource investment, evaluation is generally least effective at the end of a developing program. Of course, people involved with education and other public sector programs have found that it's never too late to begin evaluating, even if a program has been in place for years. The decisions are simply different.

The management-oriented evaluation approach is probably the preferred choice in the eyes of most managers and boards. This is hardly surprising given the emphasis this approach places on information for decision makers. By attending directly to the informational needs of people who are to use the evaluation, this approach addressed one of the biggest criticisms of evaluation in the 1960s: that it did not provide useful information.

The CIPP model, in particular, is a useful and simple heuristic tool that helps the evaluator generate potentially important questions to be addressed in an evaluation. For each of the four types of evaluation (context, input, process, and product), the evaluator can identify a number of questions about an undertaking. The model and the questions it generates also make the evaluation easy to explain to lay audiences.

The management-oriented approach to evaluation supports evaluation of every component of a program as it operates, grows, or changes. It stresses the timely use of feedback by decision makers so that the program is not left to flounder or proceed unaffected by updated knowledge about needs, resources, new developments, the realities of day-to-day operations, or the consequences of program interventions.

potential weakness

A potential weakness of this approach is the evaluator's occasional inability to respond to questions or issues that may be significant—even critical—but that clash with or at least do not match the concerns and questions of the decision maker who, essentially, controls the evaluation. In addition, programs that lack decisive leadership are not likely to benefit from this approach to evaluation.

Another potential weakness of management-oriented evaluation is the preference it seems to give to top management. If great care is not taken, the evaluator can become the "hired gun" of the manager and program establishment. Thus, one potential weakness of the management-oriented approach is the possibility that the evaluation can become unfair and possibly even undemocratic. Critics argue that the management-oriented approach disenfranchises other stakeholders who have less power and resources (House and Howe, 1999).

This point is relevant to the policy uses of evaluations by what Cronbach and others (1980) called the *policy-shaping community*. The policy-shaping community includes: (1) public servants, such as responsible officials at the policy and program levels and the actual operating personnel, and (2) the public, consisting not only of constituents but also influential persons such as commentators, academic social scientists, philosophers, gadflies, and even novelists or dramatists. Few policy studies have been found to have a direct effect on the policy-shaping community, but evaluations can and do influence these audiences over time. Policy, as a reflection of public values, may be seen as never-ending in that it continues to be molded or revised as issues, reforms, social causes, and social values change or come to the forefront of attention. We need to remember, as Cronbach has noted, that one important role of the evaluator is to illuminate, not to dictate, the decision. Helping clients to understand the complexity of issues, not to give simple answers to narrow questions, is a role of evaluation.

Another limitation is that, if followed in its entirety, the management-oriented approach can result in costly and complex evaluations. If priorities are not carefully set and followed, the many questions to be addressed using a management-oriented approach can clamor for attention, leading to an evaluation system as large as the program itself and diverting resources from program activities. In planning evaluation procedures, management-oriented evaluators need to consider the resources and time available. If the management-oriented approach requires more time or resources than are available, another approach may have to be considered.

As a case in point, consider the program manager who has to make decisions about next week's production schedule. Because of his time limitations, and the limited information that is readily available to him, this manager may be able to use only the CIPP or UCLA models informally, as an armchair aid. As with any approach, the management-oriented evaluator needs to be realistic about what work is possible and must not promise more than can be delivered.

Finally, this evaluation approach assumes that the important decisions can be clearly identified in advance, that clear decision alternatives can be specified, and that the decisions to be served remain reasonably stable while the evaluation is being done. All of these assumptions about the orderliness and predictability of the decision-making process are suspect and frequently unwarranted. Frequent adjustments may be needed in the original evaluation plan if this approach is to work well.

Major Concepts and Theories

1. The major impetus behind the management-oriented approach to evaluation is to inform decision makers about the inputs, processes, and outputs of the program under evaluation. This approach considers the decision maker's concerns, informational needs, and criteria for effectiveness when developing the evaluation.

2. Stufflebeam's CIPP evaluation model incorporates four separate evaluations (i.e., context, input, process, and product) into one framework to better serve managers and decision makers. Each of these evaluations collects data to serve different decisions (e.g., context evaluations serve planning decisions) by progressing through a series of evaluation steps that provide structure to the evaluation.

3. In the CIPP model, a context evaluation helps define objectives for the program under evaluation.

4. To facilitate the design of program procedures, the CIPP model's input evaluation provides information on what resources are available, what alternative strategies to the program should be considered, and what plans will best meet the needs of the program.

5. A process evaluation is used in the CIPP model to determine how well a program is being implemented, what barriers to success exist, and what program revisions may be needed.

6. Product evaluation is used in the CIPP model to provide information on what program results were obtained, how well needs were reduced, and what should be done once the program has ended.

7. Alkin's UCLA model is similar to the CIPP model in that it provides decision makers information on the context, inputs, implementations, processes, and products of the program under evaluation.

Discussion Questions

1. In addition to being categorized as an objective-oriented approach, Provus's Discrepancy Model has also been discussed as a management-oriented approach to evaluation. Discuss the elements of Provus's model that enable it to be discussed under the aegis of the management-oriented approaches.

2. Compare and contrast the methods of data collection employed in the context, input, process, and product evaluations.

3. Stufflebeam and Alkin's evaluation models have often been discussed as being quite similar. Identify the elements unique to each model and present the justification for including such elements.

4. Discuss how the management-oriented approach can be used for both formative and summative evaluative purposes.

Application Exercises

1. Using what you have just read about the management-oriented approach to evaluation, identify one or two decisions to be made about a program at your workplace or one with which you are familiar. Who are the decision makers? What information do *you* think they need to make the decisions? What information do *they* think they need to make the decisions? What will influence their decisions? Do you think an evaluation could help them in making these decisions? What kind of evaluation, using the CIPP model, would be most appropriate for each decision?

2. Describe how decisions about programs are typically made in your organization. Would a management-oriented approach work in your organization? Why or why not?

3. A public school system successfully demonstrated its need for federal support for an elementary compensatory education program. They received a $500,000 grant to be spent over a period of three years from July 1, 2002, to June 30, 2005. On March 15, 2002, the superintendent convened a meeting of the assistant superintendent of elementary instruction and thirty principals of elementary schools eligible to participate in the proposed program. It was their decision that a thorough evaluation of the reading and mathematics programs in these schools should be completed by September 30, 2002, to identify needs. Alternative strategies for solving needs would then be evaluated and a program chosen for the elementary compensatory education project. They also decided to establish an evaluation team that would be responsible for:
   a. Conducting the evaluation of the reading and mathematics programs of the eligible schools;
   b. Evaluating alternative programs to meet the needs of the thirty schools;
   c. Continually monitoring the program, which would be implemented starting in 2002; and
   d. Collecting information to be reported annually (on June 30 for each year of the grant) to the U.S. Department of Education.
   Using what you have just learned about management-oriented evaluation approaches, advise the evaluation team members about how they should proceed (assuming that it is now March 2002). Be as detailed in your planning as you can be.

4. Consider an existing affirmative action program for a state university. The program is designed to recruit a more diverse student body to the university without lowering academic standards. The program has two phases: recruitment of potential minority students and instructional assistance once students matriculate. Using your knowledge of your own university, develop evaluation questions that would be considered at each of Stufflebeam's stages, e.g., the context, the input, the process, and the product stages. What managers would be interested in the answers to each

of these questions? (Identify the level of manager from chancellor to dean of students to the affirmative action director.) Would other managers (e.g., deans, department chairs) be interested in the results of any question?

5. The federal government is turning responsibility for welfare and other social services over to states and counties. You're the director of social services in your county and have been operating a welfare-to-work program for selected welfare recipients for about a year. Now, you're working with your staff to determine what you should do to expand this program. You're given a lot more flexibility than in the past. The primary criterion is that welfare recipients must be off welfare within two years of the start date. What context, input, process, and product questions might you ask during the stages of this evaluation? How might you collect data to address each question?

6. Identify an evaluation that was conducted in your organization or university and answer the following questions: Who initiated the evaluation (e.g., management, mandated by the federal government)? What was the purpose of the evaluation? What questions were answered by the evaluation? What types of data were collected? Were nonmanagement stakeholders provided with the evaluation results? What was management's level of receptivity to the evaluation? Were the evaluation findings used? Next, consider whether management would have been more or less receptive to the evaluation and whether they would have used the evaluation findings if the management-oriented approach had been employed. Discuss your answers.

Suggested Readings _____

Alkin, M. C. (1991). Evaluation theory development: II. In M. W. McLaughlin & D. C. Phillips (Eds.), *Evaluation and education: At quarter century.* Ninetieth Yearbook of the National Society for the Study of Education, Part II. Chicago: University of Chicago Press.

Sanders, J. R. (2000). *Evaluating school programs: an educator's guide* (2nd ed.). Thousand Oaks, CA: Corwin.

Stufflebeam, D. L. (2000). The CIPP model for evaluation. In D. L. Stufflebeam, G. F. Madaus, & T. Kelleghan (Eds.), *Evaluation models: Viewpoints on educational and human services evaluation* (2nd ed., pp. 274–317). Boston: Kluwer.

Stufflebeam, D. L., & Shinkfield, A. J. (1985). *Systematic evaluation.* Boston: Kluwer-Nijhoff.

Wholey, J. S. (1983). *Evaluation and effective public management.* Boston: Little, Brown.

Wholey, J. S., Hatry, H. P., & Newcomer, K. E. (Eds.). (1994). *Handbook of practical program evaluation.* San Francisco: Jossey-Bass.

6

Consumer-Oriented Evaluation Approaches

Orienting Questions _____

1. Consumers of educational and other human services products (e.g., curriculum materials or training materials) often use product evaluations done by others. If someone were doing a product evaluation for you, what criteria would you want that person to use?

2. What educational or other human services products do you use? How are purchasing decisions made? What criteria seem to be most important in the selection process?

3. What does the consumer-oriented evaluation approach suggest for those involved in curriculum or program development?

4. How has the consumer-oriented evaluation approach been used?

5. What are some major strengths and limitations of the consumer-oriented evaluation approach?

Independent agencies or individuals who have taken responsibility to compile information on educational or other human services products, or assist others in doing so, have promoted the consumer-oriented evaluation approach. Educational and other human services products include a range of materials available in the marketplace: curriculum packages, workshops, instructional media, in-service training opportunities, staff evaluation forms or procedures, new technology, software and equipment, educational materials and supplies, and even services to agencies.

Sales of educational products in the United States alone are approaching $1 billion annually. As competition has grown in the educational and human services product industry, marketing strategies have become creative, but often they are not calculated to serve the best interests of the consumer or client. For this reason, some evaluators have actively urged consumer education, independent reviews of products patterned after the Consumers Union approach, and requirements for objective evidence of product effectiveness. Checklists for rating products and product evaluation reports are two typical outgrowths of this approach.

The consumer-oriented approach to evaluation is predominantly a summative evaluation approach. Developers of products have come to realize, however, that using the checklists and criteria of the consumer advocate while the product is being created is the best way to prepare for subsequent public scrutiny. Thus, the checklists and criteria proposed by "watchdog" agencies have become tools for formative evaluation of products still being developed.

Developers of the Consumer-Oriented Evaluation Approach and Their Contributions

The importance of consumer-oriented evaluation seems to have been first recognized during the mid- and late 1960s as new educational products began to flood the market. Prior to the 1960s, most materials available to educators were textbooks. With the influx of federal education funds earmarked for product development and federal purchases, however, the marketplace swelled.

Scriven's Concerns and Checklists

Scriven (1967) made a major contribution to this approach with his distinction between formative and summative evaluation. The summative role of evaluation, he said, "[enables] administrators to decide whether the entire finished curriculum, refined by use of the evaluation process in its . . . [formative] role, represents a sufficiently significant advance on the available alternatives to justify the expense of adoption by a school system" (pp. 41–42). Criteria that Scriven suggested for evaluating any educational product included the following:

- Evidence of achievement of important educational objectives
- Evidence of achievement of important noneducational objectives (for example, social objectives)
- Follow-up results
- Secondary and unintended effects, such as effects on the teacher, the teacher's colleagues, other students, administrators, parents, the school, the taxpayer, and other incidental positive or negative effects
- Range of utility (that is, for whom it will be useful)
- Moral considerations (unjust uses of punishment or controversial content)
- Costs

Later, Scriven (1974b) published a product checklist that expanded his earlier criteria. This new product checklist was the result of reviews commissioned by the federal government, focusing on educational products developed by federally sponsored research and development centers and regional educational laboratories. It was used in the examination of over ninety educational products, most of which underwent many revisions during that review. Scriven stressed that the items in this checklist were *necessitata*, not *desiderata*. They included the following:

1. *Need:* Number affected, social significance, absence of substitutes, multiplicative effects, evidence of need

2. *Market:* Dissemination plan, size, and importance of potential markets

3. *Performance—True field trials:* Evidence of effectiveness of final version, with typical users, with typical aid, in tropical settings, within a typical time frame

4. *Performance—True consumer:* Tests run with all relevant "consumers," such as students, teachers, principals, school district staff, state and federal officials, Congress, and taxpayers

5. *Performance—Critical comparisons:* Comparative data provided on important competitors such as no-treatment groups, existing competitors, projected competitors, created competitors, and hypothesized competitors

6. *Performance—Long-term:* Evidence of effects reported at pertinent times, such as a week to a month after use of the product, a month to a year later, a year to a few years later, and over critical career stages

7. *Performance—Side effects:* Evidence of independent study or search for unintended outcomes during, immediately following, and over the long-term use of the product

8. *Performance—Process:* Evidence of product use provided to verify product descriptions, causal claims, and the morality of product use

9. *Performance—Causation:* Evidence of product effectiveness provided through randomized experimental study or through defensible quasi-experimental, ex post facto, or correlational studies

10. *Performance—Statistical significance:* Statistical evidence of product effectiveness to make use of appropriate analysis techniques, significance levels, and interpretations

11. *Performance—Educational significance:* Educational significance demonstrated through independent judgments, expert judgments, judgments based on item analysis and raw scores of tests, side effects, long-term effects and comparative gains, and educationally sound use

12. *Cost-effectiveness:* A comprehensive cost-analysis made, including expert judgment of costs, independent judgment of costs, and comparison to competitors's costs

13. *Extended Support:* Plans made for postmarketing data collection and improvement, in-service training, updating of aids, and study of new uses and user data

These are stringent standards, to be sure, but defensible and important, although few textbooks or curriculum packages now on the market would satisfy all of them. Perhaps no one product will ever be judged successful on all these criteria, but producers' efforts to meet these standards have a marked effect on improving the efforts of product developers. Scriven also developed a checklist to use as a guide for evaluating program evaluations, titling it the **Key Evaluation Checklist** (KEC) (Scriven, 1991c, 2002). This checklist can be found at www.wmich.edu/evalctr/checklists.

Scriven continues to be the most avid and articulate advocate of the consumer-oriented evaluation approach, although he is not unaware of weaknesses in some of its applications, as noted in the following observation:

> We should add a word about what may seem to be the most obvious of all models for a consumerist ideologue, namely *Consumer Reports* product evaluations. While these serve as a good enough model to demonstrate failures in most of the alternatives more widely accepted in program evaluation, especially educational program evaluation, it must not be thought that the present author regards them as flawless. I have elsewhere said something about factual and logical errors and separatist bias in *Consumer Reports*. . . . Although *Consumer Reports* is not as good as it was and it has now accumulated even more years across which the separatists/managerial crime of refusal to discuss its methodologies and errors in an explicit and nondefensive way has been exacerbated many times, and although there are now other consumer magazines that do considerably better work than *Consumer Reports* in particular fields, *Consumer Reports* is still a very good model for most types of product evaluation (Scriven, 1984, p. 75).

Other Checklists and Product Analysis Systems

In the mid-1960s, Ken Komoski was a leader in establishing the Educational Products Information Exchange (EPIE) as an independent product-reviewer service modeled after the Consumers Union. Through its newsletter (*EPIE Forum*) and published reports (see www.epie.org), EPIE has provided much-needed evaluative information to state departments of education and school districts that subscribe to its service. EPIE checklists and analysis guides have also been valuable tools for the educational consumer.

Likewise, the Curriculum Materials Analysis System (CMAS) checklist developed by Morrisett and Stevens (1967) includes the following useful guidelines for product analysis:[1]

1. *Describe the characteristics of the product:* media, materials, time needed, style, costs, availability, available performance data, subject matter and content, dominant characteristics of curriculum forms

2. *Analyze its rationale and objectives:* description and evaluation of rationale, general objectives, specific objectives, behavioral objectives

---

[1]These categories are drawn from the CMAS outline, which is not reproduced here in its entirety. We take full responsibility for any distortions of intent or content that may result from our selective presentation.

3. *Consider antecedent conditions in using this product:* pupil characteristics, teacher capabilities and requirements, community and school characteristics, existing curriculum and curriculum organization (vertical and horizontal)

4. *Consider its content:* cognitive structure, skills to be taught, affective content

5. *Consider the instructional theory and teaching strategies used in this product:* appropriateness of teaching strategies, forms, modes, or transactions

6. *Form overall judgments:* other descriptive data, reported experiences with the product, pilot tryouts, and outside recommendations.

A variety of product evaluation checklists have been developed and used over the past several years by individual evaluators and agencies. Many serve as valuable guides from which one might develop a checklist tailored for one's own situation. The checklist in Figure 6.1, developed by Patterson (n.d.), provides a good example of a concise review form useful for heuristic purposes.

An array of evaluation checklists, including Scriven's Key Evaluation Checklist, are listed on the Western Michigan University Evaluation Center Web site (www.wmich.edu/evalctr/checklists).

How the Consumer-Oriented Evaluation Approach Has Been Used

As mentioned previously, the consumer-oriented approach to evaluation has been used extensively by government agencies and independent educational consumer advocates, such as EPIE, to make information available on hundreds of products. As products begin to be developed for use in communities to address youth and other human needs, similar efforts will be needed to sort out the champions from the charlatans.

The Program Effectiveness Panel in the U.S. Department of Education (previously called the Joint Dissemination Review Panel) established a classic example of a consumer-oriented evaluation system by setting standards (Tallmadge, 1977) for new educational programs that must be met before the panel would recommend any program for adoption. Those programs that passed the panel's review were approved through the National Dissemination Network for dissemination to school systems throughout the United States.

A role that state departments of education or other governmental agencies could play in consumer protection by using this evaluation approach has been discussed but never implemented. Rather than evaluate products themselves and then disseminate their findings to consumers or merely list available products, governmental agencies could use standard forms to compile and then disseminate evaluation information about any new product. Guidelines developed for this purpose could address four aspects of any product: its processes, content, transportability, and effectiveness. In each case the central concern is, "What does one

Instructional Materials Review Form:

Marvin Patterson
Center for Studies in
    Vocational Education
Florida State University

Title(s) _____

_____

Author(s) _____

_____

Publisher _____

_____

Latest Copyright Date _____

☐ Retain for Committee Review

☐ Bibliography Only

☐ Reject (Comments):

Use the following code to rate materials:

+ means yes or good quality

0 means all right, but not of especially good quality

– means no or poor quality

NA means not applicable

						Committee Members
						1. Does the content cover a significant portion of the program competencies?
						2. Is the content up-to-date?
						3. Is the reading/math level appropriate for most students?
						4. Are objectives, competencies, or tasks stated in the student materials.
						5. Are tests included in the materials?
						6. Are performance checklists included?
						7. Are hands-on activities included?
						8. How many outside materials are required? **+** means 0–1 materials **0** means 2-3 materials **–** means 4+ materials
						9. Would you use these materials in your training program?
						If the materials to this point appear to be a possible choice for selection, continue with your review. Stop if the materials appear to be too poor for further consideration.
						10. Is a Teacher's Guide included that offers management suggestions for the materials?
						11. Is the material presented in a logical sequence?
						Quality Judgments. Use **+**, **0**, **–** to rate the quality of the products.
						12. Quality of objectives, competencies, and/or tasks
						13. Degree of match between learning activities and objectives
						14. Quality of test items and degree of match with objectives
						15. Quality of performance checklists and degree of match with objectives
						16. Quality of directions for how students are to proceed through the materials
						17. Quality of drawings, photographs, and/or other visuals
						18. Overall design of the learning activities for individualized instruction
						19. Emphasis on safety practices (when needed)
						20. Degree of freedom from bias with respect to sex, race, national origin, age, religion, etc. (see provided guidelines)
						21. Quality of management procedures for teachers (teacher's guides, etc.)
						22. (Optional) List the career-map competencies covered by these materials.

Comments:

FIGURE 6.1 *Sample Checklist for Evaluations*

Source: The form is from M. Patterson, n.d., Tallahassee, FL: Center for Instructional Development and Services, Florida State University.

need to know about a product before deciding whether to adapt or install it?" Questions posed within each category include the following:

Process Information

1. What is the nature and frequency of interactions among students or clients/teachers or service delivery staff/administrators/relevant others? Have these interactions been evaluated?
2. Is the strategy to be employed described so that its appropriateness can be determined? Has the strategy been evaluated?
3. Is the delivery schedule required by the program or product described so that its feasibility can be determined? Has the schedule been evaluated?
4. Are the equipment and facilities required by the program or product described so that their feasibility can be determined? Have they been evaluated?
5. Are the budget and human resource requirements of the program or product listed so that their feasibility can be determined? Have the following requirements been included?
   a. Start-up and continuation budget requirements
   b. Administration, staff, parent, or advisory committee resource requirements
   c. In-service program requirements
6. Is evaluation an integral part of (a) the development and (b) the implementation of the program or product?

Content Information

1. Does this program or product have basic elements, such as those listed below?
   a. Clearly stated outcome objectives
   b. Sufficient directions
   c. Other materials required
   d. Prerequisite knowledge/attitudes required
   e. Fit with knowledge base and existing programs
2. Have the above elements been evaluated?
3. Has the content of the program or product been evaluated by recognized content specialists?
4. Is there sufficient information about the program or product rationale and philosophy to permit a decision about whether it is within the realm of school or agency responsibility or consistent with the organization's philosophy? (For example, school responsibility has traditionally encompassed such areas as intellectual development, personal development, citizenship and social development, educational and personal adjustment, physical growth and development.)
5. Do the objectives of the program or product have cogent rationales? Are they compatible with the school or agency philosophy and the values of the community?

Transportability Information

Three elements relating to transportability appear critical (1) geography and setting, (2) people, and (3) time.

1. What information is available regarding *settings* in which the program or product has been used effectively, in terms of the following factors?
   a. Size/numbers
   b. Organization
   c. Political factors
   d. Legal issues
   e. Facilities
   f. Wealth
   g. Occupational factors
   h. Geographical indices (for example, rural/urban)
   i. Cultural factors
   j. Public/nonpublic factors
   k. Philosophical issues
2. What information is available concerning the *individuals* or *groups* with whom the program or product has been used effectively in relation to the variables listed below?
   a. Age/grade
   b. Experience
   c. Entrance knowledge, skills, and behaviors
   d. Expectations/preferences/interests
   e. Ethnic/cultural makeup
3. What information is available regarding the *time of year* in which the program or product has been used effectively?
4. Does the program or product have *special requirements* in areas such as the following?
   a. Training
   b. Organization or facilities
   c. Additional materials or equipment
   d. Research people/specialists

Effectiveness Information

1. Has technically sound information about the effects of the program or product on its target population been obtained using one or more of the following procedures?
   a. Comparison to established base (pre-/post-)
   b. Prediction (making success estimates using regression techniques or subjective estimation)
   c. Comparison to local or state groups
   d. Comparison against objectives or predetermined criterion levels
   e. Comparison to competing programs or products

2. Is there evidence that the program or product has eliminated a documented need, in addition to management gains such as the following?
   a. Cost savings
   b. Improved morale
   c. Faster improvement rate
3. Is good immediate and follow-up effectiveness information available?

These questions could easily be made into a checklist formed by using the following response categories.

Yes	*No*	*Implied*	*Not Applicable*
Information available:			

Although not necessarily a product evaluation enterprise, the *Mental Measurement Yearbooks* published by the Buros Institute at the University of Nebraska (www.unl.edu/buros/index.html) must be mentioned as a form of consumer-oriented evaluation. These yearbooks contain critical reviews of commercially available tests marketed in the United States and other English-speaking countries. As educational products, these tests deserve the same scrutiny any product receives, and the *Mental Measurement Yearbooks* have provided a valuable service in this regard to educators, psychologists, personnel directors, and any others who use tests or other measurement devices.

Strengths and Limitations of the Consumer-Oriented Evaluation Approach

Developers of the consumer-oriented approach to evaluation have provided a valuable service in two ways: (1) they have made available evaluations of products as a service to those who may not have the time or information to do the job thoroughly, and (2) they have increased consumers' knowledge about the criteria most appropriate to use in selecting educational or service-delivery products. The checklists that have evolved from years of consumer-oriented product evaluations are useful and simple evaluation tools. They have been especially useful in addressing the Values Identification Standard (Standard U4) in *The Program Evaluation Standards* (Joint Committee, 1994).

Consumers have become more aware of commercial sales ploys thanks to the efforts of consumer-oriented evaluators. Consumers are (or should be) less vulnerable to sales tactics than they were twenty years ago. They are (or should be) more discriminating in the way they select products.

The product development industry has a long way to go, however, in being responsive to consumers' needs. Just ask a textbook sales representative for information about the performance or proven effectiveness of her product, and see what kind of information you get. Most of the time it will be either anecdotal testimony and sales information or scanty, poorly conceived product evaluation. Very seldom do corporations spend the time or money needed to acquire acceptable information about their products' performance. Consumers must insist on such information if the product development industry is to take product evaluation seriously.

The consumer-oriented approach to evaluation is not without drawbacks (although they seem small compared to its benefits). It can increase the cost of products. The time and money invested in product testing will usually be passed on to the consumer. Moreover, the use of stringent standards in product development and purchase may suppress creativity because of the risk involved. There is a place for field-trial programs before products are fuller adopted. By developing long-term plans for change, educators and other service providers can give untested products a chance without consuming large portions of the budget. Cooperative trial programs with developers may be in the best interests of all.

Finally, the consumer-oriented approach to evaluation threatens local initiative development because local practitioners may become increasingly dependent on outside products and consumer services. Service providers need to place the purchase of outside products in perspective so that they are not overly dependent on the availability of other people's work. We agree with those who contend that we need to be less concerned with developing and purchasing practitioner-proof products and more concerned with supporting product-proof practitioners—those who think for themselves and who take the initiative in addressing human needs.

Major Concepts and Theories

1. The increase in federal funding allocated for educational products and materials since the 1960s spurred the development of the consumer-oriented evaluation approach, which provides potential consumers with information regarding a variety of product factors. This information is provided to help consumers become more knowledgeable about the products they purchase.

2. The most widely used methods of collecting data in consumer-oriented evaluations are stringent evaluation criteria and checklists, which provide consumers with defensible results on a wide variety of product factors.

Discussion Questions

1. What was the major reason for the development of the consumer-oriented approach?

2. Identify some examples of consumer-oriented evaluations. What was the purpose behind these evaluations? What were the evaluations' major audiences? Secondary audiences? What types of data were collected? What decisions were made based on evaluation findings?

3. How can a consumer-oriented evaluation be formative? Summative? What kind of information would each type of evaluation provide to developers, manufacturers, and consumers of products?

4. What kind of questions would evaluators ask if they were interested in the transportability of a product? In its effectiveness? In its content? In the process associated with its implementation?

Application Exercises

1. A company's catalog of resources available to community leaders who work with youth claims that those who apply their approach to youth development will see decreases in alcohol and other drug use, early sexual activity, violence, and school failure. Using what you have learned about consumer-oriented evaluation, what information would you seek before you ordered resource materials from this catalog?

2. Teachers in each academic department of a senior high school are given a choice of curricular programs to use in their classrooms. This policy is designed to take full advantage of the range of capabilities of individual faculty members. All faculty members are required to prepare an evaluation of their program and circulate these reports among their colleagues. These evaluations are to be conducted in keeping with the evaluation guidelines established by the curriculum council, which require:
   - A statement from all teachers at year-end about the goals for their courses and an assessment of the extent to which these goals were met using the selected program;
   - Submission of information from all teachers about how their pupils' performance compares to that of pupils using a different curricular program;
   - An outside assessment of the appropriateness of the selected program for each teacher's stated goals;
   - A comparison of student performance on standardized tests to national norms; and
   - A complete list of test items that are used during the year. Results for each item are to be reported.

   Using what you have just learned about consumer-oriented evaluation, what changes in the evaluation process could you suggest to the curriculum council? How could faculty reports be structured so that other schools could benefit from their consumer reports?

3. You have recently graduated from your master's or doctoral program, and now that you don't have to spend all that money on tuition, you are in the market for a new automobile. You have seen all the flashy and seductive commercials for new cars and trucks and, although you are enticed by the commercials, you are determined to make the best decision about which car or truck to purchase (after all, money does not grow on trees!). What information is going to be most important

to you in making your decision? Where will you go to find this information? Is there anything your information source needs to provide so that you can be assured that its data collection, analysis, and reporting procedures were sound?

4. As a member of the New York City School Board, you have been asked to determine which science textbooks to purchase for the next school year. As with most districts, yours is faced with budget cuts and you will be unable to buy more than one textbook. Thus, your first decision needs to be the best one for your students.

   Given the information provided about the consumer-oriented evaluation approach in this chapter, what kinds of questions will you be asking the publisher, teachers, and students who have been exposed to the books? Will you involve experts in your decision-making process? Will you rely on data collected by an outside firm? Do you want to perform a content analysis?

Suggested Readings

Scriven, M. (1974). Standards for the evaluation of educational programs and products. In G. D. Borich (Ed.), *Evaluating educational programs and products*. Englewood Cliffs, NJ: Educational Technology Publications. Also in W. J. Popham (Ed.), (1974), *Evaluation in education*. Berkeley, CA: McCutchan.

Scriven, M. (1991). Key evaluation checklist. In M. Scriven, *Evaluation thesaurus* (4th ed.). Newbury Park, CA: Sage.

Tallmadge, G. K. (1977). *Ideabook: JDRP* (ERIC DL 48329). Washington, DC: U.S. Government Printing Office.

www.epie.org

www.wmich.edu/evalctr/checklists

7

Expertise-Oriented Evaluation Approaches

Orienting Questions

1. What are the arguments for and against using professional judgment as the means for evaluating programs?
2. Under what conditions would accreditation, blue-ribbon panels, or connoisseurship be methods of choice for conducting an evaluation?
3. What criteria would you use to screen experts to select the best for an expertise-oriented evaluation?
4. What differences exist between formal and informal professional review systems?
5. What are some major strengths and limitations of the expertise-oriented evaluation approach?

The expertise-oriented approach to evaluation, probably the oldest and most widely used, depends primarily on professional expertise to judge an institution, program, product, or activity. For example, the worth of a drug-prevention curriculum would be assessed by curriculum or subject-matter experts who would observe the curriculum in action, examine its content and underlying learning theory or, in some other way, glean sufficient information to render a considered judgment about its value.

In another case, the quality of a hospital could be assessed by looking at its special programs, its operating facilities, its emergency room operations, its in-patient operations, its pharmacy, and so on, by experts in medicine, health services, and hospital administration. They could examine facilities and equipment/supplies of the hospital, its operational procedures on paper and in action, the qualifications of its personnel, patient records, and other aspects of the hospital to determine whether it is meeting appropriate professional standards.

Although subjective professional judgments are involved to some degree in all the evaluation approaches described thus far, this approach is decidedly different because of its direct, open reliance on subjective professional expertise as the primary evaluation strategy. Such expertise may be provided by the evaluator(s) or by someone else, depending on who offers most in the substance or procedures being evaluated. Usually one person will not own all of the requisite knowledge needed to do the evaluation adequately. A team of experts who complement each other are much more likely to produce a sound evaluation.

Several specific evaluation processes are variants of this approach, including doctoral examinations administered by a committee, proposal review panels, professional reviews conducted by professional accreditation bodies, reviews of institutions or individuals by state or national licensing agencies, reviews of staff performance for decisions concerning promotion or tenure, peer reviews of articles submitted to "refereed" professional journals, site visits of educational programs conducted at the behest of the program's sponsor, reviews and recommendations by prestigious "blue-ribbon" panels, and even the critique offered by the ubiquitous expert who exists to serve in a self-appointed watchdog role.

To impose some order, we choose to organize and discuss these various manifestations of expertise-oriented evaluation within four categories: (1) formal professional review systems, (2) informal professional review systems, (3) ad hoc panel reviews, and (4) ad hoc individual reviews. Differences in these categories are shown in Table 7.1, along the following dimensions:

1. Is there an existing structure for operating the review?
2. Are published standards used as part of the review?
3. Are reviews scheduled at specified intervals?
4. Does the review include opinions of multiple experts?
5. Do results of the review have an impact on the status of whatever is reviewed?

TABLE 7.1   *Some Features of Four Types of Expertise-Oriented Evaluation Approaches*

Type of Expertise-Oriented Evaluation Approach	Existing Structure	Published Standards	Specified Schedule	Opinions of Multiple Experts	Status Affected by Results
Formal review system	Yes	Yes	Yes	Yes	Usually
Informal review system	Yes	Rarely	Sometimes	Yes	Usually
Ad hoc panel review	No	No	No	Yes	Sometimes
Ad hoc individual review	No	No	No	No	Sometimes

To this we have added a fifth category, namely educational connoisseurship and criticism, to discuss an interesting expertise-oriented approach that does not fit neatly into the other categories or dimensions shown in Table 7.1.

Site visitation, frequently the mode for conducting expertise-oriented evaluations, is not itself an approach to evaluation; rather, it is a method that might be used not only here but also with other evaluation approaches. Site-visit methods and techniques are discussed in Chapter 16, along with other techniques often used by expertise-oriented evaluators. A more comprehensive and detailed discussion of guidelines and procedures for site visits and proposal reviews also appears in Worthen and White (1987).

Developers of the Expertise-Oriented Evaluation Approach and Their Contributions

It is hard to pinpoint the origins of this approach, for it has long been with us. It was formally used in education in the 1800s, when schools began to standardize college entrance requirements. Informally, it has been in use since the first time an individual to whom expertise was publicly accorded rendered a judgment about the quality of some endeavor (and history is mute on when that occurred). Several movements and individuals have given impetus to the various types of expertise-oriented evaluations.

Formal Professional Review Systems

We would define a formal professional review system as one having: (1) structure or organization established to conduct periodic reviews; (2) published standards (and possibly instruments) for use in such reviews; (3) a prespecified schedule (for example, every five years) for when reviews will be conducted; (4) opinions of several experts combining to reach the overall judgments of value; and (5) an impact on the status of that which is reviewed, depending on the outcome.

Accreditation.   To many, the most familiar formal professional review system is that of *accreditation,* the process whereby an organization grants approval of institutions such as schools, universities, and hospitals. Beginning in the late 1800s, national and regional accreditation agencies in education gradually supplanted in the United States the borrowed western European system of school inspections, and these became a potent force in education during the 1930s. Education was not alone in institutionalizing accreditation processes to determine and regulate the quality of its institutions. Parallel efforts were underway in other professions, including medicine and law, as concern over quality led to wide-scale acceptance of professionals' judging the efforts of fellow professionals. Perhaps the most memorable example is Flexner's (1910) examination of medical schools in the United States and Canada in the early 1900s, which led to the closing of numerous schools he cited as inferior. As Floden (1983) has noted, Flexner's study was not accreditation in the strict sense, because medical schools did not participate voluntarily, but it certainly qualified as accreditation in the broader sense: a classic example of private judgment evaluating educational institutions.

Flexner's approach differed from most contemporary accreditation efforts in two other significant ways. First, Flexner was not a member of the profession whose efforts he presumed to judge. An educator with no pretense of medical expertise, Flexner nonetheless ventured to judge the quality of medical training in two nations. He argued that common sense was perhaps the most relevant form of expertise.

> Time and time again it has been shown that an unfettered lay mind, is . . . best suited to undertake a general survey. . . . The expert has his place, to be sure; but if I were asked to suggest the most promising way to study legal education, I should seek a layman, not a professor of law; or for the sound way to investigate teacher training, the last person I should think of employing would be a professor of education (Flexner, 1960, p. 71).

It should be noted that Flexner's point was only partially supported by his own study. Although he was a layman in terms of medicine, he was an *educator* and his judgments were directed at medical *education*, not the practice of medicine, so even here appropriate expertise seemed to be applied.

Second, Flexner made no attempt to claim empirical support for the criteria or process he employed because he insisted that the standards he used were the "obvious" indicators of school quality and needed no such support. His methods of collecting information and reaching judgments were simple and straightforward: "A stroll through the laboratories disclosed the presence or absence of apparatus, museum specimens, library, and students; and a whiff told the inside story regarding the manner in which anatomy was cultivated" (p. 79).

Third, Flexner dispensed with the professional niceties and courteous criticisms that seem to typify even the negative findings yielded by today's accreditation processes. Excerpts of his report of one school included scathing indictments such as this: "Its so-called equipment is dirty and disorderly beyond description. Its outfit in anatomy consists of a small box of bones and the dried-up, filthy fragments of a single cadaver. A cold and rusty incubator, a single microscope, . . . and no access to the County Hospital. The school is a disgrace to the state whose laws permit its existence" (Flexner, 1910, p. 190).

Although an excellent example of expertise-oriented evaluation (if expertise as an educator, not a physician, is the touchstone), Flexner's approach is much more like that of contemporary evaluators who see judgment as the sine qua non of evaluation and who see many of the criteria as obvious extensions of logic and common sense (e.g., Scriven, 1973). But today's accreditation systems seem for the most part to have grown up differently. Whereas Flexner's review used the same process and standards for all medical schools reviewed, there is much more variability in contemporary national and regional accreditation systems. Agencies in the United States, such as the North Central Association (NCA) for accrediting secondary schools, the Joint Commission on Accreditation of Healthcare Organizations (JCAHO), or the National Council for the Accreditation of Teacher Education (NCATE), have developed dualistic systems that include some minimum standards deemed important for all institutions, along with an internal self-study component in which institutions can present their unique mission and goals, defend their reasonableness and importance, and report on how well that self-study approach is accomplishing its goals and what capabilities it offers for the foreseeable future. These two facets of accreditation are emphasized to greatly different degrees in various accreditation systems, leading Kirkwood (1982) to criticize accreditation for lacking "similarity of aims, uniformity of process, or comparability among institutions" (p. 9), whereas others complain that the imposition of external standards by accrediting agencies denies institutions the opportunity of developing unique strengths.

Current accreditation systems also depend on the assumption that only members of a profession are qualified to judge the activities of their peers. Not only are accreditation site-visit team members drawn from the profession or occupation whose work they will judge, but also the standards and criteria are developed solely by members of that professional fraternity.[1] For example, "The standards of techniques for accreditation of schools of teacher education have been determined by committees, comprised mainly of practicing teachers and teacher educators" (Floden, 1983, p. 262).

Although accreditation has historically focused on the adequacy of facilities, qualifications of staff, and perceived appropriateness of the processes used, rather than assess the outcomes of programs, several current accreditation systems aspire to justify their criteria and standards on the basis of empirical links of inputs and processes to outcomes. In large part such efforts are reactions to critics of accreditation who have typified accreditation as (in private correspondence from an unnamed colleague) "a bunch of anachronistic old fogies who bumble about with meters, measuring lighting and BTUs and counting the ratio of children per toilet, but failing to measure anything which could be conceived by any stretch of the imagination as related to what children are learning." Though obviously far overdrawn, such a caricature strikes a sensitive nerve among people responsible for accreditation systems, and such criticisms may account, at least in part, for a gradual de-emphasis on such quantitative indicators as square footage per student or number of volumes in the library and a move toward more qualitative indices dealing with purposes of schooling. The same issue appeared in a mental health setting where an accreditation team member observed that an organization that received a "solid C" was probably providing better services than one that received an A. His reasoning was that the accreditation focused so much on time-consuming paperwork irrelevant to patient outcomes that an organization that did well on those issues was probably not spending sufficient time for its professionals to provide good therapy.

---

[1]Floden (1983) has noted that jurisdictional disputes *within* professions exist, as with the long-standing tension over who should control accreditation of teacher education programs, elementary and secondary school teachers or faculties of teacher education institutions. Though beyond the scope of this chapter, issues of who should participate in and who should control accreditation processes are obviously important.

Some movement has been seen in recent years toward including outcomes in the accreditation process. Regional school accreditation agencies are developing outcomes-based accreditation procedures. Several state commissions on higher education are trying to include outcome standards such as graduation rates, job placement, withdrawal rates, and ratios of the costs of education to eventual salaries of graduates. These efforts have not yet stood the test of long usage, but they do appear promising.

As accreditation systems have matured, they have taken on commonalities that extend to the accreditation of most institutions, permitting Scriven (1984) to describe the distinctive features of contemporary accreditation as including (1) published standards; (2) a self-study by the institution; (3) a team of external assessors; (4) a site visit; (5) a site-team report on the institution, usually including recommendations; (6) a review of the report by some distinguished panel; and (7) a final report and accreditation decision by the accrediting body. Although not every accrediting system follows this prescription completely, this is an excellent description of most accreditation systems today.

Although viewed by some as not truly an evaluative system, others see accreditation as very much evaluative. Regardless of which view one holds, most would agree that accreditation has played an important role in institutional change. It is true that accrediting agencies have little real power over agencies who fail to take their recommendations seriously, as Floden (1983) states:

> If accreditors instruct an institution to make particular changes, three options are open. First, officials may amass the necessary funds and make the changes. Second, they may decide the changes cannot be made and close their doors. Third, they may decide not to worry about what the accreditors say and make no changes. If an institution exercises either of the first two options, the aims of accreditation have been realized. When the third option is taken, the process of accreditation has failed to achieve its main purpose (p. 268).

Yet, in our experience, the third option is only infrequently exercised. Fully accredited status is, if nothing more, a symbol of achievement highly valued by most institutions. Although there may be much room for improvement in the accreditation process, it appears to be a formal review process that will be with us for a long time and, if the upsurge of thoughtful analyses of accreditation issues, problems, and potential is any indication, there is reason to be optimistic that its impact can be positive.

Other Formal Review Systems. Despite the wide reach of accreditation, there are those who feel it is an incestuous system that often fails to police itself adequately. As House (1980) has stated:

> At one time it was sufficient for an institution to be accredited by the proper agency for the public to be assured of its quality—but no longer. Parents are not always convinced that the school program is of high quality when it is accredited

by the North Central Association. In addition, political control of accrediting activities is shifting to state governments (p. 238).

Because of such concerns over accreditation's credibility, coupled with the pervasive feeling that decisions "closer to home" are preferable, many state boards or departments are conducting their own reviews of institutions. Although these typically supplement rather than supplant reviews by private accrediting bodies and generally use similar review strategies, they seem of greater consequence to institutions and programs reviewed because negative reviews result not only in loss of status but also possible loss of funding or even termination.

Informal Professional Review Systems

Many professional review systems have a structure and a set of procedural guidelines and use multiple reviewers. Yet some lack the formal review system's published standards or specified review schedule. For example, in the United States, state departments of education were required by federal law, over a period of two decades, to establish a system to evaluate all programs and projects funded under a specific funding authorization designed to increase innovation in schools. Compliance varied widely, but those states that conscientiously complied established an evaluation system in which at least a sample of districts receiving such funds were reviewed annually by site-visit teams and the results used to determine future funding levels and program continuation. However, few states had anything resembling published standards, and most site-visit teams were left to develop their own evaluation procedures without the benefit of any guidelines. Clearly, these were informal review systems.

A graduate student's supervisory committee, composed of experts in the student's chosen field, is an example of an informal system for conducting expert-oriented evaluation. Structures exist for regulating such professional reviews of competence, but the committee members determine the standards for judging each student's preparation and competence. Few would question whether results of this review system affect the status and welfare of graduate students.

Some may consider the systems for obtaining peer reviews of manuscripts submitted to professional periodicals to be examples of informal professional review systems—perhaps. Many journals do use multiple reviewers, chosen for their expertise in the content of the manuscript and, sometimes, empaneled to provide continuity to the review board. In our experience, however, the review structure and standards of most professional journals shift with each appointment of a new editor, and reviews occur whenever manuscripts are submitted rather than on any regular schedule. In some ways, journal reviews may be a better example of the ad hoc professional review process discussed below.

Ad Hoc Panel Reviews

Unlike the ongoing formal and informal review systems discussed above, many professional reviews by expert panels occur only at irregular intervals, when circumstances demand. Generally, these reviews are related to no institutionalized structure for evaluation and use no predetermined standards. Such professional reviews are usually "one-shot" evaluations prompted by a particular, time-bound need for evaluative information. Of course, a particular agency may, over time, commission many **ad hoc panel reviews** to perform similar functions without their collectively being viewed as an institutionalized review system.

Funding Agency Review Panels.   Many funding agencies and foundations use peer-review panels to review competitive proposals. Reviewers read and comment on each proposal and meet as a group to discuss and resolve any differences in their various perceptions.[2] Worthen and White (1987) provided a set of proposal review guidelines and instruments for use by external review panels, including (1) preparing for the proposal review (selecting reviewers, structuring review panels, preparing and training reviewers in the use of review instruments); (2) conducting the proposal review (individual evaluation procedures, total panel evaluation procedures, methods for eliminating bias); and (3) presenting results of proposal reviews (summarizing review results). Justiz and Moorman (1985) and Shulman (1985) have also discussed particular proposal review procedures that depend on the professional judgment of panels of experts, but expert professionals are not the only ones who can be used as evaluators. Many community volunteers review proposals for United Way and other funding agencies that use committees of volunteers as reviewers. While these reviews are done conscientiously, new, unstated considerations and criteria are often injected into the funding decisions, and the committees are often criticized as not being qualified to judge the funding proposal. If community volunteers are viewed as "experts in the needs of the community," and if they are assisted by subject-matter consultants in some way, then the evaluation process may come closer to the expertise-oriented approach as defined in this chapter.

Blue-Ribbon Panels.   A prestigious "blue-ribbon panel," such as the National Commission on Excellence in Education in the early 1980s, discussed in Chapter 1, is an example of an ad hoc review panel. Members of such panels are appointed because of their experience and expertise in the field being studied. Such panels are typically charged with reviewing a particular situation, documenting their observations, and making recommendations for action. Given the visibility of such panels, the acknowledged expertise of panel members is important if the panel's findings are to be credible. On more local scales, where ad hoc review panels are frequently used as an evaluative strategy for many endeavors ranging from economic development and environmental policies to school governance expertise of panel members is no less an issue, even though the reviewers may be of local or regional repute rather than national renown. Although recommendations of ad hoc panels of experts may have major impact, they also may be ignored, for there is often no formalized body charged with the mandate of following up on their advice.

---

[2]"Field readers" who respond individually from afar may collectively make up a panel if they or their opinions are later brought together to arrive at a group judgment concerning that which is evaluated.

Ad Hoc Individual Reviews

Another form of expertise-oriented evaluation resides in the ubiquitous individual professional review of any entity by any individual selected for his expertise to judge its value. Employment of a consultant to perform an individual review of some educational, social, or commercial program or activity is commonplace. Such expert review is a particularly important process for evaluating textbooks, training programs, media products, job-placement tests, program plans, and the like. Such materials need not be reviewed on site, but can be sent to the expert. A good example is the review of commercially available tests used by the Buros Institute of Mental Measurements (see Plake and Impara, 2001).

Educational Connoisseurship and Criticism

The roles of the theater critic, art critic, and literary critic are well-known and, in the eyes of many, useful roles. Critics are not without their faults (as we shall discuss later), but they are good examples of direct and efficient application of expertise to that which is judged. Indeed, few evaluative approaches are likely to produce such parsimonious and pithy portrayals as that of one Broadway critic who evaluated a new play with a single-line summary: "The only thing wrong with this play is that it was performed with the curtain up!"

Although not championing one-line indictments, Eisner (1991) does propose that experienced experts, like critics of the arts, bring their expertise to bear in evaluating the quality of programs in their areas of expertise. Eisner does not propose a scientific paradigm but rather an artistic one, which he sees as an important qualitative, humanistic, "nonscientific" supplement to more traditional inquiry methods.[3]

Eisner (1975, 1991) has written that this approach requires *connoisseurship* and *criticism*. Connoisseurship is the art of appreciation—not necessarily a liking or preference for that which is observed, but rather an awareness of its qualities and the relationships between them. The connoisseur, in Eisner's view, is aware of the complexities in real-world settings and possesses refined perceptual capabilities that make the appreciation of such complexity possible. The connoisseur's perceptual acuity results largely from a knowledge of what to look for (advance organizers or critical guideposts) gained through a backlog of previous relevant experience.

The analogy of wine tasting is used by Eisner (1975) to show how one must have many experiences[4] to be able to distinguish what is significant about a wine, using a set of techniques to discern qualities such as body, color, bite, bouquet, flavor, aftertaste, and the like, to judge its overall quality. The connoisseur's re-

---

[3]This is an important point lost on some who employ Eisner's notions as the *sole* evaluation of the evaluation object, overlooking the fact that Eisner never proposed his approach as sufficient in and of itself.

[4]We add that Eisner doubtlessly had *quality* of experience in mind as much or more than *quantity*. The connoisseur of wine and the lush are worlds apart.

fined palate and "gustatory memory" of other wines tasted is what enables him to distinguish subtle qualities lost on an ordinary drinker of wine and to render judgments rather than mere preferences. Connoisseurship does not, however, require a public description or judgment of that which is perceived, for the latter moves one into the area of criticism.

"Criticism is the art of disclosing the qualities of events or objects that connoisseurship perceives" (Eisner, 1979a, p. 197), as when the wine connoisseur either returns the wine or leans back with satisfaction to declare it of acceptable, or better, quality. Evaluators are cast as critics whose connoisseurship enables them to give a public rendering of the quality and significance of that which is evaluated. Criticism is not a negative appraisal, as Eisner presents it, but rather an educational process intended to enable individuals to recognize qualities and characteristics that might otherwise have been unnoticed and unappreciated. Criticism, to be complete, requires description, interpretation, and evaluation of that which is observed. "Critics are people who talk in special ways about what they encounter. In educational settings criticism is the public side of connoisseurship" (Eisner, 1975, p. 13). Program evaluation, then, becomes program criticism. The evaluator is the "instrument," and the data collecting, analyzing, and judging are largely hidden within the evaluator's mind, analogous to the evaluative processes of art criticism or wine tasting. As a consequence, the expertise—training, experience, and credentials—of the evaluator is crucial, for the validity of the evaluation depends on his perception. Yet different judgments from different critics are tolerable, and even desirable, for the purpose of criticism is to expand perceptions, not to consolidate all judgments into a single definitive statement.

Kelly (1978) has also likened evaluation to criticism by using literary criticism as his analogy. Although different in some features from Eisner's approach, it is similar enough to be considered another example of the expertise-oriented evaluation approach.

How the Expertise-Oriented Evaluation Approach Has Been Used

As we noted earlier, this evaluation approach has been broadly used by both national and regional accreditation agencies. Two rather different types of accreditation exist. One is *institutional accreditation,* whereby the entire institution is accredited, including all of its more specific entities and activities, however complex. In essence, such institutional endorsement means the accrediting body has concluded that the institution, in general, meets acceptable standards of quality. The second type is *specialized* or *program accreditation,* which deals with various subunits in an institution,[5] such as particular academic or professional training programs. As Kirkwood (1982) has noted, "institutional accreditation is not

---

[5]Obviously, in single-purpose institutions, such as a dental school with no other programs, this distinction is meaningless.

equivalent to the specialized accreditation of each of the several programs in an institution" (p. 9). Rather, specialized accrediting processes are usually more specific, rigorous, and prescriptive than are those used in institutional accreditation. Most specialized accreditation bodies are national in scope and frequently are the major multipurpose professional associations (e.g., the American Psychological Association or the American Medical Association), whereas institutional accreditation is more often regional and conducted by agencies that exist solely or primarily for that purpose (e.g., in the United States, the North Central Association or the New England Association).

A good example of how accreditation by private professional agencies and government-sponsored professional reviews are combined comes from Bernhardt's (1984) description of the evaluation processes of state, regional, and national education agencies, which collectively oversaw teacher education programs in California:

> Colleges and Universities in California must be accredited or approved by at least three agencies to offer approved programs of teacher education. Private institutions must first have the approval of the State Department of Education's Office of Private Postsecondary Education (OPPE) to offer *degree* programs. Public institutions must be authorized by their respective California State University and University of California systems. Second, institutions must be accredited by the Western Association of Schools and Colleges (WASC). Then, institutions must submit a document that states that the program is in compliance with all CTC guidelines in order to gain the approval of the Commission on Teacher Credentialing (CTC).
>
> In addition to OPPE, WASC, and CTC accreditation, educational institutions often choose to be accredited by the National Council for Accreditation of Teacher Education (NCATE) (p. 1).

Other uses of expertise-oriented evaluation are discussed by House (1980), who noted the upsurge of university internal-review systems of colleges, departments, and programs. He noted that such professional reviews were not only useful in making internal decisions and reallocating funds in periods of financial austerity but also may have deflected suggestions that such programs should be reviewed by higher education boards.

Uses (and abuses) of peer review by governmental agencies have been discussed by scholars in many disciplines (see Anderson, 1983). Some funding agencies have also used panels of prestigious educators to evaluate the agencies to which research and development awards had been made. For example, the U.S./Department of Education has empaneled review teams to visit and evaluate each member within its federally funded network of regional laboratories and university-based research and development centers, even though the evaluation focused on only some important outcomes.

As for uses of Eisner's educational criticism approach, we are familiar with few applications beyond those studies conducted by his students (Alexander, 1977; McCutcheon, 1978; Vallance, 1978).

Strengths and Limitations of the Expertise-Oriented Evaluation Approach

Collectively, expertise-oriented approaches to evaluation have emphasized the central role of expert judgment and human wisdom in the evaluative process and have focused attention on such important issues as whose standards (and what degree of publicness) should be used in rendering judgments about programs. Conversely, critics of this approach suggest that it often permits evaluators to make judgments that reflect little more than personal biases. Others have noted that the *presumed* expertise of the reviewers is a potential weakness. Beyond these general observations, the various types of expertise-oriented evaluation approach have their own unique strengths and weaknesses. Formal review systems such as accreditation have several perceived advantages. Kirkwood (1982) lists accreditation's achievements:

> (1) in fostering excellence in education through development of criteria and guidelines for assessing institutional effectiveness; (2) in encouraging institutional improvement through continual self-study and evaluation; (3) in assuring the academic community, the general public, the professions, and other agencies that an institution or program has clearly defined and appropriate educational objectives, has established conditions to facilitate their achievement, appears in fact to be achieving them substantially, and is so organized, staffed, and supported that it can be expected to continue doing so; (4) in providing counsel and assistance to established and developing institutions; and (5) in protecting institutions from encroachments that might jeopardize their educational effectiveness or academic freedom (p. 12).

The thoroughness of accreditation agencies has prevented the sort of oversimplification that can reduce complex educational systems to unidimensional studies. Other desirable features claimed for accreditation include the external perspective provided by the use of outside reviewers and relatively modest cost.

Of all these advantages, perhaps the most underrated is the self-study phase of most accreditation processes. Although it is sometimes misused as a public relations ploy, self-study offers potentially great payoffs, frequently yielding far more important discoveries and benefits than does the later accreditation site visit. Together, internal self-study and external review provide some of the advantages of an evaluative system that includes both formative and summative evaluation.

Formalized review systems also have nontrivial drawbacks. We have already commented on public concerns over credibility and increasing public cynicism that professionals may not police their own operations very vigorously. Scriven (1984) has called accreditation "an excellent example of what one might with only slight cynicism call a pseudo-evaluative process, set up to give the appearance of self-regulation without having to suffer the inconvenience" (p. 73). The steady proliferation of specialized accrediting agencies suggests that there may indeed be truth to the suspicion that such processes are protectionist, placing professional self-interest before the interests of the institutions or publics they serve. Further, proliferation of review bodies, whether for reasons of professional self-interest or governmental distrust of private accreditation processes, can place unbearable financial burdens on institutions. Bernhardt (1984) suggests that the California system, which was described earlier, is too expensive to operate under current budgets, that it is not efficient, and that it is effective for determining only institutional compliance, not educational quality. Perhaps one accreditation visit may be relatively cost-efficient, as noted above, but multiple reviews can boost costs to unacceptable levels. Scriven (1984) has cited several problems with accreditation: (1) no suggested weighting of a "mishmash" of standards ranging from trivial to important, (2) fixation on goals that may exclude searching for side effects, (3) managerial bias that influences the composition of review teams, and (4) processes that preclude input from the institution's most severe critics.

Informal peer-review systems and ad hoc professional reviews reflect many of the advantages and disadvantages discussed above for accreditation. In addition, they possess unique strengths and limitations. Some pundits have suggested that such expert reviews are usually little more than a few folks entering the program site without much information, strolling through the facilities with hands in pockets, and leaving the site with precious little more information but with firm conclusions based on their own preconceived biases. Such views are accurate only for misuses of expert-oriented evaluations. Worthen and White (1987) have shown, for example, how on-site ad hoc panel reviews can be designed to yield the advantages of cross-validation by multiple observers and interviewers while still maximizing the time of individual team members to collect and summarize a substantial body of evaluative information in a short time span. Such ad hoc review panels can also be selected to blend expertise in evaluation techniques with knowledge of the program and to avoid the naive errors that occur when there is no professional evaluator on the review team (Scriven, 1984).

Disadvantages of expert-oriented peer reviews include the public suspicion that review by one's peers is inherently conservative, potentially incestuous, and subject to possible conflict of interest. If evaluators are drawn from the ranks of the discipline or profession to be evaluated, there are decided risks. Socialization within any group tends to blunt the important characteristic of detachment. Assumptions and practices that would be questioned by an outsider may be taken for granted. These and other disadvantages led us (Worthen & Sanders, 1984) to point to serious problems that can occur if a program is evaluated only by those with expertise in program content.

House (1980) has noted that confidentiality can be another problem because professionals are often loath to expose their views boldly in the necessary public report. This normally results, he says, in "two reports, one an inside confidential report revealing warts and blemishes, the 'real' report, and a public report which has been edited somewhat. This dual reporting seems to be necessary for professional cooperation, but of course it makes the public distrustful" (pp. 240–241).

Obviously, the question of interjudge and interpanel reliability is relevant when using expert-oriented evaluation because so much depends on the professionalism and perception of the individual expert, whether working alone or as a team member. The question of whether a different expert or panel would have made the same judgments and recommendations is a troublesome one for advocates of this approach for, by its very definition, replicability is not a feature of expertise-oriented studies. Moreover, the easy penetration of extraneous bias into expert judgments is a pervasive concern.

Finally, the connoisseurship–criticism approach to evaluation shares, generally, the strengths and limitations of the other expertise-oriented evaluation approaches summarized above, in addition to possessing unique strengths and weaknesses. Perhaps its greatest strength lies in translating educated observations into statements about program quality. Prior training, experience, and "refined perceptual capabilities" play a crucial role in every expertise-oriented approach to evaluation, but they are perhaps best explicated in Eisner's connoisseurship–criticism approach. One cannot study his proposals and still lampoon expertise-oriented evaluation as a mere "hands-in-pocket" stroll through the program site.

The connoisseurship–criticism approach also has its critics. House (1980) has cautioned that the analogy of art criticism is not applicable to at least one aspect of evaluation:

> It is not unusual for an art critic to advance controversial views—the reader can choose to ignore them. In fact, the reader can choose to read only critics with whom he agrees. A public evaluation of a program cannot be so easily dismissed, however. Some justification—whether of the critic, the critic's principles, or the criticism—is necessary. The demands for fairness and justice are more rigorous in the evaluation of public programs (p. 237).

R. Smith (1984) is perhaps the harshest critic of the "educational criticism" approach to evaluation, fearing that "educational criticism will be esteemed more for its quality as literature and as a record of personal response than for its correct estimates of educational value" (p. 1). He continues by attacking Eisner's conception of criticism on philosophical and methodological grounds, and two of Smith's points are germane here. First, he quarrels with Eisner's contentions that connoisseurs require no special preparation for their role by noting that anyone wishing to be a connoisseur–critic must possess the skills of literary criticism, knowledge of the theories of the social sciences, and knowledge of the history and philosophy of the programs they are evaluating, as well as sensitivity and perceptiveness—no small feat for the person whose primary training may be, for example, as a social worker. How many could really qualify as connoisseurs is an important question. Second, Smith questions whether the same methodology is useful for judging the wide array of objects Eisner includes as potential objects of criticism. "Do the same nondiscursive techniques serve the criticism of classroom life, textbooks, and school furniture?" (p. 14). Can we extend such techniques even further to judge shelters for the homeless, food distribution systems, and nursing homes?

Major Concepts and Theories

1. The hallmark of the expertise-oriented evaluation approach is its direct reliance on professional judgment (either one expert or a team of experts) in the area of the program being evaluated.

2. Expertise-oriented evaluations vary in the extent to which they are formalized or informal. Characteristics to be considered include whether the evaluation uses an existing structure and a specific schedule for review, has published standards, uses the opinion of multiple experts, and has results that directly affect the status of the program or organization.

3. The formal review system (e.g., accreditation) has an existing structure, published standards, a specific schedule, and the opinion of multiple experts; also, the status of a program or organization is usually affected by evaluation results.

4. The informal review system (e.g., graduate student committees) has an existing structure and the opinions of multiple experts; the status of the thing being evaluated is usually affected by evaluation results, but standards are rarely published, and only sometimes is there a specified schedule.

5. Ad hoc panel reviews (e.g., blue-ribbon panels) do not have existing structures, published standards, or specified schedules, but they do incorporate the opinions of multiple experts, and the status of the thing being evaluated is sometimes affected by evaluation results.

6. Ad hoc individual reviews (e.g., Buros Institute of Mental Measurements) do not have existing structures, published standards, specified schedules, or opinions of multiple experts, and the status of the thing being evaluated is only sometimes affected by evaluation results.

7. Educational connoisseurship and criticism involve the description, interpretation, and evaluation of the thing being evaluated in order to expand one's perception of the thing under evaluation, rather than reaching consensus among several experts or connoisseurs.

8. Institutional accreditation involves evaluation of the entire institution's activities and entities, whereas program accreditation evaluates only institutional departments or subsystems.

Discussion Questions

1. Identify two occasions when you were evaluated by a formal review system on one hand, and by an ad hoc panel review on the other. How did these two evaluations differ? Which evaluation did you prefer and why? Did both evaluations yield the same information? How were decisions made based on information collected from these two evaluations?

2. Compare and contrast formal and informal review systems. What are the major differences between the two? Similarities? Provide examples of both types of evaluations.

3. What are the reasons behind conducting in-house accreditation or reviews rather than relying on outside accreditation agencies to conduct the analysis?

4. In which category of expertise-oriented evaluation would professional journal reviews most likely be put? Provide justification for your response.

5. Provide an example of connoisseurship. How does connoisseurship differ from formal review systems? From ad hoc panel review systems?

Application Exercises

1. The Metropolitan Community Action Organization of Los Angeles received federal funds to establish a one-year education program for adults who have been unable to find employment for eighteen consecutive months. A program was implemented that had two major components: (1) the teaching of basic skills, such as reading, mathematics, and English as a foreign language, and (2) the teaching of specific vocational skills, such as computer skills, carpentry, and set design. The program was designed by adult education specialists from a local university and representatives of the employment-training task forces of local unions. Adults were tested as they entered the program by using standardized test batteries in reading and mathematics. Entrants scoring below a grade equivalent of 8.0 were assigned to appropriate levels of reading and/or mathematics instruction. Individual instruction was also provided for students who were not comfortable using the English language. Vocational offerings varied and depended on the unions' assessment of potential job openings in the Los Angeles area. Many of the vocational classes were held on the premises of places of business or industry. A few were conducted in the facility provided for the adult education program.

 Using what you have learned about expertise-oriented evaluation approaches, indicate how these approaches might be used in the evaluation of this program. What purposes could they serve? What could they contribute that other approaches might neglect or not address well? What process and criteria would you use to select your experts and to evaluate their performance?

2. What outside experts review your program or organization?
 a. If you work in an organization that is accredited, review the standards used for accreditation. Do you feel the standards get at the real quality issues of the program or organization? What other standards might you add? Does the accreditation tell the organization's staff something they didn't already know? How are the accreditation findings used?
 b. What other outsiders review your program or organization? How expert are they in your program or organization's context, process, and outcomes? What are the characteristics of the most helpful and least helpful reviewers?

3. The city jail in a mid-size Florida city has experienced two suicides of inmates in the last few months. As a result, the city council has hired a new director for the jail. The new director recognized that the jail has quite a few problems with officers' and

guards' morale, physical facilities, training, security, and other issues and has decided to call in experts to advise him on the status of the jail. You've been hired to coordinate the evaluation.

Provide detailed information on the types of evaluation questions you will be asking, what types of data will be collected, and your justification for the type of expertise-oriented evaluation model you will employ. If your model depends on the opinions of multiple experts, provide information on which experts you will ask to evaluate the jail and whether you will have independent expert analyses or analyses from teams of experts.

4. Your high school is going to be visited by an outside accreditation team. What issues do you think they should attend to? What do you think they might miss in a short visit? What information do you think they should collect? What should they do while they're visiting? Do you think such a team could make a difference for your school? Why or why not?

5. If you participate as an expert reviewer for an accreditation agency, or if you have ever had an opinion about a movie, glass of wine, or hotel room, consider the following questions: How might your expert opinion differ from someone else's within your department (or family)? How might your expert opinion differ from someone else's outside your department (or family)? Do you consider your opinion to be biased? How do you ensure that your opinion will not be biased by your personal preferences? How might your bias impact an evaluation of an institution or glass of wine?

Suggested Readings

Eisner, E. W. (1991a). *The enlightened eye: Qualitative inquiry and the enhancement of educational practice.* New York: MacMillan.

Eisner, E. W. (1991b). Taking a second look: Educational connoisseurship revisited. In M. W. McLaughlin and D. C. Philips (Eds.), *Evaluation and education: At quarter century,* Ninetieth Yearbook of the National Society for the Study of Education, Part II. Chicago: University of Chicago Press.

Floden, R. E. (1980). Flexner, accreditation, and evaluation. *Educational Evaluation and Policy Analysis, 20,* 35–46.

Kells, H. R., & Robertson, M. P. (1980). Post-secondary accreditation: A current bibliography. *North Central Association Quarterly, 54,* 411–426.

Kirkwood, R. (1982). Accreditation. In H. E. Mitzel (Ed.), *Encyclopedia of educational research* (Vol. 1, 5th ed., pp. 9–12). New York: Macmillan and Free Press.

National Study of School Evaluation (1978). *Evaluative criteria.* Arlington, VA: Author.

8

Participant-Oriented Evaluation Approaches

Orienting Questions _____

1. What led to the development of participant-oriented evaluation approaches?
2. What are some of the fundamental principles that participant-oriented evaluators follow when they conduct their evaluations?
3. What problems might a naturalistic evaluator have with a client who wants a detailed evaluation plan in hand before allowing the evaluation to begin? How could the evaluator deal with this requirement?
4. Should naturalistic evaluations limit their practice to qualitative methods? Why?
5. Which can be used most flexibly and eclectically, responsive evaluation or empowerment evaluation? Why?
6. How has each of the evaluation approaches described in this chapter been used?
7. What are the major strengths and limitations of participant-oriented evaluation approaches?

In the previous four chapters, we have described evaluation approaches that have focused, respectively, on (1) the objectives of the program being evaluated, (2) the information needs of program managers, (3) program consumers' ratings of program features and quality, and (4) judgments experts make about programs. We see each of these evaluation approaches as useful. However, they all share a common characteristic: their primary focus is *not* on serving the needs of those who participate in the program who are, in fact, the *raison de'être* for the program. Not that these four prior approaches are unconcerned about the participants' opinions or welfare, for advocates of any of these four general approaches could, if pressed, point out how their approach might ultimately benefit those who participate in the program they evaluate. The key, however, lies in the qualifying word "ultimately." None of the four general approaches we have described thus far *begin* with the program participants. This began to trouble some evaluators as early as 1967, but each succeeding decade has seen more voices raised to propose various types of participant-centered or participant-oriented evaluation approaches, until, by the turn of the century, these had become the most widely discussed approach in current evaluation journals.

We should note that popularity is a fickle criterion by which to choose friends, music, or evaluation approaches. The fact that participant-oriented approaches to evaluation are widely discussed does not mean that we advocate them over other approaches, for we see each as useful for its purposes. Indeed, we present in these chapters a wide array of approaches, finding that in our practice none of them serve as a recipe we follow, but rather as heuristic suggestions and reminders we draw upon as we tailor our own approach with snippets from each that we find useful for our purposes. That disclaimer is made here lest readers assume, from the relative brevity of Chapters 4 through 8, that the greater length of this chapter tips one to our private preference. Not so. Instead, it reflects the rich abundance of differing ways that have been suggested to approach evaluations with the programs' participants as the primary focus and orientation of the evaluation. It also reflects the fact that, whereas some of the prior chapters have addressed more unified, nearly singular views about that approach, here there is a wide array of participant-oriented approaches that must be described.

Evolution of Participant-Oriented Evaluation Approaches

In its early years after evaluation was first mandated by U.S. governmental agencies, most evaluation theorists understandably adopted or adapted the philosophy of conventional nomothetic science and the methods of social science and educational research. But not all. As early as 1967, several evaluation theorists began to react to what they considered to be the dominance of mechanistic and insensitive approaches to evaluation in the field of education. These theorists expressed concerns that evaluators were largely preoccupied with stating and classifying objectives, designing elaborate evaluation systems, developing technically defensible objective instrumentation, and preparing long technical reports, with the result that evaluators were distracted from what was really happening in the programs they evaluated. Critics of traditional evaluation approaches noted that many large-scale evaluations were conducted without the evaluators ever once setting foot on the participating program site(s). What began as a trickle of isolated comments grew to a deluge that flooded evaluation literature in education and the social sciences. More and more practitioners began publicly to question whether many evaluators really understood the phenomena that their numbers, figures, charts, and tables were intended to portray. An increasing segment of the education and human services communities argued that the human element, reflected in the complexities of everyday reality and the different perspectives of those engaged in providing services, was missing from most evaluations.

Consequently, a new orientation to evaluation arose, one that stressed first-hand experience with program activities and settings and involvement of program participants in evaluation. This general approach, which grew quickly after the early 1970s, is aimed at observing and identifying all (or as many as possible) of the concerns, issues, and consequences integral to the human services enterprise.

In large part a reaction to perceived deficits in other evaluation approaches, this orientation encompasses a wide variety of more specific proposals that might be generally tied together by their acceptance of the intuitionist–pluralist philosophy of evaluation (see Chapter 3). Many of those who contributed to the development and use of participant-oriented approaches to program evaluation prefer naturalistic inquiry methods as described later in this chapter. Moreover, most advocates of this approach see participants in the endeavor being evaluated as central to the evaluation, hence the descriptor *participant*-oriented as a label for this approach.

The evaluator portrays the different values and needs of individuals and groups served by the program, weighing and balancing this plurality of judgments and criteria in a largely intuitive fashion. (By intuitive, we do not mean that the evaluator cannot approach this task in a systematic manner but rather that there is no algorithm she can follow in doing so; her intuition about what weight to put on each criterion will determine how the judgment is shaped.) What is judged "best" depends heavily on the values and perspectives of whichever groups or individuals are judging. By involving participants in determining the boundaries of the evaluation, evaluators serve an important educative function by creating better-informed program staff.

Developers of Participant-Oriented Evaluation Approaches and Their Contributions

In an important sense, Stake (1967) was the first evaluation theorist to provide significant impetus to this orientation in the field of education. His paper "The Countenance of Educational Evaluation," with its focus on portrayal and processing the judgments of participants, was to alter dramatically the thinking of evaluators in the next decade. Along with his later writings (Stake, 1975a, 1975b, 1978, 1980, 1988, 1991, 1994, 1995), he provided conceptions and principles that have guided the evolution of this approach. Stake's early writings evidenced his growing concern over dominance of program evaluation by parochial, objectivist, mechanistic, and stagnant conceptions and methods.

Guba's (1969) discussion of the "failure of educational evaluation" provided further impetus at the time to the search for an alternative to the rationalistic approach to evaluation. Parlett and Hamilton (1976) complained that the predominant "agricultural-botanist" research paradigm was deficient for studying innovative educational programs, and they presented an alternative "illuminative evaluation" approach that followed a social anthropology paradigm. Rippey (1973) decried the insensitivity of existing evaluation approaches to the impact of an evaluation on the incumbents in roles within the system being evaluated; he proposed "transactional evaluation" as a more appropriate evaluation approach for systems undergoing evaluation and resultant changes. MacDonald (1974, 1976) expressed concern over existing evaluation approaches' misuses of information for questionable political purposes, opting instead for "democratic evaluation," designed to protect the rights and informational needs of the whole "community" involved.

Guba and Lincoln (1981) reviewed the major approaches used in program evaluation and rejected all except Stake's notion of **responsive evaluation** (described later in this chapter), which they incorporated with naturalistic inquiry to create an evaluation approach they proposed as superior to all alternatives for education. Their subsequent work (Guba & Lincoln, 1989) further delineated an approach that not only rejected the positivist paradigm in favor of that of the constructivist but also focused on evaluation as a means of empowering stakeholders they deemed as disenfranchised with other evaluation approaches.

Since the 1970s, many others have argued for greater involvement of stakeholders in evaluation. See, for example, Cousins and Earl's strong argument for evaluators and practitioners to work in partnership in program evaluation (1995), as well as the writing of Whitmore (1998) and Greene and Abma (2001). House and Howe (1999) have extended this further in their description of their deliberative democratic approach to evaluation, noting that their approach is ". . . one of inclusive, dialogical deliberation in evaluation. By inclusive, we mean that all relevant interests are represented in the evaluation and given full expression. Representation of views and interests should not be dominated or distorted by power imbalances, such as powerful interests curtailing the less powerful in the evaluation . . . evaluative conclusions should emerge from deliberation, from careful reasoning, reflection, and debate" (p. 409).

Other intriguing participant approaches have been suggested. Patton (1994) proposed development evaluation, which he defined as:

> Evaluation processes and activities that support program . . . or organizational development (usually the latter). The evaluator is part of a team whose members collaborate to conceptualize, design, and test new approaches in a long-term, ongoing process of continuous improvement, adaptation, and intentional change. The evaluator's primary function in the team is to elucidate team discussions with evaluative data and logic, and to facilitate data-based decision-making in the developmental process (p. 317).

Bryk (1983) and Mark and Shotland (1985b) proposed stakeholder-based evaluation, in which selected stakeholders representing all legitimate groups were consulted at the planning and data-interpretation phases of the evaluation.

advocacy evaluation

Fetterman's (1994) empowerment evaluation and Mertens's (1999) emancipatory evaluation are proposed to free those persons who are the most marginalized, oppressed, or with the least power, and empower them to control their own destiny by use of the results of the study.

Many of these proposals for democratic, transactional, collaborative, participatory, empowerment, or emancipatory evaluation are not only obviously related, but in a loose way could all be subsumed under the label "advocacy evaluation." As early as 1989, Guba and Lincoln had proposed that evaluators become advocates for the voiceless and powerless of society. Each of these participant-oriented approaches contains an element of advocacy which distinguishes them from the approaches presented in the four previous chapters, where the general assumption in all of them is that of evaluator "neutrality." In contrast, those who have proposed the approaches summarized in this chapter would doubtlessly agree with Greene's (1997) argument that advocacy in evaluation is inevitable, and that the question is not whether evaluators *should* advocate, but rather for *what* and *whom* they should advocate.

Diverse as these widely arrayed proposals are for variants of this general evaluation approach, two threads seem to run through all of them. The first, as Wachtman (1978) notes, is

> disenchantment with evaluation techniques which stress a product-outcome point of view, especially at the expense of a fuller, more holistic approach which sees education as a human endeavor and admits to the complexity of the human condition. Each author argues that instead of simplifying the issues of our humanity we should, in fact, attempt to understand ourselves and human services in the context of their complexity (p. 2).

Second, in most of these writings, value pluralism is recognized, accommodated, and protected, even though the effort to summarize the frequently disparate judgments and preferences of such groups is left to the intuitive sagacity and communication skills of the evaluator. (See, for example, Abma & Stake, 2001.)

Those who use participant-oriented approaches to evaluation typically prepare descriptive accounts—"portrayals," as they have come to be called—of a person, classroom, school, agency, site, project, program, activity, or some other entity around which clear boundaries have been placed. Not only is the entity richly portrayed but it is clearly positioned within the broader context in which it functions.

In addition to commonalities noted above, evaluations that use this approach generally include the following characteristics:

1. *They depend on inductive reasoning.* Understanding an issue or event or process comes from grassroots observation and discovery. Understanding emerges; it is not the end product of some preordinate inquiry plan projected before the evaluation is conducted.

2. *They use a multiplicity of data.* Understanding comes from the assimilation of data from a number of sources. Subjective and objective, qualitative and quantitative representations of the phenomena being evaluated are used.

3. *They do not follow a standard plan.* The evaluation process evolves as participants gain experience in the activity. Often the important outcome of the evaluation is a rich understanding of one specific entity with all of its idiosyncratic contextual influences, process variations, and life histories. It is important in and of itself for what it tells about the phenomena that occurred.

4. *They record multiple rather than single realities.* People see things and interpret them in different ways. No one knows everything that happens in a school or in any but the tiniest program. And no one perspective is accepted as *the* truth. Because only an individual can truly know what she has experienced, all perspectives are accepted as correct, and a central task of the evaluator is to capture these realities and portray them without sacrificing the program's complexity.

Of the many authors who have proposed participant-oriented evaluation approaches, we have selected for further description here a few who have made unique or especially noteworthy contributions.

A Caution about Semantics and Labels

Before discussing in more detail a few examplars of approaches we believe fall comfortably within this chapter, we must insert a caution about placing too much trust in our labels for these approaches—or anyone else's, for that matter. Use of descriptive titles for these various approaches are anything but univocal. Various authors pin the same descriptive label to significantly differing strategies. One might use the label "participatory" to encompass every approach we discuss in this chapter, while another uses it to describe only a particular subset of those approaches. Some authors think of all approaches in this chapter as "collaborative" evaluations, whereas others restrict that title to a specific approach they propose. Thus, we can hardly claim that the labels we use to impose order on the many specific approaches we describe reflect standard usage in evaluation terminology, for there really is no such standard. Rather, we have simply used the labels under which we have clustered the proposals of different evaluators in ways that (1) generally conform to what seems to be "majority usage" and (2) will be helpful to the reader.

Stake's Countenance Framework

Stake's (1967) early analysis of the evaluation process had a major impact on evaluation thinking and laid a simple but powerful conceptual foundation for later developments in evaluation theory. He asserted that the two basic acts of evaluation are *description* and *judgment* (the "two countenances" of evaluation). Thus the two major activities of any formal evaluation study are full description and judgment of that which is being evaluated. To aid the evaluator in organizing data collection and interpretation, Stake created the evaluation framework shown in Figure 8.1.

Using this framework, the evaluator (1) provides background, justification, and description of the program rationale (including its need); (2) lists intended

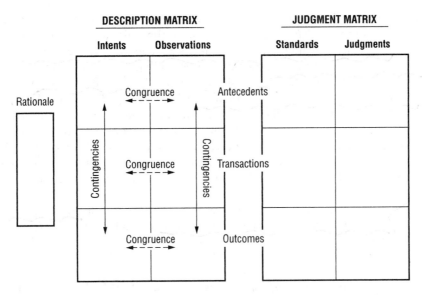

FIGURE 8.1   *Stake's Layout of Statements and Data to Be Collected by the Evaluator of an Educational Program*

Source: From "The Countenance of Educational Evaluation" by R. E. Stake, 1967, Teachers College Record, *68,* p. 529. Reprinted by permission.

antecedents (inputs, resources, existing conditions), transactions (activities, processes), and outcomes; (3) records observed antecedents, transactions, and outcomes (including observations of unintended features of each); (4) explicitly states the standards (criteria, expectations, performance of comparable programs) for judging program antecedents, transactions, and outcomes; and (5) records judgments made about the antecedent conditions, transactions, and outcomes. The evaluator analyzes information in the description matrix by looking at the congruence between intents and observations, and by looking at dependencies (contingencies) of outcomes on transactions and antecedents, and of transactions on antecedents. Judgments are made by applying standards to the descriptive data.

The countenance structure thus gives evaluators a conceptual framework for thinking through the data needs of a complete evaluation. In reviewing his countenance paper twenty-five years later, Stake (1991) noted that it underemphasized the process of describing the evaluation, a shortcoming that he addressed later in his responsive evaluation paper.

Responsive Evaluation

During the early 1970s, Stake began to expand his earlier (1967) writing more obviously into the realm of participant-oriented evaluation. Although the seeds of this explication lie in his earlier work, Stake's subsequent conceptions of responsive evaluation (1972, 1975b, 1978, 1980) are implicitly less formal and explicitly more pluralistic and process-focused than his earlier countenance model.

Responsive evaluation's central focus is in addressing the concerns and issues of a stakeholder audience. Stake (1972) noted that he was not proposing a new approach to evaluation, for "responsive evaluation is what people do naturally in evaluating things. They observe and react" (p. 1).[1] Rather, Stake saw this approach as an attempt to develop a technology to improve and focus this natural behavior of the evaluator. Stake stressed the importance of being *responsive* to realities in the program and to the reactions, concerns, and issues of participants, rather than being *preordinate*[2] with evaluation plans, relying on preconceptions and formal plans and objectives of the program. Stake (1975a) defined responsive evaluation as follows:

> An educational evaluation is responsive evaluation if it orients more directly to program activities than to program intents; responds to audience requirements for information; and if the different value perspectives present are referred to in reporting the success and failure of the program (p. 14).

A major reason for proposing responsive evaluation is Stake's perception that the ultimate test of an evaluation's validity is the extent to which it increases the audience's understanding of the entity that was evaluated. Improved communication with stakeholders is a principal goal of responsive evaluation. "The responsive approach tries to respond to the natural ways in which people assimilate information and arrive at understanding" (p. 3).

The purpose, framework, and focus of a responsive evaluation emerge from interactions with constituents, and those interactions and observations result in progressive focusing on issues (similar to the progressive focusing in Parlett and Hamilton's [1976] illuminative evaluation described earlier). Responsive evaluators must interact continuously with members of various stakeholding groups to ascertain what information they desire and the manner in which they prefer to receive such information. Stake (1975b) described the responsive evaluator's role this way:

> To do a responsive evaluation, the evaluator of course does many things. He makes a plan of observations and negotiations. He arranges for various persons to observe the program. With their help he prepares for brief narratives, portrayals, product displays, graphs, etc. He finds out what is of value to his audience. He gathers ex-

---

[1]Stake's assertion is confirmed by personal experience. After being skeptical for several years about the usefulness of responsive evaluation, one of the authors of this text was asked to describe in print how he would evaluate a particular curriculum (Worthen, 1981). This expedition into "logic-in-use" (see Kaplan, 1964) was revealing because it forced recognition that Stake's description of responsive evaluation had indeed captured those activities and procedures so long used by many experienced evaluators as to become second nature. Stake has served the practice of evaluation well by articulating and bringing to a level of public discourse and analysis procedures that have previously existed largely at the subconscious level of practicing evaluators.

[2]"Preordinate" evaluation refers to evaluation studies that rely on prespecification, when inquiry tends to follow a prescribed plan and does not go beyond the predetermined issues and predefined problems.

pressions of worth from various individuals whose points of view differ. Of course, he checks the quality of his records. He gets program personnel to react to the accuracy of his portrayals. He gets authority figures to react to the importance of various findings. He gets audience members to react to the relevance of his findings. He does much of this informally, iterating, and keeping a record of action and reaction. He chooses media accessible to his audiences to increase the likelihood and fidelity of communication. He might prepare a final written report; he might not—depending on what he and his clients have agreed on (p. 11).

As one might infer from the above description, responsive evaluators are relatively disinterested in formal objectives or the precision of formalized data collection; they are more likely to be at home working within the naturalistic or ethnographic paradigm, drawing heavily on qualitative techniques. Feedback to the various stakeholders is more likely to include portrayals and testimonials rather than more conventional evaluation data. Such portrayals will frequently feature descriptions of individuals in **case studies** based on a small sample of those affected by the program or process being evaluated. Reports to audiences will underscore the pluralism within the program setting. A single set of recommendations is highly improbable; recommendations are more likely to be of the conditional sort where judgments about the "best" program or the "preferred" course of action will vary, depending on who is doing the judging and what criteria she uses to ascertain value. Maxwell (1984) has published a rating scale that could be used to assess the quality of responsive evaluations.

Stake (1975b) used the "clock" shown in Figure 8.2 as a mnemonic device to reflect the prominent, recurring events in a responsive evaluation. Although the evaluator might best begin the evaluation at twelve o'clock and proceed clockwise, Stake has emphasized that any event can follow any other event, and at any point the evaluator may want to move counterclockwise or cross-clockwise, if events warrant such flexibility. Further, many events may occur simultaneously; many will occur several times during an evaluation. The "clock" serves to remind evaluators that flexibility is an important part of using this participant-oriented approach.

One revealing comparison of responsive and **preordinate evaluation** approaches was provided by Stake's (1975b) analysis of what percentage of time evaluators of each persuasion would spend on several evaluation tasks (p. 20):

	Preordinate (%)	Responsive (%)
Identifying issues, goals	10	10
Preparing instruments	30	15
Observing the program	5	30
Administering tests, etc.	10	—
Gathering judgments	—	15
Learning client needs, etc.	—	5
Processing formal data	25	5
Preparing informal reports	—	10
Preparing formal reports	20	10

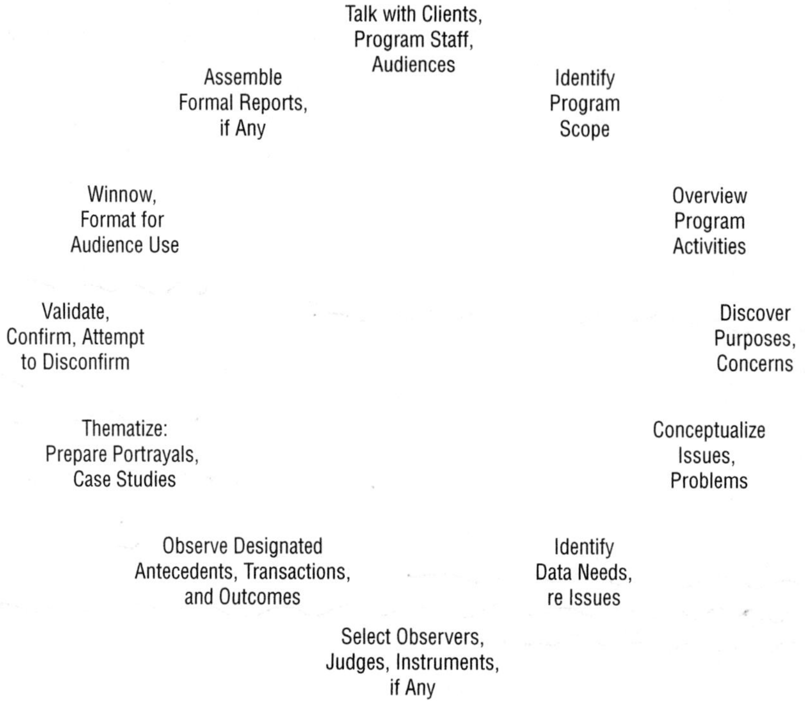

Talk with Clients,
Program Staff,
Audiences

Assemble
Formal Reports,
if Any

Identify
Program
Scope

Winnow,
Format for
Audience Use

Overview
Program
Activities

Validate,
Confirm, Attempt
to Disconfirm

Discover
Purposes,
Concerns

Thematize:
Prepare Portrayals,
Case Studies

Conceptualize
Issues,
Problems

Observe Designated
Antecedents, Transactions,
and Outcomes

Identify
Data Needs,
re Issues

Select Observers,
Judges, Instruments,
if Any

FIGURE 8.2   *Prominent Events in a Responsive Evaluation*

Source: From *Program Evaluation, Particularly Responsive Evaluation* (Occasional Paper No. 5, p. 19) by R. E. Stake, 1975b, Kalamazoo, MI: Western Michigan University Evaluation Center. Adapted by permission.

Stake (1978) also advanced the participant-oriented approach to evaluation by elaborating its rationale. This approach, he said, has appeal for the following reasons:

1. It helps audiences for the evaluation understand the program if evaluators pay attention to the natural way in which audiences understand and communicate about things.

2. Knowledge gained from experience (tacit knowledge) facilitates human understanding and extends human experience.

3. Naturalistic generalizations, which are arrived at by recognizing similarities of objects and issues in and out of context, are developed through experience. They serve to expand the way in which people come to view and understand programs.

4. By studying single objects, people accumulate experiences that may be used to recognize similarities in other objects. Individuals add to existing experience and human understanding.

We have given more space to responsive evaluation than to other participant-oriented evaluation approaches because, as eclectics, we believe that responsive evaluation can be included in all other approaches. The focus of responsive evaluation is on audience concerns and issues—on the information they want the evaluator to provide. One audience may desire information about program outcomes, another may wish to know about how to improve some process, and a third may be concerned with information that would show stakeholders whether the program is being implemented correctly. Any or all of these needs could be addressed by a responsive evaluator, for her evaluation is tailored to fit ("respond to") whatever informational need the evaluation's clients wish to have addressed.

One might question whether or not responsive evaluation, so broadly defined, may lose its uniqueness and meaning. Such a broad claim for responsive evaluation, misunderstood, could also result in less able evaluators attempting to pass off inferior evaluations, which would be rejected as examples of any other evaluation approach, by labeling them as "responsive" evaluation. That prospect tempts one to narrow the definition of responsive studies to exclude atrocities that do not deserve inclusion under any rubric. But one may as well rail against use of the term "creativity" because of the largely abortive efforts to define and measure that construct as to argue for limiting the broad perspective of responsive evaluation because those incapable of doing quality evaluation work, by any definition, may try to creep under the shelter of the broader conceptions that Stake and Guba and Lincoln have proposed. In the final analysis, each evaluation must be judged by its usefulness, not its label. Used intelligently and competently, responsive evaluation methods have great potential for enhancing the quality of any evaluation study.

Before leaving this section, we should correct any misperception we may have created by mostly citing Stake's earlier writing. Responsive evaluation is still used implicitly or explicitly by many evaluators. For example, Spiegel, Bruning, and Giddings (1999) incorporated one style of responsive evaluation into a unique evaluation of an education effort in Nebraska. Also, Greene and Abma (2001) recently devoted an entire issue of *New Directions for Evaluation* to responsive evaluation. Moreover, Stake reaffirms his ongoing faith in this approach, musing in a published interview thirty years after he conceived it, that ". . . the rhetoric and the ethic of responsive evaluation is to be open, to come to understand what's going on there, to find more than your initial issues" (Abma & Stake, 2001, p. 9). He goes on to say that he is ". . . always concerned about diversity, the particular, and the local, the practitioners and others most close to the program, the problems of standardization" (p. 9). This would seem a good summary statement from the author of the responsive approach to evaluation.

Naturalistic Evaluation

In *The Flame Trees of Thika*, Elspeth Huxley (1982) astutely observed:

> The best way to find things out is not to ask questions at all. If you fire off a question, it is like firing off a gun—bang it goes, and everything takes flight and runs

for shelter. But if you sit quite still and pretend not to be looking, all the little facts will come and peck round your feet, situations will venture forth from thickets, and intentions will creep out and sun themselves on a stone; and if you are very patient, you will see and understand a great deal more than a man with a gun does (p. 272).

Huxley's words sum up the spirit of the **naturalistic evaluation** approach better than could any academic description. Yet it is important to move beyond the prosaic to try, as House (1983a) has done, to understand the structure of reality underlying this approach. He labeled as "naturalistic" evaluation any evaluation that

aims at naturalistic generalization (based on the experience of the audience); is directed more at non-technical audiences like volunteers or the general public; uses ordinary language and everyday categories of events; and is based more on informal than formal logic (p. 57).

Although House and others had written of naturalistic approaches to evaluation, Guba (1978) provided the first comprehensive discussion of the merits of introducing naturalistic methods into program evaluation. He differentiated between naturalistic inquiry, rooted in ethnography and phenomenology, and "conventional" inquiry, based on the positivist, experimental paradigm. He not only outlined several reasons for preferring naturalistic inquiry but also analyzed major methodological problems confronting naturalistic inquirers. His monograph contributed greatly toward formulation of naturalistic evaluation methodology.

The most significant work in this area, however, is the work of Guba and Lincoln, which carefully linked naturalistic inquiry to Stake's responsive evaluation and then described procedures for implementing this approach (Guba & Lincoln, 1981, 1989; Lincoln & Guba, 1985).

According to Guba and Lincoln, the major role of evaluation is one of responding to an audience's requirements for information in ways that take account of the different value perspectives of its members. By taking a naturalistic approach to evaluation, the evaluator is studying the program activity in situ, or as it occurs naturally, without constraining, manipulating, or controlling it. Naturalistic inquiry casts the evaluator in the role of a learner, and those being studied in the role of informants who "teach" the evaluator. The dominant perspective is that of the informant, because the evaluators learn their perspectives, learn the concepts they use to describe their world, use their definitions of these concepts, learn the "folk theory" explanations, and translate their world so the evaluator and others can understand it.

Guba and Lincoln stress that the criteria used to judge the rigor of scientific inquiry also hold for naturalistic inquiry but require some reinterpretation. For instance, if one were concerned about the "truth" of an evaluation for particular subjects in a particular context, the naturalistic evaluator would be concerned with the *credibility* of findings rather than internal validity. Corroboration of data through cross-checking and **triangulation** are two methods used by the naturalistic evaluator to establish credibility.

If one were concerned with the *applicability* of an evaluation in other contexts or for other subjects, the naturalistic evaluator would look at the fit of the evaluation findings rather than external validity. Applicability is enhanced through the use of working hypotheses that should be tested in other contexts, and through the use of "thick description," which is a "literal description of the entity being evaluated, the circumstances under which it is used, the characteristics of the people involved in it, the nature of the community in which it is located, and the like" (Guba & Lincoln, 1981, p. 119).

If one were concerned with the *consistency* of evaluation findings (that is, whether the same finding would result if the study were repeated), the naturalistic evaluator would consider the study's *auditability* rather than reliability. By having a second team review the documentation and reasoning underlying the evaluation, the evaluator can determine whether agreement on the findings can be reached. Halpern (1983) has developed an extensive model for auditing naturalistic inquiries.

Finally, if one were concerned about the *neutrality* of the evaluation, the naturalistic evaluator would look at the evaluation's *confirmability* rather than its objectivity. Data should be factual and confirmable. The naturalistic evaluator will require that the information generated by the evaluation can be confirmed.

The naturalistic evaluator proceeds by first identifying stakeholders. Their value positions are important, for it is their perspectives that should be reflected in the evaluation. Concerns and issues are elicited from interviews with the stakeholders and from naturalistic observations by the evaluator.

The naturalistic evaluator's data-collection task is defined by certain kinds of information that are sought:

- Descriptive information about the object of the evaluation and its context
- Information responsive to concerns (documenting concerns, seeking **causes** and consequences, and identifying possible actions)
- Information responsive to issues (clarifying issues, identifying potential courses of action to resolve them)
- Information about values (clarifying values, finding out about their source and degree of conviction)
- Information about standards to be used in the evaluation (identifying criteria, expectations, and needs)

Through the use of interviews, observations, nonverbal cues, documents, records, and **unobtrusive measures,** the naturalistic evaluator uses field notes and records as the sources of this information. Descriptions are used not only as data but also as a reporting technique.

Participatory Evaluation

Another set of loosely confederated suggestions for evaluation might be thought of, in their simplest form (and after all, this *is* an introductory evaluation text), as "participatory." One might expect from our label that we see the evaluation suggestions summarized in this section as the purest examples of "participant-oriented" evaluation. Not necessarily. We believe all the approaches we describe in this chapter fit that description. Rather, we use this term because it is the term used by those whose proposals are described in this section.

Origins of this approach seem to be rooted in the popular participatory action research movement of the 1980s and early 1990s (e.g., Tandon, 1981; Whyte, 1991), aimed largely at providing community input to research/evaluation of social and human-services programs that affected them. But it was perhaps Cousins and Earl (1992, 1995) who began to popularize it enough to draw it into the mainstream of program evaluation. In their anthology of readings on participatory evaluation in education, Cousins and Earl (1995) defined participatory evaluation as evaluation that involves trained evaluation personnel and practice-based decision makers working in partnership. It is best suited, in their view, to formative evaluations that help to inform and improve program implementation. The approach they propose includes training key organizational personnel in the technical skills of evaluation while they are working in partnership with evaluators. This form of capacity building in organizations is intended to prepare key organization members to take on evaluation coordination in continuing and new projects. The evaluator then moves into the role of consultant on technical issues and tasks.

In this collection, Cousins and Earl describe the uniqueness of participatory evaluation in two ways:

1. Participatory evaluation seeks to use evaluation data for practical problem solving, not theory development or empowerment of individuals or groups, or rectification of social inequities.

2. Participatory evaluation has evaluators working in partnership with practitioners. A few key partners are involved in all aspects of the evaluation. The evaluator is the coordinator with responsibility for technical support, training, and quality control. Conducting the study is a joint responsibility.

These authors also claim special advantages for participatory evaluation, specifically that:

> Participatory evaluation is likely to be responsive to local needs, while maintaining sufficient technical rigor so as to satisfy probable critics, thereby enhancing use within the local context. This feature differentiates participatory evaluation from other similar practice-based research activities (p. 9).

In 1998, Cousins and Whitmore held to the same general definition of participatory evaluation as voiced in Cousins and Earl's earlier collection.

> Participatory evaluation implies that, when doing an evaluation, researchers, facilitators, or professional evaluators collaborate in some way with individuals,

groups, or communities who have a decided stake in the program, development project, or other entity being evaluated.

Unlike Cousins and Earl's earlier rejection of "empowerment of individuals or groups" as a role of participatory evaluations, however, Cousins and Whitmore (1998) differentiate between two "themes" of participatory evaluation, one the "transformative" participatory evaluation—empowerment of less powerful or dominated community groups[3]—and the other, "practical" participatory evaluation, which is generally consistent with the first of Cousins and Earl's numbered points above.

While many find this evaluation approach very useful (e.g., King, 1998), some see both pitfalls and potential in it (e.g., Mathison, 2001), while others believe it is an excellent exemplar of program, professional, or organizational development, but fails to qualify as genuine evaluation (e.g., Smith, 1999).

Utilization-Focused Evaluation

According to Patton (1997, p. 20), "utilization-focused evaluation begins with the premise that evaluations should be judged by their utility and actual use; therefore, evaluators should facilitate the evaluation process and design any evaluation with careful consideration of how everything that is done, from beginning to end, will affect use."

This is a theme repeated in such influential evaluation guides as Fetterman's *Empowerment Evaluation* (1996), Sonnichsen's *High Impact Internal Evaluation* (2000), and The Joint Committee on Standards for Educational Evaluation's *Program Evaluation Standards* (1994). By involving intended users of the evaluation in decisions about the evaluation design, including its focus and methods choices, evaluators increase the likelihood of users buying into and using evaluation findings. In addition, evaluators are seen to have a responsibility for training users in evaluation processes and the uses of information.

Empowerment Evaluation

Much like participatory evaluation, the approach frequently referred to as Empowerment Evaluation had its roots in the same soil of community psychology and community-based action research (e.g., Rappaport, 1987) as did its "participatory" cousin. From that soil sprang strongly held views that evaluators should not only facilitate citizen participation in evaluation, but also become advocates for societies' disenfranchised and voiceless minorities. Concerns of advocacy-inclined evaluators about involvement, participation, and empowerment echo the strong concerns expressed in other disciplines and societal sectors over stakeholders' participation, advocacy, social actions, and teamwork. These concerns

---

[3]This empowerment-focused use of participatory evaluation will not be discussed further here, but is relevant to a later section of this chapter on "empowerment evaluation."

have also been well articulated in the field of management (McKinley, 1998; Mitroff, 1998), where similar concerns about social justice, fairness, and participation are highlighted.

Application of this orientation to evaluation was suggested by Brunner and Guzman (1989) and McGee and Starnes (1988). However, empowerment evaluation was vaulted onto evaluation's center stage by Fetterman's (1994) presidential address delivered to the American Evaluation Association the previous fall. In it, he urges evaluators to help program participants to take "... evaluation into their own hands and conduct self-evaluations ...," seeking "... assistance of an evaluator to act as coach ..." (p. 10). While acknowledging that this approach is the anathema of objectivity, Fetterman argues that it is "... obvious ... that science and specifically evaluation have never been neutral. Empowerment evaluation is explicitly designed to serve a vested interest—program participants ... to help them become self-determined" (p. 10).

The several advantages Fetterman claims for empowerment evaluation are viewed by him as inherent in the following facets of this approach:

1. *Training:* "... evaluators teach people to conduct their own evaluations and thus become more self-sufficient" (p. 3).

2. *Facilitation:* "Evaluators can serve as coaches or facilitators to help others conduct their evaluation" (p. 4).

3. *Advocacy:* "Evaluators may ... serve as direct advocates—helping to empower groups through evaluation" (p. 6). .... "Advocate evaluators write in public forums to change public opinion, embarrass power brokers, and provide relevant information at opportune moments in the policy decision making forum" (p. 7).

4. *Illumination:* "Empowerment evaluation can also be illuminating" (p. 7). "This process creates a dynamic community of learners as people engage in the art and science of evaluating themselves" (p. 8).

5. *Liberation:* "Empowerment evaluation can ... [help] individuals take charge of their own lives—and find useful ways to evaluate themselves—[liberating] them from traditional expectations and roles" (p. 9).

Not every evaluator thinks that these advantages are all that advantageous. Stufflebeam (1994), perhaps concerned at Fetterman's missionary zeal for this approach (Fetterman had closed his presidential address with a section entitled, "Spreading the Word"), expressed concern at what he saw as its inherent relativism and lack of regard for objectivity. He applauded everything Fetterman proposed doing as an eminently useful and appropriate societal undertaking, stating "While his commitment to '... helping people help themselves' is a worthy goal, it is not a fundamental goal of evaluation. Surely this is a valuable role that evaluators and all citizens should play, but it is not evaluation" (p. 323).

Fetterman's (1995) response in defense of his position did not end the debate over empowerment evaluation (see also Fetterman, 1997; Patton, 1997a,

1997b; and Scriven, 1997a, 1997b for extended dialog about this approach). Perhaps Patton put his finger on a problem that has contributed significantly to differing views of empowerment evaluation, namely its lack of a clear definition to distinguish it from other participant-oriented approaches.

> Fostering self-determination is the defining focus of empowerment evaluation and the heart of its explicit political and social change agenda. However, empowerment evaluation overlaps participatory, collaborative, stakeholder-involving, and utilization-focused approaches to evaluation. . . . A critical question becomes how to distinguish empowerment evaluation from these other approaches. Making such distinctions has become critical as the field debates the boundaries and implications of empowerment evaluation (1997b, p. 147).

Some efforts have been made to examine the empowerment evaluation approach empirically (see, for example, Lackey, Moberg, and Balistrieri, 1997; Schnoes, Murphy-Berman, & Chambers, 2000). The only conclusion one can draw from such studies, however, is that the empowerment approach is a useful tool, but one that must be used carefully and thoughtfully if it is to be maximally effective. Whether or not it is evaluation is a debate we will leave for another venue.

Looking Back. The participant-oriented evaluation approaches we have described in this chapter collectively reflect a growing emphasis in the field of program evaluation. They are similar in important ways, yet each has unique features. A 1977 review of a collection of actual evaluations that follow this general orientation is still relevant today. The authors of the review noted that . . . they display "a family resemblance, not an enclosed orthodoxy guided by a tacit uniformity of practices" (Hamilton, Jenkins, King, MacDonald, & Parlett, 1977, p. 235). Hamilton (1977) provided a general description of "pluralist evaluation models" that still serves to summarize the participant-oriented approaches we have discussed.

> In practical terms, pluralist evaluation models . . . can be characterized in the following manner. Compared with the classic models, they tend to be more extensive (not necessarily centered on numerical data), more naturalistic (based on program activity rather than program intent), and more adaptable (not constrained by experimental or preordinate designs). In turn, they are likely to be sensitive to the different values of program participants, to endorse empirical methods which incorporate ethnographic fieldwork, to develop feedback materials which are couched in the natural language of the recipients, and to shift the locus of formal judgment from the evaluator to the participants (p. 339).

How Participant-Oriented Evaluation Approaches Have Been Used

In one sense, given the breadth of this general evaluation approach, one could almost include as examples any program evaluation that has involved participants in the evaluation or made use of naturalistic methods. We will resist that temptation, recognizing that many studies may use some of the apparatus of participant-oriented evaluation without being good examples of this approach. Rather, we would point to a few examples that reflect conscious efforts to follow this evaluation approach.

Rippey (1973) has described how the concept of transactional evaluation has been used to aid in the process of change in different types of organizations. Likewise, Parlett and Dearden (1977) provided examples of the use of illuminative evaluation in evaluation of higher-education programs.

The arts was the focus of an extensive evaluation project using the responsive evaluation approach (Stake, 1975a). In this project and an earlier one, which evaluated a program for talented youth (Stake & Gjerde, 1974), responsive evaluation procedures were used to address issues of immediate interest to evaluation audiences.

Malcolm and Welch (1981) provide an example of a naturalistic case study of a Catholic junior college in Minneapolis, Minnesota. Of particular interest are the authors' personal reactions to such topics as the evaluators' preparations, note taking in the field, phases in planning for the study, interviewing, data analysis and report writing, and final editing and validation.

Other uses of the participant-oriented approaches have been reported by Wolcott (1976), Wolf and Tymitz (1977), Guba and Lincoln (1981), Spindler (1982), Williams (1986), Patton (1994, 1997), Fitzpatrick (1992), Stake (1992, 1994), Cousins and Earl (1995), Schnoes, Murphy-Berman, and Chambers (2000), and Fetterman (2001). King (1998) discusses three examples that illustrate her work with social-services programs, high schools, and leadership development programs. Coupal and Simoneau (1998) provide an interesting illustration of the application of participatory evaluation in an international context, evaluating community projects in Haiti. In addition, Independent Sector (1995) has produced a useful guide to getting people involved in evaluations. A recent issue of *New Directions for Evaluation* (Greene & Abma, 2001) describes several recent applications of responsive evaluation and describes the changes that have occurred in this model since its beginnings.

Strengths and Limitations of Participant-Oriented Evaluation Approaches

Introduction of evaluations using this approach has prompted more acrimonious debate than almost any development in evaluation within the last two decades. Critics of these approaches discount it as hopelessly "soft-headed" and argue that few, if any, program evaluators are either virtuous or intellectually agile enough to wield masterfully the seductively simple yet slippery and subtle tools that this approach requires. Champions of pluralistic, responsive approaches reply that they can be readily used by any sensitive individual and that they are infinitely richer and more powerful than other approaches and, indeed, can subsume them, because they are flexible and do not preclude the use of other approaches within them, should that be desired by the evaluator's sponsor. Our intent here is not to add to the debate but rather to summarize briefly some of the pros and cons thus far advanced for this approach.

It is important to distinguish between participant-oriented approaches to evaluation and qualitative methodologies used in data collection. Participant-oriented approaches can and do use both qualitative and quantitative methods. There is, however, more use of qualitative methods in participant-oriented evaluations than is typical in, for example, objectives or management-oriented evaluations.

Few would argue against the claim that participant-oriented evaluation has emphasized the human element in evaluation. It directs the attention of the evaluator to the needs of those for whom an evaluation is being done, and it stresses the importance of a broad scope: looking at the program from different viewpoints. Those who use this approach view programs as a complex human undertaking and attempt to reflect that complexity as accurately as possible so that others may learn from it. The potential for gaining new insights and usable new theories about our educational, social, or corporate programs by using this approach stands among its greatest strengths. Other advantages of this method are its flexibility, attention to user training in evaluation as part of the evaluation process, attention to contextual variables, and encouragement of multiple data-collection techniques designed to provide a view of less tangible but crucial aspects of human and organizational behavior. In addition, this approach can provide rich and persuasive information that is credible to audiences who see it as reflecting genuine understanding of the inner workings and intricacies of the program. Finally, evaluators from the participant-oriented school succeed in establishing dialogue with and empowering the quiet, powerless stakeholders who are often left out of the evaluation process (Fetterman, 2000; House & Howe, 1999; Mertens, 1999).

As with other approaches to evaluation, the strengths of this approach may also prove to be its limitations. Attempts to simplify the evaluation process have proven popular and effective in the past, as evidenced by the fifty-year dominance of the objectives-oriented evaluation method. Thus, an approach that stresses complexity rather than simplicity may ultimately prove more popular with theorists than with practitioners, however sound it may be on other grounds.

More than any other approach to program evaluation that we have examined, participant-oriented approaches add a political element inasmuch as they foster and facilitate the activism of recipients of program services. Today many citizens seek an active role in governance. Parents have become active participants in school policy making. Citizens are involved in crime-prevention programs and are involved in developing programs to improve their environment and their communities. Programs intended to serve AIDS patients, the homeless, the chronically mentally ill, and tenants in public housing programs more often are carved out of a politicized climate. Programs such as these often receive much national and local media attention and have interest groups that are quite well organized.

In today's participatory culture, these models provide a means for empowering and educating stakeholders, particularly those with less access to power, to make informed choices and become involved in decision making.

Critics of the participant-oriented approach have argued that its subjectivity is a serious limitation, even though its proponents have helped make us aware of how values inevitably enter into methodological and evaluative decisions (Guba & Lincoln, 1981). Because of their reliance on human observation and individual perspective, and their tendency to minimize the importance of instrumentation and group data, advocates of this approach have been criticized for "loose and unsubstantiated" evaluations. For example, Sadler (1981) discussed intuitive data processing as a potential source of bias in naturalistic evaluations. Others have noted that ethnographic field work can take so much time to complete that the situation often changes or the administrator has to make a decision before the evaluation findings are available. Moreover, some have claimed that excluding judgment from the evaluator's role makes some participant-oriented approaches nonevaluative. In fact, some have expressed concern that such approaches minimize the central role evaluators play in judging merit or worth and worry that these approaches confuse with evaluation the many roles that evaluators can play outside of evaluation (e.g., Mayeske, 1995; Stufflebeam, 1994).[4]

The cost of using participant-oriented approaches to evaluation has been viewed by some as a serious limitation, especially during times of tight budgets. This approach can be labor-intensive, often requiring full-time presence of the evaluator in the field over an extended period. The time it takes to prepare field notes and reports using this approach is at least as long as it takes for the initial observations.

The labor intensity of participant-oriented approaches to evaluation limits the number of cases that can be studied intensively. Consequently, it is critical that cases be selected carefully and, even then, that conclusions not be extended beyond what those cases will allow. On the whole, evaluators using this approach are well advised to be cautious in making interpretations and drawing conclusions. Most results might best be considered contextually anchored facts on which to base—and then test—tentative generalizations.

Finally, a dilemma confronting any of these approaches that promote advocacy as a goal of evaluation lies in the danger that evaluators who advocate for and become enamored with societal trends may lose the ability to provide unbiased evaluations of programs that touch or are touched by those trends. Yet one cannot expect (or even wish) for evaluators to become recluses, foregoing all chances to be active participants in society so as to be sure to retain a clear (unbiased) view if called upon to evaluate programs pertinent to (or based on the values of) the societal trend in question. Finding a way to have the simultaneous cake-having and cake-eating of evaluators being both involved citizens and dispassionate evaluators will tax our ingenuity in the years ahead, and how we re-

---

[4]It should be noted that recent advances in the methodology of naturalistic and participant-oriented approaches have largely neutralized these latter concerns, however.

solve this dilemma will help to shape the future of participant-oriented evaluation approaches.

Major Concepts and Theories

1. In the participant-oriented evaluation approaches, evaluators work to portray the multiple needs, values, and perspectives of program stakeholders to be able to make judgments about the value or worth of the program being evaluated.

2. Evaluations that follow the participant-oriented approach often depend on inductive reasoning, use multiple data sources, do not follow a standard plan, and describe multiple rather than single realities.

3. Stake's Countenance Framework attempts to describe the thing being evaluated and render judgment about the thing's value or worth. This framework assists the evaluator in making data collection and interpretation decisions, and it affords the evaluator the information needed to analyze the level of congruency between intended and actual outcomes, the dependency of outcomes on transactions and antecedents, and the dependency of transactions on antecedents.

4. The Illuminative Evaluation model focuses more on description and interpretation than on rendering judgments of value and worth, and on intensive study of a program as a whole rather than on manipulation and control of factors that may impact program success.

5. Responsive evaluations incorporate the concerns of stakeholder groups into the evaluation plan through continuous interaction with stakeholders. This allows evaluators to be responsive to stakeholder concerns and to increase communication and stakeholder understanding of the object of evaluation.

6. The primary concern of the naturalistic evaluator is evaluating the program as it occurs. The evaluator is in the role of a learner, and the stakeholders serve as teachers. The goal is to describe a program fully while taking into account the different value perspectives of its stakeholders.

Discussion Questions

1. When would a participant-oriented evaluation be particularly appropriate? Provide a few examples from your own experience.

2. What kinds of risks does an evaluation entail by involving many different stakeholder groups?

3. Compare and contrast participant-oriented evaluation with objectives-oriented evaluation. What are the major differences between these two approaches? Similarities?

4. What do we mean by multiple perspectives of a program? Why would different groups have different perspectives? Shouldn't the evaluation just describe the one "real" program?

5. Is it useful to a manager to know about different perspectives of a program? Why? What can a manager (or other stakeholders) do with such information?

6. Describe the ways in which naturalistic evaluators determine which questions should be asked in an evaluation and which data collection methods are most appropriate to employ.

7. How might a naturalistic evaluator establish the credibility of evaluation findings? Determine applicability findings to other settings or subjects? Establish the finding's level of consistency? Examine the neutrality of the evaluation?

8. Who are the common stakeholders for evaluations in your field?

Application Exercises

1. What current program are you involved with that would benefit from a participant-oriented evaluation? Who are the stakeholders for this program? How would you proceed with the evaluation? How could "thick description" be used?

2. As newly appointed director of student activities for the John F. Kennedy High School, you decide to conduct an evaluation of the student activities program in the school. The most current information about the program is found in the faculty handbook, published at the opening of each school year. This description reads as follows:

   The John F. Kennedy High School offers a wide range of activities for its 2,000 students. Among the various activities are clubs, intramural and varsity sports, band, choir, orchestra, and various service programs such as Red Cross. Clubs are organized by students and assigned a faculty advisor by the dean of students. Meetings are scheduled on Monday to Thursday evenings and held in the cafeteria, auditorium, or gymnasium of the school. Varsity sports activities are directed by members of the physical education faculty. Intramural sports are organized by home rooms and directed by a faculty member appointed by the dean of students. Band, choir, and orchestra are under the direction of members of the music department. Service programs are organized by students who must also find a faculty member who is willing to advise them.

   Feeling that this description does not provide you with sufficient insight into the program, you decide to conduct an evaluation of the current program before undertaking any modifications or restructuring of the program. As a participant-oriented evaluator, how would you proceed to plan and conduct the evaluation?

3. Describe briefly similarities and differences among responsive, participatory, and empowerment evaluation.

4. a. In your own work, identify two evaluation questions that would be most appropriately answered with a participant-oriented approach. Identify two questions or issues that might be inappropriate to address with a participant-oriented approach. Why do you think the first lend themselves to a participant-oriented approach and the second ones do not?

   b. Take one of the questions you identified as appropriate to address with a participant-oriented approach. What stakeholder groups would you involve in the evaluation? How would you involve them? At what stages? Would you take a case study approach? How would your data collection differ from that used in a more "objective" approach?

5. Use a participatory approach to evaluate the following program: Arvada Hospital has begun an aggressive program to screen men over fifty years old for prostate cancer. Their first efforts involved a saturation advertising program using billboards and radio and newspaper advertisements with well-known local men advocating screening and describing their experience. The hospital has hired you to use a participant-oriented approach to evaluate this effort. What do you do? What stakeholders do you involve? How? How do you make use of qualitative or naturalistic methods? What quantitative methods might you use? How appropriate are they?

Suggested Readings

Cousins, J. B., & Earl, L. M. (Eds.). (1995). *Participatory evaluation in education*. Bristol, PA: Falmer Press.

Fetterman, D. M. (1994). Empowerment evaluation. *Evaluation Practice, 15*, 1–15.

Fetterman, D. M. (2000). *Foundations of empowerment evaluation*. Thousand Oaks, CA: Sage.

Greene, J. C., & Abma, T. A. (Eds.). (2001). *Responsive evaluation*. New Directions for Evaluation, No. 92. San Francisco, CA: Jossey-Bass.

Guba, E. G., & Lincoln, Y. S. (1989). *Fourth generation evaluation*. Thousand Oaks, CA: Sage.

Lincoln, Y. S., & Guba, E. G. (1985). *Naturalistic inquiry*. Beverly Hills, CA: Sage.

Patton, M. Q. (1994). Developmental evaluation. *Evaluation Practice, 15*, 311–320.

Patton, M. Q. (1997). *Utilization-focused evaluation* (3rd ed.). Thousand Oaks, CA: Sage.

Stake, R. E. (1967). The countenance of educational evaluation. *Teachers College Record, 68*, 523–540.

Stake, R. E. (1975). *Program evaluation, particularly responsive evaluation*. (Occasional Paper No. 5). Kalamazoo, MI: Western Michigan University Evaluation Center.

Stake, R. E. (1995). *The art of case study research*. Thousand Oaks, CA: Sage.

Sonnichsen, R. C. (2000). *High impact internal evaluation*. Thousand Oaks, CA: Sage.

Whitmore, E. (Ed.). (1998). *Understanding and practicing participatory evaluation*. New Directions for Evaluation, No. 80. San Francisco, CA: Jossey-Bass.

9

Alternative Evaluation Approaches: A Summary and Comparative Analysis

Orienting Questions

1. What are some cautions to keep in mind when considering alternative evaluation approaches?

2. Did you find one evaluation approach that you feel most comfortable with, or did you find useful ideas coming out of each approach?

3. Would you miss much if you ignored all but one approach, which you then used for all evaluations? What are some dangers of always using the same evaluation approach?

4. What negative metaphors underlie certain evaluation models? Why is that a concern?

5. What has each of the alternative evaluation approaches contributed to the conceptualization of evaluation?

6. What are some of the major contributions that the various evaluation approaches, viewed collectively, make to the practice of program evaluation?

7. How might the various evaluation approaches be used together in an actual evaluation?

In Chapter 3 we presented a variety of ways to classify evaluation approaches, including our schema, which organizes the proposed approaches into five categories: objectives-oriented, management-oriented, consumer-oriented, expertise-oriented, and participant-oriented evaluation. Together these five represent major current schools of thought about how to approach program evaluation. Collectively, Chapters 4 through 8 summarize the theoretical and conceptual underpinnings of most of today's program evaluations. It is therefore appropriate to ask how useful these frameworks are. The answer is "Very useful indeed," as we shall discuss shortly, but first we feel compelled to offer several cautions.

Cautions about the Alternative Evaluation Approaches

Five cautions about the collective conceptions of evaluation presented in Chapters 4 through 8 are worthy of consideration here.

The Significant Writings in Evaluation Are neither Models nor Theories

In a young field there is inevitably a good bit of conceptual floundering as notions are developed, circulated, tried out, refined, and challenged by new alternatives. Until a solid knowledge base begins to guide practice, any new field is likely to be guided by the positions, preferences, and polemics of its leaders. Some may argue that this is inappropriate, but the point is that it is also inevitable, for no new field or discipline is born full grown. Yet, it is also appropriate to ask how far the conceptions of leaders have led the field, and in what direction.

Given the fact that program evaluation grew in part out of scientific inquiry, it is not surprising that many evaluators have aspired to be scientists. As evaluators turned toward the various evaluation "frameworks" as sources of guidance, many began asking how close program evaluation was to becoming a science or discipline in its own right. Perhaps political, social, or situational naïveté fosters the hope that evaluation will one day grow into a full-grown discipline. That day, if attainable, would seem far off. As Scriven (1991a) has noted, the more appropriate conception is that evaluation is a transdiscipline.

Neurath, Cernap, and Morris (1955) noted decades ago that advancement in any field is often directly related to the existence of a "univocal language," one in which there is one and only one term for each construct and where each important construct is so named. The semantic undergrowth in the field of evaluation could hardly be termed univocal; some clearing of redundant verbiage is clearly called for.

If one applies standard criteria for scientific models, the various evaluation approaches do not seem to qualify in any but the loosest sense. Even the less rigorous dictionary definitions of *models* seem ill-suited for the current evaluation literature. The most relevant definition is "something eminently worthy of imitation, an exemplar, an ideal," but without clearer operational guidelines and procedures, most evaluation *models* are so vague and general as to elude emulation in any strict sense.

If not models, then what about theories? Here again, our conceptions in evaluation seem not to fit. What we have come to call the theoretical underpinnings of our field lack important characteristics of most theories. Our evaluation writings are not axiomatic or deductive bodies of knowledge. They do not enable us to develop, manipulate, or interrelate laws and explanations. They do not permit us to predict or explain. They are not tested in the empirical crucible or interrelated with or validated against other relevant bodies of knowledge. In short, they are not theories.

If not models or theories, what are those influential conceptions about evaluation we have used five chapters of this book to present? Quite simply, they are individuals' conceptions about the field of evaluation, their efforts to order the content of a new and partial field into some kind of logical structure. They are sets of categories, lists of things to think about, descriptions of different kinds of evaluation, and exhortations to (perhaps) be heeded. Useful? Very. But theories? Models? No, clearly not.

"Discipleship" to a Particular Evaluation "Model" Is a Danger

> Into the street the Piper steps,
>   Smiling first a little smile,
> As if he knew what magic slept
>   In his quiet pipe the while;
> —*Robert Browning*, "The Pied Piper of Hamelin"

Every evaluation approach described in this book has adherents who believe that a better evaluation will result from that orientation than from alternatives. Fair enough. We have no quarrel with those who follow particular persuasions, just so they do so intelligently, knowing when and where their preferred approach is not applicable, as well as when and how to apply it.

What is troublesome, however, is that every evaluation approach also has some unthinking disciples who are convinced that a particular approach to evaluation is right for every situation.[1] There really are evaluators who are CIPP loyalists, or unswerving adherents of theory-based evaluation, or those who hold the tenets of responsive evaluation as articles of faith. Many evaluators unthinkingly follow a chosen evaluation approach into battle without first making certain the proposed strategy and tactics fit the terrain and will attain the desired outcomes of the campaign. Insisting that an outcome-based approach be used for an internal formative evaluation when the issues, not to mention the program, are vague and amorphous is as foolish as mounting a cavalry attack across a swamp.

Ideally, evaluation practitioners are sufficiently at home using these approaches as heuristic tools, selecting from a variety of evaluation approaches one appropriate for the situation rather than distort the interests and needs of the evaluation's audience(s) to make them fit a preferred approach. For an illustrative example, see the interview with Fetterman in which he discusses departing

---

[1]Readers are reminded of Kaplan's (1964) "law of the instrument" analogy to show the fallacy of such thinking (see Chapter 4).

from his empowerment approach in a particular evaluation because of the context (Fitzpatrick & Fetterman, 2000).

Calls to Abandon Pluralism and Consolidate Evaluation Approaches into One Generic Model Are Unwise

The proliferation of proposals for how to do evaluation has frustrated some writers, resulting in calls for consolidating the different approaches to program evaluation into one omnibus, generic model that would encompass all others (e.g., Gephart, 1978). The arguments for consolidation stem from a desire to simplify the task of evaluation. In his call for a synthesis of the alternative evaluation approaches, Gephart lamented that "the multiple model mess has become dysfunctional!" and argued that the only real difference in the models "is the verbiage used to describe the elements of the 'different' models" (pp. 2–3).

On the surface, such calls for synthesis are appealing because they address the desire of many practitioners and clients just to get to the point, namely, "Skip the academic discussions and just tell us how to do program evaluation!" Were it possible to achieve, a synthesis would unravel evaluation's currently tangled literature, especially if the purpose of the synthesis were limited to identifying similarities in approaches. One might profitably analyze the various evaluation approaches in terms of their concepts and constructs, assumptions and orientations, terminology and (when provided) proposed methodology, and then ask to what extent these approaches really look at different but related evaluation phenomena. Perhaps, with all approaches viewed in aggregate, a more complete portrayal of evaluation would emerge. If a synthesis accomplished nothing more than to bring into the present jungle of terminology some semblance of semantic cultivation, the effort would be useful.

Yet, there are inherent dangers in attempting to synthesize alternatives, especially if the intent is to create the "one model" (of which Gephart speaks) generally applicable in program evaluation. Indeed, we would argue against such reductionism for several reasons. First, the alternative evaluation approaches described in the preceding chapters are based on widely divergent philosophical assumptions. Although some are compatible enough to be fruitfully combined, integrating all would be a philosophical impossibility, for key aspects of some approaches are directly incompatible with central concerns of others.[2] One might "synthesize" diverse ethnic cultures in a societal "melting pot," but, as with evaluation models, we have found the recognition and contribution of different ethnic cultures to be enriching and, thus, have moved to sustain them. The analogy to program evaluation is quite apt. It would be unfortunate if efforts to synthesize diametrically opposed approaches into one "model" resulted in so much philosophical dilution that the whole was truly less than the sum of its parts.

---

[2]We view this, not lack of interest or effort, as the most likely reason that no synthesis has been forthcoming since the profession-wide discussion of that issue in 1977. We should also note that this does not negate the possibilities of eclectically combining compatible portions of different approaches, as discussed later in this chapter.

Second, moving toward one omnibus model at this time could bring premature closure to expansion and refinement within the field. Our conceptions are still too untried and our empirical base too weak for us to be very certain of which notions should be preserved and which discarded. It would seem far more preferable to tolerate our contradictory and confusing welter of ideas and make of them what we can than to hammer them into a unified but impoverished conception of evaluation. "The dangers are not in working with models, but in working with too few, and those too much alike, and above all, in belittling any efforts to work with anything else" (Kaplan, 1964, p. 293). Just because we can synthesize does not mean that we should. As Kaplan puts it, consolidation would impose a premature closure on our ideas and, thus, limit

> our awareness of unexplored possibilities of conceptualization. We tinker with the model when we might be better occupied with the subject-matter itself . . . incorporating it in a model does not automatically give such knowledge scientific status. The maturity of our ideas is usually a matter of slow growth, which cannot be forced. . . . Closure is premature if it lays down the lines for our thinking to follow when we do not know enough to say even whether one direction or another is the more promising (p. 279).

A final concern has to do with whether we would really be enriched if the multitude of approaches and recommendations for how to do an evaluation could somehow be streamlined into one or two more sophisticated guidelines. Evaluation contexts are so different that it is difficult to conceive of any one or two models that would be relevant to all. For all their imperfection, diverse frameworks offer a richness of perspectives and serve as heuristics, especially if one uses evaluation approaches eclectically (when philosophical compatibility permits), as we shall propose later.

The Choice of Evaluation Approach Is Not Empirically Based

If one accepts our view that it is useful to have a variety of evaluation approaches, the next logical question is, How will one know which approach is best for a given situation? That question is devilishly difficult to answer because of one simple fact: There is almost no research to guide one's choice.

Over the years many evaluators have called for a program of research on evaluation (e.g., Shadish, et al., 1991; Stufflebeam, et al., 1971; Worthen, 1972, 1977). For the most part, their calls have fallen on deaf ears. The lack of an adequate empirical base is probably the single most important impediment to development of a more adequate evaluation theory and models. In the absence of relevant evidence about which approach works best under which circumstances, adherence to any one model rather than another is largely a statement of philosophy or a profession of faith. As Scriven (1976) observed many years ago,

> There has been a good deal of work on "evaluation models" which are hybrids between ways of conceptualizing evaluation and reminders as to how to do it. These

range from the highly relativistic and value free approaches of many Tyler students and Malcolm Provus' Discrepancy Evaluation, through the touchy-feely school of transactional and responsive evaluation (Rippey and Stake respectively) to the extremely far reaching and absolutistic approach that I have espoused. Each can, I believe, contribute something of value to most clients, but beyond that I can hardly make a dispassionate judgment (pp. 28–29).

Years after he first pointed out the need for such research, Stufflebeam (1981) was forced to conclude that "there has been very little empirical research on the relative merits of different approaches to evaluation. Clearly, the field of evaluation could profit from systematic examinations of the feasibility, costs, and benefits of competing conceptualizations" (p. 4). In the ensuing years, this situation has not changed much. Until we have solid information about the relative effectiveness of the numerous evaluation approaches, choices among alternatives will remain a matter of the evaluator's preference.

Negative Metaphors Underlying Some Approaches Can Cause Negative Side Effects

In Chapter 3 we discussed how different evaluation metaphors have led to widely diverse evaluation approaches. This leads us to a disquieting fact about these underlying metaphors, namely, that they are predicated on negative assumptions that fall into one of two categories.

First, several metaphors tacitly assume there is something wrong in the system being evaluated: a patient has died and the cause of death must be discovered (e.g., forensic medicine or pathology); a scandal has emerged and the truth must be uncovered (investigative journalism or investigative social research); or allegations have been made and must be investigated (criminal investigations and judicial proceedings). Such an indictment mentality is shortsighted and should be discouraged.

Second, several metaphors are based on assumptions that people will lie, evade questions, or withhold information as a matter of course. For example, in Douglas's (1976) volume on investigative social research, he notes that most social research techniques are based on a cooperative methodology that assumes candor and honesty once one builds rapport with interviewees, informants, and so forth. Instead, he proposes an alternative confrontive methodology for handling dishonesty and evasion, which he asserts are typical in situations fraught with anxiety and threat. If we accept the premise that evaluation is basically anxiety-provoking to those being evaluated, then we could readily conclude that Douglas's methods would be appropriate for collecting data in most program evaluations. But that would be tantamount to saying that individuals whose programs are being evaluated are prone to be deceitful, dishonest, and evasive, which is an absurd generalization on its face. To champion any evaluation methodology that leads to mutual distrust between evaluators and practitioners would not only be wrongheaded but also self-defeating.

Which brings us to a critical question: Can one draw on metaphors such as investigative journalism, investigative social research, congressional hearings, and the like without their serving as Trojan horses to carry insidious assumptions into the precepts and practice of evaluation? We have uneasy visions of evaluators marching in the wake of Ralph Nader, evaluating enterprises with no more care than that shown in Nader's assault on the Educational Testing Service and the school testing industry. Cohen (1978) tells of how irresponsible distortions of his own research by a *National Inquirer* reporter led to a congressional request for the formal report of Cohen's research from the sponsoring National Science Foundation. The specter that evaluation could become a degenerate example of tabloid journalism is frightening—and perhaps not so far-fetched as we'd like to think. It would be unfortunate to try broadening evaluators' perspectives and succeed only in creating a muckraker mind-set.

One way to avoid some of these problems would be to evoke more positive metaphors, such as the health maintenance approach to medicine. Diagnoses and prescriptions (however unpalatable) are likely to be accepted more gracefully if it is apparent from the outset that the primary objective is not only to uncover and eradicate what is wrong but also to identify and strengthen what is working well. Rallis and Rossman's conception of evaluation as a critical friend (2000) and the adaptation of techniques of appreciative inquiry (AI) to evaluation reflect this more positive approach.

Contributions of the Alternative Evaluation Approaches

If, as argued earlier, the evaluation approaches suggested in the literature are not models or theories, and if there is no empirical basis for deciding which to follow when designing and conducting a particular evaluation, then of what worth are they? Of considerable worth, actually. A novice evaluator may not use Scriven's (1972) goal-free method of evaluation, but probably no month passes when that evaluator does not somehow make conscious use of the concepts of formative or summative evaluation that Scriven introduced to our thinking. Individuals may spend years as evaluators and never once use Stufflebeam's (1971) CIPP model of evaluation, but most likely they have checked one or more of their evaluation designs against Stufflebeam's (1973a) list of steps in designing evaluations or his checklists (www.wmich.edu/evalctr/checklists). In similar ways, most of the evaluation approaches summarized in prior chapters influence the practice of evaluation in important ways.

Thinking back to evaluations we have done, our colleagues' work was used in this way in almost every study. As one of us noted in earlier editions of this textbook,

Although I have developed some preferences of my own in doing evaluations, probably 75 percent of what I do is application of what I have distilled from others' ideas. Doubtlessly, all who have been repeatedly exposed to the evaluation literature have absorbed much "through the pores," as it were, and now reapply it without cognizance of its source. Although few of us may conduct our evaluations in strict adherence to any 'model' of evaluation, few of us conduct evaluations which are not enormously influenced by the impact of our colleagues' thinking on our own preferences and actions (Worthen, 1977, p. 12).

The alternative conceptions about how evaluation should be conducted—the accompanying sets of categories, lists of things to think about, descriptions of different strategies, and exhortations to heed—influence the practice of program evaluation in sometimes subtle, sometimes direct, but always significant ways. Some evaluation designs adopt or adapt proposed approaches. Many evaluators, however, conduct evaluations without strict adherence (or even purposeful attention) to any "model," yet draw unconsciously in their philosophy, plans, and procedures on what they have internalized through exposure to the literature. So the value of the alternative approaches lies in their capacity to help us think, to present and provoke new ideas and techniques, and to serve as mental checklists of things we ought to consider, remember, or worry about. Their heuristic value is very high; their prescriptive value seems much less.

Comparative Analysis of Characteristics of Alternative Evaluation Approaches

So many new concepts have been presented in Chapters 4 through 8 that the reader might be feeling challenged to assimilate all of it. The matrix in Table 9.1—a comparative analysis of the characteristics, strengths, and limitations of the five approaches—should help. The aspects of each approach that we have chosen to highlight are as follows:

1. *Proponents*—Individuals who have written about the approach
2. *Purpose of evaluation*—The intended use(s) of evaluation proposed by writers advocating each particular approach or the purposes that may be inferred from their writings
3. *Distinguishing characteristics*—Key descriptors associated with each approach
4. *Past uses*—Ways in which each approach has been used in evaluating prior programs
5. *Contributions to the conceptualization of an evaluation*—Distinctions, new terms or concepts, logical relationships, and other aids suggested by proponents of each approach that appear to be major or unique contributions
6. *Criteria for judging evaluations*—Explicitly or implicitly defined expectations that may be used to judge the quality of evaluations that follow each approach
7. *Benefits*—Strengths that may be attributed to each approach and reasons why one might want to use this approach (what it can do for you)
8. *Limitations*—Risks associated with the use of each approach (what it can do to you)

TABLE 9.1   *Comparative Analysis of Alternative Evaluation Approaches*

	Objectives-Oriented	*Management-Oriented*
1. *Some proponents*	Tyler Provus Metfessel and Michael Hammond Popham Taba Bloom Talmage	Stufflebeam Alkin Provus Wholey
2. *Purpose of evaluation*	Determining the extent to which objectives are achieved	Providing useful information to aid in making decisions
3. *Distinguishing characteristics*	Specifying measurable objectives; using objective instruments to gather data; looking for discrepancies between objectives and performance	Serving rational decision making; evaluating at all stages of program development
4. *Past uses*	Program development; monitoring participant outcomes, needs assessment	Program development; institutional management systems; program planning; accountability
5. *Contributions to the conceptualization of an evaluation*	Pre-post measurement of performance; clarification of goals; use of objective measurements that are technically sound	Identify and evaluate needs and objectives; consider alternative program designs and evaluate them; watch the implementation of a program; look for bugs and explain outcomes; see if needs have been reduced or eliminated; metaevaluation; guidelines for institutionalizing evaluation
6. *Criteria for judging evaluations*	Measurability of objectives; measurement reliability validity	Utility; feasibility; propriety; technical soundness
7. *Benefits*	Ease of use; simplicity; focus on outcomes; high acceptability; forces objectives to be set	Comprehensiveness; sensitivity to information needs of those in a leadership position; systematic approach to evaluation; use of evaluation throughout the process of program development; well operationalized with detailed guidelines for implementation; use of a wide variety of information
8. *Limitations*	Oversimplication of evaluation and problems outcomes-only orientation; reductionistic; linear; overemphasis on outcomes	Emphasis on organizational efficiency and production model; assumption of orderliness and predictability in decision making; can be expensive to administer and maintain; narrow focus on the concerns of leaders

160

TABLE 9.1 *Continued*

	Consumer-Oriented	Expertise-Oriented
1. *Some proponents*	Scriven Komoski	Eisner Accreditation Groups
2. *Purpose of evaluation*	Providing information about products to aid decisions about purchases or adoptions	Providing professional judgments of quality
3. *Distinguishing characteristics*	Using criterion checklists to analyze products; product testing; informing consumers	Basing judgments on individual knowledge and experience; use of consensus standards, team/site visitations
4. *Past uses*	Consumer reports; product development; selection of products for dissemination	Self-study; blue-ribbon panels; accreditation; examination by committee; criticism
5. *Contributions to the conceptualization of an evaluation*	Lists of criteria for evaluating educational products and activities; archival references for completed reviews; formative–summative roles of evaluation; bias control	Legitimation of subjective criticism; self-study with outside verification; standards
6. *Criteria for judging evaluations*	Freedom from bias; technical soundness; defensible criteria used to draw conclusions and make recommendations; evidence of need and effectiveness required	Use of recognized standards; qualifications of experts
7. *Benefits*	Emphasis on consumer information needs; influence on product developers; concern with cost-effectiveness and utility; availability of checklists	Broad coverage; efficiency (ease of implementation, timing); capitalizes on human judgment
8. *Limitations*	Cost and lack of sponsorship; may suppress creativity or innovation; not open to debate or cross-examination	Replicability; vulnerability to personal bias; scarcity of supporting documentation to support conclusions; open to conflict of interest; superficial look at context; overuse of intuition; reliance on qualifications of the "experts"

(continued)

TABLE 9.1 *Continued*

	Participant-Oriented
1. *Some proponents*	Stake Patton Guba and Lincoln Rippey MacDonald Parlett and Hamilton Cousins and Earl
2. *Purpose of evaluation*	Understanding and portraying the complexities of programmatic activity, responding to an audience's requirements for information
3. *Distinguishing characteristics*	Reflecting multiple realities; use of inductive reasoning and discovery; firsthand experience on site; involvement of intended users; training intended users
4. *Past uses*	Examination of innovations or change about which little is known; ethnographies of operating programs
5. *Contributions to the conceptualization of an evaluation*	Emergent evaluation designs; use of inductive reasoning; recognition of multiple realities; importance of studying context; criteria for judging the rigor of naturalistic inquiry
6. *Criteria for judging evaluations*	Credibility; fit; auditability; confirmability
7. *Benefits*	Focus on description and judgment; concern with context; openness to evolve evaluation plan; pluralistic; use of inductive reasoning; use of a wide variety of information; emphasis on understanding
8. *Limitations*	Nondirective; tendency to be attracted by the bizarre or atypical; potentially high labor-intensity and cost; hypothesis generating; potential for failure to reach closure

Eclectic Uses of the Alternative Evaluation Approaches

The purpose in the foregoing comparative analysis is to provide key information on the strengths, limitations, and primary uses of each approach. The information in Table 9.1 is not intended to imply that any one approach is "best"; rather, it is our contention that each approach can be useful. The challenge is to determine which approach (or combination of concepts from different approaches) is most relevant to the task at hand.

Perhaps an experience of one of the authors in attempting to answer a question of a student in a graduate evaluation seminar will help make the point.

We were conducting a several-week-long examination of various authors' evaluation approaches and how each might be applied to do an evaluation, when one student asked, . . . "What approach do you usually use?" . . . I pointed out that I did not believe there was one best approach, that each has its strengths, and that I simply used whichever approach was most appropriate to the situation at hand.

"How do you know which one is most appropriate?" she queried. I . . . talked about things like looking at the purpose of the evaluation, the kind of decision needed, limitations of the approach, and so on, . . . and concluded . . . that a lot of it was in experience and, although a little tough at first, they would all get the hang of it once they had done a few evaluations.

"Maybe it would help," she stated, "if you could give us a few examples of where you've used one of the approaches and then show us why you picked it."

That seemed like a very useful suggestion, . . . so I began to sort through my mental files to find the very best examples of where I had used one of the evaluation approaches. Then I began to sort to find *any* examples of where I had used one of the approaches. I discarded evaluation after evaluation because I really had not used the approach, whatever it was, fully. There were truncated CIPP evaluations . . . , because I seldom seemed to be called on early enough to do much with context or input evaluations. There were applications of responsive evaluation through involving stakeholders in different ways. Each was incomplete as an example of use of the approaches, and I struggled for more pure examples to offer.

Finally, I remembered using Stake's "countenance" framework in its entirety in evaluating an administrators' training program. That one was memorable because it had been a class project that two students and I had taken on . . . so they could get the experience. . . . That one brought others to mind and before long I was able to give examples of using several of the frameworks in the way they were intended to be used. The intriguing realization was that every one of those examples came from class projects conducted jointly with students, when I had intentionally adhered to the models to demonstrate their features. I could not recall a single "lone-wolf" evaluation of my own for which I had consciously selected any single approach to guide the study. Instead, for several years I had been designing each evaluation de novo, pulling pieces of different frameworks in as they seemed relevant. Certain features of some models I used frequently, others seldom or never.

That realization seemed worth sharing, although in the process I felt a twinge of disloyalty toward some of my esteemed colleagues and friends for never really using their frameworks in my work. . . . The class was slightly taken aback at first by my heretical revelation, but they seemed comforted when I pointed out that there were distinct advantages in eclecticism, because one was free to choose the best from diverse sources, systems, or styles. Warming to the idea, I argued that one could choose the best features of each approach and weave them into a stronger overall approach—really a classic bit of cake-having and cake-eating. . . .

We talked for the remainder of the class about why each evaluation required a somewhat different mix of ingredients, how synthesis and eclecticism were not identical, and why an eclectic approach could be useful (Worthen, 1977, pp. 2–5).

The authors of this text are all self-confessed eclectics in our evaluation work, choosing and combining concepts from the evaluation approaches to fit the particular situation, using pieces of various evaluation approaches as they seem appropriate. In very few instances have we adhered to any particular "model" of evaluation. Rather, we find we can ensure a better fit by snipping and sewing together bits and pieces of the more traditional ready-made approaches and even weaving a bit of homespun, if necessary, rather than by pulling any existing approach off the shelf. Tailoring works.

Obviously, eclecticism has its limitations (after all, it has been derided as the discipline of undisciplined minds), and one obviously cannot suggest that we develop an "eclectic model" of evaluation, for that would be an obvious non sequitur. The uninformed could perform egregious errors in the name of eclecticism, such as proposing that a program's objectives be evaluated as a first step in conducting a goal-free evaluation or laying out a preordinate design for a responsive evaluation. Assuming that one avoids mixing evaluation's philosophically incompatible "oil and water," the eclectic use of the writings presented in the preceding chapters has far more potential advantages than disadvantages, whether that eclecticism means combining alternative approaches or selectively combining the methods and techniques inherent within those approaches.

In fact, many evaluators are more eclectic in their approaches than one might believe. Fitzpatrick's interviews with individual evaluators over the last few years in the *American Journal of Evaluation* have illustrated that, like us, when confronted with a specific evaluation, many evaluators make choices drawing from a variety of approaches. (See her column on exemplary evaluations from 1997 to 2002.)

Eclecticism is more common in education, however, than in some other areas. This is partly due to the fact that education has been the primary field in which different approaches have been discussed. Other fields, such as sociology, criminal justice, and mental health, have erred in not considering those approaches for evaluation. By failing to consider these approaches, evaluators in these fields have often failed to consider sufficiently the critical components of their evaluation, such as audiences, purposes, and uses. The evaluations in those fields have remained more applied research than evaluation and have been more summative than formative. Much of evaluation's potential lies in the scope of strategies it can employ and in the possibility of selectively combining those approaches. Narrow, rigid adherence to single approaches must give way to more mature, sophisticated evaluations that welcome diversity. Admittedly, this will be a challenging task, but that does not lessen its importance.

Drawing Practical Implications from the Alternative Evaluation Approaches

All the evaluation approaches we have presented have something to contribute to the practicing evaluator. They may be used heuristically to generate questions or uncover issues. The literature contains many useful conceptual, methodological, political, communicative, and administrative guidelines. Finally, the approaches offer powerful tools that the evaluator may use or adapt in his work.

Later in this book we will look at practical guidelines for planning and conducting evaluations. Many of these guidelines have been developed as part of a particular approach to evaluation. Fortunately, however, they are generalizable, usable whenever and wherever needed. Just as a skilled carpenter will not use only a hammer to build a fine house, so a skilled evaluator will not depend solely on one approach to plan and conduct a high-quality evaluation.

Let us now turn in the next section of this book to practical uses of the tools that evaluation practitioners, theorists, and methodologists have generated. But first, pause a moment to apply what you have learned in this chapter.

Major Concepts and Theories

1. Through application of standard scientific criteria, evaluation approaches are viewed neither as scientific nor theories, yet the field of evaluation is still young and these approaches are undergoing refinement on a continual basis.

2. Despite the call for synthesis of evaluation terminology and consolidation of all evaluation models into one framework, each of the evaluation frameworks offers a different perspective on evaluation that can be applied to some, but not all, evaluation situations.

3. The way in which evaluators determine which approach(es) to employ in a given situation is not based on scientific inquiry or empirical testing; rather, it is based on philosophical, methodological, and client preferences. Often, evaluators will not adhere to one specific approach, but instead will opt for a combination of several approaches in a more eclectic approach to evaluation.

Discussion Questions

1. Why is it important to learn about the different evaluation approaches?

2. How would you go about selecting an evaluation approach to employ? What considerations would you have to make? Would you adhere to one approach? Would you adapt several approaches and create your own synthesis?

3. Is there one evaluation approach that you particularly like or feel more comfortable with than another? Why?

4. Discuss why evaluation approaches are considered scientific models or theories.

5. What would be the advantages and disadvantages of consolidating all evaluation approaches into one?

Application Exercises

1. Identify five evaluation studies in a journal of interest to you or, better yet, collect in-house reports on five evaluation studies. These might be from your own welfare agency, from your school or university, from a city, county, state, or federal office, or from a nonprofit agency. After reading the report, discuss what approach the author used. Is it eclectic or does it follow one model predominantly? What elements of each approach seem to be most useful in guiding the authors in identification of purpose, audiences, data-collection methods, and presentation of results?

   Using each of the five evaluation approaches discussed in Chapters 4 through 8 in this book, decide whether you agree or disagree with the evaluation plan just described. For each approach, describe how that approach might lead you to proceed differently with the evaluation. Do you see any combination of approaches that would be particularly useful in evaluating this program?

2. Below is a list of evaluation purposes. Which approach would you choose to use in each of these examples? Why? What would be the advantages and disadvantages of this approach in each setting?
   a. Determining whether to continue a welfare-to-work program designed to get full-time, long-term employment for welfare recipients
   b. Describing the implementation of a distance-learning education program for college students
   c. Making recommendations for the improvement of a conflict-resolution program for middle-school students
   d. Determining whether reading levels of first graders at the end of the year are appropriate

3. The fitness center has sent out requests for evaluation proposals to conduct a full analysis of its organization. The center recently opened and is the only full fitness club available in the area. This club offers its members an Olympic-size swimming pool, six indoor tennis courts, four indoor racquetball courts, two full-size basketball courts, several aerobics and water aerobics classes, cardiovascular and weight-lifting equipment, a tumbling facility for children, dance classes, and fitness and tennis instructors. The analysis will need to include an examination of the fitness center's organizational structure and its political and cultural environment with emphasis on customer and employee satisfaction.

   Select one of the approaches to develop an evaluation plan to assess the fitness center. Discuss how you would use this plan to develop the evaluation and why you view it as the most desirable approach.

4. Adams Elementary School has started a volunteer program in which parents are encouraged to help out in the classroom. The goal of the program is not only to provide the teacher with assistance but also to get parents more involved in the school and their children's education. The principal hopes to boost the learning of the low-achieving students in the school by getting their parents more involved in their children's education through volunteer efforts in the classroom. Contrast using a management-oriented, objectives-oriented, and participant-oriented approach.

Suggested Readings

Madaus, G. F., Scriven, M., & Stufflebeam, D. L. (Eds.). (1983). *Evaluation models: Viewpoints on educational and human services evaluation.* Boston: Kluwer-Nijhoff.

McLaughlin, M. W., & Phillips, D. C. (Eds.). (1991). *Evaluation and education: At quarter century,* Ninetieth Yearbook of the National Society for the Study of Education. Chicago: University of Chicago Press.

Scriven, M. (1993). *Hard-won lessons in program evaluation.* New Directions for Program Evaluation, No. 58. San Francisco, CA: Jossey-Bass.

Shadish, W. R., Cook, T. D., & Leviton, L. C. (1991). *Foundations of program evaluation.* Thousand Oaks, CA: Sage.

Stufflebeam, D. L. (2001). *Evaluation models.* New Directions for Evaluation, No. 89. San Francisco, CA: Jossey-Bass.

Stufflebeam, D. L., & Shinkfield, A. J. (1985). *Systematic evaluation.* Boston: Kluwer-Nijhoff.

Part III

Practical Guidelines for Planning Evaluations

In Part One we discussed the purpose and uses of evaluation, presented some basic evaluation concepts and distinctions, and described the history of program evaluation. In Part Two we examined factors that led to alternative conceptions of evaluation, summarized the key characteristics and the strengths and weaknesses of the five general evaluation approaches most commonly used in evaluation today, and argued for thoughtful use of those approaches, including eclectic combination of features of the alternative approaches, when doing so would be advantageous.

Which brings us to the heart of this book: practical guidelines. In this part we begin to provide guidelines that we believe will be helpful to evaluators, regardless of which evaluation approach or combination of approaches they might elect to use. In Part Three we present guidelines for clarifying, focusing, and planning evaluation efforts. (In Part Four we present guidelines for conducting and using evaluations.)

We begin Part Three by examining in Chapter 10 reasons that lead to initiation of program evaluations, considerations in deciding when to evaluate ("always" is a common but incorrect answer), and how to determine who should conduct the evaluation. In Chapter 11 we discuss the importance of the evaluator's understanding the setting and context in which the evaluation will take place, as well as the importance of accurately describing that which is to be evaluated. Two crucial steps in evaluation planning—identifying and selecting evaluative questions and criteria, and planning the information collection, analysis, and interpretation—are examined in detail in Chapters 12 and 13. We also include in Chapter 13 a few guidelines for developing management plans for evaluation studies, stressing the importance of establishing evaluation agreements and contracts.

The focus of the chapters that follow is decidedly practical. Although we will continue to quote or reference other sources, these chapters are not intended as scholarly reviews of the content covered. Were such reviews to be included, several of these chapters could each fill a textbook. Our intent is only to introduce enough information to give both the evaluator and user of evaluation (1) an awareness of how to proceed and (2) direction to more detailed coverage of many (especially technical) topics in other textbooks. Experience and further study will have to suffice to teach the rest.

Introduction of Case Study

To help readers apply the content of the chapters in this and the following section, we have included a case study, which we will thread through the chapters. At the end of each chapter (in Chapters 10 to 18) is a section titled "Case Study Application," in which we attempt briefly to describe how we would apply some of the content of that chapter to one particular evaluation of a public school curriculum. It is important to point out that not *all* of the content in *any* chapter can be applied to the case study; such an attempt would double the length of this book. We have selected only those few concepts to discuss within the case study that we think will be most helpful in making or clarifying our points. We hope that this case study will help to show how at least some of the guidelines we discuss could be applied to a real evaluation.

Setting the Stage: The Radnor Case Study

The case study we will use here appeared in Worthen and Sanders (1987), the predecessor to this book, and has been retained because of positive feedback on it from students and faculty who have used it previously. It describes the "Radnor humanities curriculum," a real curriculum that existed in the Radnor Middle School in Wayne, Pennsylvania (and may still exist, for all we know). A brief description of the Radnor humanities curriculum is provided below, in the form of a short description of an imaginary report of the Radnor humanities curriculum review committee. Beginning in Chapter 10 of this book, and extending through Chapter 18, an account of a fictional evaluation of that curriculum is presented, drawing on an earlier, hypothetical description of how such a program could be evaluated.[1]

Three introductory comments are appropriate. First, in this case study, the imaginary evaluator has chosen to apply the rather eclectic "multiple-method" approach we have come to favor to our imaginary evaluation of the Radnor curriculum. If readers wish to see how their other preferred evaluation approaches (such as participant-oriented, expertise-oriented, or decision-oriented evaluation) could be applied to the Radnor curriculum, other chapters in Brandt (1981) illustrate how a variety of evaluation approaches might be applied to a single cur-

[1]Originally from Worthen (1981), in Brandt (1981), used by permission of the Association for Supervision and Curriculum Development, and adapted and extended to fit the needs of this text.

riculum. We strongly endorse Brandt's entire book as excellent supplemental reading to this text.

Second, students and faculty who are not educators should not be "put off" by use of this example; a school curriculum is clearly an educational program, and those from other fields should be able to transfer important learnings from this case study to programs in their own fields.

Third, we have left the evaluation case study in the informal, singular, first-person form in which it first appeared because it was originally written only by the senior author of this present text. However, it has been modified and updated slightly by all the authors, to parallel changes we have made in this edition and to fit with currently emerging trends and issues in evaluation.

THE RADNOR HUMANITIES CURRICULUM

"How have you evaluated this program?" asked the president of the board of education. She seemed determined to maintain an air of objectivity, but the atmosphere was growing tense in the school library where the board was meeting.

The main business of the evening was a report on the middle school's humanities program. Prepared by a committee of eleven educators and six parents, the report was the product of more than thirty committee meetings plus discussions with students, staff, and citizens. It explained philosophy, listed goals and objectives, described the curriculum in detail, made specific recommendations, and included a rationale for each recommendation. It even listed a number of alternatives that had been considered but rejected as undesirable.

All students in the sixth, seventh, and eighth grades were required to take the humanities course, which was taught two days a week by four teachers, including an artist and a musician, all members of a separate humanities department. The arts—everything from literature and drama to architecture and the visual arts—were used to develop the students' "understanding of all that it means to be human." Looking at a van Gogh painting of a Flemish mining family at dinner, for instance, students might be asked, "Would you like to be invited to dinner here?" as well as, "What tones and colors did the painter use?" They might listen to Humperdink's opera *Hansel and Gretel* or "She's Leaving Home" by the Beatles. Examples were drawn from many different cultures including European, American, Hispanic, Asian, and African.

The program should be continued, the report said, with some modifications, including a new organizational framework based on the concepts and skills being taught, and increased emphasis on writing and other language skills. Several board members and parents were not satisfied. A woman who was a member of the study committee, but who had not attended most meetings, read a statement expressing concern about the general direction of American education and objected to "values clarification" and "secular humanism" in the program. (The teachers insisted they did not use techniques such as those advocated by proponents of values clarification.)

Others said a humanities course would be more appropriate for older students, who would have the background to appreciate it, but that students in the middle school needed more basic knowledge first. One board member asked what impact the program was having on students and how it could be measured. Another was concerned that the time being used could be better spent on content that addressed the state standards tests.

Pointing out that the program had been in limbo for more than a year, the principal, assistant superintendent for curriculum, and the superintendent offered strong personal endorsements and asked for an immediate decision. Several parents added their support. But when the meeting ended at 11:00 P.M., the board had postponed acceptance of the committee's report until they could talk privately with the principal about how the program could be scheduled and staffed in light of declining enrollments.

Ten days later, a majority of the board members voted to permit continuation of the humanities course. Still, evaluation remained an issue. In reply to the question about measurement, the principal had said it couldn't be done statistically; the course did not teach children *what* to think and feel, it taught them *to* think and feel.

Evaluation of the Radnor Humanities Curriculum

In Chapters 10 through 18, practical guidelines for various aspects of evaluation will be discussed and then applied, in turn, at the end of each chapter, to an imaginary evaluation of the preceding humanities curriculum.

10

Clarifying the Evaluation Request and Responsibilities

Orienting Questions

1. Suppose you received a telephone call from a potential client asking if you would do an evaluation. What are some of the first questions you would ask?

2. Are there times you would decline a request for evaluation? If so, under what conditions?

3. How can an evaluability assessment help determine whether an evaluation will be productive?

4. What are some advantages and disadvantages in having an evaluation conducted by an external evaluator? By an internal evaluator?

5. What criteria would you use to select an external evaluator?

In the preceding chapters we discussed evaluation's promise for improving programs. The potential and promise of evaluation may create the impression that it is *always* appropriate to evaluate and that every facet of every program should be evaluated.

Such is not the case. The temptation to evaluate everything may be compelling in an idealistic sense, but it ignores many practical realities. In this chapter we discuss how the evaluator can better understand the origin of a proposed evaluation and judge whether or not the study would be appropriate.

To clarify the discussion, we need to differentiate here among several groups or individuals who affect or are affected by an evaluation study: sponsors, clients, stakeholders, and audiences.

An evaluation's **sponsor** is the agency or individual that authorizes the evaluation and provides necessary fiscal resources for its conduct. Sponsors may or may not actually select the evaluator or be involved in shaping the study, but they generally have ultimate authority concerning the evaluation. In some circumstances, the sponsor may delegate that authority to the client.

The **client** is the specific agency or individual who requests the evaluation. In many instances, the sponsor and client are synonymous—but not always. For example, in an evaluation of a domestic violence treatment program operated by a nonprofit agency, the agency (client) requests and arranges for the actual study, but the requirement and funding for the evaluation may both originate with a foundation that is the funding source for the program (sponsor).

Stakeholders consist of many groups. Essentially stakeholders include anyone who has a stake in the program to be evaluated or in the evaluation's results. Sponsors and clients are both stakeholders, but so are program managers and staff, the recipients of program services and their families, other agencies affiliated with the program, interest groups concerned with the program, elected officials, and the public at large. As we will discuss, it is wise to consider all the potential stakeholders in a program when planning the evaluation. Each group may have a different picture of the program and different expectations of the program and the evaluation.

Audiences include individuals, groups, and agencies who have an interest in the evaluation and receive its results. Sponsors and clients are usually the primary audiences and may occasionally be the only audiences. Generally an evaluation's audiences will also include all stakeholders, although that is not always so. For example, elementary school students might be participants in an evaluation of their school's reading program, being observed, tested, or interviewed, but only in some circumstances would they likely display much interest in the results of that evaluation. Sometimes it is appropriate to prepare a community report based on the evaluation findings for a program. In that case, the audience can include the community at large. More will be said about evaluation audiences in Chapter 11.

Understanding the Reasons for Initiating the Evaluation

It is important to understand what prompts an evaluation. Indeed, determining the purpose is probably the most important decision the evaluation sponsor will make in the course of an evaluation. Understanding that purpose is probably the most important insight the evaluator can have. If some problem prompted the decision to evaluate, or if some stakeholder has demanded an evaluation, the evaluator should know about it.

Presumably, the decision to evaluate stemmed from someone's need to know. Whose need? What does she want to know? Why? How will she use the results? The evaluator's first questions should begin to identify these reasons.

Sometimes the evaluation client can answer such questions directly and clearly. Unfortunately, that is not always the case, and the evaluator's task is made more difficult when the client has no clear idea about what the evaluation should accomplish. It is not uncommon to find that the clients or sponsors are unsophisticated about evaluation procedures and have not thought deeply about possible ramifications or results. Sometimes even the people who commission the evaluation study are not clear about why the evaluation is being planned. Frequently, the purpose of the evaluation is not clear until the evaluator has carefully read the relevant materials, observed the evaluation object, and probed the aspirations and expectations of stakeholders.

Such probing is necessary to clarify purposes and procedures. Where sponsors or clients are already clear about what they hope to obtain, it is no less crucial for the evaluator to understand their motivations. She can often do so by exploring—with whoever is requesting the evaluation—such questions as the following:

1. Why is this evaluation being requested? What is its purpose? What questions will it answer?

2. To what use will the evaluation findings be put? By whom? What others should be informed of the evaluation results?

3. What is to be evaluated? What does it include? Exclude? During what time period? In what settings? Who is the intended client for the program? What are the goals and objectives of the program? What problem or issue is the program intended to address? Who is in charge of it? Who will deliver it? What are their skills and training? Has it ever been evaluated before?

4. What are the essential program activities? How do they link with the goals and objectives? What is the program theory?

5. How much time and money are available for the evaluation? Who is available to help with the evaluation? Is certain information needed right away?

6. What is the political climate and context surrounding the evaluation? Will any political factors and forces preclude a meaningful and fair evaluation?

The foregoing questions are only examples, and evaluators might add or subtract others. What is important is that, through careful questioning and listening, the evaluator comes to understand the purpose for the evaluation. Not all purposes are equally valid.

By listening closely to the client's reasons for initiating the evaluation and talking with other stakeholders to determine their information needs and perceptions of the study, the evaluator can learn much about the program that will help ensure that the evaluation is appropriately targeted and useful. The evaluator can also take a proactive role during this phase by suggesting other reasons for evaluating that may prove even more productive (Fitzpatrick, 1989). This strategy is particularly useful when the stakeholders are new to evaluation and unsure of their needs. Such clients may assume that evaluations should only measure whether objectives are achieved (the objectives-oriented approach) when other critical information needs exist that could be served by evaluation. Other clients may want to rush into data collection and see the evaluator's role as "helping us with a survey" or "analyzing some test scores." They are unfamiliar with the critical planning phase and how the evaluator can help them to focus the evaluation to determine what they want to know. Thus, this phase begins the important two-way communication process essential to evaluation, in which the evaluator learns as much as she can about the program through careful questioning, observing, and listening and, at the same time, educates the stakeholders about what evaluation can do.

Cronbach and his colleagues (1980) emphasize the importance of the educative role of the evaluator in helping the client determine the directions of the evaluation. They note that "the evaluator, holding the mirror up to events, is an educator. . . . The evaluator settles for too little if he simply gives the best answers he can to simple and one-sided questions from his clients. He is neglecting ways in which he could lead the clients to an ultimately more productive understanding" (pp. 160–161). Thus, before proceeding with the evaluation, the evaluator must spend a significant period of time learning about the program, its stakeholders, the decision-making process, and the culture of the organization in order to accurately determine the purpose of the study.

Informational Uses of Evaluation

Evaluation is intended to enhance our understanding of the value of whatever is evaluated. Yet, as we noted at the beginning of this text, evaluation has many different uses. Examples of some of the informational uses of evaluation by policy makers, program managers, and program staff include:

1. Determining whether sufficient need exists to initiate a program and describing the target audience;
2. Assisting in program planning by identifying potential program models and activities that might be conducted to achieve certain goals;
3. Describing program implementation and identifying whether changes from the program model have occurred;
4. Examining whether certain program goals or objectives are being achieved at desired levels; and
5. Judging the overall value of a program and its relative value and cost compared to competing programs.

Each of these five uses of evaluation may be directed to an entire program or to one or more of the smaller components of a program. The first two uses are frequently parts of planning and **needs assessment** (McKillip, 1987; Witkin & Altschuld, 1995). These tasks generally take place during the early stages of a program but may occur at any stage when program changes are being considered. The third use is often described as a **monitoring** or **process study.** The fourth use can be characterized as an **outcome study.** The final use is achieved through conducting **cost-effectiveness** or **cost-benefit studies.** All of these studies serve legitimate uses for evaluation because each one serves an important, informational use: enhancing our understanding of the value of the program.

Noninformational Uses of Evaluation

In addition to the direct "informational" uses described in the previous section, evaluation also has noninformational uses. Cronbach and his colleagues (1980) first noted this use in arguing that the very incorporation of evaluation into a system makes a difference. They conclude that "the visibility of the evaluation mechanism changes behavior" (p. 159), citing as an analog how drivers' observance of speed limits is affected by police officers' patrolling the highways in plainly marked patrol cars. They also suggest that the existence of evaluation may help convince stakeholders that the system is responsive, not impervious, to their feedback. More recently, Kirkhart (2000) has argued for an expanded understanding of evaluation use that conceptualizes use as "influence." (See Chapter 16 for more on the many positive, noninformational uses of evaluation.)

An important use of evaluation is its role in educating others, not simply about the program being evaluated, but also about alternative means for decision making. Smith (1989) writes that one of the most important benefits of evaluability assessment, a method of determining whether the program is ready for evaluation, is improving the skills of program staff in developing and planning programs. Through participating in an extensive series of structured discussions to develop the program model, staff gain skills that can be used in the next program they develop, even if evaluation is not involved. Such changes are an example of the positive influence of evaluation on a process within the organization (Kirkhart, 2000; Preskill & Torres, 2000).

Evaluation can also educate stakeholders by empowering them to become active in evaluations, helping them gain skills in questioning and learning about programs in which they have a stake. Fetterman's model of empowerment evaluation (Fetterman, Kaftarian, & Wandersman, 1996) and Preskill and Torres (Preskill & Torres, 1999), writing on learning organizations, both illustrate how evaluation can be used to educate and change the views and skills of various groups. (See Chapter 8 for a discussion of these approaches.)

Others (House & Howe, 1999) propose that evaluation can be useful in encouraging what they call deliberative democracy. They note that evaluators often inform those stakeholders who have more power, such as policy makers, school boards, and legislators, because these are often the stakeholders with the resources to commission an evaluation. But, evaluators can stimulate deliberative democracy by including other, less powerful stakeholders in the questions and discussions that emerge in evaluation.

However, some noninformational uses are undesirable. In her seminal treatise on evaluation, Weiss (1972) noted that evaluation also has several noninformational uses that are seldom acknowledged. Some of the more covert, nefarious, and patently political uses she cites are:

> *Postponement.* The decision maker may be looking for ways to delay a decision. Instead of resorting to the usual ploy of appointing a committee and waiting for its report, he can commission an evaluation study, which takes even longer.
>
> *Ducking responsibility.* . . . There are cases in which administrators know what the decision will be even before they call in the evaluators, but want to cloak it in . . . legitimate trappings. . . .
>
> *Public relations.* . . . The administrator believes that he has a highly successful program and looks for a way to make it visible. . . . The program administrator's motives are not, of course, necessarily crooked or selfish. Often, there is a need to justify the program to the people who pay the bills, and he is seeking support for a concept and a project in which he believes. . . .
>
> *Fulfilling grant requirements.* . . . Many federal grants . . . are tagged with an evaluation requirement. . . .the operators of a project . . . tend to neglect the evaluation [and] . . . see it mainly as a ritual designed to placate the funding bodies, without any real usefulness to them.
>
> Evaluation, then, is a rational enterprise sometimes undertaken for nonrational, or at least noninformational, reasons (pp. 11–12).

Recent work by Worthen (1995) suggests, however, that such noninformational uses may be more common in federal or national evaluations than in evaluations of programs administered at the state or local level. In an analysis of 108 evaluations, Worthen found that over two-thirds of the evaluations of state and local programs served informational purposes, while only 15 percent of those conducted at the federal level served such purposes. While these results are based on a sample of studies conducted by only one institute, the Western Institute for Research and Evaluation (WIRE), and the number of national programs sampled is relatively small, the results do fit rather well our collective experiences in other evaluations. If one can assume that the political tides run stronger in national programs than at lower levels, then these results may be attributable to the impact political forces have on evaluation, as we discuss in Chapter 17.

Conditions under which Evaluation Studies Are Inappropriate

Except for some uses cited by Weiss, the foregoing examples all represent *appropriate* uses of evaluation studies. But evaluations are not always used appropriately. Smith (1998) has outlined several reasons for declining an evaluation contract. He groups these reasons into two broad categories: (1) when the evaluation could harm the field of evaluation, or (2) when it would fail to support the social good. These problems may arise when it is likely that the ultimate quality of the evaluation is questionable, major clients are alienated or misled concerning what evaluation can do, resources are inadequate, or ethical principles are violated. Building on Smith's typology, we outline below several circumstances in which evaluations are, at best, of dubious value.

Evaluation Would Produce Trivial Information

Heretical as this may sound to some, sometimes a program simply lacks sufficient impact to warrant the expense of formal evaluation. Some programs are one-time efforts with no potential for continuation. Some are provided at such low cost to so few people that the need for more than informal evaluation is unlikely. Evaluability assessment or other evaluation planning activities may indicate the program's theory or model is inadequate to achieve the desired impact. In other words, program activities simply have insufficient connections to the program goals or are too weak, due to duration or intensity, to achieve desired outcomes. Needs assessments or formative evaluations *may* be of use in improving the program if the emphasis in the evaluation is formative, but summative or outcome evaluations are probably not worth the cost unless there is a need to demonstrate failure. Common sense must dictate when a program has enough impact to warrant formal evaluation of its effectiveness.

Evaluation Results Will Not Be Used

Too often the professed "need" for an evaluation is merely an unreasoned assumption that every program must be evaluated. Evaluation is of dubious value unless there is commitment by someone to use the results. There may be some value in a "decision-free Nader's Raiders" type of evaluator capability, but, given the scarcity of evaluation resources (both financial and human) and the demand for evaluation information to inform important decisions, it seems a questionable investment at present.

Sometimes there are important decisions or choices to be made, but it is clear that they will be made for reasons unrelated to evaluative data. A program may, for instance, have sufficient political appeal or public support that administrators are simply unwilling to discontinue or change it drastically, no matter what problems an evaluation study may reveal. For example, Drug Abuse Resistance Education programs, better known as D. A. R. E., have enjoyed wide public support in spite of the failure of repeated, rigorous evaluations to find an effect on subsequent drug use (Lyman, Milich, Zimmerman, Novak, Logan, & Martin, 1999; Rosenbaum, 1998; Sullivan, 2000).[1] In this case, evaluation can play no meaningful role except—assuming the data cooperate—to justify program continuation, a dubious "whitewash" function at best. Evaluators should

[1]The Robert Woods Johnson Foundation is currently sponsoring a large evaluation of a substantially revised D. A. R. E. program based on a social norms strategy that may be more successful than the traditional program.

avoid meaningless, ritualistic evaluations or pro forma exercises in which evaluation only appears to justify decisions actually made for personal or political reasons.

Of course, such dubious (and, one hopes, rare) motives are not always apparent. One of the most frustrating situations the evaluator will confront is to learn, *after* the evaluation has been completed, that the client or sponsor was not really open to information that contradicted preconceived notions. If the evaluator learns during the evaluation that certain conclusions are inevitable, it would be best to find ways to truncate the evaluation "sham" at the earliest opportunity. (In some cases, evaluation can have effects on the organizational culture or views of stakeholders that can make conducting an evaluation worthwhile when direct instrumental use is unlikely. See Chapter 16 on Reporting and Using Evaluation Information.)

Evaluation Cannot Yield Useful, Valid Information

Sometimes, despite an important pending decision, it appears highly unlikely that an evaluation study will produce any relevant information. For example, consider a decision about whether to continue a school dropout-prevention program. Here information about the program's effects on dropout rates, graduation percentages, and so forth would be relevant. But what if the program only started one month before the school board must make its decision? The probability of obtaining dependable information (even predictive information) about the program's effectiveness in that length of time is so slight that it would seem wiser to spend one's energies convincing the school board to delay the decision. Similarly, a variety of constraints beyond the evaluator's control (e.g., inadequate resources, lack of administrative cooperation or support, limited time in which to collect decent evaluation data, impossible evaluation tasks, and inaccessible data essential to the evaluation) can prevent the evaluator from providing useful information. Well-intentioned but naive clients may request "mission impossible" evaluations that yield only wasted efforts and disappointment. The evaluator needs to recognize when an evaluation is doomed to fail from the beginning. If unreasonable constraints preclude a professionally responsible evaluation, the evaluator should decline the evaluation. A bad evaluation is worse than no evaluation at all; poor evaluation data can readily mislead and lull administrators into the false security of thinking the misinformation they have really portrays their efforts.

The Type of Evaluation Is Premature for the Stage of the Program

Programs that are in a tryout phase nearly always benefit from well-conducted formative evaluation (barring reasons listed hereafter). But one cannot be so quick to conclude that a summative evaluation would always be appropriate. Premature summative evaluations are among the most insidious misuses of evaluation, prompting concerns such as those expressed by Campbell (1984):

Another type of mistake involved *immediate evaluation,* evaluation lon
grams were debugged, long before those who were implementing a
lieved there was anything worth imitating.

When any one of them, after a year or so of debugging, feels they
something hot, a program worth others borrowing, we will worry about program
evaluation in a serious sense. Our slogan would be, "Evaluate only proud programs!" (Think of the contrast with our present ideology, in which Washington
planners in Congress and the executive branch design a new program, command
immediate nationwide implementation, with no debugging, plus an immediate
nationwide evaluation.) (pp. 35–37).

Today, the emphasis on assessing outcomes in education and many nonprofit programs funded by foundations often leads to premature summative evaluations. Programs with potentially effective models may be scuttled because of
too-early summative judgments when fine-tuning those programs might result in
their success. Money spent in more careful needs assessment and formative evaluation during program development and early delivery can lead to programs that
are prepared for summative evaluations. Tharp and Gallimore (1979) illustrate a
more effective approach to evaluation. Their approach requires a long-term commitment to using evaluation for decision making and the development of evaluation questions that are appropriate for the stage of the program and the current
information needs of program developers. The process is an iterative one. Results
of one study are used to make changes and refinements with the next study examining whether these changes have succeeded.

Propriety of Evaluation Is Doubtful

Evaluations are undertaken for many reasons—some noble and some not. When
the evaluator can discern that the reasons for undertaking the study are honor-
able and appropriate, the chances that the evaluation will be a success are enhanced. But the evaluator must also be able to recognize less noble reasons,
including those that strain or violate professional principles. It would be unwise
to proceed with any evaluation if its propriety is threatened by conflict of interest, jeopardy to participants in the study, or any other factors.

Propriety is one of the four attributes of an ethical evaluation as defined by
the Joint Committee on Standards for Educational Evaluation (1994). The identification of this area, along with accuracy, feasibility, and utility, indicates the
high importance professional evaluators place on propriety. The standards outlined under propriety by the Joint Committee are designed to insure that the evaluation will protect the rights of those involved in the evaluation, whether they
be program recipients (students, clients, patients, the general public), staff, managers, or other stakeholders. An evaluation that is conducted with propriety respects the rights and dignity of those from whom data are collected and works to
help organizations to address the needs of all their clients. (See Chapter 18 on ethical aspects of evaluation.)

Determining When an Evaluation Is Appropriate: Evaluability Assessment

In the early 1970s, Joseph Wholey and his colleagues at the U.S. Department of Health, Education, and Welfare (now Health and Human Services) saw that the proliferation of program evaluation in the 1960s had not resulted in an increase in the use of program evaluation for decision making (Buchanan & Wholey, 1972). In fact, many of the potential users of evaluation were unhappy with such studies, believing that they often failed to provide useful information.

Wholey and his colleagues developed **evaluability assessment** as a tool to remedy this situation. They saw evaluability assessment as a means for facilitating communication between evaluators and stakeholders, for determining whether a program was "evaluable," and for focusing the evaluation study itself.

The developers of **evaluability assessment** believed that many evaluations had failed because of discrepancies between "rhetoric and reality" (Nay & Kay, 1982, p. 225). As Nay and Kay point out, different levels of policy makers and program managers have different rhetorical models of the program. The models of high-level policy makers may be quite general, reflecting their role in advocating for resolution of the problem and gaining funding. The rhetorical models of managers closer to program delivery become more specific and closer to reality. Yet, even the models of managers relatively close to the program may fail to match reality. Many policy makers and managers may continue to cling to their rhetorical models because they perceive their particular model as necessary for public consumption. In any case, the varying rhetorical models and the gap between rhetorical models and reality make program evaluation difficult. The evaluator is unsure which program "reality" to assess.

Other common barriers to a program's being evaluable include nebulous or unrealistic goals and objectives, failure to link program activities to these goals and objectives, and managers who are unable or unwilling to make program changes on the basis of evaluation information (Horst, Nay, Scanlon, & Wholey, 1974). Other problems Wholey and others have discussed in more recent work include: (1) the failure of evaluators and managers to agree on goals, objectives, and performance criteria for measuring these objectives; (2) the inability to obtain data on program performance; and (3) problems with the particular purposes and uses of the evaluation itself (Wholey, 1983, 1987; Wholey, Hatry, & Newcomer, 1994). Wholey and his colleagues wanted to develop a way to remedy these problems.

Evaluability assessment was devised to help programs meet three criteria they deemed necessary for meaningful evaluation:

1. Program objectives, important side effects, and priority information needs are well defined (that is, program managers have agreed on a set of measurable objectives and program performance indicators to be used in managing and assessing the program).

2. Program objectives are feasible to achieve with the intended target audience, the knowledge and skills of program deliverers, and the resources provided.

3. Intended uses of information are well defined (that is, program managers have agreed on intended uses of program performance information) (Wholey, 1983, pp. 39–40).

Evaluability assessment was first developed as a precursor to a summative evaluation; if the evaluability assessment revealed that the program did not meet the criteria, the summative evaluation would not proceed. Over the past twenty-five years the uses of evaluability assessment have expanded. It is now frequently employed to clarify the purposes of a formative study or as a planning tool in its own right (Smith, 1989). It can serve as an effective method for clarifying the evaluation request for many types of evaluation study. Developing program theory, using theory-based evaluation, can also serve as a method for determining the need and focus of the evaluation. (See Chapters 4 and 5.)

How Does One Determine Whether a Program Is Evaluable?

The major steps to determining whether a program is evaluable are:

1. Clarify the intended program model or theory.
2. Examine the program in implementation to determine whether it matches the program model and could, conceivably, achieve the program goals and objectives.
3. Explore different evaluation approaches to determine the degree to which they meet stakeholders' information needs and are feasible to implement.
4. Agree on evaluation priorities and intended uses of the study.

These steps are achieved not by the evaluator alone but in conjunction with the intended users of the study. A working group is established to clarify the program model or theory and to define their information needs and expectations for the evaluation. The role of the evaluator is to facilitate these discussions and to listen and learn about the program and the stakeholders. Wholey (1994) writes: "evaluators do not hypothesize the program design. Instead, they *extract* the program design . . . from relevant documentation and key actors in and around the program" (p. 20, italics ours). An evaluation can really miss the mark if the evaluators develops their model of the program and simply assume stakeholders agree.

What methods are used to accomplish these tasks? In addition to the facilitation of the working group, the evaluator uses *personal interviews* with stakeholders, reviews of *existing program documents* (proposals, reports, brochures, etc.), and *site visits* to observe the program's implementation. The interviews and program documents help the evaluator facilitate the early discussions of the working group to achieve consensus on the program model or theory.

The program model or theory should delineate the goals and objectives of the program and the principles that link program actions to these goals and objectives. Frequently, a model will take the form of a flowchart linking program actions and assumptions to the program goals and objectives. Alternative models may be developed as necessary to facilitate communication. Closure occurs when stakeholders achieve consensus on a particular model that is sufficiently detailed for the evaluator to conduct a study.

Site visits and further study of program documents (quarterly reports, resource allocations, other evaluation studies) can then help the evaluator examine (1) whether the program is being implemented according to the model, and (2) whether the implementation can feasibly achieve the desired goals. If problems occur in either of these areas, the evaluator should then return to the working group. She can help the working group determine whether the model should be revised to match program reality or program changes should occur so that the program implementation corresponds to the current model. The working group can then also address whether and when the evaluation should proceed. In cases where major adaptations need to be initiated, any outcome or summative evaluations might best be postponed until program stability is achieved.

Instead, if program implementation appears to be going smoothly and the activities appear to have some chance of achieving intended outcomes, the working group can then turn to examining various evaluation questions. The evaluator would also facilitate this discussion to provide guidance about what evaluation can accomplish, at what cost, and in what time frame. By this time, the evaluator also should have learned, from her interviews, of different stakeholders' needs. Alternative evaluation plans can be developed, specifying the questions the evaluation will answer, data to be collected, time and resources required, and potential outcomes and uses. The working group then needs to select a plan.

At any stage the group and/or the evaluator can conclude that an evaluation is inappropriate at this time or that a quite different evaluation is required. Evaluations might be postponed if:

- Consensus cannot be achieved among major stakeholders on the program model;
- Program actions differ greatly from the program model;
- Program actions could not feasibly achieve any stated goals or objectives of the model;
- Major stakeholders cannot achieve consensus on the direction of the evaluation;
- The desired evaluation plan is not feasible given data availability and resources;
- Intended uses of the evaluation are too ambiguous.

The above conditions might lead to the conclusion that the intended evaluation is inappropriate at that time. However, the process may have led to another type of evaluation. Specifically, the working group and/or the evaluator may conclude that, although the originally intended outcome study is inappropriate due to lack of agreement on the program model or failure in program implementation, a needs assessment or monitoring study would be useful at this time. The needs assessment study could be used to better define the program model. The monitoring study could determine whether proposed changes in the implementation of the program occur. Thus, this process of determining when an evaluation is appropriate may result in a relatively simple "go" or "no-go" or may result in a changed evaluation focus. In either case, the evaluator, through this planning effort, has made a major step toward conducting an evaluation that makes a difference in organizational effectiveness.

Checklist of Steps for Determining When to Conduct an Evaluation

The checklist in Figure 10.1 should help the evaluator decide when to initiate an evaluation. However, when the decision is "yes," the evaluator may still choose to adopt some of the methods discussed to assist in focusing the evaluation.

Using an Internal or External Evaluator

In the previous section we discussed when to conduct an evaluation. We now consider who will conduct the evaluation. The first decision to be made may be choosing whether to use an external or **internal evaluator.** When the decision to be made is summative—whether to continue, expand, or drop a program—an **external evaluator** (also called a third-party evaluator, independent evaluator, evaluation consultant, or evaluation contractor) may be preferable to an internal evaluator. However, as evaluation has grown as a field, some have observed that few evaluations are purely summative (Smith, M. F., 1994). Most evaluations, however, have implications for formative and summative decisions, and internal and external evaluators can present distinct differences. Note that, with the growth of performance monitoring, internal evaluators are becoming a much more common fixture in many organizations.

Advantages of External Evaluations

The advantages of using an external agency or individual to conduct the evaluation can be summarized as follows:

1. The external evaluation is likely to be viewed as more impartial and objective because the external evaluator has more distance from the program and those involved in its planning and implementation than the internal evaluator.

2. The external evaluation is likely to be more credible to outside audiences, especially if the program is controversial and evaluation findings are to be used in settling a dispute.

3. External evaluation enables an agency to draw on evaluation expertise beyond that possessed by agency staff. Many school systems and other public and nonprofit organizations simply do not find it feasible to hire sufficient numbers

FIGURE 10.1 *Checklist for Determining When to Conduct an Evaluation*

	Check one for each item	
	Yes	*No*

Step 1. *Is there a legal requirement to evaluate?* (If yes, initiate the evaluation; if no, go to step 2.)

Step 2. *Does the object of the evaluation have enough impact or importance to warrant formal evaluation?* (If yes, go to step 3; if no, formal evaluation is unnecessary, and you should discontinue further use of this checklist.)

Step 3. *Is there sufficient consensus among stakeholders on the model for the program? its goals and objectives?* (If yes, go to step 4; if no, consider a needs assessment study.)

Step 4. *If the program has begun, are its actions consistent with the program model? Is achievement of goal(s) feasible?* (if yes, go to step 5; if no, consider a needs assessment or monitoring evaluation to study program modifications.)

Step 5. *Is the proposed evaluation feasible given existing human and fiscal resources and data availability?* (If yes, go to step 6; if no, find more resources before proceeding or revise the scope of your plan.)

Step 6. *Do the major stakeholders agree on the intended use of the evaluation?* (If yes, go to step 7; if no, discontinue or focus on fewer stakeholders who can use the information effectively.)

Step 7. *Are the stakeholders in a position to use the information productively?* (If yes, go to step 8; if no, discontinue or focus on other stakeholders who can use the information to make decisions or take action.)

Step 8. *Will the decisions of your primary stakeholders be made exclusively on other bases and be uninfluenced by the evaluation data?* (If yes, evaluation is superfluous, discontinue; if no, go to step 9.)

Step 9. *Is it likely that the evaluation will provide dependable information?* (If yes, go to step 10; if no, discontinue.)

Step 10. *Is the evaluation likely to meet acceptable standards of propriety?* (See Chapter 18.) (If yes, go to summary. If not, consider other means of data collection or discontinue.)

Summary:
Based on steps 1–10 above, should an evaluation be conducted?

of evaluation specialists to conduct the evaluations needed in the system, but they can obtain the necessary expertise through external evaluators. Moreover, external evaluators fit into more flexible staffing arrangements because there is no need for continuing financial commitment, as is the case with internal evaluators. Thus, the particular skills of several individual external evaluators might be employed at appropriate stages, with each being paid only for the specific services needed.

4. External evaluators bring with them a fresh, outside perspective. Unlike the internal evaluator, they see both the forest and the trees and may detect unwarranted assumptions that are accepted by insiders.

5. Sometimes persons associated with a program are more willing to reveal sensitive information to outsiders (if trust exists) than they are to on-site evaluators, who they fear may inadvertently breach their confidentiality because they are continually on-site and in contact with others involved in the program.

6. External evaluators can feel more comfortable than internal evaluators in presenting unpopular information, advocating changes in the audiences for the study to maximize use, and working to disclose findings broadly. Specifically, because their future salaries and promotions do not depend on people in the organization, external evaluators can be as blunt and honest as the situation merits. Internal evaluators can be inhibited by future concerns. (This perceived advantage of the external evaluator can, however, be overstated. External evaluators are often interested in further work with the organization and good references, if not permanent employment.)

Advantages of Internal Evaluations

Internal evaluations may be conducted by staff whose full-time responsibilities and training are in the evaluation area or, in small organizations, by people whose primary responsibilities and training are in other areas. Obviously, the internal person with more evaluation expertise is preferable to her counterpart whose expertise lies less in evaluation and more in other areas. Nevertheless, both types of internal evaluators share some advantages.

1. Internal evaluators have more knowledge of the program model and its history. This advantage can make internal evaluators quite useful in needs assessment and monitoring studies or in assessing immediate outcomes for formative purposes.

2. Internal evaluators are more familiar with the various stakeholders and their interests, concerns, and influence. This knowledge can help increase the use of the evaluation. Further, if the evaluator has formed positive relationships with management and staff, this relationship can help ease anxiety and build trust regarding evaluation (Love, 1991).

3. Internal evaluators know the history of the organization, its clients, funders, and other stakeholders, the environment in which it operates, and the typical dynamics involved in decision making. Thus, they can more readily and accurately identify persons who will make productive use of the study and can time and present the study to maximize its use.

4. Internal evaluators will remain with the organization after the evaluation and can continue to serve as advocates for use of its findings.

5. Given that internal evaluators are already employed by the organization and oriented to it and the program, start-up times for the evaluation can be quicker than searching for, selecting, and hiring an external evaluator who will need to take time to learn its dynamics unless she has worked with the organization in the past.

6. Internal evaluators are a known quantity. Their strengths and weaknesses are known to the organization and can be analyzed in reference to the project under consideration.

The definition of an internal evaluator becomes less clear in larger organizations and governmental units. Evaluators from the General Accounting Office (GAO) would probably be considered external evaluators when they evaluate an Executive Branch program in response to a congressional request, even though they are federal employees evaluating a federal program. Is an employee of a state evaluation unit, analogous to the GAO, considered an internal or external evaluator when she evaluates a program in another state organization? What if the evaluator is part of an evaluation unit within the state organization she is evaluating? Now, she would be more likely to be considered an internal evaluator, especially if the organization were a small one.

The prototypical internal evaluator is an employee of a small organization who works daily with program planners and providers; moderate-size nonprofit organizations and many units of local government are examples of organizations that would include such internal evaluators. Conversely, the prototypical external evaluator is an independent consultant or an employee of an organization whose function is to conduct evaluations by contract. Many evaluators lie somewhere between these two extremes. Nevertheless, the contrasts between internal and external evaluators, as with the distinctions between summative and formative evaluations, help us to examine the strengths and weaknesses of the various alternative evaluators we could select to conduct the study. We also can use the continuum from internal to external evaluator to ameliorate some of our concerns. Thus, the concern regarding impartiality or bias of the internal evaluator may be partially remedied by selecting an internal evaluator who is relatively distant, on an organizational chart, from the program. Note, however, that this distance, while improving impartiality, diminishes the internal evaluator's typical advantage of knowing the program and its stakeholders.

Sonnichsen (2000), the Director of the FBI's Office of Planning and Evaluation, describes how internal evaluation units can be established and organized to maximize impact. He sees internal evaluators as having the potential to "build an organizational tradition of systematic, critical review and reflection on organizational issues and problems with positive consequences in terms of improved performance" (Sonnichsen, 2000, p. 2). He proposes five preconditions in order for internal evaluators to have high impact on an organization: supportive top management, availability of competent evaluators, an organizational culture of internal review, reliable data systems, and unlimited access by evaluators to the organization's data and personnel. His successful internal evaluator is very much oriented to improving the decision-making process within organizations. (See also Love, 1991, for more on internal evaluation.)

Advantages of Combining Internal and External Evaluation

Internal and external evaluation are far too often viewed as mutually exclusive. They need not be. Combining the two approaches can compensate for several of the disadvantages of each mentioned previously. The external evaluator's lack of familiarity with the program and its stakeholders is less of a problem if she works in tandem with an internal evaluator who can provide the necessary contextual information. Travel costs can be greatly reduced by having the internal evaluator collect the bulk of the necessary data and actively communicate evaluation plans and results to significant internal audiences. Finally, after the external evaluator is gone, the internal evaluator will remain as an advocate for the use of the evaluation.

The external evaluator can then be used to ensure impartiality and credibility as well as to provide specialized knowledge and skills that are not routinely needed in-house. The external evaluator can assist with key tasks when bias might inadvertently occur, such as designing the evaluation, selecting or developing instruments, drawing conclusions from data, and the like. The external evaluator can interpret and present sensitive results to stakeholders.

External evaluators can also be used to "audit" internal evaluation studies to certify that they are methodologically sound and unbiased (Chen, 1994; Sonnichsen, 2000). Such partnerships incorporate the advantages of external evaluation without requiring that the entire evaluation be conducted externally. Further, through the resulting teamwork, internal evaluators can learn new evaluation methods to be used by the organization in the future.

Checklist of Steps for Determining Whether to Use an External Evaluator

Figure 10.2 is proposed as a checklist for deciding whether or not to use an external agency or individual to conduct the evaluation.

Hiring an Evaluator

Hiring an evaluator, whether she is to be a permanent internal employee or an external consultant, is neither simple nor trivial. There is no better way to guarantee a bad evaluation than to turn it over to someone who is inept. Relationships with stakeholders can be irreparably harmed by an insensitive or unresponsive evaluator. Misleading or incorrect information is easy to generate and disseminate but

FIGURE 10.2 *Checklist for Determining Whether to Use an External Evaluator*

	Check one for each item	
	Yes	No
Step 1. *Is there a legal requirement that the evaluation be conducted by an external evaluator?* (If yes, initiate the search for an external evaluator; if no, go to step 2.)	_____	_____
Step 2. *Are financial resources available to support the use of an external evaluator?* (If yes, proceed to step 3; if no, discontinue use of this checklist and conduct the evaluation internally.)	_____	_____
Step 3. *Does the evaluation require specialized knowledge and skills beyond the expertise of internal evaluators who are available to do the evaluation tasks?* (If yes, initiate the search for an external evaluator; if no, go to step 4.)	_____	_____
Step 4. *Is the evaluation concerned with measuring major or highly politicized goals for summative purposes?* (If yes, initiate the search for an external evaluator; if no, go to step 5.)	_____	_____
Step 5. *Is an outside perspective of particular importance to the study?* (If yes, initiate the search for an external evaluator; if no, go to the summary.)	_____	_____

Summary
Based on steps 1–5 above, *should this evaluation be conducted by an external evaluator?*

difficult to eradicate. Therefore, great care should be exercised in hiring evaluators. Before summarizing some criteria that have been suggested for hiring evaluators, it is necessary to consider briefly what competent evaluators must be able to do.

Competencies Needed by Evaluators

There have been several conceptual and/or empirical efforts to identify the tasks required of evaluators and more specific competencies (knowledge, skills, and sensitivities) required to perform those tasks well (e.g., Anderson & Ball, 1978; Covert, 1992; King, Stevahn, Ghere, & Minnema, 2001; Mertens, 1994; Worthen, 1975). Recent efforts to consider the certification of evaluators have inspired more work in this area (Altschuld, 1999). Worthen (1999) writes, "Evaluation competencies—skills and knowledge that enable an individual to conduct a quality evaluation study—represent the *sine qua non* in performance as an evaluator" (p. 546).

The overlap among various lists is reassuringly high. We would be concerned if there were substantial disagreement among professional evaluators regarding critical competencies, but that is not the case. In fact, in their recent study of professional evaluators' consensus on competencies, King et al. (2001) found substantial agreement.

The few areas where the lists of competencies do not overlap result, we believe, from: (1) different publication dates (new issues and needs in evaluation are being discovered continually); (2) differences in level of detail; and (3) differences in the evaluation philosophy or setting of the authors. For example, King et al. (1999) found that the areas in which consensus did *not* emerge often reflected differences in the context and role of the different evaluators taking part in their study and, thus, may reflect different *types* of evaluation practice. For example, conflict-resolution skills were viewed as more important by evaluators who work closely with stakeholders.

Critical competencies for any evaluator include the ability to work with audiences to formulate key evaluation questions; skills in research design, data collection, analysis, and interpretation; the planning and management skills to carry out a study in a timely, cost-effective fashion; the ability to conduct the study in an ethical manner; the communication skills to convey results to varying audiences through oral and written venues; and, finally, the sensitivity to work with a variety of stakeholders in a manner that meets their needs and facilitates the use of results.

Possible Approaches to Hiring an Evaluator

What are the means by which an agency can determine whether an evaluator has these skills? As in any personnel process, selection methods should be matched to the knowledge and skills needed for the job. A résumé and/or past evaluation reports can be useful in judging whether the candidate has the necessary methodological expertise and writing skills. An interview with the candidate—if possible, conducted by representatives of different stakeholders—can be used to assess the candidate's oral communication skills and ability to work with different audiences. An interview can be particularly successful in determining an evaluator's ability to explain complex issues clearly (in describing previous work) and to listen and learn. The candidate's questions and comments during an interview can be judged in terms of the applicant's interest in the program and the evaluation, sensitivity to different stakeholders, and overall oral communication skills. Finally, talking with others who have used the evaluator can be invaluable in discovering more about the candidate's skills in managing an evaluation responsibly and ethically. Such references can also provide useful information about the personal style and professional orientation of the evaluator as can samples of any report produced for prior clients who are willing for them to be shared.

Checklist of Questions to Consider in Selecting an Evaluator

Figure 10.3 is proposed as a checklist of criteria to consider in selecting an evaluator. Each can be answered with a simple "yes" or "no," or qualified as necessary.

FIGURE 10.3   *Checklist of Questions to Consider in Selecting an Evaluator*

	Evaluator qualifications (Check one for each item)		
	Yes	No	?
Question 1. *Does the evaluator have the ability to use the methodologies and techniques that may be required in the study?* (Consider education and training, past experience, and philosophical orientation.)			
Question 2. *Does the evaluator have the ability to help articulate the appropriate focus for the study?* (Consider communication skills, ability to work with stakeholder groups, content specialization.)			
Question 3. *Does the evaluator have the management skills to carry out the study?* (Consider education and training, past experience.)			
Question 4. *Will the evaluator maintain appropriate ethical standards?* (Consider education, training; talk with references.)			
Question 5. *Will the evaluator be interested in and able to communicate results to desired stakeholders in such a way that they will be used?* (Examine previous evaluation documents; talk with references.)			

Summary
Based on questions 1–5 above, *to what extent is the potential evaluator qualified and acceptable to conduct the evaluation?*

How Different Evaluation Approaches Clarify the Evaluation Request and Responsibilities

How would the proponents of the different models reviewed in Chapters 4 to 9 approach the clarification of the evaluation request? Most proponents of the models described in those chapters would not object to the methods discussed above. All except Scriven's goal-free evaluation would include at least some interviews with stakeholders and reviews of existing documents during the planning stage to clarify the request.

An evaluator subscribing to an objectives-oriented model would focus primarily on the specification of objectives or program theories during this stage. Contemporary evaluators would be more likely to be theory-based. Such an evaluator would assume that the evaluation questions would be designed to test normative or research theories regarding the program. In contrast, the management-oriented evaluator would focus more on the decisions to be made and the information needs of the managers who will make those decisions. If these decisions concern program theories or objectives, the evaluator would focus on those; however, if the decisions concern other issues, she would readily adapt. In contrast to the management-oriented approach, the consumer-oriented evaluator would clarify the request through working with the consumers of the program and identifying their concerns. Similarly, the expertise-oriented evaluator might limit the evaluation by relying on established areas of concern in the discipline of the program (e.g., medical, education, or environmental standards). The clarification might have little focus on the needs of actual stakeholders, as the evaluator would assume that she was hired to define the criteria based on her personal expertise in the discipline of the program.

The participant-oriented evaluator would involve many more stakeholders than would adherents of other models in the clarification of the evaluation request. The values of such a diverse group of stakeholders are more likely to differ than are those of more homogeneous groups (such as managers or funders). Thus, meetings of diverse working groups, as proposed by Wholey in evaluability assessment, may be more acrimonious and achieving consensus more difficult. Further, if the gap between managers and other stakeholders were too great, an external evaluator (because an external evaluator would be less likely to be perceived as a "tool of management") with strong conflict-resolution skills might be more appropriate. However, such working groups could succeed in identifying issues that might not have been raised in managerial meetings and, in such a way, further communication between managers and other stakeholders. As an alternative, the participant-oriented evaluator might clarify the evaluation request through interviews with different stakeholder groups, reviews of program documents, and observations of the program, without trying to achieve consensus through a working group of all stakeholders. The participant-oriented evaluator who is of a constructivist bent is looking for multiple realities, not necessarily consensus.

All models can be implemented by either internal or external evaluators; however, internal evaluators are more likely to be management oriented. Their primary purpose is to assist managers in decision making. Because of their ongoing presence, their focus is more on organizational improvement than on any individual program. They would be less likely to take a consumer-oriented or expertise-oriented approach because their primary stakeholder is unlikely to be a consumer and they have been hired for evaluation expertise, not expertise in the content of the particular program. External evaluators, in contrast, are typically hired to evaluate a specific program or policy. They may be hired by consumers, managers, or any group of stakeholders. They may be hired for their evaluation expertise or their expertise in the content of the particular program they are to evaluate. Within that context, elements of theory-based and participatory approaches may be adapted by either internal or external evaluators, given the particular circumstances of the evaluation and needs of the stakeholders.

CASE STUDY APPLICATION

At first, I was fooled by ASCD's (the Association for Supervision and Curriculum Development) request that led to this "case study."[2] The task appeared straightforward enough. "Would you," ASCD editor Ron Brandt had asked over the telephone, "be willing to write a chapter for a book on evaluation? We will give you a description of a real program—sort of a case study—and would like you to explain, in a general way, how you would go about evaluating it." Straightforward. Simplicity itself. So I agreed.

Then the case study arrived; it was a description of a humanities curriculum in a middle school in the Radnor Township (Pennsylvania) School District. It contained the report of the Humanities Curriculum Review Committee and a brief overview that provided an introduction (pp. 188–190). I read the material quickly, worried vaguely that the description was so incomplete that it might not provide much focus for an evaluation, and then dropped the missive into my ASCD file; the deadline was still months away.

Months passed. So did the deadline. A skillfully worded reminder from the editor prodded my conscience, and I retackled the task, beginning by rereading the program description. I had been right. The writing was lucid; it provided a general outline of the humanities program, gave the general context and some issues surrounding it, and even provided some details about rationale, objectives, schedules, and the like. But it struck me as not nearly enough. Somehow I have never learned to design an evaluation that is really "on target" without knowing a good bit about not only the program but also the context in which it is embedded, the personnel who operate it, the population it is intended to serve, availability of resources for the program (not to mention the evaluation), and so on. Without such information, deciding how to aim the evaluation is largely guesswork, and the odds are high that it will miss the mark. How, I wondered, could ASCD expect any evaluator to make a clean hit on such an obscure target?

To put it bluntly, I felt frustrated at the realization that it simply was not feasible to extract, from what I had received, a clear enough picture of the program and the factors influencing it to permit me to design an evaluation I would feel comfortable defending. So I continued to fret about the ambiguity of the request.

Then suddenly the realization hit me. The fuzziness of that target was no accident. By providing purposely incomplete information about the Radnor humanities curriculum, ASCD was forcing each author to fill in the gaps, and, in so doing, to reveal clearly the personal preferences and predilections that make each evaluator's approach unique and render evaluation still more of an art than a science.

Finally, I decided to take the liberty of imagining that the evaluation has already been planned and conducted, thus permitting a description of what has already happened. This shift in tense is important, because it allows exploration of the interactive, iterative nature of evaluation design, which is difficult to see when one looks only at the artificially one-dimensional evaluation plan.

I have chosen to use imaginary journal entries and file artifacts to communicate many of my thoughts about how the evaluation might be conducted. In doing

---

[2]This section and parallel sections that follow at the end of chapters are taken from Worthen (1981) with adaptations and expansions as necessary for our purposes today. The Radnor humanities curriculum, which is evaluated in this "imaginary" evaluation, is described in the Part Three introduction.

so, I have liberally interpreted the Radnor context; I have made many assumptions about what went on as the evaluation unfolded; I have invented fictional characters and events to suit my purposes; and, in the process, I have probably unintentionally maligned at least some of the principal actors in the Radnor drama. If so, it is hoped that I have at least done so equitably. My sincere apologies are extended to Principal Claire Janson and others for any violence I may have done to their school system or sensibilities.

My journal entries cover a twelve-month period during the design, conduct, and reporting of the evaluation of the humanities program. I have also annotated these entries and artifacts under "author comments" to help underscore important points.

Journal Entry: August 11. Today was the first of three days I've agreed to spend here in Battle Creek, Michigan, serving as a member of a panel of evaluators helping the Kellogg Foundation's Evaluation Director refine his concept of "cluster evaluation." Tonight at dinner, Harriet Millman, another of the panelists, told me she had recently been asked to recommend an evaluation consultant to do an evaluation for a school district in Pennsylvania she worked with a couple of years ago. I'm not quite clear on what it's about, except I believe it's some kind of middle-school art program that is drawing fire from some folks who want a more traditional approach to learning; at least that's what she thinks. Not sure I want to get involved, even should they ask me, which is a long shot, because Harriet says they're considering several possible consultants but only have the resources to hire one and may not want to fly someone in.

Guess I'm a bit reluctant because, from what I can gather, the school is being pressured to have the evaluation done, and I'm a bit wary of being brought into situations where the locals have been forced to set up an evaluation but want to let you know that they're not going to be forced to like it. Being unwanted and unwelcome is "unfun," and it makes establishing rapport a real upstream swim. Maybe I'm jumping at shadows, though, because of some prior experiences I'm not eager to repeat, like the time a faculty member in a college several of us were evaluating stood up in a public meeting and defined waste as "a busload of evaluators going over a cliff—with two empty seats"! Quaint sense of humor, that.

All I really know about this Pennsylvania art program, however, is that the decision to evaluate it has been made. Anyway, I told Harriet I would be willing to talk about it if they should contact me.

Author Comments.   Sometimes the evaluator is identified and selected early enough to help determine whether or not it is appropriate to evaluate a particular educational endeavor. More often, however, the decision has been made before the evaluator is ever contacted. In such cases, the client has presumably made the right choice in deciding to evaluate or else the decision to evaluate has been made at a higher administrative or governing level (in an equally rational way, one would hope). All the evaluator can do is to be sensitive to the possibility that evaluation may be premature or unwarranted for reasons discussed earlier in this chapter. Should that be the case, the professionally responsible evaluator will so advise, urging that the evaluation not go forward until or unless it is appropriate.

August 19.   Received an interesting call today from a Ms. Janson, principal of a middle school in Radnor Township (somewhere near Philadelphia). She asked if I might be willing to consider undertaking an evaluation of the program Harriet Millman told me about. Turns out that it's a somewhat controversial humanities curriculum in her school. Seems board of education members have asked for the evaluation. She made it clear to me that she wasn't asking me to do it but only asking if I'd be interested, because they're still deciding who they want. Harriet gave my card to the superintendent, and Ms. Janson (Claire) says she has inherited the job to call several evaluators to find out who might be interested and available to do the study.

She didn't seem at all hostile toward having part of her school's curriculum evaluated, so maybe it's not as hot an issue as I'd thought. Besides, she said no one would believe the results of the evaluation unless it were conducted by an outsider. Anyway, I told her I would be interested—tentatively, at least—and sent her the résumé she requested. I hoped she might mention who else she was considering, but she didn't. No reason why she should, because I guess this could be viewed as a "competitive" situation, although I'm not really panting over the opportunity. It's been a while since I've been asked to throw my hat into the ring, but no harm, I guess.

August 24.   Claire Janson's secretary called from Radnor today and asked if I had a graduate transcript I could send. I told her no, saying I doubted if it would be helpful even if I had one, because those courses were taken twenty years ago. She asked if I had much coursework or background in the humanities. I told her no, not much. She seemed a bit flustered asking those questions, until I offered to send her copies of a couple of evaluation reports I had done and a few names of folks for whom I had done evaluation work in the past four to five years. I suggested she ask Ms. Janson if that wouldn't suffice, because it seems a lot more relevant and a whole bunch easier to locate. I've no idea where to look for my transcript.

Author Comments.   Some wisdom should guide the rigor with which information about evaluators might be pursued. The relevance of formal academic preparation fades with the passage of time, and intervening experience becomes more important. Asking for documents or information not only of dubious utility but also not convenient for the evaluator to provide may discourage interest, unless the evaluator is salivating over the opportunity. Of course, if the evaluation is in Tahiti, or the contract is large and lucrative, one can ask for nearly outrageous information and some evaluators will try to provide it. No evaluator should object, however, to being asked for a few work samples or references of clients previously served. If they do object, that should raise a red flag regarding further discussions.

August 31.   Harriet called from Penn State today and said she'd been at Radnor yesterday and heard I was going to be doing the external evaluation. That's news to me; I've not heard a word since I sent the stuff to them last week. Sounds as if they may have made a decision. Harriet said she didn't know who else they were considering, but guessed they may not have had many well-qualified persons interested in the job. I had hung up the phone before I realized what she'd said! Reminds me of my old psychometrics prof who was fond of saying one could always look good if compared to a norm group made up of stuffed owls.

Major Concepts and Theories

1. Evaluations can be used by the sponsor, client, audience, or stakeholders. Each group has its own needs and concerns and informational requirements for the evaluation. The evaluator should identify each group and, as appropriate, incorporate their concerns in the evaluation plan.

2. Determining and understanding the purpose for an evaluation is probably the most important activity to be completed before the evaluation begins.

3. Evaluation can serve many uses including direct information use, educating users about alternative ways to make decisions, stimulating dialogue among stakeholders, and raising awareness of program issues or stakeholder views.

4. It may be inappropriate to conduct an evaluation if the client is using it to avoid responsibility, for public relations purposes, or to postpone making a decision; resources are inadequate; trivial or invalid information will be produced; the evaluation could lead to unethical practices; or audiences will be misled.

5. Evaluability assessment can be used to determine if it will be effective to proceed with an evaluation. This includes working with program managers to determine if goals and program models or theories are clearly articulated and feasible and if identified audiences will use the information.

6. Internal or external evaluators can conduct evaluations. Internal evaluators have the advantage of knowing the organization, its history and decision-making style and will be around to encourage subsequent use. External evaluators can bring greater perceived objectivity and specialized skills for a particular project.

Discussion Questions _____

1. Why is it important to clarify the evaluation requests? What do we mean by that?

2. How might the typical information needs of sponsors, clients, audiences, and different groups of stakeholders differ?

3. How do you think evaluability assessment might help the evaluator? The users?

4. Under what circumstances would you prefer to use an internal evaluator? Name a program or issue that you would prefer an internal evaluator to address. Do the same with an external evaluator. What concerns would you have about each?

Application Exercises _____

1. What questions might you want to ask if you were being considered to perform an evaluation?

2. Consider a program you know. Does it meet Wholey's criteria for evaluability? If not, what changes need to occur? Are there any steps you could take as an evaluator to help achieve these changes?

3. Considering the program you identified in Exercise 2 and a probable need for information, would an internal or external evaluator be preferable for this evaluation? Justify your choice.

4. What knowledge and skills would be necessary to evaluate the program you are considering? How would you go about hiring a person to conduct this evaluation (internal or external)?

Relevant Evaluation Standards

The evaluation standards we see as relevant to this chapter's content are the following. These standards are described in Chapter 18.

U1—Stakeholder Identification
U2—Evaluator Credibility
F2—Political Viability
P1—Service Orientation
P7—Conflict of Interest
A1—Program Documentation
A2—Context Analysis
A3—Described Purposes and Procedures

Suggested Readings

Cronbach, L. J., Ambron, S. R., Dornbusch, S. M., Hess, R. D., Hornik, R. C., Phillips, D. C., Walker, D. F., & Weiner, S. S. (1980). *Toward reform of program evaluation.* San Francisco: Jossey-Bass.

Joint Committee on Standards for Educational Evaluation. (1994). *The program evaluation standards* (2nd ed.). Thousand Oaks, CA: Sage.

King, J. A., Stevahn, L., Ghere, G., & Minnema, J. (2001). Toward a taxonomy of essential evaluator competencies. *American Journal of Evaluation, 22,* 229–247.

Love, A. J. (1991). *Internal evaluation: Building organizations from within.* Newbury Park, CA: Sage.

Smith, M. F. (1989). *Evaluability assessment: A practical approach.* Boston: Kluwer Academic.

Smith, N. (1998). Professional reasons for declining an evaluation contract. *American Journal of Evaluation, 19,* 177–190.

Sonnichsen, R. C. (2000). *High impact internal evaluation.* Thousand Oaks, CA: Sage.

Wholey, J. S. (1983). *Evaluation and effective public management.* Boston: Little, Brown.

Wholey, J. S. (1994). Assessing the feasibility and likely usefulness of evaluation. In J. S. Wholey, H. P. Hatry, & K. E. Newcomer (Eds.), *Handbook of practical program evaluation.* San Francisco: Jossey-Bass.

11

Setting Boundaries and Analyzing the Evaluation Context

Orienting Questions _____

1. Who are the potential audiences for an evaluation? When and how should they be involved in the evaluation?

2. Why is it important to describe the object of the evaluation?

3. What tools does the evaluator use to describe the object of the evaluation?

4. How can presenting more than one budget be useful to the evaluator? What are some ways that costs can be reduced?

5. What should the evaluator consider in analyzing the political context in which an evaluation will occur? What impact would political considerations have on the conduct of the study?

In the preceding chapter we dealt with determining whether to conduct an evaluation, deciding whether to use an internal or external evaluator, and judging the qualifications of competing evaluators. In this chapter we turn our attention to four other important considerations: identifying evaluation audiences, setting boundaries on whatever is evaluated, analyzing available resources, and analyzing the political context.

Identifying Intended Audiences for an Evaluation

During the planning stage of an evaluation, it is essential that the evaluator identify all the various stakeholders and audiences for the evaluation. Involving the stakeholders during the planning stage helps insure that the evaluation addresses appropriate concerns and assists the evaluator in identifying potential users. Further, involving stakeholders at an early stage can help to reduce their anxieties about the evaluation and allow the evaluator to learn how different groups perceive the program. Recognition of audiences beyond the immediate stakeholders can help the evaluator to consider future dissemination of results. In this section we discuss the identification and involvement of appropriate evaluation audiences.

Identifying the Multiple Audiences for an Evaluation

An evaluation is adequate only if it collects information from and reports information to all legitimate evaluation audiences. An evaluation of a school program that answers only the questions of the school staff and ignores questions of the school board, parents, students, and relevant community groups is simply a bad evaluation. The evaluator should identify and communicate with each audience to learn its perceptions and concerns about the program and the evaluation. Obviously, because some audiences will usually be more important than others, some weighting of their input will be necessary. In almost all evaluations, however, the final **evaluation plan** will include questions that address the information needs of several different stakeholder groups. So, how does one identify all the legitimate audiences?

At the outset, the evaluator must realize that the sponsor and client usually represent a primary audience, yet there are almost always additional important audiences for the evaluation's results. Indeed, the evaluation's sponsor often supports the study to provide information for other audiences such as the evaluated program's staff.

Working with the evaluation client and/or sponsor, the evaluator must strike a reasonable balance in deciding whether to define audiences broadly or narrowly. Few evaluations hold sufficient interest to warrant news releases in the *Wall Street Journal* or the *London Times,* but the more frequent mistake is settling on too narrow a range of audiences. Policy makers, managers, and representatives of those working in the "trenches" are usually selected to guide evaluations and consume their products. Community members and representatives of other influence groups are increasingly numbered among the evaluation's audiences. There is still a regrettable tendency, however, to respond to the squeaking wheel, targeting evaluation studies to those who are vociferous, strident, or powerful. What about the folks without school-age children, who are uninvolved in the PTSA and often regarded only when their numbers and approaching school bond issues or other tax increases make it prudent to ignore them no longer? What of the high school students and their parents? In their model of deliberative democracy in evaluation, House and Howe (1999) argue that the evaluator has a responsibility to "use procedures that incorporate the views of insiders and outsiders [and] give voice to the marginal and excluded" (p. xix). While they acknowledge their view as an ideal, their point is that evaluators can play a powerful role in bringing about a "democratic dialogue" or a discussion between groups that often don't exchange views by considering the way the evaluation is planned and implemented.

Increasing the number and diversity of stakeholders can add to the complexity and cost of the evaluation. However, for political, practical, and ethical reasons, the evaluator can ill afford to ignore certain constituents. Thus, the question of who the audiences are and how they are to be served is a crucial one.

Guba and Lincoln (1981) have developed a set of questions to assist the evaluator in identifying potential audiences. Their questions distinguish among audiences involved in supporting or developing the program to be evaluated, audiences potentially benefiting from the program, and audiences for whom the program may present disadvantages or decrements. We have adapted their questions in modifying the checklist shown in Figure 11.1.

It is doubtful that any one evaluation would have all the audiences listed in Figure 11.1, but the viability of each of these audiences should be considered during the planning stage. The evaluator should review these audiences with the client to identify representatives of each group and then meet individually with these representatives to learn their perceptions of both the program to be evaluated and the evaluation itself. What does each audience perceive as the purpose of the program? How well do they think it works? What concerns do they have about it? What would they like to know about it? What have they heard about the evaluation? Do they agree with its intent? What do they hope to learn from the evaluation? What concerns do they have about it? The evaluator should attempt to meet with audiences with diverse opinions of the program not only to include all audiences but to give them a complete picture of the program.

After meeting with representatives of all potential audiences, the evaluator can then make decisions, possibly with the client, about the import and role of each audience in the evaluation. Important audiences might be involved in an advisory group to the study and consulted frequently; some might become involved in data collection and interpretation of results; others might be briefed on a more intermittent basis. Other audiences may have little or no interest in the study, given its focus.

The checklist in Figure 11.1 is intended to help evaluators and clients think broadly of the audiences for the evaluation and the purpose that might be served in involving them in the study or providing them with the evaluation information. Once the appropriate evaluation audiences have been identified, the list should be reviewed periodically as the evaluation progresses because audiences can change.

FIGURE 11.1   *Checklist of Evaluation Audiences*

Evaluation Audience Checklist

Entity to Be Evaluated   *(Check all appropriate boxes)*

Individuals, Groups, or Agencies Needing the Evaluation's Findings	*To Make Policy*	*To Make Operational Decisions*	*To Provide Input to Evaluation*	*To React*	*For Interest Only*
Developer of the program					
Funder of the program					
Person/agency who identified the local need					
Boards/agencies who approved delivery of the program at local level					
Local funder					
Other providers of resources (facilities, supplies, in-kind contributions)					
Top managers of agencies delivering the program					
Program managers					
Program deliverers					
Sponsor of the evaluation					
Direct clients of the program					
Indirect beneficiaries of the program (parents, children, spouses, employers)					
Potential adopters of the program					
Groups excluded from the program					
Groups perceiving negative side effects of the program or the evaluation					
Groups losing power as a result of use of the program					
Groups suffering from lost opportunities as a result of the program					
Public/community members					
Others					

Of course, as data collection plans are developed and data are collected and analyzed, it is important to consider what information each audience needs and will use. All audiences are not interested in the same information. Program deliverers and primary managers will be interested in more detail than the general public or policy makers. Differing interests and needs often require that evaluation reports be tailored for specific audiences, in ways discussed further in Chapter 17.

Importance of Identifying and Involving Evaluation Audiences

The aggregated viewpoints of various evaluation audiences provide focus and direction to the study. Unless evaluators direct the evaluation clearly at their audiences from the outset, results are likely to have little impact. Discussing who will use evaluation results, and how, is essential to clarify the purpose of the study.

As noted in Chapter 10, most evaluators have at some time been misled (perhaps inadvertently) into undertaking an evaluation, only to find at some point that its underlying purpose was quite different from what they had supposed. Such misunderstanding is much more likely if an evaluator talks only to one audience. Dialogue with multiple audiences also clarifies the reasons behind an evaluation (except for the rare case in which a manipulative individual may intentionally obscure the real purposes; in those cases even contact with multiple audiences would be less useful than truth serum in discerning the real reasons for the evaluation). Vroom, Colombo, and Nahan (1994) report a fascinating case study of such an evaluation.

Describing What Is to Be Evaluated: Setting the Boundaries

Setting boundaries is a fundamental step in gaining a clear sense of what an evaluation is all about. No evaluation should be conducted without a detailed description of the program being evaluated. Such a description establishes the boundaries of what is to be evaluated. Poor or incomplete descriptions can lead to faulty judgments—sometimes about entities that never really existed. For example, the concept of team teaching fared poorly in several evaluations, resulting in a general impression that team teaching is ineffective. Closer inspection showed that what is often labeled as "team teaching" provides no real opportunities for staff members to plan or work together in direct instruction. Obviously, better descriptions would have precluded these misinterpretations. One can only evaluate adequately that which one can describe accurately.

The importance of good description increases in proportion to the complexity and scope of what is evaluated. Evaluators are frequently asked to help evaluate entities as vague as "our Parks and Recreation program." Does that include all programs across all seasons, only the summer recreational programs, or only swimming programs? Would such an evaluation focus on training of part-time summer employees, public use of parks, maintenance of parks, or all of the above? Would it determine whether the goals of Parks and Recreation meet the need of the community, whether the program managers are correctly and effectively implementing the policies determined by elected officials, or both? Answering such questions establishes boundaries that help the evaluation make sense.

A **program description** is a description of the critical elements of the program to be evaluated. Such a description typically includes goals and objectives, critical components and activities, and descriptions of the target audience. It may also include characteristics of personnel delivering the program, administrative arrangements, the physical setting, and other contextual factors. Descriptions often include models or flowcharts depicting the theory of the program or why it is expected to achieve the proposed outcomes. Many descriptions are extensive, delineating critical factors in the history of the program and reasons for choices made at various stages. Others are briefer, but still convey a picture of the essence of the current program. The critical factor in a program description is that it is sufficiently detailed to provide the evaluator with an understanding of why the program is supposed to achieve its desired impacts and to serve as a foundation for identifying evaluation questions. However, some descriptions are so microscopically detailed and cluttered with trivia that it becomes difficult for the evaluator to identify critical elements and linkages between program activities and outcomes. An accurate final description agreed upon by all stakeholders provides a common understanding of the program for all the parties involved, permitting the evaluation to proceed with some consensus concerning the entity to be examined.

Factors to Consider in Characterizing the Object of the Evaluation

The evaluator can demarcate the object of the evaluation and the study itself by answering a series of questions:

• What problem was the program designed to correct? What need does the program exist to serve? Why was the program initiated? What are its goals? Whom is it intended to serve?

• What does the program consist of? What are its major components and activities, its basic structure and administrative/managerial design? How does it function? What research exists to link the activities of the program and characteristics of the clients with the desired outcomes?

• What is the program's setting and context (geographical, demographic, political, level of generality)?

• Who participates in the program (direct and indirect participants, program deliverers, managers and administrators, policy makers)? Who are other stakeholders?

• What is the program's history? How long is it supposed to continue? What critical decisions are key stakeholders facing in regard to the program? What is the time frame for these decisions?

• When and under what conditions is the program to be implemented? How much time is it intended to take? How frequently is it to be used?

• Are there unique contextual events or circumstances (e.g., contract negotiations, budgetary decisions, changes in administration, elections) that could affect the program in ways that might distort the evaluation?

- What resources (human, materials, time) are consumed in using the program?

- Has the program been evaluated previously? If so, what were the findings? How were they used?

The evaluator should also seek to clarify what is *not* included in the program to be evaluated.

Other models also exist to characterize the object of the evaluation. As discussed in Chapter 10, through his development of the process of evaluability assessment, Wholey (1983, 1987, 1994) has written of the need to develop a program model that conveys the linkages between program goals and objectives and program actions. Thus, he would suggest developing a model that links the program activities described in the second question in the preceding list with the goals identified in the first question. The model would describe how these activities could conceivably achieve the stated goals. If no clear linkage between program activities and goals and objectives emerged, the program might not be ready for evaluation.

Using Program Theory to Describe the Program

Theory-driven evaluation, suggested briefly by Weiss (1972) and Fitzgibbon and Morris (1975), but developed more fully by Chen, Donaldson, and Bickman (Bickman, 1987; Chen, 1990; Chen & Rossi, 1983; Donaldson, 2002), uses program theory as a tool for (1) understanding the program to be evaluated, and (2) guiding the evaluation. Chen (1990) defines **program theory** as "a specification of what must be done to achieve the desired goals, what other important impacts may also be anticipated, and how these goals and impacts would be generated" (p. 43). Program theory consists of two parts: normative and causative theory. Normative theory describes the program as it should be, its goals and outcomes, its interventions and the rationale for these, from the perspectives of various stakeholders. Causative theory makes use of existing research to describe potential outcomes of the program based on characteristics of the clients and the program actions. The information gained from these theories can then be used to develop a plausible program model.

Chen's work was prompted by the often atheoretical approach of evaluators to a program. By failing to understand the program theory, or the complex assumptions that link the problem to be resolved with the characteristics and actions of the program and the characteristics and actions with desired outcomes, evaluations have sometimes tended to be black-box studies. Such studies measure inputs and outputs but, due to lack of understanding of the program theory itself, fail to explain program failures or successes. What aspects of the program prompted failure? Success? Why did these components fail or succeed? By articulating the theory of the program, the evaluator begins the evaluation with an understanding of how the program is supposed to achieve its goals.

Rossi's (1971) impact model illustrates a simple method for beginning to develop the theory of the program. He proposes three steps: a causal hypothesis, an intervention hypothesis, and an action hypothesis.

1. The **causal hypothesis** links the problem to be solved or reduced by the program (A) to a purported cause (B). For example: teenagers abuse drugs (A) because they think drug use is very common among their peers (B).[1]

2. The **intervention hypothesis** links program actions (C) to the purported cause (B). Thus: educating teens about the actual occurrence of drug use among their peers (C) will help teens see that drug use is not very common and, in fact, large proportions of teens like them do not use drugs (B).

3. Finally, the **action hypothesis** links the program activities with the reduction of the original problem. Thus, the action hypothesis would be: educating teens about drug use among their peers (C) will decrease teen drug abuse (A).

The evaluator can work with stakeholders to develop an impact model that specifies problems, causes, and program activities and links between these. The initial impact model will be primarily normative, based on the perceptions and experiences of the stakeholders and program developers. A causative model can then be developed that links research to each of the hypotheses or raises questions when empirical evidence is lacking. In some cases, program sponsors, managers, or providers may have previously identified research that supports their normative model. In other cases, the evaluator might conduct a literature review to find research that supports, or challenges, the assumptions of the program model. If existing research causes questions to be raised about the existing model, the evaluator may work with program personnel and other stakeholders to revise the model. These actions, while part of the evaluation planning process, can provide immediate benefits to the organization before the evaluation has even begun.

The final program model then provides the framework for the subsequent evaluation. Thus, a causal hypothesis can lay the foundation for needs assessment questions such as: To what extent does teen drug abuse really exist among our target population? What is the nature of the problem? What drugs are abused? Under what circumstances? Do inaccurate beliefs regarding peers' drug use contribute to students' beginning to use drugs? The intervention hypothesis or hypotheses can help identify important components of the program to monitor or describe in formative studies. (Most models will have several intervention hypotheses connecting different parts of the program with various causes of the problem.) The action hypothesis makes the final link between the problem and the program. It exemplifies the question many black-box studies address, namely, did the program achieve its goal? However, without the important causal and in-

---

[1]This causal hypothesis, that teens overestimate the use of drugs by other teens and this prompts them to use drugs, is the foundation for the revised D.A.R.E. curriculum currently being funded by the Robert Woods Johnson Foundation. There is research support for this hypothesis.

tervention hypotheses, the evaluator may fail to understand and explore the underlying theory of the program.

Methods for Describing the Object of the Evaluation

Developing a program description, model, or theory can be accomplished in a variety of ways. Three basic approaches to collecting the necessary information are: (1) reading documents with information about the object, (2) talking with various individuals familiar with the object, and (3) observing the object in action. Each is discussed briefly here.

Descriptive Documents.   Most programs are described in proposals to funding agencies, planning documents, reports, minutes of relevant meetings, correspondence, publications, and so on. Taking time to locate and peruse such documents is an important step in understanding any entity well enough to describe it correctly.

Interviews.   Helpful as they are, written documents cannot provide a complete or adequate basis for describing the object of the evaluation. It is relatively common for a program to have changed, intentionally or unintentionally, from the plans on paper to actual implementation in the field. The evaluator should talk at length with those involved in planning or delivering the program, with people (students, clients, teachers) who receive the program, and with those who may have observed it in operation. Stakeholders with different perspectives should be interviewed. In evaluating a treatment program for domestic violence perpetrators, for example, the evaluator would be well advised to learn how the program is (and is supposed to be) operating, not only from the therapists and administrators responsible for delivering the program but also from the state department responsible for providing funding for the program, the participants in the program and their families, judges who make referrals to the program, and so on. It is important to interview representatives of all the relevant audiences to develop a model on which consensus can be reached *and* to understand the different perspectives of the audiences.

Observations.   Much can be learned by observing programs in action. In addition to personally observing the program, the evaluator may wish to ask relevant content or process experts to make observations. Often observations will reveal variations between how the program *is* running and how it is *intended* to run that an evaluator may not discover through interviews or reading. In fact, differences between written documents, interviews, and observations can provide the foundation for much learning at this stage. The evaluator should be alert to differences and attempt to learn how these differences have emerged. For example, when observations indicate a program is being delivered in a way that differs from written documents and information gained from interviews, a first useful step is talking with the deliverer to learn the rationale for changes. If appropriate, these differences can then be confirmed with managers or policy makers who have been previously interviewed.

Having described the object of the evaluation, the evaluator must insure that the stakeholders agree that the description accurately characterizes the program. Confirmation of this agreement may be achieved through ongoing meetings with a work group that has been involved in developing the program description (as in evaluability assessment), through distribution of a formal description to different audiences, or through meetings with various stakeholders. Recall, however, that the purpose of this stage is also to set boundaries for the evaluation by clarifying exactly what is to be evaluated. To achieve a full understanding of the context of the evaluation, the description may have involved a larger portion of the program than the evaluation will address. If the evaluation is to focus on a smaller piece of the overall program, clarification about the object of the evaluation should occur at this time.

Clarifying what is to be evaluated reduces the chances that the evaluator will later be accused of evaluating the wrong thing, of conducting an evaluation that was too narrow in scope, or of failing to take important factors into account.

Dealing with Different Perceptions

The above discussion assumes that, in general, consensus on both the program itself and the boundaries of the evaluation exists. Such is not always the case.

As a case in point, Vroom, Colombo, and Nahan (1994) describe how differences in perceptions of goals and program priorities among managers, staff, and sponsors led to a very problematic evaluation. In an innovative program to use cable technology to help the unemployed find jobs, these stakeholders differed in the priority they attached to the technology and the direct service components of the program. The sponsor was concerned with measuring the direct impact on the unemployed, but the agency staff members were concerned with implementing the new, sophisticated cable technology. While other organizational problems also contributed to the failure of the evaluation, the authors believe that more extensive ongoing discussions and meetings with the stakeholders could have clarified the differences in perspective and helped the evaluation.

House (1988) describes the problems that occurred in the evaluation of Jesse Jackson's PUSH/Excel program when the evaluators' perceptions differed from those of the program administrators and staff. The federal evaluators saw the program as having clearly defined, specific components. When they found that each site did not have these components, they attributed the variations to program failure. Program developers, however, had anticipated adaptation to local concerns; they saw PUSH/Excel as a far less structured entity than did the evaluators. The failure to communicate these differences clearly led to a failure in the evaluation.

When disagreements over the nature of the evaluation object exist, the evaluator can take one of two routes. If the differences are relatively minor and reflect the values or position of the stakeholder, the evaluator can choose to learn from these different perceptions, but not push toward consensus. The different perceptions can provide the evaluator with an opportunity to learn more about each stakeholder and the program if he takes the opportunity to carefully learn about each group's perception or interpretation. Then, by permitting each group to attach whatever meaning they wish to the object and following through by focusing on results that are relevant to that meaning, the evaluator can address the information needs of multiple audiences. Moreover, he can educate audiences by helping them look beyond their particular perspectives.

However, if the differences of perception are major and occur among the primary audiences for the study, the evaluator should attempt to achieve some sort of consensus description before moving on with the evaluation. He may want to establish a working group of members of the differing audiences to reach an agreement on a program description and the boundaries of the evaluation. If consensus cannot be achieved, the evaluator may conclude that further evaluation should be delayed. (See Chapter 10 for discussion of evaluability assessment.)

Sometimes it is important for evaluators to obtain formal agreement from the client that a description is accurate. Such agreements can help avoid later conflicts between stakeholders and the evaluator about whether or not the evaluator has really understood the evaluation object.

Redescribing the Object as It Changes

It is important to portray the actual character of the object not only as it begins but also as it unfolds. A critical point for evaluators to remember is that the object to be evaluated frequently changes during evaluation. As House (1993) has written, a program is not "a fixed machine." The nature of a program varies and this variation is caused by many factors (McClintock, 1987). The changes may be due in part to the responsiveness of program managers to feedback that suggests useful refinements and modifications. It is also often the case that an object, whether it is a curriculum, a training program, providing a service, or instituting a new policy, is not implemented by users in quite the way its designers envisioned. Some adaptations may be justifiable on theoretical grounds, some may result from naïveté or misunderstanding, and some may stem from purposeful resistance on the part of users determined to expunge something objectionable from the original conception. Regardless, the evaluator must describe at the end of the evaluation what was actually evaluated, and that may be quite different from what was originally planned.

Guba and Lincoln (1981) provide an excellent discussion of reasons why changes in the evaluation object (which they call the "evaluand") might occur.

> The evaluator who assumes that an implemented evaluand will be substantially similar to the intended entity is either naive or incompetent. Thus, field observations of the evaluand in use, of the setting as it actually exists, and of the conditions that actually obtain are absolutely essential.
>
> Variations in the entity, setting, and conditions can occur for a variety of reasons. In some cases the reluctance or resistance of the actors in the situation

produces unwanted changes. Adaptations to fit the evaluand to the local situation may have to be made. The simple passage of time allows the action of various historical factors to make their contribution to change. Most of all, the continuing activity of the evaluator himself, if it is taken seriously by the actors and if it produces meaningful information, will contribute to a continuously changing set of circumstances (p. 344).

A Sample Description of an Evaluation Object

To help illustrate the key points in this section, we include a discussion of a program evaluated by one of the authors (Fitzpatrick, 1988). The program to be described is a treatment program for people convicted of driving under the influence (DUI) of alcohol. The description is organized around the first two bulleted items listed on page 204, under "Factors to Consider in Characterizing the Object of the Evaluation." Program descriptions or models can be organized in many different ways. This presentation is designed to illustrate what might be learned in regard to each factor.

The first set of questions is: What problem was the program designed to correct? What need does the program exist to meet? Why was it initiated? What are its goals? Whom is it intended to serve?

> This particular treatment program is designed for offenders who are considered problem drinkers or incipient problem drinkers due to a number of different criteria, including number of DUI arrests, blood-alcohol level at the time of arrest, scores on a measure of alcoholism, and whether an accident was involved in the arrest. The program exists to reduce deaths and accidents due to drunk driving. As with many programs of this type, it was initiated due to public attention to this issue and recognition that some sort of cost-effective treatment might be needed for certain offenders to contain the problem. Its goals are to help offenders to recognize that they have a drinking problem and to seek further treatment. The designers of the program recognize that resources for the program are insufficient to stop problem drinkers from drinking. Thus, the following program theory contains a more immediate, implicit goal. The theory or model of the program is (a) problem drinkers drive under the influence of alcohol because they have problems with alcohol and are not aware of the extent of their problem; (b) if these offenders are exposed to information regarding alcohol use and participate in group discussions regarding their own use, they will recognize their own alcohol problem; (c) the treatment program will refer them to places where they can receive extended therapy; (d) by receiving extended therapy, the offenders will reduce their consumption of alcohol and, hence, their frequency of driving under the influence of alcohol. A secondary competing model to achieve the goal is to get participants to use alternative means of transportation and avoid driving when they have been using alcohol. (See below.)

The second set of questions is: What does the program consist of? What are its major components and activities, its basic structure and administrative/managerial design?

How does it function? What research exists to link the activities of the program and the characteristics of the clients with the desired outcomes?

> The curriculum and methods used in the treatment program were developed, outlined, and disseminated to treatment sites by the state agency that funds and administers the program. The program is twenty to thirty hours in length delivered over eight to twelve sessions. The content consists of a combination of lectures, films, group discussions, and exercises. The manual for the treatment is quite specific about the content for each session; however, interviews with the treatment deliverers, who are independent practitioners in the alcohol abuse area, indicate that they often adapt the content based on their perceptions of the group's needs. Observations of a few programs suggested experiential activities may be more limited than expected. The theory on which the treatment is based requires a heavy emphasis on experiential methods rather than didactic approaches to achieve the goal of recognizing their own program with alcohol. Offenders who meet the criteria to be classified as problem drinkers are sentenced by the judges to complete the program at the site closest to their home. (Offenders have lost their driver's licenses as part of their punishment.) If they fail to complete the program, they are then sentenced to time in jail.

Another critical component of the program description is characterization of the stakeholders.

> Prominent stakeholders in this program include the judges (who initially sponsored the study), Mothers Against Drunk Driving (MADD, who lobbied the judges to sponsor the study), the program deliverers, and the state division that oversees the program. Other stakeholders include the clients, their families, victims of traffic accidents in which arrests are involved and their families, insurance companies, alcohol treatment centers, and the public at large. The judges are interested in improving their sentencing by learning what kinds of offenders are least likely to complete treatment successfully. MADD is interested in the degree to which the program achieves its goals. The program deliverers are persons with expertise in treating alcohol offenders both through these programs and others. They are most interested in ending alcohol abuse. The state funding source agrees that alcohol abuse is part of the problem and should be remedied but also advocates alternative methods of transportation. Research suggests that treatments that decrease the frequency of driving (removal of license and increase in insurance costs) are more effective at decreasing deaths due to driving under the influence than treatments that address the alcohol abuse itself. However, as most professionals in this field are from the alcohol treatment area rather than the transportation area, the alcoholism treatment approach tends to be the dominant focus.
>
>   Much research has been conducted in this area nationally, and the state division responsible for overseeing the program collects some routine data from sites. However, little systematic research has been performed on this state program. Current data collection focuses on attendance and change on pre-post knowledge and attitude measures administered at the beginning and end of the programs. No monitoring studies or follow-up outcome studies have been conducted.

The preceding description is designed to illustrate some of the critical factors that an evaluator might note in characterizing the object of the evaluation during the planning phase. To describe the program, the evaluator made use of printed material (state manuals and proposals, local site materials); interviews (judges, MADD, deliverers, state administrators); observations of the program; and a review of literature on treatment programs and solutions for people convicted of drunk driving. With the information obtained from answering the first two questions, a model can be developed for the program. The model can be depicted with a flowchart or in a narrative manner, as illustrated in this example. Empirical research that both supports and weakens the model should be described. Site visits to the program can then help bring this model to life and assist the evaluator in determining whether program activities correspond to the model. This description, then, can provide the foundation for further communication with audiences in planning the focus of the evaluation.

Analyzing the Resources and Capabilities That Can Be Committed to the Evaluation

Very often, program managers, deliverers, and, sometimes, clients themselves view resources committed to evaluation as resources taken away from the program itself. If those dollars were only available we could educate more students, treat more patients, serve more clients, create more parks, and so on. However, others in the public and nonprofit sectors have come to recognize that evaluation can be very useful to them. Evaluation can help program managers and deliverers adapt programs to better meet the needs of their clients. The use of Total Quality Management (TQM) in the private sector to assess client satisfaction and delivery of products persuaded many others that evaluation might, in fact, pay for itself. Hodgkinson, Hurst, and Levine (1975) first introduced the doctrine of cost-free evaluation to argue that evaluation is not an "added-on-extra" but a means for identifying "cost-saving and/or effectiveness-increasing consequences for the project" (p. 189). Evaluators should recognize that their purpose is to improve productivity and the quality of the product, either through formative recommendations for program improvement that will lead to better products or result in lower costs or summative recommendations that will result in maintaining or expanding successful, cost-effective programs or eliminating unsuccessful ones.

Analyzing Financial Resources Needed for the Evaluation

Even when the client is converted to the doctrine of cost-free evaluation, determining what resources can be devoted to evaluation is difficult. As Cronbach and others (1980) have noted, "deciding on a suitable level of expenditure is . . . one of the subtlest aspects of evaluation planning" (p. 265).

Ideally, this decision should be made in consultation with the evaluator, whose more intimate knowledge of evaluation costs would be of great help. Unfortunately, there may not be sufficient rapport between evaluator and client to foster such collaborative planning, though such collaboration is much more likely to occur when the evaluation is conducted by internal evaluation personnel. However, in many situations where external evaluators are hired, the client may initially proceed independently to set budgetary limits for the study. Sometimes the evaluator is informed about how much money is available for the evaluation. Frequently, however, the amount of money available is not made clear. In such cases, we recommend that the evaluator propose two or three different levels of evaluation that differ in cost and comprehensiveness—perhaps a "Chevrolet" and a "Cadillac" evaluation, for example—from which the client can select. Internal evaluators can have more dialogue with decision makers at the budgeting stage, but may also develop several budgets to reflect different alternatives. Clients new to evaluation are often unaware of the possibilities of evaluation design, of what information evaluations might be able to produce, or of the cost of evaluation services. Faced with decisions about trade-offs and budget limitations, the client also needs to know about alternatives and their consequences in order to make a good decision. Budgeting could be the last step in planning an evaluation. On the other hand, if budget limits are known at the beginning, they will affect (and usually enhance) planning decisions that follow.

Ideally, evaluation plans and budgets should remain flexible, if at all possible. Circumstances will change during the study, and new information needs and opportunities will unfold. If every dollar and every hour of time are committed to an inflexible plan, the results will fail to capitalize on the new insights gained by evaluator and client. Even the most rigid plan and budget should include provisions for how resources might be shifted, given approval of the client or decision maker, to accomplish evaluation tasks that take on new priority through changing circumstances.

Analyzing Availability and Capability of Evaluation Personnel

Budget is only one consideration affecting the design of an evaluation study. Personnel is another. Both internal and external evaluators can be assisted by employees whose primary responsibility is to perform other functions. Program deliverers may be able to collect data. Administrative assistants can work preparing documents, searching records, making arrangements for meetings, interviews, or the like, at no cost to the evaluation budget.[2] Graduate students from local universities seeking internship experience or working on dissertations or course-related studies can undertake special assignments at minimal cost to the evaluation budget. Volunteers from neighborhood associations and other community groups,

---

[2]This is not to say there is no cost for such personnel services, only that it may be possible to obtain some assistance with evaluation tasks from on-site personnel within existing operating budgets.

parent–teacher associations, church groups, or advocacy groups associated with the project can often perform nontechnical evaluation tasks. Clients themselves can also help. Calls for volunteers from among these various groups often pay off, and involving volunteers not only helps contain costs but also sparks interest in the evaluation among stakeholders.

Whenever people who are not evaluation specialists conduct or assist with evaluation tasks, the evaluator faces unique responsibilities that cannot be neglected: orientation, training, and quality control. Evaluation personnel who lack specialized training or relevant experience require orientation to the nature of the study, its purposes, and the role they will be asked to play. They must understand their responsibilities, not only in completing evaluation tasks in an effective and timely manner, but also in representing the evaluation team and its sponsoring organization. Naive and unprepared evaluation staff (volunteers or otherwise) can play havoc with an evaluation if they interact abrasively with others, misrepresent the nature or purpose of the study, betray anonymity or confidentiality, or even dress inappropriately for the setting. Evaluation volunteers or assistants must also be trained in the skills required to do the tasks assigned. They must follow protocols or misleading, inaccurate information or other types of errors may result. Supervision and spot-checking can be very helpful, especially in the early stages, to ensure that non-evaluation personnel understand their tasks and responsibilities.

If non-evaluation personnel are used to expand an evaluation effort at low cost, the risk of bias is present. Personal considerations must not influence the way in which these volunteers conduct their evaluation tasks. It is easy to allow presuppositions to color one's perceptions. Evaluators are trained to recognize their biases and adjust; people new to evaluation are unlikely to be aware of their biases or the effects they may have on the evaluation. Although few seem likely to be so unprincipled, it is also possible to alter or distort the data to make it fit one's prior conclusions. Thus, to protect the study's validity and credibility it is essential that an evaluator using non-evaluation personnel exercise caution and judgment in determining which tasks the volunteers will perform. If they are assigned tasks that would expose them to confidential information, they should be carefully trained in the meaning of confidentiality and the importance of maintaining the dignity and privacy of clients or others from whom data are collected. Given conscientious supervision, monitoring, and auditing, local staff or volunteers can make a valuable, cost-effective contribution to an evaluation.

Some evaluations, however, have been greatly enhanced by using people not originally trained in evaluation to assist in the project. Mueller (1998) won an American Evaluation Association award for the work of her team in evaluating Minnesota's Early Childhood Family Education (ECFE) program. Part of the impetus for the award was the effective training and use of program staff at all stages of the evaluation. Staff were involved in identifying families for different phases of the study, videotaping and interviewing clients, analyzing data, and developing reports. Through her efforts she was able to conduct a relatively comprehensive evaluation with a small budget and to achieve her goal of building internal evaluation capacity within the organization by training and using ECFE staff to perform the evaluation. Given appropriate training, volunteers who are part of the client population can sometimes collect more sensitive and valuable qualitative information through interviews than well-trained, but culturally different evaluators. Empowerment evaluation is founded on the principle of training others to evaluate their own programs.

Analyzing Technological and Other Resources and Constraints for Evaluations

The availability of existing data, including files, records, previous evaluations, documents, or other data-collection efforts to which the evaluation may be attached, is an important consideration. The more information that must be generated de novo by the evaluator, the more costly the evaluation.

The availability of needed support materials and services is also important. Existing testing programs, computer services, routine questionnaires, or other information services are all possible resources that could be drawn on at little or no cost to the evaluation if they already exist for other purposes.

Also, advances in technology have provided opportunities for both collecting more useful information and for reducing costs. Although face-to-face communication, particularly with new stakeholders during the planning stage, can never be replaced, E-mail among groups and individuals can be used to increase communication and reduce time and travel costs by replacing or supplementing meetings involving people from different locations, sometimes scattered across a state or country. Conference calls, with video accompaniment, can sustain the dynamics of face-to-face meetings while also reducing costs. Technology can be used to share drafts of data collection measures, results, or reports and seek input from various stakeholders who might not have been included in the past. Surveys can be conducted with target audiences who are on-line and results analyzed as data are accumulated. Videos or photographs of program activities, stakeholders, clients, or other pertinent evaluation- or program-related information can be posted on the Internet for others to view and comment. Finally, it has become almost commonplace for many final evaluation reports to be posted on Web sites for foundations or organizations in order for these results to reach wider audiences. (See Fitzpatrick & Fetterman, 2000, for a discussion of Fetterman's use of technology in the evaluation of the Stanford University teacher-training program.)

The evaluator should also take into account the relevance of existing evaluation approaches and methods for the specific study being considered. The methodological or technological state of the art necessary to respond successfully to a particular evaluation request may be so underdeveloped or new that a major research and development effort will be required before the evaluation can be launched. Pioneering can require considerably more time, effort, and money than either evaluator or sponsor can afford to spend.

Time must be considered a resource. The evaluator does not wish to miss opportunities for making the evaluation useful because of tardy reports or data collection and analysis. Knowing when to be ready with results is part of good planning. It is ideal to have sufficient time to meet all information needs at a pace that is both comfortable and productive. Limited time can diminish an evaluation's effectiveness as much as limited dollars.

Analyzing the Political Context for the Evaluation

Evaluation is inherently a political process. Any activity that involves applying the diverse values of multiple constituents in judging the value of some object has political overtones. Whenever resources are redistributed or priorities are redefined, political processes are at work. Consider the political nature of decisions regarding whose values are attended to, how they are weighted, what variables are studied, how information is reported and to whom, how clients and other audiences intend to use evaluative information, what kind of support is given to the evaluation and by whom, what potentially embarrassing information is hidden, what possible actions might be taken to subvert the evaluation, and how the evaluator might be co-opted by individuals or groups. Political processes begin to work with the first inspiration to conduct an evaluation and are pivotal in determining the purpose(s) to be served and the interests and needs to be addressed. Political considerations permeate every facet of evaluation from planning through the reporting and use of evaluation results.

We have reserved our more extensive discussion of political factors in evaluation for Chapter 17, but we cannot leave this chapter without saying a few words about the importance of analyzing the political context in which the evaluation will be conducted while there is still time to recognize and retreat from a political debacle that could render an evaluation useless.

On receiving any new request to undertake an evaluation, the evaluator might consider the following questions:

1. Who would stand to lose/gain most from the evaluation under different scenarios? Have they agreed to cooperate? Do they understand the organizational consequences of an evaluation?

2. Which individuals and groups have power in this setting? Have they agreed to sanction the evaluation? To cooperate?

3. How is the evaluator expected to relate to different individuals or groups? As impartial outsider? Advocate? Organizational consultant? Future consultant or subcontractor? Confidante? Facilitator? What implications does this have for the evaluation and its ability to provide useful results in an ethical manner?

4. From which stakeholders will cooperation be essential? Have they agreed to provide full cooperation? To allow access to necessary data?

5. Which stakeholders have a vested interest in the outcomes of the evaluation? What steps will be taken to give their perspective a fair hearing without allowing them to preclude alternative views?

6. Who will need to be informed during the evaluation about plans, procedures, progress, and findings?

7. What safeguards should be incorporated into a formal agreement for the evaluation (e.g., reporting procedures, editing rights, protection of human subjects, access to data, metaevaluation, procedures for resolving conflicts)?

Answers to these questions will help the evaluator determine whether it will be feasible and productive to undertake the evaluation study, a decision we will address shortly. First, it may be helpful to consider briefly how the activities and issues discussed so far in this chapter would be influenced by the evaluation approach being used.

Variations Caused by the Evaluation Approach Used

The participant-oriented model has had an important influence on evaluators. Few evaluators today would conduct an evaluation without considering the perceptions and needs of other stakeholders and the context in which the evaluation is to be conducted. However, as in Chapter 10, the models differ in emphasis.

An evaluator using a pure objectives-oriented approach, a rare case today among trained evaluators, might involve different audiences in defining program objectives but, in his single-minded focus on objectives, might fail to obtain an adequate description of the program and an understanding of the political context in which it operates. An objectives-oriented approach tends to be relatively linear and can fail to acknowledge the multiplicity of views about the program, the clients it serves, and the context in which it operates. However, the development of logic models or the specification of program theory, as advocated by those using a contemporary objectives-oriented approach, can avoid that problem. The development of program theory or logic models, especially when conducted as a dialogue with different stakeholders, can illuminate program operations and hidden assumptions.

Similarly, a management-oriented approach is often criticized for its focus on the manager as the primary decision maker and on providing information only for identified decisions to be made. While sophisticated users of this model would certainly identify and learn about the concerns of other audiences, these audiences would be viewed as secondary. If such audiences were outside the organization (e.g., clients, interest groups), they would almost certainly not be seen as a primary audience because the evaluator following this approach would tend to see them as lacking the power to make decisions that could affect the program dramatically. (Obviously, such evaluators would have failed to consider boycotts!)

Similarly, a management-oriented evaluator might focus on defining the decisions to be made and the context for those decisions rather than the context for the program itself. Today's performance monitoring and use of standards falls within the management-oriented model because these devices are used for internal management decisions. However, often the decisions to be made are not specified and, like early objectives-oriented models, the means for achieving the standard or performance may remain unspecified.

The consumer-oriented approach will, of necessity, define the program from the perspective of consumers. In this case, other audiences and other views of the program or products may be neglected. Thus, a consumer-oriented evaluation of the national forests might choose to focus on the satisfaction of campers in these forests. How pleased are they with the camping facilities? The beauty of the site? The access to the campground? Such a focus would neglect other audiences such as ranchers, nonusers who want the land protected, and future generations of users and nonusers.

The expertise-oriented evaluator is likely to be the most narrow in identifying and considering audiences and their descriptions and views of the program. The expertise-oriented evaluator is hired more for his knowledge of the content of the program than for his expertise in evaluation. Such knowledge, and the criteria for the evaluation, typically arise from professional education, training, experience in the field, and, often, standards developed by the same profession in which the "expert" is educated. Thus, the audience for the program and the means for describing the program are rather narrowly circumscribed by the profession the program represents (e.g., education for schools, health for hospitals, criminal justice for prisons). The expertise-oriented evaluator may collect data on the program from many different audiences but rarely would consider these audiences' information needs for the evaluation. This evaluator would view his role as reflecting the standards of his field, not those of others.

The participant-oriented model is certainly the most ardent in advocating the inclusion of many different audiences and perspectives in the planning of the evaluation. The evaluator using this model would constantly seek the multiple perspectives of different audiences. He would argue that no one view of the program reflects truth and, thus, he must seek many different perspectives to understand the program in its totality. Such an approach is, of course, likely to consider the most audiences and the largest number of program descriptions. The question becomes one of synthesis. Who makes this synthesis? The evaluator may become an important decision maker with this approach if he is the sole person responsible for such synthesis. Or, alternatively, the evaluator may work with a committee of different users to guide the synthesis or serve as a facilitator to help groups achieve a synthesis of their own. The management-oriented evaluator might accuse the participant-oriented evaluator of being naive about the political sphere. The evaluator is betting that the manager he targets as the primary decision maker is the one most interested and most able to make decisions based on the results of the evaluation. The participant-oriented evaluator might retort that few decisions emerge directly from an evaluation. By involving and informing many audiences, his evaluation, he would argue, is most likely to make a difference in the long run.

Determining Whether to Proceed with the Evaluation

In Chapter 10 we talked about identifying reasons for the evaluation; such reasons provide the best indicators of whether an evaluation will be meaningful. In this chapter we have discussed the importance of understanding who will use the evaluation information and how, and we have suggested ways to identify relevant audiences. We have stressed the importance of describing and setting boundaries for what is evaluated and analyzing fiscal, human, technological, and other resources to determine feasibility. We have cautioned evaluators to consider whether any political influences might undermine the evaluation effort as well.

At this point, the evaluator must make a final determination—having accumulated sufficient information on the context, program, stakeholders, and resources available—of whether to continue the evaluation. In Chapter 10, we reviewed conditions under which an evaluation might be inappropriate. Now, the evaluator has learned even more about the boundaries and feasibility of the evaluation and the needs and views of stakeholders. With this information, the evaluator should again consider whether to proceed.

Unfortunately, we can offer no simple algorithm for balancing all these factors in making a final decision about whether to proceed with the evaluation. Thoroughness in considering the factors outlined in this and the preceding chapter, insight, thoughtfulness, and common sense are the ingredients essential to a sensible decision about when to agree to do an evaluation. Yet, even the most insightful evaluator with considerable experience will sometimes make an unwise decision, which is our cue to return to the case study we left at the end of Chapter 10.

> ### CASE STUDY APPLICATION
>
> ***September 2.*** Claire Janson, the Radnor principal, called today and told me I'd been picked by the committee to do their evaluation, if I would. I agreed tentatively, but told her I couldn't make a final commitment without knowing more about the program, precisely why they want it evaluated, what use they would make of the evaluation findings, the resources available for the evaluation study, and so on. She promised to send some written materials for me to review.

Author Comments.   To agree to undertake an evaluation without first knowing a bit about the program to be evaluated strikes me as a potential disservice to both the program and the evaluator. Only an evaluator who is naive, avaricious, or supremely confident that his evaluation skills or approach will solve any evaluation problem would plunge in with so little information. Having once met all three of those criteria, I have more recently repented, and during the last decade have insisted on learning enough about the program, prior to committing to evaluate it, to be certain I can be of some help.

> *September 8.* Spent a few minutes this evening reading through materials I received from Radnor Township School District. They sent a brief report of their Humanities Curriculum Review Committee, which listed committee membership; outlined their activities; gave goals, objectives, and rationale for the curriculum; and included an outline of the content of the program and the schedule for implementation. They also listed other alternatives they had considered and rejected, even explaining why, which is a helpful inclusion. No clue in the materials, however, concerning some of the more important things I need to know before I decide whether I can be of any real help to them. Spent a while jotting down some questions I want to ask the principal.

Author Comments.   Later examination of artifacts in my Radnor School District Evaluation file would reveal the following list of questions (Artifact 1).

> **ARTIFACT 1**
>
> 1. How old is the humanities curriculum in the Radnor School District? The Humanities Curriculum Review Committee was launched in 2001, just a few years ago, but what about the curriculum? Is it well established or new? Entrenched or struggling to find root?
> 2. Have there been any previous efforts to evaluate the humanities program? If so, by whom? When? What were the findings? How did they affect the program?
> 3. Why does the board want the program evaluated now? What are the political forces at work? If it is controversial, who are the advocates (beyond the obvious)? The opponents? What sparks the controversy?
> 4. What decision(s) will be made as a result of the evaluation? Will the evaluation really make a difference, or is it merely for show?
> 5. How broadly did the curriculum committee sample opinions of the public, the students, teachers, administrators, outside specialists? To what extent did those groups really have a chance to give input? Were they well enough informed for their input to be on target? How much do they feel they were really listened to? Did their input really shape the outcome?
> 6. How well is the humanities department at Radnor School integrated with the other departments? Is the relationship congenial? Competitive? Any problems here?
> 7. What are the costs of the humanities program (dollars, time)? Any problems here?
> 8. What resources are available to conduct the evaluation? How good a job do they really want? (If evaluation budget is inadequate, are there staff members in the school or district who might be assigned to spend time helping collect some of the data, working under my supervision? Perhaps I could use some staff for interviews or program observation? The principal might be able to recommend central office staff who do not have a stake or interest in the program and who would be interested in gaining these skills.)
> 9. What access will I have to collect data I need? Are there any problems with the teachers' association or contracts, policies on testing students, and so forth, that would constrain me if I wanted to observe classrooms, interview teachers, or test students? What about policies concerning control of the evaluation report(s), review or editorial rights they may insist on, my rights to quote, release, and so on?

10. Are there any other materials that might give me a better feel for the program? What are the activities and major components? What methods are used? How do these activities and methods link to the goals and objectives of the program?
11. What do the teachers and curriculum planners see as the theory or model for the program? How do they think the activities and methods of the program lead to achievement of the goals? Have they modeled the program on other programs they are familiar with?
12. And, lest I forget, rhetoric aside, are they really serious about attaining all the goals they have laid out, in a mere two hours per week over three school years? Or are those goals just window dressing to sell the program?

Author Comments.   Most of these questions simply seek descriptive information essential to knowing how (or whether) to conduct the evaluation. Questions 3, 4, 5, 7, 8, and 12 may also suggest a hint of cynicism or suspicion, yet the failure to ask and answer such questions has sent more rookie evaluators baying down wrong trails, en route to unproductive thickets of irrelevant findings, than any other single oversight. I don't really expect Ms. Janson to be able to answer all these. Many will require talking with others involved in the project, but at least I can get her point of view and see how sensitive they might be to such questions.

September 9. Called Claire Janson, who responded to several of my questions. As we got into the discussion, however, it became apparent that she couldn't really answer some of them without presuming to second-guess the board or others. After a bit, she asked, in view of all the questions I was posing, how much information I really thought I would need before I could sit down and outline an evaluation design that would tell them what they needed to know. I pointed out that was precisely the problem. I wasn't yet certain just what it was they needed to know; hence, all my questions. I suggested to Ms. Janson that the most feasible way to proceed would be for me to visit the school for two or three days, talk with her and some other members of the committee (including a few parents and students), visit with some board members, observe some humanities classes, review the written units, and see if I couldn't get my questions answered, along with a lot of other questions that will probably occur to me in the process. I suggested that I could then leave with her a rough draft of some issues the evaluation might address and next steps to be taken; they could review it and decide whether they want me to proceed with any or all of it. That way they would know in advance how I intend to carry out the evaluation and what data I propose to collect rather than discover at the end of the evaluation that they didn't really place much stock in the approach I had used or that I had omitted information they viewed as critical. Ms. Janson immediately saw the wisdom and advantage in my suggestions. She seems delightfully perceptive! I arranged to visit Radnor next week. Before I go, I want to have a graduate student do a quick review of literature on such programs so I can learn a little about methods that have been found to achieve such goals with children this age.

Author Comments.   In reaching agreements about the conduct of an evaluation, the evaluator should not be the only person to exhibit caution. Evaluation clients should also look carefully at what is proposed before they commit precious resources to the evaluation. Although most evaluators of my acquaintance are well intentioned and competent, it remains a new field and there are still too many charlatans and hucksters who lack the ethical principles and/or the skills necessary to do good evaluation work. Atrocities committed by such have gone far to breed skepticism that many program staff extend undeservedly to well-qualified, reputable evaluators. Even with well-intentioned, competent evaluators, potential clients can have no assurance a priori that their particular approach to evaluating the program will be very helpful.

It is for these reasons that I generally suggest that the evaluator and client interact enough to clarify in some detail what the evaluator is proposing before they "plight their troth." This might require the client to invest a small amount of resources to cover out-of-pocket expenses and a day or two's time for the evaluator (or more than one evaluator) to talk with representatives of the various audiences for the evaluation, probe areas of ambiguity, and provide at least a rough plan to which the client can react. In my judgment, that small investment will yield important returns to the client and avoid the later disenchantment that often occurs as an evaluation unfolds in ways never imagined by a client (but perhaps envisioned all along by the evaluator).

The best possible results of such a "preliminary design" stage are sharper, more relevant focusing of the evaluation and clarity of understanding that will undergird a productive working relationship between evaluator and client throughout the study. The worst that can happen is that a small proportion of the resources will be spent to learn that there is a mismatch between what the evaluator can (or is willing to) deliver and what the client needs. That is small cost compared to discovering the mismatch only after the evaluation is well under way, the resources largely expended, and an untidy divorce the only way out of an unsatisfactory relationship.

Of course, with an internal evaluator the client is familiar with the evaluator's skills and approach to evaluation. Nevertheless, even an internal evaluator must take time to consider the proposal to evaluate a new object, review documents, talk with users, and consider whether the evaluation is appropriate at that time.

The quick review of literature can be supplemented and better focused after the visit, but it is useful to learn a little about what has been found to work, and what *doesn't* work. This information can help the evaluator to ask good questions when talking with the clients about the model for the program. If they're using methods that the literature shows have not been too successful, the evaluator can probe to learn more about why they have chosen that method, whether they know about others' failures with it, and how open they are to hearing about potential failures of some program components.

> *September 14.* I just completed an interesting day and evening in the Radnor School District trying to get a fix on their humanities program. Had informative discussions with Claire Janson, Ron Holton (chairman of the committee), two humanities teachers, and one parent who served on the committee. All are staunch "loyalists" for the program, but they don't seem closed-minded about it. Not that they are really clam-

oring for an evaluation—I gather that interest comes mostly from the board—but they seem open to looking at the program and have been candid in responses to my questions. The humanities teachers were the most guarded; not too surprising, I suppose, for it appears they may have a lot at stake. They and Claire Janson were all quick to record their skepticism about using tests and statistics to measure something as ethereal as the humanities. The humanities teachers seemed dumbfounded to learn that my Ph.D. is not in some branch of the humanities. One asked how anyone except an expert in humanities could presume to evaluate a humanities curriculum. I countered by pointing out that I write doggerel, publish an occasional short story, and once even tried to sell an oil painting. She wasn't easily impressed. I debated whether to trot out my well-practiced arguments about why evaluators need not be specialists in the content of what they evaluate but decided the moment was not right for conversion.

I asked each person I talked with what she or he saw as the major goals of the program and how they thought the program achieved those goals. For those who were hazy on this, I asked them what problems they felt students had before this curriculum began and what caused those problems. I then asked them to talk about how the humanities program could mediate these problems. Many talked about how much rote learning was in the school, and I had to work to get them to focus on the students. However, many noted the program was to help students become more creative and to appreciate the arts and abstract concepts. Some work will be needed to explore what they mean by "understanding of all that it means to be human," but I am beginning to get a better understanding of the model for the program. I also asked people what they would like to learn about the program, what they hoped the evaluation would provide, and how they would use the evaluation. I'll do the same tomorrow and try to refine the model and make up a master list of potential questions. For me, this is a crucial step.

Also read lesson plans for several of the units. No obvious clues there, except that some units appear to focus more on stuffing students with facts than engaging them in higher-level mental processes that the literature indicated was needed to achieve the goals. I'll need to look at some other lesson plans to see whether I just pulled a biased sample. Also observed a humanities class in action, much of which focused on varying styles used by artists in the different art periods.

What have I learned so far? Quite a bit, I think, but I'll wait until I complete my observations tomorrow before I try to summarize them.

Author Comments.   Although this journal entry may not really reflect a full day's work for the ambitious evaluator, it reflects some of the types of information the evaluator might try to obtain in informal interviews and perusal of written information and other materials. Whereas the evaluator's thoughtfully prepared questions might be the core of such interviews, often the most useful information comes from probing leads that open during the conversation. Rogerian counseling[3] may yet contribute useful skills to program evaluation.

---

[3]A counseling technique that elicits information by reflective, open-ended questions such as, "Tell me more about that," or "So you feel the program is not working well; can you tell me more about why you think that is the case?"

The discovery that the evaluator is not a specialist in the content or processes at the heart of the program being evaluated is often a rude shock to the client who is honestly confused as to how such a neophyte in the relevant subject matter could possibly be of help. Having concluded that evaluators need not be content specialists, except when certain evaluation approaches (e.g., expertise-oriented evaluation) are used, I used to try to convert clients with repeated and lengthy appeals to reason. Experience (and exhaustion) have convinced me of the wisdom of eschewing such appeals in favor of simple promises to obtain judgments of relevant substantive experts as part of the evaluation. Invoking patience is infinitely easier than persuasion and, in this case, seems as productive, because I have never had a client continue to worry this point after the client has seen how relevant content expertise plays a part in the evaluation design.

> *September 15.* Met with three members of the board of education for lunch. Found them all frankly skeptical, in varying degrees, about the value of the middle school's humanities curriculum. Radnor has done okay on the recently initiated Pennsylvania standards test, but content that doesn't directly address the standards can cause a little worry among board members and principals even in the highest-scoring schools. (It's interesting that Claire Janson has been able to avoid the pressure most principals feel on standards. This might be worth exploring to better understand the politics of the situation.) One board member, an engineer, really seemed to have her mind made up. She described the humanities curriculum as a "puff course" and argued that there was greater need for more formal reading instruction and work in the sciences at this age level and that the "interdisciplinary frills" could wait until students had mastered the basics. She forecast the outcome of "any honest evaluation" with such certainty that I suspect she may be impervious to any evaluative data that may show the program to have merit.
>
> The other board members seemed less definite, but both called for rigorous, tough evaluation that will "tell it like it is." The board president indicated the program had never been formally evaluated and she felt it was difficult to defend continuation of a program, about which serious questions were being raised, in the absence of objective measurements that show it is working. We talked at length about program costs, what decisions will result from the evaluation, and who will make them. A most useful interview, especially when I got them to list the questions they would like to see addressed by the evaluation. I think board members are leaning but have not yet made up their minds.
>
> Spent the morning reviewing another set of lesson plans. No fact sheets these; on the contrary, they contained much that strikes me as esoteric for the seventh grader. But I'll await the judgment of humanities experts on that one.

Author Comments.   Before beginning any evaluation that relates to continuation or termination of a program, I always try to ferret out whether there is really any need to evaluate; that is, have those who hold the power to make the decision already made up their minds (with little probability they will change them), regardless of the results of the study? That perspective stems from the sad realization that perhaps 75 percent of my first several years as an evaluator was spent generating methodologically impeccable but altogether useless evaluation reports—

useless because I wasn't sharp enough to recognize the symptoms of ritualistic evaluation.

This doesn't mean that one aborts every evaluation when the decision makers are found to be tilted toward one view or another. To take that stance would be to eliminate evaluations of most programs governed by human beings. But it does mean that one should check and be convinced there really are views or perspectives, if not immediate decisions, that the evaluation can influence. If not, I can muster little defense for the expenditure of time and money to carry out the study.

> *September 15 (continued).* This afternoon I met again with Ms. Janson, then with a third humanities teacher, and finally with two teachers, one each from the English and social science departments. Now I feel a need to boil down all the rough notes I've taken to try to see what I have learned and what I still need to learn about the program (Artifact 2). That should help me be ready for the special session the principal has arranged with the committee tomorrow.

> **ARTIFACT 2**
>
> Memo to the File
> September 15
> Re: Radnor Humanities Program: Summary of Information
>   Learned On-Site, September 14–15
>
> 1. Radnor Township School District has had a humanities curriculum for ten to eleven years, but it has evolved and mutated several times. With the exception of the additional structure and more skill emphasis, the current program has not changed greatly in the past three years.
> 2. The goal of the program appears to be to introduce students to the range of human creativity and, in so doing, to inspire them to be more creative and to have a greater interest and appreciation for the arts and how they enhance our lives. Activities linked to this goal appear to include both review of different artists, architects, musicians, and writers and their work, and students' creation of their own individual projects in various areas of the arts.
> 3. The humanities curriculum has never been formally evaluated.
> 4. During the past year or two, community concerns have risen about the need for more academic content, more basic skills development, and so forth, and the humanities curriculum has come to be viewed increasingly as a frill by important segments of the community, including some board members. Achieving state standards doesn't seem to be a concern among personnel and parents at Radnor, but may be a board concern.
> 5. "Values clarification" does not appear to be a real issue, except in the minds of a strident few (including one committee member). The real issue seems to be that of devoting more time to the basic subjects versus spending it on an interdisciplinary program aimed at using the arts to help students "understand and appreciate all that it means to be human." The differences appear to be honest ones of philosophy and conviction, not those of convenience or self-interest, at least for the most part. Although there is no public outcry evident, the skepticism reflected by the board seems to reflect the trend in the community (as perceived by those involved).

6. The curriculum committee made no systematic effort to obtain input from a broad or representative sampling of parents or others prior to their report. They did hold public meetings attended by some parents, and parents on the committee reported conversations they had with other parents, but community input was really quite limited.

7. The humanities department is isolated physically in a separate building from other departments with which it might be expected to be integrated. There does not appear to be much integration across the departments.

8. The fiscal costs of the humanities program really reside in the collective salaries of the four humanities teachers (close to $170,000 in total). There are no texts or other significant dollar costs. There does appear to be an interest on the part of some board members in the possible savings if the program were eliminated, because the board has expressed interest in making any staff reductions that might be made without reducing the quality of schooling offered to its students.

9. "Opportunity costs" are a key issue for those in the community who favor courses concentrating more intensely on state standards. Within the school, faculty members in science and social science are particularly concerned about opportunity costs, for time spent on their subjects was cut back to make room for the required humanities courses.

10. Within the school, faculty members in the science and social science departments are reported to be generally unenthusiastic about the program, those in the reading department about evenly split for and against it, and those in the English department generally favorable. The latter may relate to the fact that some of the humanities teachers apparently have good credentials in English plus more seniority in the district than the current staff in the English department. If humanities folds, those staff members might be given jobs in the English department, putting jobs of some of the English faculty on the line. Support under those circumstances may be more pragmatic than idealistic.

11. The board really wants to make a "go–no go" decision and is asking for a summative evaluation to provide them with information to help them decide intelligently. All my instincts tell me that, if there were no evaluation, or if the evaluation were not credible to the board, they would ultimately discontinue the program. I am equally convinced, however, that an evaluation showing that the program is producing the benefits its sponsors claim for it could yield a positive board decision to allow its continuation.

12. There is apparently about $60,000 available for the evaluation this school year, with any subsequent follow-up funding (if necessary) to be decided by the board. The district is willing to assign some of its staff to assist in collecting data I might specify.

13. District policy will permit me access to whatever data sources I need. The district would not restrict my rights to quote, use, or release the report at my discretion.

14. Other units' lesson plans are available for review, but some may not be currently in use. Other lessons may be being delivered that do not have completed plans.

15. The staff does seem genuine about the program's goals, although some awareness seems to be creeping in that it may be difficult to help students understand "all that it means to be human" in a lifetime, let alone two hours a week for 27 months.

16. The primary audiences for the evaluation seem to be (1) the board, (2) the Humanities Curriculum Review Committee, and (3) district and school staff not included on the committee but influenced by the outcomes. Important secondary audiences would include parents and students.

17. There is a sharp difference in the type of data preferred by the various audiences. The principal represented the point of view of the humanities department staff and a majority of the committee when she said, "Numbers won't tell the story—this type of program defies quantitative evaluation." Board members called for hard data, however, with one saying, "If you can't quantify it somehow, it probably doesn't exist." Others noted they found testimonials unconvincing and would hope for something more substantial. When informed of those sentiments and asked to react to them in light of her own pessimism about quantitative measurement of student outcomes in humanities, Claire Janson said she would love to see some good "numerical" proof that the program was working, for she wasn't sure anything else would convince the board. She acknowledged that testimonials were likely to fall on deaf ears, but she was skeptical that anything else could be produced.

18. Radnor has only one middle school. If one wished to find the most comparable students for a possible control group comparison, the Welsh Valley or Balla Cynwyd Middle Schools in the Lower Merion Township School District, also in the west Philadelphia suburbs, would be the best bets. Or might there be some way to relax temporarily the requirement that all students in the middle school must go through the humanities curriculum, so that some might spend that time in the more traditional subject matter? That may not be feasible, but I need to probe this more. Without some sort of comparison, I worry that we might pick up student gains (losses) and attribute them to the curriculum, whereas they really stem from maturation or the *Classes for Youth* series on Channel 7.

Author Comments.   These simulated conclusions are what I believe, reading between the lines, one might find if one spent a couple of days working in the Radnor School context. Although these conclusions may be inaccurate, they represent the types of information that should be gleaned in an initial visit to a program. In one sense, the evaluation has already begun, and some of these conclusions represent evaluation findings. Yet many are still impressionistic and would need further confirmation before I would lean on them too heavily. For now, their primary utility would be to focus my design and further my data-collection efforts. More important, much of what has been collected constitutes the basic stuff of "program description" and prepares me for working with different stakeholders, identifying their concerns, and working with their anxieties about the evaluation.

Without using space to comment on each item in my "memo," let me draw attention to two things. First, specification of audiences for the evaluation findings is an essential, often neglected, part of evaluation design. Let us hope memo items 16 and 17 help make that point, if only on one dimension. Second, memo 1item 18 alludes to the possibility of finding an appropriate comparison group. Space does not permit me to create enough of the context to outline in any sensible way what such a design might look like, for it could take many forms, dependent on the conditions, or might prove inappropriate altogether. The specifics of any comparative design are less important here, however, than the fact that I would probably *try* to include a comparative element in any evaluation of a program such as this one, if feasible. Such an approach can get to the heart of the issues of effectiveness and opportunity cost, whereas most other approaches are weaker or even speculative in this regard. If one chooses, for whatever reason, to evaluate a program without looking at whether it produces the desired outcomes more efficiently or humanely than alternative programs (or no program at all), one never knows just what has been gained by choosing that particular program or lost by rejecting other, possibly better, alternatives.

Now, lest I be accused of falling prey to the "law of the instrument," let me hasten to note that I probably use a comparative evaluation design in fewer than half of the evaluations I conduct. Often they are irrelevant to the evaluation issues of concern. When such designs do suit the purpose, sometimes they simply are not feasible; sometimes I find it too much of an uphill struggle to disabuse program staff of the widely held view that comparative experiments are irrelevant or harmful; and sometimes I'm simply not creative enough to come up with one that makes sense. But none of these facts dissuades me from the feeling that one should look carefully at the power of the comparative element in evaluation. Were this a real-life evaluation, I would work hard to see whether a reasonable comparison could be included to get at issues such as relative effectiveness and cost of students' spending time in the humanities curriculum versus other alternatives.

> *September 16.* Held a half-day meeting with Claire Janson, six other members of the curriculum committee, and the president of the board of education. Spent the first hour checking my perceptions about the program to make sure I was on track, and the next hour was devoted to discussing and resolving issues.
>
> We talked at length about the polarization that seemed to be developing over the program. Another problem that emerged is some of the teachers asked whether I really understood the program well enough to evaluate it. Would the program I evaluated really be *their* program or my misconception of it? I'm afraid I may have led them into thinking that this visit would be it and now I would move on to develop an evaluation from my university office!
>
> I discussed with the group my desire to have a more participatory evaluation involving not just them, but many other stakeholders. We decided to establish an advisory group for the evaluation composed of representatives of several stakeholder groups including a humanities teacher, a science teacher, a couple of parents with different takes on the program, a member of the curriculum committee, a representative of the Board, and a community representative, perhaps a parent with an elementary school child and/or a retired educator or community leader. I want to work with this group to flesh out the theory for the program and achieve consensus on what the program is and what it's designed to do. From that theory, we can derive different evaluation questions for the study to address. The more I can involve these different stakeholders in dialogue concerning the evaluation, the more likely I am to find both camps are responsive to the results in the end. While the impetus for the evaluation is summative (should the program be continued or not?), like most evaluations, this focus can change. If the final outcome is to continue the program, I want to have some results that are acceptable to the teachers who deliver the program that will help improve and focus the program. Even the best program can benefit from some good formative findings!

Author Comments.   This has just been a quick trip. Evaluating at a distance can always be problematic, but Radnor has no in-house evaluation staff. Given the controversy over this program, it's important that I involve all the stakeholder groups in the evaluation. I don't want the teachers to think it's a set-up by the board, and hashing out different issues as a group can help me learn more about different perspectives of the program and different concerns. I can't develop a program description from this brief visit, though I have learned a lot. I think I know what the program theory is, but I don't want it to be *my* theory. I want it to be one they have developed together and agree on. From their discussions, and my facilitation, commonalities and differences—and evaluation questions—will emerge. In facilitating, I can help them learn a little bit about program theory and models. Sometimes those intimately involved with a program have difficulty summarizing the program theory because their knowledge keeps them from "seeing the forest for the trees."

Major Concepts and Theories

1. A first step in analyzing the evaluation context is learning the needs and perceptions of the evaluation from different potential audiences. Identify, interview, and, as appropriate, involve different users in the planning stage.

2. The second means for setting boundaries and understanding the context of the evaluation is developing a program description. This description can include goals and objectives, program activities and their links to goals and objectives, and characteristics of target audiences. The description can be developed through interviews with stakeholders or as a group, but should ultimately be shared with the users for confirmation or discussion.

3. Program theory is a type of program description that includes normative theory, the theories of people involved with the program, and causative models or research-based theories. These theories, and the knowledge gaps within them, can provide clues as to appropriate evaluation questions.

4. To describe the program fully, review existing information (e.g., organizational reports, proposals, previous evaluations); interview managers, staff, clients, and other important stakeholders; review literature in areas related to the program; and observe the program in operation.

5. Consider available resources and the potential costs associated with the evaluation. Program staff or volunteers may be used to reduce costs.

6. Consider how the political context may affect the approach of the evaluation, the nature of information collected, and the interpretation and use of results.

Discussion Questions

1. Why is it important to consider all the different audiences for an evaluation? Which audiences do you think are typically viewed as most important? Which are most likely to be neglected? How could ignoring these latter audiences lead to a problem?

2. Why is it important to understand the context of the object being evaluated? The program theory?

3. What role do you think research on program-related issues plays in understanding the context of a program?

4. What are some of the advantages and risks in using program staff to assist in an evaluation? In using volunteers?

5. Why is evaluation inherently a political process?

Application Exercises

1. Consider a program with which you are familiar. Who would be the audiences for the evaluation of this program? Use Figure 11.1 to identify potential audiences. Whom might you choose to interview? What might be the perspectives of each? Do you think it would be advisable to select some representatives of the audiences to serve as an advisory committee for the evaluation? If so, whom would you select and why?

2. What critical political factors might the evaluator in the above situation need to be aware of?

3. Through either a literature review or through contact with an agency, find a report describing a program. What is the model for this program? What are the goals and objectives? What are the critical components and activities? Is it feasible that these goals and objectives could be achieved with the specified clients using the described activities? Why or why not? Does the literature review or program description provide any evidence for why the model should work? For why it might fail? Does it provide an accurate description of the model? What questions would you like to ask program staff to learn more about the model?

4. Consider the problem of teacher turnover or employee turnover in your agency. Develop an impact model for this problem with a causal hypothesis, intervention hypothesis, and action hypothesis. First, develop such a model based on your knowledge of the problem. Next, interview people in your community school or agency and develop a normative theory of the problem. Finally, review the research literature and determine the validity of the normative model based on the research you find. What alternative causative models might you develop?

Relevant Evaluation Standards

The evaluation standards we see as relevant to this chapter's content are the following. These standards are described in Chapter 18.

U1—Stakeholder Identification
F1—Practical Procedures

F2—Political Viability
A1—Program Documentation
A2—Context Analysis

Suggested Readings

Chen, H. (1990). *Theory-driven evaluations.* Newbury Park, CA: Sage.

Donaldson, S. I. (2002). Theory-driven program evaluation in the new millennium. In S. I. Donaldson & M. Scriven (Eds.), *Evaluating social programs and problems: Visions for the new millennium.* Hillsdale, NJ: Erlbaum.

House, E. R., & Howe, K. R. (1999). *Values in evaluation and social research.* Thousand Oaks, CA: Sage.

McClintock, C. (1987). Conceptual and action heuristics: Tools for the evaluator. In L. Bickman (Ed.), *Using program theory in evaluation.* New Directions for Program Evaluation, No. 33, 43–57. San Francisco: Jossey-Bass.

Mueller, M. R. (1998). The evaluation of Minnesota's Early Childhood Family Education Program: A dialogue. *American Journal of Evaluation, 19,* 80–99.

12

Identifying and Selecting the Evaluation Questions and Criteria

Orienting Questions

1. What is the function of evaluation questions? Criteria? Standards? When is each necessary?

2. What are good sources for evaluation questions?

3. What role should the evaluator play in determining what questions will be addressed in the evaluation? What role should the client play?

4. In identifying and selecting evaluation questions, what different concerns and activities are involved in the *divergent* and *convergent* phases?

5. Should standards be absolute or relative? What kinds of standards can be specified?

Evaluations are conducted to answer questions concerning program adoption, continuation, or program improvement. The **evaluation questions** provide the direction and foundation for the evaluation. Without them, the evaluation will lack focus, and the evaluator will have considerable difficulty explaining what will be examined, how, and why. This chapter will focus on how these evaluation questions can be identified and specified to provide the foundation for the evaluation study and to maximize the use of the results. The evaluator's primary responsibility is to gather and interpret information that can help key individuals and groups improve efforts, make enlightened decisions, and provide credible information to the public.

The process of identifying and defining the questions to be answered by the evaluation is critical. It requires careful reflection and investigation, for if important questions are overlooked or trivial questions are allowed to consume evaluation resources, the result could be

- Little or no payoff from the expenditure for the evaluation,
- A myopic evaluation focus that misdirects future efforts,
- Loss of goodwill or credibility because an audience's important questions or concerns are omitted,
- Disenfranchisement of legitimate stakeholders, or
- Unjustified conclusions.

If the evaluation is to take a summative focus, judging the overall success of the program to make decisions about program continuation or expansion, the evaluator must also identify the factors or **criteria** that will be used to judge the success of the program and may work with others to specify the **standards** the program must achieve on these criteria to be considered successful. Without such specifications, it can be difficult to translate the information obtained from the evaluation into value judgments about the worth of the program. For example, attendance is often identified as one criterion in a voluntary program. Standards can then be established to indicate the level of attendance necessary to be considered successful. Is an in-service program for supervisors successful if 50 percent of the supervisors attend? That all depends on the rationale for the program and the attendance standard that would signal success or failure. What about a 70 percent attendance rate in a high school mathematics class? Is that good or bad? Again, it depends on the standard. If it is a college preparatory class with high attendance expectations—say a standard of 95 percent—70 percent is very poor. If it is a remedial mathematics class for dropouts who are returning to school on a part-time basis, the expectation might be considerably lower—say 70 percent— and an attendance rate of 95 percent might be noteworthy. These oversimplified examples should underscore the point that identifying the criteria and standards to be used to judge a program's success can be very useful in summative evaluations. By working with different groups to identify criteria and standards, the evaluator can improve communication concerning expectations about program performance.

Cronbach (1982) uses the terms *divergent* and *convergent* to differentiate two phases of identifying and selecting questions for an evaluation. We will adopt these helpful labels in the discussion that follows.

In the **divergent phase,** as comprehensive a "laundry list" of potentially important questions and concerns as possible is developed. Items come from many sources, and little is excluded, for the evaluator wishes to map out the terrain as thoroughly as possible, considering all possible directions.

In the **convergent phase,** evaluators select from the "laundry list" the most critical questions to be addressed. Criteria are then developed for these questions.

As we shall see later in this chapter, the process of setting priorities and making decisions about the specific focus for an evaluation is a difficult and complex task.

During the evaluation, new issues, questions, and criteria may emerge. The evaluator must remain flexible, allowing modifications and additions to the evaluation plan when these seem justified. Now let us consider the divergent, and then the convergent, phase in some detail.

Identifying Appropriate Sources of Questions and Criteria: The Divergent Phase

Cronbach (1982) summarizes the divergent phase of planning an evaluation as follows:

> The first step is opening one's mind to questions to be entertained at least briefly as prospects for investigation. This phase constitutes an evaluative act in itself, requiring collection of data, reasoned analysis, and judgment. Very little of this information and analysis is quantitative. The data come from informal conversations, casual observations, and review of extant records. Naturalistic and qualitative methods are particularly suited to this work because, attending to the perceptions of participants and interested parties, they enable the evaluator to identify hopes and fears that may not yet have surfaced as policy issues. . . .
>
> The evaluator should try to see the program through the eyes of the various sectors of the decision-making community, including the professionals who would operate the program if it is adopted and the citizens who are to be served by it (pp. 210, 212–213).

If the evaluator is to obtain genuinely diverse viewpoints, she must "throw a broad net" to encompass a wide variety of sources.

1. Questions, concerns, and values of stakeholders
2. The use of evaluation "models," frameworks, and approaches (such as those in Part Two of this book) as heuristics
3. Models, findings, or salient issues raised in the literature in the field of the program
4. Professional standards, checklists, guidelines, instruments, or criteria developed or used elsewhere
5. Views and knowledge of expert consultants
6. The evaluator's own professional judgment

Each of these sources will be discussed in more detail in the following pages.

Identifying Questions and Concerns of Stakeholders

Generally, the single most important source of evaluation questions is the project or program's stakeholders: its clients, sponsors, participants, and affected audiences. Today, most models of evaluation emphasize the importance of consulting concerned stakeholders, but, at the same time, many fail to articulate how these stakeholders should be involved. We cannot overemphasize the importance of garnering the questions, insights, perceptions, hopes, and fears of the evaluation study's stakeholders, for such information should be primary in determining the evaluation's focus.

To obtain such input, the evaluator needs to identify individuals and groups who are influenced or affected by whatever is being evaluated. This can be a tough but not impossible task, as Weiss (1984) observes:

> No procedural mechanisms appear capable of identifying, let alone representing, the entire set of potential users of evaluation results or the questions that they will raise. But in the normal course of events, adequate representation of stakeholders seems feasible (p. 259).

Identifying stakeholders may be easier if one uses a checklist that includes the following: (1) *policy makers* (such as legislators or governing board members); (2) *administrators* or *managers* (those who direct and administer the program or entity evaluated); (3) *practitioners* (those who operate the program); (4) *primary consumers* (those intended to benefit, such as students, clients, or patients); and (5) *secondary consumers* (citizen and community groups that are affected by what happens to primary consumers). These five groups represent types of stakeholders who are associated with almost any program, and several distinct stakeholders or groups of stakeholders may emerge in each category. For example, administrators and managers for a school program will often include assistant principals, principals, and people affiliated with the program in the central administration, cluster coordinators, and so on. The superintendent may be considered a policy maker or an administrator depending on her relationship to the program. By considering each of the five categories, the evaluator can identify many potential stakeholders.

The checklist of potential evaluation audiences presented in Chapter 11 can also be useful in helping to identify potential stakeholders. That list of audiences is more extensive than the above list because audiences include groups who have no particular stake in the program but would be interested in the results of the evaluation. Nevertheless, audiences should include all relevant stakeholders.

Once stakeholders are identified, they should be interviewed to determine what they would like to know about the object of the evaluation. What questions or concerns do they have? What is their perception of the program to be evaluated? What do they think it is designed to do, and how well do they think it is doing that? How would they change the program if they had the opportunity?

Dynamics of Involving Stakeholders to Achieve Validity and Equity.
Evaluation has moved in an increasingly participative direction since its beginnings. Today, stakeholders are involved in evaluations for many reasons, but the primary reasons are to encourage use and to enhance the validity of the study (Brandon,

1998; Cousins & Earl, 1995). For many years participative evaluators have been persuasive in arguing that involving users at every stage of the evaluation will increase use of the results. Involving stakeholders increases the chances that they will use the results because it helps reduce their anxiety about the evaluation and improves their understanding of its purposes and intent, as well as insuring that at least some of the evaluation questions address their concerns. But, as noted above, involving stakeholders has the further advantage of increasing the validity of the study (Brandon, 1998).

Evaluators, especially external evaluators, may be new to the program; stakeholders are not. Huberman and Cox have written: "The evaluator is like a novice sailor working with yachtsmen who have sailed these institutional waters for years, and know every island, reef, and channel" (1990, p. 165). Involving stakeholders in describing the program, setting program boundaries, identifying evaluation questions, and making recommendations about data collection, analysis, and interpretation adds to the validity of the evaluation because stakeholders are program "experts." While the expertise of stakeholder groups will vary, each group has a particular view of the program that is different, and often more knowledgeable, than that of the evaluator. Students or clients have experienced the program intimately as recipients. Staff have delivered the program. Managers have helped fund and plan it. However, the evaluator must be careful to use stakeholders in the right way. The stakeholders are program experts, but the evaluator is the evaluation expert. She knows what is needed for a good evaluation; they know the characteristics and context of the program and its participants and their own values and information needs.

Smith (1997) has developed three broad procedural rules for using stakeholders to improve evaluation:

- Stakeholders differ in their knowledge and expertise. Use stakeholders for the areas in which they have expertise and experience.
- Consider carefully the methods used to tap that expertise.
- Insure that participation is equitable, in particular that stakeholders with less power are able to provide information and views in a safe, comfortable, and equitable fashion.

Brandon (1998), Greene (1987), and Trochim and Linton (1986) describe some specific methods for achieving useful and valid input from stakeholders. Ask stakeholders about what they know. For example, teachers know why they made changes in the planned curricula; students or program participants do not. Participants know what they understood and how they felt about a program or curriculum; teachers or program staff may not be the best source for such information. The evaluator must consider what each group knows and learn more about its perspective. Brandon (1998) describes an excellent way for involving teachers, the group with most expertise in appropriate expectations for their students, in setting standards for an evaluation.

When stakeholder groups differ in power, as is the case in almost all evaluations, using small groups, trained facilitators, and other methods to hear the voices of less powerful stakeholders can be important. In educational evaluations, many parents who have not had successful experiences with the school system (e.g., parents who struggled in school themselves, immigrants, non-English-speaking parents) are unlikely to feel comfortable voicing their concerns in a large group where teachers and educational administrators, often of a different social class, are present. Students are likely to feel similarly disenfranchised. Yet the views of these groups are important, not only for democratic and social purposes, but to improve the validity of the evaluation itself. These groups can provide important and different perspectives on the evaluation questions and methods of data collection. The manner in which their input is sought must be carefully considered and planned.

Eliciting Evaluation Questions from Stakeholders.   Many stakeholders who are unfamiliar with evaluation may have difficulty expressing what they would like the evaluation to do because they do not know what evaluations can do. It is, therefore, important that the evaluator collect information in ways that are meaningful to the stakeholder. Rather than focus on the evaluation, the evaluator can begin with the stakeholders' area of expertise—their knowledge of the program, their experience with it, and their concerns about it. The evaluator may translate these concerns into evaluation questions at a later point.

In many cases, as relationships with significant stakeholders evolve, the evaluator may move into an educative role to help the stakeholders learn of the different questions the evaluation could address or to acquaint the stakeholders with relevant research findings or evaluation approaches that would be appropriate. However, at the initial stage, it is important for the evaluator to spend more time *listening* than educating. By listening to the stakeholders' perceptions and concerns, the evaluator will gain an enormous amount of information about the program, its environment, typical methods of decision making, and the values and styles of the stakeholders. Asking why they are concerned about a particular aspect of the evaluation object, why they would value particular outcomes, what other methods they think would be useful for achieving the outcomes, or what they would do with the answers to particular questions can help the evaluator judge the thoughtfulness and importance of particular questions.

There is no single technique for eliciting evaluation questions from stakeholders, but we believe a simple and direct approach works best. Before attempting to identify these questions, however, it is useful to first establish a context that will help to make them more meaningful. For example, we might begin this way: "As you know, I've been hired to do an evaluation of the X program. I would like the information that I collect to be useful to people like yourself. At this stage, I'm interested in learning about your perceptions of the program and what the evaluation can do for you. Could we begin by your telling me what you know about the program?"

We find it useful to begin in this rather *general* way. What the stakeholder chooses to tell the evaluator reflects her priorities. Making the initial questions more focused can result in your missing her major concerns. After you have learned about the stakeholder's general concerns, some probing may enable you to learn her *perception of the model or theory of the program.* For example, if a theory-based approach seems appropriate, you might ask questions such as: "What do you see as the major changes that will occur in students or clients as a result of participating in this program?" Then, "How do you think the program activities lead to those outcomes?" Or, "Which activities do you see as most critical for achieving the goals?"

Having learned of the stakeholders' perceptions about the program, you need to determine what questions they want the evaluation to answer. There is no more important, or more frequently neglected, step for assuring that the evaluation will be used by its stakeholders. You might begin by asking: "If I could collect information to answer any question about the program that you would like this evaluation to answer, what question would that be?" Like pickles in a jar, evaluative questions are easier to get out after the first one has been extracted. Some probing may help clients focus their thinking, using questions such as "What information would be most helpful to you to better manage or deliver the program? To decide whether to continue your support? Your participation in it? Which program components or activities do you consider most critical to the program's success? Which program components or activities don't work as you thought they would? What questions do you have about program operations?"

If stakeholders overlook areas of obvious importance, you might ask, "Are you interested in X (fill in the area)?" The question "What else would you like to know?" often produces abundant responses. This is no time to be judgmental or to point out that some suggested questions may currently be unanswerable. This is the time for generating all the evaluation questions possible. The time for weighing and selecting the subset of questions to be ultimately pursued is later, in the convergent stage. You should, however, briefly describe the process to each stakeholder so that she recognizes that the questions will later be winnowed.

Figure 12.1 illustrates a possible sequence of questions in a stakeholder interview, leading from general questions intended to identify stakeholder views of the program, to more focused questions intended to identify their major evaluation questions. Additional specific procedures for guiding evaluator–participant interactions can be found in the writings of advocates of responsive and participative evaluation and others (e.g., Abma & Stake, 2001; King, 1998; Lincoln & Guba, 1985; Stake, 1980; Trochim & Linton, 1986; Wadsworth, 1997). Patton's (1996) utilization-focused evaluation provides additional guidance for the evaluator in learning of the information needs of stakeholders. By grounding the evaluation plan in the concerns of key people, the evaluator takes steps to ensure that the evaluation will be useful and responsive to constituents who may have differing points of view. For example, consider a leadership training program funded by an external foundation. Interviews with stakeholders of such a program might produce the following questions:

1. (From the program administrator) Are we running on time and within our budget? Are we meeting foundation expectations for this program? Is the pro-

FIGURE 12.1   *Information to Be Obtained in Interviews with Stakeholders*

1. What is your general perception of the program? What do you think of it? (Do you think well of it? Badly of it? What do you like about it? What do you not like? Why?)
2. What do you perceive as the purposes (goals, objectives) or guiding philosophy of the program? (Do you agree with these purposes or philosophy? Do you think the problems the program addresses are severe? Important?)
3. What do you think the theory or model for the program is? (Why/how do you think it works? How is it supposed to work? Why would the program actions lead to success on the program's objectives or criteria? Which program components are most critical to success?)
4. What concerns do you have about the program? About its outcomes? Its operations? Other issues?
5. What do you hope to learn from the evaluation? Why are these issues important to you?
6. How could you use the information provided by the answers to these questions? (Would you use it to make decisions, to enhance your understanding?)
7. What do you think the answer to the question is? (Do you already know it? Would you be concerned if the answer were otherwise?)
8. Are there other stakeholders who would be interested in this question? Who are they? What is their interest?

gram being implemented as planned? What changes have occurred and why? Are participants achieving needed leadership skills?

2. (From program staff) What materials and procedures have been developed in other programs that we might use? How are trainees reacting to the program? Which sessions/methods work best? Worst?

3. (From participants toward whom the program is aimed) Have the leadership skills of participants really improved? What portions of the program are most useful to participants?

4. (From the top managers in the organization) What evidence is there that the program is working? What continuing expenses are going to exist once foundation support terminates? Is this program having the desired impact on the units in which the trainees work? Would this program serve as a model for other change efforts? How is this program changing our organization?

5. (From the foundation) Is the program doing what it promised? What evidence is there that variables targeted for change have actually changed? How cost-effective is this program? Could the program be established in other settings? What evidence is there that the program will continue once foundation funds are terminated?

Using Evaluation Models, Frameworks, and Approaches as Heuristics

In exploring different approaches to evaluation in Part Two of this book, we noted that the specific conceptual frameworks and models developed under each approach play an important role in generating evaluation questions. This is one place in the evaluation process where the conceptual work done by the different evaluation theorists pays considerable dividends.

In reviewing the evaluation literature summarized in Part Two, the evaluator is directed toward certain questions. Sometimes a framework fits poorly and should be set aside, but usually something of value is suggested by each approach, as the following examples illustrate.

The objectives-oriented approach guides us to ask whether goals and objectives are defined and to what extent they are achieved. Have the goals and objectives been evaluated? Are they defensible? Achievable? Under what conditions or in what settings? What would prevent their achievement? Theory-based models raise questions concerning whether specific program activities lead to program success or whether certain participant characteristics lead to differential success.

The particular management-oriented approach developed by Stufflebeam generates questions about the context (need), input (design), process (implementation), and product (outcomes) for a program. Management-oriented approaches also remind us to learn about the decisions that are to be guided by the evaluation, for example, what do decision makers need to know, and when do they need to know it?

The participant-oriented approach reminds us that we should be sure to consider all stakeholders and should listen to what each group and individual has to say even during informal conversations. The process of the program is critical and we should try to understand the different ways that people view it or the different meanings placed on it. Portraying the program in its full complexity as a means of educating audiences should be of utmost concern. Stake's (1967) Countenance Model offers a framework for us to ask questions about rationale, intents, actual events, and standards. We are reminded that full descriptions of the actual object of the evaluation and the context in which it operates should be included in our evaluation.

The consumer-oriented approach has generated many checklists and sets of criteria that may be of considerable value to us when considering what components or characteristics to study in an evaluation or what standards to apply. The expertise-oriented approach has produced standards and critiques that reflect the criteria and values used by contemporary experts in education, mental health, social services, criminal justice, and other fields.

To the extent that these conceptual frameworks can stimulate questions that might not emerge from other sources, they are important sources for evaluators to consider in the divergent phase of focusing the evaluation. As noted, many stakeholders are not familiar with the variety of issues an evaluation can address.

We have found that stakeholders will sometimes focus only on outcomes, assuming that an evaluation must measure outcomes. This is especially true in today's "outcome mania." While in many cases such a focus is appropriate, often other concerns are more paramount, given the stage of the program and the needs of stakeholders. Posavac (1994) describes a case in which stakeholders' limited understanding of evaluation led to their advocacy for a summative evaluation when a formative evaluation was a more appropriate strategy. He argues that evaluators must "take an active role in helping their clients to understand what they really need" (p. 75). Evaluation models can help the evaluator consider other areas of focus for the evaluation and educate the stakeholder as to the myriad issues that evaluation can investigate.

Using Research and Evaluation Work in the Program Field

Many evaluators focus their work in a limited number of content areas or fields. Some evaluators work entirely in the field of education; others in mental health, health education, criminal justice, social services, training, nonprofit management, or some other area. In any case, the evaluator should be conversant with the salient issues in the area and consider their relevance to the present evaluation.

For example, enthusiastic sponsors and participants of a merit pay program for teachers may need to be reminded of the potential impact of the system on teamwork. Or advocates for low-cost housing dispersed throughout the community may fail to address adequately the concerns of existing homeowners regarding the impact of such housing on their property values or quality of life. The evaluator has a responsibility to raise such questions.

Commissions and task forces are sometimes formed by national, regional, or local governments to study particular issues of interest to governmental leaders. The report of the National Performance Review (1993), *From Red Tape to Results: Creating a Government That Works Better and Costs Less,* is a good example. Such reports raise provocative questions and, although they occasionally make unsubstantiated claims, they usually reflect current social concerns, issues, and beliefs. They may also serve to draw an informed evaluator's attention to issues that should be raised during a particular evaluation. Questions about important current issues may be omitted if the evaluator fails to raise them, with the result that the evaluation may be considered informative but devoid of information on the "real issues facing the field today." Obviously, we are not proposing a faddish "bandwagon" approach to determine what questions will be addressed by an evaluation study, but it would be naive indeed not to even consider the relevance of educational and social issues permeating current professional literature and other media.

In addition to being familiar with current issues in the field, the evaluator should make use of existing research to help develop causative models and questions to guide the evaluation. Chen (1990) and Donaldson (2002) advocate using existing theory and research to develop program models to guide the evaluation. Existing research and theory can be used to identify causes of the problem the program is designed to address, to discover successes and failures in remedying these problems, and to examine conditions that can enhance or inhibit program success with specific kinds of students or clients. The research literature can shed light on the likelihood that the program to be evaluated can succeed. It can be useful for the program evaluator to compare models in the research literature with the existing normative program model. Discrepancies between these models can suggest important areas for evaluation questions. Published evaluations of similar programs can suggest not only questions to be examined but also methods that might be productive for the evaluation study. The evaluator who has worked in this area extensively may be familiar with existing research. Nevertheless, a literature search can be a useful start to any planning process.

Using Professional Standards, Checklists, Guidelines, and Criteria Developed or Used Elsewhere

In many fields, standards for practice have been developed. Such standards can often be useful either in helping to generate questions or in specifying criteria. As with existing research and evaluation, standards can signal areas that may have been overlooked in the focus on the existing program. Standards can be helpful for generating questions or criteria that are pertinent to a particular evaluation. They are important resources for evaluators to have in their tool kits.

One caution is important. As Tittle (1984) has pointed out indirectly in her thoughtful analysis of contextual influences on professional standards, standards set by autonomous professional groups are in and of themselves likely to be more convergent than divergent. Tittle states:

> Professional standards codify acceptable practice for a field. In professions which are autonomous, the standards are set by the members of the profession. Such standards are a product of general consensus within the profession, and often represent the results of much negotiation and compromise (p. 3).

Thus, compromise and consensus in developing sets of professional standards may rob them of diversity; using them as only one source in conjunction with others justifies their inclusion in a discussion of the divergent phase of evaluation planning. The same would be true for several of the other sources of evaluative questions and criteria discussed below.

Asking Expert Consultants to Specify Questions or Criteria

Evaluators are often asked to evaluate a program outside of their area of content expertise. The evaluator's expertise in evaluation is needed, but the specific content of the program is relatively new for most evaluators. For example, an evaluator may be called on to evaluate a school's reading program, even though she knows little about such programs. As noted, the stakeholders can provide valuable expertise in helping orient the evaluator to the particulars of the program. But, in some cases, the evaluator may also want to make use of consultants with expertise in the content of the program to provide a more neutral and broader view than she may gain from program staff. Such consultants can be helpful in suggesting evaluation questions and criteria that reflect current knowledge and practice.

That evaluation specialists must elicit input from content experts is widely recognized. Scriven (1973) asks that serious consideration be given to subject-matter experts' opinions of the quality of curriculum materials. Stake (1967) proposes that evaluators seek out, process, and report opinions of "persons of special qualification," presumably including content specialists. Stufflebeam and his colleagues (1971) point out that the evaluator often appropriately plays an "interface role" between content experts and audiences for the evaluation, and The Joint Committee on Standards for Educational Evaluation (1994) recommends using teams of experts for most evaluations.

In the case of evaluating a school reading program, for example, the consultant could be asked not only to generate a comprehensive list of questions to be addressed but also to identify previous evaluations of reading programs, standards set by professional organizations such as the International Reading Association, and research on the criteria and methods for evaluating reading programs. If there is concern about possible ideological bias, the evaluator might employ more than one independent consultant.

Using the Evaluator's Professional Judgment

The evaluator should not overlook her own knowledge and experience when generating potential questions and criteria. Experienced evaluators are accustomed to describing the object of the evaluation in detail and looking at needs, costs, and consequences. Perhaps the evaluator has done a similar evaluation in another setting and knows from experience what questions proved most useful. Professional colleagues in evaluation and the content field of the program can suggest additional questions or criteria.

Evaluators are trained, at least in part, to be skeptics, to raise insightful (one hopes) questions that otherwise might never be considered. This training is never more valuable than during the divergent phase of identifying evaluation questions and criteria, for some important questions may be omitted unless the evaluator raises them herself. House and Howe (1999), though advocating deliberative democracy in evaluation to give a voice to less powerful stakeholders, make it quite clear that, in their view, the evaluator has the authority and responsibility to make use of her own expertise. Certainly, evaluators are inclusive in bringing in, and balancing, the values and views of different stakeholders. Yet, the evaluator plays a key role in leading the evaluation and, as such, must make use of her expertise in both group dynamics and methodology. Other evaluators, even in the context of an empowerment evaluation, note the importance of the evaluator's role at that stage.

In their interesting case study of an empowerment evaluation, Schnoes, Murphy-Berman, and Chambers (2000) work hard to empower their users, but, ultimately, they note, "Whose standards of accountability should prevail in defining project outcomes, particularly if the clients' understanding and notions of what consists of valid measurable results are at variance with the standards endorsed by evaluators?" (p. 61). Evaluators are hired for their knowledge and expertise, and adding to the generation of evaluation questions based on that knowledge and experience is not only appropriate, but mandatory in many situations.

An experienced and insightful evaluator looking at a new project might raise questions like the following:

- Are the purposes the project is intended to serve really important? Is there sufficient evidence of need for the project as it is designed? Are other more critical needs going unattended?
- Are the goals, objectives, and project design consistent with documented needs? Are scheduled activities, content, and materials consistent with needs, goals, and objectives?
- Have alternative strategies been considered for accomplishing the project's goals and objectives?
- Does the program serve the public good? democratic goals? community goals?
- What are some of the unintended side effects that might emerge from this program?

The evaluator might ask herself:

- Based on evaluations of other, similar, projects, what questions should be incorporated into this evaluation?
- Based on my experience with other, similar, projects, what new ideas, potential trouble spots, and expected outcomes or side effects can be projected?
- What indicators of project success will be accepted by different stakeholders? Can such indicators be assessed or described adequately?
- What critical elements and events should be examined and observed as the project develops?
- Should we monitor critical events to determine if they occur on time and within budgetary guidelines?

Summarizing Suggestions from Multiple Sources

Somewhere in the divergent process the evaluator will reach a point of diminishing returns, when no new questions are being generated. Assuming each available resource has been tapped, the evaluator should stop and examine what she has obtained: usually, long lists of several dozen potential evaluation questions, along with potential criteria. So that the information can be more readily assimilated and used later, the evaluator will want to organize the evaluation questions into categories. Here certain evaluation frameworks, such as Stufflebeam's (1971) CIPP model, Stake's (1967) Countenance Model, Rossi's program theory (see Chapter 11) may be useful. The evaluator might adopt labels from one of these frameworks or create a new set of categories tailored to the study. Regardless of the source, having a manageable number of categories is essential in organizing potential questions and communicating them to others. Here is a sample of possible questions that might arise in the divergent phase for planning an evaluation of an existing conflict-resolution program in the schools:

Needs Assessment or Context
1. What kinds of conflict occur among students in the schools? Who is most likely to be involved in a conflict (age, gender, characteristics)? What is the nature of the conflict?
2. How were conflicts resolved without conflict resolution? What kinds of problems occurred as a result of this strategy?
3. What communication skills do the students have that conflict resolution could build on? What problems do the students have that might hinder the learning or use of conflict-resolution skills?
4. How many conflicts currently occur? How frequent is each type?
5. What effects do the current conflicts have on the learning environment? The management of the school? The motivation and abilities of the teachers?

Process and Monitoring
1. Are the conflict-resolution trainers sufficiently competent to provide the training? Have the appropriate personnel been selected to conduct the training? Should others be used?
2. Do the students selected for training meet the specified criteria?
3. What proportion of students participate in the complete training program? What do these students miss by participating in the training (opportunity costs)?
4. Does the training cover the designated objectives?
5. Do students participate in the training in the intended manner?
6. Where does the training take place? Is the physical environment for the training conducive to learning?
7. Do the teachers encourage use of the conflict-resolution strategies? How? Do the teachers use these strategies themselves? How? What other strategies do they use?

Outcomes
1. Do the students who have received the training gain the desired skills? Do they believe the skills will be useful?
2. Do the students retain these skills one month after the completion of training?
3. What proportion of the students have used the conflict-resolution strategies one month after program completion? For those who have not used the

strategies, why not? (Were they not faced with a conflict, or were they faced with a conflict but used some other strategy?)

4. Under what circumstances were students most likely to use the strategies? Under what circumstances were they least likely to use them?
5. How did other students support or hinder the students' use of the strategies?
6. Did the students discuss/teach the strategies to any others?
7. Was the incidence of conflicts reduced at the school? Was the reduction due to the use of the strategies?
8. Should other students be trained in the strategy? What other types of students are most likely to benefit?

It will be obvious to thoughtful evaluators and stakeholders that it is not feasible to address all identified questions in any one study. Practical considerations must limit the study to what is manageable. Some questions might be saved for another study; others might be discarded as inconsequential. Such winnowing is the function of the convergent phase.

Selecting the Questions, Criteria, and Issues to Be Addressed: The Convergent Phase

Cronbach (1982) introduces well the need for a convergent phase of evaluation planning:

> The preceding section [the divergent phase] spoke as if the ideal were to make the evaluation complete, but that cannot be done. There are at least three reasons for reducing the range of variables treated systematically in an evaluation. First, there will always be a budget limit. Second, as a study becomes increasingly complicated, it becomes harder and harder to manage. The mass of information becomes too great for the evaluator to digest, and much is lost from sight. Third, and possibly most important, the attention span of the audience is limited. Very few persons want to know all there is to know about a program. Administrators, legislators, and opinion leaders listen on the run.
>
> The divergent phase identifies what could possibly be worth investigating. Here the investigator aims for maximum bandwidth. In the convergent phase, on the contrary, he decides what incompleteness is most acceptable. He reduces bandwidth by culling the list of possibilities (p. 225).

No evaluation can answer responsibly all the questions generated during a thorough, divergent planning phase. So the question is not whether to winnow these questions into a manageable subset, but who should do it and how.

Who Should Be Involved in the Convergent Phase?

Some evaluators write and behave as if selecting crucial, practical evaluation questions were the sole province of the evaluator. Not so. In fact, under no circum-

stances should the evaluator assume sole responsibility for se
to be addressed or the evaluative criteria to be applied. This ta
teraction with stakeholders. The sponsor of the evaluation, key
dividuals or groups who will be affected by the evaluation shou

Indeed, some evaluators are content to leave the final sele
to the evaluation sponsor or client. Certainly this lightens the e\
our view, however, taking that easy course is a disservice to th\   ....ng
the advantage of the evaluator's special training and experience, ...e client may
well wind up posing a number of unanswerable questions for the study.

How Should the Convergent Phase Be Carried Out?

How can the evaluator work with the multiple stakeholders to select the questions for the evaluation? To begin with, the evaluator can propose some criteria
to be used to rank the potential evaluation questions. Cronbach and others (1980)
suggest the following criteria:

> So far we have encouraged the evaluator to scan widely; only in passing did we
> acknowledge that all lines of inquiry are not equally important. How to cut the list
> of questions down to size is the obvious next topic.
>
> . . . simultaneous consideration is given to the criteria . . . [of] prior uncer-
> tainty, information yield, costs, and leverage (that is, political importance). These
> criteria are further explained as follows: The more a study reduces uncertainty, the
> greater the information yield and, hence, the more useful the research.
>
> Leverage refers to the probability that the information—*if* believed—will
> change the course of events (pp. 261, 265).

We draw on Cronbach's thinking in proposing the following six criteria for
determining which proposed evaluation questions should be investigated:

1. *Who would use the information? Who wants to know? Who will be upset if this evaluation question is dropped?* If limitless resources were available, one could argue
that (except for invading rights of privacy) anyone who wishes to know has, in a
democratic society, the right to information about what is evaluated. Rarely are
resources limitless, however, and even if they were, prudence suggests a point of
diminishing returns in collecting evaluative information. Therefore, if no critical
audience will suffer from the evaluator's failure to address a particular question,
one might well give it a lower ranking or delete it. What is a critical audience?
That audience will vary with the context of the evaluation. In some cases, critical
audiences are decision makers because a decision is imminent and they are uninformed. In other cases, previously uninvolved or uninformed stakeholders (program participants, family members of participants, emerging interest groups) may
be critical audiences by virtue of their previous lack of involvement.

2. *Would an answer to the question reduce present uncertainty or provide information not now
readily available?* If not, there seems little point in pursuing it. If the answer already

exists, then the question can be addressed easily with little cost to the evaluator or client.

3. *Would the answer to the question yield important information? Have an impact on the course of events?* Some answers satisfy curiosity but little more; these are what we call "nice to know" questions. Important questions are those that provide information that might inform action. They may address areas considered problematic by stakeholders with the motivation or means to make or influence changes. When limited resources force choices, the importance of an answer should be an obvious criterion for inclusion.

4. *Is this question merely of passing interest to someone, or does it focus on critical dimensions of continued interest?* Priority should be given to critical questions of continuing importance. Program theory can help illuminate critical dimensions of the program.

5. *Would the scope or comprehensiveness of the evaluation be seriously limited if this question were dropped?* If so, it should be retained, if possible. In some cases, however, comprehensiveness, evaluating every aspect of the program, is less important than evaluating certain areas of uncertainty in depth, but the evaluator and stakeholder should consciously consider the issues of breadth versus depth in their selection of evaluation questions.

6. *Is it feasible to answer this question, given available financial and human resources, time, methods, and technology?* Limited resources render many important questions unanswerable. Better to delete them early than to breed frustration by pursuing impossible dreams. Not all questions are equally costly to answer. Perhaps this seems obvious, but it is so commonly ignored that Cronbach's (1982) reminder is important.

> The evaluator, working within fixed resources, reduces the initial list of questions to a manageable subset; then he budgets resources unequally over the survivors (holding back some reserves). Not many questions drop entirely out of consciousness. . . . It is sensible to pick up inexpensive information. Recording incidental observations costs almost nothing, while it costs somewhat more to cull data from records produced by normal operations and still more to collect fresh data (p. 239).

The six criteria just noted can be cast into a simple matrix (see Figure 12.2) to help the evaluator and client narrow the original list of questions into a manageable subset. Figure 12.2 is proposed only as a general guide and may be adapted or used flexibly. For example, one might expand the matrix to list as many questions as exist on the original list, then simply complete the column entries by answering yes or no to each question or, alternatively, assigning some numerical rating. Numerical ratings offer the advantage of helping to weight or rank questions.

However the matrix is used, the evaluator and client (and representatives of other stakeholder groups, if possible) should work together to complete it. Although the evaluator may have the say on what is feasible, the relative importance of the questions will be determined by the client and other stakeholders. Scanning the completed matrix reveals quickly which questions are not feasible to answer, which are unimportant, and which can and should be pursued.

FIGURE 12.2 *Matrix for Ranking or Selecting Evaluation Questions*

	Evaluation Question					
Would the evaluation question . . .	*1*	*2*	*3*	*4*	*5*	*. . .*	*n*
1. Be of interest to key audiences?						
2. Reduce present uncertainty?						
3. Yield important information?						
4. Be of continuing (not fleeting) interest?						
5. Be critical to the study's scope and comprehensiveness?						
6. Have an impact on the course of events?						
7. Be answerable in terms of						
A. Financial and human resources?						
B. Time?						
C. Available methods and technology?						

Of course, this is only one way to narrow down the original list. The evaluator may simply wish to go through the organized laundry list and, for each potential question, jot down a few words or phrases, keeping in mind the criteria summarized in Figure 12.2. The evaluator might place an asterisk (*) beside each question that appears to be a sure candidate for selection, then review the overall scope of selected questions and the feasibility of answering all of them in a quality manner. Has the potential utility of the evaluation been compromised in any way so far? Is feasibility still a concern?

At this point, the evaluator should sit down with the sponsor, client, or appropriate group of stakeholders to review what could have been addressed in the evaluation (the laundry list), what seems most reasonable (those with asterisks), and what issues still exist in making selections (feasibility, scope, potential utility, any concerns the sponsor or client may have).

Whether the evaluator prefers to work directly from the original laundry list or to use a matrix like that in Figure 12.2, we cannot stress too strongly the importance of conducting this activity—which will focus the entire evaluation study—interactively with the evaluation client. The sponsor or client will likely want to add or subtract selected questions, possibly negotiating an increased or reduced scope for the study or debating rationales for adding or dropping certain questions. The evaluator may find it necessary to defend her own professional judgment or the interests of unrepresented stakeholders. This can be difficult. If the sponsor or client demands too much control over the selection of evaluation questions (e.g., requiring inclusion of unanswerable questions or those likely to yield one-sided answers or denying the needs of certain stakeholder groups), the evaluator must judge whether the evaluation will be compromised. If it is, it is probably in the best interest of all concerned to terminate the evaluation at this point, though certainly the evaluator should take this opportunity to educate the sponsor on what evaluation can do and the ethical guidelines of evaluation practice. Conversely, the evaluator must refrain from insisting on her own preferred questions and overriding legitimate concerns of the sponsor or client.

Usually the evaluator and client can agree on which questions should be addressed. Reaching a congenial consensus (or compromise) goes far toward establishing the sort of rapport that turns an evaluation effort into a "partnership" in which the client is pleased to cooperate. A feeling of "shared ownership" greatly enhances the probability that evaluation findings will be used.

In many evaluations today, this process will take place with an advisory group consisting of individuals representing the stakeholder groups that are important to the evaluation and the program itself. Under such circumstances, the process of winnowing the evaluation questions begins the dialogue that will be an important part of the evaluation. However, sometimes the initial winnowing of questions is conducted solely by the evaluator and the client or sponsor. If that is the case, it is important to then check the acceptability of the winnowed evaluation questions with other stakeholders.

To facilitate this dialogue, the evaluator provides a list of questions to be addressed with a short explanation indicating why each is important. If the matrix (Figure 12.2) is used, a copy should be provided. The list of questions and/or matrix should be shared with all important stakeholders in the evaluation. They should be informed that this tentative list of questions is being given to them for two reasons: (1) to keep them informed about the evaluation, and (2) to elicit their reactions, especially if they feel strongly about adding or deleting questions. Sufficient time should be set aside for their review before the final list is produced.

Concerned comments merit a direct response. The evaluator should meet with any stakeholders who are dissatisfied with the list of questions and with the sponsor, if need be, to discuss and resolve concerns to everyone's satisfaction before continuing. To push for premature closure on legitimate issues surrounding the scope of the evaluation is one of the worst mistakes the evaluator can make. Unresolved conflicts will not go away, and they can be the undoing of an otherwise well-planned evaluation.

One caution: A timeworn but effective ploy used by those who wish to scuttle an unwanted evaluation is to raise unresolvable objections. The astute evaluator should recognize strident insistence on including biased or unanswerable questions. This is where an advisory committee of stakeholders, including the conflicting parties, can be particularly useful. The committee can be given the task of hearing and making recommendations on the evaluative questions to be addressed. Other stakeholders, and the evaluator, can then work to clarify the objections, modify the questions or design as appropriate, and move toward consensus.

Specifying the Evaluation Criteria and Standards

Having identified the evaluation questions, the evaluator, in concert with the stakeholders or advisory group, may proceed to specify standards for each question that requires a final judgment. If these questions do not make explicit the criteria being used to judge the program, criteria for such judgments should also be developed at this point.

To insure that the questions have incorporated the desired criteria, the evaluator should discuss with the group the object to be judged. If the purpose of the study is summative, it is critical that the important criteria for judging a program be conveyed in the evaluation questions. The evaluator should ensure that criteria found in the literature to be critical to program success are included. She should insure that the group agrees that the criteria conveyed through the evaluation questions are appropriate. If the purpose of the study is formative, an overall judgment regarding the program may be inappropriate, but a judgment of a particular portion of the program may be required. In a manner similar to that used for the overall program, the evaluator can then help the group to consider whether the questions adequately convey their criteria for judging this portion of the program and its operations.

The specification of standards of performance can be a complex area fraught with uncertainty. In some cases, the program is too new or the specification of standards is too divisive to specify realistic and valid standards. The evaluator should be sensitive to the fact that staff, when pushed into developing standards, may feel defensive and develop standards that they feel certain to achieve. Such standards may not reflect others' goals for the program. Nevertheless, in many cases, these discussions of expectations, moving to a development of standards, can be quite useful.

Where similar programs exist, such programs can be examined for standards of performance. With new programs, or questions that address process concerns, less information is available to guide the decision. Nevertheless, it is important for the evaluator and the stakeholder group to have some idea of levels of performance that are acceptable. Achieving such consensus can prevent later disagreement. Without a consensus on expected levels of performance, program advocates can claim that the obtained level of performance was exactly the one desired and program detractors can claim that the same level of performance is insufficient for program success. Agreeing on standards prior to obtaining results can be very useful in helping groups to be clear, realistic, and concrete concerning what expectations are acceptable for program success.

A standard should be developed to reflect the degree of difference that would be considered sufficiently meaningful to adopt the new program. Such a standard might be absolute or relative.

Absolute Standards. Sometimes policy will require the specification of an absolute standard. Today, 49 of the 50 states make some use of standards to assess students' educational progress. These standards are absolute, not relative. That is, they reflect an amount of knowledge expected of students at various grade levels. If these standards overlap with the goals of the program, as will frequently be the case in educational settings, the standards may be appropriate to use in the evaluation. (This would only be the case in circumstances when the standards are feasible for the client population. In some cases, state standards have been established primarily for political purposes and do not necessarily reflect feasible, or genuine, outcomes. See the American Evaluation Association's statement [2002] on high-stakes testing at www.eval.org/hstlinks.htm.) Similarly, accreditation requirements or standards for care of patients can lead to the need for absolute standards.

When existing performance standards are absent, the evaluator can begin with seeking input from knowledgeable stakeholders about their expectations on each question. As the evaluator learns the range of expectations, she can then lead a discussion of proposed standards with the key stakeholders or an advisory group. Standards should be specific to each criterion. Thus, if attendance were an important criterion for success, the evaluator might ask, "What proportion of students do you expect to complete the program? 100 percent? 90 percent? 75 percent?" or "How much of a reduction in disciplinary incidents do you expect to occur as a result of the program? 75 percent? 50 percent? 25 percent?" Such questions can prompt a frank discussion of expectations that will be invaluable in judging program results.

Sometimes, the answer that stakeholders may come up with is an honest "We don't know." If the research literature has reported on similar programs, results of these programs may provide some answers, but caution should be used in applying these standards to new target audiences with different characteristics and new staff with different competencies and skills. In some cases, experience implementing the program may be needed before standards can be established. If standards are established, the evaluator should avoid having program staff purposely set standards too low (to insure program success) or having program opponents set them too high (to guarantee failure). Working with a group of stakeholders with different perspectives can help avoid such a situation.

Relative Standards.   Some argue that absolute standards such as those discussed above are unnecessary when the study will involve comparisons with other groups. Thus, Light (1983) argues that outcomes superior to those achieved with a placebo control or comparison group are sufficient to demonstrate program success. Scriven (1980) advocates comparing programs with available alternatives. Such comparisons can be useful in determining program impact and, hence, value. The standard in such cases may be that the new program is significantly better than the alternative method. Care should be taken, however, to define the term *significant*. A statistically significant difference may still be too small to have any practical significance. Many evaluators use **effect size,** a measure of the magnitude and practical significance of between-group differences, because they see it as more meaningful than the traditional statistically significant difference. While traditional statistical significance focuses on the probability of the null hypothesis being true (a "true–false" approach), the effect size conveys the size of the difference in a manner similar to that of a Z-score or standard deviation units. The term *effect size* is drawn from the literature on meta-analysis, which is designed to combine results from across a number of studies (Durlak & Lipsey, 1991;

Glass, McGraw, & Smith, 1981). It is typically calculated by dividing the difference between the means of the two groups (control and experimental groups) by the pooled, within-group standard deviation. Thus, when evaluations involve the comparisons of two programs, effect size can be used to specify standards. The effect size essentially conveys the degree to which differences between the two groups differ beyond, and in comparison to, the ordinary variability among individuals. As such, the effect size can provide a standard that is relative to typical group performance. Thus, using effect size to specify a standard can be useful when it is difficult, or unnecessary, to specify an absolute standard. (See Kellow [1998] for a discussion of different ways to estimate effect sizes, including examining simple mean differences, calculating standardized mean differences as described above, or using estimates of the proportion of variance explained [PVE] in the variable of interest.)

Remaining Flexible during the Evaluation: Allowing New Questions, Criteria, and Standards to Emerge

Evaluations can be flawed by evaluators who relentlessly insist on answering the original questions, regardless of intervening events, changes in the object of the evaluation, or new discoveries. During the course of an evaluation, many occurrences—for example, changes in scheduling, personnel, and funding; unanticipated problems in program implementation; evaluation procedures that are found not to work; lines of inquiry that prove to be dead ends; new critical issues that emerge—require new or revised evaluation questions. Because such changes cannot be foreseen, Cronbach and his associates (1980) propose that

> Choice of questions and procedures, then, should be tentative. Budgetary plans should not commit every hour and every dollar to . . . the initial plan. Quite a bit of time and money should be held in reserve (p. 229).

When changes in the context or object of the evaluation occur, the evaluator must ask whether that change should affect the list of evaluation questions. Does it make some questions moot? Raise new ones? Require revisions? Would changing questions or focus in the middle of the evaluation be fair? The evaluator should discuss any changes and their impact on the evaluation with the sponsor, client, and other stakeholders. Allowing questions and issues to evolve, not committing to an evaluation carved in stone, fulfills Stake's (1975b) concept of responsive evaluation discussed in Chapter 8.

A word of warning, however: Evaluators must not lose track of questions or criteria that—despite possible changes—remain important. Resources should not be diverted from vital investigations just to explore interesting new directions. Flexibility is one thing, indecisiveness another.

Once the evaluation questions (and/or criteria, standards) have been agreed upon, the evaluator can complete the evaluation plan. The next steps in the planning process are covered in Chapter 13.

CASE STUDY APPLICATION

Reprise: The reader is reminded that, on September 14 and 15, the evaluator, during on-site interviews, had asked all those interviewed (the school principal, three humanities teachers, the Humanities Curriculum Review Committee chairperson, one teacher each from the English and social science departments, one parent, and three members of the school board) what questions they would like the evaluation study to answer. This helped get people thinking about what they'd like to know and gave the evaluator some sense of their theories about the program, potential disagreements, and the different camps of stakeholders. The visit closed with a meeting on the last day with Claire Janson, a board member, and some members of the curriculum committee. This helped finalize some observations and we agreed to establish an advisory group for further planning.

After this visit, the evaluator worked with Claire Janson and the board member to nominate and recruit members for the advisory group. The evaluator then spoke by phone with each of them, giving them an orientation to their roles and indicating that he would be sending them some information by E-mail and then planning a group meeting for his second visit in mid-October. A day's planning session was planned for October 15th.

September 18. Back home at last! I've had a chance to reflect on how to balance the views of different stakeholder groups. Even experienced teachers like these Humanities teachers can still be intimidated by board members and, in group settings with educators, parents often can feel like a fish out of water. So, I'm going to have them give me some feedback by E-mail first. I'll start with a few open-ended questions asking what they're interested in. Then, I'll feed all the questions I receive back to them to stimulate more ideas and reactions. I suspect that the teachers and parents will feel more comfortable with the relative anonymity of E-mail. All are on-line, so this should be no problem. Before my second visit, I can send them the laundry list of questions for them to reflect on. While some are impatient to get on with the study ("Why can't we just start collecting data?!" said the board member), there's no bigger mistake than having a great evaluation study, but answering the wrong questions! I want people to have time to reflect on the program and what they want to know and to learn what evaluation can do.

September 30. I've received quite a bit of feedback from these E-mail exchanges. Some wanted the evaluation to focus on the curriculum goals and objectives, using those as organizers for collecting and reporting the data, but the community representative, a woman who heads a nonprofit counseling center for at-risk teens, noted that the objectives were only part of the program, and she listed several important questions she felt would be overlooked if we were bound by the objectives. That was tremendous! It usually takes a fair bit of time to get people to look beyond their written objectives, so I was pleased to be able to take the opportunity to tout the advantages of using evaluative questions as key organizers in an evaluation study and broadening our focus to meet real information needs. This opened a flood of questions. I told them to continue sending questions, concerns, and comments until today, when I would synthesize what I had received from them and send it back so they could reflect on priorities for our October meeting.

Before I finalized the list of questions, I told them I would review some other professional sources for additional questions we may want to add. I'm sure glad I had Denise do the literature search! I went through those articles, and also considered some evaluation models to identify areas we might have missed.

Several additional questions occurred as I started thinking about Stake's and Eisner's approaches to evaluating the arts, so now I've inserted some questions on how the various stakeholders view the process of education and teaching middle-school students, as well as what expert humanities "connoisseurs" might say about this program. I also pulled a couple of relevant questions from the Commission on Excellence report. In the review of literature I found one article that described models for using the arts to broaden students' perspectives in middle school. Two others described evaluations of programs in other states that had attempted to achieve similar outcomes.

The smartest thing I did was to put Denise in touch with Dewey Pitcher, associate dean of the College of Humanities on campus. He had pointed her in the right direction to find some of these evaluations and models. Seeing how helpful he had been, I decided to pump him a little further. I know he used to do a lot of accreditation and site-visit work, and wondered if he could tune me in to any sets of written standards for humanities programs that might be floating around in some relevant professional group. He was really helpful, even though he didn't cite any standards, as such, because he reeled off about two dozen questions he'd want answered about any humanities program and pointed out some of the controversial issues in the area. Even though we had already thought of most of the evaluation questions, there were three or four that were new and struck me as important. Also, there does seem to be disagreement in the field about how receptive middle-school students are to such knowledge, given their stage of moral development. He suggested I attend carefully to the ages of the students and past educational experiences. Now I feel ready and armed for the October meeting. I've sent off a summary of questions and a proposed agenda to the people on the advisory group.

Author Comments. It is paramount to include representatives of all important audiences in the design of an evaluation study. Without that step, it is your evaluation design; with their involvement, there is an excellent chance they will see it as their design. What better way to have someone understand an evaluation and use its results than to get that person involved as a partner in its conduct?

For me, an easy first step is to ask everyone directly or indirectly involved in the program what questions he would like to see answered by the evaluation study. Evaluators should feel free to inject their questions (and may need them for "pump priming" so others get a feel for what is meant by "evaluation questions"), but a major portion of these questions should be drawn from those with a stake in the outcome of the study.

By examining the relevant research and evaluation literature and perusing the professional writings that describe good and not-so-good humanities programs, I can gain a greater understanding of why the program may or may not work and what its critical components are. This also helps me find seeds to still more evaluative questions. I always ask an expert in the field—someone who "knows the territory"—to help start the literature review. Computer searches often provide too much information. You can't separate the wheat from the chaff! If the expert is knowledgeable, sometimes she can provide a reasonable shortcut to help you identify key issues, questions, models, and important articles and evaluations that would not be feasible for you to ferret out on your own.

The examples used in this hypothetical case study may not suffice in a real evaluation, but they should illustrate some of what goes on in the divergent phase of identifying evaluative questions. Now to the convergent phase.

October 15. It's good to be back on-site at Radnor. The advisory group representatives seemed anxious to get going. I think the E-mail exchanges worked well to orient them to the task and their work as a group, though I began the meeting talking about what we would do today and during the course of the evaluation, using them to suggest data sources, react to proposed methods for collecting data, get involved in observing some classes and interviewing some students or looking at some papers, helping synthesize findings and reviewing draft reports, and so forth. I want them to buy into this project and feel like real partners. We talked a while about questions and concerns they have. They're a pretty active group. Most have experienced some type of evaluation before, but that can be more of a hindrance than a help if their experience wasn't good.

They had all received the final list of questions synthesized from their input, the review of literature, evaluation models, Dewey Pritchard's thoughts, and my experience. I listed several criteria on the blackboard and we used those as yardsticks to determine whether or not to include each question. This is a pleasant group; usually someone has apoplexy over one or more of the questions that threatens some particular sacred cow. Not so this time, except when I asked, "What evidence exists that the goals of the curriculum are really important?" That one raised dust for a minute or two, but they accepted it after the shock wore off that anyone would presume to ask it. After a bit they almost seemed to relish the answer, presuming I'd get the answer they would predict.

I had someone in the group talk briefly about each question and why it would be useful or informative. Then, I talked a little about what answering that question might mean in terms of data collection, costs, and my impression of the usefulness of the findings in judging the quality of the program and whether to continue it. Because the board is the one making the decision, I wanted to make sure we can meet their needs in addition to informing others.

The discussion was really useful though, as always, it took longer than I thought. I tend to forget that it takes time, even with stakeholders who have a little experience with evaluation, to acquaint them with what can be done and the implications of it, but this early communication is critical for the group to learn to work together and to reach a consensus on what will constitute a useful evaluation.

After the discussion of each question, I asked people to write down their top three to five evaluation questions considering the criteria. I tallied the results and put them on the board. The top questions showed a surprising amount of agreement across the group. We reordered the remaining questions by grouping similar ones together. I encouraged different group members to argue for or against certain questions in regard to how they addressed the criteria. Ultimately, we agreed on six questions that are crucial, plus three others we'll try to answer if resources permit. Most focused on some critical changes in students, but it won't be a "black-box" study. Some questions remained that will allow us to examine the process of the program to make sure the critical elements occur (that program theory does come in handy!). The board representative had a tough time letting go of one pet question that was just not feasible without a $200,000 study, but finally made it.

Once we got set and agreed on the questions, I suggested we spend our remaining time trying to get the group to help me identify where to begin to look for answers to the questions.

Author Comments.   The criteria mentioned in the above journal entry are those shown earlier in Figure 12.2, which I always find useful and prefer to use if possible. Jim Sanders feels more at home with his laundry list and asterisks. Jody Fitzpatrick uses the laundry list and asterisks but with a few criteria designed for that organization. All work. The key is to find the approach that you can use to help stakeholders in the evaluation converge on the subset of evaluation questions that are (1) of most importance, and (2) feasible. The importance of narrowing the focus to a reasonable number of important, answerable questions that are satisfactory and interesting to key audiences is so obvious that one might wonder why we trouble to state it. Actually, it really is not so obvious to many evaluation practitioners. We have witnessed numerous studies that were launched with long lists of unranked, unselected evaluation questions, only to end up months later frustrated and confused because they have only produced answers to a few, and those were not the questions the clients cared about most. Indeed, if we had $50 for every case like that we have seen, we would be basking in the Bahamas rather than penning these pages.

Major Concepts and Theories

1. Evaluation questions help give focus to the evaluation. They may specify the standards and criteria for judging the program. They guide choices for data collection.

2. Criteria specify those characteristics of the program that are critical to a program's success. Standards, then, indicate the level of performance a program must reach on the criteria to be considered successful.

3. The divergent phase of question development is conducted with all key stakeholders and results in the development of a comprehensive list of potential evaluation questions and concerns.

4. Other sources for questions include evaluation models, existing standards in the field, the research literature, and the evaluator's own experience.

5. The convergent phase concerns winnowing down the questions for the final evaluation. Questions that are retained should have high, direct potential use to important and/or many stakeholders. Questions may be further culled based on the cost and feasibility of providing valid answers.

6. If the evaluation is summative, criteria and standards should be considered. If used, standards may be absolute or relative.

Discussion Questions

1. What can an evaluator do in the question development phase to help ensure that evaluation findings will be used, in some fashion, by stakeholders?

2. What benefits derive from applying evaluation models reviewed in Part Two to a comprehensive list of questions?

3. As an evaluator, what would you do if a client or other stakeholder were to push adamantly for a biased or an unanswerable question?

4. Discuss the potential advantages and disadvantages of using expert consultants to generate evaluation questions and criteria.

Application Exercises

1. Consider an evaluation that would have meaning for you and your organization or employer. If you're at a loss for a program you know, you might select your graduate program. Or try some recent, highly publicized program or policy being considered by city or state officials. Using what you now know about generating and then selecting questions, criteria, and standards for the evaluation, generate a list of evaluation questions you would want to address.

2. What method would you use to cull the above questions in the convergent phase, knowing your organization and the issues involved? Do the criteria in Figure 12.2 serve the purpose? Would you modify them? Are there questions that you know must be answered and the laundry list with asterisks would suffice? How would you involve the other stakeholders in the convergent phase?

3. Which of your questions would benefit from criteria and standards? If the evaluation is summative, do the questions convey all the important criteria for the program? Should other questions or criteria be added? Now, set standards for each question as appropriate. Discuss your rationale for each standard.

4. Interview a fellow student about a program with which he is familiar. If possible, interview someone else knowledgeable about the same program. What differences do you discover? Why do you think these differences exist?

5. Obtain a copy of a report from a completed evaluation study. (If you don't have access to an evaluation report, go to one of the Web sites listed in the appendix.) Consider the questions that were addressed. Were there any critical oversights? Was the evaluation formative or summative? Was the focus on needs assessment, monitoring program activities, or examining outcomes? Were criteria and/or standards explicitly stated? If not, was their omission acceptable? Why or why not? If

they were stated, on what grounds were they developed? Do you agree with the criteria? Would you have added others? Were standards set at the appropriate level?

Relevant Evaluation Standards

The evaluation standards we see as relevant to this chapter's content are the following. These standards are described in Chapter 18.

U1—Stakeholder Identification
U3—Information Scope and Selection
U4—Values Identification
F1—Practical Procedures
F2—Political Viability

F3—Cost-Effectiveness
P1—Service Orientation
P5—Complete and Fair Assessment
A3—Described Purposes and Procedures
A12—Metaevaluation

Suggested Readings

Cronbach, L. J. (1982). *Designing evaluations of educational and social programs.* San Francisco: Jossey-Bass.

Lincoln, Y. S., & Guba, E. G. (1985). *Naturalistic inquiry.* Beverly Hills, CA: Sage.

Mertens, D. M. (2001). Inclusivity and transformation: Evaluation in 2010. *American Journal of Evaluation, 22,* 367–374.

Patton, M. Q. (1997). *Utilization-focused evaluation: The new century text* (3rd ed.). Thousand Oaks, CA: Sage.

Whitmore, E. (Ed.). (1998). *Understanding and practicing participatory evaluation.* New Directions for Program Evaluation, No. 80. San Francisco: Jossey-Bass.

Witkin, B. R., & Altschuld, J. W. (1995). *Planning and conducting needs assessments.* Thousand Oaks, CA: Sage.

13

Planning How to Conduct the Evaluation

Orienting Questions _____

1. What are some activities or functions common to all evaluations that must be considered in planning any evaluation study? (*Hint:* One of them is "collection of information.")

2. What should be specified in the evaluation plan?

3. What is the role of the client and other stakeholders in developing the plan?

4. How can you organize time, responsibilities, and resources so that all evaluation tasks are accomplished in a first-rate and timely manner?

5. What resources must be considered when developing evaluation budgets?

6. Why would a formal evaluation contract or agreement between evaluator and client be useful?

Much has been said in earlier chapters about the need to "focus" the evaluation study—to understand what is to be evaluated, why the evaluation has been proposed, what the evaluation's sponsor, client, and other stakeholders want to learn, and what criteria they would use to make judgments. But is this evaluation planning? Yes. When the focus of a study has become clear, is the evaluation plan complete? No, for focusing is only one part of developing an evaluation plan.

To explain the relationship between focusing and planning an evaluation, we turn to the earlier work of Stufflebeam (1968, 1973b). He proposes that one first *focus the evaluation* to determine what information is needed. He also proposes four functions common to various kinds of evaluation, namely, information *collection, organization, analysis,* and *reporting.* To develop an evaluation design, Stufflebeam maintains one must plan how each of these functions would be carried out. Finally, he proposes that developing a plan for *administering the evaluation* is an integral part of an evaluation design. Stufflebeam's (1973a) resultant structure for developing evaluation designs includes these six activities/functions:

1. *Focusing* the evaluation
2. *Collecting* information
3. *Organizing* information
4. *Analyzing* information
5. *Reporting* information
6. *Administering* the evaluation

In Chapters 10 through 12 we dealt with various aspects of *focusing the evaluation* (phase 1 in the list). Understanding the origin and context of a proposed evaluation and identifying and selecting the evaluation questions, criteria, and standards most appropriate for the study are the major aspects of focusing the evaluation. In this chapter we discuss how phases 2 through 6, collecting, organizing, analyzing, and reporting information and administering the evaluation, need to be considered in the evaluation plan. (Chapters 14 through 18 will then provide more detail on carrying out these phases.) Before addressing these topics, we wish to remind the reader of two important points:

1. *Evaluations should be conducted in a flexible manner.* One should not infer that the steps involved in evaluation are sequential and linear. We might have almost as conveniently used here Stake's (1975b) "clock" (shown as Figure 8.2), which emphasizes that one may move back and forth among evaluation functions, from data analysis to more data collection, to reporting, back to reanalysis, and so on. Whatever schematic is used to portray them, all evaluations have in common these facts: (a) they involve data collection, analysis, and interpretation, and (b) the evaluator must plan how these functions will be fulfilled.

2. *The evaluator should have a clear understanding of the purpose and role of the evaluation.* In earlier chapters we outlined several different approaches to evaluation and described how each might be used to perform different evaluation roles. Then we provided practical guidelines (especially in Chapters 11 and 12) to help the evaluator focus the evaluation study. It would seem difficult for an evaluator to go through activities such as we have proposed without developing a fairly clear notion of the role the evaluation will play and a general idea of the type of evaluation study that will best suit that role. Such conceptual clarity is essential to any good evaluation plan.

Yet, far too often evaluators arrive at this point, after considerable interaction with the client and other stakeholders, still unable to articulate clearly the purposes or focus of the evaluation. By now, the evaluator should exhibit a clear understanding of the particular evaluation he is proposing. Is he planning a formative or summative evaluation? Is the focus on needs assessment, monitoring, or outcomes? Is it comparative or descriptive? Is the evaluation to be decision-oriented, with the design built around some key decisions, or theory-based, with the design built around testing key components of the program theory? Answers to questions such as these should be apparent in any good **evaluation plan.** If they are not, the evaluator should settle them in his mind (and that of the client) before proceeding further. Without clarity on these points, the focus for the evaluation is fuzzy indeed, and it would be an accident if the remainder of the evaluation were anything but a muddle.

Identifying Design and Data Collection Methods

In Chapter 12 we dealt with identifying and selecting those evaluation questions that the evaluation study should answer. Once the evaluation questions are known, the next logical step is to determine what information is needed to answer each question. For example, consider the monitoring question "Have the critical program activities occurred on time and within budget?" To answer this question, the evaluator would need to know, among other things, which activities were identified as critical; the program time frames and budget, by activity; when each critical activity began and ended; and the total cost of each critical activity.

The information needs in the preceding example seem very straightforward, but in practice they are often much more complex. For example, consider the outcome question, "What impact does the computer-based WANDAH program have on the writing performance of high school students in the Jefferson High WAN-DAH writing classes?" To answer the question it would be necessary to first choose the appropriate design. Is the program at a pilot stage and, therefore, the design should be descriptive? Is a summative decision to be made, making a causal design more appropriate? Having determined the design, the evaluator would then need to specify the means for measuring "writing performance." Writing performance could be viewed either holistically or analytically, or both. Holistic measures of students' writing ability might involve judgments made by panels of the overall quality of students' papers, before and after exposure to WANDAH. An analytic approach might include measures of syntactic density, numbers of T-units, percent of *to be* verbs, or average sentence length before and after using WAN-DAH. Or, students' writing performance might be measured according to the extent and effectiveness of revisions from one draft to another. In this armchair example, we can avoid the choice, but were we actually conducting the study we would be required to decide which type of design would be best and precisely what constructs and measures should be used to answer the question.

The evaluator should obviously involve the client and other stakeholders in deciding what information would best answer each evaluation question. But the evaluator plays an active and pivotal role, as Cronbach and his colleagues (1980) have observed.

> The evaluator, then, should be far more than a passive note taker trying to locate variables to study. From his own knowledge or from his consultation with experts,

he should come to understand the problem area and the history of similar programs well enough to suggest likely points of breakdown and possible unfortunate side effects. He can reasonably become devil's advocate, imagining the complaints that opponents might voice about the program. The evaluator can also suggest outcome variables that others have failed to mention, so that his clientele can decide whether data are wanted on these (p. 170).

Selecting Designs for the Evaluation

Designs specify the organization or structure for collecting data. The design selected generally has implications for the sources and methods of data collection. Thus, the evaluator should consider what types of designs may be appropriate for each evaluation question and discuss related issues with the stakeholders in the development of the evaluation plan. Many evaluators conceptualize designs as descriptive or causal. When the evaluation question is causal, evaluators will often use experimental or quasi-experimental designs (see Bickman, Noser, & Summerfelt, 1999, and Riccio & Orenstein, 1996, for good examples). Others may make use of descriptive case studies to examine changes that occur (see Datta, 1995, and Michalski & Cousins, 2001, for good examples). In examining the impact of policies that affect whole groups (changes in laws or regulations), evaluators may use multiple regression or other statistical methods to help in answering the evaluation question (see Folz & Hazlett, 1991; Freeman, Klein, Townsend, & Lechtig, 1980).

More often the evaluation question is a descriptive one—to show a trend, to illustrate a process, to convey the status of something, or to describe and analyze a program, process, or procedure. *Time series* designs may be selected to show a trend, as reflected in the question, "Are high school graduation rates declining?" A *cross-sectional* design may be used to assess public opinions of a program. A *case study* design may be used to describe the critical components of a successful child-abuse prevention program. Guba and Lincoln (1981) have used the term *thick description* to refer to certain types of descriptive case studies, and such thick description can be most useful in informing stakeholders about what is actually happening in a program. Descriptive designs are commonly used in needs assessments and monitoring or process studies. They also can be useful in impact studies designed to determine whether participants' final performance is at the desired level or to describe performance at critical stages of the program. (See Spiegel, Bruning, & Giddings, 1999, for an innovative evaluation of an assessment conference for teachers.) Many summative evaluations consist of a mix of causal and descriptive designs to avoid a black-box solution that fails to describe connections between the clients and the program.

The evaluator and stakeholders should examine each question carefully to identify any important research design issues relevant to the question. Most evaluations use several designs or combinations of designs to address different questions. Nevertheless, it is important to consider design at this stage. Agreements may need to be reached on the availability of comparison groups, the appropriateness of random assignment, the time for collecting data from multiple sources, the specification of the cases, the timing of measures, and other issues relevant to implementing the evaluation.

At this stage the evaluator may be ready to specify the exact design to be used if the intent of the question is quite clear and the limitations and flexibility permitted in data collection have been explored. For example, if the question is specifically to examine a trend—"Has the number of pregnant women receiving prenatal care in the first trimester increased over the last five years?" "Has the number of high school graduates pursuing education at community colleges increased over the last decade?"—it may be perfectly appropriate to designate a simple time-series design at this point. However, if there is some interest in exploring the *whys* of the trends, the evaluator might need to explore further to determine the extent to which case study or cross-sectional components need to be added. In some cases, the evaluator may be content with simply specifying whether the design will be causal or descriptive and delaying the selection of a specific design until the details of information needs, feasibility of different designs and methods, costs, and time lines are further developed. Design concerns should, however, be addressed before the conclusion of the planning process.

The designation of the appropriate design for each question enhances communication between the stakeholders and the evaluator and helps the stakeholders envision how the study will actually be implemented. Through learning the details of the design, the stakeholders can raise any concerns they have about data collection or issues that might constrain the study. Changes can then be made at that point rather than in the middle of data collection.

Identifying Appropriate Sources of Information

Each evaluation question requires the collection of information on at least one variable, if not more. For each variable, the evaluator and stakeholders can consider who or what might be the source(s) for that information. For example, let us say that, to answer the question "Have the critical program activities occurred on time and within budget?" it was agreed that needed information would include program time frames and budget by activity, costs for each activity, and documentation of when each critical activity began and ended. The primary information source for such items would typically be the program administrator and existing program documents. Secondary sources (used as necessary to supplement or cross-check information and perceptions) might be the organization's accountant or budget officer, funding agency officials of the program if externally funded, or program participants (for information on timing and direction of activities).

To answer the question "What impact does the computer-based WANDAH program have on the writing performance of high school students in the Jefferson High WANDAH writing class?" let us assume that it had been decided that information was needed on one holistic measure (teachers' judgments of overall writing quality on one assignment) and one analytic measure (percent of *to be* verbs). The source of information for both would be the students in the WANDAH classes (and students in some non-WANDAH classes, if a comparison group were used).

The source is not the teacher or the rater who counts the *to be* verbs; they only judge, score, or transmit information about writing performance, and that information obviously emanates from the students. The source is the group of individuals or the location of existing information that can answer the question.

Using Existing Data as an Information Source. Evaluators (and clients) sometimes overlook the fact that not every question must be answered by collecting original data. Evaluators would be wise to see whether information relevant to any of the evaluation questions already exists in readily available form. For example, are there extant evaluation reports, status reports, or data collected for other purposes that might provide complete or partial answers to some evaluation questions? Much of the information necessary to answer the first question posed above—"Have the critical program activities occurred on time and within budget?"—might be available in existing organizational documents. Before moving to collecting new information, the evaluator should always ask the client, program managers, and deliverers of the program whether there are existing sources that might meet the information needs. He then needs to judge the appropriateness of these sources. Internal data, specific to the organization, may or may not be collected and organized in a valid and reliable manner. Such data may, however, provide much information about the environmental context of the program.

Public documents and databases are another major source of existing information. Examples of such data include the reports developed by the U.S. Census Bureau (including the Census of Governments, the Decennial Census of Population and Housing, the monthly Current Population Survey, and Survey of Income and Program Participation); statistics collected by the U.S. Department of Labor and other federal departments; the City-County Data Book; reports and databases of various state, local, and nonprofit organizations; and the like. Most state departments of education maintain extensive data on schools' performances on standards, enrollment, disciplinary incidents, and the like. Today, much data are available on-line. Searching the names of agencies that may hold such data can reveal a wealth of information!

Such data are typically intended to be used by others. As such, the information is generally collected in a careful, standardized fashion and is likely to be more reliable and valid than much internal existing data. While it is reliable and valid for the purposes for which it is collected, such information may not, however, be reliable and valid, or sufficiently sensitive, for the program evaluation at hand. The evaluator should be certain to learn about the manner in which the information is collected, the definitions of the constructs, the sampling methods used, and the time frame and population sampled to determine whether the data will be appropriate for the current program evaluation.

One word of caution: Just because data exist does not mean the data must be used. We have no sympathy for the evaluator who permits evaluation questions to be wrested into nearly unrecognizable form only so they can be answered by available information. Such distortion of an evaluation's intent is not excusable by claims of heightened efficiency. In such cases, the evaluator has committed what Patton (1986) calls a "Type III error," answering the wrong question!

Commonly Used Information Sources.   Within each evaluation study, information sources will be selected to answer the particular questions posed. Obviously, information sources may be as idiosyncratic as the related questions. As discussed above, existing data are one important information source. If original information must be collected, the most common sources are these:

- Program recipients (e.g., students, patients, clients or trainees)
- Program deliverers (social workers, therapists, trainers, teachers, physicians, nurse practitioners)
- Persons who have knowledge of the program recipients (parents, spouses, coworkers, supervisors)

Other frequent sources include:

- Program administrators
- Persons or groups who might be affected by the program or who could affect its operation (the general public, future participants, organizations or members of interest groups involved in the program)
- Policy makers (boards, CEOs, executive and legislative bodies)
- Persons who planned or funded the program (state department officials, legislators, federal funding agency officials)
- Persons with special expertise in the program's content or methodology (other program specialists, college or university specialists)
- Existing data and documents (existing databases, files, and public documents such as written reports)
- Program events or activities that can be observed directly

Policies That Restrict Information Sources.   It is important to identify, early in planning an evaluation, the organizational policies that may affect the collection of information. For example, contracts or agency policies may restrict how employees can be involved in the evaluation. Employees may be restricted from data collection or other tasks beyond their immediate job responsibilities. Most organizations have policies concerning collecting data from clients or existing files. Such policies are often designed to protect the interests of clients; however, the evaluator needs to be aware of such policies to learn how they may limit or restrict data collection. Many organizations require that surveys or interview questions be approved prior to use. Often, permission of parents or guardians must be obtained before collecting information from children or those unable to give permission themselves. Many constraints exist around the use of personnel information.

In addition to organizational constraints, evaluators have certain ethical principles they must follow to protect those from whom information is collected. (See Chapter 17 on ethics.) Evaluators need to protect confidentiality or anonymity, if that has been promised, and avoid invasion of privacy. If certain potentially harmful information may be subpoenaed later, the evaluator should consider whether it is necessary to collect it in the first place. Protection of Human Subjects committees, established in the United States by the National Research Act of 1974, should have time to review plans and instruments used in the evaluation.

Some evaluators try to ascertain whether any existing policies will affect their study even before they identify the major evaluation questions their study will address. We prefer not to be constrained by policy considerations quite so early, however. Restrictive or enabling policies will become apparent quickly enough if the evaluator identifies the best possible sources of information needed for the study and then asks the client whether there are any policies restricting use of those sources to gather information.

If reconsideration of the policy is deemed inappropriate, the evaluator will have to obtain information from secondary sources or forgo collecting it altogether. Questions that become unanswerable because of policy constraints needn't be tossed out. Retaining them in the evaluation plan can be instructive in reminding the evaluator and stakeholders of information needs.

Client Involvement in Identifying Information Sources. The client's role in identifying information sources is nearly as important as client involvement in determining what information is needed. The evaluator will often, by dint of experience, be able to identify good sources of information that might not have occurred to the client. Almost as often, the client will be able to identify useful sources of information that might otherwise escape the evaluator's attention. It is simple enough to ask the client, "Do you have any suggestions about where we might best obtain information on teachers' use of discussion groups [or the like]?" This sort of collaboration not only yields helpful answers but further enhances the shared ownership of the evaluation by the client and evaluator.

Identifying Appropriate Methods for Collecting Information

Once the evaluator has specified where or from whom the needed evaluation information will be obtained, the next step is to specify the particular methods and instruments for collecting the needed information. Returning to our earlier examples, information about the timeliness and cost of critical program events might be obtained through personal interviews with the program administrator, budget officer, and program participants or through perusal of program budget and schedule documents. Information about the impact of the WANDAH program on students' writing ability might be collected by the previously mentioned holistic measure (teachers' judgments of overall writing quality on a given assignment) or analytic measure (percentage of *to be* verbs in one writing assignment).

There are countless ways to classify data collection methods and instruments. Although not exhaustive, we have found the following classification scheme[1] useful in prompting neophyte evaluators' thinking about possible methods of data collection.

I. Data collected directly from individuals identified as sources of information
   A. Self-reports
      1. Paper-and-pencil methods (e.g., structured questionnaires, unstructured surveys, checklists, inventories, rating scales)
      2. Interviews (structured or unstructured, personal or telephone)
      3. Focus groups
      4. Personal records kept at evaluator's request (e.g., diaries, logs)
   B. Personal products
      1. Tests
         a. Supplied answer (essay, completion, short response, problem solving)
         b. Selected answer (multiple-choice, true–false, matching, ranking)
      2. Performances (simulations, role-playing, debates, pilot competency testing)
      3. Samples of work (portfolios, work products of employees)
II. Data collected by an independent observer
   A. Narrative accounts
   B. Observation forms (observation schedules, rating scales, checklists)
III. Data collected by a technological device
   A. Audiotape
   B. Videotape
   C. Time-lapse photographs
   D. Other devices
      1. Physical devices (blood pressure, air quality, blood-alcohol content, traffic frequency or speed)
      2. Graphic recordings of performance skills
      3. Computer collation of participant responses
IV. Data collected with unobtrusive measures
V. Data collected from existing information resources or repositories
   A. Review of public documents (federal, state, or local department reports, databases, or publications)
   B. Review of organizational documents or files (files of client records, notes or products of employees or program deliverers, manuals, reports, audits, publications, minutes of meetings)
   C. Review of personal files (correspondence or E-mail files of individuals reviewed by permission of correspondent)

[1]This set of categories is drawn from Worthen, Borg, and White (1993).

Numerous other ways of categorizing methods for collecting information have been developed; of these, the listing of multiple measures provided by Brinkerhoff, Brethower, Hluchyj, and Nowakowski (1983) and Posavac and Carey (1991) are useful examples.

Reviewing the Adequacy of Methods for Collecting Information.   Many evaluators choose data collection techniques or instruments more for their familiarity than for their appropriateness. Evaluators may frequently find familiar techniques applicable, but, equally often, new approaches must be sought. Stufflebeam (1981) makes a similar observation.

> Only recently have evaluators begun to realize that evaluation needs a respectable methodology that is built from the ground up. That is, the techniques of evaluation must be built to serve the information needs of the clients of evaluation (p. 5).

In addition to making sure the information collected matches the construct of interest, the evaluator should ensure that sufficient information will be collected on each construct. Some phenomena are sufficiently clear-cut (e.g., height, number of children in a classroom, dollars spent) that only one measure is needed. Others, such as writing ability or parenting skills, require multiple measures because no one measure is sufficient to capture the totality of the phenomenon. In such cases, multiple measures, using different sources and/or different methods, are necessary to insure the evaluation question is answered completely.

Once information collection techniques have been specified for each evaluative question, the evaluator should review them, as a set, to assess their technical soundness, availability, relevance, and utility, asking these questions:

- Will the information to be collected provide a comprehensive picture of what is evaluated?
- Are the procedures for collecting the information legal and ethical?
- Will the cost of any data collection procedure be worthwhile, given the amount and kind of information it will provide?
- Can the information be collected without undue disruption of the project?
- Can the procedures be carried out within the time constraints of the evaluation?
- Will the information collected be reliable and valid for the purposes of the evaluation?
- Does the data collection plan make use of already existing data when appropriate information is available?

Role of the Client in Identifying Methods.   Typically, the evaluator will have more expertise regarding the array of possible methods than will the client or members of the advisory group. However, it can be useful to involve the client or advisory group in the selection of methods to receive their feedback. These stakeholders can often provide a fresh perspective on the measures and insights concerning how those from whom data are to be collected might react. The wording of questions, the focus of the observation, the means for building rapport and alleviating anxiety in focus groups and interviews, the feasibility of physical measures can all be elements for useful discussion. Finally, the methods for collecting information will form the foundation of the evaluation. If the client does not find them to be credible, the ultimate usefulness of the evaluation may be in question.

In most instances, collecting the evaluation information is the province of the evaluator, not the client, for reasons discussed in earlier chapters (e.g., conflict of interest, technical competence). It is, after all, the evaluator who must guarantee the ultimate quality of the evaluation information—the core of the evaluation. While the evaluator has the responsibility to ensure that data collection procedures are designed and implemented to ensure quality information, clients may be involved in the data collection. In recent years, many evaluators have moved to involve stakeholders more at this stage. Fetterman (1994) cites many studies that have used evaluations to empower clients to become change makers in their own organizations or communities. In any case, when others are involved it is the evaluator's responsibility to insure that they have the training to carry out the data collection in a responsible manner. (See Chapter 12 for more on involving clients in data collection.)

Determining Appropriate Conditions for Collecting Information

It is not enough to specify only the methods and instruments for collecting information. As noted above, the evaluator must also insure that the conditions within which those methods and instruments are employed are appropriate. Perhaps the most common concerns are these: (1) Will sampling be used in collecting the information? (2) How will the information actually be collected? and (3) When will the information be collected? A few words about each of these concerns may be helpful.

Specifying Sampling Procedures to Be Employed.   Some innocents have stated that researchers use sampling because they are concerned with generalizing their findings to large populations, whereas evaluators do not use sampling procedures because they are concerned only with describing and judging what exists in the particular case. Such logic misses the key point: Sampling can be as useful and efficient for drawing inferences about more circumscribed populations as for large populations.

For example, if an evaluator were asked to evaluate the effect of HMOs on health costs and patient health in California, it is unlikely that he would propose collecting information on every person enrolled in an HMO in California. The cost would likely be prohibitive and probably unjustified as well. Careful use of systematic sampling procedures permits the evaluator to select and test a much smaller group while still generalizing with a high degree of confidence about the likely impact of HMOs in California. Similarly, no sane educational evaluator, charged with evaluating the effect of a districtwide, ninth-grade math curriculum on student achievement in a large metropolitan school district would propose testing on every ninth grader (though he might make use of data from existing tests if the test items reflect the goals of the curricula).

However, when the sample is very small, it is advisable to try to collect data from the entire population. In such circumstances, sampling methods are not as likely to result in a sample representative of the population. For example, in an evaluation of an employment-training program with 118 trainees, it would be helpful (depending on budget and time) to administer a paper-and-pencil test to each of the 118 trainees enrolled in the program. If the test were group-administered, this could easily be warranted. However, if data collection is costly, sampling might be used for cost purposes. If data needed to be collected through interviews with supervisors or observations of performance on the job, it would not be practical to collect information on all 118 trainees.

Sampling, then, is a tool to be employed by the evaluator whenever resources or time are limited and whenever the group of interest is sufficiently large to permit selecting a sample that meets the purposes of the evaluation. Some may insist on collecting data from everyone, but such endeavors inevitably cut back the amount of information that can be collected in other ways. Thus, if surveying or interviewing everyone leads to eliminating other methods of data collection that might yield important information, sampling should be considered. We would usually prefer to see sampling employed to allow resources to be expanded on multiple sources and methods of collecting information than see all the resources for an evaluation expended to collect data from the entire population on a single measure.

Specifying How Information Will Be Collected. For each type of data collection it is necessary to specify *who* will collect the data as well as the *conditions* under which it will be collected.

- Who will collect the information? For methods such as interviews, observations, and focus groups, how will the characteristics of the evaluator influence the behavior of participants?
- What training should be given to the people collecting the data? What sorts of checks need to occur as data collection proceeds?
- In what setting should data collection take place? Is the setting conducive to the respondents' providing the desired information?
- How can anonymity and confidentiality be protected?
- Does the data collection pose any threat to the respondents? What type of debriefing is needed?
- Is any special equipment or material needed for the collection?

If the evaluator is using a method or measure new to him, it is critical that he examine the literature on methods for using such methods accurately and talk with others who have used the method to get their suggestions. If the method is quite new to the evaluator, he should not implement it without training or assistance from others. Evaluators need a bigger "bag of tools" than researchers because they are examining a wider variety of phenomena than most researchers. As such, it is imperative for the evaluator to reassess continually the methods he knows and seek training concerning new techniques.

Specifying When the Information Will Be Collected.   It seems almost a truism to say that evaluation information collected too late to bear on the relevant course of events is not useful. Timeliness is essential. In determining when information should be collected, the evaluator must consider three criteria:

1. When will the information be needed?
2. When will the information be available?
3. When can the information conveniently be collected?

Knowing when information will be needed establishes the latest allowable date for collecting it because time must be allowed to analyze, interpret, and report results. Availability is also an issue. It is patently absurd to schedule student "posttesting" for early June if the school year ends in late May, yet we have seen evaluators who have discovered this fact too late. Similarly, mailing surveys in mid-December when many people are too busy with holiday activities is not wise planning. It is also inefficient to return repeatedly to the site to collect data that could have been collected only once, given better planning. If the evaluator specifies the time for each data-collection technique, it is easy to see whether data pertaining to other evaluation questions might be conveniently collected at the same time, using the same technique. It seems obvious, doesn't it? Yet this simple bit of planning is often overlooked.

Determining Appropriate Methods and Techniques for Organizing, Analyzing, and Interpreting Information

Evaluators must plan the format in which information will be collected in addition to designating means for coding, organizing, storing, and retrieving it (Stufflebeam, 1973a). An example might underscore this point. A consultant of our acquaintance was once called by a school district to help analyze "some evaluation data we have collected and would like to analyze in the next week or two." After asking to see the data, our friend was led to a room nearly half the size of a normal classroom. There were the data—thousands of students' notebook diaries bound in bundles, by classroom and school, filling the room and stacked floor to ceiling, except for passageways. Our friend's first fear was that the data might topple over on him; his second was that district officials might really believe all that data could be analyzed adequately in such a short time. After some discussion with our friend, school officials realized that analyzing a random sample of the data was all that was possible. It also occurred to them that they could have greatly simplified the lives of the students and spared their time (not to mention the forests of the Northwest) if that had been all the data they had collected in the first place.

Specifying How Information Is to Be Analyzed.   For each evaluation question, the evaluator should describe the way in which collected information will be analyzed. This requires two steps: (1) identifying the statistical or summarizing *techniques* to be employed for analyzing both quantitative and qualitative information, and (2) designating some *means* for conducting the analysis. For instance, in the example above, central tendency and dispersion descriptive statistics could be used with quantitative data, or content analysis for qualitative data. The "means" might refer to the computer and necessary software to be used to analyze the data.

Interpreting the Results.   Statistical reports do *not* speak for themselves. Different people looking at the same results may attach very different interpretations to them, depending on their values, past experiences, and personal expectations. For this reason it is useful to share the results of data analyses as they become available with the evaluation client and other key audiences to elicit their interpretations of what those results mean. For some evaluation questions, the criteria and standards developed will serve as a guide to the interpretations. However, the evaluation plan should allow for the recording of multiple or conflicting interpretations, and all interpretations should take multiple perspectives into consideration.

In later chapters we discuss at greater length helpful procedures for interpreting data-analysis results as well as some common misinterpretations of evaluation findings. Here our concern is only with pointing out the importance of carefully planning interpretation procedures.

Determining Appropriate Ways to Report Evaluation Findings

For each evaluation question selected, the evaluator should specify when answers and interpretations should be prepared and for whom. For some questions, frequent periodic reports may be appropriate; for others, a single report may suffice. Some reports should be formal technical documents; others may take the form of memoranda, informal discussions, oral presentations, or meetings.

A good way to plan the reporting of evaluation findings is to use a matrix that specifies for each evaluation question: (1) the audience, (2) the content to be included, (3) the reporting format, (4) the date of the report, and (5) the context in which the report will be presented. An example is shown in Figure 13.1.

Once the evaluator has planned reports for each evaluation question, he should review the reports, as a set, to see whether collectively they provide the needed information in a usable form. In Chapter16 we discuss evaluation reporting at some length. At the planning stage, however, we cannot improve on a very useful set of questions suggested by Brinkerhoff and colleagues (1983):

1. Are report audiences defined? Are they sufficiently comprehensive?
2. Are report formats, content, and schedules appropriate for audience needs?

FIGURE 13.1   *Sample Work Sheet for Planning the Evaluation Reporting*

Evaluation Question	Audience for the Report	Report Content	Report Format	Reporting Schedule	Context for Presenting Report
1. Have the critical program events occurred on time and within budget?	Program staff	Progress to date; problems needing attention	Memorandum and verbal presentation	Beginning of each month	Presentation at staff meeting, with one-page written summary
2. What impact does WANDAH have on students' writing ability?	School principal, language arts faculty, school board	Findings of student performance on holistic and analytic measures	Written report, with oral briefing, plus executive summary	Preliminary report on March 15; final report on May 1	Briefing and discussion of preliminary report with faculty and principal; written final report to them and executive summary to board, with oral briefing as requested by board

3. Will the evaluation report balanced information?
4. Will reports be timely and efficient?
5. Is the report plan responsive to rights for knowledge and information with respect to relevant audiences? (p. 48)

Use of Simple Work Sheets to Summarize an Evaluation Plan

It may be useful to summarize briefly our discussion of those items that collectively form the outline of an evaluation plan. For each evaluation question used to focus the study, it is important to specify the following:

1. *Information required* to answer the question (constructs or variables on which information will be collected)
2. *Design(s)* to be used to collect information
3. *Source(s)* of that information
4. *Method(s)* for collecting the information

5. *Information-collection arrangements,* including
   a. Sampling procedure (if any)
   b. Collection procedure (who collects information; under what conditions)
   c. Schedule for collection
6. *Analysis procedures*
7. *Interpretation procedures* (including standards as appropriate)
8. *Reporting procedures,* including
   a. Audience(s) for report
   b. Report content
   c. Report format
   d. Schedule for reporting
   e. Context for reporting

An efficient way of completing these steps is to use a matrix with the first column listing the evaluation questions and subsequent column headings corresponding to each important element of the plan, as shown in Figure 13.2. Naturally, nowhere is it written that one must use every column of the matrix for it to prove useful. Nor is there anything magical or immutable about the headings we have provided; they can be modified to suit the evaluator. For example, a more simplified matrix such as that shown in Figure 13.3 has proven useful in many evaluation studies. This simpler version is especially useful with clients, who can more readily assist in completing this "short form," and with funding agencies, who have found such matrixes useful in understanding what is proposed by the evaluator. The evaluator can, of course, subsequently add columns and detail as desired, for his own purposes. A simple device of this type is among the most useful tools an evaluator can employ for summarizing or communicating an evaluation plan to clients and other audiences.

Specifying How the Evaluation Will Be Conducted: The Management Plan

The final task in planning the evaluation study is describing how it will be carried out. A **management plan** is essential to help in overseeing the project. Who will do what? How much will it cost? Will it be within budget? Conducting a thorough and systematic evaluation study is a complex undertaking. To make the effort successful, the evaluator must effectively manage not only the evaluation activities but also the resources allocated to carry them out.

Evaluation management is multifaceted. An evaluation manager must supervise other staff; serve as liaison to evaluation clients, participants, and other evaluation stakeholders; and identify and cope with political influences. Effective management also demands communication and reporting skills. Needed resources must be identified, allocated, and monitored. Periodically, the manager must review all evaluation activities to insure that schedules are being respected and that all activities meet the high technical standards expected.

FIGURE 13.2   *Sample Work Sheet for Summarizing an Evaluation Plan*

Evaluation Question	Information Required	Design	Information Source	Method for Collecting Information
What types of employment did welfare mothers find after completing their employment training? Did it include health benefits? Was the compensation adequate to bring about self-sufficiency?	Job title, responsibilities, sector of employment (public, private, nonprofit), number of hours per week, salary, health benefits, length of time employed, other components as they arise	Descriptive, cross-sectional, possible case study elements	Graduates of employment training who found employment	Survey, interviews, possible focus group

Sampling	Information-Collection Procedures	Schedule	Analysis Procedures
Survey to all (*n* = 50), interview with sample of 20; focus group with 10	Surveys distributed when client picks up graduation diploma; interviews arranged then and conducted in their home by trained research assistants; focus group conducted by consultant, 15 randomly recruited with compensation of $25 and babysitting provided	Surveys—October; interviews—November; focus group—early December	Descriptive stats and chi square for surveys. Use results for interview. Summarize major themes of interviews. Use results to plan focus groups. Use taped transcript of focus groups for analysis. Integrate all results to describe trends and solutions.

		Reporting Procedures		
Interpretation Procedures	Audience(s)	Content	Format	Schedule
Are at least two-thirds of those who are employed earning a sufficient amount to sustain their family? Are they able to afford adequate child care? Are health benefits provided? For those whose employment does not establish or appear to lead to self-sufficiency, what solutions are recommended?	Funding sources (city and state departments), project administrators, program deliverers (especially employment counselors), clients, public at large	Help answer question: What is the program doing well? What changes are needed?	Technical report to funding sources and project administrators with one meeting with each funding source to discuss results; several meetings with project administrators and deliverers to discuss their interpretation of results and possible changes; meeting with clients to report results and receive their input; press release to general public	Meetings to discuss results—January; release report—mid-February with press release

FIGURE 13.3   *Sample Work Sheet for Summarizing an Evaluation Plan: Abbreviated Form*

Evaluation Questions or Objectives	Infor-mation Required	Inform-ation Source	Method for Collecting Information	Information Collection Arrangements			Analysis Procedures	Interpre-tation Procedures and Criteria	Reporting of Information		
				By Whom	Condi-tions	When			To Whom	How	When

This sample worksheet (reduced in size from the original) is suggested for use in compiling information needed to prepare an evaluation plan. When completed, all the essential ingredients of an evaluation plan or design are present and can be summarized to communicate key features of the plan to clients and coworkers.

An evaluation, whether a team or single-person effort, cannot afford to be disorganized or haphazard. As the Program Evaluation Standards (Joint Committee, 1994) remind us, professional evaluators are responsible for planning cost-effective evaluations. A management plan is needed to structure and control resources, including time, money, and people. As with the evaluation plan, the management plan must be open to change in response to fluctuating circumstances, but the need for flexibility in no way diminishes the need for a plan.

A good management plan must specify for each evaluation question the following: (1) the tasks to be performed and the time lines for each task, (2) the personnel and other resources required to complete the task, and (3) the cost. Each column builds on the next. Once tasks and time lines are specified, the personnel and resources to perform the tasks can be identified. Complex tasks will require higher-level personnel; time-consuming tasks will require more hours. When tasks are compressed into a short time frame, more personnel will be required. Finally, with the specification of personnel and resources, costs for each question can be determined. Figure 13.4 presents a sample management plan. The sections below will describe how it is developed.

FIGURE 13.4   *Sample Management Plan Work Sheet*

Evaluation Question	Tasks	Estimated Task Beginning and Ending Dates
1. Have the critical events of the program occurred on time and within budget?	1a. List program's critical events, time schedule for each, and budget for each.	1a. First month of program.
	b. Monitor progress and expenditures for critical events.	b. Beginning to end of each month of program.
	c. Prepare and present monthly reports.	c. Last week of each month of program
2. Is there sufficient evidence of need for the program as it is designed? Are there other, more critical, needs that are not being addressed?	2a. Search of assessment of needs.	2a. First day of program or before.
	b. If no needs assessment exists, plan and conduct needs assessment.	b. First month of program.
	c. Prepare written report for project administrator.	c. Fourth week of program
	d. Meet with program administrator.	d. End of fourth week of program

Estimating and Managing Time for Conducting Evaluation Tasks

Among the most common techniques used for estimating time on tasks are **PERT charts** and **Gantt charts**. PERT is an acronym for "Program Evaluation and Review Technique" and was developed by the U.S. Department of Defense as a management tool for complex military projects. It has since been used in many other settings to examine the interrelationships among tasks and the time required to complete both subsets of tasks and entire projects (Cook, 1966; Sylvia, Meier, & Gunn, 1985). PERT charts are most useful in large, complex studies when over-

FIGURE 13.4 *Continued*

Personnel Involved and Estimated Costs	Other Resources Needed and Costs	Total Task Cost
1a. Evaluator, 5 days at $400 per day = $2,000	1a. None	1a. $2,000
b. Evaluator, 2 days at $400 per day = $800 per month of program	b. None	b. $800 per month
c. Evaluator, 2 days at $400 per day = $800 per month of program	c. .5 day of clerical time = $35 per month of program	c. $835 per month
2a. Evaluator, 1 day at $400 per day = $400	2a. None	2a. $400
b. Evaluator, 10 days at $400 per day = $4,000	b. Consultants, 1 for 3 days at $400 = $1,200; research assistant, 10 days at $150 = $1,500; reimbursement to focus group participants: 4 groups with 10 members, $30 each = $1,200; rooms and refreshments for focus groups at $50 each = $200; secretarial costs for transcribing tapes, 2 days at $75 per day = $150	b. $8,250
c. Evaluator, 2 days at $400 per day = $800	c. Clerical time, .5 day at $75 = $35	c. $835
d. Evaluator and program administrator, 2 hours at $50 per hour = $100	d. None	d. $100

looking details may create unresolvable problems. For many evaluations, however, PERT may be more cumbersome and time-consuming than it is enlightening. In most evaluation studies, a simplified version of PERT, in which one estimates the time required for each task and links the task with others to be performed either simultaneously or before or after the task at hand, is sufficient. An example of a simplified PERT chart is shown in Figure 13.5.

Gantt charts (Clark, 1952) are simple displays that include proportionate, chronologically scaled time frames for each evaluation task. A Gantt chart lists tasks on the vertical axis and a time scale on the horizontal axis. A horizontal line is drawn for each task to show how long it will take. An evaluator (or anyone)

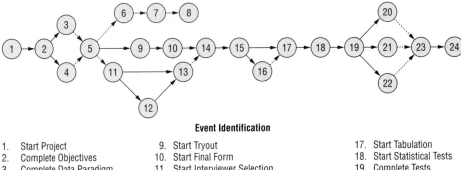

Event Identification

1. Start Project
2. Complete Objectives
3. Complete Data Paradigm
4. Complete Hypothesis
5. Start Item Construction
6. Start Universe Definition
7. Start Sampling
8. Start Sample Selection

9. Start Tryout
10. Start Final Form
11. Start Interviewer Selection
12. Complete Administration Procedures
13. Complete Schedules
14. Start Field Interview
15. Start Data Coding
16. Complete Follow-Up

17. Start Tabulation
18. Start Statistical Tests
19. Complete Tests
20. Complete Interpretation
21. Complete Tables
22. Complete Charts
23. Start Narrative
24. Complete Narrative

FIGURE 13.5   *Summary Network for Survey Research Project*

Source: From *Program Evaluation and Review Technique: Applications in Education* (Monograph No. 17, p. 43) by D. L. Cook, 1966, Washington, DC: U.S. Office of Education Cooperative Research. Reprinted with permission.

can look at a Gantt chart and tell at a glance when activities will begin and how long each will continue. Gantt charts are easy to prepare and, in addition to their management benefits, are effective in communicating evaluation plans. A sample Gantt chart is shown in Figure 13.6.

Charts can help highlight important interim deadlines (or "milestones," as they are often called by funding agencies) that must be met if the overall evaluation study

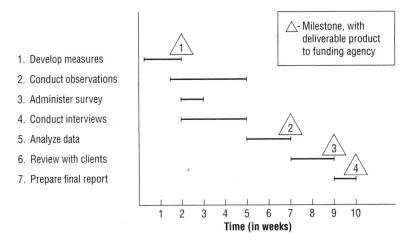

FIGURE 13.6   *Example of Showing Milestones on a Gantt Chart*

is to be completed on time. Even if a formal PERT or Gantt chart is not used, the evaluator should develop a list of critical tasks for each piece of data collection and estimate the time required to perform each task. He should then consider which tasks can or should occur simultaneously in order to meet the overall time constraints of the project. Start and end times for each task should then be specified. This time line can then be used for effective monitoring of projects.

Bell (1994) observes that well-specified milestones are essential to monitor projects adequately. Monitoring should not be time-specific, such as monthly, but based on identified milestones on the tasks to be completed. Complex or lengthy tasks, or work completed by a new staff person, will require more milestones than other types of task. Milestones for monitoring a large project should not simply be the beginning and end points of information collection but should include key interim steps during which the evaluation managers can discuss progress and findings with the staff person.

As more time is required for certain tasks, the evaluator should adjust the overall project time line. This might be accomplished by reducing the time required for future tasks through adding more personnel, reducing the scope of work, or determining whether the time frame for the study can be extended. The time line is a tool, not a taskmaster. It gives the evaluation manager a means for organizing and monitoring progress, but, as unanticipated events occur, such as unforeseen difficulties in data collection, the need for greater depth or additional collection of information due to ambiguities in results, or a client's requests for additional information, the evaluator can and should adjust the time line to meet these needs.

It is essential that sufficient time be allowed for all aspects of the evaluation, from focusing the evaluation study through final reporting. Good evaluation management never places key actors under unrealistic constraints that jeopardize the quality of their performance.

Analyzing Personnel Needs and Assignments

The quality of any evaluation depends heavily on the capability and energy of those who carry it out. In some instances, only one individual—the evaluator—may be responsible for everything. Most typically, others—secretarial personnel, evaluation assistants, consultants, or evaluation colleagues—will also be involved.

Perhaps the first concern of any evaluation manager is whether qualified individuals are available to carry out the various evaluation tasks. Answering this question demands specifying clearly the roles and responsibilities of each individual. In proposing how to develop an implementation plan for evaluation, Suarez (1981) outlines "personnel role specifications" as the first step: Specify who would manage the study, complete the evaluation design, select or develop instruments, collect data, analyze data, write summary reports, and so on.

To determine who will do what, consider the skills required for completing each task. Who has these skills? Who has experience and interest in this area?

Who has training and experience in content analysis? In recruiting participants for focus groups? In analyzing data with path analysis techniques? In writing clear, interesting reports for the public? For a small project, choices may be among the evaluator and one or two assistants or consultants. For larger projects, the skills of the existing professional staff, and their existing workloads, should be reviewed to determine who is available and most appropriate for each task. Even with a large existing staff, consultants may need to be hired in specialized areas.

For internal evaluators, many choices exist among the current organizational personnel who perform different duties. Consider how publications editors or public relations personnel can be of assistance in disseminating evaluation information. Computer and technology personnel may be able to provide assistance in on-line data collection, accessing and storing data, purchasing new software as necessary, and data analysis.

In many participatory—and certainly in empowerment evaluations—program personnel and clients are involved in collecting, analyzing, and interpreting data. Consider the relevant skills, strengths, and risks each group or individual brings to the evaluation and use them accordingly. (See Chapter 11, "Analyzing Availability and Capability of Evaluation Personnel," for more on using clients and volunteers to assist in the evaluation.)

Estimating Costs of Evaluation Activities and Developing Evaluation Budgets

There are many nonmonetary and indirect costs of evaluation, such as opportunity costs or political costs. In the interest of simplicity, we limit our discussion here to direct dollar costs; Alkin and Solmon (1983) provide a more complete treatment of other evaluation costs and benefits.

Typical Resources and Their Costs.   An evaluation budget usually includes the following ten categories (Sanders, 1983):

1. *Evaluation staff salary and benefits.* Personnel costs typically consume the largest part of the evaluation budget. The amount of time that staff members must spend on evaluation tasks and the level of expertise needed to perform particular evaluation tasks both affect costs. Decisions must be made about who will perform various tasks and the amount of time the tasks will require. Benefits have become an increasingly costly portion of the budget as health insurance costs have risen. Costs in this category are estimated relatively easily by using existing salary and benefit figures. Once the proportion of a person's time devoted to the evaluation is determined, that portion of the staff member's salary and benefits can be charged to the evaluation budget. Most organizations have a set benefit rate that is a percentage of the salary. If a new person must be hired, salaries for the proposed position can be determined by consulting with other organizations with like employees, perusing advertisements and notices in publications advertising for similar positions, and so on.

2. *Consultants.* As noted, consultants are frequently needed either (a) to provide skills not currently reflected among project staff and not permanently needed in the organization, or (b) to provide an independent perspective on the program or the evaluation. Consultants also have the advantage (to the budget, at least!) of not receiving benefits. Costs for consultants can be calculated using their daily or hourly rate.

3. *Travel and per diem (for staff and consultants).* Costs depend on the amount of field work and the degree of personal interactions required to design and conduct an evaluation. Some contracts apply restrictions on travel costs (e.g., no billing for travel within the catchment area of the organization). Travel costs can include estimates of automobile mileage for meetings, training, observations, data collection, and other activities outside of the catchment area. Airfare, ground transportation, and per diem costs for lodging and meals should be calculated for long-distance travel.

4. *Communications (postage, telephone calls, etc.).* This category includes both fixed costs (e.g., continuing monthly billings for telephone lines, computer networking, and Internet access) and variable costs (for special communication efforts, such as long-distance calls, faxes). Fixed costs can be budgeted by multiplying the length of the contract by the proportion of work the organization devotes to that contract. (Many of these elements may already be counted in indirect or overhead costs.) Variable costs should be estimated based on the nature of the tasks involved. Thus, postage costs will be much higher if mailed surveys are part of the study. These postage costs should be calculated directly based on the number of mailings, postcards, and return envelopes.

5. *Printing and duplication.* Costs cover preparation of surveys, protocols for observations and interviews, evaluation reports, and any other documents. Routine costs may be estimated by comparison with past projects or discussions with others who have overseen similar projects. Often clerical staff can be helpful in estimating budget costs in this area. Costs of printing and duplicating final reports, binding, or any special graphics should be checked with copying centers. Remember that disseminating reports via E-mail or posting them on the Internet, if these methods will reach the intended audience and attract their interest as well as other methods, can save print production costs, though costs for associated Web-design issues should be considered and included as necessary.

6. *Data processing.* Consider whether new software will need to be purchased for data analysis, storage, or retrieval.

7. *Printed materials.* This category includes the costs for purchasing existing data collection instruments and library materials. Publishers of books or measures can provide costs for possible budget items.

8. *Supplies and equipment.* This category covers the costs of specific supplies as well as equipment that must be purchased or rented. If the primary supplies to be used are routine (pencils, pens, paper, etc.), typical office estimates should be obtained and prorated for the length of the contract. Occasionally, special purchases or rentals are necessary. These could include videotaping equipment, specialized software or hardware required for the project, purchases of existing databases or fees for using existing data, or mechanical devices for collecting data (blood-pressure monitors). Costs of purchasing or renting such special equipment should be obtained from suppliers. In some cases, contracts may require rentals rather than purchases of costly equipment.

9. *Subcontracts.* This category includes expenditures for any contracted services, such as accounting, legal services, test development, and so forth. All subcontracts must be negotiated with the subcontractor before the evaluation budget is completed. Each subcontractor may submit an independent budget. Agencies and institutions often include these costs in their overhead rates. However, small or new agencies may need to bill for these services.

10. *Overhead (facilities, utilities).* The greater the use of external personnel and services, the lower the overhead costs. Typically, however, an institution must bear certain fixed overhead costs (i.e., those of maintaining an adequately equipped physical plant) regardless of what arrangements are made for the evaluation. Most organizations have fixed percentages of a total budget, or of personnel salaries and benefits, that they charge as operating overhead. Check to see what overhead covers to make sure you are not double-billing. Thus, if overhead includes fixed costs for communication, computers, accounting, or legal services, these should not be billed separately.

Once costs in each budget category have been calculated, a total cost for the evaluation can be determined. This first estimate often exceeds the evaluator's or client's expectations. When this happens, review each line item and ask how the work could be completed at less cost. Some effective cost-saving measures include:

- Using available volunteers or low-cost workers to reduce staff salaries and benefits;
- Using local specialists for data collection to reduce travel costs if evaluation staff are at a distance;
- Training less-costly personnel to perform selected tasks;
- Borrowing (equipment, people, materials, and supplies);

- Seeking "in-kind" contributions from the organization in which the external evaluator is employed (often done for good public relations) or the sponsoring agency;
- Reducing the scope of the evaluation, perhaps deferring some parts for the future;
- Using existing measures, data, or reports;
- Using inexpensive data collection when precision can be sacrificed without severe consequences;
- Using public media to disseminate results;
- "Piggybacking" on other studies;
- Increasing efficiency through good management.

Establishing Evaluation Agreements and Contracts

Many potential problems that arise during evaluation can be more readily solved if client and evaluator share a firm understanding. Even among administrators and evaluators with the highest possible professional standards and ethics, conflicts can and do arise—usually in the absence of well-documented agreements concerning important procedures. As Guba and Lincoln (1981) note:

> Evaluations are done for clients who commission the evaluation, provide for its legitimization, and pay for it. Since he who pays the piper calls the tune, the evaluator must have a firm understanding with the client about what the evaluation is to accomplish, for whom, and by what methods. The evaluator also needs to be protected against certain arbitrary and possibly harmful or unethical actions by the client, just as the client needs to be protected against an unscrupulous evaluator. The means for achieving these understandings and establishing these safeguards is the evaluation contract (pp. 270–271).

Anderson and Ball (1978), quoting Samuel Goldwyn's wry comment that "oral agreements aren't worth the paper they're written on," add the following:

> For major evaluation efforts, a formal, legal contract should be negotiated; not to have one would be foolish for both parties. In smaller evaluation efforts, a formal contract might be unnecessary, but even then a letter of agreement . . . makes excellent sense. In either case, the agreement should spell out not only the financial arrangements but also the main elements and requirements of the planned evaluation (p. 155).

The Joint Committee's Program Evaluation Standards includes Formal Agreements as a specific standard: "Obligations of the formal parties to an evaluation (what is to be done, how, by whom, when) should be agreed to in writing, so that these parties are obligated to adhere to all conditions of the agreement or formally to renegotiate it" (Joint Committee, 1994, p. 87). They suggest guidelines for the agreement and note common errors in drafting such agreements. Stufflebeam (2000) analyzes two relatively similar evaluation projects he conducted, one of which "went sour" while the other received commendation. He attributes the differences in the outcomes of the evaluations to differences in the contracting procedure.

Another agreement between clients and evaluators that should occur at this point concerns ethics and standards. The evaluator should share either the Guiding Principles or the Program Evaluation Standards or both with the client and other stakeholders. This information can help the audiences for the study to know what to expect from the evaluation. Both the Guiding Principles and the Standards can be examined and downloaded at www.eval.org or brochures may be ordered from that site for distribution to clients. (See Chapters 17 and 18 for more on the Guiding Principles and the Program Evaluation Standards.)

We began this chapter with a list of Stufflebeam's six activities in evaluation. We will close it with another reference to Stufflebeam—his checklists. We have described many of the essential steps to planning in this chapter, but Stufflebeam's checklists for developing an evaluation plan and evaluation contracts can serve as useful guides or final checks. These checklists are available on the Western Michigan University Evaluation Center's Web site: www.wmich.edu/evalctr.checklists/.

CASE STUDY APPLICATION

October 15 (continued). With the time remaining in our meeting, I proposed we use the evaluation questions we had agreed on to flesh out an evaluation plan. We took a few of the questions and, using a matrix I offered, went through the exercise of identifying information we would need to answer them, listing where and how we would obtain the information, and so on. It was great to see the enthusiasm of several of the group when they began to realize how simple and straightforward it was. Once they had the hang of it, I suggested they fill out as much of the matrix as they could for the remaining questions and send a draft to me. They scheduled a meeting for the following week. I'm going to participate by conference call at the end, but I want to give them time at the beginning to talk about the evaluation among themselves without my presence hindering them.

I feel good about what we were able to accomplish even though we didn't finish the plan. The important thing is this isn't going to be *my* evaluation plan. It is at least *ours*, if not *theirs*, built on questions they posed and answered by information from sources they specified.

November 3. I spoke with the Radnor Advisory Group a few weeks ago when they met. It seems they're moving along very well as a group. Yesterday, I received the draft of their effort to fill out the matrix for the remaining evaluation questions for their study. They got most of it filled out and had some interesting ideas I may not have thought of. Think I'll save a copy and use it in my evaluation seminar to prove my point that much of evaluation planning, sans its mystique, is simple logic and should be shared by the client, with the evaluator providing technical help as and where it's needed.

Author Comments.   Perusal of my handout for spring quarter would reveal the document appearing as Artifact 3, of which only a few samples, and only a few columns of those, are shown here in the interest of space.[2]

Yes, I do think it useful to have the client and other stakeholders help identify not only possible sources of information but also possible ways to collect it. Methodological expertise notwithstanding, the evaluator seldom has the stakeholders' feel for the program, such as who is really involved, who knows what, and even how certain groups or individuals might respond to proposed data collection strategies. Obviously they should not be left to focus the evaluation alone, but there seems little reason for failing to involve at least some stakeholders, including the client, as partners.

A few comments about the matrix are in order. First, these sample evaluation questions do not pretend to be complete. Several key questions are obviously omitted, for example, questions about students' learning of concepts presented in the curriculum and how that learning coincides, or fails to coincide, with the goals of the program.

Second, this simulated (but realistic) example of how the matrix might look obviously reflects a first draft in need of considerable refinement. Questions should be raised about whether other sources of information should be included or present sources excluded. Strategies for data collection and instruments are still vague in some instances and need to be checked for cost and feasibility.

Third, even when it is refined, there is no claim that this is the only way a good evaluation could be designed. I would argue, however, that it is a systematic way to produce a good evaluation design because the evaluator can ensure it is technically sound and the client can be sure it is acceptable on other grounds.

Finally, the matrix contains "pieces" of the evaluation that still need to be summarized to yield the real evaluation design. For example, summarizing the columns on methods and arrangements for collecting information will normally identify several questions to be posed to the same source (e.g., teachers), using the same method (such as a mailed questionnaire). Economy of time and effort (and the respondent's patience) will generally result from collecting all the information in a single instrument. Such summarization also quickly reveals inconsistencies and proposals in the draft that are not feasible.

[2]Even these samples are only partial, providing the first four columns of a matrix. Subsequent columns that would need to be completed for each evaluation question include *at least* the following: arrangement for collecting information (by whom, when, under what conditions), analysis of information, and reporting of information (to whom, when, how).

ARTIFACT 3   *Sample Items from the Radnor Township Draft Evaluation Design*

Evaluation Questions	Information Required	Source of Information	Strategy/Method of Collecting Information
1. To what extent are the program objectives shared by important groups?	Ratings of importance of objectives	a. Board of education b. Hum. Curr. Review Comm. c. Teachers d. Parents e. Other community members	a–b. Individual interviews c–e. Mailed questionnaire to all teachers, samples of others, using Phi Delta Kappa goal-ranking procedure.
4. Is the content of the lesson plans faithful to the humanities?	Substantive adequacy of lessons and other materials	External humanities experts	Expert review of lesson plans and materials
5. How do teachers, parents, and community members view the program?	Attitudes of teachers, parents, and community members	a. All teachers b. Parents c. Community leaders	Survey Focus group Interviews
9. Do the teachers use appropriate methods to deliver the program?	Methods teachers use	Expert in instructional methods Teachers	Observation of classes Review of lesson plans
13. Do student attitudes demonstrate that the curriculum is producing the desired results?	Attitudes of students toward the values and concepts taught in the curriculum	Students	a. Comparative design, using attitude scales, observation, and unobtrusive measures; and . . . ? b. Simulated situations, role-playing to get at real student attitudes (e.g., attitudes toward cultural differences)

November 6. Completed the evaluation design for the Radnor humanities curriculum today. In the process, I realized we had never explicitly agreed on the criteria or standards the board would use in determining whether or not to continue the program, even though we had discussed them in relationship to the evaluation questions and I had talked individually with some board members about them. So I called Nancy Reese, the board president, and asked her if she might be able to help me with that. We agreed she should go to her colleagues on the board with the list of evaluation questions and ask them, "Do these evaluation questions cover all the important criteria you will use in judging the value of the program? Which criteria are most important?" Then, to help define standards: "What kind of answer to this question would convince you to continue the program? To discontinue it?" Given an-

swers to those questions, we can make sure we're covering all the important criteria and have some sense for the standards they will apply to each. Their answers will help me decide what emphasis to place on the various kinds of data.

Author Comments.   There are many ways one might go about identifying criteria and setting standards for determining whether an entity like this humanities curriculum should be continued or jettisoned. The example offered here is admittedly somewhat tardy if you believe that the only criteria of importance are those held by the formal decision makers. Yet, I find formal decision makers seldom work in a vacuum and are often influenced by the standards other groups use to judge the program. Once I tended to blurt out, within moments of an introductory handshake with a decision maker, "Okay, now what criteria do you intend to use to determine whether or not to continue the program?" I am now more patient. Indeed, I like to share the full range of questions various groups hold to be important with the formal decision makers—in this case, the board—and ask them, in essence, whether the answer to that question would influence them either to continue or to scrap the program. Not only can one generate criteria in this way but there is also the possibility of expanding the horizons of those who must make difficult decisions.

> ***November 13.*** Nancy Reese called back today after polling the board members on criteria. She reported that she and one other member of the board think all the questions should be used to decide whether to keep the humanities curriculum, but consensus of the board is that the most important criteria relate to three areas: (1) how well students are performing in basic skills (writing and other language skills)—in particular whether the program improves scores on the state writing test; (2) whether students are attaining the general and specific goals of the curriculum (critical thinking, appreciation of cultural, ethnic, and social diversity); and (3) whether the parents and other supporters of the school wish to see the curriculum continued. On the first criterion, Ms. Reese indicated the board hoped students would be performing at least as well as students from similar schools while their abilities on the second should be much better. They would like a solid majority of parents to support the curriculum. With that information, I can complete the evaluation plan and send a copy off to Claire Janson tomorrow.

Author Comments.   Nancy Reese may not have reported formalized standards per se, but she has given the stuff of which standards are made. Further, I now know which questions address the most important criteria. I have nothing against decision makers who tell me they intend to continue a program only if "75% of the students exceed the 'proficient' level on the state standards test," just as long as they can defend their rationale and the standards tests is an appropriate measure of the desired outcomes. Sometimes such standards are based on criteria relating to political pressures, program funding, or other such practical considerations. However, I do like to explore the degree to which such criteria are purely arbitrary. In addition to being unfair, this can cut off discussion of important issues. I would much rather have a glimmer of what stakeholders really think important (and some future opportunity to help them reflect more specifically on how they intend to apply the criteria) than deal with the artificial precision built into too many of today's so-called standards.

> *November 14.* Completed the Radnor evaluation plan tonight (Artifact 4). Was disappointed to find I had to cut out some things I feel are important because there simply isn't enough time and/or money to do them. Alas. Still, I think the plan is a good one, given the constraints we're operating under. I did list, in a section on "limitations of this evaluation," those things I deemed important but had to sacrifice due to shortage of resources.

ARTIFACT 4   *Outline of the Humanities Program Evaluation*

I. Introduction
  A. History and description of the humanities curriculum
  B. Purposes of the evaluation
  C. Audiences for the evaluation
  D. Constraints and policies within which the evaluation must operate
II. Evaluation plan
  A. Overview
    1. Possible comparative elements
    2. Sequencing and interrelationship of components
    3. Evaluation questions to be addressed by the study
    4. Criteria for judging the program
  B. Work unit 1.0: curriculum analysis
    1. Expert review: humanities specialists
    2. Expert review: instructional design specialist
  C. Work unit 2.0: collection of extant data
    1. Lesson plans and program documents
    2. Minutes of faculty meetings, newsletters to parents, student products and activities
  D. Work unit 3.0: mailed questionnaire to teachers
    1. Survey whole population
    2. Develop survey and pilot test
    3. Follow-up with focus group
    4. Nonresponse bias checks
  E. Work unit 4.0: student measures
    1. Paper-and-pencil measures
      a. Cognitive measures (standards test and measures of humanities content specific to program)
      b. Affective measures
    2. Interviews
    3. Focus group
  F. Work unit 5.0: evaluation team on-site visit
    1. Classroom observation
    2. Interviews
      a. Students
      b. Teachers

    c. Parents
    d. Board members
  III. Reporting of results
    A. Preliminary report: exit interview of on-site team
    B. Monthly communications with Advisory Group
    C. Develop draft reports
    D. Review of draft reports
    E. Disseminate (meetings with board, PTSA, teachers and staff)
  IV. Personnel
    A. External evaluation team
    B. Radnor staff (supervised by evaluation team)
  V. Schedule
    A. Work flow
    B. Deadlines
  VI. Budget

Author Comments. Space prohibits commentary on each of the points in this sketchy outline of the plan, but elaboration may be helpful on a few points that may not be self-evident.

First, for reasons outlined earlier, I would try to get comparative snapshots of the students in the program and other comparable youngsters. Without more information about the availability of other comparison groups and willingness to allow their use, however, one could only temporize at this stage, laying out a possible comparative design in II-A and promising, should that not prove feasible, to direct the resources assigned to that effort into more intensive data collection within Radnor on those variables.

Second, within each "work unit" proposed, I would preview *briefly* the methods proposed for collecting information (listing specific instruments if they are already in existence) and the proposed data analysis.

Third, in work unit 1.0, I would propose sending program goals and lesson plans to the humanities specialists and having them conduct their analyses first from afar, unsullied by the rhetoric of the enthusiastic program staff, but I'll have to remember they're only reviewing *plans*. Our observation data will help us determine the extent to which these plans are implemented. On the other hand, I am going to have the instructional design specialist do some on-site observation as well. It's too difficult to judge teaching from afar.

Fourth, in work unit 2.0, I would envision collection of information on variables such as discussions in faculty meetings on directions for the program; information provided to parents and community through newsletters; and information that might suggest changes in students, e.g., instances of in-school problems among different ethnic groups; membership in elective dance, drama, or art classes; participation in extracurricular arts events, and the like.

Fourth, in work unit 3.0, I am interested in learning more about how the teachers *actually* deliver the program, what changes they've made, what thoughts they have about the program, and changes they observe in students. I'll develop one survey for the teachers involved in the program. I might even see if they're willing to keep a log or diary for a period. Then, I'll develop another survey for other teachers in the school to learn more about their perceptions of the program and their observations of students, their needs, changes observed, and so forth.

Fifth, in work unit 4.0, I would first examine the state standards tests to see if they address some of the basic skills that the board members are concerned with and compare scores on these with other schools in the state. Fortunately, the state standards test isn't *too* time-consuming, so Radnor is still using a norm-referenced test to see how they do compared to kids across the nation. I'll try to use both of these sources of existing data so I don't have to pile on too much additional assessment. In addition, I would want to sample students' written and creative or artistic products, given the emphasis the curriculum places on that area. In the humanities content, local criterion-referenced measures should be constructed, working cooperatively with the humanities faculty to make certain the items reflect important concepts. In addition, I would want to select a good measure of critical thinking to get at those ambitious program goals.

In the affective area, I would look for existing measures of appreciation of the arts and sensitivity to others and talk with stakeholders to see whether they met our needs. There's a lot of research in this area, so there could be something that works. If not, I would again work closely with teachers to design measures that matched the Radnor curriculum. As a supplement, I would structure simulated situations and role-playing opportunities so that a smaller sample of students could react directly to stimuli, making choices that reveal relevant attitudes (e.g., stereotypic perceptions of the elderly).

Sixth, I would use an intensive on-site visit of two or three days' duration as one of the major sources of data. For all its limitations, there is a great deal to be said for good old-fashioned professional judgment by those who know the territory, so I would be certain to include both humanities experts and evaluation specialists on a team of four or five people. With careful advance scheduling, orientation of the team to the evaluative questions and the interview schedules, splitting the team up to conduct individual interviews, and then coming back to debrief and synthesize findings, a good bit can be accomplished in a reasonably short time.

Seventh, interviews and observations will play a major role in data collection despite the number of instruments we're considering above. I want to give the board members and others (other teachers, parents) a feel for what's happening in the best classrooms where this program is being delivered. This is going to require some funds for observation, but I might be able to make use of some students at the local college to train in observational methods. I want to interview some teachers and students myself but, having gotten a sense for trends, I might train some of these students in interviewing strategies to conduct more extensive interviews. I might even be able to get some Radnor staff involved in interviewing parents about their reactions to the program and expectations for their child.

Of course, I'll need to train them in interviewing skills. It will be important to teach them to listen and probe carefully and, most importantly, not to influence the interview with their own points of view.

Eighth, once the instruments and instructions for their use were completed, I would rely heavily on Radnor district staff to assist with much of the on-site data collection and data entry, thus greatly amplifying the data that can be collected on a small evaluation budget. The training requirements here are less than those with interviewing, but still must be accomplished. I'll need to make sure the staff distributing or administering the instruments know how to do that in a standardized fashion: again, not inserting their points of view, which can influence responses. On data entry, it's possible, or even likely, that some staff at Radnor will know the software I'm using. They will almost certainly know Excel. Perhaps I could have them enter the data on Excel and then transfer that into my statistical software. I'll have to think about that.

Finally, this evaluation plan proposes what might be called an eclectic, "multiple-source, multiple-method" evaluation, with all the advantages inherent in such an approach.

> *November 15.* Now, for the management plan! As I worked out how I was going to accomplish all this, I could see that some questions could be asked in one operation. For example, some of the questions involve external experts in the humanities and I could have them responding to both evaluation questions for the same consulting fee. Such efficiency!
>
> As I worked out my management plan, it became obvious that I should line up a part-time research assistant right away. Otherwise the good students would be unavailable when I need them.

Author Comments. Again, in the interest of space and simplicity, the document appearing as Artifact 5 is limited to a management plan for the first question listed in Artifact 3.

> *November 15 (continued).* The Gantt chart for the main evaluation questions listed in the plan revealed the following pattern of project activities. (See Artifact 6.) This chart should be a useful tool to communicate the evaluation plan to the folks at Radnor. I didn't break it down by task because the chart got to be too cluttered. I can later develop a Gantt chart for each question to guide me and the research assistant.

> *November 15 (continued).* It appears that a part-time research assistant and a part-time administrative assistant will serve the needs of this project nicely. Now that my research assistants and I do most of our own word processing on the computer, I find our need for clerical help is greatly reduced. Nevertheless, the assistant is essential for keeping track of paper work on budgetary issues in the university bureaucracy and for coordinating mailings of surveys and the like. I may want to delegate some of my load to boost up the time of the research assistant on the project while lightening my

ARTIFACT 5 *Summary of the Management Plan*

Evaluation Question	Tasks	Estimated Task Beginning and Ending Dates	Personnel Involved and Estimated Costs	Other Resources Needed and Costs	Total Task Cost
1. To what extent are the program objectives shared by important groups?	1a. Develop and pilot-test questionnaire and cover letter to be used for surveys and plan for interviews	1a. January 1– January 15	1a. Evaluator, 2 days at $400 per day = $800; research assistant, 1 day at $150 = $150.	1a. 2 hrs. of clerical time at $75 per day = $20.	1a. $970
	1b. Develop sampling plan.	1b. January 1– January 15	1b. Evaluator, .25 day at $400 per day = $100; research assistant, .75 day at $150 per day = $113.	1b. None	1b. $213
	1c. Develop follow-up and nonresponse bias check procedures.	1c. January 1– January 15	1c. Evaluator, 1 day at $400 per day = $400.	1c. None	1c. $400
	1d. Conduct interviews and mail survey with follow-up.	1d. January 20– February 15	1d. Evaluator, 5 days at $400 per day = $2,000; research assistant, 5 days at $150 per day = $750.	1d. Travel expense = $50; postage = $100; duplication = $125; paper = $40; clerical time, 2 days = $150.	1d. $3,215
	1e. Analyze data.	1e. February 20– March 1	1e. Research assistant, 5 days at $150 per day = $750.	1e. None	1e. $750
	1f. Prepare reports.	1f. March 1– March 15	1f. Evaluator, 5 days at $400 per day = $2,000.	1f. 1 day of clerical time = $75; duplication = $125.	1f. $2,200

294

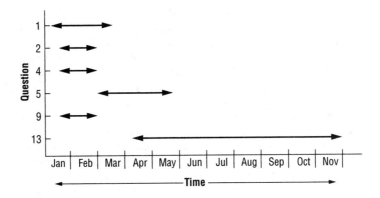

ARTIFACT 6

own. Depends on the reaction to the budget I proposed and the quality of my research assistant (Artifact 7).

ARTIFACT 7

Evaluation staff salaries (evaluator, research assistant, secretary)	$52,208

Consultant
    (humanities experts—4,
    instructional theory experts—2,
    case study researchers—2)
	10,000

Travel	1,243
Postage	340
Telephone	100
Duplication	432
Supplies (tapes)	100
Total direct costs	$64,423
Indirect costs (28% of Direct Costs)	$18,038
Budget total	$82,461

November 15 (continued). When I added up this budget, I was utterly amazed—I had no idea it would add up so fast. All the costs are well grounded on detailed planning for this project, but Claire Janson may have a stroke, yet I realized that I had not even budgeted for some little things like normal office supplies, and my travel budget was low and would only allow me to use fairly local external consultants.

November 21. Claire Janson called today and indicated the board and committee had given the go-ahead on the plan I submitted, with the only suggested changes coming in the deadline and budget. The board has decided they cannot delay a decision about the humanities curriculum as long as they had originally planned. Instead, they want to make a decision by May 15 so they will have time, should they decide to discontinue the program, to plan for its phaseout and provision of alternative curricular offerings for the students. Because the time line is tighter, they've agreed to let the budget go up to $75,000.

The reduced time frame disappoints me, for it will be a real hurry-up job to develop the instruments, supervise the data collection, coordinate the on-site visit, and orchestrate the expert reviews of the materials by that deadline. Fortunately, most of the design can still be implemented and completed within the deadline, although it will be tight. The greatest problem this new deadline causes is the loss of any chance to look at changes in students over time—something I had intended with the cognitive, affective, and unobtrusive measures of student behavior. So I have taken out the pretest-posttest stuff and will depend much more on the site visit, the observations, and the comparison with other schools on the basic skills. That weakens the evaluation, but one hopes the combination of perspectives left in the study will still be strong enough to yield solid findings. One good thing came from this. They agreed to fold the consultant review into the site visit, using a team that includes both humanities experts and us evaluators, so that should help.

Anyway, I cut out those activities that couldn't be completed by May, revised the Gantt chart and budget accordingly, ready to send it back to Radnor as an appendix to the evaluation agreement I'll draft tomorrow. It does shave the budget a bit, which is good, but not too much, what with increasing the travel budget some.

Author Comments.   The best-laid plans of mice and evaluators often go awry. (That is why evaluators need to be not only intellectually flexible but also emotionally resilient.) It is not uncommon for deadlines to be abruptly shifted for reasons far less reasonable than that which I invented as the rationale of the Radnor board. Let me strike another blow for eclectic, multiple-method evaluation designs; they are considerably more robust to changes than are their more single-minded counterparts. If one depends on a single strategy for collecting information and it so happens that changing circumstances disrupt that strategy, there is much less likelihood that the evaluation will succeed.

November 22.   Spent a while this morning trying to draft a written evaluation agreement to send to Claire. Frankly, I couldn't get my heart into it. I'm glad I shared the Program Evaluation Standards and Guiding Principles for Evaluators with the Advisory Group when we began our planning. These give them a great sense for what they can expect from me and the product. The only problem is specifying what I expect from them?

Maybe I'm a bit cowardly, but I can't get my nerve up to send a stiff, legalistic contract to Radnor and ask those people to sign it. I feel like they'd suspect they'd hired a lawyer, not an evaluator. The last thing I want to do is go into this evaluation with them feeling like I don't trust them. I'm already an outsider, and an evaluator, so that's two strikes against me. I'm not about to waste my third strike by creating the impression with them that there is no basis for good, old-fashioned trust. Maybe I'm suffering from an overdose of Thanksgiving turkey, but I think I'll let a brief letter suffice (Artifact 8).

ARTIFACT 8

November 22

Ms. Claire Janson, Principal
Radnor Middle School
13 Ideal Circle
Radnor, PA 19087

Dear Ms. Janson:

I was pleased to learn from you earlier today that you and your colleagues have generally accepted my evaluation plan, subject to the modifications in activities, schedule, and costs on which we have agreed. I have made the necessary alterations and a revised copy is enclosed.

    If you would be comfortable with a fairly informal agreement, I see no need for much formality. Will it suffice to say that I will do the evaluation for the $75,000 outlined in the budget attached to my revised plan? Also, let's agree that I'll follow the plan attached, and we can incorporate it by reference into this letter of agreement.

    Anything else we need to agree to or modify can be worked out comfortably as necessary, I am sure.

    If this is agreeable, please countersign this letter below, retain one copy for your records, and return one to me.

    I look forward to working with you.

Sincerely yours,

Author Comments. The evaluation plan provides a good basis for finalizing the agreement between evaluator and client, but there should be some form of written agreement or letter of understanding that incorporates the plan, agrees on reporting deadlines, budget, and the like. I would urge development of such an agreement in virtually any significant evaluation enterprise. Some may see seeds of distrust in such urging. I agree, but the distrust is not of the motives or character of the principal parties; it is merely distrust of their total recall of an understanding made months earlier. In larger evaluation studies, a more detailed and formal contractual agreement will be necessary.

    The above entry represents two "cop-outs." The first is by our mythical evaluator who would rather be comfy than safe, friendly than correct. I used to feel just like him, until I'd been "burned" a few times. Now I get tempted to write down and obtain my teenager's signature on agreements to replace gasoline in the family car. Well, almost tempted. We'll have to wait and see how our evaluator fares and whether his casual approach to evaluation contracting comes back to haunt him at a later date.

    Meanwhile, the second cop-out is letting my evaluator cop out, not just to make an instructional point but also to keep the number of pages for this section within bounds. My rationalization is that the reader who really wants to peruse sample evaluation contracts can find several—even one laced liberally with "whereas" and "wherefore"—elsewhere (www.wmich.edu/evalctr.checklists/).

Major Concepts and Theories

1. Evaluation consists of the following major functions: focusing the evaluation; collecting, organizing, analyzing, and reporting information; and administering the evaluation.

2. During the planning phase, the evaluator should begin to consider which design is most appropriate for conducting the evaluation. Evaluations can be characterized as primarily descriptive or primarily causal. Many evaluations involve elements of both, but individual evaluation questions tend to be either causal or descriptive. For each question, consider whether it is causal or descriptive and the types of designs that would be most appropriate for addressing the question.

3. Next, the evaluator should consider possible data sources. First, he should determine whether there are existing data to address each question. Such data can be relatively inexpensive to retrieve and may be quite valid and reliable.

4. Generally, existing data will not completely answer all evaluation questions. When original data must be collected, the evaluator should determine who is the best source for such data. Who knows this information? Potential sources include program recipients, deliverers, administrators, policy makers, those with knowledge of the program recipients, and the general public.

5. Having identified appropriate sources for the data, the evaluator should consider what methods will be most feasible and cost-effective for collecting information from these sources. Common methods include interviews, paper-and-pencil measures (surveys or knowledge tests), telephone interviews, observations of program activities or individuals, and focus groups. Multiple methods should be used if one method is insufficient for tapping the construct of interest.

6. Sampling is often used if the number of people from whom data are to be collected is large. Whether sampling will be used, and which sampling methods should be considered at the planning stage.

7. Procedures should also be considered for conducting the study. Who will collect the data and when will it be collected? Under what conditions? What training will be necessary for data collectors?

8. A management plan should be developed specifying the tasks to be completed, and the time line, personnel, and cost associated with each task. The management plan serves as a guide for overseeing the evaluation but should be adapted for changing circumstances. GANTT and PERT charts can assist the evaluator in estimating and managing time.

9. In developing the budget, the evaluator needs to consider evaluation staff salary and benefits, consultants, travel and per diem, communication, printing and duplication, supplies and equipment, and overhead. Each of these is dependent on the type of evaluation and data collection methods used as well as the nature of the evaluation reporting that will be carried out.

10. Finally, the evaluator should work out a contractual agreement with the client that indicates clearly the purpose of the evaluation, the activities to be completed, and responsibilities for each.

Discussion Questions

1. Discuss the considerations an evaluator must make when deciding who will collect evaluation data and when and under what conditions data will be collected.

2. What are some ways evaluators can decrease the costs associated with an evaluation?

3. Why is a contractual agreement between the evaluator and the client useful?

Application Exercises

1. Using the evaluation questions you developed at the conclusion of Chapter 12, develop an evaluation and management plan to address those questions. What further information do you need to do that? (Subsequent chapters will tell you more about methods.) What stakeholders should you involve in planning the evaluation design? What tasks are involved in each step? Who should do them? When?

2. Select a recent article describing an evaluation from *American Journal of Evaluation, New Directions for Program Evaluation,* or *Evaluation Review.* Reconstruct an evaluation plan from that article. What were the evaluation questions the study answered? What information was collected? What designs, sources, and methods were used? Were multiple methods used? How were data analyzed and interpreted? How were stakeholders or clients involved in the planning of the evaluation?

3. Interview someone who has conducted an evaluation study. Ask him how he developed his design. What issues were most troublesome at the planning stage? How did he involve stakeholders on the issues? On which issues did stakeholders play a major role? On which did the evaluator hold more decision-making power? Why? How would you have developed the study differently? What aspects of his plan would you now incorporate into your own matrix?

4. During your interview for exercise 3, ask how the evaluator managed the study. What did professional evaluators do? Research assistants? Clerical staff? What kinds of tasks were accomplished by internal staff? What was their connection to the program and how were they trained? How did he monitor the time line? Finally, see if he will give you a copy of the budget and ask him how he determined some of the costs. Did costs change as the project developed? Bring the budget to class and compare it with budgets obtained by other students.

Relevant Evaluation Standards

The evaluation standards we see as relevant to this chapter's content are the following. These standards are described in Chapter 18.

U1—Stakeholder Identification
U2—Evaluator Credibility
U3—Information Scope and Selection
F2—Political Viability
F3—Cost-Effectiveness
P1—Service Orientation
P2—Formal Agreements
P3—Rights of Human Subjects
P4—Human Interactions
P5—Complete and Fair Assessment
P6—Disclosure of Findings
P7—Conflict of Interest
P8—Fiscal Responsibility
A1—Program Documentation

U4—Values Identification
U6—Report Timeliness and Dissemination
F1—Practical Procedures
A2—Context Analysis
A3—Described Purposes and Procedures
A4—Defensible Information Sources
A5—Valid Information
A6—Reliable Information
A7—Systematic Information
A8—Analysis of Quantitative Information
A9—Analysis of Qualitative Information
A11—Impartial Reporting

Suggested Readings

Brinkerhoff, R. O., Brethower, D. M., Hluchyj, T., & Nowakowski, J. R. (1983). *Program evaluation: A practitioner's guide for trainers and educators.* Boston: Kluwer-Nijhoff.

Morris, M., Scheirer, M. A., & Eastmond, N. (1998). Ethical challenges: The design. *American Journal of Evaluation, 19,* 381–395.

Posavac, E. J., & Carey, R. (1991). *Program evaluation: Methods and case studies.* Englewood Cliffs, NJ: Prentice-Hall.

Stufflebeam, D. L. (2000). Lessons in contracting for evaluations. *American Journal of Evaluation, 21,* 293–314.

Wholey, J. S., Hatry, H. P., & Newcomer, K. E. (Eds.). (1994). *Handbook of practical program evaluation.* San Francisco: Jossey-Bass.

Part IV

Practical Guidelines for Conducting and Using Evaluations

In Part Three we provided guidelines for getting an evaluation started, including how to determine what should be evaluated, how to be certain the evaluation is focused on the right things, and how to plan the specifics of an evaluation. In Part Four we focus on guidelines for actually conducting and using evaluations, beginning in Chapter 14 with suggestions for making choices about designs and sampling strategies for collecting data. In Chapter 15, we examine many different qualitative and quantitative methods and techniques for collecting, analyzing, and interpreting information. Chapter 16 deals with various aspects of reporting and using evaluation results, while Chapter 17 provides suggestions for dealing with the critical political, ethical, and interpersonal aspects of evaluation. Finally, Chapter 18 brings a close to our section on practical guidelines for conducting evaluations by providing important standards and procedures for evaluating evaluation plans, activities, and reports.

None of the chapters in this section purport to treat completely their respective topics. A textbook could be devoted to each chapter (and, indeed, many texts do exist on several of those topics). Each chapter is intended only to introduce the topic and provide practical suggestions for how to use the material in an actual evaluation. References to more extensive discussions of each topic are provided for those who wish more detailed information.

14

Collecting Evaluative Information: Design, Sampling, and Cost Choices

Orienting Questions

1. What steps does one take to plan and carry out data collection for an evaluation?
2. How does using mixed methods and drawing from different paradigms increase the quality of an evaluation? How are mixed methods used most effectively?
3. How does the evaluator decide what to collect information on?
4. What are the purposes of each type of design? Under what circumstances would each be used?
5. When is sampling important in an evaluation? What steps would one take to select appropriate cases in a case study? To select a sampling strategy when the purpose is generalizing to a larger group?
6. How does cost–benefit differ from cost-effectiveness?

The government is very keen on amassing statistics. They collect them, add them, raise them to the nth power, take the cube root, and prepare wonderful diagrams. But you must never forget that every one of these figures comes in the first instance from the village watchman, who just puts down what he pleases (Sir Josiah Stamp, as quoted by Light & Smith, 1970).

The collection of information is fundamental to evaluation. Although a policy maker or citizen may joke about "data-free" or "fact-free" evaluations, no reputable evaluator would presume to make evaluative judgments without first assembling a solid base of evidence.

Still, information is situational and changes with every evaluation. Similarly, the methods evaluators use to collect information also change to match the evaluation questions and information needs and proclivities of stakeholders. Rarely is there one clear choice. Even the most experienced evaluator must make tough choices about sources, methods, and means for collecting information. The evaluator must consider cost, precision, stability (reliability), relevance, and validity of measurements, as well as feasibility, political advisability, and acceptability to various audiences.

In most evaluation studies the essential steps to collecting information are:

1. Study the evaluation questions that have been developed in the evaluation plan and determine what information needs to be collected. What information is necessary to answer the questions? What are the constructs that must be assessed or described?

2. Develop or select a design(s) for collecting the necessary information. What design or designs are most appropriate for answering each question? How should the design be adapted for the specific circumstances of the study?

3. If appropriate, consider sampling strategies. Will you collect information from everyone or every site, or are the number of people or sites sufficiently large that sampling might be cost-effective? If so, what sampling strategy is most appropriate for your purposes?

4. Identify appropriate sources and methods for collecting the information and areas where multiple measures are necessary. Who has this information (source or sources)? What is the most appropriate method for collecting it?

5. Develop procedures for collecting the information. Who will collect it? When? How? With what training and instructions?

6. Collect the information using appropriate checks.

7. Analyze the information. Are statistical methods appropriate? If so, what statistical tests will be used? How should qualitative information be organized and interpreted? What software is needed?

8. Interpret the results and draw evaluative conclusions.

Entire books have been written on a single data collection technique, instrument, or procedure. We could not hope to cover in comparable detail the many data collection methods that evaluators have come to use and value. Instead, we devote two chapters to these topics. In this chapter we will discuss the steps evaluators take to answer questions 1–3 above. We will review issues concerning data collection, analysis, and interpretation in Chapter 15.

Using Mixed Methods

During the 1980s and early 1990s, evaluation was consumed by controversy over the use of qualitative or quantitative methods. The controversy over methods, while sometimes divisive, was useful for the field in informing evaluators from different backgrounds and disciplines of the alternative approaches and measures available and encouraging evaluators to consider multiple sources and methods. Evaluators address many different types of questions, from needs assessments to outcome and cost studies, and measure a wide array of concepts, from blood pressure to self-esteem, from computational skills to quality of life. Given the breadth of their tasks, evaluators must have a broad array of "tools" that encompasses both qualitative and quantitative methods.

Most evaluators now agree that no one method or approach is always appropriate. Rather, the method must be selected based on the evaluation question or questions one is trying to answer, the context of the evaluation, and the values and perspectives of the various stakeholders. Further, because many of the phenomena we study are amorphous or difficult to measure directly, these phenomena will require multiple measures to adequately assess the issue. Such multiple measures should not all be of the same type; the purpose of multiple measures is to observe the phenomenon from different perspectives so as to be certain it is accurately perceived. Thus, when multiple measures are used, those measures will often include a combination of qualitative and quantitative approaches. As Cronbach (1982) has noted, "Evaluations should not be cast into a single mold [scientific]. For any evaluation, many good designs can be proposed, but no perfect ones" (pp. 1–2).

Choices and Types of Mixed Methods

Mixed methods are used in evaluation for a variety of purposes. Initially, researchers and evaluators chose multiple methods to improve the validity of their measurement. *Triangulation* was the term coined to refer to the process of using multiple methods to measure a construct validly. (Picture the construct as the area of the triangle and the sides as various measures.) Greene, Caracelli, and Graham (1989) have since described other purposes for mixed methods, including *complementarity* and *expansion*. More recently Greene and Caracelli (1997) have defined other types of mixed method designs focusing on *integrated* designs that draw from different paradigms to enrich judgments and interpretations of the program or policy being evaluated. (See "Mixed Method Designs" later in the chapter for more on this issue.)

In the positivist or scientific tradition, the focus has been on use of mixed methods for increasing validity of measurement, in other words, to obtain a more accurate picture of the construct. If the purpose is to increase validity in measuring a construct or individual variable, the evaluator should select measures with different biases (Shotland & Mark, 1987). Two different paper-and-pencil tests would, in all likelihood, be insufficient in breadth to provide a full picture. Similarly, individual interviews and focus groups with the same individuals over a short time frame would provide some useful information, but the methods fail to differ sufficiently to constitute a complete assessment of the phenomenon of interest.

Shadish (1993) builds on Shotland and Mark's suggestions using the concept of critical multiplism originally developed by Cook (1985). Shadish recommends identifying the strengths, biases, and assumptions associated with different methods and proposes that, "when it is not clear which of several defensible options for doing a task is least biased, select more than one to reflect different biases, avoid constant biases, and overlook only the least plausible biases" (p. 19). When results using different measures are similar, this convergence provides additional support for the evaluative conclusions. When results differ, the evaluator should attempt to explain the differences or collect additional information to explore the apparent contradictions.

The complementarity and expansion designs described by Greene, et al. (1989) represent other common reasons for using mixed methods. In fact, in their review of 57 evaluations that used mixed methods, Greene and her coauthors found these designs to be more common in practice than the use of mixed methods for triangulation. Rather than increasing validity, mixed methods used for a *complementarity* purpose are designed to gain a fuller understanding or picture of the construct of interest. Methods with different biases may still be selected, but not with the hope of results converging and increasing validity. Instead, the hope is for somewhat different results that, when combined across methods, will provide a fuller picture of the abstract constructs we tend to examine in evaluation. *Expansion* designs use mixed methods to study a program rather than a single construct. Often, qualitative methods are used to describe the implementation and character of the program and more quantitative methods used to assess outcomes. Use of mixed methods in an expansion design provides a fuller picture of the program, but not of any individual construct.

With the passing of the quantitative–qualitative debate, Greene and Caracelli (1997) note that mixed-method evaluations must be planned and considered at three levels: (1) the political level; (2) the philosophical level; and, (3) the technical level. As we noted earlier, Greene and Caracelli conclude that, at the technical level, the quantitative–qualitative debate has essentially been resolved. They write, "Currently, there is wide consensus that mixing different types of methods at the technical level, or the level of method, is not problematic and can often strengthen a given study. . . . Different kinds of methods are best suited to learning about different kinds of phenomena. All methods have limitations and biases; using multiple methods can help to counteract some of these biases" (p. 7). It is at the philosophical or paradigm level, they argue, that differences still exist. These differences concern alternative approaches to knowing and studying the world.

In reviewing the practice of evaluation, Greene and Caracelli identify three different stances to mixing paradigms in mixed-method evaluation: (1) a purist stance (paradigms cannot be mixed because they have fundamentally different and incompatible assumptions); (2) a pragmatic stance (paradigm differences do exist, but decisions about data collection can be made independently of paradigms based on the particular circumstances of the evaluation); and (3) a dialectical position (paradigm differences do exist and are important, thus, methodological decisions should be made using the paradigms to enhance understanding of the phenomenon of interest). We strongly encourage readers to read Greene and Caracelli's volume, *Advances in Mixed-Method Evaluation: The Challenges and Benefits of*

Integrating Diverse Paradigms, for discussion of these issues and some excellent examples to illustrate these different approaches. Our chapters will take a primarily pragmatic stance to assist the new evaluator in selecting the methods most appropriate for the context of the evaluation; however, drawing on the dialectic stance, we will point out when mixed-methods choices can be used to improve our understanding and possibly revise our thinking on an issue.

Designs for Collecting Causal and Descriptive Information

Design is currently in a period of transformation in the field of evaluation. Causal designs articulated by Campbell and Stanley (1966) and Cook and Campbell (1979), and case study designs described by Stake (1967; 1978) in the 1960s and 1970s, are no longer used as templates. Instead, mixed methods have led evaluators to adapt these designs and others to meet the purpose of the study and to shed light on the meaning of the program or phenomenon being investigated. To be fair, Campbell never intended his designs to be used as templates, but rather to serve as starting points for development. In practice, however, many were reluctant to deviate from proscribed designs, especially when establishing causality was viewed as paramount. Work by evaluators and researchers of a more interpretivist bent have prompted evaluators to move ahead in adapting and developing new approaches.

We will begin this section with reviewing commonly used designs, but conclude with a discussion of means for integrating these designs to achieve different purposes. These designs and some ways to mix methods effectively for different purposes will be summarized in Figures 14.1 and 14.2 (on pages 319 and 321, respectively).

Case Studies

The **case study** is one of the most frequently used designs in evaluation. It draws heavily on qualitative methods, but can employ both qualitative and quantitative methods. Yin (1994) and Stake (1995), each of whom have written textbooks on the case study method, serve as examples of how evaluators can approach case studies from different perspectives. Stake relies on a more interpretivist approach with a strong qualitative emphasis (see Chapter 8). His interest is in describing and understanding an individual case, while Yin's emphasis is on extending from that case to build knowledge or theory. Yin approaches case studies from a postpositivist tradition, mixing qualitative and quantitative approaches to achieve the three purposes he articulates for case studies: description, explanation, and exploration.

Case studies are particularly useful when the purpose of the evaluation is to describe something—a case—in depth. Very often, evaluations are concerned with exploring the "hows" and "whys" of a program or policy. How did a program achieve certain outcomes in clients? How was the program adapted in the field?

Why did parents develop a charter school? Why do good teachers leave our district? How can we best train first-year teachers? Case studies can be an excellent method for answering these types of questions because they encourage a deeper exploration of the issues, recognizing that there are many different perspectives on each.

While case studies are often used when the purpose of the evaluation is descriptive, they can also be quite successful for examining outcome issues. Consider case studies you have read that illustrated how a program or curriculum was implemented—the factors that influenced program adoption, early stages of implementation, problems encountered, frustrations endured, surprises experienced, adaptations that were made, successes achieved, staff and participant reaction, environmental influences, and the like. Such studies give the reader a real understanding of the program and the many different ways it might be viewed. The voices and perspectives of many different stakeholders involved with the program are heard. Explanatory case studies may explore outcomes describing the links between program actions and outcomes, examining differences among cases to help the reader better understand how outcomes are achieved. Case studies can also be useful in exploring needs of clients or students for an organizational needs assessment. Exploratory case studies may be conducted to identify needs of students, clients, or the community or to explore problems in implementing a program or achieving outcomes. Exploratory case studies are merely less defined and more open-ended than descriptive and explanatory case studies.

The focus of a case study is on the case itself. Such an approach may be particularly appropriate in evaluation when there is a need to provide in-depth information about the *unit*, or case, at hand, and not so much to generalize to a larger population. Because evaluation is typically intended to be situation-specific, a case study design provides the opportunity to discover the unique attributes of an individual case. Generalization to other settings or other times, often the focus of research, is not the goal. Stake (1995) writes: "The real business of case study is particularization, not generalization. We take a particular case and come to know it well, not primarily as to how it is different from others but what it is, what it does" (p. 8). Lincoln and Guba (1985), also prominent advocates of case studies and conducting evaluation in natural settings, argue that the goal is to develop "thick descriptions," or a thorough, complete understanding of the case, to help others understand and judge the program's worth and the context within which it has operated. Yin (1989) notes that concerns about generalizing results from a case study could also be applied to generalizing from a single experiment. Neither cases nor units of analysis are randomly selected in experiments. With each, we generalize not by statistical generalization, but by "analytic generalization" or using the case study to test propositions from a theory. Whether your purpose is thick description or explaining the linkages in a theory, a case study can serve as the appropriate tool.

Case studies are characterized by three features: (1) a focus on a selected case or cases; (2) a desire for in-depth understanding of an issue; and (3) collecting data in many different ways, but with a focus on qualitative methods such as observations, interviews, and the study of existing documents. The first challenging step can be selecting the case. Stake (2000a) observes that a case can be as broad or narrow as desired: "A case may be simple or complex. It may be a child, or a classroom of children, or an incident such as a mobilization of professionals to study a childhood condition" (p. 436). A case might consist of one large unit (a city, a school district, a hospital) or a few small units (classrooms, wards), or individuals themselves (students, clients, managers, providers). Cases might be selected because they are considered "typical" or because they are "unusual." The choice is up to the evaluator and others involved in planning the study, but the rationale for the choices should be clearly articulated.

Some examples may prove useful here: Consider a multisite program in which many sites are struggling to implement a program or achieve certain outcomes, but some have succeeded in adverse circumstances. An evaluator might conduct a case study in one or more of the sites that have succeeded to explore the factors that facilitated that success. Best practices studies, identifying units or organizations that do well at something and describing them intensively, are broader examples of instances in which the case selected is not intended to be typical. One can see such choices in case studies of schools that have received high scores on state standards tests with at-risk kids. Other evaluations may select cases that are typical or may reflect the range of behaviors. An evaluation conducted by one of our authors included case studies of four women substance abusers to learn more about the difficulties they faced and the strategies they used in their transition to the community after staying in a residential substance-abuse facility. In the first example, the case is an organization, a school, that succeeded. In the second example, the cases are individuals and they were selected to represent some typical outcomes.

Unlike quantitative designs, a case study does not have a clearly delineated method. In fact, people even differ in how they label case studies. Some may call it a design; others, a method; others, an approach (Patton, 2002). Stake (1994) has written: "Perhaps the simplest rule for method in qualitative case work is this: Place the best brains available into the thick of what is going on" (p. 242). He writes that the person doing the case study should make use of her observational and reflective skills to obtain a greater understanding of the case at hand.

While the methods used in case studies are not as proscribed as for some other types of designs, case study methods can be characterized by the use of multiple methods and a greater emphasis on qualitative methods such as observations, interviews, and the study of documents. The design is descriptive, but unlike the cross-sectional study or the time-series study, there is an emphasis on depth of description. The methods of the case study may be selected or adapted as the evaluator achieves a better understanding of the case. That is, the design is *responsive* to the case and the circumstances at hand. It is adaptive and continues to adapt until the evaluator believes she has a good understanding of the case. While the focus is on qualitative methods to attain that depth of description and understanding, case studies do make use of quantitative methods as well; surveys, statistical analysis of existing data, and the like, can be used to supplement what the evaluator has learned through observations and interviews. Methods may be selected as the study moves along and the evaluator identifies directions of uncertainty, areas where more information or understanding is needed. The evaluator can then select the method that is appropriate to examine an issue at some stage of the design.

The writing of the results becomes an integral part of the case study as results should be conveyed in a way that "focuses the reader's attention and illuminates meanings" (Guba & Lincoln, 1981, p. 376). Guba and Lincoln describe the case study as "holistic and lifelike. It presents a picture credible to the actual participants in a setting, and it can easily be cast into the 'natural language' of the involved audiences" (p. 376). Such case studies can lead to greater utilization because the report is both more easily understood and more compelling than the typical report. Yin (1989) proposes six structures for writing a case study that can be selected and adapted for the purposes of an evaluation: linear–analytic (akin to a traditional research format); comparative (comparing different cases); theory-building (contrasting findings with a theory or model); suspense structures (beginning with an outcome and proceeding to explain how it was attained); and, finally, unsequenced structures (often used for descriptive evaluations). For more information on case studies, see Stake (1995) and Yin (1994). Lincoln and Guba (1985) discuss the case reporting format, and Hebert (1986) provides an example of the case study in the qualitative style. Stake (1995) presents a very useful example of a case study, with his own commentary, as the last chapter in his book.

Experimental Designs

Anyone who reads the newspaper is familiar with experimental designs, even if the person doesn't know the appropriate labels. Studies on the effectiveness of various drugs or medical treatments reported in the news frequently contrast findings from the group that received the new drug or treatment with those who received a placebo or an older, established treatment. Patients are randomly assigned to the groups. Health-care providers and patients are "blind" to the group they are in. Treatments are delivered, data are collected and analyzed, and conclusions are drawn. A recent study received much attention because it was the first controlled study of its kind. It compared the mood of a group receiving the herbal anti-depressant St. John's Wart with two groups receiving either the commonly used prescription antidepressant or a placebo. While St. John's Wart did not fare well, neither did the prescription drug. The group receiving the placebo reported the most improvement! Such designs are commonplace in the medical literature and we, as health consumers, expect such rigorous, FDA-approved studies.

If such designs are considered appropriate, even desirable, when our health is at stake, why not when the issues are learning, job training, counseling, child care, or the air we breathe? Because applying the medical model without thought to social policy issues is a mistake. Misuses of experimental designs have been legitimately criticized (House, 1990; Johnston & Swift, 1994; Lincoln & Guba, 1985; Patton, 1986). Rejecting such designs out of hand as infeasible, unethical, or uninformative, however, can needlessly limit our bag of tools. The medical model—and experimental designs—have limitations for studying human service programs because human behavior and "treatments" for human behavior are often much more complex and variable than a drug or surgical intervention. A colleague of ours once remarked disparagingly, "This [studying public policy] isn't brain surgery!" To which one of us responded, "No, it's tougher. Human bodies are relatively similar. Behavior is not. So, studying educational and social phenomena is much more difficult!"

Experimental and quasi-experimental designs can be appropriate when the primary purpose of the evaluation is to answer questions of effectiveness by comparing the program outcomes achieved by one program with those of another program that is being actively considered as an alternative. Such decisions arise frequently. Again, in recent news, we have read about the failures of DARE and the successes of Early Head Start. Both of these programs were evaluated using experimental and quasi-experimental designs. Principals ask, "Should we adopt a new drill-and-practice approach to math learning or continue with our hands-on, exploratory curriculum?" Health administrators ask, "Is our new outreach program for pregnant teens resulting in earlier prenatal care than the old method?" To make this choice, these stakeholders want information that compares the outcomes of the two programs in a responsible way. Ideally, the new programs have had time to "work out the kinks" and formative evaluation has been used to monitor program actions and outcomes and work for improvement. After this period of pilot-testing and revising to maximize the model, an outcome study may be appropriate to help administrators and other stakeholders make the summative choice of which program to continue and expand. Such designs are not a magical way to attribute causality. No design can completely prove causality. But these designs, along with theory building and the collection of descriptive information about program implementation, can be quite helpful in demonstrating the effects of various programs. (See Lipsey, 2000, for an argument for using social science methods in evaluation.)

Experimental designs, *if feasible,* are preferable to quasi-experimental designs in that they can counter more threats to the internal validity of the study. Experimental designs include pre-post and posttest-only designs. Each of these designs involves randomly assigning program participants to a group. Through random assignment of a sufficient number of people to each group, experimental designs maximize the probability that the groups are equal on the factors that could influence their response to the program, namely, individual characteristics and attitudes, past history, things going on in their lives currently, and so on. While individuals in the groups are not equal, the groups as a whole are viewed as equivalent. Thus, differences that emerge between the groups on measures taken after the program can be more validly attributed to the program itself rather than to other causes.

Posttest-only designs are the least complicated of the experimental designs and require simply the following. First one must decide what comparisons are desired and meaningful. For example, will the program of interest (e.g., an experimental educational program, which we will call X) be compared to an alternate educational program, Y, that attempts to achieve in some alternate way the same goals as those sought for Program X? Or will students in group X be compared only to those in another group that has received *no* similar or alternate program with goals similar to X?

Second, steps must be taken to assure that those students in the two (or more) comparison groups are similar. If group X contains intellectually gifted students while those in the comparison group had learning disabilities, the experiment would obviously be biased in favor of Program X. To assure comparability, the post-test only design randomly assigns those participating in the experiment to the different groups. This may be accomplished using a random numbers table or computer-generated random numbers. The participants are assigned numbers and those whose numbers appear are assigned to receive the new experimental program. The remaining participants receive the alternative.

Third, one must collect information after the program ends (the posttest) to determine whether differences occurred. The name of the design, posttest-only, does not dictate the measure to be used. Post-treatment measures can be surveys, interviews, observations, tests, or any other measure or measures deemed appropriate for getting a full picture of the outcomes. The term *posttest-only* refers only to the time at which information will be collected. No pretest information is collected with the posttest-only design because it is assumed the two groups are equivalent due to the random assignment of individuals or units (offices, schools, classrooms) to the programs or treatments.

The **pre-post design** is employed when a pretreatment measure can supply useful information. For example, if the groups are small, there may be concern about their equivalence. A pretest can help confirm their equivalence, though only on the measures collected. If there is concern that many participants may drop out of the program, and, thus, scores on the posttest may not represent equivalent groups, pretest scores can be used to examine differences in the two groups as a result of dropouts. For example, dropouts would be a legitimate concern in evaluating a training program for the hard-core unemployed, but would probably not be a concern in a month-long program for fourth graders at a school with stable enrollment. Thus, pretests can provide useful information with small groups or groups in which dropout rates may be high.

Many use pretests as benchmarks to report the change that has occurred in those participating in the program from before the program to its conclusion. These reports are often appealing to stakeholders; however, pre-post comparisons can be misleading because the change from pre to post can be due to the program and/or other factors in the participants' lives (e.g., natural changes that occur with the passage of time, other learning, and intervening events). Instead, the post measure of the comparison group is generally the more appropriate comparison because it better represents what the treatment group would have been like—*at that point in time*—if they had not received the new curriculum or program. In other words, the comparison group experienced the same other factors and passage of time that contributed to change from the pre to the post measure in the group receiving the new program; they simply did not experience the program. So, the difference between the comparison group and the treatment group more clearly reflects the effect of the program than does a comparison of the change from the pre to post measures.

If the decision to be made is whether to deliver a new program or an old one, the comparison group should receive the old intervention, and the stakeholders should focus on the differences between the posttest scores of the two groups. The posttest score of the comparison group represents what the treatment group would have achieved if they had been assigned to that treatment. The real choice for stakeholders is between one program and another, as represented by the post scores of the two groups, not between their previous state and their current state. If, in fact, the choice to be made is between no program and an existing or new one, a comparison group can be constructed to receive no special alternative treatment. The posttest scores of this comparison group will then reflect how participants in the treatment group would have changed if they received no formal treatment at all. (See Cook and Campbell [1979] or O'Sullivan and Rassel [1995] for more discussion of internal validity and experimental designs.)

In response to those who argue that comparative experiments are not feasible in field studies, Cook and Campbell (1979) list several situations when randomized experiments or quasi-experiments are appropriate and possible:

- When lotteries or other chance drawings are expected
- When demand outstrips supply
- When an innovation cannot be delivered in all units at once
- When experimental units can be temporarily isolated
- When experimental units are spatially separated or interunit communication is low
- When change is mandated and solutions are unknown
- When a tie can be broken
- When some people express no preference among alternatives

It is not uncommon for a new program to be costly either in terms of materials or training of personnel to deliver the program. For these reasons, or others, it often is not practical to deliver a new program or curriculum to all students or consumers. In other cases, a new program may be controversial. Some stakeholders, including staff who deliver the program, may disagree on its merits relative to other options or the present mode of delivery. In such circumstances, random assignment to the new treatment can be a viable option.

Many argue against random assignment to treatments on an ethical basis. Such concerns can be very legitimate. Often new programs have been carefully planned, have a firm theoretical foundation, and offer great promise to participants. However, we often fail to consider the ethical issues involved in failing to study the new curriculum, policy, or program thoroughly. Is it ethical to expose people to treatments or programs that may, in implementation, be *less successful* at achieving the goal than the currently accepted method? Is it right to raise the expectations of those in need and then dash them with an untried, untested program? In a time of declining resources for those in need, is it ethical to continue expenditures on an untested approach when these resources could be used to effectively meet needs in proven ways? There are no easy answers to these questions. The consequences of randomization need to be considered carefully for each circumstance. What are the *risks* to each group? How much do we know about the new treatment? About the old? How long will the study period last? Under what circumstances could the data collection be halted and the better treatment delivered to all? Dennis and Boruch (1989) present a set of threshold conditions that should be attained before considering randomized experiments. While their conditions are applied to developing countries, they can be easily extrapolated to other settings. Passamani (1991) provides a thoughtful discussion of the ethics of random assignment, or clinical trials, in medical settings. For more information on implementing experimental designs in the field, their effects on construct validity, and the ethical and personal issues faced by evaluation and program staff in such designs, see Conrad (1994).

Quasi-Experimental Designs

For many evaluations concerned with establishing effects, random assignment is neither feasible nor desirable. In such cases, a **quasi-experimental design** can be more appropriate. These designs do not involve random assignment but can be useful in countering some explanations for change other than the program. The most commonly used quasi-experimental designs are the interrupted time-series design and the nonequivalent comparison group design.

The **interrupted time-series design** involves collecting data many times prior to the program and then many times after its introduction. This design is used frequently when the intervention, or program, is a law or policy that must apply to everyone in the district, city, state, or nation. New clean air standards cannot be randomly assigned to some households and not others. Changes in the laws for prosecuting juveniles cannot be applied to some juveniles and not others. However, for each of these "programs," information is routinely collected on phenomena of interest prior to and after the new laws or standards are imposed. Environmental agencies routinely collect data on air quality; juvenile justice agencies collect such data on juvenile crime. These existing data can be analyzed to assess program effects.

Theoretically, an interrupted time-series design can be used in many settings. In fact, its most frequent application is with existing data that have been collected routinely prior to the intervention. The value of the interrupted time-series study lies in the measures made prior to the intervention. These measures help demonstrate trends or typical variations that occurred *before the program was initiated.* The more measures that can be collected before the policy is implemented, the better one can assess the typical ups and downs of the construct being examined, whether it is high school graduation rates, cancer survival rates, housing costs, or drug arrests. Having established the usual trend, one can then examine the line to determine if the trend changes after the introduction of the program or policy. If so, the change may be due to the program (or some other phenomenon that occurred at the same time). If, instead, the post-measures simply reflect the usual variation, the results would suggest the policy or program had no effect.

Note that we used the word "suggest" in our last sentence. It is possible that the interrupted time-series design can cause a Type II error, failing to show a program effect when there is one. This would occur when the trend line *would* have changed at that point due to some other policy or environmental change, but remains the same because of our new treatment. For example, time-series data in many states showed that increasing highway speed limits from 65 to 75 mph did not increase deaths. However, the increased prevalence of air bags in automobiles at the time may have caused a decline in the trend line if speed limits had not been increased.

Observe that with this type of design establishing the pre-program trend is critical, and this trend can only be estimated by having many data points prior to the intervention. One pre-measure is *not* sufficient. One pre-measure may be an aberration caused by measurement error, an exceptional group or time, or a combination of all three. In fact, new programs are often initiated in response to an extremely poor previous year. The next year may have resulted in improvement by chance because the prior year was atypical. Nevertheless, if you examine data from only the prior year and the first year of the program, the program will look successful, simply because it's moving back to the norm (or regressing to the mean, for the statistically sophisticated!). A current mistake of this nature is the tendency for most states to report changes in scores on school standards based on comparisons only with the previous year. No prior trend is established and, therefore, it is impossible to determine whether the increase or decline is due to real changes in teaching methods, changes in the student population, changes in staff, or measurement error. Yet, the general public and many elected officials believe these annual changes reflect real change in each and every case.

Even when used correctly with ample pre-intervention data, a drawback remains to the interrupted time-series design. A change in the trend line certainly may indicate a program or policy effect, but the change may have been caused by something else occurring at the same time. Let's say we've introduced a program for new teachers to improve retention and use an interrupted time-series design to examine annual turnover of new teachers for the past 15 years. And, let's say that, after two years, our chart shows a decline in turnover compared to the trend prior to the orientation program. This change could be due to our orientation, but what if the economy in our school district had taken a serious downturn during that time and jobs were scarce. The scarcity of jobs may have discouraged new teachers from changing jobs and, thus, improved our retention rate. A related issue: Very often in the public sector, we institute a package of several reforms to deal with a serious problem. This package may help us to address the problem comprehensively, but it hinders us in discovering which aspects of the package worked.

One other caution: An interrupted time-series design is most appropriate with programs that expect a relatively quick change. If the change is gradual, the change in the trend line will be gradual and it will be more difficult to attribute any observed changes to the program. Of course, one can lengthen the time between points of data collection to attempt to have the trend line show a more immediate effect, but the longer the time between points, the more likely it is that other factors may have caused the change.

In summary, consider an interrupted time-series design when the following conditions can be established:

- Random assignment is inappropriate or impractical
- Existing data are available that have consistently measured the construct of interest
- Quite a few data collection points exist to establish a trend prior to the new program or policy
- Few, if any, other factors are anticipated to occur concurrently that could also change the construct
- The program or policy should have a relatively quick impact

A **nonequivalent comparison group design** is similar to the experimental pre-post design, but participants or students are not randomly assigned to groups. Instead, we try to find an existing group very similar to the one that will receive the new program. The pretest is a more important component of this design than it is in the experimental designs because it helps us examine similarities between the groups. Of course, the goal is to establish the equivalence of the groups, if only on the pre-measure. (It would be wise to collect other descriptive data to compare the two groups and further explore their equivalence.) If intact groups in large organizations are being studied (e.g., offices, classrooms, schools, wards) and the program is short-lived, it may be relatively easy to find a comparable comparison group. However, if the organization is small (a single elementary school with three classrooms per grade or a school district with two high schools), it is likely that the different units will have some significant differences. If the program is long, the groups may begin as relatively equal, but other differences may occur through the course of the program (e.g., different teachers or staff with different motivations, skills, and emphases) that could contribute to differences on the final measure. (See McCall, Ryan, & Green [1999] for a useful discussion of nonrandomized constructed comparison groups for evaluating age-related outcomes in children.)

Another quasi-experimental design is the **regression-discontinuity design.** This design is particularly useful when eligibility for the program to be studied is determined by a person's "scoring" above or below a certain point on the eligibility criterion (e.g., high blood pressure or cholesterol levels). Thus, patients may be eligible for a special weight-reduction program based on being at least 30 percent above standard weight guidelines for their height and gender. The design then compares outcomes for these patients with outcomes for people who were not eligible for the program, using regression methods. A "discontinuity" in the line, or a difference in the regression line, for the two groups suggests a program effect. This design can be useful when programs are limited to those most in need or most qualified, such as a program for highly gifted students, and eligibility is determined by a clearly defined cut point. See Trochim (1984) and Reichardt, Trochim, and Cappelleri (1995) for more information on this design.

Shadish, Cook, and Campbell (2002) provide more information on design in general and quasi-experimental designs in particular. One of the newer issues in experimental designs concerns the failure to adequately consider statistical power in planning designs. As a result, Type II errors, or failure to find significant differences between groups when such differences really exist, occur far more frequently than we are aware. Such errors can cause us to reject beneficial programs because we believe they make no difference when, in fact, small sample sizes and/or large group variability may have limited our ability to detect differences. Lipsey (1990) discusses methods for planning designs to avoid such problems.

Some Selected Descriptive Designs

Case studies are often used for descriptive purposes when the desire is to examine an issue from many different perspectives. Two other designs, more quantitative in their approach, can form a part of a case study or can stand alone to provide a quick impression of an issue: the cross-sectional design and the time-series design. Unlike the qualitative case study design, these designs do not provide in-depth descriptions. They are fairly simple designs but are used frequently to answer rather straightforward questions.

The **cross-sectional design** is intended to show a "snapshot in time." A political poll is a common example of such a design. The attitudes collected are considered true for that point in time. Subsequent polls show changes in attitudes. This design typically makes use of a survey approach to collect information on the attitudes, behaviors, opinions, or lives of various groups, either total populations or subgroups sampled from those populations. The purpose of the cross-sectional design is both to describe trends across all groups and to identify any differences among the subgroups. (Recall how political polls, as reported in the media, help us learn both who might win—the overall trend—and which subgroups favor which candidates.) In fact, most organizations occasionally, or routinely, survey their clients to obtain feedback. Annual surveys of parents are mandated in most schools. Hospitals survey former patients. But, such routine practices often don't make full use of the design because they fail to consider the evaluation questions that could be explored by such routine data collection or to identify subgroups that might be of particular interest for analysis.

A cross-sectional design might be used to answer any one of the following questions: A principal asks, "What do parents think of our school? What do they see as the strengths and weaknesses of the school environment, facilities, curriculum, personnel? Do parents differ in their opinions based on the grade their child is in? Their child's performance? Their ethnicity? The parents' education and expectations?" The director of an outpatient unit of a mental health center asks, "How do our clients hear of us? What are their expectations about mental health treatment? What problems typically prompt their first visit? Do these opinions differ by the age, income, education, or ethnicity of clients? By the nature of their presenting problem?" These questions might be posed in the context of a needs assessment or formative evaluation. At this initial stage, the primary interest is in identifying problems or priorities. Further evaluation may move into a case study mode to explore the viability of solutions to problems discovered through the cross-sectional design.

A **time-series design** is intended to demonstrate trends or changes over time. Unlike the interrupted time-series design, the purpose of the design is not to examine the impact of an intervention, but simply to explore and describe changes in the construct of interest. The results of a time-series design can be very useful at the beginning stage of a case study if the evaluator explores with stakeholders their interpretations of the ups and downs exhibited in the results. Their perspectives may point the way to the next steps in data collection.

As with the cross-sectional design, the questions to be answered with a time-series design are relatively simple and straightforward. A health administrator might ask, "Is the number of premature births in our hospital declining?" A high school principal may ask, "Is the proportion of our student body needing ESL classes increasing or decreasing?" A police chief might ask, "What is the trend of juvenile crime in our city? Which juvenile crimes are increasing? Which are decreasing? Which are remaining stable? How do these trends compare with the number of juveniles in our population? Will the number of juveniles remain the same in the next decade?" The latter includes a number of different questions that will help the chief and her staff in planning, but all would be addressed through simple time-series designs. As with interrupted time-series designs, the time-series design generally makes use of existing information in order to obtain enough observations over time. Key decisions involve the time ranges to use (quarterly, semiannually, yearly) and the number of data collection points to obtain. As the evaluator collects information from points increasingly further back in time, she must make sure the data collection methods themselves have not changed. Changes in the manner of data collection or definition of terms (What is a juvenile? What is a felony? Which crimes are recorded? What is an ESL class? What is a premature birth?) can make it appear that there is a change in the phenomenon being studied, when in fact the change is due to a change in the manner in which data are collected or categorized. See O'Sullivan and Rassel (1995) for more information on time-series and cross-sectional designs.

Figure 14.1 summarizes some of the key characteristics of the designs discussed in this section.

Mixed Method Designs

The designs described above, the case study, experimental and quasi-experimental designs, and the cross-sectional and simple time-series designs, are all models or

FIGURE 14.1 *Characteristics of Designs*

Design	Characteristic	Purpose
Case Study	Focus on case	In-depth description, understanding (Stake)
	Multiple measures	Description, explanation, exploration (Yin)
	Qualitative emphasis	
Experimental		
Post-only	Random assignment	Purpose is causal
Pre-post	Random assignment	Dropouts are a concern
Quasi-Experimental		
Interrupted time-series	Examining trend for change/cause	Use existing data, program or policy applies to all, quick effect
Comparison group	Pre-post, intact, similar groups	Have similar comparison group
Other Descriptive		
Cross-sectional	Quantitative, survey	"Snapshot in time" of a large group
Time-series	Examine trend	To look for changes over time

archetypes that the astute evaluator can use to craft a design or designs appropriate for the evaluation questions of interest in a specific evaluation. There is no one design that is best for all settings. A good design is one that matches the evaluation questions developed during the planning phase, the context of the evaluation, and the information needs and values of stakeholders. As evaluation has developed, evaluators have adapted these designs to different settings.

When using mixed methods, the evaluator should consider her purpose or purposes in using those mixed methods and select the design or approach most appropriate for achieving that purpose. As noted earlier in this chapter, Shotland and Mark (1987) and Shadish (1993) have emphasized that, when mixed methods are used for triangulation, methods with different biases should be used. Greene, Caracelli, and Graham (1989) found *complementarity* and expansion were the most common uses of mixed methods. If the purpose is to gain a fuller picture of a construct of interest, complementarity, then the evaluator should consider which facets of the construct she is failing to measure with her initial or firsts measures and identify other approaches to capture the construct. Using in-depth interviews to enhance results from a survey would be a common example. The survey provides breadth, but not depth. The intensive interviews provide depth, but those interviewed are not necessarily representative. Together the two methods shed more light on the issue, for example, reading interests of high school students. *Expansion* designs use different methods to measure different program components. Often quantitative measures are used for outcomes and qualitative measures are used to describe implementation. These designs are common, and do expand our knowledge of the program, but are not necessarily the best use of mixed methods designs because the contrasting methods focus on such different issues. As such, evaluators fail to make use of the unique qualities of different methods through counterbalancing different methods.

Caracelli and Greene (1997) have more recently moved to describing ways in which methods and designs can be integrated across paradigms. They describe two broad classes of designs: component and integrated designs. Triangulation, complementarity, and expansion designs are examples of component designs. In such designs the methods coming from different paradigms (interpretivist and postpositivist) are relatively distinct, coming together only when the evaluator comes to the stage of combining results to draw conclusions. Integrated designs mix methods and paradigms at many different stages. Caracelli and Greene see these designs as more desirable, writing that they "have the potential to produce significantly more insightful, even dialectically transformed, understandings of the phenomenon under investigation" (1997, p. 23).

A common design of this type is the *iterative* design. With an iterative design, the evaluator uses different methodologies, from different paradigms, in sequence with the results of each informing the next stage of data collection and interpretation. Thus, interviews might be conducted to begin tapping the construct and to provide information for constructing a survey or some other paper-and-pencil measure such as a test. This measure could be given to a broader sample of people to further explore perspectives gained from the initial interviews and study the degree to which such views are held across many different people and subgroups. These results might then be used to conduct focus groups or more intensive interviews with subsets of the population tested or surveyed. This stage of data collection can probe for greater understanding of the survey results. Caracelli and Greene describe several effective examples of this and other integrative designs. (See Figure 14.2 for a summary of these designs.)

Sampling

Sampling refers to the method the evaluator will use to select the units (people, classrooms, schools, offices, counties, etc.) to study. In a statewide evaluation of immunization rates, if we were to test only a portion of the children in the state, we would be sampling. If our sample were constructed using some randomized procedure, we might then be able to use the information collected from the sample to make inferences about immunization rates and patterns of the entire target population (in this case, all the children in the state). But, if generalization is not our purpose, using such a mode of sampling would be inappropriate and a different sampling strategy should be used.

Sampling is not necessary in all evaluations. If the population of interest, or the group to which the results of the study will be extended, is small, it would be wise to collect information from the entire group. If the population is large, how-

FIGURE 14.2   *Characteristics of Mixed Method Designs*

Design	Characteristic	Purpose
Component Designs		
Triangulation	Measures same thing w. different biases	To increase construct validity Hope for same results
Complementarity	Measure different facets of same thing	To increase understanding of thing
Expansion	Measure different components of program	To better understand program
Integrated Designs		
Iterative/spiral	Each stage of data informs next	To increase understanding, depth, richness of results
Embedded	Different methods are embedded within each other	"
Holistic	Use program theory or concept mapping as structure for integrating mixed methods throughout	"
Transformative	Mix methods, values, stakeholders Use participatory, empowerment, action-oriented	To transform the dialogue across different stakeholders with ideological differences

ever, sampling can reduce the costs of collecting information. We would never attempt to conduct intensive interviews on 300 clients. Similarly, we would typically not survey 30,000 former graduates. In *basic research* and in *polling*, sampling is almost always appropriate because the population of interest is very large (i.e., all children in the United States, all voters).[1] Evaluators, however, should not immediately assume sampling is called for in all studies, especially if the population is small.

If sampling is required, the evaluator must determine the appropriate sample size. The variability of the phenomenon to be examined and the desired degree of accuracy both affect the sample size. Henry (1990) emphasizes that, in

---

[1]Though random sampling is appropriate in much basic research because the purpose is to extend the results to a much larger population, it is, in fact, rarely used. Scan research journals in various fields and one rarely finds a study in which random sampling was used, much less one in which the sample was selected randomly from the population of interest. When random sampling is used in basic research, the researcher tends to sample from an available subset of the population. In such cases, the random sampling only permits the empirical generalization to the subset from which the sample was drawn. The researcher, then, must use reasoning (logic, argument, statistics comparing the available group to the entire population) to generalize the results to the population of interest. Sampling from the true population of interest (e.g., all four-year-olds in the United States or all children at risk for drug abuse) is generally not feasible.

addition to the statistical techniques for estimating the desired sample size, evaluators should also consider the credibility of the size of the sample to significant stakeholders. He gives an example of a study in which evaluators selected a sample of sixty licensed homes for adults. After collecting detailed data, the evaluators found that the administrators using the study viewed the sample as too small. After further extensive data collection from 240 more homes, the final results were within 3% of the initial results with the smaller sample. The problem, therefore, was not the validity of the sample size, but the credibility of the size to the central audience for the study. Henry cautions, "Prior planning and attention to factors that may serve to undermine sample credibility may thwart undue attacks" (p. 126). His advice and examples illustrate how involvement of significant stakeholders, even on these more technical decisions, is important.

Not all methods of sampling are equally successful. One common method of sampling is haphazard or convenience sampling. With convenience sampling, individuals or other units from whom data will be collected are selected on the basis of accessibility, with little concern for the composition of the sample as a whole. If we were to select the first four people coming into an agency for our sample, regardless of who they were, we would be drawing a convenience sample. Convenience sampling is usually inappropriate. In case studies, convenience sampling is not effective because the researcher does not have the opportunity to carefully define and select her cases to achieve the purposes of her study. In studies designed to generalize the results to a larger population, convenience sampling fails to provide a sample that is representative of the population of interest. Conclusions based on a convenience sample are very likely to be erroneous. Nevertheless, mall surveyors and television "man-on-the-street" interviews seem quite happy with this method!

Judgment or **purposive sampling,** however, is used successfully in case studies. As noted above, with case studies the purpose is not to generalize to a larger group, but rather to understand and explore some issues with a small group, a case or cases. The goal is thorough understanding of that group or case. Efforts that could be spent on drawing a representative sample are wasted; instead, the evaluator's work should be focused on determining the types of cases she wants to explore and how to identify and select those cases. With purposive sampling, a sample is drawn based on particular purposes or judgments. Students who are deemed the greatest discipline problems by teachers might be selected to describe the types of discipline problems teachers encounter. Or a group of "typical" clients in a budget-counseling program might be selected to determine the types of problems these "typical" clients encounter in applying information from the program. When using a case study methodology, the critical issue is to describe the rationale for your sample. What types of students or clients did you select, and why? Were the cases identified through provider or teacher nominations, archival records, peer recommendations, observation, or what other means? Document the procedures and criteria used for selecting cases so that the reader can understand the context. Involve other stakeholders in considering the cases to select. Which cases will best illustrate and add to knowledge on the issue of concern? How can those cases best be identified?

If the evaluator, however, is sampling to save costs and the ultimate desire is to describe a larger group, *probability sampling,* in which each unit in the population has a known probability of being selected, may be in order. With simple **random sampling,** a type of probability sampling, each unit has an equal and independent chance of being selected. Samples drawn in this method, if large enough, are more likely to represent the population than samples drawn through convenience or purposive sampling. Most large assessment projects (e.g., the U.S. National Assessment of Educational Progress [NAEP]) and public opinion polls use probability sampling.

What does probability sampling involve? First, let us define a few terms. A *sampling unit* is an element or collection of elements in the target population. Sampling units could be individuals; classrooms, offices, departments or like units; or entire institutions such as schools, hospitals, or prisons. Care must be taken to select a sampling unit that is consistent with the element about which one would like to make inferences. That is, if we want to draw conclusions about individual schools, we should use schools as the sampling unit, not classrooms or individual pupils.

A *sampling frame* is the list, map, directory, or other source in which sampling units are defined or listed and from which a set of units is selected. If the target population were all small elementary schools (fewer than 200 children) in Iowa, our sampling frame would be a list or directory of those schools. In selecting a sampling frame, the evaluator should consider the degree to which the sampling frame includes all the population of interest. (Are all elementary schools with fewer than 200 children in Iowa included in the list? Have some new schools started since the list was developed?) Conversely, it is important to determine whether the sampling frame includes units that are not currently part of the population of interest. (Does the list contain schools that have grown to be larger than 200 pupils since the publication of the document?) The degree to which the sampling frame includes the entire target population, and no others, greatly influences the accuracy of the sampling process.

To draw a random sample, the evaluator must first define the population of interest for the evaluation and specify the sampling unit. Then, she must find the sampling frame that contains all the population, and no others, in the unit of interest. Some adjustments to the sampling frame may be required to exclude units no longer in the population and add units new to the population. If *simple random sampling* is to be used, the evaluator could use a table of random numbers to select those from whom information will be collected from the sampling frame. Computer programs are also available to assist in this process.

Two common variants of simple random sampling are stratified random sampling and cluster sampling. **Stratified random sampling** is used when the evaluator is interested in examining differences among subgroups in the population, some of which are so small that they may not be represented in sufficient numbers in a simple random sample. (If all subgroups of interest are large, stratifying is unnecessary. Sufficient numbers will be attained through random sampling.) Thus, if an evaluator were examining parents' attitudes about schools, she might stratify the sample on the dimension of whether or not parents had children in special needs classes. Such stratifying would help ensure that such parents are sufficiently represented for the evaluator to be able to confidently report the attitudes of this important subgroup. Often, samples are stratified for race or ethnicity if it is believed that racial or ethnic minorities may have different opinions and they represent only a small proportion of the population. Company surveys might stratify for level of position to make sure that administrators are sampled in sufficient numbers. Stratified random sampling divides the population into "strata" representing the subgroups of interest. Simple random sampling is then used to select units within each strata.

Cluster sampling serves a different purpose and is most commonly used for cost-saving purposes in studies covering rather large geographic regions. Cluster sampling involves drawing a series of random samples of geographic clusters (i.e., blocks or voter precincts rather than individual units). If your population of interest were the entire midwestern United States, simple random sampling would result in extensive travel for each individual unit (household, person) sampled. Cluster sampling can condense that travel and cost by permitting more intense data collection in each geographic area selected. Of course, cluster sampling is *only* useful if the method of data collection requires face-to-face data collection. The costs for mailed surveys or phone surveys would not be reduced through cluster sampling. Random digit dialing has largely replaced traditional sampling methods in conducting phone surveys.

A comprehensive discussion of sampling appears in Henry (1990). We also recommend that the evaluator study the well-designed sampling procedures used by large-scale assessment projects such as the NAEP, or survey studies such as those conducted by the Institute for Social Research at the University of Michigan. Many existing sampling designs can be adopted or adapted by the evaluator.

Figure 14.3 summarizes some key steps for selecting an appropriate sampling method.

Cost Analysis

Most program managers are not econometricians and should not be expected to be skilled in identifying all the financial, human, or time costs associated with programs they operate. That leniency cannot extend to the evaluator, however, for it is her job to bring precise information on costs to the attention of developers, deliverers, and administrators who are responsible for their products or programs. Educators and other public administrators are sometimes faulted for choosing the more expensive of two equally effective programs because the expensive one is packaged more attractively or advertised more widely. The real fault lies with the program evaluation's having failed to consider cost along with the other variables.

FIGURE 14.3   *Checklist for Selecting a Sampling Procedure*

1. Is the design a case study? (If not, proceed to step 2.)
   a. What unit is of interest (individuals, classrooms or offices, organizations)?
   b. How many units are necessary to achieve the desired depth and understanding?
   c. Should the units represent a range of characteristics, a typical unit, or unusual units on one or more dimensions?
   d. What characteristics are of interest in selection?
   e. By what means will the cases be identified?
2. Is generalizing the results beyond the sample a priority?
   a. How would you define the sampling unit (type of unit, critical characteristics)?
   b. Is there a sampling frame that might contain most, if not all, of the sampling units? How can units in the sampling frame that do not represent the sample be eliminated? How can you identify units that may have been omitted from the sampling frame?
   c. Are you interested in examining the responses of small subgroups? If so, consider stratifying to insure obtaining a sufficient number of the subgroup.
   d. Will respondents be interviewed face-to-face? Are they spread apart geographically? If yes to both, consider cluster sampling.
   e. If no to c. and d., consider simple random sampling.

As any insightful administrator knows, sound decision making depends on knowing how much program X will accomplish *at what cost.*

Analyzing costs and benefits for public sector programs can be a complex undertaking. Public administrators, elected officials, and the public at large are very concerned with the cost of public programs today. Thus, cost studies are important. However, it is essential to distinguish among the different types of cost studies that can be conducted. Each type is useful but serves different questions, choices, and program stages. We have found Levin and McEwan's (2001) discussions of cost–benefit, cost-effectiveness, cost–utility, and cost–feasibility analyses to be a useful guide to what is possible.

Cost-benefit analysis is defined as the analysis of well-defined alternatives by comparing their costs and benefits when both costs and benefits are expressed in monetary terms. Each alternative is examined to see whether benefits exceed costs, and the ratios of the alternatives are compared. The alternative with the highest benefit-to-cost ratio is then selected.

Conducting a cost-benefit study essentially involves identifying all costs and all benefits associated with a program and translating any nonmonetary costs or benefits into dollars. While determining all costs and monetizing them (converting them to dollars) can be difficult, monetizing benefits is often more problematic. The outcomes of most public sector programs are difficult to convert to dollar terms. What is the monetary value of better mental health? Clean air? An additional year of education? One less murder? Educational benefits are often translated into projected gains in earnings or into the amount of money one would have to pay for educational services if they were not provided. Other outcomes that contribute to greater longevity (health programs, clean air) or greater productivity (training, better mental health) also make use of earnings to monetize benefits. Benefits for national parks have been monetized by determining the amount people pay to travel to and visit them (Mills, Massey, & Gregersen, 1980). The evaluator is advised to review the literature on cost–benefit studies in the discipline of the program to be evaluated to identify the commonly accepted benefits used and means for converting these benefits to dollars.

The disadvantage in cost–benefit analysis, of course, is that it can be very difficult to translate all benefits into dollar terms. While gains in earnings are one benefit of education, other benefits are accrued through the impact of education on the quality of life and the educational aspirations of the next generation, to name only two. Further, cost–benefit studies can involve quite technical issues, using *discounting* to put all costs in the same time frame ($1,000 in 1950 is not worth the same amount in 1997) and *opportunity* costs to convey the costs of not pursuing other options. (Yes, you may earn more after going to college, but be sure to consider also the income lost due to not working full-time during that period of attending school, and lesser seniority and experience once one enters the job market.) These methods can improve the accuracy of the final ratio but add further to the complexity and estimation or judgment involved in conducting such a study. Levin and McEwan (2001) caution that cost–benefit analysis should only be used "when the preponderance of benefits could be readily converted into pecuniary values or when those that cannot be converted tend to be unimportant or can be shown to be similar among the alternatives that are being considered" (p. 15).

One of the most important things for evaluators to remember, and to convey to stakeholders, about cost–benefit studies is that, in spite of the fact that the study ends with nice, neat numerical ratios, these numbers are quite fallible. Many judgments and estimates are involved in determining the costs and benefits to be included and how to transform these costs and benefits into dollars. Good studies often present several ratios (called "sensitivity analysis") to show how changes in assumptions will change the ratios.

The term *cost–benefit* has become popular and, on more than one occasion, the authors have been asked to conduct a cost–benefit study when, in fact, such a study would not address the information needs of the client. Often, simple cost analyses will suffice to satisfy the client. Given their costs, cost–benefit studies are only cost-effective when stakeholders are trying to make summative decisions about programs with quite different outcomes. Should we rebuild the playground or purchase new books? Which program deserves more funding: public television or children's immunizations? When a choice is to be made among programs with like outcomes, other types of cost studies that do not require monetizing benefits can be more appropriate.

Cost-effectiveness analysis involves comparing the costs of programs designed to achieve the same or similar outcomes. When the task for the administrator or stakeholder is to choose from among several different ways to achieve the same goal, this method would be the correct choice. Like cost–benefit analysis, cost-effectiveness analysis results in a ratio. However, the benefits side of the ratio is not expressed in monetary terms. Instead, it is expressed as one unit of outcome that would be desired for the programs being compared. The outcome might be one additional year of life, one year's increase in reading ability, an employment or college placement, or one less violent crime. The ratio then shows the cost of each program per outcome achieved. Programs can then easily be compared for their cost-effectiveness in achieving the desired outcome.

The advantage of cost-effectiveness analysis is that benefits do not have to be converted to monetary terms. In addition, cost-effectiveness ratios more appropriately reflect the decisions that most administrators have to make, i.e., which program to pursue to achieve a particular goal. However, compared to cost–benefit analysis, there are disadvantages. Only programs with common goals and common measures of effectiveness can be compared using this method. The final ratio does not inform us as to how the program costs are offset by the benefits. In other words, with a cost–benefit ratio, we are provided with information on whether the benefits are more than the costs. We cannot make this assessment with cost-effectiveness ratios. Finally, cost–benefit studies allow us to convey many, if not all, of the benefits in one ratio. Each cost-effectiveness ratio conveys the costs for only one benefit.

Because many programs have multiple goals, judgment is involved in determining the goal to focus on in the ratio. Several ratios may be calculated to reflect the different goals of the programs. A cost-effectiveness study of two reading programs might, quite appropriately, calculate one ratio with the outcome of gains in reading ability and another ratio with the outcome of books read voluntarily in the next year to measure the success of the programs in instilling a desire to read. While several ratios may complicate the decision to be made, such ratios can be useful in conveying the comparative values of programs. An advantage of cost–benefit ratios is that they have the potential to include all program benefits or outcomes on the benefit side of the ratio through monetizing. The cost-effectiveness study must develop different ratios for each benefit. However, if the benefits are difficult to translate to monetary terms and the program has only two or three major outcomes, several cost-effectiveness ratios may be preferable.

Many excellent examples of the use of cost-effectiveness analysis are available. Levin, Glass, and Meister (1987) use cost-effectiveness analysis to compare several different methods of improving math and reading performance in elementary education. They find peer tutoring to be more cost-effective than the options of computer-assisted instruction, smaller classes, and longer days. McBride, Bertrand, Santiso, and Fernandez (1987) demonstrate the use of cost-effectiveness analysis to compare five methods of service delivery for contraceptive services in rural Guatemala. The last two cost-analysis methods are used prior to the implementation of a program. Thus, estimates of costs and benefits are made rather than relying on actual program expenditures and outcomes. These analyses involve even more assumptions than the studies reviewed above but can serve useful needs assessment decisions.

Cost–utility analysis is used to analyze alternatives by comparing their costs and their utility as perceived by users. This method has been used primarily in the health field. Utility can be measured by assessing users' preference for or satisfaction with each option. The results are ratios quite similar to cost-effectiveness ratios except the ratio reflects cost for satisfaction, not effect.

Cost–feasibility analysis concerns only one side of the ratio, the costs. This method is used during the planning phase of a program to determine probable costs. The costs of one program or several alternatives may be estimated to determine which to pursue. Cost–feasibility studies should be conducted before too much has been invested in program development.

We hope this brief discussion of cost analysis provides a sufficient overview to help the reader understand basic approaches and necessary steps. Extensive discussions of cost analysis of education may be found in Levin and McEwan (2001), Scriven (1974a, 1984), and Thompson (1980). Yates (1996) discusses ways to conduct cost-effectiveness and cost–benefit analyses in human service settings and provides useful examples of its application to substance abuse, suicide prevention programs, residential programs, and other settings. Williams and Giardina (1993) provide an interesting discussion of cost–benefit analysis as approached internationally; they include examples from the areas of health and transportation. Layard and Glaister (1994) review methods and problems in cost studies using cases in the environmental, health, and transportation fields. Scott and Sechrest (1992) discuss cost studies from Chen's theory-driven approach. Skaburskis (1987) discusses the ethics and problems of using cost–benefit analysis in studying rapid transit decisions.

CASE STUDY APPLICATION

November 25. I'm beat tonight, having spent all day working on methods for gathering the data we agreed to collect for the Radnor evaluation. Thinking is tiring work.

But the day was productive. I was able to think through the design a little more carefully. While our purpose is generally causal—to demonstrate the effect of the humanities curriculum—an experimental design is not feasible. The program is already going for the year. Too bad, because some of those board members probably would have responded well to that type of evidence. The teachers would have objected to random assignment initially, I suspect, but if I could have had a chance to persuade them that this is the best way to show the advantages of their program *and* that the students taking the traditional approach could take the humanities curriculum next semester, I think it could have worked. But time is a problem! So, a quasi-experimental design is my best solution for that component of the evaluation. An interrupted time-series design is out; there are no existing data on the issues we're concerned with. I'll have to compare the program with performance in some similar schools. The nonequivalent comparison group design will have to do. I'll have to have another look at that Welsh Valley Middle School in the next school district. Radnor is the only middle school in its district, but the Welsh Valley district has similar demographics among its students and teachers, but hasn't tried a special humanities program. It might work.

Many of the evaluation questions concerning the content of the curriculum, the instructional methods used, and community attitudes are descriptive. A lot of people simply don't understand what this program is about. Different stakeholders hold conflicting views about what schools are supposed to do and what education is all about. We need a case study to really stimulate dialogue between these groups about the nature of the program portraying these multiple perspectives. Our unit of analysis, of course, is the program itself, but I'm going to select a few classes to study. I don't know whether to focus my case on a few teachers and how they have changed their teaching or a few students and how they have changed and learned. I'm going to talk with the advisory group about that on my next visit or in a conference call with them. I'd like to do some observations of the humanities classes and then select some teachers or students or both for some intensive interviews and follow-up. I don't need to plan this too intensively at this stage. I might start with some interviews of a few teachers and recent graduates and use an iterative design to consider the next phase. But, I don't want to get ahead of myself here. The advisory group will be a big help in conceptualizing this case study and helping select cases because they know the territory.

Author Comments.   Many people underestimate the feasibility of experimental designs. In this case, time is a problem. But, given the importance of the issue and the controversy surrounding it, many audiences might have been willing to accept a short-term, one-semester random assignment of students to the options to permit a more fair comparison than the nonequivalent comparison group design will allow. Because there's only one middle school in the town, it at least contains all the middle-school students. In towns where there are two or three middle schools, people sometimes want to use one of the other middle schools for a comparison, but there are almost inevitably demographic differences across schools. If the adjacent school district is a similar suburban or small town, its single middle school may be comparable.

Like many evaluation studies, most of the questions of interest do not call for a complicated causal design. I've found that the vast majority of questions stakeholders want answered are descriptive: What was the program like? Was it implemented as planned? What changes were made? What did participants think of it? What does the public (or other stakeholders) think of the program? How did it affect teachers' approach to learning? Students' perspectives on society and learning? Policy makers might argue that, while the majority of questions evaluations respond to are descriptive, the *most important* ones for their uses are causal. And, depending on the decision, that might be the case. For summative decisions about ending, continuing, or expanding programs, one of the most important criteria is certainly whether the program has the intended effect. However, politicians and administrators are not immune to public opinion. If all governmental decisions were based on whether programs achieved their intended effects, we would undoubtedly have quite different programs. Unfortunately, those making the decisions are faced with a public who wants decisions based on effectiveness *and* what they believe in or want. So, values are a very important influence. Because influential supporters can be found for every existing government program, results based on causality are often secondary concerns.

For *formative* decisions, however—which many evaluations serve—descriptive questions are often the most useful. I need to remember that the board hired me to make a decision about continuation, but there's a critical need for the evaluation to stimulate a dialogue about what middle-school education is about at Radnor. Using an iterative case study design for exploratory purposes will help us both describe the program and explain some of the outcomes, or absence of outcomes. Even if the board ends the program, the discussion the case stimulates will help in planning curricula at Radnor in the future.

> *November 25 (continued).* I've also given some thought to sampling strategies. For questions concerning student outcomes, the population is too small to draw a sample of students in the Radnor humanities program. We'll have to collect data from each student for questions concerning learning. However, purposive sampling can be used in answering some of the other questions, especially those addressed by the case study.
>
> We don't have the budget to conduct interviews with every student. If we focus on students, which I would like for at least some cases, I think we should select the students for interviews based on teacher recommendations and scores on some of the achievement measures. I'd like to interview some students who are doing well in the program and others who are doing poorly, to get their reactions. In sampling classroom sessions to observe, because I have a concern about whether the instructional methods being used are sufficiently interactive and not simply didactic lectures, I would like to select sessions that should have much interaction and instruction geared to high-level objectives. I'll look over the curriculum and also ask the external reviewers to recommend some sessions they think should be most interactive.
>
> Probability sampling for the community surveys to parents and other stakeholders will work; however, I think stratified sampling will be necessary. Because the number of community leaders is small, relative to the other groups, I will probably survey all of them and analyze their data separately. However, I want to stratify for the other groups to make sure I get a sufficient number of questionnaires back from parents with students in the program and the minority population. Radnor has relatively small Asian and Hispanic populations. Because the curriculum deals with diversity, I want to make sure I get enough returns from these groups to determine accurately their responses. I considered using the student directory as the sampling frame so I can use surnames to identify Hispanic and Asian students and their parents. However, reflecting on how diverse our culture has become, I realized this wouldn't work—not all people have last names that match their ethnicity. Perhaps I'll just ask the school to give me names of all children and their ethnic identification. Schools are required to keep that. I'll use the enrollment lists for the humanities classes to identify the parents with students enrolled.

Author Comments.   When groups are small, as with the students enrolled in the program, it is best to collect information from all of them. However, when data collection becomes costly, as with interviews or observations, sampling is necessary. Some might think that random sampling should always be used. However, random sampling for interviews and observations could result in data that are representative but not very useful for the intended purpose. The purpose in the interviews and observations is to enhance our understanding of the effects of the program and how it accomplishes those effects. Thus, selecting students who have done well and poorly will help in exploring these issues. One must be careful not to assume that these results can be generalized to all students.

Some might think that selecting those sessions *most likely* to have interactive activities is biasing the study. It certainly won't give us a representative sample. However, that's not our purpose. Some sessions don't lend themselves to interaction. Our concern is whether those sessions *most likely to have interaction* really do have it. We could waste a lot of time observing a random sample of sessions and find nothing interactive going on in most. Instead, we can observe those that are most likely to include such activities. If they don't, it's unlikely that others will. If they are interactive, it shows it can be done and can provide information for those teachers in the program struggling to encourage interaction.

Major Concepts and Theories

1. Evaluators use many designs and methods in their evaluation studies. The choice should be based on the methods that are most appropriate for answering the question at hand. Often, that requires multiple methods.

2. The evaluator chooses among experimental, quasi-experimental, and descriptive designs to consider how to structure the study. Different designs may be used to address the different questions of the study. Causal questions are often addressed using experimental or quasi-experimental designs, although case studies may be used to accumulate evidence for causal relationships. Experimental designs, involving random assignment, may be used when the stakes are high, establishing causality by empirical means is preferred, and random assignment is possible. Quasi-experimental designs can be useful when random assignment is difficult or inappropriate. Interrupted time-series designs are commonly used when existing data are available and the program is a policy or law that applies to everyone.

3. Descriptive designs are the most common design in evaluation and serve many useful purposes. Cross-sectional designs provide useful quantitative information on large numbers of individuals and groups. Case studies are invaluable for exploring issues in depth, providing "thick descriptions" of programs in implementation, different outcomes, contextual issues, and needs and perspectives of various stakeholders.

4. Newer components designs encourage use to consider our purposes in using mixed methods. These designs include expansion, iterative, and transformative designs. Each uses mixed methods for different purposes.

5. To answer most evaluation questions, data will be gathered from the entire population because the population of interest is relatively small and external validity, or generalizability, beyond the group of interest is not a priority. Methods of random sampling can be used when the group is large and generalizability is important. Purposive sampling is useful when information is being collected from small numbers of individuals or units. In these cases, the purpose is not generalizability, but description and generation of new ideas.

6. Cost studies help determine if the program outcomes are worth the cost. The most common methods are cost–benefit analysis, used to compare programs with different outcomes, and cost-effectiveness analysis, which can be useful in comparing the costs of programs with like outcomes.

Discussion Questions

1. What designs are most commonly used in your field? What are the strengths and weaknesses of these designs? Having read about many different types of designs, which do you think could be used more frequently in your organization?

2. Some people argue that random assignment is unethical, that everyone should receive the benefits of a new program. What are the arguments against this position? In what circumstances would you feel comfortable with random assignment? Not comfortable? Why?

3. Compare and contrast convenience sampling, purposive sampling, and random sampling. Give an example of when you would use each.

Application Exercises

1. Recheck your evaluation plan worksheets from Chapter 13. Are there plans that you would like to change, using what you just learned in this chapter? Would you want to reconsider design or sampling issues? Add cost-related questions? Approach things a little differently?

2. Consider a problem or issue in your organization that is currently controversial. Which design or mix of designs would be most appropriate to address that issue? What evaluation question(s) would your design answer? How would you implement the design?

3. Find a cost–benefit study in your field. Read it and consider the assumptions made. How were benefits quantified? What costs were considered? Whose perspective was used in the ratio (the client, the public)? Were sensitivity analyses conducted? What types of decision was the study to serve? Would cost-effectiveness analysis have been a more appropriate approach?

4. Find an evaluation study that uses one or more of the evaluation designs or sampling strategies reviewed in this chapter. How does the method or methods shed light on the program? What types of questions do the methods answer? (Example: Read "Of snakes and circles: Making sense of classroom group processes through a case study," a classic case study by Valerie Janesick published in *Curriculum Inquiry, 12,* pp. 161–185, in 1982.)

5. Read Chapter 2, "Crafting Mixed-Method Evaluation Designs" by Caracelli & Greene in Greene, J. C., & Caracelli, V. J. (Eds.), (1997), *Advances in mixed-method*

evaluation. (See citation below.) Use Caracelli and Greene's framework to critique your own evaluation plan as developed in Question 1 and the study you reviewed in Question 4. What is the primary purpose of your evaluation? Of the one you critiqued? How would you modify your design, or the one you read, based on Caracelli and Greene's discussion and examples?

Relevant Evaluation Standards

The evaluation standards we see as relevant to this chapter's content are the following. These standards are described in Chapter 18.

U3–Information Scope and Selection   P4–Human Interactions
U4–Values Identification   P5–Complete and Fair Assessment
F1–Practical Procedures   A1–Program Documentation
F2–Political Viability   A3–Described Purposes and Procedures
F3–Cost-Effectiveness   A5–Valid Information
P3–Rights of Human Subjects   A10–Justified Conclusions

Suggested Readings

Denzin, N. K., & Lincoln, Y. S. (Eds.). (2000). *Handbook of qualitative research*. Thousand Oaks, CA: Sage.

Gall, M. D., Borg, W. R., & Gall, J. P. (1996). *Educational research: An introduction* (6th ed.). White Plains, NY: Longman.

Greene, J. C., & Caracelli, V. J. (Eds.). (1997). *Advances in mixed-method evaluation: The challenges and benefits of integrating diverse paradigms.* New Directions for Program Evaluation, No. 74. San Francisco: Jossey-Bass.

Henry, G. T. (1990). *Practical sampling.* Newbury Park, CA: Sage.

Levin, H. M., & McEwan, P. J. (2001). *Cost-effectiveness analysis: Methods and applications.* Thousand Oaks, CA: Sage.

O'Sullivan, E., & Rassel, G. R. (1995). *Research methods for public administrators* (2nd ed.). White Plains, NY: Longman.

Shadish, W. R., Cook, T. D., & Campbell, D. T. (2002). *Experimental and quasi-experimental designs for generalized causal inference.* Boston, MA: Houghton Mifflin.

Stake, R. E. (1995). *The art of case study research.* Thousand Oaks, CA: Sage.

15

Collecting Evaluative Information: Data Sources and Methods, Analysis, and Interpretation

Orienting Questions _____

1. What are the strengths and weaknesses of different sources of data? Different methods of collecting data?

2. What considerations are important in planning our procedures for collecting, organizing, and storing data?

3. How can the results obtained from qualitative and quantitative methods be synthesized?

4. How does analysis differ from interpretation? Who should be involved in interpreting results?

In the previous chapters we described how evaluators work with stakeholders to make some important decisions about what information needs to be collected, and possible designs and sampling strategies that can be used to collect such information. In this chapter we discuss the next choices involved in data collection: selecting sources of information and methods for collecting it; planning procedures for gathering the data; and, finally, collecting, analyzing, and interpreting the results.

Just as with design and sampling, there are many important choices to be made. The selection of methods is influenced by the nature of the questions to be answered, the perspectives of the evaluator and stakeholders, the characteristics of the setting, budget and personnel available for the evaluation, and the state of the art in data collection methods. Nevertheless, using mixed methods continues to be helpful to obtain a full picture of the issues. Remember, the evaluator's bag of tools is much larger than that of the traditional, single-discipline researcher because he is working in a variety of natural settings, answering many different questions, and working and communicating with stakeholders who hold many different perspectives. As in Chapter 14, we will discuss critical issues and choices to be made at each stage, along with references to more detailed treatments of each method.

Before discussing specific methods, we will again comment briefly on the choice between qualitative and quantitative methods, in this case referring specifically to methods of collecting data. Few, if any, evaluation studies would be complete if they relied solely on either qualitative or quantitative measures.

As noted in Chapter 14, we believe that the evaluator should select the method that is most appropriate for answering the evaluation question at hand. He should consider the best source for the information, which can usually be identified by asking, "Who knows the most about the issue to be addressed? Who is in possession of the information?" Having chosen the source, he should select the most appropriate method for collecting information from that source. The goal is to identify the method that will produce the highest quality information, provide the most insight into the program, be most informative to stakeholders, involve the least bias and intrusion, and be both feasible and cost-effective to use.

Qualitative methods such as content analysis of existing sources, in-depth interviews, focus groups, and direct observations, as well as more quantitative devices such as surveys, tests, and telephone interviews should all be considered. Each of these, and other methods more difficult to categorize will be discussed. In practice, many methods are difficult to classify as qualitative and quantitative. Some interviews and observations are quite structured and are analyzed using quantitative statistical methods. Some surveys are very unstructured and analyzed using themes that make the data-gathering device more qualitative in orientation. Our focus will not be on the paradigm or label attached to the method, but, rather, on how and when each method might be used and the nature of the information it generates.

Common Sources and Methods for Collecting Information

Existing Documents and Records

The evaluator's first consideration for sources and methods of data collection should be existing information, or documents and records. We recommend considering existing information for three reasons: (1) using existing information can be considerably more cost-effective than original data collection; (2) such information is *nonreactive* or not changed by the act of collecting or analyzing it; other methods of collecting information typically affect the respondent and may bias the response; (3) way too much information is already collected and not used sufficiently. In our excitement to evaluate a program, we often neglect to look for existing information that might answer some of the evaluation questions.

Documents include personal or agency records that were not prepared specifically for evaluation purposes. **Records,** in contrast, are official documents or statistics prepared for use by others (Lincoln & Guba, 1985). Records are typically collected more carefully because they are intended for use by others. On the other hand, documents, because of their more informal or irregular nature, may be better at revealing the perspectives of various individuals or groups. Content analyses of minutes from meetings; correspondence between teachers, principals, and parents; manuals of state educational standards; lesson plans or hospital charts can help identify and clarify values in an objective way no other source can match. Guba and Lincoln (1981) also distinguish between documents and records because of their different uses. Records are typically used statistically, for tracking, such as employment records or data from the U.S. Census Bureau or county Departments of Social Services. Documents, because of their nature, generally require more qualitative methods for analysis, such as content analysis of a therapist's notes or of the minutes of a staff meeting. Evaluators should actively consider using existing textual documents as a data source. Such documents can include newspaper articles, proposals, annual reports, curricula, texts, and other publications. Text documents can be scanned onto the computer and analyzed with existing qualitative software using content analysis procedures. (See Analysis of Qualitative Data at the end of this chapter.)

Remember that, while existing information can be cheaper, the cost will not be worth the savings if the information is not valid for the purposes of the *current* evaluation study. Unlike data collected originally for the study, this information has been collected for other purposes. These purposes may or may not match those of your evaluation. (See Chapter 13 for a discussion of existing data and records which can be useful to evaluators.)

Other perspectives on using existing data are offered by Chelimsky (1985), who discusses the use of existing statistical data in national studies and describes concerns over funding cuts for maintaining such data, and Elder, Pavalko, & Clipp (1993), who describe ways for using archival data to study people's lives.

Observations

Observations are essential for almost all evaluations. At minimum, such methods would include site visits to observe the program in operation and making use of one's observational skills to note contextual issues in any interactions with stakeholders. Observation can be used more extensively to learn more about the program operations and outcomes, participants' reactions and behaviors, interactions and relationships among stakeholders, and other factors vital to the study. Observation methods for collecting evaluation information may be quantitative or qualitative, structured or unstructured, depending on the approach that best suits the evaluation question to be addressed.

Unstructured Observations.   Unstructured methods are especially useful during the initial phase of the evaluation. The evaluator should make use of his observational skills to note critical features during his first interactions with stakeholders. Jorgensen (1989) writes:

> the basic goal of these largely unfocused initial observations is to become increasingly familiar with the insiders' world so as to refine and focus subsequent observation and data collection. It is extremely important that you record these observations as immediately as possible and with the greatest possible detail because never again will you experience the setting as so utterly unfamiliar (p. 82).

Unstructured observations remain useful throughout the evaluation if the evaluator is alert to the opportunities. Every meeting is an opportunity to observe stakeholders in action, to note their concerns and needs, and their methods of interacting with others. If permitted, informal observations of the program being evaluated should occur frequently. Such observations give the evaluator a vital picture of what others (e.g., participants, deliverers, administrators) are experiencing, as well as the physical environment itself. Each member of the evaluation staff should be required to observe the program at least once. Those most involved should observe frequently to note changes and gain a greater understanding of the program itself. Too many evaluations occur with the evaluator only having a brief glimpse of the program in action or, worse yet, a paper description of the delivery model. When two or more members of the evaluation team have observed the same classes, sessions, or activities, they should discuss their perspectives on their observations. All observers should keep notes to document their perceptions at the time. These notes can later be arranged into themes as appropriate. (See Fitzpatrick and Fetterman [2000] for a discussion of an evaluation with extensive use of program observations or Fitzpatrick and Greene [2001] for a discussion of different perceptions by observers and how these can be used.)

Structured Observations.   Structured and quantitative observation methods become useful when the evaluator desires to observe specific behaviors or characteristics. What specific behaviors or characteristics might be observed? For many public sector programs, critical characteristics may be *physical* in nature: the size and arrangement of classrooms, park maintenance, road quality, playground facilities, library collections, physical conditions and/or density of program facilities, and so forth. Other observations can involve *interactions* between program deliverers and participants: teacher–student interactions, teacher–administrator interactions, student–administrator interactions, physician–nurse–patient interactions, social worker–client interactions, therapist–client interactions, receptionist–client interactions, and so on. Of course, many such observations may be confidential or require informed consent, and the evaluator should be aware of any ethical violations that observations may produce.

A final category of interactions involves participants' *behaviors.* What behaviors might one observe? Imagine a school-based conflict-resolution program designed to reduce playground conflicts. Observations of playground behaviors provide an excellent method for observing outcomes. Imagine a new city recycling program for which there are questions about the level of interest and nature of participation. The frequency of participation and the amount and type of refuse recycled can be easily observed. Students' attention to task has been a common measure observed in educational research. While many programs focus on outcomes that are difficult to observe, i.e., self-esteem, drug-abuse prevention, many others lead to outcomes that can be observed. This is particularly the case when the target audience or program participants are congregated in the same public area (e.g., hospitals, schools, prisons, parks, or roads).

Structured methods of observation typically involve using checklists or forms for recording observations, often called **observation schedules.** Simon and Boyer (1974) have collected observation instruments that may be used to study educational processes. As with attitude measurement, the procedures required for developing good observation checklists and schedules can be complex and costly. Whenever quantitative observation data are needed, we advise reviewing the literature for existing measures and adapting an instrument that already exists. Other concerns in structured observation involve training observers, insuring inter-rater reliability among observers, selecting sites and participants for observation, and avoiding reactivity, or changes in the participants, due to their being observed. Structured observations can also be a costly endeavor if a large number of observations are desired or if participants are geographically dispersed. Sechrest (1985) also discusses instances in which structured observations can be useful and describes the means for using these methods in the field. He notes examples with evaluations of the performance of emergency medical technicians and the implementation of programs for developmentally disabled persons. For more information on structured observations see Greiner (1994).

Qualitative Observation Methods.   Qualitative observation depends less on available instruments and more on the evaluator or observer. Checklists may be used, but typically they are less structured. Denzin (1978) has distinguished among the following arrangements for qualitative observation: the complete participant, the participant as observer, the observer as participant, and the complete observer. These terms convey in words the extent to which the observer may become, or desire to become, involved in the program itself. The observer-as-participant role is frequently taken in anthropological research, but may also be used in evaluating, for example, adult learning programs when the evaluator needs to experience the curriculum as a participant. An observer in a training program may often choose the observer-as-participant role to minimize trainees' reactivity to the observation. The assistant in a focus group, however, is typically the complete observer, making no effort to blend in with the group, but instead focusing on carefully observing the verbal and nonverbal cues of the participants. One should carefully consider which role will be most appropriate for collecting the desired information.

In circumstances where those being observed will be inhibited or otherwise influenced by the observation, more participative roles can be desirable. Such participation can also help the observer appreciate the position of those being observed.

Guba and Lincoln (1981) make the following recommendations regarding the means for organizing and recording one's observations:

1. *Running notes:* a pad may be used to jot down observations as they occur
2. *Field experience log or diary:* detailed notes on a particular concern, such as how an administrator organizes a staff meeting or how a staff member delivers a service to a client
3. *Notes on themes:* detailed notes on a particular theme, such as how teachers work together to revise a curriculum or how participants respond to a particular part of the program
4. *Chronologs:* a step-by-step running account over a unit of time (for example, a day)
5. *Context maps:* a diagram of the context in which observations take place
6. *Taxonomies or category systems:* predetermined categories for which instances are sought in open-ended fashion
7. *Schedules:* specified place, times, duration of observation, and method of notation for the observation
8. *Sociometrics:* relational diagrams indicating social intercourse
9. *Panels:* periodic observations of the same people over time
10. *Debriefing questionnaires:* completed by the observers, not the subjects of the observation
11. *Unobtrusive methods:* use of concealed devices or indirect measures

The stages of qualitative observation often include: (1) thorough preparation through reading or "chatting" with informants; (2) articulating the purpose of your observations; (3) looking *at* (not *for*) what occurs; (4) listening; (5) asking questions (*after* listening and observing); (6) assimilating and synthesizing information; (7) checking working hypotheses; and (8) triangulating, confirming, and cross-checking.

Let us focus for a moment on what we mean by these steps. First, as with all evaluation, talk with stakeholders and read documents and records to learn more about what you might observe and why. What do they hope to learn from the evaluation? Next, articulate to yourself the purposes of your observation. These purposes might be relatively unstructured: to see what the classroom looks like, to watch what patients or clients do during the program. Or, they may be more pointed: to examine how trainees interact in a small group and whether a leader emerges or groups remain leaderless. In any case, with the purpose articulated, one can then go observe. Point three is important: Look *at* not *for* what occurs. Observe the clients or group participants. What happens? Who speaks first? What does he say? What is his tone? Does he make eye contact? What other body language occurs? What is the response? Take detailed notes of what you are seeing. Don't look *for* "friendliness" or "warmth." Look *at* the people interacting and note your observations. Listen to what occurs. If you are surprised by what you observe, ask questions either of those observed or those knowledgeable about their actions. Assimilate and synthesize what you've learned. Look at your notes across many observations. What trends do you observe? How do these match your expectations? Those of others? Finally, seek other data to confirm or cross-check your hypotheses. For more information on unstructured observational methods see Jorgensen (1989), Adler and Adler (1994), Patton (2002), and Angrosino and Mays de Perez (2000).

Site Visits.   A special category of observational methods is the **site visit,** when such a visit constitutes the primary method of evaluation. This method is a primary example of the application of the expertise-oriented evaluation approach discussed in Chapter 7. Regulatory agencies, such as accrediting bodies, frequently use site visits as a method for evaluation or a requirement for funding. Though most frequently used for summative evaluation, or for educational or financial audits, site visits can also be very useful for formative evaluation (Worthen & White, 1987). Stake has noted that, although site visits have been criticized as observers frequently see the best sides of programs, site visits remain an excellent method of evaluation because they make use of "the most sensitive instruments available—experienced and insightful [people]" (Stake, 1970, p. 193). He recommends using training of site visitors and careful planning of observations to strengthen the process.

Inadequate preparation limits the usefulness of many site visits. Completing the following activities will greatly enhance the success of the visit itself.

1. *Identifying specific information needed*
2. *Developing evaluation questions to be posed during on-site interviews*
3. *Developing on-site instruments* (for example, interview forms, checklists, or rating scales)
4. *Selection of on-site visitor(s)*
5. *Previsit communications and arrangements*
6. *Conducting the on-site evaluation visit,* considering:
   a. Amount of time to be spent on site
   b. An initial on-site team meeting, prior to meeting with on-site administrators or staff, to reemphasize the purpose, procedures, and expected products of the visit
   c. An initial briefing by site administrator(s) and/or staff to orient the team to specific nuances or idiosyncratic information not readily available in previsit materials
   d. Efficient interviewing and observation by splitting the team up to cover more activities or interviewees, having the entire team together only for key events or interviews with key personnel
   e. Interspersed team meetings to debrief and share impressions, and a final team formulation of their overall evaluation
   f. Exit interview with the site administrator(s) and, if appropriate, site staff
7. *Writing, disseminating, and using the final report of the on-site evaluation.*

For a comprehensive, detailed discussion of on-site evaluation guidelines and procedures, evaluators are referred to Worthen and White (1987). That text includes examples of on-site evaluation interview forms, rating scales, previsit information forms, team-training materials, and sample exit and final reports.

Surveys

Surveys (sometimes referred to as questionnaires)[1] are often used in evaluation to measure attitudes, opinions, behavior, life circumstances (income, family size, housing conditions, etc.) or other issues. Braverman (1996), in his review of surveys in evaluation, notes that, "Surveys constitute one of the most important data collection tools available in evaluation" (p. 17). Surveys can be administered face-to-face through oral questioning, by telephone, or in paper-and-pencil format delivered through the mail or in person. (This section will focus on paper-and-pencil surveys. Subsequent sections will describe differences when surveys are administered by telephone or face-to-face.)

Henry (1996) has noted that evaluators tend to use surveys to measure relatively small and specific groups, for example, students or clients served, or groups that might be served. He argues for wider use of surveys of the general public in evaluation to involve the public further in policy issues and improve democratic discourse. Those of us who complain that the public is misinformed by the media about our work might take his recommendation to heart. Henry also addresses how surveys of the public could be used to: (1) help frame evaluation questions during the planning stage; (2) provide a context for the recommendations of the evaluation by informing policy makers of likely public reaction; and (3) communicate evaluation information to the public. Certainly, most organizations make use of satisfaction surveys with clients, parents, and the like. Often these are conducted in a rote and superficial way. We should both consider surveying other audiences for input and make wise use of the surveys we routinely conduct to retrieve more than general satisfaction information.

Most surveys solicit relatively structured responses and are typically analyzed statistically. Item types include open-ended items for which content analysis is used; short-answer open-ended items (e.g., number of children); multiple-choice items; items with adjectival responses (e.g., rating items using a five-point scale of excellent [1] to poor [5]); items with adverb responses (always, frequently, etc.); and Likert-scale items, to be discussed later in this section.

As with any type of information to be collected, the evaluator should first consider whether there are existing questionnaires that would be appropriate to use in the current study. *The Mental Measurements Yearbook* series has published independent reviews of commonly used tests and other measures for many years. The fourteenth edition (Plake & Impara, 2001) includes reviews of 430 measures including achievement tests, and personality, vocational, and behavioral measures.

---

[1]*Survey* more appropriately refers to the general method, while *questionnaire, interview protocol,* and the like refer to instruments used to collect the actual data.

The Handbook of Tests and Measurement in Educational and the Social Sciences presents measures on topics ranging from change, conflict, self-esteem, stress, burnout, supervisors' behavior, teacher attitudes, job satisfaction, leadership, and so on (Lester & Bishop, 2000). This handbook includes the actual items for each measure as well as references, commentary, and reliability and validity information. Another useful resource is the *ETS Test Collection Catalogue* (1991), which reviews 16,850 tests and measurement devices over five volumes. Volumes are devoted to achievement; vocational measures; measures for special populations; cognitive, aptitude, and intelligence measures; and attitude scales. The volume on attitudes presents 1275 measures on a wide variety of issues including multicultural education, student attitudes toward school, health care professionals' opinions of organizational effectiveness, teachers' attitudes towards principals, managers' opinions of management style, organizational climate, attitudes toward computers, and so forth. The ETS Test Collection is also on-line. Users can search through over 20,000 tests and research measures (www.ets.org/testcoll/index.html). Another way to learn of recent, commonly accepted measures is through the review of literature conducted by the evaluator during the planning stage. Note the measures used by other researchers and evaluators in these studies and consider their appropriateness for your own purposes.

When the purpose of the survey is to measure opinions, behaviors, attitudes, or life circumstances quite specific to the program to be evaluated, the evaluator is likely to be faced with developing his own instrument. In this case, we recommend developing a design plan for the questionnaire analogous to the evaluation design used for the entire evaluation. In the first column, list the questions (not the item) to be answered by the survey. That is, what questions should the results of this survey answer? In the second column, indicate the item type(s) that should be used to obtain this information. A third column may be used after items are developed to reference the numbers of the items that are to answer this question. A fourth column can then specify the means of analysis. Figure 15.1 provides an illustration. This design then becomes a guide for planning the survey and ana-

FIGURE 15.1   *Sample Design Plan for Questionnaire*

Question	Item Type	Item Number	Analysis
1. What is clients' overall opinion of the agency?	Likert 5-point scale	2–20	Descriptive for each item and total score
2. How did clients first learn of the agency?	Multiple-choice	21	Percentages
3. What type(s) of services do they receive from the agency?	Checklist	22–23	Percentages
4. Do opinions differ by type of service required?		Score on 2–20 with 22–23	t-tests and ANOVA, explore

lyzing the information obtained. It helps the evaluator to make sure he includes a sufficient number of items to answer each question. (Some questions need more items than others.) The design also helps avoid items that sound interesting but, in fact, don't really address any of the evaluation questions. The evaluator may decide to include such items, but their purpose should be further explored. Items that do not answer a question of interest lengthen the questionnaire and show disrespect for the time and privacy of the respondent.

In selecting a type of item, consider that many variables can be measured with several different item formats. Yet attitudes are probably most appropriately measured with **Likert-scale items.** These items consist of sentences that reflect an attitude on the construct of interest. Responses are made on a "strongly agree—strongly disagree" continuum. Behaviors are perhaps best measured with multiple-choice items (to select a behavior) or adverbial items (to report frequency of behaviors), while opinions might best be obtained by using adjectival items (for ratings of favorability) or multiple-choice items (for preference of options). Information concerning life circumstances might best be measured with multiple-choice items (presenting numeric ranges, alternatives, or yes–no responses) or short-answer, open-ended items. If the questionnaire is to be mailed, open-ended items should be used sparingly unless the audience is quite motivated; requiring much writing can greatly decrease the response rate. Nevertheless, open-ended items at the conclusion of the questionnaire can provide useful additional information and give the respondents an opportunity to voice alternative views.

Careful development of the questionnaire draft, instructions, and cover letter (if distributed by mail) then follow. A first draft of the questionnaire should meet these criteria:

1. *Sequencing questions*
   a. Are later responses biased by early questions?
   b. Does the questionnaire begin with easy, unthreatening, but pertinent questions?
   c. Are leading questions (ones that "lead" to a certain response) avoided?
   d. Is there a logical, efficient sequencing of questions (e.g., from general to specific questions; use of filter questions when appropriate)?
   e. Are closed- or open-ended questions appropriate? If closed, are the categories exhaustive *and* mutually exclusive? Do responses result in the desired scale of data for analysis (i.e., nominal, ordinal, interval)?
   f. Are the major issues covered thoroughly while minor issues are passed over quickly?
   g. Are questions with similar content grouped logically?
2. *Wording questions*
   a. Are questions stated precisely? (Who, what, when, where, why, how? Don't be too wordy.)
   b. Does the questionnaire avoid assuming too much knowledge on the part of the respondent?

    c. Does each item ask only one question?

    d. Is the respondent in a position to answer the question, or must he make guesses? If so, are you interested in his guesses?

    e. Are definitions clear?

    f. Are emotionally tinged words avoided?

    g. Is the vocabulary at the reading level of the audience? If any technical terms, jargon, or slang are used, are they the most appropriate way to communicate with this audience?

    h. Are the methods for responding appropriate? Clear? Consistent?

    i. Are the questions appropriately brief and uncomplicated?

3. *Establishing and keeping rapport and eliciting cooperation*

    a. Is the questionnaire easy to answer? (Questions are not overly long or cumbersome.)

    b. Is the time required to respond reasonable?

    c. Does the instrument look attractive (i.e., layout, quality of paper, etc.)?

    d. Is there a "respondent orientation"?

    e. Does the cover letter provide an explanation of purpose, sponsorship, method of respondent selection, anonymity?

    f. Is appropriate incentive provided for the respondent's cooperation?

4. *Giving instructions*

    a. Are the respondents clearly told how to record their responses?

    b. Are instructions for return clear? Is a stamped return envelope provided?

In 1996, *New Directions in Evaluation* published its first major issue on survey research in over a decade, "Advances in Survey Research" (Braverman & Slater, 1996). This issue should be reviewed by readers considering surveys as part of their evaluation. In particular, Braverman (1996) reviews major sources of survey error and their implications for evaluation studies with specific suggestions to avoid bias or error by administrators, by the measures itself, and by the mode of collection (face-to-face, telephone, or self-administration).

More information on constructing surveys can be found in Fowler (1988), Fink (1995), Peterson (2000), and Salant and Dillman (1994). Many evaluators make use of the "total design method" developed by Don Dillman of the Survey Research Laboratory at Washington State University to increase return rates (Dillman, 1978, 1983). He provides specific suggestions for formatting, length, cover letters, follow-ups, and inducements. Others have provided additional, experimentally-based evidence on the effect of altering these dimensions (Moss & Worthen, 1991; Rogers & Worthen, 1995; Worthen & Valcarce, 1985).

Telephone Interviews

As many of you know—especially those who have been greeted by a phone call from a professional survey firm during the middle of cooking dinner and juggling children and homework—telephone interviews have become a much more commonly used method of collecting information. While the information obtained from telephone interviews can be qualitative and analyzed in such a manner, in practice a telephone interview is typically more akin to a questionnaire administered orally than to a personal interview. Like a survey, it must be brief to encourage participation and the questions rarely require long responses. Unlike the personal interviewer, the telephone interviewer has difficulty in establishing rapport due to the lack of eye contact and other nonverbal cues. While branching is often used in telephone interviews to skip questions inappropriate for the current respondent, the interviewer is seldom encouraged to adapt questions as in an unstructured personal interview. Instead, standardization is encouraged.

The questions asked in telephone interviews are often quite similar to those one would use in a questionnaire except that items with long stems or response alternatives that may be difficult to comprehend when received orally are discouraged. But open-ended items can be more frequent in telephone interviews than in mailed questionnaires because respondents are more willing to *speak* a sentence or even a paragraph than to write one. Telephone interviews can result in obtaining information more quickly than questionnaires distributed through the mail although, if questionnaires can be distributed to intact groups (employees, students, clients), questionnaires may be the more efficient and effective method.

In spite of disputes over costs, the costs of each method can be relatively similar, depending on the number of respondents, the length of the questionnaire or interview, and the availability of staff to administer telephone surveys. The categories of costs are simply different. Costs in mailing questionnaires include clerical time, paper, copying, postage, postcards, and envelopes. Costs in telephone surveys are primarily the costs of staff involved in conducting and monitoring the surveys. Long-distance charges, the rental of facilities for telephoning and training, and the purchase of phones may also be factors.

Telephone surveys should be considered as preferable to mailed surveys when: (a) there is a need for speed, (b) respondents may be reluctant or unable to complete written surveys but can be reached by telephone, and (c) the questions lend themselves to being answered over the phone. Dillman, Sangster, Tarnai, and Rockwood (1996) review research on differences in results with telephone surveys versus those delivered by mail or otherwise self-administered. They review seven propositions that have been researched concerning differences in responses and find that, while more research is necessary, the primary difference is that responses to telephone interviews are somewhat more likely to produce socially desirable answers, presumably because the respondent is answering to a person in contrast to the anonymity provided by paper. They cite a study in which people were asked the same question concerning driving while under the influence of alcohol by telephone and by mailed survey. Eleven percent more respondents by mail (48%) than by phone (37%) admitted to drinking and driving (Dillman & Tarnai, 1991). They note that face-to-face administration of the questions results in an even higher incidence of socially desirable responses. These findings emphasize the importance of attending to the mode of delivery and considering the characteristics of each in regard to the item content and the characteristics of the interviewers and respondents (see also Braverman, 1996).

Good references for telephone surveys include Dillman (1978) and Lavrakas (1987).

Electronic Surveys and Interviews

As more and more people have access to E-mail and the Web on a daily basis, on-line surveys or interviews are becoming increasingly common. Surveys that would typically be distributed on paper can be administered via E-mail or posted on Web sites. Care must be taken, however, to insure that those who complete the survey are not systematically different from nonrespondents because they are more likely to use computers for communication. When the sample consists of people who work in the organization to be evaluated though, using the in-house E-mail system can be quite successful. Caution must be used to protect confidentiality. Directing respondents to a Web site where the survey can be completed under more anonymous circumstances is recommended.

While surveying on-line has its risks, especially if significant groups within the population will be underrepresented, Shaefer and Dillman (1998) found that on-line surveys result in response rates similar to those achieved with mailed surveys, but provide superior data because people type in more complete answers to open-ended items than they are willing to write on mailed surveys. Their article presents Dillman's recommended procedures for conducting surveys by E-mail.

Fontana and Frey (2000) see electronic interviewing as one of the new trends in qualitative data collection. They note that most current electronic interviews are structured, quantitative measures and, when used for qualitative purposes, present significant disadvantages. The absence of face-to-face contact and the anonymity of computer communications can make it difficult to establish rapport and can increase the likelihood of false responses from the interviewee. Obviously, it is also impossible to make use of nonverbal cues. Interestingly, while on-line responses to surveys can be more detailed than those to mailed surveys, on-line responses for qualitative interviews are shorter and provide less depth than responses given face-to-face. Nevertheless, on-line interviewing can be cheaper, quicker, and provide the interviewer with more time to consider follow-up questions and prompts (Markham, 1998).

Face-to-Face Surveys

Some surveys are administered by an interviewer for a variety of reasons: to gather information from clients who have literacy problems or may have difficulty understanding the questions, to stimulate or motivate responses, or to permit occasional probing by the interviewer to increase the quality and nature of the response. Conducting surveys face-to-face is more costly than self-administered surveys and can be more costly than telephone surveys if visits need to be made to the respondents' homes. Nevertheless, this method of data collection remains a viable option in many cases.

Few differences exist between the nature of questions developed for face-to-face surveys and telephone interviews, though some exist. In face-to-face interviews, interviewers are better able to establish rapport with the respondent. The introduction to the interviewee should be planned carefully to accomplish that purpose. Interviewers should introduce themselves and explain the purpose of the interview. Confidentiality and anonymity should be clarified, and the introduction should put respondents at ease while respecting their privacy.

Typically, the interviewer can quickly mark the responses given by the person interviewed because the questions are very structured, but if the responses are anticipated to be more open-ended, tape-recording the interview can be considered. (Evaluators differ in their views regarding the use of tape recorders. Some feel it frees the interviewer to make more eye contact and establish rapport, while still documenting the dialogue; others prefer hand-writing notes, believing that the presence of the tape recorder can inhibit discussion by intimidating the interviewee.)

Give interviewees time to ask any questions they may have, and use eye contact and body language to establish rapport. Typically, interviewees are most responsive to people they perceive to be like them, so try to match interviewers to critical characteristics of interviewees, e.g., gender, race and ethnicity, age. Interviewers' dress and demeanor, while remaining professional, should match that of the respondent.

As noted above, a drawback to face-to-face interviews can be the tendency of the respondents to provide more socially desirable responses because they are answering to a person and, thus, losing the anonymity of a self-administered survey (Dillman, et al., 1996). However, a well-trained interviewer, appropriately matched to the respondent, can be more successful at eliciting more detailed responses from some stakeholder groups than a self-administered or telephone survey might. In cases where the people to be interviewed are found in a central location, such as coming to an agency or organization, or attending a meeting, the costs of face-to-face interviews may be quite comparable to telephone interviews and more successful because of the opportunity for building rapport.

If interviews are to be conducted by several people, careful consideration should be given to training. Because the results of face-to-face surveys are typically analyzed quantitatively, there is an assumption that the means of administration is standardized and that the interviewer has little personal impact (See Braverman [1996] for a discussion of survey errors occurring based on interviewer bias.) Yet, to take advantage of the face-to-face format, some probing must be permitted. So, interviewers need to be trained in standardized methods for delivering the questions including using probes, pauses, and prompts, methods for recording the information, and means for establishing and maintaining rapport (Bernard, 2000).

Qualitative Interviews

Interviews are often a key to qualitative data collection. Observations are typically the core element of qualitative evaluation, but there is so much that the evaluator cannot observe and, even when observing, the evaluator's perspective differs from that of others experiencing that same phenomenon. Thus, qualitative interviews are used for learning the perspectives, attitudes, behaviors, and experiences of others. Stake (1995) remarks that "The interview is the main road to multiple realities" (p. 64). In other words, only through hearing and interpreting the stories of others through interviews can the evaluator learn the multiple realities and perspectives that different groups and individuals bring to an object or experience.

A major difference between surveys and collecting data through personal interviews is that interviews allow clarification and probing, and permit exploration and discovery. Interviews are useful when the nature of the information to be collected is more ambiguous and greater depth in information is needed than would be permitted with a survey. Personal interviews require more time than surveys and can, therefore, cost more if many people are to be interviewed. However, they can provide a wealth of information. Exploratory interviews with a variety of stakeholders during the beginning of the evaluation process can be invaluable in shedding light on stakeholder's perspectives and concerns. Later in the evaluation, interviews designed to answer particular evaluation questions or continue exploration can be used.

However, good interviewing *is* a skill. While the interviewer is encouraging people to talk and tell their stories, he is guiding the discussion or talk, through questions and probes, to learn more about the evaluation questions of interest. At the same time, as McCracken (1988) notes, the interviewer must demonstrate that he is "a benign, accepting, curious (but not inquisitive) individual who is prepared and eager to listen to virtually any testimony with interest" (p. 38). Kvale (1996) recommends that evaluators consider their role and purpose and provides two metaphors of the interviewer: the interviewer as a miner, who uses interviews to "unearth" knowledge that may be facts or "nuggets of essential meaning" (p. 3), and the interviewer as a traveler who "wanders through the landscape and enters into conversations with the people encountered" (p. 4). The traveler–interviewer reflects the more qualitative approach. The metaphor reveals the role of the interviewer in wandering, learning, possibly changing, and "returning" to interpret what he has learned to people in his home country. Kvale develops his concept of interviews as conversations designed to learn and understand the "life world" of the interviewee in respect to the object being evaluated. He discusses and provides numerous examples of interviews to achieve this purpose.

While the questions asked in each qualitative interview will differ, Stake (1995) reminds us that

> the interviewer needs to have a strong advance plan. It is terribly easy to fail to get the right questions asked, awfully difficult to steer some of the most informative interviewees on to your choice of issues. They have their own. Most people are pleased to be listened to. Getting acquiescence to interviews is perhaps the easiest task in case study research. Getting a good interview is not so easy (p. 64).

When planning your questions, consider the evaluation question you are trying to answer. What information do you need to answer the question? What experiences or opinions do you want them to describe? What linkages, thoughts, or explanations of theirs do you want to elicit? To explore and probe? Develop a brief list of broad questions and be prepared with prompts.

One of the most common errors of an interviewer is to talk too much. After rapport is successfully established, the interviewer is present primarily to listen and encourage responses. A good interviewer should become comfortable with pauses and not feel compelled to fill gaps hurriedly. Respondents often pause to convey difficult or sensitive information. If the interviewer rushes in to break the silence, such information is lost. Similarly, the interviewer should be prepared with prompts and phrases to continue discussion: "tell me more about that," "that's interesting," "oh, yes," or, even "uh-huh" show you are listening and encourages the interviewee to continue without the interviewer determining the direction. Reflecting on the last statement of the interviewee can be helpful in encouraging the respondent to continue though the interviewer should be careful not to add his own interpretation, but only to reflect the comments of the respondent: "You say you were concerned when you couldn't understand the instructions?"

Following are some helpful hints for developing interview questions:

1. Begin with simple, informational or "chatty" questions to establish rapport and learn more about the style and manner of the interviewee.

2. Keep the language pitched to the level of the respondent. Questions posed to specialists can rely on the terminology with which they are familiar and show the interviewer's own expertise on the issue. This use of "technical jargon" can encourage the specialist to talk in more depth, but questions posed to the general public *must* use language more commonly understood. Special care should be taken in interviewing individuals or groups whose language may differ from the typical evaluator's frame of reference. Agar (2000) discusses the language/culture he discovered within an organization in an ethnographic evaluation of a tuberculosis screening program.

3. Avoid long questions. They often become ambiguous and confusing.

4. Consider whether you're seeking facts, opinions, or broader perspectives with each question and phrase your question accordingly. Use prompts or follow-up questions to obtain the type of information you are seeking.

5. Do not assume that your respondent possesses factual or firsthand information. Parents may be able to report what books their children read, but only the children can tell you accurately how much they enjoy reading.

6. Listen for implicit assumptions or biases that may be as important as the answers to your questions. Consider whether the interviewees' comments suggest certain orientations or perspectives and decide whether to probe those perspectives. For example, if the interviewee is complaining about school vouchers, the interviewer might want to probe to see whether the interviewee is against the vouchers for personal or political reasons and, once that is determined, to learn more about the nature of these reasons.

7. Decide whether you need a direct question, an indirect question, or a combination. An example of a direct question is, "Do you ever steal on the job?" An indirect question might be, "Do you know of anyone ever stealing on the job?" A combination might be, "Do you know of anyone ever stealing on the job?" followed by "Have you ever taken anything while on the job?"

8. Frame the question so that, to the degree possible, you communicate what you want to know. For example, if interested in reader preferences in magazines, don't ask, "*How many* magazines do you read?" Ask, "*Which* magazines do you read?"

9. Protect your respondent's ego. Don't ask, "Do you know the name of the Chief Justice of the Supreme Court?" Ask, "Do you happen to know the name of the Chief Justice of the Supreme Court?"

10. If you are interested in obtaining negative, or critical, information, give your respondent a chance to express his positive feelings first so that he feels comfortable being critical. First ask, "What do you like about X?" Then ask, "What don't you like about X?" or "What bothers you about X?"

A final issue in interviewing concerns how to record the information obtained. As noted above, in face-to-face surveys evaluators disagree on whether to use tape recorders or to take notes during the interview. For qualitative interviews, in which eye contact and developing rapport are critical to helping the respondent feel comfortable in telling his story, decisions about procedures should be made very carefully. Taking extensive notes can make respondents uncomfortable and certainly detracts from the body language that would encourage honesty and sharing of experiences. If tape recording is inappropriate because it would also reduce respondents' comfort levels, jot a few notes or key words as the interview proceeds. Then, immediately after the interview, make extensive notes on the respondent's remarks. Share these notes with the respondent to insure his agreement (or disagreement) with your interpretation.

There is disagreement on this issue. Stake (1995) writes:

> Getting the exact words of the respondent is usually not very important, it is what they mean that is important. . . . Interviewees often are dismayed with transcripts not only because of the inelegance of their own sentences but because they did not convey what they intended. And the transcript arrives long after context and innuendo have slipped away (p. 66).

On the other hand, others view taping interviews as the norm and even recommend videotaping to capture nonverbal cues in certain circumstances (Kvale, 1996; McCracken, 1988; Patton, 2002). Patton (2002) writes

> No matter what style of interviewing you use and no matter how carefully you word questions, it all comes to naught if you fail to capture the actual words of the person being interviewed. The raw data of interviews are the actual quotations

spoken by interviewees. Nothing can substitute for these data: the actual things said by real people (p. 380).

Taping permits the interviewers to study the remarks, provides more detail for data analysis, and remains to attest to the veracity of the process.

Patton (2002), Kvale (1996), Fontana and Frey (2000), and McCracken (1988) all provide useful guidance to conducting qualitative interviews. Babbie (1992) and Bernard (2000) discuss interviewing methods from a more traditional research perspective. These sources are highly recommended for evaluators who plan on using interviews to collect information.

Focus Groups

Focus groups have become an increasingly popular method of obtaining qualitative information from a group of individuals. Focus groups are like an interview in that they involve face-to-face interaction, but they build on the group process. A skilled focus group facilitator will make use of ideas or issues raised by participants in the focus group to obtain reactions from others in the group. Discussion in focus groups is not always interviewer to interviewee, but often dialogue continues among focus group participants themselves. Thus, the interview is very much of a *group* process.

Focus group techniques emerged from the field of marketing where such techniques were used to gauge potential customers' reactions to new products and to learn more about customers' needs and wants in regard to the product. Focus group methods have now been adapted to be used in many different settings where there is a need to obtain information on how individuals react to either planned or existing services, policies, or procedures or to learn more about the needs and circumstances of participants or potential clients. Thus, in addition to reacting to issues, focus group participants may suggest new methods or describe circumstances that pose problems with existing programs or policies. Focus groups are particularly useful in needs assessments and monitoring studies and for formative evaluations. Participants can describe their experiences or their reactions to proposed new programs or changes, changes they would recommend, and beliefs or attitudes or life circumstances that they have that might facilitate or hinder the success of the program. Focus groups can help confirm or disconfirm program theories during the planning stages of programs. They can raise novel ideas based on participants' *own* experiences. Focus groups can also be useful in discovering more about program outcomes, such as how participants have used what they gained, what barriers they faced, or what changes they would make in the program.

Focus groups typically consist of eight to twelve individuals who are relatively homogeneous, but unknown to each other. Some focus group specialists recommend smaller groups of five to seven for complex topics (Krueger & Casey, 2000). Homogeneity is desired to facilitate group interaction; noticeable differences in education, income, prestige, authority, or other characteristics can result in hostility or withdrawal by those who are lower on those dimensions. Where input from different groups is desired, it is best to compose focus groups for each distinct group. (See Brown [2000] for a discussion of gender dynamics in mixed-sex focus groups.)

The role of the leader is to facilitate discussion by posing initial and periodic questions, moderating the responses of more vocal members, and encouraging responses of quieter members. The leader may also ask questions to clarify ambiguities or get reactions from other group members. Participating in groups can be intimidating for some. Sensitive topics can be difficult and there can be a tendency for individuals to acquiesce by agreeing with the majority of the group, i.e., group think. Fontana and Frey (2000) note that the skills required for leading a focus group are similar to those required for a good interviewer, but the leader must also be knowledgeable about methods for managing group dynamics. As such, leading an effective focus group can be a challenging task.

One frequent error in focus groups is to rely too extensively on short, forced-choice questions (e.g., yes or no) or to have group members respond by raising hands. The focus group then really becomes a structured group interview, not a focus group, because it has lost the key focus group characteristics of member interaction, openness, and exploration.

In selecting a moderator, consider how that moderator's characteristics and background can enhance or impede group discussion. Employees, or someone known to the focus group participants, should *never* be used as a focus group leader. The position or attitudes of the leader can influence such discussions in undesirable ways. It can be desirable, though not always necessary, to match moderator and group characteristics on critical demographic variables such as age, gender, race, or ethnicity. At minimum, the moderator should have a good knowledge of the culture or lifestyles of the participants in order to understand and interpret comments and effectively facilitate interactions.

Groups are typically led by one moderator with an assistant to observe body language and interactions and to assist in interpreting the session. Sessions are usually tape-recorded, and participants are reimbursed for their time. Sessions generally last one-and-a-half to two hours. The environment for the focus group is important. Generally, refreshments are available and the room is arranged to be conducive to conversation. Results are interpreted through analysis of transcripts from tapes. The results may be analyzed by themes in more open-ended discussions or by responses to groups of questions posed by the moderator.

Though focus groups have been used widely in many fields, Flores and Alonso (1995) note that qualitative evaluators in education have neglected focus groups for interviews and observations. They show how focus groups can be used successfully to obtain teachers' perspectives on change. Vaughn, Schumm, and Sinagub (1996) have developed a useful guide to conducting focus groups in educational and psychological settings. They give particular attention to conducting focus groups with children and adolescents. Basch (1987) discusses how focus groups can be used more effectively in the health field. Hoppe, Wells, Morrison, Gillmore, and Wildson (1995) describe ways to use focus groups to discuss sensitive topics with children. For more information on focus groups, see Krueger and Casey (2000) or Morgan (1997).

Tests

Tests are a common method used for collecting evaluative information in education and training programs. Knowledge acquisition is often the primary objective of educational programs, and the acquisition of knowledge is generally, but not always, measured by tests. Evaluators in other fields also make use of tests, though less extensively than educational evaluators. Evaluators in training settings may use tests, though their ultimate objective is often application on the job or effect on the organization. Evaluators in the health field may make use of tests for the many educational programs conducted for clients or for health education programs for practitioners. Evaluators in social services may make use of tests to measure outcomes in employment or parenting programs. Thus, all evaluators need to have some knowledge of tests as a data-collection instrument.

Four approaches to achievement testing have emerged: norm-referenced testing (NRT), criterion-referenced testing (CRT), objectives-referenced testing (ORT), and domain-referenced testing (DRT). These four strategies have many elements in common, but, depending on which strategy is chosen, the procedures for test development and interpretation can be quite different. **Norm-referenced tests** are intended principally to compare students' performance against others taking the same test. They are the tests routinely administered in many school districts to assess progress. The California Achievement Test, the Comprehensive Test of Basic Skills, and the Iowa Test of Basic Skills are common examples. The strength of such tests is that they permit comparison with established norm groups; as such, they can be helpful in answering questions such as "How is our school doing in conveying commonly accepted knowledge and skills compared to other schools in the nation?" Their chief weakness is that the content may not be valid for the curriculum being evaluated. To be useful, care should be taken to ensure that the content of the NRT items and the knowledge and skills required to respond correctly match reasonably well the instructional objectives of the program to be evaluated.

Norm-referenced tests may be useful in descriptive time-series designs for examining changes across time to explore causes for problems and identify needs. The results of norm-referenced tests can also be useful if considered as the instrument in a cross-sectional design. In other words, the norm-referenced test is a "snapshot" in time of how students in that school are doing at that particular point. Then, the evaluator can make use of the results to explore performance differences or changes among different subgroups, for example, fifth graders who have attended the school throughout elementary school versus those who have not or students from one neighborhood compared with those from another. Or the evaluator can combine a time-series design with cross-sectional elements and examine how specific groups of students' scores have changed over time. For example, it can be useful to graph and contrast changes in scores for the top one-third, middle one-third, and bottom one-third of students over eight or ten years to see how the school is succeeding with different groups.

In contrast to norm-referenced tests, **criterion-referenced tests** are developed specifically to measure performance against some absolute criterion. The most common example of such tests today is the standards tests used by 49 of the 50 states in the United States. (See Chapter 2 for a discussion of "Performance Measurement and Standards-Based Education.") The items on standards tests are typically written to assess standards that have been set by the state. Standards-based tests are used by most states to judge the performance of schools or school districts. (See Fitzpatrick and Henry [2000] for a discussion of some of the issues around standards-based testing.) Traditional criterion-referenced tests are designed to address a particular program or curriculum. The tests can then be used to judge students' progress on a particular curriculum or program. These measures, designed to assess a particular program, are useful for many program evaluations because the content of the items reflects the curricula.

Objectives-referenced testing and domain-referenced testing do not provide standards such as a norm group or a criterion for judging performance. Instead, they yield descriptive data about student performance with no judgments attached. **Objectives-referenced tests** make use of items keyed to specific instructional objectives in an educational or training program. Such tests are useful for formative evaluation feedback for teachers or trainers to help them examine areas in which objectives are being achieved and areas that need improvement as well as for summative decisions about program success in achieving certain learning changes. **Domain-referenced tests** are used to estimate a student's knowledge of a specific content or domain. The items are not linked to a curriculum but rather to the content domain being measured (e.g., American history, comparative anatomy). These items, too, can be useful for evaluative purposes, though such tests are costly to develop compared to objectives-referenced and criterion-referenced tests. They can, however, be used to answer questions such as "How much do our graduates know about X content?" Standards can be developed to reflect the school's or organization's expectations regarding the amount of knowledge a graduate or a student finishing a course should have.

As discussed in Chapter 2, the standards-based tests are now administered in 49 of the 50 states.[2] President George W. Bush has discussed establishing national standards and, possibly, a national test. Given the prominence of this reform movement, many schools concentrate heavily on their scores on these tests (see the American Evaluation Association statement on high-stakes testing at www.eval.org).

As might be expected, the quality of standards-based tests varies from state to state. Some tests have been carefully constructed and validated. Others have not. Scores on these tests may provide useful information for the evaluator

---

[2]Iowa, a state that has traditionally been strong in education, has rejected statewide tests to permit local districts to develop measures appropriate to their own information needs.

working in K–12 settings, but should be judged by the evaluator like any other existing data. Consider whether the items on the test are adequate measures of the concepts that need to be measured to answer the evaluation questions at hand. In some cases, the standards-based test can serve as an important and useful measure. Consider also using subscores or even individual items if these portions of the test are better indicators of the constructs stated in the evaluation question. Always remember and remind others that the goal is not to "raise test scores," as we so often hear, but to improve student learning. Consider what elements of student learning are the focus of the program or curriculum you are evaluating. If scores, subscores, or items on standards-based tests can provide information about that learning, by all means use them! If not, consider other measures, which can include other traditional tests, tests developed specifically for the program or curriculum, or authentic assessment. (See the following section for more on authentic assessment.)

The series of *Mental Measurements Yearbook* volumes and Tests in Print (developed originally by O. K. Buros and currently managed by the Buros Institute at the University of Nebraska) are invaluable reference works when selecting a test for data collection. The most recent of these is Plake and Impara's (2001) *Fourteenth Mental Measurements Yearbook,* which reviews over 400 tests and attitude scales described under "Surveys" in this chapter for its attitude measures.

Alternative Assessment Methods

In schools, standardized achievement tests and standards-based tests are routinely used to measure learning. However, in recent years there has been a move away from using only standardized tests to measure progress. Significant stakeholders, including many parents, teachers, and administrators, question whether such tests measure students' abilities accurately and comprehensively. Further, many teachers and administrators have not found the information useful to them in revising or managing the educational process. A national study of the use of tests in science education found that "existing standardized and text-embedded tests (publisher-supplied tests) are inadequate to support reform in science and mathematics education" (Harmon, 1995, p. 32). Alternatives Harmon sees emerging are changing the content of multiple-choice tests (she cites the National Assessment of Educational Progress as an example of a test that measures higher-order thinking in science), open-ended written items, structured interviews, and performance assessment. Standards-based tests in many states have moved beyond multiple-choice items and require written responses to assess thinking processes and writing performance.

Several labels have been used to describe alternatives to standardized tests, with the most common being *direct assessment, authentic assessment, performance assessment,* and the more generic *alternative assessment.* Although these various descriptors reflect subtle distinctions in emphasis, the several types of assessment all reflect two central commonalities. First, they are all viewed as *alternatives* to traditional multiple-choice, selected-answer achievement tests. Second, they all refer to *direct* examination of student *performance* on significant tasks relevant to life outside of school.

Some of these alternatives reflect the positive influence advocates of qualitative methods have had on the measurement field. These alternatives also remind us that testing can be accomplished both by paper-and-pencil measures and by performance measures. (See the list of data collection methods in Chapter 13.) Paper-and-pencil tests that are criterion-referenced, objectives-referenced, or domain-referenced can be included in an evaluation to inform stakeholders about progress and strengths and weaknesses. But performance measures, such as simulation devices, student portfolios, or oral debates, can also be appropriate, given the content to be measured, in assessing knowledge or skills. As with any evaluation, the key is to select the method or methods that provide the best match to the content to be measured and the purpose of the evaluation. In measuring conversational ability in a foreign language, a structured language proficiency interview would clearly be more appropriate than a paper-and-pencil test. In measuring the skill to use scientific equipment to perform an experiment, a performance assessment in the lab would probably be most appropriate. In measuring the ability to recognize and correct grammatical and spelling errors, a paper-and-pencil test may be most efficient.

A recent issue of *New Directions for Teaching and Learning* focuses on alternative ways for measuring student performance, including chapters on involving students in the assessment process, measuring class participation, oral presentations, written assignments, portfolios, cooperative projects, and performance in real-world settings (Anderson & Speck, 1998). O'Sullivan and Tennant (1993) have developed a guide to evaluating programs for at-risk students that includes discussion of many of the types of measures reviewed in this chapter including using focus groups, attitude scales, observation checklists, interviews, and alternative assessment measures. For detailed discussions of alternative assessment methods, including development of assessment measures and scoring rubrics, see Worthen, White, Fan, & Sudweeks (1999).

Figure 15.2 summarizes the data collection methods we have reviewed in this section and some of the important characteristics of each.

Planning and Organizing the Collection of Information

Data collection methods must be sanctioned by the proper authorities. These authorities can include Protection of Human Subjects committees or other review committees within the organization, the client, administrators of the program to be evaluated, program staff and program participants, or clients, depending on the nature of the data collection. In addition to seeking approval through proper channels and following organizational policies, it is important that the evaluator seek

FIGURE 15.2 *A Review of Various Means of Data Collection*

Data Collection Method	Characteristics
Documents	Nonofficial papers: minutes, notes, plans Reveals actions, thinking, perceptions uninfluenced by the study
Records	Official documents: census, attendance, salaries More valid and reliable than documents
Observation	Observations of program context and activities, participant behaviors, and environments Can be structured or unstructured Useful in some way in almost every evaluation
Site Visits	A subset of observation, used by regulatory agencies
Surveys	Reports of attitudes, opinions, behavior, life circumstances Can be administered in person or by mail
Telephone Interviews	Purposes are similar to those of a survey, but questions can be more open-ended, but must be shorter Can develop rapport and use verbal prompts
Electronic Interviews or Surveys	Questions delivered and answered using computer technology Items may be constructed as open or closed
Interviews	Qualitative interviews are useful for eliciting values, perspectives, experiences, and more detailed responses Can be structured (face-to-face surveys) or qualitative
Focus Groups	Useful when group interaction can encourage and enhance responses
Tests	Used to examine knowledge and skills Primarily used in education and training
Alternative Assessments	Examines knowledge and skills in a direct way Viable alternative to paper-and-pencil measures

the input of those who will be involved actively or passively in the collection of information (e.g., responding to surveys, helping to administer tests, observing activities or being observed, and the like). These audiences' cooperation can be vital to successful data collection. If they object to the data collection methods or procedures or fail to understand the purpose, they can sabotage the collection of valid information by providing false or misleading information or encouraging others to do so. Others simply may not take the data collection seriously. Explaining the importance of their cooperation can prevent many potential problems. Guaranteeing confidentiality or anonymity can be helpful. Rewards, such as released time or feedback from the study, may also encourage full cooperation. Adherence to ethical practices that protect participants' rights is also essential to insure access to data sources.

Technical Problems in Data Collection

The evaluator's version of Murphy's Law goes something like this: "If anything can go wrong in collecting information, it will." A comprehensive list of potential problems would fill this chapter, but here are a few of the major ones:

- Unclear directions lead to inappropriate responses, or the instrument is insensitive or off-target. (Always pilot-test your methods.)
- Inexperienced data collectors reduce the quality of the information being collected. (Always include extensive training and trial runs. Eliminate potential problem staff before they hit the field. Monitor and document data-collection procedures.)
- Partial or complete loss of information occurs. (Duplicate files and records; keep records and raw data under lock and key at all times.)
- Information is recorded incorrectly. (Always check data collection in progress. Cross-checks of recorded information are frequently necessary.)
- Outright fraud occurs. (Always have more than one person supplying data. Compare information, looking for the "hard to believe.")
- Procedures break down. (Keep logistics simple. Supervise while minimizing control for responsible evaluation staff. Keep copies of irreplaceable instruments, raw data, records, and the like.)

Analysis of Data and Interpretation of Findings

Evaluations involve processing mountains of information that, if not organized in a form that permits meaningful interpretation, is often worthless or, worse, misleading. The aim of *data analysis* is to reduce and synthesize information—to "make sense" of it—and to allow inferences about populations. When considering alternative methods for data analysis or interpretation, the evaluator should ask two questions:

1. What methods of data analysis and interpretation are appropriate for the *questions* I am trying to answer, the *information* that I plan to collect, and the *method* I will use to collect information?
2. What methods of data analysis and interpretation are most likely to be *understood* and to be *credible* to the audiences who will receive reports?

Involve stakeholders in data analysis from the beginning. Meeting with the client or important stakeholders to review results can demystify the data-analysis stage and actively involve the user. The evaluator can learn the types of information that are of most interest to the client or different stakeholders and the most effective ways of presenting that information. Working with the client or group, the evaluator will often learn new questions and issues that the data analysis can address.

Analysis of Quantitative Data

One major choice in data analysis will be whether to use descriptive or inferential statistics to answer the question of interest. Before moving immediately into high-powered inferential techniques, the evaluator should spend much time exploring the data that have been collected using descriptive statistics and graphics. Always know your data thoroughly before moving to summarize with scores or comparisons. What are the central tendencies with each item? What are the frequencies or, for continuous data, the shape of the distribution? Who are the "outliers"? What is the spread of the distribution? Are the respondents very homogeneous or quite different in their responses? Which options were selected more than anticipated? Which were selected less? In addition to looking at overall trends, spend some time analyzing the responses of subgroups. Do younger respondents differ from older ones? Do those with families differ from single respondents? Are there differences by geographic region? By where or when services are received? By the nature of service delivered?

Many things can be discovered (including errors in data collection, coding, or entry) by carefully exploring the data. More than once, we have been asked to help an agency with a complex statistical problem, only to discover that the in-house data analyst, concerned about being "sophisticated," has failed to use adequate descriptive methods to learn about the information he has. The evaluator's goal should not be to impress with complexity but to convey information that will help the stakeholder know more about the program. Many important questions of concern to stakeholders can be answered with descriptive statistics or graphs. (See Henry, 1997, for a discussion and examples of using graphs to convey different types of evaluation data.)

For questions concerned with causality or relationships, inferential statistics are appropriate. Here, the evaluator should select the method that matches the scale of data collected and make sure the data meet the assumptions of the statistic. Chi-square and other nonparametric methods can be useful for examining relationships between ordinal and nominal variables. ANOVA and t-tests can be used to examine relationships between nominal and interval or ratio variables. Finally, multiple regression methods and their extensions can be useful in exploring relationships among variables or in exploring the independent effects of many variables on one dependent variable.

Analyzing differences in outcomes between particular groups of students or clients and between different classrooms, schools, or sites can be a useful way to learn more about why the program works. Pawson and Tilley (1997) recommend doing these types of subgroup analyses to learn more about program theory. For example, learning that the program works at one site and not at another can lead the evaluator to explore differences between the sites that may have contributed to these different outcomes. These discoveries help shed light on what parts of the program are most critical and with whom. This is the type of integrated, iterative evaluation design that leads to a fuller, more complete understanding of the program and its effects.

Useful texts on quantitative data analysis methods have been prepared by Jaeger (1990) and Giventer (1996). Brinkerhoff, Brethower, Hluchyj, and Nowa-kowski (1983) have provided a succinct summary of data-analysis techniques that are frequently employed in evaluation.

In using inferential statistics, the evaluator should remember to caution clients that statistics do not establish causality but simply demonstrate relationships. Statistics, logic, and design must all be used synergistically to establish cause-and-effect relationships.

Another common error is to confuse statistical significance with practical significance. Finding that a particular program produces statistically significant reductions in drug use by students only means that the difference between the compared scores of the two groups is not due to chance. The reductions may or may not be sufficient to be considered meaningful by different groups of stakeholders.

Statistical significance is influenced by many factors, not the least of which is the sample size. The more observations or measurements included in the analysis, the more likely it is that differences not due to chance will be found. The more critical question in evaluation is whether these differences are sufficiently large to be meaningful for program decisions. Effect sizes are frequently used to enhance significance testing and convey more about the practical significance of the difference. Standards developed during the planning stage can be helpful in determining the programmatic significance of the findings. Such determination is a judgment and should rarely be made by the evaluator alone. The client and other stakeholders who know what they want from the program are often in a better position to determine practical significance of the findings. See Lipsey (1990) for more information on determining practical significance and Kellow (1998) for methods of estimating effect size.

Analysis of Qualitative Data

Stake (1995) observes that qualitative and quantitative techniques are most different from each other at the stage of data analysis. "The qualitative researcher concentrates on the instance, trying to pull it apart and put it back together again more meaningfully—analysis and synthesis in direct interpretation. The quantitative researcher seeks a collection of instances, expecting that, from the aggregate, issue-relevant meanings will emerge" (Stake, 1995, p. 75). As qualitative data are collected, analysis is also beginning. The evaluator is formulating categories, revising categories, reviewing field notes, and collecting more information until different perspectives begin to be more fully revealed. But, how does the evaluator summarize the vast amounts of information he has collected? How does he verify it and ensure that it has credibility to the stakeholders and other users? At some point, the evaluator begins to consider how to amass his qualitative data and use it to tell the multiple stories he has learned.

The method of analysis of qualitative data depends on the nature of the data and the conceptual framework employed in the analysis. Methods for qualitative data analysis can range from narrative description to quantitative analyses of narrative components as in **content analysis.** Patton (2002) has developed these options for organizing and reporting qualitative data:

Storytelling approaches
- Chronology and history
- Flashback

Case Study Approaches
- People
- Critical Incidents
- Various Settings

Analytical Framework Approaches
- Processes
- Issues
- Questions
- Sensitizing Concepts, e.g., leadership versus followership (p. 439).

Searching for patterns and categories is part of the analytic induction that undergirds all qualitative analysis. This search "builds levels of confidence" in the evaluation's ultimate conclusions through these steps:

1. *Exploring and forming impressions,* recorded in field notes

2. *Identifying patterns or themes,* recorded in memos or short concept statements

3. *Focusing and concentrating,* using "working hypotheses" as focal points for further observation and documentation. As these "working hypotheses" are "tested," those that are supported receive further attention, whereas those that are not supported are noted, along with the evidence used to reject them. Meanwhile, the exploring and forming of impressions (step 1 above) continues.

4. *Verification.* "Working hypotheses" are given the status of tentative conclusions; scenarios and thick, detailed descriptions are developed to make them come alive. These tentative conclusions are then tested for authenticity by the subjects in the study. Confirmation checks and triangulation are used to increase the certainty that these conclusions are accurate.

5. *Assimilation.* Conclusions are placed in the broader context of what else is known about the object of the evaluation.

The initial stages of data analysis are typically approached using "open coding" (Strauss & Corbin, 1998). In other words, the evaluator is examining the data, field notes, text, interviews, observations, and so on, looking for patterns and themes. In this inductive approach, the evaluator does not begin the data analysis with set categories, but instead explores the data to see what patterns or themes emerge.

The next major step is developing a coding scheme for categorizing content or data. Remember that codes are designed to *reduce* data to manageable proportions, so don't develop too many codes. Codes generally are related to program models or theories or to evaluation questions, but beginning with open coding allows the evaluator to find themes not identified during the planning stage.

Data can then be analyzed using these codes. Many software programs that make qualitative data analysis much more manageable are now available. These software programs essentially provide a means for storing, coding, and managing the data. Passages or incidents that convey similar themes can be compared and linked. Noteworthy stories or quotations that illustrate themes can be readily identified. Fielding (2000) describes a wide array of software packages for analyzing qualitative data. If the evaluation will accumulate sufficient qualitative data to make software useful (and this is often the case), it can be advisable to select a software package *before* beginning data collection so that the collection procedures will lend themselves to entry.

Grounded theory is a common approach to the analysis of qualitative data. It makes use of an iterative process, alternating inductive and deductive methods, to explore for patterns and confirm findings. An inductive, open approach is used as the first step in examining the data. The evaluator then builds some tentative hypotheses or theories about the data and then changes to a deductive approach, examining the data to see if it confirms the theories. This process of back-and-forth inductive and deductive examination of the data is used to allow the evaluator to become "grounded" in the theory implicit in the qualitative data (Strauss & Corbin, 1998).

Content analysis is a special type of analysis of qualitative information collected in textual form (e.g., field notes, narrative interviews, newspaper articles, minutes of meetings). These procedures may be used to describe, analyze, and summarize the trends observed in these documents. It makes use of procedures similar to those used in any qualitative analysis. That is, patterns and themes are identified; coding schemes are established; and, then, selected "chunks" of the textual information (sentences, paragraphs, pages) are coded, counted, and analyzed. Coding categories may focus on either the actual content of the document ("what is said") or underlying motives, emotions, or points of view ("how it is said") (Guba & Lincoln, 1981). A sample set of categories (Sanders & Cunningham, 1974) reflecting themes in newspaper articles on sex education is shown in Figure 15.3. Paragraphs in the article, if that were the unit of analysis, would be read and tallies made for each category reflected in the paragraph.

Various methods are used to confirm the findings from qualitative analysis, including:

- Weighting the evidence to give stronger data more weight;
- Looking for and examining rival or competing themes;
- Trying to find negative cases that do not conform to the theory or hypothesis and considering whether they disprove or refine the theory;
- Studying extreme cases for enhancing descriptions and theories;
- Considering an attempt to replicate the findings with another case;

FIGURE 15.3 *Sample Set of Content Analysis Categories*

Newspaper:	Date:	Story Source:

– (Negative)	+ (positive)
Expressions of opposition to sex education	Expressions favoring sex education
Actions in opposition to sex education	Actions in support of sex education
Statements attacking proponents of sex education	Statements supporting proponents of sex education
Statements listing opponents of sex education	Statements listing proponents of sex education
Provisions of alternate plans	Statements opposing alternate plans
Some other plan satisfactory	Authorities insist on current objectives
Miscellaneous –	Miscellaneous +

0 (Neutral)	Other themes
School board to discuss issue	
School board vote to be close	
Possible areas of compromise	
Miscellaneous	

Content totals	Headline	Headline Content
+ _____	Head size _____	(+1, –1, or 0)
– _____	Location on page _____	
0 _____	Length _____	
	Total score and direction _____	

Source: From "Techniques and Procedures for Formative Evaluation" by J. R. Sanders and D. J. Cunningham, 1974, in G. D. Borich (Ed.), *Evaluating Educational Programs and Products*, Englewood Cliffs, NJ: Educational Technology. Reprinted by permission.

- Looking for triangulation of findings across different methods;
- Using another evaluator or a selected informant to provide feedback on your analysis and to act as a devil's advocate against your theory.

For detailed discussions of qualitative data analysis methods, the reader is referred to Miles and Huberman's (1994) text detailing methods for qualitative data analysis. Fielding and Lee (1998) and Fetterman (1998) describe some of the computer methods and software for organizing and analyzing qualitative data. Strauss and Corbin (1998) discuss and provide examples of grounded theory in practice. Finally, Denzin and Lincoln's (2000) *Handbook of Qualitative Research* provides much useful information in this area.

Components of Interpreting Data Analyses

Data analysis focuses on organizing and reducing information and making statistical inferences; interpretation, on the other hand, attaches meaning to organized information and draws conclusions. Analysis may be thought of as organizing and verifying facts; interpretation as applying values, perspective, and conceptual ability to formulate supportable conclusions.

Interpretation should be characterized by careful, fair, open methods of inquiry. Anyone who claims that the "numbers speak for themselves" is either naive or a shyster. Interpretation means judging the object of the evaluation and considering the implications of those judgments. Recall that Stake's countenance model (discussed in Chapter 8) includes in the "judgment matrix" both *standards* and *judgments*. These are part of interpretation, but there is more.

The evaluator's perspective also influences his interpretation of the data. Perspective is a result of experience, of unique views and orientations developed over idiosyncratic life histories, and of a tendency to attend to certain details. Thus, all interpretations, to some extent, are personal and idiosyncratic. Consequently, not only interpretations but the *reasons* behind them should be made explicit.

Conceptual ability can also affect interpretation. Each evaluator looks at the evaluation information, twists it around, discovers nuances, and generates insights—things that others may never have seen without the evaluator's help— in an individual way that affects the outcomes of the evaluation. If evaluation is to serve an educational function, as Cronbach and his associates (1980) claim, results must be interpreted so that audiences know how best to use or consider them.

Guidelines for Interpreting Findings

Evaluators are just beginning to develop systematic methods of interpretation, and new methods will likely be generated in the future. Among those interpretation methods that have served well in the recent past are the following:

1. Determining whether objectives have been achieved;
2. Determining whether laws, democratic ideals, regulations, or ethical principles have been violated;
3. Determining whether assessed needs have been reduced;
4. Determining the value of accomplishments;
5. Asking critical reference groups to review the data and to provide their judgments of successes and failures, strengths and weaknesses;
6. Comparing results with those reported by similar entities or endeavors;
7. Comparing assessed performance levels on critical variables to expectations of performance or standards;
8. Interpreting results in light of evaluation procedures that generated them.

Interpretation of data analyses is not the sole province of the evaluator. No one is omniscient. Most evaluators have learned that interpreting and summarizing results in isolation is generally an unsound practice. The evaluator brings only one of many pertinent perspectives to bear and, in fact, is sometimes less well prepared to offer insightful interpretations than others who can look at the data through fresh eyes.

One method for bringing multiple perspectives to the interpretation task is to use *stakeholder meetings*. Small groups of five to eight people meet for several hours to discuss their interpretations of printouts, tables, charts, and other information collected and analyzed during the evaluation. Stakeholders can be supplied in advance with the results, along with other pertinent information such as the evaluation plan and the list of questions, criteria, and standards that guided the evaluation; that way, meeting time can be devoted to discussion rather than presentation. At the meeting, findings are systematically reviewed in their entirety, with each participant interpreting each finding: for example, What does this mean? Is it good, bad, neutral? Consequential or inconsequential? What are the implications? What, if anything, should be done?

Besides contributing his own interpretations, the evaluator serves as transcriber so that all interpretations and the reasons for them can be recorded and included in the evaluation reports. These interpretative sessions not only capture diverse perspectives and original thinking but they also frequently disclose values previously undetected. All this contributes to the utility of the evaluation while assuring that those who should be involved are.

Other methods of interpretation suggested by the Joint Committee on Standards for Educational Evaluation (1981) include:

1. Having different teams write advocacy reports representing the various perspectives;
2. Conducting a jury trial or administrative hearing to review evidence concerning the object of the evaluation;
3. Seeking convergence of opinion about interpretation of results through use of a Delphi study.

Some additional useful guidelines suggested by Brinkerhoff and others (1983) for interpreting the results of analysis include the following:

1. Seeking confirmation and consistency with other sources of information;
2. Dealing with contradictory and conflicting evidence; not forcing consensus when none exists;
3. Not confusing statistical significance with practical significance;
4. Considering and citing limitations of the analysis.

CASE STUDY APPLICATION

November 25 (continued). I have some ideas for how I want to collect data. Certainly, we will need to construct parent questionnaires. Because I don't have the staff in Radnor to conduct phone interviews and I *do* have the time it takes to wait for mailed surveys with postcards and two distributions to be returned, I will probably go with that method of distribution. Materials sent home by the school will provide a low-cost way of letting parents know a questionnaire is coming. However, I think I will distribute them by regular mail rather than through school folders. Middle-school students are notorious for forgetting to share information with their parents! Such distribution can create a quite biased sample!

December 10. I've been working several days planning data collection, considering sources and methods. Of course, we can make use of quite a bit of existing documents and records: lesson plans, student papers and projects and participation in extracurricular creative activities, minutes of staff meetings in which curricula were discussed, and last years' scores on standards and achievement tests. For original data, our primary sources are school board members, parents, and other community members who will be telling us about their views of the program objectives; teachers who will not only tell us their views about the objectives, but also their methods for delivering the materials and their observations on its merits; and, of course, students! A review of *Mental Measurements Yearbook* and some research on creative thinking helped me identify some existing measures which I'd like to pass by the Advisory Board. Even if we don't use those measures, it can give us some ideas, but, for the most part, it looks like a do-it-yourself instrument development effort. So far I have completed a first draft of the following:

> Interview schedules for students, teachers, parents, and board members, using the questions I know so far to be important. I'll probably add others suggested by the site-visit team of experts, once they're selected.

> A classroom observation instrument. This is somewhat open-ended. I'm wanting to get a sense for the method of instruction used and how students respond. Dewey Pitcher, my humanities expert, cautioned me that classroom involvement is critical for achieving the kind of goals they have outlined.

> A survey to students with a lot of Likert-scale items to get at some of the attitudinal stuff. I borrowed some of the items from existing attitude measures for adults, but I want to review these with the Radnor staff to make sure these items address their concerns and are appropriate for middle-school kids. I've adapted the vocabulary a little, but I'll of course need to pilot-test them with kids this age first. I wonder if I could use one of my son's classrooms for pilot-testing?

> A very rough draft of some criterion-referenced tests, mostly useful, I suspect, as a starting place to work with the Radnor humanities faculty. Even though I pulled the concepts from their materials, I'm not certain my items reflect the concepts they view as important.

> Variations of the parent and community survey that I hope will get at a lot of opinions and factual information that might otherwise fall through the cracks. People who dash off casual questions surely fall under the "ignorance is bliss" rubric. By the time I'd torn up my third draft today, I was almost wishing I had never minored in sociology.

We're also going to be able to make use of quite a few existing documents and records. We've decided to compare absenteeism in these classes with those of others as a measure of student interest. We're going to look at student participation in humanities-related extracurricular activities and elective classes—things like enrollments in drama, music, and art electives, participation in clubs, Odyssey of the Mind, Inter-Scholastic League writing competitions, and so on. We'll compare Radnor's participation in such events with those of the other school. We can't attribute all differences to the program, but these indicators do reflect the real goal of getting students to have a lifelong interest in the humanities and they will help us get a better picture of the broader effects of the program. We're going to review some teacher products (curriculum revisions, faculty meeting minutes) to get a sense of the evolution of the program. And, finally, it looks like we'll be able to examine some student products that occur throughout the program, a major paper and a humanities "creation" of the students' choice—art, music, an essay or fictional piece—to actually describe the outcomes occurring among students. We'll have our site visitors look at these things as well as do some detailed content analysis ourselves.

Author Comments. Were I actually to conduct this evaluation, I would turn quickly to the *Mental Measurements Yearbook* volumes or other collections that may contain well-developed instruments for attitude measures. I would also contact the authors of some of the published evaluation studies in this area to inquire about instruments they had used. Even though I am never too optimistic about finding just the right instrument, I suspect useful instruments on variables such as critical thinking, writing and language arts, and attitudes toward different cultural groups and ethnicity could be located in these sources. Even if one did not find usable instruments, there is a high probability of finding useful strategies and formats for asking questions that will make developing the measures an easier task.

Where no measures exist—and I suspect that would be the case for most of the specific content of the humanities curriculum—homemade (do not misread that as *carelessly* made) cognitive measures would need to be fashioned. I would work closely with the humanities faculty and members of the Humanities Curriculum Review Committee in designing those instruments. That not only ensures relevance but also is an excellent way to build rapport and trust with those whose program is being evaluated. I would also pilot drafts of the resulting criterion-referenced instruments with small samples of students. The strategy for designing affective measures would be similar.

While the questions of the evaluation lead us to several paper-and-pencil measures, qualitative data collection will be an important part of this study. We need qualitative data—observations of the program itself; interviews with students, teachers, and parents; the site visit—to help us judge the overall program and make recommendations concerning its strengths and weaknesses. Finally, we need this information to be able to *describe* the program and convey to the board members and members of the public what the program really Is. They may not really have a sense for what the program is and may be reacting to political issues and superficial labels. The observations, interviews, and, most importantly, the student products will help us provide a picture of that. While decision makers want numbers (remember the engineer!), they also want stories. Many scholars in the management field today are talking about how managers learn by stories. They're right! People remember a telling anecdote more than a figure. The qualitative data will be more than an anecdote; it will convey the whole picture of the program.

April 20. Sorry, journal, for the neglect, but the past few months have been hectic. But, things are nearly back to normal, and I'm catching up. The Radnor evaluation is almost on schedule, and the data-collection effort is nearly completed. The site visit is the only major evaluation activity still ahead, and the other classroom observations are coming to a close. The interviews with parents and students were quite informative.

No hitches in the testing or attitude measurement, and the second follow-up on the mailed questionnaire to parents and community leaders has boosted the response rate to over 70 percent and still climbing. Guess there is some genuine interest in this program to get that good a response rate (or perhaps those Dillman strategies for increasing response rates really do work!). I'd rather work to get a good response rate than have to fall back on checking nonresponse bias any day.

Anyway, as soon as we get the last data in, we'll be able to start thinking about analysis and reporting. Of course, we're getting a pretty good picture already about opinion data, and so forth, from the interviews, and we'll soon know what the experts think. But I'll try to keep an open (don't read that as empty) mind until all the data are in and analyzed.

Author Comments.   Most of the information-collection activities I might actually have conducted in an evaluation of this type can be readily inferred from the evaluation plan outlined in Artifact 4 in Chapter 13, but three comments may be helpful.

First, it is important to capitalize on what is known about survey methods if one intends to obtain an adequate response rate to a mailed questionnaire. There exists a body of literature on how to increase response rates (see Dillman, 1983; Dillman & Sangster, 1991; Worthen & Valcarce, 1985, for information and references in this area). In addition, it would be important to know and use appropriate techniques for assessing whether respondents and nonrespondents differ significantly on relevant variables that might bias the results.

Second, little has been said about observation within classrooms, yet I would see that as a pivotal part of the study. Here, I would want the humanities specialist(s) to work with the evaluation assistants I would hire to do periodic observations. The assistants would be able to get a fairly good feel for the classroom climate, the effectiveness of the instruction, whether the curriculum objectives are being translated into learning activities for students, and how students react to those activities. The humanities expert is needed, however, to get at the more subtle nuances and to judge whether what students are learning in the classroom is really the essence of what is important for them to know about the humanities.

Finally, although I may nowhere label it as such, a data-collection effort such as that outlined here is obviously an instance of multiple-method, multiple-source evaluation.

May 4. For once, I believe I did something right. Remember all the time I spent last year planning for the analysis of all of the data that I would collect on the Radnor evaluation? Well, it's paying off now. There is nothing more frustrating than to get to the end of a long and expensive data-collection effort only to find that you can't analyze the data in important ways because of the methods used to collect them (e.g., the scale of data is inappropriate for certain analyses, or the categories and methods used for observation and interview data don't match the evaluation questions). It's usually too late to go back and do it again by the time data analysis is begun, but this time things worked out well.

I've collected both quantitative and qualitative data in this evaluation and, thus, used a variety of procedures for data analysis. Claire Janson asked how I would be analyzing the data, so I summarized that briefly and sent it off to her today (see Artifact 9).

ARTIFACT 9

Data	Quantitative or Qualitative?	Techniques Used for Analysis
1. Interviews with students, teachers, parents, and board members	1. Qualitative and quantitative	1. Descriptive statistics (means, standard deviations, frequency distributions) were used for the structured, standard questions. A pattern analysis and summary of response types with their frequencies were done for the qualitative, probing, and follow-up questions.
2. Classroom observations	2. Quantitative and qualitative	2. Percentages, means, and standard deviations were used to convey the proportion of time spent on interactive exercises in each session observed. In addition, I had asked observers to write short, descriptive narratives about what went on in each classroom so that we could get a sense of what it was like to be there. I had two independent readers read these accounts and then list what they thought were important events or transactions. They then compared their analyses and resolved any differences between them. Both the full descriptions and the readers' analyses will be used in our reports.
3. Survey data on Likert-scale items; data on attitudes toward values and concepts taught in the curriculum	3. Quantitative	3. There is some debate over whether data collected with such scales should be considered interval or ordinal. I consider each item ordinal. Thus, I reported medians and percentages responding to each option on the item-by-item analysis. But, to give some sense of the overall trend, I also calculated overall scores and subscores on a few dimensions identified through factor analysis. I consider these scores "approaching interval," as they include many data points. Thus, I reported means for these.

(continued)

ARTIFACT 9 (*Continued*)

Data	Quantitative or Qualitative?	Techniques Used for Analysis
		In comparing the scores of students in the program with the comparison group, I used t-tests. I must be a little cautious in reporting these results, as these were homemade measures and more research is needed to validate them. My factor analysis of the instruments revealed that several possible dimensions were present. It was tempting to report summary, summated ratings for each resulting dimension, but without further research on the instruments I was uncertain enough about stability of these dimensions so that I avoided using them in the analysis.
4. Criterion-referenced test results	4. Quantitative	4. I had spent a lot of time pilot-testing the CRT items and was relatively confident that every item correlated highly with total test scores. My internal consistency (KR_{20}) for the test was high. I used the test to collect pre- and posttest data on participating classrooms and the comparison school. I used an analysis of covariance to determine whether the scores of the two groups differed using the pretest scores as the covariate. This helps control for differences between the groups—at least on the pretest. I also calculated an effect size to provide some information on the practical significance of the change. Finally, I compared the change and the posttest scores with the standards we had set during the planning stage.
5. Survey questionnaires	5. Qualitative and quantitative	5. For the structured items, I used frequencies and percentages to

ARTIFACT 9 (*Continued*)

Data	Quantitative or Qualitative?	Techniques Used for Analysis
		report responses on each individual question. I also looked at cross tabulations, using chi-square tests for certain demographic variables crossed with the responses for certain questions. A content analysis was conducted of responses to the open-ended items. Percentages of respondents making each type of response were calculated. We also saved some sample responses to illustrate the nature of the comments.
6. Faculty analyses of curriculum; expert reviews of lesson plans and materials (from site visit)	6. Quantitative and qualitative	6. I used a standard analysis form for these analyses and then allowed reviewers to provide open-ended comments as well. Responses to the structured questions were summarized with frequency distributions and with the appropriate measure of central tendency and dispersion for each question (e.g., mode/median/mean, semi-interquartile range/standard deviation). There were so few on-site reviewers that I reported their open-ended comments verbatim in the report of my analyses.

Author Comments. Several precautions are in order as the raw data from the instruments are prepared for data analysis. With the advent of laptop computers, it is possible to do most of the analyses right in the field. Before any data can be entered, a coding handbook should be developed and checked by a colleague. After each form has been coded and entered, a printout of the entered data should be prepared and checked for accuracy. (I'm grateful that some software will now check the accuracy for you.) As a last safeguard, the numbers on the printouts should be checked to make sure they are reasonable and within the range of possibilities.

There is nothing (well, almost nothing) more embarrassing than to discover that some particular point I am stressing heavily in the report is wrong, attributable to human error in the analysis. My credibility is also at stake, and no evaluator can afford to lose that.

Confidentiality is also a concern at this point, and I need to make sure that the raw data are stored in a secure area. I promised my respondents that their names would never be associated with their responses. Their trust and my professional integrity are at stake here, so I must be careful. The data entered into the computer only had ID numbers associated with the responses—I am safe there. But the raw data are going to be locked in a data-storage cabinet, never to be opened (unless a reanalysis is in order) for several years to come. My rule of thumb is not to discard any raw data from projects for at least three years.

> *May 10.* The data have been analyzed and summaries developed. Enough copies have been made of each for me to distribute them to the advisory group for their review and interpretation. These aren't reports—just illustrative quotes, critical incidents in the classroom, tables, and graphs. And, of course, the site-visit information is missing, because that occurs later this week.
>
> A half-day meeting has been scheduled with the advisory group to go through the results, instrument by instrument, question by question, and to get their reading and interpretation of the preliminary findings. What do they mean to us? What conclusions can we draw? I am doing my homework now, and I am sure each of the stakeholders will also. This step is important to all of us because it insures a place for our values to be reflected in the report. So much the better if we all agree on an interpretation, but if we don't, there is a place for multiple interpretations of the same results. This is part of the educational process—when people learn about differing perspectives and expectations. I am really looking forward to this meeting.

Major Concepts and Theories

1. Evaluators make use of many different data sources and methods. The selection of sources and methods is dependent on the nature of the evaluation question(s) and the context for the program to be evaluated.

2. The evaluator should consider a wide array of methods to collect information. These include interviews, observations, documents and records, tests, questionnaires, telephone interviews, and focus groups.

3. Quantitative data are analyzed using descriptive and inferential statistical methods as necessary to answer the evaluation question of interest.

4. Qualitative data are analyzed for patterns and themes. Categories are formed and revised as information is accumulated and new considerations emerge.

5. Data must be interpreted, not simply analyzed. Clients and other stakeholders can be actively involved in this interpretation to permit different perspectives to emerge.

Discussion Questions _____

1. How might an evaluator encourage full participation of the evaluation client, stakeholders, and people from whom data are collected? What advantages does this participation provide? What limitations might be considered?

2. Give an example of when you would consider a telephone interview to be superior to either a paper-and-pencil measure or a face-to-face interview. When would the interview be preferable? What about the paper-and-pencil measure?

3. Discuss the advantages and disadvantages associated with collecting observational data. Consider a program you know. What information might be usefully collected through observation? What important program outcomes would be difficult to measure using observational methods?

Application Exercises _____

1. Examine your worksheets from Chapter 13. How would you revise the sources and methods for data collection that you considered then? What method(s) are most appropriate for answering each evaluation question?

2. Plan an interview to be conducted with fellow students on their reactions to this course. How does it meet their needs? How will they use the information in the future? Design the interview to answer these questions and two others of your own formulation. Develop the questions to ask in the interview. Then interview, individually, three other students. What differences do you find in responses? Does your interviewing style change? Improve? How? Is an interview the best way to answer this question? How does it compare to the use of a survey or focus group? Under what circumstances would you use each approach? Both approaches?

3. Consider your place of work. What documents and records exist there that might be useful for evaluation? How are the documents different from the records? What problems might you encounter in accessing either type of information?

4. In small groups, plan and develop a survey to measure attitudes toward your university. First, develop the questions the survey is to answer. (This may be done as a large group before going into small groups or as part of the small-group exercise.) Then, consider the appropriate item types to answer each question. Develop draft items complete with an introduction and instructions. "Pilot-test" your questionnaire on another group and discuss their responses and interpretations. How would you revise your instrument? Was a questionnaire the best way to gain this information? Why or why not?

5. What methods of data collection would you use to answer the following questions:
   a. Do the methods used by teachers at Smith High School correspond to the principles of block scheduling introduced last fall?
   b. Did the new reading curriculum result in improved reading abilities among second graders? Increased interest in reading?

    c. What types of recruitment strategies are most effective in involving fathers in Early Head Start?

    d. What do different stakeholder groups—parents, students, teachers, counselors, and coaches—think of changing the high school schedule to 9:00 A.M. to 4:00 P.M.?

    e. What strategies were most useful in helping children of new immigrants in their transition to Haley Middle School?

Relevant Evaluation Standards

The evaluation standards we see as relevant to this chapter's content are the following. These standards are described in Chapter 18.

U3–Information Scope and Selection	A3–Described Purposes and Procedure
U4–Values Identification	A4–Defensible Information Sources
F1–Practical Procedures	A5–Valid Information
F2–Political Viability	A6–Reliable Information
P3–Rights of Human Subjects	A7–Systematic Information
P4–Human Interactions	A8–Analysis of Quantitative Information
P5–Complete and Fair Assessment	A9–Analysis of Qualitative Information
A1–Program Documentation	A10–Justified Conclusions
A2–Context Analysis	

Suggested Readings

Braverman, M. T., & Slater, J. K. (Eds.). (1996). *Advances in survey research.* New Directions for Evaluation, No. 70. San Francisco: Jossey-Bass.

Denzin, N. K., & Lincoln, Y. S. (2000). *Handbook of qualitative research* (2nd ed.). Thousand Oaks, CA: Sage.

Krueger, R. A., & Casey, M. A. (2000). *Focus groups: A practical guide for applied research* (3rd ed.). Thousand Oaks, CA: Sage.

Kvale, S. (1996). *InterViews: An introduction to qualitative research interviewing.* Thousand Oaks, CA: Sage.

Miles, M. B., & Huberman, A. M. (1994). *Qualitative data analysis: A sourcebook of new methods.* Thousand Oaks, CA: Sage.

Patton, M. Q. (2002). *Qualitative research & evaluation methods* (3rd ed.). Thousand Oaks, CA: Sage.

Salant, P., & Dillman, D. (1994). *How to conduct your own survey.* New York: John Wiley.

Stake, R. E. (1995). *The art of case study research.* Thousand Oaks, CA: Sage.

16

Reporting and Using Evaluation Information

Orienting Questions

1. What considerations are important in tailoring the reporting of evaluation results to audience needs?
2. What are some of the different ways results can be communicated to stakeholders?
3. How can a written evaluation report be designed to be most effective for users?
4. How should oral reports of evaluation results be organized and presented?
5. What types of influence can evaluation have?

In the prior two chapters we have discussed the collection, analysis, and interpretation of evaluation information. Obviously, these activities are not ends in themselves but terribly important means to making evaluation information useful. It seems obvious that such information is not likely to be used effectively unless it has been communicated effectively. Yet reporting is too often the step to which many evaluators give the least thought. That is distressing to many evaluation audiences; for example, Newman and Brown (1996) cite their earlier research that found that educational administrators and teachers perceive inadequate reporting as a pervasive problem in program evaluation.

In the past decade, evaluators have realized that it isn't enough to craft a good evaluation report. Indeed, evaluators have become increasingly aware that one can work hard to maximize the quality of their report and still find that the impact and influence it has on its stakeholders, programs, or policies is at best negligible and at worst, zero. Thoughtful evaluators now contemplate at the outset how their evaluation reports may be used and consider ways to assure that they are useful. There is a burgeoning body of literature on ways in which evaluations influence not only the programs that are evaluated but also the people and organizations that operate those programs. Designing, preparing, and presenting an evaluation report is the *very essence of* evaluation, but if that report does not prove useful or influential, then that "essence" quickly evaporates into an empty exercise. Thus, we conclude this chapter with a thorough analysis of how evaluations are used and the multiple types of influence they may have, many beyond the uses intended at the outset.

In this chapter we will review various methods for communicating results to different audiences. These include clarifying evaluation purposes; tailoring reports to meet the needs of each audience; protecting clients' and participants' rights and sensitivities; avoiding common reporting failures; and understanding factors that influence the use of evaluation reports.

Purposes of Evaluation Reports

We noted in Chapter 1 that evaluations can have many different purposes, and the information produced can be put to very different uses. We noted, for example, that formative evaluation information is typically used by those wanting to improve a program they are developing or operating, whereas summative evaluation information is typically used by funders and potential consumers, as well as program staff, to certify a program's utility.

The purpose of an evaluation report is directly linked to the use intended for the evaluation. If the evaluation is formative, its overall purpose is to improve the program, and the report should inform program staff early about how the program is functioning and what changes must be made to improve it. If the role of the evaluation is summative, the report should provide information and judgments about the mature program's value to those who (1) may wish to adopt it, (2) will determine resource allocation for its continuation, or (3) have a right to know about the program for other reasons.

Given that the purpose of an evaluation report follows naturally from the role the evaluation plays, it is apparent that evaluation reports can serve many different purposes. Henry and Mark (2003), Brinkerhoff, Brethower, Hluchyj, and Nowakowski (1983), Patton (1986), Cousins and Leithwood (1986), and King (1988) have all discussed the range of ways evaluation findings can be used. Among the purposes they identify are:

- Demonstrating accountability;
- Assisting in making a decision;
- Bringing an issue to the attention of others;
- Helping stakeholders elaborate or refine their opinion of an issue;
- Convincing others to take action;
- Exploring and investigating issues;
- Involving stakeholders in program planning or policy development;

- Gaining support for a program;
- Promoting understanding of issues;
- Changing attitudes;
- Changing individual behaviors;
- Changing the nature of dialogue or interaction among groups;
- Influencing policy;
- Introducing those involved to new ways of thinking through evaluation.

Indeed, evaluation reports serve many purposes. Central to all of them, however, is that of "delivering the message"—informing the appropriate audience(s) about the findings and conclusions resulting from the collection, analysis, and interpretation of evaluation information.

Important Factors in Planning Evaluation Reports

In Chapter 11 we discussed the importance of identifying the multiple audiences for an evaluation and suggested procedures for doing so. An evaluation report obviously cannot be well targeted without clear definition of its audience(s) and the types of questions that audience is likely to raise about findings. Writing an evaluation report before defining the audience is like firing a gun blindfolded, then hurrying to draw the bull's-eye in the path of the speeding bullet. As Lee and Holly (1978) note, "Identify your audience" may be an obvious, overworked platitude, but unfortunately it is often an overlooked step. They cite some common mistakes that have particular relevance for evaluation reports.

> Most evaluations have many audiences. Not identifying all of them is a common mistake. An ignored audience can on occasion get pretty testy and introduce a lot of undesired commotion into the situation. More typically, an audience who needs certain information but never gets it, will make its decisions in ignorance of some perhaps vital information. . . .
>
> Another mistake you can make in identifying your audience is to identify too broad or too narrow an audience. An example of this would be for an evaluator to think a parent committee is the evaluation audience, when the actual audience is the committee chairperson. (She is the respected opinion leader of the group and always determines the action the committee will take on any issue.) Therefore, the majority of the evaluator's dissemination efforts toward the committee should be directed at informing and persuading the chairperson of the validity and implications of the evaluation information (p. 2).

Tailoring Reports to Their Audience(s)

Different audiences have different informational needs. Knowledge of the values held by those who receive information can help the evaluator shape communications effectively. We suggest that an *audience analysis* be completed for all pertinent stakeholders for the evaluation. Such an analysis would involve determining what information each audience should be receiving or is interested in receiving, the values of the audience, and the best channels and approaches to transmit such information.

For example, when an evaluator completes an evaluation, her methodologically oriented colleagues will be interested in a complete, detailed report of the data-collection procedures, analysis techniques, and the like. Not so for the typical policy maker, manager, client, or public interest group. Neither school superintendents, parole officers, corporate trainers, nor immunization staff will be interested in wading through descriptions of an evaluation's methodology. These audiences do not necessarily share the evaluator's grasp of or interest in technical details. The evaluator will have to tailor reports for these groups so that the language and level of technical detail are appropriate to the audience. Yet she still needs to satisfy those who would not view her study as credible without knowing all of its technical aspects. Thus, an evaluation might end up with one omnibus technical evaluation report that includes all the details and several nontechnical evaluation reports aimed at different audience(s). In preparing an evaluation report, the evaluator should consider what type of evidence her audiences will find most compelling, as well as the particular medium, format, and style they are likely to appreciate.

Tailoring Report Content to the Evaluation's Audience(s).   Because of their diverse backgrounds, interests, preferences, and motivations, those who receive and use evaluation reports look for different things. The evaluator who neglects to identify her audiences' needs and preferences will generally find that audiences respond by neglecting her evaluation reports.

In addition to including the specific content important to each audience, the evaluator must also account for differences in the ways audiences interpret and accept evaluation reports. One group may find inferences drawn from certain information credible and useful, whereas another group may scoff at the same conclusions (no matter how "scientifically" defensible). In evaluating a school program, testimonials of students and teachers may be the most persuasive information possible for some audiences, whereas others would insist on statistical summaries of student test performance. The evaluator must also take into account the criteria various audiences will use to make judgments and what standards they will employ to determine the success or failure of that which is evaluated. Evaluation reports must present results in a believable way.

Evaluators can learn from the research of Weiss and Bucuvalas (1980), who state that evaluation reports are most likely to be heard and used by policy makers if they meet two criteria: those of truth value and utility value for the recipient. *Truth value* refers to the technical quality of the study and to whether the findings correspond to policy makers' previous understanding and experience with how the world works (expectations). *Utility value* refers to the extent to which the study provides explicit and practical direction on matters the policy makers can do something about and challenges the status quo (with new formulations and approaches).

Tailoring Report Format, Style, and Language to the Evaluation Audience(s).
Evaluation reports are often thought of as written documents, but, actually, evaluation reports can be delivered in many different ways. They can be written, oral, or presented in many alternative formats (for example, videotapes, Web site-based presentations, PowerPoint). For our purposes, "report" refers to any means by which evaluation findings are communicated. The means *may* be a formal, lengthy bound report, but today's world of evaluation requires the evaluator to consider many other methods as well. Shorter, targeted written reports may be developed for different audiences. Findings can be summarized and reported through brochures, posters, slide-tape shows, E-mail communications, or established Web sites. Interim reports may be delivered frequently with updating occurring at meetings or drafts distributed through E-mails requesting feedback from stakeholders. Oral communications of results, from formal presentations to briefings at meetings, can be a very effective way of communicating information, largely because oral reports engage the audience and encourage dialogue. Ripley (1985) found that audiences who received evaluation information only in a written report were less likely to agree with the conclusions and recommendations than were those who only received information in a nonwritten form.

In short, good evaluations seldom depend solely on the printed word. An important challenge for the evaluator is to present the report in the medium and format that will both appeal to and convince the evaluation's audience(s).

Whatever the form of the report, it is also important to tailor the language and level of sophistication so that evaluation findings can be clearly understood. The evaluator must decide whether the report should be general or specific, technical or nontechnical. Cousins and Leithwood (1986) found that a combination of oral and written reports, delivered in nontechnical language, had a higher impact on the evaluation's audience(s) and led to their being more aware of the evaluation and having greater appreciation of its results.

In tailoring the presentation of findings to audience needs, the evaluator might choose from many different media and modes of display.

- Written reports
- Photo essays
- Audiotape reports
- Slide-tape presentations
- Film or videotape reports
- Multimedia presentations
- Dialogues/testimonies
- Hearings or mock trials
- Product displays
- Simulations

- Scenarios
- Portrayals
- Case studies
- Graphs and charts
- Test score summaries
- Questions/answers

E-mail Reports.   The advent of E-mail and the increasing use of the Internet has added an entirely new dimension to evaluation reporting. The obvious advantages of E-mail include its potential for instant and frequent communication between individuals or among members of a group networked by a common list server. Its capacity for ongoing dialogues and its flexibility make it a prime medium not only for routine evaluation reporting, especially interim reports and preliminary drafts of final reports, but also for atypical reporting. For example, evaluators can send preliminary findings and conclusions to the client(s) in bite-size segments, asking for their prompt reactions. Clients can thus be involved in how evaluation results will be used. David Fetterman (Fetterman, 2001; Fitzpatrick & Fetterman, 2000) has made use of the Internet to share information (field notes, photographs, quantitative data) with members of far-flung evaluation teams to keep each member up-to-date with evaluation findings and to continue a dialogue among the evaluation team members concerning their activities, discoveries, and interpretations. He posts film-strips of evaluation sites on the Internet so that any user of his evaluation findings can gain a picture of the setting and context for the study. (See his Web site at www.stanford.edu/~davidf/.) Much more could be said about the great potential for electronic messaging for evaluation reporting, but E-mail is doubtlessly so well-known to today's students that it would be superfluous. You will likely conceive of innovative uses of E-mail in evaluation reporting in ways we had never dreamed of.

Audiences Can Help Tailor Reports to Fit Their Needs.   Patton (1986) points out that evaluation data are used more if the evaluator discusses and negotiates the format, style, and organization of evaluation reports with primary users. Brinkerhoff and his colleagues (1983) suggest some ways audiences might be involved in influencing the evaluation reports: (1) suggesting dates on which they need information, (2) stating in advance what information would be of interest, (3) requesting specific kinds of recommendations, and (4) suggesting displays and graphs they would find useful. It is beyond the scope of this book to discuss specifics of all the alternative reporting schedules, types, and formats the evaluator might use, but we will deal in the following sections with the issue of timing of reports and the two most common types of reports: written and oral.

Timing of Evaluation Reports

As purposes and audiences for evaluation reports vary, so obviously will the timing of those reports. Formative evaluation reports designed to inform program administrators of needed improvements in a developing pilot program obviously cannot be delivered after the program has been completed (although that might be appropriate for a summative evaluation report to the program's sponsors or regulatory agency). An evaluation report that is limited in scope and perhaps even in rough draft form, but presented prior to relevant decisions, is preferable to a polished, comprehensive report that is delivered after those decisions have been made. Informal verbal briefings that serve an early warning function are preferable to formal but tardy reports. Timeliness is critical in evaluation.

The scheduling of evaluation findings must be guided in a general way by the role of the study. It is obvious, for example, that early reporting will be more customary in a formative evaluation than in a summative study. But it would be an error to conclude that summative reporting is restricted to formal, written reports. Indeed, too much formality may well lessen the likelihood that evaluation findings will be used, for an evaluation's primary audience often will not take the time to study a report. Higher-level administrators and policy makers often hear evaluation findings only from underlings or others who have read the report and distilled from it the particular message they prefer. The evaluator who wishes her message to be heard by managers has to rely largely on informal interim reports, using "nonprint" strategies such as these:

- Being around and available to provide information that managers request
- Talking to those trusted people on whom the manager relies
- Using examples, stories, and anecdotes to make succinct, memorable points
- Talking often, but briefly, and in the audience's language

These suggestions are compatible with Cousins and Leithwood's (1966) report that use of evaluation results is enhanced by ongoing communication and/or close geographical proximity between evaluator and decision maker.

Scheduled Interim Reports. Throughout the planning and implementation of the evaluation, the evaluator should schedule times to meet with stakeholders to share results and seek reactions. Remember that users are most likely to use findings that conform, generally, with their own perceptions (Weiss & Bucuvalas, 1980). When findings are counter to potential users' conceptions or values, discussing interim findings with these users during periodic, regularly scheduled meetings can be helpful in preparing them for final results, providing opportunities to explore their perceptions of the findings, changing attitudes, increasing the credibility of the evaluation and the evaluator, and, ultimately, increasing the influence of the evaluation.

Reports can be scheduled at milestones in either the evaluation (e.g., conclusion of interviews, completion of data analysis on tests) or the program (e.g., near the end of budget cycles, semesters, or program cycles) or at regular intervals corresponding to routine meetings of clients or stakeholders (e.g., PTSA meetings, staff meetings). Internal evaluators may have an advantage here as they are likely to be present or aware of occasions when results might be useful, but all evaluators should be alert to such occasions.

Unscheduled Interim Reports.   The need for interim evaluation reports cannot always be seen in advance. No matter how carefully interim reports have been scheduled, there will be additional times when available evaluation information should be shared. In a formative evaluation, for example, the evaluator may discover a major problem or impediment, such as the fact that video monitors used in an experimental program designed to train federal meat inspectors are too small for trainees beyond the third row to see the critical indicators of possible contamination. It would be a gross disservice to withhold that information until the next *scheduled* interim report, which might be weeks away, and then deliver the not-too-surprising message that a majority of the new generation of meat inspectors did not seem to be learning much from the experimental program that would serve the cause of public health. Helpful evaluators will deliver many unscheduled interim reports, as the information is needed, whenever unexpected events or results pop up. Of course, unscheduled sharing of evaluation information is not limited to formative evaluation; as was noted earlier, the summative evaluator who wishes to see her results used by managers learns to "be around" to share the emerging results of the evaluation informally and frequently.

Final Reports.   Final reports are so familiar as to require no further comment here except to note that (1) they may be incremental (i.e., a preliminary final report released for review and reaction by stakeholders, followed by a later *final* report) and (2) they need not necessarily be written, depending on the desires of the client. Because most clients *do* still request a written final report, however, we turn our attention to that topic.

Key Components of a Written Report

No one best outline or suggested table of contents fits all written evaluation reports. Evaluation roles, objects, and contexts are simply too diverse to permit that. Each evaluation contains idiosyncrasies peculiar to itself, and reports must be tailored to reflect such uniqueness.

Yet there are some important items that should be included in almost every written evaluation (at least every formal, final evaluation report, and interim reports as appropriate). These items are the core of most good written evaluation reports.

We believe that one must worry much more about the form of formal reports intended for external audiences. We see the following outline as applicable in other situations as well, however, and offer it as a heuristic checklist evaluators might consider as they prepare any written evaluation report.

In our judgment, a written, comprehensive, technical evaluation report will typically contain the sections listed in the following "generic" table of contents:

   I. Executive summary
  II. Introduction to the report
      A. Purpose of the evaluation
      B. Audiences for the evaluation report
      C. Limitations of the evaluation and explanation of disclaimers (if any)
      D. Overview of report contents
 III. Focus of the evaluation
      A. Description of the evaluation object
      B. Evaluative questions or objectives used to focus the study
      C. Information needed to complete the evaluation
  IV. Brief overview of evaluation plan and procedures
   V. Presentation of evaluation results
      A. Summary of evaluation findings
      B. Interpretation of evaluation findings
  VI. Conclusions and recommendations
      A. Criteria and standards used to judge evaluation object
      B. Judgments about evaluation object (strengths and weaknesses)
      C. Recommendations
 VII. Minority reports or rejoinders (if any)
VIII. Appendices
      A. Description of evaluation plan/design, instruments, and data analysis and interpretation
      B. Detailed tabulations or analyses of quantitative data, and transcripts or summaries of qualitative data
      C. Other information, as necessary

A brief discussion of each of these major sections and their contents follows.

Executive Summary

One feature of many evaluation reports that makes them so formidable is their organization, which often requires that the busy reader ferret out from a compulsively detailed report why and how the study was conducted and what important information it yielded. Sometimes a brief summary of essential information is wedged somewhere between the presentation of the findings and the appendices, but often readers are left to sift out the most valuable nuggets of information for themselves.

    Most evaluation audiences do not have (or will not take) the time or energy necessary to read a thick report laden with tabular information or narrative details. It makes good sense, therefore, to provide a brief executive summary in one of the following forms.

Executive Summary within a Report.   For most evaluation studies, an executive summary might best be included within the report itself, preferably right up front where it is the first thing the busy administrator sees when the report is opened. We also propose that the executive summary be printed on a different color paper to draw attention to it. This summary should usually be somewhere between two and six pages in length, depending on the scope and complexity of the evaluation. In addition to a very brief description of the study's purpose, and a very brief word about how data were obtained (e.g., "Data were collected with questionnaires mailed to plant workers and a focus-group interview with plant managers"), the summary should contain the most important findings, judgments, and recommendations, perhaps organized in a simple question-and-answer format or with major findings or recommendations bulleted or numbered. The summary should also contain references directing the reader to further information on salient points. If the evaluation report is large and interest in it broad, then it is sometimes more economical to distribute a *separately bound executive summary* similar in all other respects to what we've just described.

Executive Abstract.   With a large evaluation audience, it may be necessary to condense the executive summary to a one- or two-page abstract that contains only the major findings and recommendations without any supporting documentation. Such abstracts are often useful in communicating evaluation results to large legislative bodies, parents, citizens, community leaders, members of professional associations, and the like.

In one statewide evaluation of a controversial program conducted by one of the authors, three interrelated written evaluation reports were prepared: (1) a large, detailed technical report containing most of the information called for in the earlier outline; (2) a medium-size summary of major interpretations and judgments drawn from the data; and (3) a brief executive summary of the study purposes, findings, and conclusions. Availability of these three reports was broadly announced in the newspapers and on television. Readership was estimated by the number of people who requested a copy or checked one out in the several repositories in which they were made available. Nearly 400 individuals read the executive summary, 40 read the midsize interpretive report, and only one person ever even requested the complete report (and he was an expert methodologist hired by opponents of the evaluation to see if he could find fault with it). As these results show, shorter reports will often be most widely disseminated.

Introduction to the Report

Despite its prominent placement in the report, the executive summary is only a brief abstract, not an introduction. An adequate introduction will set the stage for the remainder of the report by outlining the basic purpose(s) of the evaluation and the audiences the report is intended to serve. For example, is the evaluation intended to provide information to legislative budget analysts who will determine future funding of a statewide domestic violence program, or is it to document the performance of Mid-City's new, state-supported family violence prevention program in a true field test? Is the evaluation audience the state legislature, the administrators and staff operating the state-supported Mid-City program, or both?

One good way to ensure that a report will be relevant is to describe thoroughly the rationale for the evaluation. The rationale should address such questions as: Why was the evaluation conducted? What is the evaluation intended to accomplish? What questions was it intended to answer? Why was the evaluation conducted the way it was? Once this information is provided, audiences can determine whether the report is relevant by asking how well each question is answered.

The introduction is also one logical place to caution the reader about limitations that affect the collection, analysis, or interpretation of information. Such limitations should be openly disclosed here (or in a later section dealing with evaluation procedures). Similarly, disclaimers are sometimes placed at the beginning of a report (e.g., in the preface or on the title page) to clarify what the evaluation is and is not, thus protecting both clients and evaluators from criticisms based on misunderstandings.

It is also useful to provide in the introduction a brief "reader's guide" to the report. The table of contents only lists major topics. The reader's guide explains what each topic comprises.

Focus of the Evaluation

This section provides a focus to the evaluation, summarizing those evaluation activities we described in Chapters 10 through 13. We stressed in Chapters 10 and 11, for example, the importance of describing the evaluation object accurately, so everyone could agree on precisely what was (and was not) being evaluated. It is not only essential to agree on such a description at the beginning of an evaluation but also to share that description prominently in an early section of the report. Descriptions of evaluation objects obviously should not be limited to physical characteristics but should also include (1) rationale, goals, and objectives;[1] (2) patients, customers, students, or other recipients/participants to be benefited; (3) the program's structure, content, activities, and other characteristics; (4) strategies and procedures used for implementation; (5) operating context; and (6) human and other resource requirements needed.

It is also important to list in an early section the evaluative questions, objectives, or other organizers used to focus the evaluation. If differential priorities were assigned to the questions or objectives, that process should be explained.

Finally, it is useful to include a subsection outlining the needed information the evaluation was intended to collect, analyze, and report. Such a list helps make the rationale for the next section much more apparent.

Brief Overview of the Evaluation Plan and Procedures

Any complete evaluation report must include a detailed presentation of the evaluation plan, the data collection instruments, and the methods and techniques

[1]Unless, of course, this is a goal-free evaluation study.

used to analyze and interpret data, but they need not be in the body of the report. Early in our evaluation careers, we included all such details in this section. After a decade or two, we each concluded that a careful and complete summary would suffice in this section if detailed procedures (and possibly even the instruments themselves) were contained in supporting appendices. After another decade, we have each moved the entire description of the design, instruments, data collection, and analysis procedures to an appendix, leaving in this section of the report only a few sentences that tell very generally where the data came from and how they were obtained. Readers of the report wishing more detail are referred to the Appendix.

Presentation of Evaluation Results

This section of the report contains the results of the evaluation and represents the source of subsequent conclusions and recommendations, preferably in the form of a complete summary, using tables, displays, and quotations as appropriate, and referencing more detailed data summaries or transcripts in supporting appendices. Although some audiences are put off by too much statistical data (and factor analyses, multiple regressions, and the like should be avoided in the narrative with almost any nontechnical audience), many policy makers, managers, and others respond positively to data presented in straightforward graphs and charts because they are able to summarize data in a way that many users can understand (Alkin, Stecher, & Geiger, 1982; Henry, 1997). Henry (1997) provides a sourcebook on ways to present graphs effectively.

Remember, too, that numbers generally fail to portray or illustrate the program and its impact on others adequately. Quotations from interviews with clients or community members, pictures of program activities, and mini-case studies or stories of individual students or other recipients of services can be quite effective in giving readers a deeper understanding of the issues. (See Fischer and Wertz [2002] for a discussion of four formats they used to convey results of their study of victims of crime and their rehabilitation to policy makers.)

The interpretation of the results is as important as their presentation. Evaluation depends, after all, on the evaluator's ability to perceive and interpret. Interpreting data should not be an informal or casual activity. Rather, it should be a careful process, made as public as possible by the evaluator's careful listing of all content and steps followed to reach the particular judgments and recommendations presented.

One of the most disconcerting deficits of many evaluation reports is the lack of any organization to assist the reader in relating findings to the major evaluative questions posed. Without organization or categorization, findings often blur, becoming less understandable. We urge evaluators to relate their findings to the most logical set of organizers. We prefer to organize the findings around the evaluative questions posed for the study in a question-and-answer format. Other organizers might include the goals or objectives (if that is the evaluation's focus), various components of the program, or different groups of clients. Whatever the organizer, some structure must be given to all but the most simplistic, single-variable, single-question evaluations.

Conclusions and Recommendations

In this section of the report we would propose that the evaluator list the standards and criteria used, provide her best judgments about the quality of what has been evaluated, and provide whatever recommendations she feels follow from those judgments.

Standards and criteria should be listed explicitly. The data do not speak for themselves. The evaluator who knows those data well is in the best position to apply the standards to the data to reach a judgment of whether the evaluation object is effective or ineffective, valuable or worthless. Making judgments is an essential part of the evaluator's job. An evaluation without clear criteria is as much an indictment of its author's lack of sophistication as one in which judgments are not based on the data.

We strongly prefer organizing evaluative judgments under the headings *strengths* (presented first) and *limitations* (or the parallel and more familiar *strengths* and *weaknesses,* if client and evaluator are less squeamish). Several advantages accrue to this dichotomous presentation.

- Attention is focused on both positive and negative judgments.
- Audiences can conveniently locate the evaluator's positive or negative judgments.
- Presenting strengths first generally helps those responsible for the evaluation object to accept the weaknesses listed thereafter.

The discussion of strengths and limitations must be sufficiently complete to allow the audience(s) to see the rationale and judgments on which later recommendations are based. Another useful format familiar to planners in corporate and higher education settings is the SWOT format (strengths, weaknesses, opportunities, and threats).

Although we strongly prefer the inclusion of recommendations, there are times when they might be appropriately omitted. In some cases, a report may be used to begin a strategic planning process to generate recommendations. The evaluator might serve as the facilitator of that process or, if she lacks skills in strategic planning, should certainly be present as a resource. But, in this case, a mechanism has been established to generate recommendations. In other cases, evaluators may be better at identifying how well things are working (or not working) than they are at recommending how necessary corrections should be made. In fact, in many cases, evaluators' recommendations may urge that attention be given to correcting a problem without specifying the exact means by which the problem should be corrected. In other cases, it may be appropriate for the evaluator to work with the client, and possibly other stakeholders or an advisory group, to develop recommendations that *do* propose feasible and appropriate corrective actions. Such recommendations, developed in collaboration with stakeholders, can help increase confidence in the report.

Minority Reports or Rejoinders

Sometimes, under circumstances discussed in a later section, it may be important to include a section in which those who disagree with the evaluator's judgments, conclusions, or recommendations are provided space to share their dissenting views. Or, if one member of an evaluation team disagrees with the majority view, it seems sensible to insert any rebuttals or "minority reports" as a last section.

Appendices

Supporting appendices (bound within the report or as a separate volume) are the place where one should present any information needed to help the reader understand such things as what (if any) sampling procedures were used, how the information was collected to insure its accuracy, what specific statistical or narrative analysis procedure was used, and why. In short, this is where the evaluator provides the methodological and technical information needed not only by primary audiences but also by fellow evaluators who will decide whether the conduct of the study was adequate to make its results believable. The evaluator cannot forget that fellow evaluators keenly interested in methodological and technical adequacy will be perusing those reports. It is wise to remember Campbell's (1984) insistence on "having available (along with the data available for re-analysis) a full academic analysis for cross-examination by our applied social science colleagues" (p. 41). The appendix is the best place for such detailed descriptions of evaluation procedures, detailed data tabulations or analyses, observation logs, complete transcripts of important interviews, and other information that is relevant but too detailed to present in the body of the report. Appendices might also include the actual data-collection instruments and any other information (e.g., boundary maps of sampling units in a community survey) deemed of interest and importance to the audiences but inappropriately detailed and/or too extensive for inclusion in the body of the report. Appropriate use of appendices will make the report itself much more streamlined and eminently more readable.

Suggestions for Presenting Information in Written Reports

Written evaluation reports are nearly as varied as those who write them. But the great majority share a common characteristic: They make tedious and tiresome reading. Indeed, their variety seems limited only by the number of ways that can be found to make written information boring. Many deserve Mark Twain's waggish description of a particular book: "chloroform in print." One sometimes wonders whether such dreadful dullness reflects a purposeful design to discourage readers.

Not that all evaluation reports are awful. Now and then one appears that is both interesting and informative, both enlightening and entertaining, both comprehensive and captivating. But these, like other gems, are rare. For an example of creative ways to communicate evaluation information, we recommend *Introduction to Program Evaluation for Comprehensive Tobacco Control Programs*, a report that won the American Evaluation Association award for government service in 2002 (MacDonald, 2001).

In this and the following section, we suggest several considerations to help make the evaluator's written presentation effective, interesting, and fair.

Accuracy, Balance, and Fairness

It goes without saying that evaluation reports should not be unfair, unbalanced, or inaccurate. Yet truth is elusive, and even the most scrupulous evaluator must struggle to see that carefully collected and analyzed information is not later distorted, intentionally or unintentionally, in its presentation. As the Joint Committee (1994) states: "all acts, public pronouncements, and written reports of the evaluation [should] adhere strictly to a code of directness, openness, and completeness" (p. 109).

Similarly, the evaluator must make certain that nothing is allowed to color the presentation of information. Suppose the personality traits of a program director offend the evaluator. It is important to prevent that fact from negatively tainting the judgments and language in the evaluation report (unless, of course, the program director also offends others in ways that have a negative effect on the program). Fairness in reporting is the hallmark of a professional evaluator.

Finally, there are two or more sides to every story. It is essential that legitimate positions be reported in a balanced way. No evaluator will ever be completely free of bias, but every effort must be made to control bias in reporting. The Joint Committee, evidencing its concern in this area, provided the following as one standard of propriety:

> *Balanced Reporting.* The evaluation should be complete and fair in its presentation and recording of strengths and weaknesses of the program being evaluated, so that strengths can be built upon and problem areas addressed (p. 105).

Communication and Persuasion

Communication plays an important role in all stages of evaluation. Good communication is essential if the evaluator is to understand the origins and context for an evaluation, elicit the evaluative questions and criteria from stakeholders, reach agreements with clients concerning the evaluation plan, deal with political and interpersonal aspects of evaluation studies, maintain rapport and protocol during data collection, and so on. But nowhere is clarity of communication more central than during reporting. The quality of that communication will determine whether the evaluator's message comes through clear or garbled.

Construed broadly, communication may be thought of as all the procedures one person uses to inform another. Presenting information that cannot be understood is simply poor communication (no matter how *correct* the information). Presenting statistical summaries to lay audiences who do not understand statistics is poor communication (or noncommunication), regardless of how well a more statistically oriented audience might receive the same information. It is equally foolish to summarize rich qualitative data in prose that is truly literary and erudite when the audience consists of relatively uneducated stakeholders whose vocabulary and reading ability are badly overmatched by the evaluator's show of erudition.

It is absolutely essential that the evaluator tailor every presentation to make it understandable to its audience(s). This requires care and creativity. To present statistical evaluation results to audiences who are not schooled in statistics, Brager and Mazza (1979) suggest using (1) analogies; (2) graphs or pictorial displays; (3) well-explained summaries to highlight selected findings; (4) a television newscast format to underscore concise, important findings; and (5) a minimal number of judiciously inserted statistics.

No matter how dispassionate the presentation, if the communication seeks to bring the reader to the same conclusions the evaluator has reached, then its intent is not only to inform but also to persuade. House (1980) analyzed in one study the contrast between impersonal, neutral presentation of evaluation procedures and the dramatic use of imagery in presenting the implications for action. But, as he notes, both are used to persuade. Describing the discussion of methodology in the study as being "conducted with painstaking neutrality," he observes that

> The resulting 'scientific' style is clinical, detached, impersonal, and lacks imagery. The author presents the external world and allows it to persuade the reader. The style suggests that the observer is governed by method and by the rules of scientific integrity (p. 99).

In speaking of the study's implications for action, House notes that facts are converted to imagery; he comments:

> Imagery, dramatic structure, and mode of presentation are central considerations for the import of an evaluation. These elements, often thought of as merely cosmetic, can affect what people believe and do (p. 100).

House also relates both styles of presentation to the coherence he believes is essential, a coherence he says can be attained through "storytelling."

> Every evaluation must have a minimum degree of coherence. The minimum coherence is that the evaluation tell a story. . . .
>
> There are at least two conventional ways of telling the story. One way is to present the evaluator as a neutral, scientific observer. In this case, the story line is implied. It runs something like, "I am a detached, neutral observer who has made measurements according to the canons of science and have found certain things to be so. The program was conducted as I have described it, and I have found the

following outcomes. . . ." Usually the story line concludes that "the program was implemented, and such and such were the results." Actual description is often sparse. . . . The usual presentation is to describe the project or the goals of the project, the treatment, the results or effects, and the conclusions.

The second major way of telling the story is for the evaluator to stand closer to the program, as reflected in the narrator's 'voice,' and to tell the story by describing the events in detail. To this end the evaluator may use emotionally charged language and a narrative presentation. The story may look like a newspaper report (pp. 102–103).

The importance of telling a story through the evaluation, whether that be through careful narrative description or visual displays, cannot be overemphasized. Whatever tactic is used, it is imperative that the evaluator take pains to communicate her message clearly and persuasively in a style that will engage the audience.

Level of Detail

The notion that all evaluators suffer from obsessive-compulsive personality disorders may be an unfounded rumor, but it is probably rooted in some real-world evaluation reports. We have all seen (if not produced) such reports, two inches or more in thickness, crammed full of all conceivable (and, some inconceivable) details about the evaluation study and everything associated with it. Some evaluators confuse the call for comprehensiveness with the compulsion to collect. Cronbach and his colleagues (1980) made this wry observation:

comprehensive examination of a program does not necessarily justify an exhaustive report. . . .

Many evaluations are reported with self-defeating thoroughness. . . . A normal human being will try to assimilate only so many numbers, and not much more prose. When an avalanche of words and tables descends, everyone in its path dodges (p. 186).

How much detail should be included in an evaluation report? Only as much as the audience needs. A program's manager(s) and staff members may be interested in specifics, but that is seldom true of policy makers or other readers farther removed from the program. A particular program director may be primarily interested in a discussion of how recommendations could be used to improve the program, while community persons may simply be interested in a single sentence summarizing how the program performed on a particular objective. Thus, a written evaluation report should be organized so that various audiences can quickly assess the information of particular interest to them.

Technical Writing Style

Earlier we spoke about communication and persuasion in a broader sense. There we were concerned mostly with communicating clearly, avoiding unnecessary ambiguity, and making certain the evaluation story was clearly understood. In a written report, the use of language, as well as pictures, graphs, and tabular displays, will determine whether or not the communication is effective.

Nothing is as tiresome as reading tedious, unnecessarily convoluted, imprecise, and sometimes inconvenient and awkward expression. (See what we mean?) Wouldn't it have been better if we had said simply, "Nothing is as tiresome as reading complicated writing"?

We offer these few rules for improving writing style in evaluation reports:

- *Avoid jargon.* If users have certain "jargon," however, it can be important to use their terms for clarity and credibility to them.
- *Use simple, direct language.* Make certain the level of language is appropriate for the audience; don't ramble.
- *Use examples, anecdotes, illustrations.* Don't forget, a picture is worth a thousand words—and don't be flippant by asking why we did not illustrate this text.
- *Use correct grammar and punctuation.* And spelling should also be appropriate for the country in which the report is to be used.
- *Avoid cluttering narrative with reference notes.* Yes, we know we have done just that, but then this is a text *and reference* book, not an evaluation report, and you are not the typical evaluation audience.
- *Use language that is interesting, not dull.*

Appearance of the Report

It would be interesting to do a bit of "free-response research" to determine what is the first descriptive word that pops into people's minds when they hear "evaluation report." We cannot predict the most common responses, but we would be amazed if they included "attractive," "handsome," or "visually appealing." Concern with aesthetics has historically been as common among evaluators as compassion has been among tax collectors. Most evaluators have been preoccupied with what the report said, not with how attractively the message was packaged.

Appearance counts, however, because it will often influence how (or whether) a document will be read. Market analysts and advertising specialists know much that would be useful to evaluators who want their products used (such as how long it takes the average administrator to transmit most items from the "incoming" mailbox to the "outgoing" wastebasket or to delete a long message or attachment from their E-mail).

Until a decade or so ago, many evaluators seemed reluctant to adopt the "slick and glossy" visual tricks of advertising. Now most evaluators are concerned with the "cover appeal" of their report, as well as the attractiveness of its contents. Many evaluators frequently produce high-quality brochures and pictures when reporting evaluations of important programs to their various publics. Much knowledge from the marketing, commercial art, and publishing fields can be tastefully applied to make evaluation reports more visually appealing and readable. Five suggestions follow:

1. *Print quality.* If you have ever tried to read a faded, smudged copy of a report reproduced on some ink-dry printer or nearly worn-out copier, you know that only a rare report will be judged worth the effort. Sharp, dark printing in standard size or larger is essential.

2. *Graphics.* Evaluators (and their secretaries) are not necessarily competent in drafting or in art. Yet that is no longer an acceptable excuse for failure to include high-quality graphics and art, when appropriate, in evaluation reports. A nearly endless array of computer software packages now allows even artistically impaired evaluators to develop attractive and sophisticated graphs and art. The changes introduced by home-publishing software, the various "paintbrush" programs, and affordable color printers have left evaluators with no excuse for dull and drab reports. Visual displays should be used in evaluation reports wherever they would be helpful in telling (or better yet, *showing*) the story. Photographs and other illustrations (while not technically "graphics") can also help greatly.

3. *Page appearance.* Far too many evaluation reports are overwhelmed with a sense of "grayness"—page after page of long, uninterrupted paragraphs with nothing to relieve the monotony. (Small wonder the eye sometimes responds by closing.) Good production editors have long since learned the advantage of "breaking up the page," using strategies such as these:

- White space (to separate and relieve printed sections)
- Varied headings (regular and boldface)
- Underlining or italics (not only to give emphasis but also to add interest)
- Use of numbered or "bulleted" lists (such as this one)
- Insertion of visuals (graphs, pictures, or even cartoons)
- Boxes (or other visual displays of selected materials)

Several computer programs now have "auto-format" features that show a recommended format that incorporates several of these features.

4. *Color.* Careful use of color can make an evaluation report more attractive, as well as more functional. When the executive summary appears as the first section in an evaluation report, we prefer to print it on colored paper. This not only gives some visual appeal but also draws attention to the summary and makes it easy for the reader to locate it later. Consider printing appendices on yet another color. It will be easy to turn to, and the combination of colors with the predominantly white body of the report enhances the visual appeal of the whole.

5. *Cover.* Obviously not all written evaluation reports warrant preparing and printing a cover. A typed and stapled cover page will serve well in many formative evaluation studies, and possibly some summative evaluation studies as well, but a more attractive report cover may entice readers and suggest that the evaluator thought the information contained in the report was worthy of a professional presentation. Of course, no cover will compensate for an inadequate evaluation report.

Alternative Methods for Reporting: The Adversary Approach

In our last edition of this book (Worthen, Sanders, and Fitzpatrick, 1997), we described a category of evaluation approaches that we called adversary-oriented evaluation approaches. Although still being used in the form of hearings and debates, we no longer see this approach as a major category of evaluation practice and, therefore, have omitted it from our discussion of approaches in Part Two. However, we do see the general strategy of adversary hearings as a creative and effective way to present information to any size audience and to get them to judge the merits of the arguments.

In the broad sense, an adversary hearing is a presentation of information from opposing points of view. One presenter serves as a program advocate, presenting the most positive case for the program based on the data and deliberation, while another presenter plays an adversarial role, highlighting any deficiencies in the program. By using the opposing presentations to arrive at conclusions about the program, stakeholders become engaged in a process aimed at fairness and balance that illuminates both strengths and weaknesses of the program.

Several types of adversarial proceedings have been used to evaluate programs, policies, ideas, and other entities when choices need to be made. These include mock "judge and jury" hearings (Owens, 1971, 1973; Rice, 1915; Wolf, 1975, 1979), hearings (Levine, Brown, Fitzgerald, Goplerud, Gordon, Jayne-Lararus, Rosenberg, & Slater, 1978; Stenzel, 1982), and debates (Kourilsky and Baker, 1976; Stake and Gjerde, 1974).

Observers tend to agree that such proceedings are useful in (1) illuminating both the positive and negative aspects of a program, and (2) satisfying stakeholders' information needs in an interesting manner. Nearly everyone loves a contest. The use of broad, direct, holistic human debate is frequently cited as a strength of this way of presenting information about a program.

Despite the potential of adversary proceedings for making evaluation reporting to decision makers more interesting, there are some drawbacks. Preoccupation with the presentation itself, i.e., the "contest," may get in the way of a rational and fair deliberation. Skills of debate may introduce an unintended bias. When "winning" is at stake, seemingly rational opponents may use devious methods, such as concealing pertinent data, to sway their audience. The touchstones of debate are polemics and persuasion, not truth, which is central to evaluation.

In summary, using adversary proceedings as a way of reporting can have positive and negative impacts. When done in conjunction with other reporting strategies, they can add increased discussion of a broad set of issues, opportunities for cross-examination of both the data and interpretations of the data, and explicit and interactive discussion of the issues. Care must be taken, however, to avoid competition and showmanship from deflecting the evaluation's audiences from the study's findings.

Human and Humane Considerations in Reporting Evaluation Findings

Many evaluators become so preoccupied with preparing and presenting their messages that they forget the impact that those messages will have. If an evaluation report labels the U.S. Coast Guards's new officer-training curriculum as ill-conceived and its implementation as inadequate, the personal egos (and perhaps the professional reputations) of the curriculum designer and the trainer(s) implementing the program will not go unscathed. This doesn't mean that truth should be diluted to protect feelings, only that it be communicated as carefully, sensitively, and professionally as possible. Beyond apparent idealistic reasons for protecting the rights and sensitivities of those on whom the evaluation might reflect, there are also some obvious (if you think about it for a moment) pragmatic reasons. For example, in many evaluations, results are reported directly to those responsible for planning or running the program. Evaluators far too wise to tell any mother that her baby is ugly may tactlessly tell an administrator and staff that the program to which they have devoted three years of their lives is a disaster. Not surprisingly, the program practitioners may exercise the limits of their ingenuity in seeking ways to discount both the evaluation and the evaluator. The opportunity for the message to be of use may have been irretrievably lost.

The evaluator must take appropriate steps to protect the rights and sensitivities of all those involved in the evaluation. For the practicing evaluator, this means that raw technical facts must be buffered by sensitivity to the maxim that truth must be told with tenderness and in a context of trust. In this section we offer our suggestions for (1) delivering negative messages, and (2) providing those affected with the opportunity to review a draft report (and suggest modifications) prior to its final release.

Delivering Negative Messages

In olden days, the messenger who delivered news to the king lived a life fraught with risk. If the news was bad, the messenger might lose his tongue—or even his head. Nowadays, the bearers of bad evaluation tidings may still find themselves savaged (though in a somewhat more polite manner).

Sometimes evaluation clients (or others involved with the evaluation) are so sensitive to any criticism or any hint of imperfection that it would not matter much how negative findings were reported—the reaction would still be defensive. But more often we have observed that defensive reactions are exacerbated by the manner in which the negative results are conveyed.

Earlier we proposed one simple solution: to present the strengths of the program first. (To those who say they cannot find any strengths to report, we suggest they are not very thorough or insightful; in even the most awful program, one can usually comment sincerely on the efforts, dedication, and hard work of the staff.) We also reiterate the following steps recommended by Van Mondfrans (1985) for helping those involved in evaluation to "swallow bitter pills":

1. In an oral debriefing where the major events of the evaluation are reviewed and where the major findings are previewed, the negative information is stated in as positive a context as possible. It seems easier for clients to accept negative information in an oral form in a relatively friendly encounter.

2. A preliminary written report is presented in which the negative information is described in a straightforward factual manner but from as positive a perspective as possible. Often a personal visit needs to follow in which the preliminary report is discussed and the client allowed to propose changes if the information is viewed as unfair. If changes are needed in the preliminary report, they should not obscure negative information or allow it to be misinterpreted; however, it may be that in discussing the negative information, the client will bring up other factors not known to the evaluator at the time the preliminary report was written. These other factors may be included in the final report in juxtaposition with the negative information, thus allowing better interpretation.

3. A final written report is prepared in which the negative information is accurately and fully presented. Having undergone previous steps, the client is better prepared to deal with the negative information, having had a chance to review it several times, to think of other factors which are relevant, and present those to the evaluator. The evaluator has the opportunity to review other factors and include them in the report if they aid the interpretation of the negative information (pp. 3–4).

Benkofske (1994a, 1994b) has also suggested ways to prepare stakeholders to receive negative findings about their program's performance. In her view, this is especially important when the negative findings are distilled from qualitative data. She reports that most of her clients have heard so much about the benefits of qualitative data that they inappropriately come to expect it to yield glowing descriptions of their programs. Thus, she finds it important to engage clients early on in a discussion of what they would do if the qualitative data turn out negative. In her words:

clients all come believing their program needs a qualitative study. I have found, however, that stakeholders need to be prepared for the evaluation results if the qualitative data are not positive. It is my personal experience that qualitative data hurts; it stings like hell to see in print pages of quoted material that describes in vivid detail problems with a program. While qualitative data can "brighten the portrait" when positive, it can wound deeply when negative (p. 2).

Earlier in this chapter we mentioned that disclaimers could be inserted early in an evaluation report to protect both client and evaluator. Such disclaimers are intended to prevent misinterpretation and to put any negative messages in proper perspective. An example of such a disclaimer follows:

> This report describes the procedures and results of a (*state whether formative or summative*) evaluation of (*name of program/project*). The client, (*name of client*), reserves all rights to this information. The purpose of this evaluation was to (*state purpose*). Any other use of this report may be subject to serious errors since the information was collected with the above purpose as the sole focus. Information relevant to other purposes was either not collected or not reported.

It is often useful to expand on such cryptic disclaimers. Errors and misunderstandings can arise if evaluation results are used for purposes other than those intended.

Providing an Opportunity for Review of the Report

Only the most arrogant evaluator would assume that her work and the report that presents it are completely accurate and fair in all regards. Small factual errors can lead to nontrivial errors in judgments and conclusions. Interpretations can overlook contextual factors that the evaluator failed to understand and thus be spurious. And the evaluator's bias can creep into evaluation narratives unnoticed, especially by the evaluator.

For all of these reasons, we strongly urge that the evaluator circulate a draft of her evaluation report to the client and other key stakeholders for comments, asking that they point out (and correct where appropriate) all

- Minor errors (for example, misspellings),
- Factual errors (wrong names or titles, errors in numbers of persons participating, etc.), and
- Interpretive errors.

Reviewers should be asked not only to challenge anything that they perceive to be an error but also to provide substantiation for the alternative facts or interpretations that they propose as correct. Reviewers should be informed that the evaluator is under no obligation to accept their suggestions (the intent is not to allow clients to rewrite the report any way they wish) but only to give those suggestions serious consideration. The evaluator reserves the right to ignore suggestions and to make only those changes that are warranted.

Circulating a preliminary draft report can increase the number of individuals who read the report carefully; shared responsibility for the report's accuracy is a good motivator. Some may worry that use of drafts may lessen interest in the final report. That concerns us less than the very real possibility that many key persons who are not asked to review a draft may never read the report at all.

What if the evaluator refuses to accept a proposed change in the report, but the reviewer who suggested it continues to contend that the report is inaccurate, misleading, or unfair? Simple. Invite the reviewer to share that view, in writing, and include it in a concluding section of the report, as we proposed earlier. We see no problem with permitting reviewers to include their rebuttals, rejoinders, or contrary comments. If the evaluator's data collection, analysis, interpretation, judgments, and conclusions are on solid ground, they should not be harmed by such detraction. If they are shaky and cannot withstand such challenge, then they deserve to be challenged.

Suggestions for Effective Oral Reporting

Written evaluation reports, although very common, are not necessarily the most effective medium for evaluation reporting. Oral reports, supported by appropriate visual aids, can be even more effective.

Many of the earlier suggestions for improving written reports are pertinent for oral reports as well. Audiences who listen to oral reports need an introduction that explains the purpose of the evaluation, what was evaluated, the questions addressed, and the evaluation procedures used. Presenting positive conclusions followed by negative conclusions and recommendations is still appropriate. And the evaluator should still be as concerned about such items as the following:

- Accuracy, balance, and fairness;
- Communication and persuasion;
- Level of detail;
- Use of simple, direct, correct, and interesting language;
- Avoidance of jargon and unnecessary technical language;
- Use of examples, anecdotes, and illustrations;
- Sensitivity to the rights and feelings of those involved.

Oral reports also require particular attention to audiovisual presentation of information. Obviously the suggestions commonly offered in speech and communications courses and texts are relevant here, but the following tips are particularly relevant for making effective oral evaluation reports:

1. Begin with an outline of the message(s) you want to communicate; sequence and weave them together into the story you want to tell to your audience.

2. Decide who should tell the story. It is not essential that the lead evaluator also be the lead storyteller; what *is* essential is that the story be told well. If the lead evaluator has that capability, then she would obviously be the best choice. But using another member of the evaluation team (or even an outside "reporter") is far preferable to having a good evaluation destroyed in its telling by an evaluator who is not a strong presenter but is too egocentric to abandon center stage. Usually the lead evaluator(s) can be involved in at least a *part* of the presentation so that any awkwardness can be minimized.

3. Choose the oral report medium (verbal narrative, videotape, staged debate, etc.). Make the presentation format interesting and varied using multiple media, multiple presenters, or other variations. Don't use the format the audience expects; do something different to maintain interest.

4. Make visuals to accompany the presentation. But, notice the word *accompany.* Visuals should not dominate or lead the presentation. Many, otherwise effective, PowerPoint presentations are ruined by their being permitted to dominate the presentation. Reading a list of bullets from a PowerPoint presentation is *not* an effective use of visuals. Conversely, using PowerPoint presentations to highlight major issues, to present creative graphics, pictures, images, flowcharts, or complex tables, or to inject humor and color into a presentation can awaken the audience to the possibilities of the findings. Make sure to test the presentation at the place where it will be delivered. More than one presentation has failed because the evaluator failed to determine if the computer capabilities at the site matched those anticipated for the presentation.

5. Develop a presentation that feels natural and comfortable to you, then practice until you are at ease delivering it. Use effective highlighting techniques, such as a laser pointer or computer stylus. Practice using it. You don't want your laser beam to hit a client in the eye!

6. Involve the audience in the presentation through questions and answers, show of hands, or other interaction; give them three minutes to talk in trios or couples to identify other issues they would like you to address and the like.

7. Develop and adhere to an agenda, with appropriate breaks. Protracted oral reports will have people slumping in their seats (or worse, out of their seats).

Of course, frequent oral reporting of results—in staff meetings, forums with clients or community members, individual meetings with key managers or policy makers—is the critical way to engage audiences in the evaluation process and increase its ultimate influence. Evaluators should attempt to attend many meetings with such groups, taking the opportunity to observe the types of information each group expects, their style of interaction, and their information needs, as well as using the meeting to insert a few key pieces of information being gained from the evaluation or to remind audiences of the progress and thank them for their assistance. These frequent, more informal methods of communication prepare the audience to receive the final report with curiosity, interest, and optimism.

A Checklist for Good Evaluation Reports

Ingredients of a good evaluation report can readily be inferred from our earlier suggestions, but here, for convenience, is a checklist of things that would typify most good evaluation reports.
Check each that applies.

_____ Interim and final reports provided in time to be most useful

_____ Report content tailored to the audience(s)

_____ Report format and style tailored to the audience(s)

_____ Involvement of audiences in determining the format and style of the report

_____ An executive summary

_____ An adequate introduction to "set the stage"

_____ Mention of limitations of the study

_____ Adequate presentation of evaluation plan and procedures (primarily in appendices)

_____ Effectively organized presentation of results

_____ All necessary technical information provided (preferably in appendices)

_____ Specification of standards and criteria for evaluative judgments

_____ Evaluative judgments

_____ Lists of *both* identified strengths and weaknesses

_____ Recommendations for action

_____ Protection of clients' and stakeholders' interests

_____ Sensitivity to those affected by the evaluation findings

_____ Provision for minority reports or rejoinders

_____ Accurate and unbiased presentation

_____ Effective communication and persuasion through "telling the story"

_____ Appropriate level of detail

_____ Lack of technical jargon

_____ Use of correct, uncomplicated, and interesting language

_____ Use of examples and illustrations

_____ Attention to visual appearance and eye appeal

How Evaluation Information Is Used

The utility of any evaluation is a prime criterion for judging its worth (Joint Committee, 1994). Use is one of the factors that distinguishes evaluation from research. Evaluation is intended to have an immediate or at least a near-term impact, while research is intended to add to knowledge and theory in a field, but the results it yields may not be used for some time. If an evaluation study appears to have no effect, it will be judged harshly regardless of its technical, practical, and ethical merits whereas research is not held to the same criterion of usefulness.

Evaluators have been studying and writing about evaluation's use since the early years of the profession (Suchman, 1967; Weiss, 1972). Many respected evaluators in the 1970s and early 1980s reported that evaluation results were often disregarded (Cousins & Leithwood, 1986; Patton, 1986; Weiss, 1977). However, more recently observers have suggested that these earlier commentators underestimated the actual impact of evaluation studies. For example, Cook wrote, "in the past decade it has become clearer that instrumental use does occur and that prior accounts of its demise were exaggerated" (1997, p. 41).

Others have found evidence of use in a variety of different ways (Greene, 1988; King, 1988; Patton, 1986). Weiss (1998b) has noted that evaluation use encompasses a broad array of effects by many classes of users including the organization in which the evaluated program exists, other client groups, and even civil society at large. Some evaluators have argued that the earlier commentators perceived that evaluation was underused only because they viewed "use" through a very narrow lens, defining it very restrictively. Patton (1986) highlighted this distinction thusly:

> Our findings, then, suggest that the predominant issue of non-utilization that characterizes much of the commentary on evaluation research can be attributed in substantial degree to a definition of utilization that is too narrow in its emphasis on seeing immediate, direct, and concrete impact on program decisions (p. 37).

Kirkhart (2000) and Henry and Mark (2003) have developed models that help us to extend and define the types and nature of effects that evaluation might have in different settings. Kirkhart, building on Patton (1986) and others (Weiss, 1980), emphasizes that the language we use influences how we conceptualize evaluation use. She advocates the use of the term "influence ('the capacity or power of persons or things to produce effects on others by intangible or indirect means')" to convey evaluation's many potential effects rather than the narrower term "use" (2000, p. 7). She also proposes a model of an integrated theory of influence to depict the different potential effects of evaluation. (See Figure 16.1). Her model highlights three dimensions: the source of the influence, the intention, and the time frame.

The *source of influence* dimension makes us aware that evaluation can have an influence through either its results or its process. Traditionally, evaluators have focused on results-oriented use. That is, stakeholders use results of the study to make some immediate decision or judgment. Another type of results-oriented use involves using results not to make decisions or judgments, but simply to enlighten and inform stakeholders about issues. In addition to the effect of results, Kirkhart's model illustrates that the process of evaluation itself can have an influence on individuals and organizations. Participating in an evaluation can cause changes to occur: in one's thoughts about organizational management and programs, in drawing attention to new issues, in creating dialogues between different stakeholders.

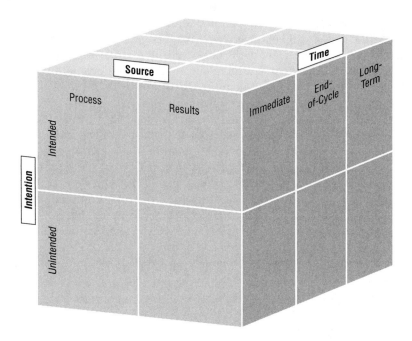

FIGURE 16.1   *Integrated Theory of Influence*

Source: From "Reconceptualizing evaluation use: An integrated theory of influence" (p. 8) by K. E. Kirkhart, 2000. In V. J. Caracelli & H. Preskilll (Eds.), *The expanding scope of evaluation use,* New Directions for Evaluation, No. 88. San Francisco: Jossey-Bass. Reprinted by permission.

Patton (1996) defines process use as "ways in which being engaged in the processes of evaluation can be useful quite apart from the findings that may emerge [from the study]" (p. 88).

The dimension of *intention* alerts us to consider unintended ways in which evaluations are used. In Chapters 10 through 12, we recommend and discuss ways to plan an evaluation by identifying the purposes of the study, the intended audiences, and the potential uses they might make of the results. All evaluations begin this way, with intentions or plans for influence.[1] Such plans can help increase the influence of evaluation by recognizing the needs of different stakeholders. But, Kirkhart notes: "Attention to the unintended influence of evaluation acknowledges both the power of ripple effects and our inability to anticipate all ramifications of our work" (2000, p. 12). She believes that unintended influences may actually exceed intended influences in many settings.

---

[1]Exceptions would include evaluations that are intended to meet the minimal requirements of a mandated evaluation.

Finally, her dimension of *time* reminds us that immediate or end-of-cycle influences are not the only occasions on which results might be used. While time is presented in the model as three discrete categories, Kirkhart observes that this dimension is actually a continuum. The recognition of long-term influence reminds us that our evaluations may have effects—intended or unintended, due to the findings of the study or the effect of participating in it—long after the evaluator has left the scene. Examples of such influence abound: the principal who makes use of an element of an evaluation process used five years earlier at her previous school to bring parents and teachers together for planning, the social worker who recalls an effect of an early intervention program on toddlers from an evaluation she participated in at a previous agency and uses it with new clients, the manager who adopts a routine use of focus groups and interviews with clients for feedback based on experience in a prior evaluation. Each of these examples illustrates the long-term influence of evaluation.

Prior conceptions of use would have constituted but one or two cubes in the integrated model of influence: intended, immediate or end-of-cycle use of results. Kirkhart's integrated theory of influence extends earlier thinking, requiring evaluators to consider the wide array of influences evaluation can have.

Henry and Mark (2003) have proposed a different model, or framework, that is intended to guide research and practice on the effects of evaluation. Like Kirkhart, Henry and Mark feel we should move beyond the term "use" to examine the *effects* of evaluation. Ironically, they believe that the emphasis on immediate use may have prevented or hindered some long-term uses and has definitely hindered our examination of other types of uses. Their model postulates three levels, or categories, of influence and, within each, they list some types of influence or change that can occur at that level. (See Figure 16.2.) These levels and types of change are drawn from research findings on change in psychology, political science, organizational behavior, and other fields.[2] Their model alerts us to consider not only evaluation's impact on individuals and their attitudes and beliefs, but also evaluation's impact on interactions and, eventually, collective actions in groups, organizations, corporations, governmental units, and the like.

In the aspects discussed so far, Henry and Mark's model is analogous to Kirkhart's integrated theory of influence in that it simply identifies other categories of influence. This, in itself, is useful. However, these authors' real emphasis is on studying *pathways* that lead to use. They argue that evaluation theory and literature have articulated different types of use, but have not examined how different types of uses are achieved. To make their point, they provide examples of two potential pathways to illustrate evaluation influence. One begins with evaluation results, the other with an influence of process.

---

[2]Henry and Mark, whose interest is in stimulating research on use, are critical of the field of evaluation for the paucity of empirical research on use and for its failure to consider research on change processes from social and behavioral sciences to inform our models. Therefore, their model is developed making use of existing research and is designed to stimulate research to determine whether the types of use they identify occur and, more importantly, what mediating variables or actions occur to facilitate or inhibit the effects of evaluation studies.

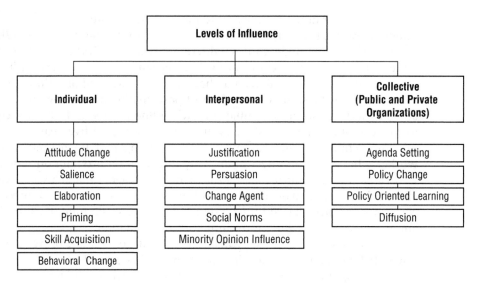

FIGURE 16.2 *Levels and Mechanisms of Evaluation Influence*

Source: From "Beyond use: Understanding evaluation's influence on attitudes and actions" by G. T. Henry & M. M. Mark, 2003. *American Journal of Evaluation,* forthcoming. Adopted by permission.

Path One: Evaluation Findings → *Minority Group Influence* →
Agenda Setting → *Opinion Elaboration* → *Policy Change*

In this hypothetical pathway, evaluation findings prompt a group whose opinion differs from that of the majority to take those findings and make others—the public, the media, or an organization—aware of the issue.[3] As the public becomes more aware of the issue, they consider it further and develop, refine, and elaborate their opinions of the issue. The evaluation findings play a role in that elaboration. Finally, the resulting, newly defined opinion held by the public prompts a policy change.

Path Two: Evaluation Process → *Attitude Change* →
Social Norms → *Behavior Change*

In this pathway, participation in an evaluation process brings about an attitude change in an individual. For example, through participating in an evaluation, an administrative leader—a principal or a manager of a nonprofit organization—may become more sensitive to the need to involve other stakeholders in decisions. She may discuss this with other managers in her organization and gradually bring about a change in social norms about participation. Ultimately, the change in so-

[3]Minority Group Influence does not refer to a demographic minority, but to a group who holds an opinion on an issue that differs from the majority opinion.

cial norms may result in a behavior change at the organizational level to include more participation in decisions.

These hypothetical pathways, and others, are useful because they help us to think of the *mediating steps* that are necessary to bring about change with evaluation. How can practicing evaluators use these ideas? They might consider what the desired end goals are and then brainstorm potential pathways to that goal. By identifying the first step in the pathway, evaluators may be able to more appropriately design the evaluation and reporting process to encourage the type of change identified in the first step (as, for example, attitude change or minority group activation in the above two pathways).

Research on Factors Found to Influence Evaluation Use

During the 1980s, much research was conducted on factors that contributed to the use of evaluation results (Alkin, Stecher, Geiger, 1982; Barrios & Foster, 1987; Cousins & Leithwood, 1986; Kennedy, Apling, & Neumann, 1980; Patton, 1991; Turner, Harman, Nielsen, & Lombana, 1988.) These evaluators defined use as direct, instrumental use rather than the expanded definitions of influence discussed above. However, these early studies inform us concerning the factors that facilitate use, partly because their results were remarkably consistent. These studies indicate that the following factors contribute to direct use of evaluation studies:

- Relevance of the evaluation to decision makers and/or other stakeholders;
- Involvement of users in the planning and reporting stages of the evaluation;
- Reputation or credibility of the evaluator;
- Quality of the communication of findings (timeliness, frequency, method);
- Development of procedures to assist in use or recommendations for action.

Little empirical research has been conducted since that time (Henry & Mark, 2003).

In the beginning of this chapter, we presented recommendations for reporting results to encourage use. Like Cook (1997), we believe that direct, instrumental use does occur and evaluators should encourage such use. We also believe that the expanded definitions of evaluation use or influence help us to consider the myriad ways our results may influence individuals and institutions. Active consideration of these influences helps us to conduct evaluations and disseminate results in such a way that evaluation can achieve its purposes of helping others make judgments of merit and worth that ultimately lead to the bettering of society.

Reporting and Influence

This chapter has focused on how to present final results using both written and oral formats to maximize stakeholders' understanding of the results. We encourage you to follow our guidelines. There is nothing wrong with working to stimulate understanding and appropriate actions at the conclusion of the study. However, remember that such actions are but one form of evaluation's influence. We remind you again to consider the pathways or means by which the outcomes desired by the clients and stakeholders of the evaluation can be achieved. Further, remember that much of evaluation's influence is unintended, based on the process rather than the results, and may not occur until long after the study is completed. The Joint Committee standards require utility, meaning the results have the *potential* to be used. They do not require immediate use because they recognize that many issues are out of the control of evaluators. Henry (2000), in fact, argues that focusing on immediate use may deter long-term, more important actions (e.g., policy changes) that take time to accomplish. We support the broader interpretation of evaluation's use by considering its influence on many different individuals and institutions in many different ways.

CASE STUDY APPLICATION

May 11. Today I had the first of the usual flurry of requests for preliminary information that come on nearly every evaluation. But we've not even held our advisory group meeting to review the preliminary data analyses yet, and anything we said at this point would be too subjective for my taste. I usually don't mind giving a few impressions, if people will remember that's all they are, but my sense is that this humanities program is controversial enough that it's likely some people might extract only the message they want to hear from whatever we say. I know we can't guard against that completely, even with the most polished final report, but if I do the best I can to present data I'm confident of, in as careful and balanced a fashion as possible, then I can sleep easier at night if someone misuses it than I can if I contribute to the misuse through casual or careless communication.

Of course, key folk on the committee are now aware of *some* of the preliminary analyses, but that's not in very "disseminable" form, even if we had finished interpreting it, which we haven't. So, there is a need for some interim information; I don't think it necessary to keep everyone waiting with bated breath right up to the final written report. I have met with the advisory group, teachers, Claire Janson, and had a working lunch with the school board during my visits. During those interactions, I have been able to keep them posted on progress and some interim findings—results from achievement test analyses and interviews—but have not hinted at any final judgments and have emphasized that each of these is just one piece of the final results. I did, however, want to see how they reacted to these interim results. I've distributed a couple of interim reports on the test data and interviews to the advisory group to get their input on how audiences might react to information, who would be interested in what, and their impressions of the results.

Author Comments.   Few evaluation reports hold such general interest that they are media events. In contexts like the Radnor humanities curriculum, however, several individuals and groups will generally press to get a preview of the findings at the earliest possible moment. The more visible the evaluation, the more curious the local folks get about the outcomes. When outside experts begin roaming through, requests for evaluation findings often spring up in their wake.

May 25. I thought I had learned not to procrastinate, but the last few days have been hectic and the final report on the Radnor program is due next week. Time to start writing. Lots of the basic stuff is already there in our data summaries, on-site visit reports, etc., but it needs to be pulled together into a cohesive, coherent report, complete with executive summary and all the trimmings. I promised Claire Janson a draft copy for review by her and the advisory group by the end of next week, so I'd best get busy. Maybe I can get the draft off to her by UPS on Monday.

Author Comments. In preparing the final report, I would produce a complete first draft, including at least the following:

1. An introduction describing the humanities curriculum, purposes and audiences for the evaluation, and an overview of the rest of the report;
2. A list of evaluative questions used to guide the study;
3. A very brief overview of the evaluation plan and procedures, with a supporting appendix to provide detail;
4. Discussion of findings, probably organized around the evaluative questions (again, detailed presentations of findings generated by each instrument could be provided in an appendix);
5. Judgments, in the form of strengths and weaknesses, along with recommendations, with sufficient rationale and linkage to findings to demonstrate that the recommendations are warranted.

Once it is completed, I would submit the draft copy of the final report to the advisory group and ask that they review it. The intent of this review would be twofold: first, to identify any factual inaccuracies; second, to challenge any inferences, conclusions, or recommendations they think are inappropriate, unwarranted, or unfair. It is important, in asking for these reviews, to communicate that you will take them very seriously and will consider carefully each suggested revision, whether it be minor editing or deletion of a major recommendation. It is equally important to make very clear that the ultimate decision for what goes into the final draft report belongs to the evaluator and that there is no guarantee that all of their suggestions will be incorporated. Failure to get these ground rules clear at the outset can lead to all manner of problems.

Having the advisory group and principal client review a draft of the report and vouchsafe its factual accuracy is good insurance against the evaluator's committing serious blunders. Helpful clients have saved me embarrassment by correcting nontrivial errors I failed to spot in draft reports (like the "typo" that turned an intended compliment of a program director as single-minded into the much less complimentary "simple-minded").

Even small factual errors, uncorrected, give comfort to the critic bent on discrediting the report. Consider, for instance, the PTA president who had opposed a new curriculum designed to teach reading through a study of local cultures, only to find that our evaluation showed clearly that the curriculum was having a very positive effect on student learning. "How," he thundered at a collective PTA and school board meeting, "can you believe anything else is accurate if the evaluator can't even spell the name of the school or its principal right!" (Now before you judge too harshly, you should try to evaluate the curriculum at Tchesinkut School, where Mr. Nakinilerak presides.) It was there, in the Alaskan bush, that I first learned the value of asking clients to review and share responsibility for accuracy of the final report.

Several references have been made previously to an executive summary. This might take the form of a parsimonious introductory chapter to the evaluation report, including a synopsis of the findings and references to other sections of the report of interest to particular audiences. Or the executive summary might be a separate, self-contained document of five to ten pages for use with interested parties who need results but are not concerned with details. In larger evaluations, when more people need to be informed, a brief evaluation abstract of one or two pages might be useful.

One ethical consideration that should not be neglected in report writing is preserving confidentiality and anonymity. Evaluators generally promise that individual responses or test scores will not be divulged (except with the individuals' express approval). Unfortunately, that promise is sometimes forgotten at the report-writing stage.

Major Concepts and Theories

1. Evaluations can have effects at three different levels: on individuals, interactions, and on collective groups or institutions. At each of these levels, different types of changes can occur. Evaluators can identify pathways between these levels and types to consider ways to achieve desired influences with a particular evaluation.

2. Evaluation reports can serve many different purposes, including: to improve programs, to make a summative decision, to draw attention to an issue, to change attitudes, to promote understanding, to encourage accountability, and to promote dialogue among different stakeholders, to name only a few. However, the purpose of any evaluation report should be determined by the needs of the intended audience.

3. The evaluator should identify the multiple audiences of an evaluation. An audience analysis can be performed to determine the information needs, perceptions and values, and the best medium for presenting information to each audience.

4. Involving audiences in decisions about timing, mode, and types of information presented can increase their receptivity to the results.

5. Findings from an evaluation can be presented in many different ways: formal, final reports; shorter, single-issue, interim written reports; oral presentations; slide-tape or PowerPoint presentations; E-mail memos or Web-site postings; and briefings at meetings. Methods should be selected to match the audience's needs.

6. Different reports and formats may be developed for different audiences. The timing, length, vocabulary, and content of each report should match each audience's needs and interests.

7. Final reports include an executive summary, an introduction, a description of the evaluation object and the questions to be answered; a brief discussion of the evaluation plan and methods; a presentation of results; and a discussion of conclusions and recommendations. Detailed technical information can be presented in an appendix.

8. Evaluation use may be better conceptualized as influence. Some evaluations result in a direct, immediate, and intended use of results, but other uses, more broadly categorized as influence, have also emerged. These include the influences of the evaluation process, unintended influences, and influences that occur long after the evaluation has been completed.

Discussion Questions

1. What types of influence does evaluation have in the setting where you work? Which types of influence do you think are most powerful?

2. How important should use be to evaluation? Considering Henry and Mark's levels and types of influence, which do you think are most important?

3. Discuss the advantages and potential disadvantages of using E-mail as your medium for communicating report findings. What audiences might you involve in this way?

4. How might an audience's level of ownership of the evaluation impact the influence of the evaluation findings?

Application Exercises

1. Apply the "good evaluation report" checklist from this chapter to an evaluation study of your choosing. Do the strengths and weaknesses of the reporting process you reviewed suggest procedures that you will want to adopt in the future?

2. List questions that you think future research on evaluation reporting and use should answer. What questions do you have for which there are no good answers?

Relevant Evaluation Standards

The evaluation standards we see as relevant to this chapter's content are the following. These standards are described in Chapter 18.

U1—Stakeholder Identification   P6—Disclosure of Findings
U2—Evaluator Credibility   A1—Program Documentation

U3—Information Scope and Selection
U4—Values Identification
U5—Report Clarity
U6—Report Timeliness and Dissemination
U7—Evaluation Impact
P5—Complete and Fair Assessment

A3—Described Purposes and Procedures
A4—Defensible Information Sources
A7—Systematic Information
A10—Justified Conclusions
A11—Impartial Reporting

Suggested Readings

Cousins, J. B., & Leithwood, K. A. (1986). Current empirical research on evaluation utilization. *Review of Education Research, 56,* 331–364.

Henry, G. T. (Ed.). (1997). *Creating effective graphs: Solutions for a variety of evaluation data.* In New Directions for Evaluation, No. 73. San Francisco: Jossey-Bass.

Henry, G. T., & Mark, M. M. (2003). Beyond use: Understanding evaluation's influence on attitudes and actions. *American Journal of Evaluation,* forthcoming.

Kirkhart, K. E. (2000). Reconceptualizing evaluation use: An integrated theory of influence. In V. J. Caracelli & H. Preskill (Eds.), *The expanding scope of evaluation use.* New Directions for Evaluation, No. 88. San Francisco: Jossey-Bass.

Patton, M. Q. (1996). *Utilization-focused evaluation* (3rd ed.). Thousand Oaks, CA: Sage.

Thompson, B. (1994, April). *The revised program Evaluation Standards and their correlation with the evaluation use literature.* Paper presented at the annual meeting of the American Educational Research Association, New Orleans.

17

Dealing with Political, Ethical, and Interpersonal Aspects of Evaluation

Orienting Questions _____

1. What types of bias can result from evaluators' interpersonal, financial, or organizational relationships? From their beliefs? How might such biases be minimized or eliminated?

2. What ethical standards and guidelines should be followed in conducting evaluation studies? What is the difference between ethical guidelines and standards of practice? Why is each important?

3. Why do we consider evaluation a political activity?

4. What types of political pressures cause the most serious problems in evaluation studies? How can evaluators cope with such pressures?

By now, we hope we have made the point that evaluation is not only—or even primarily—a methodological and technical activity. Important as methodological and technical expertise are to good evaluation, that importance is often overshadowed by the interpersonal, ethical, and political influences that shape evaluators' work. Many a good evaluation, unimpeachable in all technical details, has failed because of interpersonal insensitivity, ethical compromises, or political naïveté. It is pointless to promise to collect sensitive data (principals' ratings of teachers, for instance, or AIDS patients' reported incidence of drug use) without considering the ethical implications and the procedures that must be followed to obtain permission to collect such data. Clients have certain expectations about evaluation. Sometimes these expectations are accurate; sometimes they are not. Evaluators need to orient clients and other stakeholders to what evaluation can do. Stakeholder groups have different perspectives, different interests, and different concerns about the program and about the evaluation. Evaluators must be skilled in human relations and communication to work with different groups, to facilitate their communication as appropriate, and to make choices about how the evaluation meets the needs of different groups.

Evaluators cannot afford to content themselves with polishing and plying their tools for collecting, analyzing, and reporting data. They must consider how to deal with pressures for immediate data or oversimplified questions; how to minimize fears or misunderstandings about evaluation so that stakeholders are open to the study; how to involve different groups in the evaluation and balance their interests and needs; how evaluation reports will be received by different stakeholders; whether the results of the evaluation will be suppressed, misused, or ignored; and many other interpersonal and political issues. Ignoring these issues is self-defeating, for human, ethical, and political factors pervade every aspect of an evaluation study. It is folly to ignore them, labeling them as mere nuisances that detract evaluators from important methodological tasks. Political, ethical, and human factors are present in virtually every program evaluation, and moving ahead without dealing with them is both incompetent and unethical. Recall our discussion of the differences in evaluation and research in Chapter 1. Evaluators are working to make an impact on real people, organizations, and societies. To do so, they must not only collect good data, but they must see that intended audiences are open to using or being influenced by the data. This can be a challenging task!

In this chapter we deal with four important, interrelated topics: (1) communication between evaluator and stakeholders; (2) biases inherent in certain client–evaluator interrelationships; (3) ethical issues and considerations in evaluation; and (4) political pressures and problems in evaluation.

Establishing and Maintaining Good Communications among Evaluators and Stakeholders

The evaluation literature contains numerous pronouncements that good communications are an essential part of both evaluation and the politics that inevitably surround evaluation studies. Yet we continue to find many criticisms of evaluators' communication practices and many examples of poor communication. The tedious, voluminous (and often unread) technical report offered as the sole end product of an evaluation study is simply one example. Sometimes evaluators, who may have entered the field because of their interest in research, get too caught up in technical matters and deadlines to attend to communication. Communicating with clients and seeking out and involving other stakeholders is as critical as the data collection itself, for without involvement, participation, and effective two-way communication, the most valid data in the world will not have the intended effect. Establishing good interpersonal relations and communicating effectively takes time. Evaluators should be sure to include enough time in their evaluation plans so that communication does not get pushed aside in the press for collecting and analyzing data.

Sometimes clients need to be reminded that honest evaluation entails risk. Approval and cooperation need to be obtained from those in power. Reporting procedures must be clear to everyone at the outset, and clients and evaluators should agree on ways to maintain open communications, assure fairness and impartiality in the evaluation, and resolve any conflicts that might arise during the study.

We offer the following practical recommendations for interpersonal communications in evaluation.

1. *Prepare clients (those who sponsor the evaluation) and other stakeholders for evaluation.* Develop an "evaluation spirit" by talking with all participants about the purpose and benefits of the evaluation. Resistance to evaluation comes naturally to most people, and not knowing what to expect can only increase such resistance. If stakeholders are new to evaluation, or have had previous bad experiences with it, let them know your views about evaluation and what it can do. Learn more about their concerns and fears. As appropriate, provide stakeholders with information on other evaluations and/or approaches to learning in an organization to illustrate what evaluation and self-examination can accomplish for an organization. Current literature on continuous improvement and learning organizations can be helpful. See, for example, Preskill and Torres's writing on evaluation and its contribution to learning in organizations (Preskill & Torres, 1999, 2000).

2. *Foster stakeholder participation.* Increase the likelihood of involvement by:
- Providing multiple opportunities for involvement. Consider establishing an advisory group of stakeholders from different perspectives to work on the evaluation. This group can help in developing the evaluation plan; reacting to means for data collection, analyses, and results; considering needs for further data collection; finding meaning in the data and developing interpretations; and in considering implications of the results for different stakeholder groups. They can also provide a vital means for disseminating information in informal, nonthreatening ways;
- Raising awareness of the evaluation (presenting the evaluation's purpose and plan to stakeholders who have not been involved in that phase, clarifying what will be looked at or asked about, and sharing written evaluation documents);
- Seeking input on methods and timing for disseminating evaluation results;
- Capitalizing on various stakeholders' familiarity with the object of the evaluation (recognizing that no one person has the full range of experience with all of the program's functions) by learning more about their perspectives of the object, their experience with it, and their concerns about it;

- Encouraging constructive criticism of the evaluation. Invite stakeholders to challenge assumptions or weaknesses; encourage divergent perspectives. Model a spirit of fairness and openness when critical feedback is given. By encouraging stakeholders to provide constructive, critical feedback on their work and responding in an accepting and open manner, evaluators can demonstrate the "evaluation spirit" they hope to see in stakeholders. (See Fitzpatrick and Donaldson [2002] for a discussion of Donaldson's use of 360-degree feedback in an evaluation to provide a mechanism for program people to comment on the evaluation.)

3. *Plan adequate time for carrying out all of the evaluation.* Remember to include time for communication through meetings, interviews, and interim reports and memos to different stakeholder groups and individuals. Consider using the advisory group to schedule all planned evaluation work and to help decide if the evaluation's scope must be reduced to allow time for all planned activities.

4. *Invite and nurture outside participation.* In evaluating a school program, for example, remember that parents, school board members, and citizens in the community are all potential stakeholders. Their participation not only strengthens the evaluation but also signals that this is an important project. When evaluating programs in health and human services or in corporate settings, the external stakeholders may be different (e.g., citizen groups, families of those receiving treatment, county commissioners, service providers, corporate board members, consumer advocate groups). Learn who the stakeholders are for the program. Evaluators can play an important role in seeking to empower previously disenfranchised groups by bringing representatives of these groups into the discussion. (See our discussion of deliberative democracy in Chapter 2.)

5. *Foster a spirit of teamwork, negotiation, and compromise.* Evaluators should not make important decisions alone. While evaluators may be the most expert in methods of data collection, the client and stakeholders have expertise in the program being evaluated and their experiences with it. Their needs and views must be sought and considered.

6. *Link long-term goals to immediate actions.* People like to see results from the evaluation, so set intermediate goals as stepping stones to long-term goals, but counsel against discarding long-term goals just because they are not immediately achievable.

7. *Get stakeholders involved in conducting the evaluation.* Don't just seek the input of stakeholders. Give them responsibilities (and, of course, training, as need be, to carry out those responsibilities). Empowerment evaluation has illustrated how such involvement can work. Involving many participants fosters commitment to change and development of new plans.

8. *Put a premium on memos, meetings, and informal "chats."* People need and like to feel informed. The confidence that comes with knowing what's going on helps build an "evaluation spirit" and common understanding about the evaluation.

9. *Recognize and protect the rights of individuals.* The Joint Committee on Standards for Educational Evaluation proposes the following standard to govern human interactions: "Evaluators should respect human dignity and worth in their interactions with other persons associated with an evaluation, so that participants are not threatened or harmed" (Joint Committee, 1994, p. 99). Respect for People and Responsibility for General and Public Welfare are two of the five Guiding Principles for Evaluators developed as codes of behavior by the American Evaluation Association.

Following these recommendations can improve responsiveness to the evaluation, and, hence, subsequent use and the quality of the evaluation product itself. For example, Brandon, Lindberg, and Wang (1993) found that involving program beneficiaries in specifying which program attributes an evaluation should address enhances the validity of the evaluation findings. Other benefits of stakeholder involvement include facilitating use and understanding and instilling an ongoing learning environment.

Understanding Potential Bias Resulting from the Evaluator's Personal Values and Interpersonal, Financial, and Organizational Relationships with Others

The possibility of human beings rendering completely unbiased judgments seems very slight. There is no reason to believe that evaluators are less susceptible to bias than their counterparts in other walks of life. In fact, it is ironic that some evaluators actually could be more susceptible to bias, simply because they believe that they are completely unbiased. When biases are left undetected, to function at a subconscious level, they can have a powerful influence on evaluators' judgments, inferences, and decisions.

Perhaps the myth that evaluators are less biased than others is partly attributable to the popular view that evaluation is an "objective" enterprise, involving valid and reliable data and allowing no subjectivity. That optimistic view has been recognized as rather naive, however. Choices are, by nature, subjective, and evaluators increasingly realize that bias—inadvertent or conscious—can intrude subtly into nearly every choice they make, from selecting an evaluation approach to writing a report. Indeed, the portrait of the completely dispassionate and unbiased evaluator must be hung alongside that of the unicorn and other quaint folklore characters.

A full discussion of sources of bias in program evaluation studies transcends the scope of this book. We have discussed some sources of bias, in passing, while examining topics in earlier chapters. Perloff and his colleagues (1980) provide a provocative analysis of how various social and cognitive biases can influence evaluation. Here we will treat briefly only a few potential sources of bias. We will consider how evaluators' values and beliefs can be problematic in two different ways. We will also examine how evaluators' relationships to and dependence on others can seriously bias their judgments. Every evaluation is a reflection of the evaluator's personal beliefs, as well as a complex of interpersonal, financial, and organizational interrelationships between the evaluator and numerous other actors in the evaluation context. We shall discuss briefly how each of these factors can bias an evaluator's judgments.

The Evaluator's Beliefs and Biases

It is probably no revelation to even the newest student that evaluators' value systems and beliefs can readily bias evaluations they conduct, if they cannot keep those biases from influencing the evaluation. And they cannot. At least, not completely. While several evaluation approaches attempt to control bias, none are completely successful. The values and beliefs of evaluators enter in at every step, in the decisions about what information should be collected, how to collect it, what analyses are best, and how it should be presented. Subjectivity, a parent of bias, is possible, if not inevitable, in every such choice. Many, if not most, experienced evaluators may have found ways to enhance their neutrality and reduce the degree to which their personal values intrude into the evaluation, thus reducing their personal bias, but reducing is not eliminating. Some subjectivity and vestigial bias will always remain.

For example, an evaluator's philosophy or personal feelings about the nature or theory of a program can also bias his evaluation of it. Bilingual education is currently quite a controversial area in the United States. It would be difficult to find an evaluator who did not hold some sort of philosophical view, one way or another, about such programs. Everyone has some sort of philosophical view about a program, but evaluators need to consider how their views affect their evaluation approach. For example, we might be very positive about prevention, or we may prefer a treatment orientation. Some evaluators may prefer programs that focus on the whole child while others prefer a more standards-based approach or one that focuses on accountability for schools. Some may favor choice among consumers; others are more oriented to the cost for taxpayers. Some hold conservative views; others, more liberal. All of these belief systems have a potential for biasing the evaluation if evaluators are not alert to how their views influence an evaluation, its questions, approach, audiences, and interpretation of results.

A serious problem occurs when evaluators have become ethnocentric (believing their own group is superior to others), especially in their values and beliefs. Ethnocentric evaluators have become so blinded by their own values and beliefs that they cannot see or comprehend the divergent values of stakeholders and recognize how that has shaped their approach to the program being evaluated. This "ethnocentrism" may be racial, ethnic, gender- or age-based, or may concern social class differences. In any case, one's own experience can make it difficult to understand the experiences and perspectives of others whose experiences are quite different. Hood (2000) writes: "The evaluation community is replete with those who have limited understanding of the values that are grounded in the racial and cultural backgrounds of groups other than their own" (p. 78). Evaluators need to reflect on their own experiences and to be aware of the limitations those experiences impose. When evaluators work with groups whose experiences and views are significantly different from their own, they should work to learn more about the perceptions, values, and experiences of these other groups and be aware of how their own experiences influence and limit their perceptions of the program. They should attempt to involve evaluators and others with experiences similar to those of the clients to work with the evaluation when group differences are great.

In another concern borrowed from anthropological literature, Lincoln and Guba (1981) identified "going native" as a serious source of evaluator bias. This "evaluators-in-grass-skirts" portrayal is nearly a mirror image of ethnocentrism. "Going native" occurs when evaluators consciously or unconsciously adopt the beliefs and values of the group they are studying, resulting in their downplaying evaluation findings that would prove detrimental to the group and emphasizing positive findings. These authors point out that evaluators may intend this to benefit their "adopted" group, but their "going native" and losing perspective may actually do a disservice to the group, as well as to the cause of evaluation by causing evaluations to lose credibility.

Lincoln and Guba add that bias caused by either ethnocentrism or "going native" can be controlled, or at least lessened to a considerable degree, by three strategies:

1. Keeping careful *reflexive logs* of the evaluator's evolving perceptions, day-to-day procedures, methodological decisions, day-to-day personal introspections, developing insights and hypotheses, to help the evaluator "reflect him to himself," to better see how the evaluation design is emerging and how the evaluator is emerging as an inquirer.

2. *Peer debriefing,* to help keep the evaluator and his data collection and interpretation on track, by providing an external check. Peers can be assigned a devil's advocate role to probe and question perceptions and decisions (e.g., "Don't you think educational standards can be helpful in communicating goals to teachers, parents, and the community?" "What impact will these new environmental standards have on jobs for locals?")

3. An *audit trail* (modeled loosely on fiscal audits) designed to have an external party review the inquiry processes to determine whether the evaluation procedures used were dependable (fair and adequate, following good procedure) and confirmable (results are properly based on accurate data handling and interpretation).

Another strategy for minimizing bias is through the process of metaevaluation, or evaluation of an evaluation. This topic is addressed in detail in Chapter 18. Whatever methods are used, it is important for evaluators (and clients) to examine their personal values and beliefs and consider how they can influence their approach to the evaluation and eventual judgments. Becoming aware represents the first step in preventing bias.

Interpersonal Relationships and Bias

It is apparent to even the casual observer that individuals' feelings toward one another can color their judgments, not only about each other but about practically anything with which the other person is perceived to be associated. Hence, we have legal restrictions on testimony about one's spouse, and anti-nepotism policies that prohibit individuals from being placed in positions where they would need to make decisions about the salary, promotion, or job security of a family member.

Obviously an evaluator must decline an invitation to evaluate a displaced homemakers program directed by his sister-in-law, but a less conspicuous source of bias lies in interpersonal relationships that may influence the evaluator in more subtle but equally potent ways. Consider the school district evaluator who is assigned to evaluate a program being piloted by his weekly tennis doubles partner (a fact unknown to the superintendent who made the assignment). Or the external evaluator who finds himself unable to say anything positive about a health education program directed by an individual whose political and religious views are dramatically opposed to his own. Or the staff member assigned to evaluate nutrition counseling services provided by colleagues who share office space, coffee breaks, and membership on the office's bowling team. But relational entanglements need not be so blatant to be problematical. As Anderson and Ball noted years ago,

> These relationships . . . influence the morale of the evaluation staff and the program staff. That is, they affect not only such principled and abstract topics as bias and ethics, but also such bread and butter issues as the evaluator's mood on Friday afternoon after a week of either repeated friction or relative harmony with program personnel (1978, p. 127).

They might have gone on to say that the evaluator's mood will in turn affect such principled concerns as bias and ethics, for the impact of affect on behavior is too well known to require comment here. This does not argue for a cold, aloof evaluator, impervious to human attachments, but for awareness that myriad aspects of interpersonal relationships can color and alter the thinking and judgment of evaluators, and that these factors must therefore be thoughtfully controlled. Failure to do so will result in the evaluator being co-opted in ways that are likely to bias seriously the outcomes of the study.

Even if evaluators are entirely new to the setting—particularly if they are entirely new to the setting—they should spend time observing the program, meeting with clients and stakeholders, and developing relationships. These relationships are intended to help the evaluation to succeed—to reduce mistrust, to improve understanding, and so forth—but these relationships also introduce bias. Evaluators are likely to feel more comfortable with people whose values and beliefs are like their own, who support the evaluation and who are open to its methods and interested in its results. At the same time, evaluators learn that certain people concerned with the evaluation are more difficult. They are suspicious, accusatory, demanding, inflexible, or behave in any number of ways that are frustrating to the evaluator. These relationships, good and bad, play a role. Is the evaluator prepared to give tough, negative results—ones he knows they won't like—to people with whom he has established rapport? Who are helpful to the continuation of the study? These are tough issues, but evaluators must be prepared to deal with them, to prepare audiences for difficult results, and to prepare themselves for delivering them.

Financial Relationships and Bias

Sir Robert Walpole said that "all men have their price," the implication being that anyone can be bought. Although there are enough examples of incorruptibility and integrity around to prove Walpole's assumptions exaggerated, there are still enough corrupt individuals to give some credence to his cynical view of human nature.

Evaluators hold no claim to moral eminence. There is little reason to believe they are either more or less vulnerable than anyone else to the pressures and influences of financial advantages. We doubt there are many instances of evaluators being bribed to sway an evaluation one way or another, but financial pressures are not always so obvious and direct. For example, consider the unenviable plight of the evaluator who is employed by the very agency whose program he is evaluating. To illustrate how thorny this situation can be, let us describe an actual case.

An evaluator of our acquaintance, we'll call him John, was employed by a U.S. government-supported research center whose mission was to develop and test exemplary programs and practices for schools. Assigned to direct the center's evaluation unit, in due time John completed an evaluation of a center program designed to improve secondary school students' mathematics performance and attitudes toward math (AMP). The AMP program was expensive. Congress had invested over one million dollars in its development and, while John found that students liked the program, there wasn't a shred of evidence to suggest that it had any impact on their performance. Troubled by the implications of reporting such information to the funding agency through which Congress had initiated the program, John finally worded his draft report to convey that the evaluation was to blame for AMP's failure to produce evidence of success. The summary of his report read as follows (italics ours).[1]

> ***Summary.***   The results of this study indicate that the Accelerated Mathematics Program (AMP) was somewhat effective in developing positive attitudes toward mathematics, in the sense that students tended to like the AMP materials. The study supplied no evidence, however, from which either long- or short-term student performance changes in mathematics ability can be inferred. *The*

---

[1]The names, organizations, and titles in this summary and the following letter have been changed to provide anonymity, but the essential content has not been altered and is reproduced here verbatim.

results do not necessarily indicate that AMP was not effective in promoting change in math performance, but that a variety of shortcomings and limitations of the evaluation design did not allow for the identification and measurement of these changes.

And how did the funding agency respond to this obvious effort to soften the bad news? Their reaction to the draft report came in a letter, which is reprinted here.

Dear John:

Thank you for the three draft copies of the AMP Impact study. I look forward to the final report.

I hope that our future efforts will be structured so that statements such as those in the "summary" will not have to be made. Instead, I hope that we will be able to say something *positive* in the final report about changes in important performances. I have heard so many good things about AMP that I am disheartened by the lack of evidence that it has short-term performance effectiveness and that I cannot therefore argue for its potential for long-term effectiveness.

The issue here is straightforward. The best argument for funding centers such as yours that I can make internally here in the Department and externally with the Congress is that our products lead to measurable changes for good in American schools. Regardless of the positive "feelings" I get about AMP, it appears we cannot justify all the effort in terms of performance criteria, as per your draft report. That is a drawback, but one which I think we can overcome in future efforts, hopefully in your final report.

Sincerely,

Lawrence

Lawrence T. Donaldson
Chief Administrator

The message is blatantly clear. John better find something positive to prove AMP and its cohort programs are worth the investment, or funding could be withdrawn, the program would fold, and John himself would be looking for other employment. It would take a robust soul indeed not to feel some ethical strain in such a situation, especially when his salary comes directly from the threatened program! Fortunately, though John equivocated at first, this story eventually had a happy ending. The final report told the true story, and John was able to assume the role of evaluator (with a clear conscience) on the development staff for another program at the same center.

Even when the evaluator is external to the agency whose programs or products are being evaluated, financial dependence can be a potential source of bias. Consider, for example, the delicate balance that must be maintained by external evaluation consultants or firms who are inevitably dependent on "repeat business." Scriven (1993) points out this potential source of bias succinctly: " . . . one key economic insight about evaluation contracting is this: No one ever got rich from one evaluation contract" (p. 84). The possibility of future evaluation contracts or consulting depends on how well the client likes the most recent evaluation completed by the evaluator. No problem here if the client has a penchant for the truth, even if it might reflect negatively on the program. But what if the client goes rigid at the first hint of criticism? The evaluator who wants future work from such a person must, as Brickell (1978) puts it, bite the hand that feeds him while appearing to lick it.

Even if the evaluator is not dependent on repeat business, he may be dependent on the client for funds to complete the study at hand. Seldom is an evaluator given all the funds for an evaluation up front. Clients sometimes wish to see interim products before releasing all the dollars necessary to carry the study to completion. The apparent or unspoken desire of the client to see positive results could very well introduce bias to interim evaluation findings, so that the remaining payments will not be jeopardized.

In summary, the evaluator's financial relationship with and dependence on the client must be reviewed carefully to determine whether these factors are likely to bias the study. Scriven (1993, pp. 79–86) has offered cautions that are pertinent to such reviews aimed at detecting bias.

Organizational Relationships and Bias

Organizational relationships may be of greater concern to evaluators than immediate financial gain. The relationship between evaluators and the programs they evaluate can determine not only their present financial welfare but their future employment. Further, an organization may exert great (or total) control over the evaluator's other perquisites, such things as office space, access to secretarial resources, access to and use of facilities and record-keeping systems, even the convenience of available parking space. The way the organization exercises this control to make the evaluator's life easier or more difficult can certainly cause problems with bias.

To make this point, we present in Figure 17.1 eight possible organizational relationships between evaluators and the program being evaluated. Generally, the greatest potential of bias exists in the first row of Figure 17.1, and the least potential of bias exists in the last row.

Generally, the potential for organizational pressure is greater when the evaluator is employed by the organization whose program is being evaluated than when the evaluator is employed by an outside agency.[2] In addition, bias is more likely when the "organizationally employed" evaluator reports to the director of the program being evaluated than when he reports to someone outside that

---

[2]Organizational relationships certainly influence the amount of bias evaluators face, though there may be many subtle nuances to this issue. Morris and Cohn (1993) found that internal evaluators reported encountering fewer ethical problems than external evaluators. Mathison (1991), who has worked as an internal and external evaluator, believes the pressures encountered by internal and external evaluators are similar, but their responses differ. Sonnichsen, the director of the internal evaluation unit at the FBI, argues that internal evaluators must be placed independently (2000), separated from programs, to be effective.

FIGURE 17.1   *Organizational Relationships of Evaluator to Client*

Evaluator Employed	To Do One Evaluation or Successive Evaluations	Evaluator Reports
1. Within organization which has responsibility for the program being evaluated	1. Successive evaluations	1. Directly to director of program evaluated
2. Within organization which has responsibility for the program being evaluated	2. One evaluation	2. Directly to director of program being evaluated
3. Within organization which has responsibility for the program being evaluated	3. Successive evaluations	3. To someone outside the program being evaluated but within the same organization
4. Within organization which has responsibility for the program being evaluated	4. One evaluation	4. To someone outside the program being evaluated but within the same organization
5. By outside agency	5. Successive evaluations	5. As consultant or contractor to director of program being evaluated
6. By outside agency	6. One evaluation	6. As consultant or contractor to director of program being evaluated
7. By outside agency	7. Successive evaluations	7. Directly to outside funding agency which supports the program
8. By outside agency	8. One evaluation	8. Directly to outside funding agency which supports the program

program. And, as noted earlier, the evaluation consultant who is dependent on repeat business may be more vulnerable to bias because of a perceived need to please the client. In some large organizations, the least bias may result from having the evaluation conducted by an evaluator who is assigned to another unit within the organization, thus being "internal" to the organization, but "external" to the program being evaluated. In short, the more control the client (the unit or program being evaluated) has over the evaluator's job security, salary (or future consultant fees), and perquisites, the less candor and objectivity the evaluator is likely to demonstrate in conducting the evaluation.

Some authors (for example, Cronbach and others, 1980) are unsympathetic to concerns that the locus of the evaluator's employment may influence the results of the evaluation. Mathison (1999), who has worked as an internal and external evaluator, has observed that evaluators in these settings face similar pressures, but need to take different paths to resolve them. Lowell (1995) and Sonnichsen (2000) discuss some of the pressures internal evaluators may face and how to balance and deal with those pressures. As Lowell notes, in the long-term, the organization expects internal evaluation to pay off, i.e., to provide recommendations for improved organizational operations. Bias that produces overly positive reports on programs leads to evaluation not fulfilling its promise. Nevertheless, in the short-term internal evaluators can encounter pressures that differ from those encountered by the external evaluator. As our chart indicates, the position of the internal and external evaluator has implications for how directly organizational pressures may be brought to bear.

Bias in Formative and Summative Evaluation.   The discerning reader has probably already noted that our discussion in the preceding sections omits one important consideration: whether the evaluation is primarily formative or summative. In considering the pros and cons of an evaluator's financial and administrative dependence or independence from the client, such dependence may be not only tolerable in a formative evaluation, but even desirable, for it may prompt the evaluator to be more responsive to particular information needs of the program, information needed to improve the program. Not so for a summative evaluation, when organizational and financial dependence would seem much less tolerable, particularly if the evaluation concerns large, costly, or high-profile programs. An external, independent evaluator is generally to be preferred in summative evaluations of this type, although, as we have noted in the prior section, "independence" is defined by a variety of factors often not considered. For example, it strains credibility to argue that an external evaluator is truly independent when he is selected and paid by the client to carry out a summative study (even though independence is more likely here than if the evaluator were internal, and, hence, under even more direct client control).

Stated differently, co-optation, ego involvement, and bias are undesirable in any evaluation, but they are doubly so in summative evaluation studies, when any conflict of interest is on a direct collision course with the purpose of such studies.

Maintaining Ethical Standards: Considerations, Issues, and Responsibilities for Evaluators and Clients

In an earlier text (Worthen & Sanders, 1987) we postulated five forms of "evaluation corruptibility" that result from ethical compromises or distortions:

- Willingness, given conflict of interest or other perceived payoffs or penalties, to twist the truth and produce positive findings (Such "willingness" may be conscious or unconscious. Bias, as discussed in the previous section, is one category of this ethical problem.);

- Intrusion of unsubstantiated opinions because of sloppy, capricious, and unprofessional evaluation practices;

• "Shaded" evaluation "findings" resulting from intrusion of the evaluator's personal prejudices or preconceived notions;

• Obtaining the cooperation of clients or participants by making promises that cannot be kept;

• Failure to honor commitments that could have been honored. (p. 289)

House (1995) has listed five ethical fallacies of evaluation that address some of these problems from a somewhat different perspective:

1. *Clientism*—the fallacy that doing whatever the client requests or whatever will benefit the client is ethically correct;

2. *Contractualism*—the fallacy that the evaluator is obligated to follow the written contract slavishly, even if doing so is detrimental to the public good;

3. *Methodologicalism*—the belief that following acceptable inquiry methods assures that the evaluator's behavior will be ethical, even when some methodologies may actually compound the evaluator's ethical dilemmas;

4. *Relativism*—the fallacy that opinion data the evaluator collects from various participants must be given equal weight, as if there is no basis for appropriately giving the opinions of peripheral groups less priority than that given to more pivotal groups;

5. *Pluralism/Elitism*—the fallacy of allowing powerful voices to be given higher priority not because they merit such priority, but merely because they hold more prestige and potency than the powerless or voiceless.

In discussing the ethical problems evaluators face, House states that:

> First, they exercise powers over people that can injure self-esteem, damage reputations, and stunt careers. . . . Second, evaluators are engaged in relationships in which they themselves are vulnerable to people awarding future work. . . . Also, evaluators come from the same social classes and educational backgrounds as those who sponsor the evaluations and run the programs. These factors multiply ethical hazards (1995, p. 29).

Whether such problems as these—or the "forms of corruptibility" we listed earlier—result from the evaluator's incompetence or from more morally reprehensible causes, they still result in seriously compromised or outright discredited evaluations. It may matter greatly, on moral grounds, whether evaluation results are distorted because the evaluator is unconscionably self-serving, or because he is simply ignorant of how to discover and describe reality. In practical terms, the result is the same. Therefore, those who conduct and those who are served by evaluation studies share a responsibility for becoming informed about relevant ethical issues. Yet, in a survey of American Evaluation Association members' views on ethical issues, Morris and Cohn (1993) found that many were unaware of major ethical issues, suggesting that many evaluators would benefit from greater understanding of ethical standards for evaluation practice.

What Kinds of Ethical Problems Do Evaluators Encounter?

Although Morris and Cohn found that many evaluators were unaware of major ethical issues, nearly two-thirds of the evaluators they surveyed reported they had encountered ethical challenges in their evaluation work. These included:

- Evaluator is pressured by stakeholders to alter presentation of findings.

- Prior to the evaluation taking place, stakeholder has already decided what the findings "should be" or plans to use the findings in an ethically questionable fashion.

- Findings are suppressed or ignored by stakeholder.

- Evaluator is reluctant to present findings fully, for unspecified reasons.

- Evaluator has discovered behavior that is illegal, unethical, dangerous, and so on.

- Evaluator is unsure of his or her ability to be objective or fair in presenting findings.

- Although not pressured by stakeholders to violate confidentiality, the evaluator is concerned that reporting certain findings could represent such a violation.

- Evaluator is pressured by stakeholder to violate confidentiality.

- Unspecified misuse of findings by stakeholder.

- Findings are used to punish someone other than the evaluator.

- Findings are deliberately modified by stakeholder prior to release.

- Stakeholder declares certain research questions "off-limits" in the evaluation, despite their substantive relevance.

- Legitimate stakeholders are omitted from the planning process.

Note that many of these challenges involve pressures from stakeholders. While Morris and Cohn's sample of professional evaluators was able to identify instances of ethical challenges, they were largely unaware of major ethical conflicts they might encounter. Honea's case study (1992) of evaluators resulted in similar findings. The experienced public sector evaluators she studied seldom discussed ethics or values in their work lives. She found four factors that seemed to inhibit such discussions. Specially, her interviewees perceived that:

1. They were being ethical if they were following the model of "objective scientist," and lapses in objectivity were viewed as less an ethical than a methodological concern;

2. Participants in evaluation always behave ethically, so discussion of ethics is unnecessary;

3. Being a member of an evaluation team and engaging in team deliberations prevents unethical behavior from occurring;

4. Neither evaluators nor others involved in the evaluation have the time to confront or discuss ethical issues.

These studies suggest that more attention needs to be given to ethical issues in evaluation. In the next sections we discuss two documents that can be helpful to evaluators in raising their awareness of ethical obligations and in communicating professional obligations to stakeholders.

Ethical Standards in Evaluation

The beginning of the twenty-first century has seen corporations confronting major ethical scandals. The bankruptcy of Enron and the actions of their accounting firm, Arthur Andersen, have brought ethical issues to the attention of the public. The field of evaluation has been active, since the mid-1970s, in developing different ethical codes or standards. (See Fitzpatrick [1999] for a discussion of the history of ethical codes in evaluation and a comparison to codes in other disciplines.) Currently, the two most prominent codes for evaluation in the United States are the Program Evaluation Standards developed by the Joint Committee on Standards for Educational Evaluation (1994) and the Guiding Principles for Evaluators devised by the American Evaluation Association (1995).

These two codes differ in that the Standards are designed to assist both evaluators and consumers in judging the quality of one particular evaluation, whereas the Guiding Principles are to provide guidance for evaluators in their everyday practice. Sanders (1995) notes that the Standards are concerned with professional performance while the Guiding Principles are concerned with professional values. These are useful distinctions. The Standards focus on the product of the evaluation. The Guiding Principles focus on the behavior of the evaluator. Both, however, inform us as to ethical and appropriate ways for evaluations to be conducted. And, as Sanders observes, there are no conflicts or inconsistencies between the two documents.

Other countries, too, have been involved in developing ethical codes. The Canadian Evaluation Society (1992) and the Australasian Evaluation Society (Amie, 1995) have each developed ethical codes for evaluators. The European Evaluation Society is currently involved in such an endeavor.

It is abundantly clear that program evaluators are concerned with developing and getting evaluators to adhere to high standards of ethical conduct. Although the sets of standards or guidelines developed over the years are dissimilar in level of detail and organization, they all address the issue of ethical conduct in one way or another. (For analyses of similarities and differences in these various sets of standards and guidelines, see Covert [1995] and Sanders [1995].)

What are the ethical obligations of evaluators? We will briefly review the ethical components of the Program Evaluation Standards and the Guiding Principles here. A more complete discussion is presented in Chapter 18. We also strongly recommend that the reader become fully acquainted with the text and implications of both documents.

The Program Evaluation Standards (1994) are grouped into four categories: (1) utility, (2) feasibility, (3) propriety, and (4) accuracy. Concern for ethical conduct centers in the third category, that of "propriety." Specific standards listed in this area are:

- Service orientation
- Formal agreements
- Rights of human subjects
- Human interactions
- Complete and fair assessment
- Disclosure of findings
- Conflict of interest
- Fiscal responsibility

Each of the standards is presented, in full, in Chapter 18, "Evaluating Evaluations," but we will expand on some of the critical ethical obligations here. Service orientation is intended to assure that evaluators should serve not only the interests of the agency sponsoring the evaluation but also the learning needs of program participants, community, and society.

Formal agreements goes beyond agreement on technically adequate evaluation procedures and includes such issues as following protocol, having access to data, clearly warning clients about the evaluation's limitations, and not promising too much.

Rights of human subjects are broadly understood to include such things as obtaining informed consent, maintaining rights to privacy, and assuring confidentiality. But human rights extend also into the standard of *human interactions,* which holds that evaluators must respect human dignity and worth in all interactions associated with the evaluation so that no participants are humiliated or harmed.

Complete and fair assessment aims at assuring that both the strengths and weaknesses of a program are portrayed accurately, with no "tilt" in the study to satisfy the sponsor or appease politically potent groups. Reaching a fair balance of the strengths and weaknesses of a program does not mean, however, that an equal number of strengths and weaknesses must be identified, but that whatever strengths and weaknesses exist are accurately assessed.

Disclosure of findings reflects evaluators' obligation to serve not only their clients or sponsors but also the broader public(s) who supposedly benefit from both the program and its accurate evaluation.

Conflict of interest cannot always be resolved, but if evaluators make their values and biases explicit in as open and honest a way as possible, in the spirit of "let the buyer beware," clients can at least be alert to biases that may unwittingly creep into the work of even the most honest evaluators.

Fiscal responsibility does not end with evaluators making sure all expenditures are appropriate, prudent, and well documented. Evaluation also carries nontrivial costs to personnel involved in that which is evaluated, including time and effort in providing, collecting, or facilitating the collection of information requested by evaluators and the time and energy expended in explaining evaluations to various constituencies. Evaluators should make these costs known to clients during the planning stages, so that they know upfront what the financial costs to the organization will be.

The Guiding Principles.   The American Evaluation Association's (AEA) Guiding Principles for Evaluators are elaborations of five basic, broad principles (numbered A–E here to reflect their enumeration in the original document):

A. *Systematic Inquiry:* Evaluators conduct systematic, data-based inquiries about whatever is being evaluated.
B. *Competence:* Evaluators provide competent performance to stakeholders.
C. *Integrity/Honesty:* Evaluators ensure the honesty and integrity of the entire evaluation process.
D. *Respect for People:* Evaluators respect the security, dignity, and self-worth of the respondents, program participants, clients, and other stakeholders with whom they interact.
E. *Responsibilities for General and Public Welfare:* Evaluators articulate and take into account the diversity of interests and values that may be related to the general and public welfare (1995, p. 20). (See Chapter 18 for a more complete presentation of the Guiding Principles.)

Systematic inquiry emphasizes the distinction between formal program evaluation and the evaluations conducted in everyday life. Program evaluators, this principle asserts, use specific, technical methods to complete their evaluations. Because no method is infallible, the principle encourages evaluators to share the strengths and weaknesses of the methods and approach with clients and others to permit an accurate interpretation of the work.

Principle B, *Competence,* makes evaluators aware of the need to practice within their area of expertise and to "continually seek to maintain and improve their competencies, in order to provide the highest level of performance" (American Evaluation Association, 1995, p. 23). An emphasis on maintaining professional knowledge is a principle common to many professions' ethical codes, serving to remind their practitioners that their education is ongoing and that they have an obligation to the profession to produce work that reflects well on the reputation of the field.

The principle of *Integrity/Honesty* mirrors many of the issues articulated in the Standards. It addresses concerns regarding negotiations with clients and relevant stakeholders, conflicts of interest, sources of financial support, misrepresentation of findings, and consideration of methods. Let us highlight two issues here: The Guiding Principles explicitly state that "Within reasonable limits, they [evaluators] should attempt to prevent or correct any substantial misuses of their work by others" (p. 23). Further, Principle C.6 notes that, "If evaluators determine that certain procedures or activities seem likely to produce misleading evaluative information or conclusions, they have the responsibility to communicate their concerns, and the reasons for them, to the client" (p. 23). These two principles put evaluators in an assertive role to prevent some of the ethical challenges encountered by evaluators in the work cited by Morris and Cohn (1993).

As noted, the Standards and Guiding Principles each provide a means for evaluators to convey to clients their professional obligations. The client has hired an evaluator because of his autonomy and expertise. Part of that expertise involves the sense of professionalism that results from following ethical standards of the profession. While evaluators have an obligation to inform clients of these Standards and Guiding Principles, conforming to them can be in the clients' self-interest as well by increasing the credibility of the evaluation. (Note the consequences in 2002 to the accounting firm Arthur Andersen for failing to follow the ethical codes of the accounting profession.)

Respect for People corresponds to the Standards articulated in Rights of Human Subjects and Human Interactions. These concern expectations regarding obtaining informed consent from those from whom data are collected and advising participants regarding confidentiality. The core of this principle is drawn from the ethical codes of many social sciences concerned with collecting data from individuals, for example, the American Psychological Association, the American Anthropological Association, and the American Educational Research Association. Principle D also emphasizes the need to foster the social equity of the evaluation by helping to see that those who give to the evaluation, through data collection, receive any resulting benefits from the study as well. At minimum, these should include obtaining information on the results of the study and its implications for them. *Respect for People* also reminds evaluators of their obligation to be sensitive to ethnic, cultural, and other differences among participants and stakeholders at all stages of the evaluation, from planning the evaluation to reporting its results.

The Guiding Principles represented a change from the standards developed by the Evaluation Research Society, an earlier professional association, in 1982, by including a greater focus on nonmethodological issues (Fitzpatrick, 1999). This is nowhere more evident than in *Guiding Principle E* concerning *Responsibilities for the General and Public Welfare*. This principle mirrors the Service Orientation Standard, which states that evaluations should "look beyond educators' or organizations' self-interests to enhance development of learners and society. . . . In short, evaluations should serve program participants, community, and society" (Joint Committee, 1994, p. 83). Guiding Principle E emphasizes the obligations of evaluators to include "important perspectives and interests of the full range of stakeholders," to consider "not only the immediate operations and outcomes of whatever is being evaluated but also the broad assumptions, implications, and potential side effects of it," to "maintain a balance between client needs and other needs" and to consider the "public good . . . and the welfare of society as a whole" (American Evaluation Association, 1995, pp. 25–26). The inclusion of this principle has sparked dialogue about evaluators' obligation to the public.[3] Certainly, no evaluator has a handle on exactly what the public good is, but Principle E reminds us that our obligation is broader than our particular obligation to the client. Practicing evaluators must also consider the needs of society. Our role might be to stimulate dialogue about those needs or to involve stakeholders in considering the implications of program actions. Whatever action is taken, Principle E reminds evaluators to attend to the implications of the program for the community and society as a whole.

In fact, Principle E addresses a concern raised by Smith (1983) prior to the emergence of the Guiding Principles and the 1994 Standards. He criticized evaluation ethics for focusing solely on methodological issues. Smith wrote:

> Much of the work in evaluation ethics (i.e., the moral behavior of an individual as a professional evaluator) which has been done to date has focused on *evaluation* moral issues such as confidentiality of data, protection of human subjects, proper professional behavior, and so on. Little has been done on *program* moral issues, such as: Is this mental hospital placing the community at risk by its early release of patients? Is this nursing home meeting residents' physical needs but at the cost of their human rights of privacy, freedom of movement, and individual expression? Is this educational program for talented students enhancing cognitive skills but reinforcing their emotional dependency on special recognition and privileges? (Smith, 1983, p. 11).

Principle E extends the ethical code to argue that the evaluator has an obligation to consider these program moral issues.

House has observed that "Ethical concerns become interesting only in conflicted cases, and it is often the balance of principles that is crucial rather than the principles themselves" (1995, p. 27). While the articulation of Standards for Evaluations and Guiding Principles for Evaluators gives us a common ground for dialogue and conveys professional obligations to stakeholders and evaluators new to the field, House is right that the difficulty is in the interpretation of situations and the weighting of principles and actions. Morris has helped make us aware of these choices through his ongoing column on ethical dilemmas in the *American Journal of Evaluation.* In this column, an ethical dilemma is presented and two practicing evaluators indicate how they would respond to the issue. Distinct differences often emerge. See, for example, the disagreements between Bonnet and Schwandt (Bonnet, 1998; Schwandt, 1998). These differences help educate and sensitize evaluators to the choices they make.

---

[3]This principle emerged from the Code of Ethics of the American Society for Public Administration which cites "Serve the Public Interest" as its first ethical code. Under that code fall such behaviors as exercising discretionary authority to promote the public interest, opposing all forms of discrimination, recognizing and supporting the right to know the public's business, involving citizens in decision making, and being prepared to make decisions that may not be popular. This Ethics Code may be accessed at www.aspanet.org.

Ethics Are Not the Sole Responsibility of the Evaluator

Our emphasis on evaluators' responsibility to carry out their activities in an ethical fashion may seem to suggest that ethics is the sole province of evaluators. Obviously, such is not the case: Ethical responsibilities are shared by evaluation sponsors, participants, and audiences. A glance at the nature of the ethical challenges encountered by the evaluators surveyed by Morris and Cohn (1993) demonstrates that many of the ethical challenges begin with pressure from a client or stakeholder. This point further emphasizes the preventive benefits to evaluators of sharing the Program Evaluation Standards and/or the Guiding Principles with clients at the beginning of an evaluation. Clients then know (1) what to expect from the evaluator and the evaluation, and (2) what the evaluator expects from them.

Many ethical issues pertain directly to the programs or products being evaluated and the impact they have on the lives of those they serve and the general public. Perhaps it is appropriate to suggest that the ultimate ethical principle, "Do unto others as you would have them do unto you" is no more or less binding on evaluators than it is on the other stakeholders in every program evaluation.

Ethics beyond a Code of Ethics

The evaluation standards and guidelines described earlier are, in our judgment, singularly useful in improving the practice of evaluation in education. We urge anyone aspiring to do high-quality evaluation to become intimately familiar with those standards and guidelines and to apply them diligently. At the same time, mere adherence to ethical standards, however sound, does not ensure ethical behavior. Mabry (1999) reminds us that codes of ethics don't remove the subjectivity that is inherent in evaluation and in every human endeavor. She argues that standards and guidelines for ethical conduct cannot anticipate the wide range of particularities that are present in any evaluation. Thus, evaluators' personal standards and judgment inevitably play a role in how they apply these codes of conduct to the evaluations they conduct.

Perhaps Sieber still states it best:

> A code of ethics specifically for program evaluators . . . would be a minimum standard; it would only state what the profession expects of every evaluator in the way of honesty, competence, and decency in relation to those ethical problems that are clearly defined at present.
>
> In contrast, *being ethical* is a broad, evolving personal process. . . . Ethical problems in program evaluation are problems having to do with unanticipated conflicts of obligation and interest and with unintended harmful side effects of evaluation. To *be* ethical is to evolve an ability to anticipate and circumvent such problems. It is an acquired ability. . . . As one undertakes new and different kinds of evaluation and as society changes, one's ability to be ethical must grow to meet new challenges. Thus, *being ethical* in program evaluation is a process of growth in understanding, perception, and creative problem-solving ability that respects the interests of individuals and of society (Sieber, 1980, p. 53, emphasis added).

In her insightful discussion of future efforts necessary to solidify ethical practice in evaluation, Newman (1995) has noted another challenge: that what is ethical conduct in one culture or society may be viewed as shocking misconduct in another. Hendricks and Conner (1995) concur, citing important limitations in extending the Guiding Principles, which were designed for the United States, to evaluation practice in other countries. As Newman puts it:

> In its current state, the status of ethics in evaluation is at an early stage of development. We know we need ethics to survive; we know we, not others, must develop our ethical system; we know that we must not put off this task. We have begun the discussion; we have developed a preliminary document. We must not let the process stop at this point; we must continue the dialogue and where necessary create and recreate our own path to ethical practice (1995, p. 110).

Political Pressures and Problems in Evaluation

In the last section we focused on the importance of ethical conduct of evaluators. Rightly so. But we do not want to create the erroneous impression that the evaluator is at the root of all ethical problems encountered in program evaluations. Often the evaluator is forced to perform difficult and delicate tasks in high-pressure situations, a task little more enviable than walking a tightrope in a gale.

Chelimsky (1995) notes that evaluators are often subject to partisan attacks intended to discredit them and their evaluation, for fear of what the evaluation may reveal:

> Efforts to discredit an evaluation based on recognized standards of practice will often follow after pressures on the evaluator—varying from gentle through acute to outright intimidation—have failed. . . . It is true that the shortcomings of evaluators are real and important to address; however, in my experience, the chief barrier to producing useful evaluations lies not in the evaluator but in the evaluation milieu, which may or may not allow the evaluator to be truthful about the merits of the program or policy that has been evaluated (pp. 53–54).

We agree. Few evaluations ever completely escape the influence of political forces, and those forces are the crux and the cause of many of program evaluation's ethical dilemmas. This view was implicit in the early writings of Suchman (1967), Caro (1971), and Cronbach and his colleagues (1980), all of whom hold the view that evaluation is essentially a political activity, underscoring the fact that evaluation of publicly supported enterprises is inextricably intertwined with public policy formulation and all the political forces involved in that process. Evaluators who fail to understand this basic fact squander human and financial resources by conducting evaluations that are largely irrelevant because of their "political naïveté," however impeccably they are designed and conducted.

In this section, therefore, we discuss the political nature of evaluation and ways of coping with unwarranted political influences that can otherwise subvert evaluation efforts.

Evaluation as a Political Activity

The term *politics* has been applied so broadly to so many different phenomena that it has all but lost its meaning. It has come to stand for everything from power plays and machinations within a university department to political campaigns or relations among governmental agencies. Even Webster's *Seventh New Collegiate Dictionary* defines *politics* variously as:

- "the art or science concerned with winning and holding control . . . ,"
- ". . . activities characterized by artful and often dishonest practices,"
- "the total complex of relations between men in society" (p. 657).

And definitions of *political* are just as divergent.

Against such a permissive backdrop, we feel free to add to the proliferation of definitions two more, one more Aristotelian than the other.

1. First, we see political influence as having to do with obtaining, retaining, and exercising formal or informal control over individuals or collectives of individuals in ways that shape activities, policies, and directions of those entities.

2. Second, and more loosely, we have come to think of political influences as the sum total of everything that operated to influence an evaluation but was outside the evaluator's personal control (i.e., did not include the methods, techniques, and interpersonal capabilities of the evaluator).

Such descriptions are admittedly more practical than precise, but our discussion of evaluation's political aspects makes no pretense of "political scholarship." Rather, it draws directly on lessons learned in our collective half century of tiptoeing through the political minefields surrounding most of the many program evaluations we have conducted. When so engaged, precise definition of *politics* seem superfluous. One need not know whether the mine was a Claymore or a "Bouncing Betty" to know it would have been preferable to have trod elsewhere. And most political problems are little more predictable than buried land mines, with the only certainty being that their sudden discovery tends to ruin one's day.

Thus, no matter how one defines *politics,* many evaluators will likely view it as merely an eight-letter dirty word. That perception is perhaps forgivable, for many evaluators have come to understand political influences in much the same way as a bulls-eye learns about bullets. Yet we suggest there is a more enlightened view. Thoughtful evaluators of publicly funded programs view "politics" as the way laws and program regulations are made, the way individuals and groups influence the government, and the very essence of what enables governments to respond to the needs of those individuals and groups. Indeed, without politics, government programs would be less responsive, not more.

Even evaluators who believe they are evaluating "nonpolitical" programs and, thus, can shun the realm of politics altogether fail to perceive the highly political nature of their craft. Effective evaluators must recognize and cope with political influences as they occur. To ignore them or assume "politics can be removed from this study" is both naive and erroneous.

One of the earliest evaluators to describe how political factors influence evaluation was Weiss (1973), who described evaluation as a rational enterprise occurring within a political context. According to Weiss, political factors "intrude" on evaluations in three ways: (1) the policies and programs with which evaluation deals are, themselves, the products of political decisions; (2) because evaluation supports decision making, its reports become political documents; and (3) evaluation, by its very nature, makes implicit political statements (such as those challenging the legitimacy of certain program goals or implementation strategies). Twenty years later, Weiss (1993) reaffirmed her belief " . . . that politics impinges on evaluation in the three ways I described" and that these factors ". . . direct attention to what has come to be known as the politics of evaluation" (p. 107).

But even as Weiss was illuminating the political nature of evaluation, others were examining how shifts in the political scene were altering conceptions of evaluation. For example, Sjoberg (1975) described the evolution of "evaluation research" (his phrase, not ours) as due to societal forces. Specifically, he noted that efforts of social scientists to evaluate social programs are fraught with ethical and political dilemmas. In his view, the increasing use of evaluation as a useful tool was brought about by a fundamental shift from industrial to postindustrial economic and political systems.

In looking back on that era, Sechrest and Figueredo (1993) described how naive program evaluators initially tried to impose their view of social science onto the existing political and policy world. Rebuffed, they began to realize that the realities of the evaluation environment were quite different from their conceptions. Their dilemma was complicated still further by a social revolution from the industrial ". . . mode of management, in both business and government, to a post-industrial era, or cybernetic, mode" (p. 646) that favored multiple decision makers, an information-based society, and a blurred distinction between producer and consumer. Decentralization of policymaking led to heterogeneity of program implementation, and the formerly monolithic set of interests, objectives, and policymakers was replaced by an entire social network involved in and influenced by the social program. Faced with this new social ecology, program evaluators were forced to adapt their conceptions and processes of evaluation and, since the 1970s, there have been few evaluators who have not recognized that political processes will be an ever-present part of program evaluation.

For example, Palumbo (1987) argued that politics play a major role in the practice of program evaluation, and Patton (1988) noted that politics played a pervasive role in everything from the evaluation's theoretical orientation and design to utilization of the study's results. Perhaps Chelimsky (1987) has contributed most to understanding the political nature of evaluation of programs and policies, especially those at the national level of government. She has spoken of many lessons learned about the politics of program evaluation, including:

Evaluators have learned that they . . . must understand the political system in which evaluation operates and the information needs of those policy actors who utilize evaluation.

They have learned to more broadly conceptualize the political system and include all sectors that make the kinds of policy decisions into which evaluation feeds, including executive and legislative branch policymaking . . . (p. 17).

Taking political processes into account when conducting an evaluation transforms the way in which time is allocated. Evaluators have learned to devote much more time to negotiation, discussion, briefing, accuracy-checking, prioritizing, and presentation than before.

The use of evaluation . . . [is] growing dramatically. But if the profession is making progress, it is due largely to those who . . . focused our attention on the political environment in which evaluators expected to be useful but knew very little about (p. 19).

Canadian Senator Marsden (1991), speaking to the Canadian Evaluation Society, noted that ". . . there is a great scope and promise in program evaluations for political decision making that remains unexploited" (p. 3). She went on to urge that ". . . evaluations—or at least the clarity of some of the thinking behind program evaluations—[be] brought to bear at three stages of political work: (1) at the introduction of legislation . . . , (2) at . . . times where large cuts, large increases, etc. occur, and (3) at times of crisis" (p. 9).

Desirable as these calls are for program evaluation to be used as a tool to improve federal legislation, some evaluators worry that political forces at the national level are so strong as to threaten to swamp evaluation's ship of state. Suarez (1990) suggested that few national evaluations have as their central goal the provision of impartial information that will inform and shape national policies and decisions. The political stakes are simply so high at the federal level, she claims, that advocacy eventually inundates those who retreat to the high ground in search of valid information for use in rational decision making. Although we agree that her description fits many national evaluations, there are many notable exceptions, such as a majority of studies conducted by the U.S. General Accounting Office.

When one examines the trends in the use of evaluation at state, provincial, and local levels, there is even more room for optimism. Not that politics is absent from local and state/provincial governmental processes. Such a claim would be naive, especially when high-stakes decisions are in the offing, but despite the pervasive presence of politics at every level, there are some data (e.g., Worthen, 1995) that suggest that the political sailing is smoother on state and local tributaries than on major national flood tides where the waters are stirred up by unwanted evaluation mandates. While politically roiled programs can occur at any level, there are at least a large portion of the local and state programs that are free enough of political undercurrents to allow policymakers to use program evaluation to gather information they need to guide future program development.

Partisanship and Political Neutrality

The "politics of evaluation" also influences how evaluators deal with partisan activities meant to influence the conduct of evaluation in ways that favor one group or another. It is essential that the evaluator represent all stakeholders, following Cronbach, et al.'s (1980) advice that evaluators try to see programs through the eyes of diverse partisans, thus being multipartisan, making the best case they can for each side in turn.

The Joint Committee (1994) also recognizes the importance of the evaluator's sensitivity to the various partisan views of stakeholder groups; the committee proposes the following standard:

> *Political Viability.* The evaluation should be planned and conducted with anticipation of the different positions of various interest groups, so that their cooperation may be obtained, and so that possible attempts by any of these groups to curtail evaluation operations or to bias or misapply the results can be averted or counteracted (p. 71).

Coping with Political Pressures on Evaluation Studies

> Was it mere naïveté that accounted for the initial failure of evaluation researchers to anticipate the complexities of social and political reality? These researchers [evaluators] were mentally prepared by the dominant Newtonian paradigm of social science for a bold exploration of the icy [unchanging] depths of interplanetary space. Instead, they found themselves completely unprepared for the tropical nightmare of a Darwinian jungle: A steaming green Hell, where everything is alive and keenly aware of you, most things are venomous or poisonous or otherwise dangerous, and nothing waits passively to be acted upon by an external force. This complex world is viciously competitive and strategically unpredictable because [evaluation] information is power, and power confers competitive advantage. The Darwinian jungle manipulates and deceives the unwary wanderer into serving myriads of contrary and conflicting ends. The sweltering space suits just had to come off (Sechrest & Figueredo, 1993, p. 648).

This colorful portrayal of evaluators' first forays into the septic and unpredictable environment in which programs wait to be evaluated underscores one point that is perfectly predictable: Political pressures are inevitably part of evaluation. And the professional evaluator who prefers to eschew "politics" and deal only with technical considerations has made a strange career choice.

Some political pressures, however, can interfere with evaluation in ways that are patently unethical. It is the evaluator's responsibility to see that political forces such as these are not allowed to subvert an otherwise good evaluation study. Of course, it is easier to propose coping strategies from an armchair than from one of the hot spots just described. In reality, the difficulty of dealing with unethical political pressures is often acute. For this reason, it is often advisable for evaluators to work in teams, rather than alone. There is safety, to say nothing of commiseration, in numbers.

After offering several tongue-in-cheek rules for escaping the influence of external political factors (Do not work for anyone who has anything to do with the project you are evaluating. . . . Be independently wealthy . . .), Brickell makes the following serious suggestions for dealing with political influences in evaluation:

1. Try to understand how the client thinks. Find out what he has to gain or lose from the evaluation. . . .

2. Reassure the client at the outset that you can interpret the findings so as to give helpful suggestions for program improvement no matter what the findings of the study are.

3. Find out what the powerful decision makers—the client and those who surround him—will actually use as criteria for judging the success of the project. Gather and present evidence addressed to those criteria. You may, if you wish, also gather data on the official objectives of the program or even on objectives that happen to interest you. But never try to substitute those for data addressed to criteria the decision makers will use.

4. Try to get a supervisory mechanism set up for the evaluation contract that contains a cross-section of all the powerful decision makers. Try to get it designed so that the members have to resolve the conflicts among themselves before giving you marching orders for the study or deciding whether to accept your final report.

5. Write the report carefully, especially when describing shortcomings and placing blame, and do mention any extenuating circumstances. . . . Review the draft final report before submitting it to the client for his review, making sure in advance that you can defend any claim you make.

Following those rules will not help you escape political influences. The most they can do is help you cope with them (Brickell, 1978, p. 98).

Two decades later, Brickell's suggestions doubtlessly appear overly tilted toward placating management, while ignoring other program participants. In today's more egalitarian view, such studies would be recognized as insufficient if other stakeholder groups were not continually involved in a similar fashion. Through such means, evaluators can buffer their evaluations from political forces that could otherwise buffet it badly.

Fortunately, the Program Evaluation Standards and the Guiding Principles provide evaluators with the means to work with many of these political problems. Formal evaluation agreements and the judicious use of an outside consultant to help mediate conflicts can be invaluable. In addition, avoiding conflict of interest and insisting on open, fair, and complete disclosure of findings are two of the most important principles evaluators can remember when it comes to coping with unethical political pressures.

CASE STUDY APPLICATION

Reprise: For this chapter, let me recall an earlier note to my diary that reflects some of the ethical dilemmas that can arise in an evaluation:

January 8. I'm a tad frustrated tonight, and it's my own fault, I guess. Called Claire Janson yesterday to get her approval of the individuals I'd selected to be on the site visit team. She asked me to get the okay of the Radnor humanities faculty, saying she had no objection if they didn't. I explained that I had asked her faculty earlier this week to nominate humanities experts they thought could do a good, fair review of their curriculum, and that I had selected one of the two they proposed. But she still thought they might feel better if they reviewed the list of everyone who would be on the team, and, after reflecting for a minute, I agreed. So I asked if she might run the list past them this second time and let me know their reaction (there's more than one way to stretch a pitifully small telephone budget!).

Anyway, she called this morning and said that the faculty felt rather strongly that they wanted *both* of their nominees on the team, suggesting I drop someone else if necessary (not caring who, because they had no objection to any particular team member). I told Claire Janson I had only asked the faculty to *nominate* humanities experts, that I had honored that by choosing one of their nominees, and that I felt it was my prerogative to make the final selection of team members. Besides, I told her that I know the second humanities expert that I did list on the team, and he is excellent—not only sharp, but unbiased, plus experienced in doing curriculum reviews.

She said okay, but later today she called back and said she'd been talking with one of her faculty who was *insistent* that I use *both* nominees on the team. Claire Janson said she was uneasy, and wondered whether I might compromise a bit on this, rather than creating a fuss in the faculty before we even got the evaluation started. She said she had reviewed my evaluation plan and couldn't find anything that said I would choose the team or that their district couldn't, so she felt on shaky ground being too hard-nosed about telling her staff that I had the sole right to make final decisions about team composition.

Well, that really got to me, and I had to bite my tongue to keep from telling her that we didn't have a legalistic contract, for goodness' sake, and that she also *couldn't* find anywhere in our agreed-on plan that said I couldn't pick the team either. But I resisted. Maybe I should have drafted a more formal evaluation contract, at least laying out who makes key decisions pertaining to key aspects of the evaluation. But I hadn't. So I had to reveal something to her that I had hoped might be left unsaid, and that is the reason why I didn't include the faculty's one nominee I had dropped. I told her that when I called both proposed consultants to see if they might have the time and interest to be involved, one chap nearly panted after the opportunity, saying he would "love to get back to Radnor again." "*Again*," I asked? Turns out he was one of the people who helped set up the Radnor humanities program in the first place. So I drew a line through his name. Having him evaluate that curriculum would be a bit like having a mother evaluate her own baby.

When I explained, Claire Janson thanked me, and suggested she talk to the faculty again. A bit later she got back to me and said everyone was satisfied with the team I'd selected. She apologized for her staff, saying they hadn't thought very deeply about the fact that prior involvement as a consultant might tend to color one's judgment. So she gave me the green light to proceed.

> It still annoys me a bit that I hadn't been more precise with the evaluation agreement, but even then I may not have thought to include anything about who made the final choice of team members. Seems there are so many political or personal issues that crop up in every evaluation that I don't know how anyone would anticipate them all. Of course, that's no excuse for failing to get agreements on those you *can* anticipate, I guess.

Major Concepts and Theories

1. Evaluators can foster good communication with stakeholders by educating stakeholders on the purpose for the evaluation and their participation; by encouraging both internal and external stakeholder participation, including divergent stakeholder perspectives; and by conducting informal meetings with stakeholders.

2. Stakeholder communication can also be facilitated through the development of management plans that allow enough time to carry out all planned activities, link short-term activities and goals with long-term goals, assign responsibilities to participants, and protect the rights of participants.

3. Evaluators may hold positive or negative views about the staff, administrators, organization, program theory, or clients of a program. These views may make it difficult to control their bias and interact meaningfully with participants and stakeholders of the evaluation. These views may also bias the outcomes of the evaluation.

4. Evaluations can also be biased based on financial or organizational pressures. Consider how the position of the evaluator (e.g., internal, external, nature of relationship) can influence the evaluator.

5. The *Program Evaluation Standards* provide information for evaluators, clients, and stakeholders on how good evaluations should be conducted. Standards include utility, feasibility, propriety, and accuracy standards. Propriety standards address ethical issues such as service orientation, formal agreements, rights of human subjects, human interactions, complete and fair assessment, disclosure of findings, conflict of interest, and fiscal responsibility.

6. The Guiding Principles of the American Evaluation Association provide guidance for evaluators concerning ethical conduct. Principles are developed in the areas of systematic inquiry, competence, integrity/honesty, respect for people, and responsibilities for the general and public welfare.

7. Adherence to ethical standards involves the cooperation of the evaluator, client, sponsor, and program stakeholders because many ethical challenges are initiated when one of these groups puts pressure on the evaluator. Further, the evaluator should make others aware of ethical violations in the program. Educating users in the Standards and Guiding Principles offers evaluators a means for informing clients of expectations for ethical behavior and high-quality evaluations.

8. Evaluations are considered to be an inherently political activity in that they make political statements, albeit implicitly; they support decision making; and they are sometimes the by-product of political activity. Thus, evaluators are integrally involved in the political process, which requires that they develop some basic "evaluator survival skills" that enable them to succeed in their work without violating the professional code of conduct outlined in the Evaluation Standards and Guidelines discussed in this chapter.

Discussion Questions

1. Why is it important to maintain good communication between evaluators and stakeholders? What might happen if communication were to break down in an evaluation?

2. Explain what is meant by "going native." In which evaluation approach is "going native" most common? What are the advantages and disadvantages of "going native"?

3. If an evaluator has acknowledged a bias that will affect the evaluation findings, how might he or she control or account for this bias? Are evaluations ever totally free of bias?

4. Why is there a need for explicit ethical standards in evaluation? What benefits accrue to the evaluator and client by adhering to these standards?

5. What types of ethical violations do you think would occur most commonly in organizations with which you are familiar? How might these violations be prevented?

Application Exercises

1. Refer to the evaluation plan you developed in the prior chapters. Identify three people who might conduct the evaluation: one who is closely associated with whatever you have selected to evaluate, one who works within the same agency but is not closely associated, and one who is external to the agency. Determine how much you believe each of these three individuals' beliefs, and their financial, organizational, and interpersonal relationship (with the evaluation object) would bias the evaluation.

2. In the above situation, analyze the extent to which the evaluation will be both a political and technical activity. If you had to evaluate that program, what biases would you bring? Do you think you would be appropriate to evaluate it? Who (person or organization) might be the best alternative? Why?

3. Consider another program with which you are familiar. What "politics" are involved internally? Externally? Who would gain from potential results of the study? Who might lose? What philosophical differences exist regarding the program approach? Who makes decisions and influences decisions about this program? How might answers to these questions help you deal with problems that might arise?

Relevant Evaluation Standards

The evaluation standards we see as relevant to this chapter's content are the following. These standards are described in Chapter 18.

U2–Evaluator Credibility
F2–Political Viability
P1–Service Agreements
P2–Formal Agreements
P3–Rights of Human Subjects
P4–Human Interaction

P5–Complete and Fair Assessment
P6–Disclosure of Findings
P7–Conflict of Interest
P8–Fiscal Responsibility
A11–Impartial Reporting

Suggested Readings

Chelimsky, E. (1987). The politics of program evaluation. In D. S. Cordray, H. S. Bloom, & R. J. Light (Eds.), *Evaluation practice in review.* New Directions for Program Evaluation, No. 34. San Francisco: Jossey-Bass.

Joint Committee on Standards for Educational Evaluation. (1994). *The program evaluation standards.* Thousand Oaks, CA: Sage.

Morris, M. Ethical dilemmas. An ongoing column in each edition of the *American Journal of Evaluation.* Each column presents a case and responses from two evaluators.

Newman, D. L., & Brown, R. D. (1996). *Applied ethics for program evaluation.* Beverly Hills, CA: Sage.

Shadish, W. R., Newman, D. L., Scheirer, M. A., & Wye, C. (Eds.). (1995). *Guiding principles for evaluators.* New Directions for Program Evaluation, No. 66. San Francisco: Jossey-Bass.

Weiss, C. H. (1993). Politics and evaluation: A reprise in mellower overtones. *Evaluation Practice, 14,* 107–109.

18

Evaluating Evaluations

Orienting Questions

1. Why should evaluations be evaluated? When would you want to commission a metaevaluation?
2. What are the attributes of good evaluation?
3. What guidelines and steps would you use in carrying out a metaevaluation?
4. What are the major contributions of the Joint Committee on Standards for Educational Evaluation?

Any evaluation study is going to be biased to some extent. Decisions that evaluators make about what to examine—what methods and instruments to use, whom to talk to and whom to listen to—all influence the outcome of the evaluation. Even evaluators' personal background, biases, professional training, and experience all affect the way the study is conducted.

Both evaluators and clients must be concerned about evaluation bias: evaluators because their personal standards and professional reputation are at stake; clients because they don't want to invest (either politically or financially) in findings that are off-target. Both have a lot to lose if an evaluation is shown to be deficient in some critical aspect.

This is why *metaevaluation*—the evaluation of an evaluation—is important. Formative metaevaluation can improve an evaluation study before it is irretrievably too late. Summative metaevaluation can add credibility to final results.

In this chapter we discuss the concept of metaevaluation, standards, and criteria for evaluating evaluations, and metaevaluation procedures that can be used to enhance the quality of evaluations.

The Concept and Evolution of Metaevaluation

Not even the most enthusiastic advocate would assert that all evaluation activities are intrinsically valuable or even well intentioned. Thoughtful observers have even asked, from time to time, whether evaluation results warrant their cost in human and other resources. As Nilsson and Hogben (1983) correctly point out, *metaevaluation* refers not only to the evaluation of particular studies but also to evaluation of the very function and practice of evaluation itself.

This broader definition of *metaevaluation,* however, goes beyond the scope of both this chapter and book. By now our bias must be clear to the reader: We are thoroughly convinced of evaluation's importance. Properly practiced, evaluation has led to direct and incontestable improvements in systems, programs, and practices, improvements that would have occurred in no other way. Given the number and frequency of evaluation failures, however, we understand why some question the enterprise. When evaluation goes wrong, the fault lies, we believe, not with the concept but with the way in which the evaluation is conducted. The purpose of metaevaluation is to help evaluation live up to its potential. For this chapter, then, we restrict our discussion to evaluation of individual evaluation designs, studies, and reports.

The Evolution of Metaevaluation

In an informal sense, metaevaluation has been around as long as evaluation, for someone has had an opinion about the quality of every evaluation study ever conducted. During the 1960s, however, evaluators began to discuss formal metaevaluation procedures and criteria, writers began to suggest what constituted good and bad evaluations (e.g., Scriven, 1967; Stake, 1970; Stufflebeam, 1968), and unpublished checklists of **evaluation standards** began to be exchanged informally among evaluators. In addition, several evaluators published their proposed guidelines, or "metaevaluation" criteria, for use in judging evaluation plans or reports (Rossi, 1982; Scriven, 1974b; Stake, 1969; Stufflebeam, 1974; Stufflebeam, et al., 1971).

In general, evaluators welcomed these lists of proposed metaevaluation criteria. In addition, several authors of the criteria attempted to make them useful to evaluation consumers, thinking that perhaps, if evaluation clients were more skillful in judging an evaluation's adequacy, the number of unhelpful and wasteful evaluations might diminish. Clients can demand high quality only if they can recognize what it is that makes one evaluation better or worse than another. For this to occur, evaluators and those they serve must reach shared agreements about what constitutes a good evaluation, in terms both can understand.

However, the many different sets of proposed criteria proved disconcerting to evaluators and consumers alike. Was one set better than another? Which was best? Which was most acceptable?

No one could answer such questions well, for none of the proposed sets of criteria offered by evaluators carried any widespread consensus. Consequently, an ambitious effort was launched in the late 1970s to develop a comprehensive set of standards explicitly tailored for use in educational evaluations and containing generally agreed-on standards for quality evaluation. Development of these standards began in 1975, under the direction of Daniel Stufflebeam, at Western Michigan University's Evaluation Center. Guidance and authorization were provided by a Joint Committee on Standards for Educational Evaluation (hereafter referred to as the Joint Committee) (Ridings & Stufflebeam, 1981).[1] The result of the Joint Committee's work was the *Standards for Evaluations of Educational Programs, Projects, and Materials* (Joint Committee, 1981), which has received widespread attention in education.

These standards were revised and applied to settings beyond K–12 schools in 1994 (Joint Committee, 1994). In the introduction to the *Standards,* as we will call the book, the Joint Committee stated that development of sound standards could provide the following benefits:

> a common language to facilitate communication and collaboration in evaluation; a set of general rules for dealing with a variety of specific evaluation problems; a conceptual framework by which to study the often-confusing world of evaluation; a set of working definitions to guide research and development on the evaluation process; a public statement of the state of the art in educational evaluation; a basis for self-regulation and accountability by professional evaluators; and an aid to developing public credibility for the educational evaluation field (Joint Committee, 1981, p. 5; stated similarly in the Introduction of the Joint Committee, 1994).

The Joint Committee's Standards for Program Evaluation

The Joint Committee's *Standards* is a set of thirty standards, each with an overview that provides definitions and a rationale for the standard, a list of guidelines, common errors, illustrative cases describing evaluation practices that could have been guided by that particular standard, and an analysis of each case. The result is a work so comprehensive that it fills a book (Joint Committee, 1994). A similar set of standards—for personnel evaluation—was published by the Joint Committee in 1988.

One of the most important insights that the Joint Committee provides with the *Standards* is that the quality of an evaluation study can be determined by look-

---

[1]The following professional organizations appointed members to the Joint Committee: American Association of School Administrators, American Educational Research Association, American Evaluation Association, American Federation of Teachers, American Psychological Association, Association for Supervision and Curriculum Development, Canadian Evaluation Society, Canadian Society for the Study of Education, Council of Chief State School Officers, Council on Post-secondary Accreditation, National Association of Elementary School Principals, National Council on Measurement in Education, National Education Association, National Legislative Program Evaluation Society, and National School Boards Association. In addition, numerous professional evaluators assisted in the development of standards, testing them, and drafting instructional materials to help others apply them.

ing at its (1) utility, (2) feasibility, (3) propriety, and (4) accuracy. The 30 Program Evaluation Standards are grouped according to their potential contribution to each of these four attributes. Utility is purposely listed first for program evaluation, for the Joint Committee recognized that, without utility, a program evaluation will be judged harshly, no matter how well it focuses on feasibility, propriety, and accuracy. Following are the Joint Committee's 30 Program Evaluation Standards, with a brief explanation of each.

Summary of the Program Evaluation Standards

Utility Standards

The utility standards are intended to ensure that an evaluation will serve the information needs of its intended users.

U1 *Stakeholder Identification.* Persons involved in or affected by the evaluation should be identified, so that their needs can be addressed.

U2 *Evaluator Credibility.* The persons conducting the evaluation should be both trustworthy and competent to perform the evaluation, so that the evaluation findings achieve maximum credibility and acceptance.

U3 *Information Scope and Selection.* Information collected should be broadly selected to address pertinent questions about the program and be responsive to the needs and interests of clients and other specified stakeholders.

U4 *Values Identification.* The perspectives, procedures, and rationale used to interpret the findings should be carefully described, so that the bases for value judgments are clear.

U5 *Report Clarity.* Evaluation reports should clearly describe the program being evaluated, including its context, and the purposes, procedures, and findings of the evaluation, so that essential information is provided and easily understood.

U6 *Report Timeliness and Dissemination.* Significant interim findings and evaluation reports should be distributed to intended users, so that they can be used in a timely fashion.

U7 *Evaluation Impact.* Evaluations should be planned, conducted, and reported in ways that encourage follow-through by stakeholders, so that the likelihood that the evaluation will be used is increased.

Feasibility Standards

The feasibility standards are intended to ensure that an evaluation will be realistic, prudent, diplomatic, and frugal.

F1 *Practical Procedures.* The evaluation procedures should be practical, to keep disruption to a minimum while needed information is obtained.

F2 *Political Viability.* The evaluation should be planned and conducted with anticipation of the different positions of various interest groups, so that their cooperation may be obtained and so that possible attempts by any of these groups to curtail evaluation operations or to bias or misapply the results can be averted or counteracted.

F3 *Cost Effectiveness.* The evaluation should be efficient and produce information of sufficient value, so that the resources expended can be justified.

Propriety Standards

The propriety standards are intended to ensure that an evaluation will be conducted legally, ethically, and with due regard for the welfare of those involved in the evaluation as well as those affected by its results.

P1 *Service Orientation.* Evaluations should be designed to assist organizations to address and effectively serve the needs of the full range of targeted participants.

P2 *Formal Agreements.* Obligations of the formal parties to an evaluation (what is to be done, how, by whom, when) should be agreed to in writing, so that these parties are obligated to adhere to all conditions of the agreement or formally to renegotiate it.

P3 *Rights of Human Subjects.* Evaluations should be designed and conducted to respect and protect the rights and welfare of human subjects.

P4 *Human Interactions.* Evaluators should respect human dignity and worth in their interactions with other persons associated with an evaluation, so that participants are not threatened or harmed.

P5 *Complete and Fair Assessment.* The evaluation should be complete and fair in its examination and recording of strengths and weaknesses of the program being evaluated, so that strengths can be built upon and problem areas addressed.

P6 *Disclosure of Findings.* The formal parties to an evaluation should ensure that the full set of evaluation findings along with pertinent limitations are made accessible to the persons affected by the evaluation and to any others with expressed legal rights to receive the results.

P7 *Conflict of Interest.* Conflict of interest should be dealt with openly and honestly, so that it does not compromise the evaluation processes and results.

P8 *Fiscal Responsibility.* The evaluator's allocation and expenditure of resources should reflect sound accountability procedures and otherwise be prudent and ethically responsible, so that expenditures are accounted for and appropriate.

Accuracy Standards

The accuracy standards are intended to ensure that an evaluation will reveal and convey technically adequate information about the features that determine worth or merit of the program being evaluated.

A1 *Program Documentation.* The program being evaluated should be described and documented clearly and accurately, so that the program is clearly identified.

A2 *Context Analysis.* The context in which the program exists should be examined in enough detail so that its likely influences on the program can be identified.

A3 *Described Purposes and Procedures.* The purposes and procedures of the evaluation should be monitored and described in enough detail so that they can be identified and assessed.

A4 *Defensible Information Sources.* The sources of information used in a program evaluation should be described in enough detail so that the adequacy of the information can be assessed.

A5 *Valid Information.* The information-gathering procedures should be chosen or developed and then implemented so that they will ensure that the interpretation arrived at is valid for the intended use.

A6 *Reliable Information.* The information-gathering procedures should be chosen or developed and then implemented so that they will ensure that the information obtained is sufficiently reliable for the intended use.

A7 *Systematic Information.* The information collected, processed, and reported in an evaluation should be systematically reviewed and any errors found should be corrected.

A8 *Analysis of Quantitative Information.* Quantitative information in an evaluation should be appropriately and systematically analyzed, so that evaluation questions are effectively answered.

A9 *Analysis of Qualitative Information.* Qualitative information in an evaluation should be appropriately and systematically analyzed, so that evaluation questions are effectively answered.

A10 *Justified Conclusions.* The conclusions reached in an evaluation should be explicitly justified, so that stakeholders can assess them.

A11 *Impartial Reporting.* Reporting procedures should guard against distortion caused by personal feelings and biases of any party to the evaluation, so that evaluation reports fairly reflect the evaluation findings.

A12 *Metaevaluation.* The evaluation itself should be formatively and summatively evaluated against these and other pertinent standards, so that its conduct is appropriately guided and, on completion, stakeholders can closely examine its strengths and weaknesses.

Utility of the Standards

Evaluators and their clients may use the *Standards* in planning or reviewing evaluations, organizing preservice and in-service education in evaluation, and monitoring or auditing formally commissioned evaluations. In our judgment, the Joint Committee's *Standards* continues to be the ultimate benchmark against which both evaluations and other sets of metaevaluation criteria and standards should be judged. We are not alone in that judgment. The states of Louisiana, Hawaii, and Florida are using the Program Evaluation Standards as a guide for evaluations of education and public-sector programs.

Application of the Standards

The *Program Evaluation Standards* are not a cookbook list of steps to follow. Rather, they are a compilation of commonly agreed-on characteristics of good evaluation practice. In the final analysis, choices and trade-offs relating to each standard are the province of the evaluator. A checklist (based on the *Standards*) for judging the adequacy of evaluation designs and reports could be developed easily using a format somewhat like that shown in Figure 18.1. A checklist based on the *Standards* can be found at www.wmich.edu/evalctr/checklists.

FIGURE 18.1   *Sample Checklist for Judging Evaluation Reports and Designs*

Title of evaluation document: _____

Name of reviewer: _____

	Criterion Met?	Elaboration

Standard: **Stakeholder Identification**

Specific Criteria

a. Are the audiences for the evaluation identified? Yes No ? NA

b. Have the needs of the audiences been identified? Yes No ? NA

c. Are the objectives of the evaluation consistent
   with the needs of the audiences? Yes No ? NA

d. Does the information to be provided allow necessary
   decisions about the program to be made? Yes No ? NA

Standard: **Reliable Information**

Specific Criteria

a. Are information-collection procedures described well? Yes No ? NA

b. Will care be taken to ensure minimal error? Yes No ? NA

c. Are scoring or coding procedures influenced
   by the evaluator's own perspective? Yes No ? NA

d. Is information generated using evaluation
   instruments verifiable? Yes No ? NA

Standard: **Practical Procedures**

Specific Criteria

a. Are the evaluation resources (time, money, and
   personnel) adequate to carry out the projected
   activities? Yes No ? NA

b. Are management plans specified for conducting
   the evaluation? Yes No ? NA

c. Has adequate planning been done to support
   the feasibility of conducting complex activities? Yes No ? NA

AEA Guiding Principles for Evaluators

We cannot leave this discussion without noting the Guiding Principles of the American Evaluation Association (Shadish, Newman, Scheirer, & Wye, 1995). The AEA principles are lifestyle expectations for professional evaluators rather than a set of standards to be applied to any one specific study. The AEA principles promote a lifestyle of systematic inquiry, professional development, honesty, respect, and concern for society. As such they permeate the day-to-day activities of the evaluator over an entire career.

The Guiding Principles of the American Evaluation Association are:

A. *Systematic Inquiry:* Evaluators conduct systematic, data-based inquiries about whatever is being evaluated.
   1. Evaluators should adhere to the highest appropriate technical standards in conducting their work, whether that work is quantitative or qualitative in nature, so as to increase the accuracy and credibility of the evaluative information they produce.
   2. Evaluators should explore with the client the shortcomings and strengths both of the various evaluation questions it might be productive to ask and the various approaches that might be used for answering those questions.
   3. When presenting their work evaluators should communicate their methods and approaches accurately and in sufficient detail to allow others to understand, interpret, and critique their work. They should make clear the limitations of an evaluation and its results. Evaluators should discuss in a contextually appropriate way those values, assumptions, theories, methods, results, and analyses that significantly affect the interpretation of the evaluative findings. These statements apply to all aspects of the evaluation, from its initial conceptualizations to the eventual use of findings.

B. *Competence:* Evaluators provide competent performance to stakeholders.
   1. Evaluators should possess (or, here and elsewhere as appropriate, ensure that the evaluation team possesses) the education, abilities, skills, and experience appropriate to undertake the tasks proposed in the evaluation.
   2. Evaluators should practice within the limits of their professional training and competence and should decline to conduct evaluations that fall substantially outside those limits. When declining the commission or request is not feasible or appropriate, evaluators should make clear any significant limitations on the evaluation that might result. Evaluators should make every effort to gain the competence directly or through the assistance of others who possess the required expertise.
   3. Evaluators should continually seek to maintain and improve their competencies, in order to provide the highest level of performance in their evaluations. This continuing professional development might include formal coursework and workshops, self-study, evaluations of one's own practice, and working with other evaluators to learn from their skills and expertise.

C. *Integrity/Honesty:* Evaluators ensure the honesty and integrity of the entire evaluation process.

1. Evaluators should negotiate honestly with clients and relevant stakeholders concerning the costs, tasks to be undertaken, limitations of methodology, scope of results likely to be obtained, and uses of data resulting from a specific evaluation. It is primarily the evaluator's responsibility, not the client's, to initiate discussion and clarification of these matters.

2. Evaluators should record all changes made in the originally negotiated project plans and the reasons why the changes were made. If those changes would significantly affect the scope and likely results of the evaluation, the evaluator should inform the client and other important stakeholders in a timely fashion (barring good reason to the contrary, before proceeding with further work) of the changes and their likely impact.

3. Evaluators should seek to determine, and where appropriate be explicit about, their own, their clients', and other stakeholders' interests concerning the conduct and outcomes of an evaluation (including financial, political, and career interests).

4. Evaluators should disclose any roles or relationships they have concerning whatever is being evaluated that might pose a significant conflict of interest with their role as an evaluator. Any such conflict should be mentioned in reports of the evaluation results.

5. Evaluators should not misrepresent their procedures, data, or findings. Within reasonable limits, they should attempt to prevent or correct any substantial misuses of their work by others.

6. If evaluators determine that certain procedures or activities seem likely to produce misleading evaluative information or conclusions, they have the responsibility to communicate their concerns, and the reasons for them, to the client (the one who funds or requests the evaluation). If discussions with the client do not resolve these concerns, so that a misleading evaluation is then implemented, the evaluator may legitimately decline to conduct the evaluation if that is feasible and appropriate. If not, the evaluator should consult colleagues or relevant stakeholders about other proper ways to proceed. (Options might include, but are not limited to, discussions at a higher level, a dissenting cover letter or appendix, or refusal to sign the final document.)

7. Barring compelling reason to the contrary, evaluators should disclose all sources of financial support for an evaluation and the source of the request for the evaluation.

D. *Respect for People:* Evaluators respect the security, dignity, and self-worth of the respondents, program participants, clients, and other stakeholders with whom they interact.

1. Where applicable, evaluators must abide by current professional ethics and standards regarding risks, harms, and burdens that might be engendered to those participating in the evaluation; regarding informed consent for participation in evaluation; and regarding informing participants about the scope and limits of confidentiality. Examples of such standards include

federal regulations about protection of human subjects, or the ethical principles of such associations as the American Anthropological Association, the American Educational Research Association, or the American Psychological Association. Although this principle is not intended to extend the applicability of such ethics and standards beyond their current scope, evaluators should abide by them where it is feasible and desirable to do so.

2. Because justified negative or critical conclusions from an evaluation must be explicitly stated, evaluations sometimes produce results that harm client or stakeholder interests. Under this circumstance, evaluators should seek to maximize the benefits and reduce any unnecessary harms that might occur, provided this will not compromise the integrity of the evaluation findings. Evaluators should carefully judge when the benefits from doing the evaluation or in performing certain evaluation procedures should be forgone because of the risks or harms. Where possible, these issues should be anticipated during the negotiation of the evaluation.

3. Knowing that evaluations often will negatively affect the interests of some stakeholders, evaluators should conduct the evaluation and communicate its results in a way that clearly respects the stakeholders' dignity and self-worth.

4. Where feasible, evaluators should attempt to foster the social equity of the evaluation, so that those who give to the evaluation can receive some benefits in return. For example, evaluators should seek to ensure that those who bear the burdens of contributing data and incurring any risks are doing so willingly and that they have full knowledge of, and maximum feasible opportunity to obtain, any benefits that may be produced from the evaluation. When it would not endanger the integrity of the evaluation, respondents or program participants should be informed whether and how they can receive services to which they are otherwise entitled without participating in the evaluation.

5. Evaluators have the responsibility to identify and respect differences between participants such as differences in their culture, religion, gender, disability, age, sexual orientation, and ethnicity, and to be mindful of potential implications of these differences when planning, conducting, analyzing, and reporting their evaluations.

E. *Responsibilities for General and Public Welfare:* Evaluators articulate and take into account the diversity of interests and values that may be related to the general and public welfare.

1. When planning and reporting evaluations, evaluators should consider including important perspectives and interests of the full range of stakeholders in the object being evaluated.

2. Evaluators shuld consider not only the immediate operations and outcome of whatever is being evaluated but also the broad assumptions, implications, and potential side effects of it.

3. Freedom of information is essential in a democracy. Hence, barring compelling reason to the contrary, evaluators should allow all relevant stakeholders to have access to evaluative information and should actively disseminate that information to stakeholders if resources allow.

4. Evaluators should maintain a balance between client needs and other needs.
5. Evaluators have obligations that encompass the public interest and the public good. (The points to Principle E have been abbreviated here. The reader is encouraged to see the entire text at www.eval.org.*)

The Role of Metaevaluator

Metaevaluation was added as a standard by the Joint Committee in 1994. No longer is metaevaluation merely a nicety. It is now an expectation. Nearly everyone does informal metaevaluation. But *formal* evaluation is something else entirely. Who should do the evaluation? As Brinkerhoff, Brethower, Hluchyj, and Nowakowski (1983) state, "Not only should they [metaevaluators] be competent enough to *do* the original evaluation, but they also have to be able to tell if it was a good or bad one and be able to convince others that they know the difference" (p. 208). Often the best metaevaluators are evaluation advisory panels put together to capture different kinds of relevant expertise.

We see all of the following people as being appropriate individuals to conduct metaevaluations:

1. *Metaevaluation conducted by the original evaluator.* We discussed earlier the possible biases that can accrue from evaluating one's own work. The evaluator is not immune to personal biases, and it is always advisable to have another evaluator review one's work, even if it is only a critique by a friendly but frank colleague down the hall. Should that not be possible, however, we think it better for evaluators to measure their own evaluation work against the Joint Committee *Standards* and AEA *Guiding Principles* than to allow it to go unassessed simply because there is a risk of bias.

2. *Metaevaluation conducted by evaluation consumers.* Often the evaluation sponsor, client, or other stakeholders are left to judge the adequacy of an evaluation plan or report without assistance from a professional evaluator. The success of this approach depends heavily on the technical competence of the consumer to judge how well the evaluation meets such standards as "valid information" or "analysis of quantitative information." The Joint Committee *Standards* and the AEA *Guiding Principles,* however, do not require specialized technical training. It may be quite feasible for a client to apply most of these criteria effectively, calling on a technical expert to clarify anything that seems complex or unclear. Of course, if the evaluation is judged to be irrelevant, unintelligible, biased, or untimely, its technical adequacy may be of little concern.

3. *Metaevaluation conducted by competent evaluators.* This would seem to be the best arrangement, all else being equal. Still, there are important choices to be made. As Brinkerhoff and others (1983) remind us, (1) external metaevaluators are generally

*From "Guiding principles for evaluators," American Evaluation Association, 1995, in W. R. Shadish, D. L. Newman, M. A. Scheirer, & C. Wye (Eds.), *Guiding principles for evaluators.* New Directions for Program Evaluation, No. 34, 22–26. Reprinted with permission.

more credible than internal metaevaluators, and (2) a team may bring a greater range of skills to a metaevaluation than can an individual evaluator.

Some General Guidelines for Conducting Metaevaluations

Evaluators are well advised to plan both internal and external reviews of evaluation at critical points: once after an evaluation plan or design has been finalized, at periodic intervals during the evaluation to check progress and identify problems, and at the end of the evaluation to review findings and reports and to audit the evaluation procedures and conclusions. Many evaluators use internal and external reviews to guide their work.

The *internal review* can be conducted by an evaluation committee or advisory group. While the evaluation is in progress, the evaluator could enlist a group of stakeholders and evaluation staff, asking for their reactions to the evaluation plan, its implementation, the relative timeliness and costs of various evaluation tasks, and the need for any revisions. The minutes of such meetings provide useful progress reports for the client.

The *external review* is best conducted by a disinterested outside party with successful experience in similar evaluations. If called in early enough, the outside evaluator can review the evaluation design and offer recommendations for strengthening it. An external reviewer can also provide technical assistance during the evaluation and, at the end of the project, can review evaluation procedures, findings, and reports. The external reviewer may need to schedule a site visit at each review stage to gain full access to evaluation files, instruments, data, reports, and audiences. Such an arrangement takes both planning and knowledge of how and where to access pertinent evaluation information. The evaluator should be able to show how the evaluation has been adjusted in response to recommendations by the external reviewer.

Brinkerhoff and his colleagues (1983) provide a helpful list of procedural options (Figure 18.2) from which one might choose in focusing a metaevaluation. As noted above, one can evaluate evaluation plans, designs, activities, reports, or even the financing and management of an evaluation. We choose to emphasize in the remainder of our discussion the evaluation of the evaluation design.

In evaluation, design is critical. Poor designs do not lead to satisfactory evaluations. Yet metaevaluation has to cover more than evaluation design. It is equally important to monitor the evaluation in progress and to review reports to ensure that the promises outlined in evaluation plans have been kept. It would be foolish to wait until the report is filed to assess the adequacy of the evaluation and, thus, find it too late to correct many deficiencies that might otherwise be identified. In short, a complete metaevaluation includes:

- Reviewing the proposed design to ensure it is feasible and sound;
- Monitoring the design to see that tasks are completed as planned and within budget;

FIGURE 18.2   *Procedural Options for Doing the Metaevaluation*

	Focus of the Metaevaluation		
	Formative Uses		Summative Uses
	Evaluating Evaluation Plans	*Evaluating Evaluation in Progress*	*Evaluating Evaluation after Its Completion*
Procedures for Doing the Metaevaluation	Hire consultant (e.g, evaluator, measurement specialist, or content specialist)	Independent observers (e.g., metaevaluator, evaluation team, review panel)	Review of final reports (e.g., send reports to evaluator, consultant, advisory group)
	Review panel (e.g., advisory group) Review of evaluation plans (e.g., design, contract management plan)	Review of progress reports (e.g., logs, interim reports, budget update, management plan, collection schedule)	Metaevaluator (e.g., sponsors or funding agent, advisory panel, professional evaluator[s])

Source: From *Program Evaluation: A Practitioner's Guide for Trainers and Educators* (p. 221) by R. O. Brinkerhoff, D. M. Brethower, T. Hluchyj, and J. R. Nowakowski, 1983, Boston: Kluwer-Nijhoff. Adapted by permission.

- Checking the quality of instruments, procedures, and products (such as data and reports);
- Reviewing the design for possible midstream revisions (especially in light of the utility the evaluation has shown so far for important audiences or of problems the evaluation was running into); and
- Checking the effects of metaevaluation on the evaluation.

Because of limited space, we limit this discussion and our remaining examples to evaluating the design. Readers should easily be able to extrapolate criteria from this discussion for metaevaluations of other aspects of an evaluation.

Steps to Take in Evaluating an Evaluation Design

The following steps are proposed for conducting a metaevaluation of an evaluation design:

1. *Obtain a copy of the design in a form ready for review.* Formative evaluation of a metaevaluation is obviously desirable once the design is sufficiently formulated to make such a review productive. There is little utility in telling an evaluator that her unfinished design is incomplete.

2. *Identify who will do the metaevaluation.* Check our comments in the previous section, "The Role of Metaevaluator," for help in this decision.

3. *Ensure that authorization exists to evaluate the design.* If you are a sponsor or client and you receive a design submitted by an evaluator who proposes to contract with you to do an evaluation, you are obviously free to evaluate it, and normally there would be no professional or legal restraint on your arranging for another competent "metaevaluator" to assist you in doing so. Conversely, suppose the chair of a Concerned Citizens Against Homeless Shelters committee asks you to find flaws in an internal evaluation design the local homeless shelter proposes to use in evaluating its program. You should question the appropriateness of that role, especially if you find the design is in rough-draft form, circulated only for internal reactions, and surreptitiously spirited from the shelter to the committee by a disgruntled shelter custodian. Metaevaluators (like evaluators) can find themselves used as "hired guns," and it is important before buckling on the holster to be certain that the metaevaluation desired by your paymaster will not violate ethical or legal principles.

4. *Apply standards to the evaluation design.* The Joint Committee encourages use of the Program Evaluation Standards by appending a checklist to its publication.

5. *Judge the adequacy of the evaluation design.* No evaluation design is perfect. The question is whether, on balance, after summarizing judgments across scales, the evaluation seems to achieve its purposes at an acceptable level of quality.

A Need for More Metaevaluation

With any luck we have convinced the reader that the concept of metaevaluation is useful and that there are appropriate tools that can be used for that purpose. Despite the wide publicity, acceptance, and availability of the Joint Committee's *Standards*, however, few evaluations are being subjected to any closer scrutiny now than before their publication. Even casual inspection reveals that only a small proportion of evaluation studies are ever evaluated, even in the most perfunctory fashion. Of the few metaevaluations that do occur, most are internal evaluations done by the evaluator who produced the evaluation in the first place. It is rare indeed to see an evaluator call in an outside expert to evaluate her evaluation efforts. Perhaps the reasons are many and complex why this is so, but one seems particularly compelling: Evaluators are human and are no more ecstatic about having their work evaluated than are professionals in other areas of endeavor. It can be a profoundly unnerving experience to swallow one's own prescriptions. Although the infrequency of good metaevaluation might be understandable, it is not easily forgivable, for it enables shoddy evaluation practices to go undetected and, worse, to be repeated again and again, to the detriment of the profession.

CASE STUDY APPLICATION

June 4. My final report went to Claire Janson today, so this evaluation is completed at last! Or is it? I did suggest to the folks at Radnor that it would be in their best interest to have the completed evaluation reviewed by an outside evaluator. Masochistic as this may seem, I strongly believe that there is more to be learned by involving other eyes and ears, perspectives, experience, and, of course, expertise, in any evaluation. To the extent that we become aware of limitations and strong points in the evaluation, I and my Radnor friends can weigh how much confidence to place in the results. We can also learn something that can help us when we undertake evaluation in the future. The learning process in evaluation never stops. That's one reason why I keep at it, I guess. Of course Brad's orthodontics bill is another.

June 16. Just received a package from Radnor. Claire got a professor who teaches evaluation courses in Philadelphia to agree to review the evaluation as a volunteer service to the school district. She used the Joint Committee *Standards* as the basis for her review. Claire kindly sent me a copy of the review. Brief, but helpful.

ARTIFACT 10

Ms. Janson, my reaction to the external evaluation you had conducted for your district is summarized below, using only the category headings for the Joint Committee's *Standards* we discussed. Sorry time did not permit me to provide more detail.

1. *Utility of the evaluation.* It appears that the groundwork has been laid for producing an evaluation report that has impact. It remains to be seen, however, whether the utility of the evaluation will be worth its cost. You should follow up with the recommendations that resulted from the evaluation and should monitor changes in the program. Because the evaluator has become so knowledgeable about the program, he is a resource that might be tapped in the future for advice on follow-up reviews. My advice to you is not to look at this evaluation as a one-shot study; build on it, continue your reviews, and use further internal evaluation for planning and development. Strong points of this study related to utility were stakeholder involvement throughout the evaluation, the credibility that the evaluator established for himself and the evaluation, the scope of the evaluation, the integration of multiple value orientations into the study, and clarity and timing of the report.

A possible limitation may be the question of commitment of top administrators to the program itself as well as to using the evaluation. Although they have said they are committed, actions speak louder than words.

2. *Feasibility of the evaluation.* The evaluation was tailored to meet budget and time constraints of the client. The logistics of all phases of the evaluation were kept manageable and enabled the study to be completed on time and within budget. The evaluator did a nice job of not overpromising. He delivered what he said he would. Political viability was built by involving everyone who wanted to be involved or who had something to say about the program.

An unknown yet is the cost-effectiveness of the evaluation, and this is something you can affect. The way in which the evaluation is used should justify its cost. A lot of money and energy that might have been better spent on other work will have been wasted if this evaluation has no demonstrable impact. On the other hand, considerable cost savings could occur if the evaluation prevents investments in future unproductive program activities. This remains to be seen.

3. *Propriety of the evaluation.* This aspect of the evaluation looks fairly good. A brief agreement clarified most expectations for the evaluation, and everything that was promised was delivered in a quality manner. (But the agreement was a bit too brief and I suspect you and the evaluator must have developed a fair bit of mutual trust to get through the study without major misunderstandings.) There were no conflicts of interest evident in the evaluation. It was wise to hire an impartial and independent evaluation methodologist for the study. Reports were full, frank, and fair, and the rights of participants and informants were respected and protected. Strengths and weaknesses of the program were both addressed. Interactions during the evaluation appeared to be very professional and respectful.

4. *Accuracy of the evaluation.* The evaluator compensated well for his lack of expertise in humanities education. The use of outside experts and humanities instructors from Radnor rounded out the team of evaluators that, in my judgment, was needed to do a good job of evaluating this program. The evaluator was at somewhat of a disadvantage in that instruments for data collection were not readily available, so that several had to be developed ad hoc. This is a fairly common circumstance in evaluation, but instrument development is expensive and time-consuming. The evaluator did a good job of balancing resource allocations to instrument development with his constraints, maybe even an outstanding job, given the limitations placed on him. By using multiple methods and sources, he was able to triangulate in gathering information that is not misleading. It was evident that if he had used just one source and one method (tests, interviews, or the on-site observations), he might have been led to far different findings that would have been off target. His methods of data control, data analysis, and interpretation addressed the standards of systematic data control, analysis of quantitative and qualitative information, justified conclusions, and objective reporting.

The one limitation that I saw in the reports was the lack of thoroughness of object identification and context analysis. Although the informed reader is well informed about the program and its context, the uninformed reader of the evaluation reports is left wondering about pertinent characteristics of the school district and participating faculty and students. History and philosophy of the program received too little attention, as did implications of the evaluation for other educators who might be considering a similar undertaking. Perhaps a separate report for other educators is in order, so that they can be better informed about its transportability, processes, content, and impact.

Author Comments. Just as I thought. Well done, but not perfect. There was something to be learned from having the evaluation evaluated by an impartial expert in evaluation. There always is.

October 10. Had a telephone call from Pennsylvania today, requesting some extra copies of the evaluation report I wrote last spring. I was interested to learn that the Radnor folk did use that evaluation to make some very sensible decisions about their humanities program. That's the good news. But the bad news is that they've just launched a new districtwide, computer-assisted math curriculum, with absolutely no plans to evaluate it to see how well it works. Claire said she argued vigorously that an evaluation should be built in from the outset, but she lost out.

It beats me why evaluation isn't a regular part of every school's planning, budgeting, program development, textbook and test selection, performance reviews and staff development, educational reform, school board deliberations, mileage requests, and the like. I suspect the problem is that few leadership figures in education, in politics, and in the community have much real understanding about evaluation. There are few who are aware of the potential or who have seen the impact that evaluation can have. There are few who have seen good evaluation, in fact. And there are probably many who have seen or experienced poorly done evaluations. We have come a long way during the past 30 years in our understanding of the role and proper conduct of evaluation. We are still learning, but I shouldn't forget that we now know a lot more than we did then.

Seems to me evaluators should be working with school districts, school boards, politicians, and community groups to share what they know and to work out plans for using evaluation effectively. Wouldn't it be something if more administrators figured out how to recognize and reward exemplary evaluation efforts, or maybe even some sensible way to penalize those who spend large chunks of public funds without any effort to evaluate the quality or usefulness of those expenditures? With that kind of leadership, and real effort from the evaluation community, we should be able to make evaluation more useful so it will be used more often and more intelligently.

My word—I just reread this entry, and I wonder where I left my drums and bugle. If I'm not careful, I'll be marching forth, flags flying, to increase the esprit de évaluation! Best put a leash on my enthusiasm, I guess. I'd hate having my colleagues discount me as some wild-eyed fanatic who gets high by ranting about how evaluation can vanquish the evils of the world. That would surely be a totally exaggerated caricature. Well, at least a somewhat exaggerated caricature.

Author Comments.   And so we come to the end of our fictional evaluation. Yet I have only scratched the surface of what actually happens in carrying out any real evaluation. Most evaluation studies are complex and comprehensive enterprises. Beneath the complexity, however, lie many simple, straightforward steps on which evaluators and clients can work as partners. I hope my imaginary case study has been instructive on some of those practical guidelines. I also hope it has shown that evaluation studies are strongest when tailored specifically to meet the client's needs, drawing as necessary on multiple perspectives rather than following the prescriptions of any one evaluation model or method. It would be disappointing if my contrived evaluation failed to make that point.

I must confess that writing this fictional Radnor evaluation has been therapeutic. It is the only evaluation I have ever conducted from the comfort of my armchair, and it is the only evaluation for which no one has raised questions about my design or my motives, or even my ancestry. Yes, indeed, doing these make-believe evaluations could prove addictive.

Major Concepts and Theories

1. A metaevaluation is an evaluation of an evaluation. It helps an evaluation live up to its potential by providing judgments of the quality of the evaluation based on a set of evaluation standards.

2. The Joint Committee's Standards for Program Evaluation is a set of 30 standards used to assess the quality of an evaluation. The standards cover four areas (utility, feasibility, propriety, and accuracy). These standards can be applied by both evaluators and clients to plan or review evaluations.

3. The utility standards assess an evaluation based on how well it met the needs of its intended audience.

4. The feasibility standards provide information on how realistic, prudent, diplomatic, and frugal the evaluation study was.

5. Information about whether a program evaluation was conducted ethically, legally, and with due regard for evaluation participants and stakeholders can be found by applying the propriety standards.

6. Accuracy standards provide information regarding whether an evaluation conveyed an adequate amount of technical information to determine the quality or worth of the object of evaluation.

7. The *Guiding Principles* of the American Evaluation Association were developed to promote systematic inquiry, professional development, honesty, respect, and concern for society among evaluators.

8. Systematic inquiry refers to the technical standards evaluators apply to data collection and analysis and the evaluator interaction with the client regarding limitations of the study.

9. The competence principle provides guidelines on what evaluation skills the evaluator should possess and those skills the evaluator should obtain through additional courses or self-study.

10. The *Guiding Principles* also state that an evaluator should practice honesty and integrity throughout the entire evaluation process from contract negotiations to interpretation of findings and presentation of the final report.

11. Evaluators should have the utmost respect for the dignity and self-worth of the program participants, clients, other stakeholders, and respondents throughout the entire evaluation process.

12. Evaluators have a certain level of responsibility for the general and public welfare. They should strive to incorporate into the evaluation the diversity of interest and values of the general and public welfare.

13. Evaluators should present findings in a clear and accurate manner, maintain a balance between client and other stakeholder needs, make evaluation data available to key stakeholders, and understand the potential impact of the program outcomes.

14. Metaevaluation can be conducted by the original evaluator; by the evaluation sponsor, client, or stakeholder; or by an external and competent evaluator.

15. Metaevaluation should be conducted during evaluation planning, during intervals throughout the course of the evaluation, and once the evaluation report has been written.

Discussion Questions _____

1. Why would an evaluator want to conduct a metaevaluation of a formative evaluation? What procedures would you use?

2. Why would an evaluator want to conduct a metaevaluation of a summative evaluation? What procedures would you use?

3. Discuss the impetus for development of the Joint Committee's *Standards.*

4. How do the *Guiding Principles* affect the way you will conduct evaluations?

5. What steps would you take to conduct a metaevaluation of an evaluation design?

6. What are the advantages of having the original evaluator conduct a metaevaluation? The client? An external evaluator?

7. Why might an internal review be conducted on an evaluation? What type of evaluator would most likely conduct such a review?

8. Why might an external review be conducted on an evaluation? What type of evaluator would most likely conduct such a review?

Application Exercises _____

1. Use the Joint Committee's Program Evaluation Standards to evaluate a completed evaluation study of your choice. For what aspects of the study do you lack information? What can you learn from the strengths and weaknesses of the work of other evaluators?

2. Select a class of evaluation studies (e.g., program evaluations in a state or federal human services agency completed from 1985 until the present). Use the Program Evaluation Standards to evaluate each study. From these data, can you draw any inferences about program evaluation in the agency? Are there any patterns that emerge? You could repeat this exercise with other classes of evaluations, looking for patterns and drawing conclusions.

Relevant Evaluation Standards _____

The entire set of 30 standards is pertinent here (which should not be surprising, because this chapter focuses on metaevaluation, the very process for which the 30 metaevaluation standards were created).

Suggested Readings _____

Joint Committee on Standards for Educational Evaluation. (1994). *The Program Evaluation Standards* (2nd ed.). Thousand Oaks, CA: Sage.

Shadish, W. R., Newman, D. L., Scheirer, M. A., & Wye, C. (Eds.). (1995). *Guiding principles for evaluators.* New Directions for Program Evaluation, No. 66. San Francisco: Jossey-Bass.

Stufflebeam, D. L. (1974). *Metaevaluation* (Occasional Paper No. 3). Kalamazoo: Western Michigan University Evaluation Center.

Part V

Emerging and Future Settings for Program Evaluation

Throughout the prior sections of our text we have described how program evaluation has served important uses in a variety of public, nonprofit, and corporate settings. We have given examples of program evaluations in local school districts and national education programs, in federal and state health and human services programs, in local community programs aimed at social or environmental problems, in military and scientific endeavors, in nonprofit agencies, and in business and industrial settings. In this final section, we expand our discussion of two settings that are becoming increasingly familiar in today's evaluation scene.

First, in Chapter 19 we discuss several different ways in which multiple-site program evaluations have been used in the past, examine some pitfalls and potentials of multiple-site evaluations, and consider some new conceptions of multiple-site evaluations that are becoming more widely used.

Second, in Chapter 20 we discuss in greater detail how program evaluation is emerging as a dominant force in private and nonprofit settings and describe its role in organizational renewal and improvement of training efforts. We discuss how evaluation fits with and enhances efforts to improve quality and relevance through Total Quality Management, front-end analysis, performance appraisals, customer satisfaction surveys, and other similar corporate endeavors.

Finally, in Chapter 21 we briefly discuss what we and other commentators see as the future of program evaluation.

Because these chapters deal with a wide variety of settings, we have not attempted to extend our Radnor case study into this final section.

19

*Conducting Multiple-Site Evaluation Studies**

Orienting Questions

1. What is a multiple-site program evaluation and how does it differ from a single-site program evaluation?

2. What are the major reasons for conducting multiple-site program evaluations?

3. What are the three most common types of multiple-site evaluations?

4. What are the primary advantages and disadvantages of multisite evaluation (MSE)? What purposes does it serve?

5. What are the primary advantages and disadvantages of on-site evaluation at multiple sites? What purposes does it serve?

6. What are the primary advantages and disadvantages of cluster evaluation?

7. What major differences exist between MSE, cluster evaluation, and on-site evaluation at multiple sites?

In the preceding chapters, we have discussed procedures for planning and conducting program evaluations without devoting much attention to one very important consideration: Do the evaluation approaches and methods we have presented work equally well for evaluating (1) a program that exists at only one site, in a single agency, and (2) a program that exists at multiple sites, either within the same agency or in different agencies? For example, does the content of prior chapters apply as readily to an evaluation of Arizona's statewide, elementary school,

* Portions of this chapter draw on Worthen & Schmitz, 1997.

English as a Second Language (ESL) program as to an evaluation of the ESL program in the Frost Elementary School in Mesa? Are the evaluation approaches and methods we have presented as applicable to evaluating the Rockefeller Foundation's national, six-site Minority Female Single Parent (MFSP) program as they are to evaluating the Atlanta MFSP program? Will the processes and principles we have outlined serve as well in evaluating IBM's overall, nationwide technician training program as in evaluating the effectiveness of the technician training program operated by IBM-Memphis?

For the most part, we would answer these questions affirmatively. Most of what we have said is as applicable to a multiple-site program evaluation as to the evaluation of a single-site program. Evaluations of either a single- or multiple-site program could, for example, opt to use a management-oriented evaluation approach or an objectives-oriented approach. Either would need to be focused by determining the purposes for the evaluation, identifying precisely what aspects of the program are to be evaluated, and deciding what specific questions the evaluation is intended to answer. Either would need to be planned by deciding what specific methodology the evaluation would employ, what ethical issues exist and how they can be resolved, and who should receive reports and in what format. In short, most of the contents of this text are applicable to both multiple-site and single-site evaluations.

There are, however, some special evaluation procedures and issues that pertain to evaluation of multiple-site programs. In this chapter, we briefly discuss reasons why multiple-site evaluations can be advantageous; distinguish between three different, general types of multiple-site evaluations; and discuss some special considerations and concerns relating to each of these three types. While some forms of multiple-site evaluation have been with us for decades, others we describe in this chapter are newly emerging or evolving in ways that will likely affect how many program evaluations are conducted in the future.

Purposes and Characteristics of Multiple-Site Evaluations

There are several reasons for conducting program evaluations that span multiple sites. Some of the major reasons are:

- To determine the overall effect of the program, when effects are aggregated across all program sites;
- To evaluate the program in a sample of representative sites so as to estimate the effect of the program across all sites;
- To determine whether the program works under the variety of conditions and circumstances that exist where it has been implemented;

- To study how the program interacts with specific site characteristics (e.g., demographic differences in program participants, varying placements of the program within agencies' governing structures);
- To monitor individual site compliance in implementing the program according to its specifications or standards;
- To compare program performance across sites to identify the most effective and ineffective ways of operating the program;
- To determine which sites should be continued or discontinued in the program;
- To facilitate cross-site sharing of "effective practices," "lessons learned," and other insights gained in one site that could be beneficial to other sites;
- To have program administrators and staff at each site understand that their site may be included in an evaluation (thus serving one of evaluation's primary noninformational purposes);
- To develop collaborative evaluation efforts among evaluators at specific sites to improve evaluation at each site and across sites.

Doubtlessly there are other good reasons for multiple-site evaluations that we have overlooked. Those we have listed have contributed to a variety of specific forms of multiple-site evaluations. We will discuss the three most common in the remainder of this chapter.

Three Common Types of Multiple-Site Evaluations

Multisite Evaluations.   One of the most conspicuous uses of multiple-site evaluation is the conduct of large-scale experimental or quasi-experimental studies of major social or human services programs in areas such as health care, education, mental health, criminal justice, or public welfare. We will refer to this particular type of multiple-site evaluation as "multisite," in keeping with prominent literature on this type of evaluation (e.g., Turpin & Sinacore, 1991).

On-Site Evaluation at Multiple Sites.   A second common approach to evaluating multiple-site programs is the use of on-site evaluation teams to visit all or a sample of sites implementing the program. Typically, the purpose of such visits is to determine the value and effectiveness of the individual programs and/or the overall program, when individual site findings are aggregated as described by Worthen and White (1987).

Cluster Evaluation.   A third, emerging form of multiple-site evaluation is cluster evaluation, a multiple-site, multilevel evaluation approach developed and used within the W. K. Kellogg Foundation to evaluate "clusters" of projects either funded by a specific, targeted funding initiative or clustered together because they deal with the same theme or topic. (See Worthen & Schmitz, 1997.)

These three types of multiple-site evaluations are intended to serve rather different purposes, which may be more readily understood by examining some specific dimensions on which they differ.

Two Dimensions on Which
Multiple-Site Evaluations Differ

Sinacore and Turpin (1991) categorized multiple-site evaluations (which they termed "MSEs") into *prospective* and *retrospective*. In the former, the evaluator "intends to use multiple sites at the beginning of an evaluation," while in the latter the use of multiple sites is an afterthought "in which data from different evaluations on a similar topic are brought together for an analysis" (p. 6). These authors also distinguish between two subtypes of MSE:

> One subtype of MSE is an evaluation of a program that is implemented in the *same way* at different geographical locations . . .
>   Another subtype of MSE is an evaluation of a program that is implemented in *different ways* at different geographical locations (p. 6).

From Sinacore and Turpin's discussion of MSEs, one can conceive of four different types, as shown in Figure 19.1.[1] For now, let us merely say that the *Controlled Prospective* variant (cell 1) is perhaps the most common form of multiple-site evaluation, while the *Controlled Retrospective* variant (cell 2) is more rare, because the probability of finding program implementation the same without prior planning is not very high. It may occur, however, when evaluators become aware that they have counterparts laboring in similar vineyards where the grapes and methods of harvesting them are sufficiently similar to allow the results to be combined into an evaluation "wine" that contains a blend of the individual program evaluations. More often, however, such retrospective analyses discover that the program implementation in the various sites was so dissimilar (e.g., very dissimilar program participants) that the evaluation slides into cell 4, *Uncontrolled Retrospective* multiple-site evaluations, which is appropriately shunned by most evaluators as having little to offer in generating useful information about the program. *Uncontrolled Prospective* multiple-site evaluations (cell 3) are useful in that the clustering of sites has a thoughtful, preordinate rationale, but they are problematic in that it is difficult to sort out the effects of the specific site from the effects of the program. Yet this approach to multiple-site evaluation is preferred by advocates of cluster evaluation, as we will discuss shortly.

Multisite Evaluation (MSE)

Turpin and Sinacore (1991) have coined the term **multisite evaluations (MSEs)** to refer to common evaluations of large-scale social programs such as an evaluation of health services provided by 172 U.S. Department of Veterans Affairs medical centers dispersed throughout the nation. Based on social science research

---

[1]While the two major structuring dimensions shown in Figure 19.1 are suggested by Sinacore and Turpin (1991), the present authors have combined and juxtaposed them in new ways and are thus solely responsible if doing so has altered the meaning or significance of those dimensions.

Decision to Use Multiple Sites Is Made

		Before Evaluation Begins (Prospective)	After Evaluation Data Are Collected (Retrospective)
Program Implementation in Multiple Sites Is	**Controlled (The Same in All Sites)**	**1. Controlled Prospective** Multiple sites selected early; uniform program implementation attempted	**2. Controlled Retrospective** Retropective analysis of data from multiple sites found (after the fact) to have used the same implementation
	Uncontrolled (Different across Sites)	**3. Uncontrolled Prospective** Multiple sites selected early; no effort made to make program implementation uniform	**4. Uncontrolled Retrospective** Retropective analysis of data from multiple sites found to have been implemented dissimilarly

FIGURE 19.1   *Dimensions for a Typology of Multiple-Site Evaluations*

methods, MSEs typically use experimental or quasi-experimental designs, complete with randomization, coupled with sophisticated statistical analysis. MSEs are marked by careful efforts to standardize and control both implementation of the program and the procedures for collecting, verifying, and analyzing the evaluation data. Careful sampling of sites for inclusion in the evaluation is another attribute of most well-conducted MSEs. Thus, the MSE is the archetypical example of a *Controlled Prospective* multiple-site evaluation (cell 1 in Figure 19.1).

Greenberg, Meyer, and Wiseman (1994) define MSE as "a multisite design in which similar program features have been tested simultaneously at several different local administrative offices" (p. 679). Sinacore and Turpin (1991) state:

> The distinguishing feature of an MSE is its implementation at different sites with an analysis of *original* data. MSEs should not be confused with metanalyses in which investigators study the effects of programs by examining the summary statistics of numerous published and unpublished evaluations (p. 7).

Purposes of MSE

The most widely agreed-on purposes of MSEs are those listed by Turpin and Sinacore (1991):

> It appears that many evaluators conduct MSEs for similar reasons: to increase generalizability of findings, to maximize sample size, and to respond to a variety of political and social demands (p. 1).

These authors note that increasing the generalizability of findings greatly increases their external validity, because collecting data from multiple sites helps to pinpoint how well the program works with different types of clients in different contexts. They also point out that using multiple sites increases the sample size, thus raising the statistical power of data analyses and the reliability and validity of the results.

Cottingham (1991) points out that not only are MSEs proposed as a fast means of learning about a program's universality and replicability but, if the program works, its use in multiple sites is viewed as useful in speeding acceptance and adoption of the new program. Greenberg and his colleagues (1994) have provided, in the following quotation, a good sense of the purposes MSEs can serve. They addressed the question of why one might opt to undertake an experiment at multiple sites.

> Since it is obvious that, with a given sample size, it is more costly to conduct and evaluate a multisite experiment than a single-site experiment, a useful starting point is to ask what purposes are served by the former that cannot be served by the latter. There are at least three potential advantages of multisite experiments. First, a multisite design can be used to determine whether the program being tested "works" under a variety of conditions. For example, sites may vary in the characteristics of the population being served, economic and other environmental conditions, and program components and inputs. Second, impact estimates can be based on an evaluation sample that is pooled across sites, thereby producing measures that are "representative" of potential program effects over broad geographical areas such as a state or the nation as a whole. Third, multisite evaluations can be used to draw inferences about underlying production relationships by examining how program effects vary with cross-site differences in participant characteristics, environmental conditions, and program features (p. 680).

Issues in MSE

There are a variety of issues that must be addressed in planning an MSE. First, there is the natural tension between maintaining standardization and control of the program implementation versus the need to adapt the program to local needs and circumstances. While we have said that efforts to control implementation typify the MSE, that is not to say that all those who propose MSE advocate that programs mindlessly force each site to implement the program in the prescribed pattern if (1) it is obvious that local circumstances would cause that prescription to fail, but (2) slight adaptations would allow the program to work well. But how much adaptation can be tolerated before one no longer has an evaluation of a single program at multiple sites but rather a series of evaluations of quite different programs? If an MSE of a drug-free schools program shows poor results, is the program to blame, or was the failure due to lack of fidelity in implementing the program? This is an important issue to resolve early in any MSE. Readers who wish more depth in this area are referred to Mowbray and Herman (1991), Cottingham (1991), and Tushnet (1995).

A second issue in MSE is how sites should be selected for inclusion in the evaluation. What seems to be a straightforward issue ("just draw a random sample") turns out to be somewhat more complex. As Sinacore and Turpin (1991) put it:

> Statistically speaking, deliberate sampling for heterogeneity does not allow one to generalize in meaningful ways to a larger population. This is because selection is not random. However, the variation in participants that is created by using multiple sites allows the evaluator to examine the extent to which a program influences different types of people. For example, if it were shown that the reading program in question was successful at all the sites, it would be known that children across three socioeconomic levels were affected by the program. Given this outcome, something would be learned about the efficacy of the program relative to specific groups of different socioeconomic levels. It would not be known if the same results would be found with a stratified random sample, but at least it can be said that an effect was obtained across the particular range of children involved in the evaluation (p. 8).

Groups and organizations, like individuals, have "personalities" that can seriously affect program outcomes and cannot be ignored as mere nuisance effects. Therefore, one needs to consider such institutional dimensions before selecting specific sites, using everything that is known about the specific social, political, and organizational characteristics of sites in selecting the best cross-section of sites for the MSE. Sinacore and Turpin (1991) concur, noting that

> In sum, a high-quality MSE depends on the evaluator's knowledge about the sites—their organizations and personnel—before including them in the study. A common wisdom in the Department of Veterans Affairs states, 'When you have seen one VA, you have seen one VA.' This message should be well heeded. The wise evaluator verifies any claims regarding similarity of prospective sites while planning an MSE (p. 11).

A third issue in MSE is how to obtain adequate cooperation from each participating site. This has to do both with obtaining the necessary sanction to conduct the evaluation activities at that site and with how relationships, tasks, and arrangements for data collection can be structured to ensure that the needed access to data sources will not be closed off.

There are also many practical issues in conducting MSEs. We enumerate several such issues below, drawing on Sinacore and Turpin (1991), Hedrick and her colleagues (1991), and the authors' experience with MSEs.

1. Understanding the System. Evaluators' success in conducting an MSE will be determined to a large degree by how well they understand the system within which the program "lives."

2. Staffing the MSE. A functional staffing plan is essential to the success of any MSE. Whether each site has a separate site coordinator, whether that person has supervisory responsibility for internal program staff and/or external data collectors, whether a central staff will travel to collect all the site data, and so on will vary with each MSE. We can offer no guidelines except that careful guidelines for staffing MSEs must be developed and followed.

3. Staff Training. For MSEs to be feasible, all evaluation staff must be well trained in how to perform their various tasks. Training may depend on training manuals with separate sections for data collectors, site coordinators, and the like. Training videos may be useful. Workshops to train site evaluation staff may be held at some central location, or a traveling trainer may make a circuit ride, training site evaluators in their own local sites.

4. Budgeting. Whether an MSE costs more or less than a single-site evaluation with a similar overall magnitude of effort depends on individual circumstances. In general, however, the MSE will be more expensive because of travel costs, personnel time needed to arrange the travel, and long-distance communication (telephone, fax, mail). Budgets for MSEs can sometimes become rather complicated and must be carefully developed and applied.

5. Identifying and Overcoming Cross-Site Obstacles. The success of an MSE depends on a variety of sensitive and intricately balanced issues. One is stakeholder "buy-in" to the evaluation: Involvement of stakeholders in the MSE is important to enhance their ownership of the evaluation activities and results. Communication barriers and social gaps can scuttle the MSE, because it requires such a high degree of communication and cooperation. Nowhere is the ability to analyze and cope with political issues more important than in an MSE. As Sinacore and Turpin (1991) aptly put it:

> While most of us are aware of the political aspects of evaluation research, the multiple political environments of an MSE can be easily overlooked. Even if there is a strong central figure for the study who has influence over participation, there are frequently gatekeepers at each site who can influence data quality. Therefore, it is imperative for evaluators to become aware of the political climate at each site and to respond accordingly (p. 11).

6. Maintaining Quality Control. The greater the number of sites in an MSE, the greater the challenge is to maintaining quality of the evaluation data. Standardization across sites of some, if not all, of the evaluation data is the sine qua non of MSE. For data to be "aggregatable," the procedures for collecting, organizing, and verifying all site data must be followed carefully.

7. Conducting Appropriate Statistical Analyses. Combining data across multiple sites poses challenges not confronted by the single-site evaluator. Even a cursory discussion of those special challenges concerning units of analysis, pooling, and interaction effects would exceed our space here, but interested readers are referred to Sinacore and Turpin (1991).

8. Conducting Multi-Level MSEs. Many MSEs are already complicated enough when the evaluation of the program is all at the same level. Sometimes, however, an MSE may contain two or more levels of evaluation, such as (1) site-specific program evaluations that attempt to determine the value of specific program variations, and (2) a cross-site evaluation of the program intended to provide judgments about the program's overall quality and value.

Future of MSEs

Those who prefer to use social science research methods in their evaluations will likely continue to use MSEs to evaluate human services and other public-sector programs. According to Sinacore and Turpin (1991), MSEs are becoming more popular, and more evaluators will need to prepare themselves to conduct such studies. In their words:

> Use of MSEs is slowly on the rise. Indeed, some evaluators are presently conducting MSEs without realizing that the techniques involved are emerging as a new area of methodological expertise in professional evaluation. Therefore, evaluators who are aware of the advantages and the demands of MSEs will be prepared to conduct the best evaluations of this type. As interest in MSEs continues to grow over the next few years, we expect that many evaluators will come to recognize the potentially rich data sets that MSEs can offer (p. 17).

On-Site Evaluation at Multiple Sites

On-site evaluation, when an external evaluator or team visits the program site, collects data, and judges the program on specified evaluative criteria, is one of the most frequently used strategies to evaluate programs in education, health and human services, and nonprofit programs. The popularity of on-site evaluation is doubtless due, at least in part, to the fact that it can be a simple and straightforward approach that is not dependent on extensive technical expertise in psychometrics, statistics, or data manipulation. For those who view professional judgment as constituting the core of evaluation, on-site evaluation is often the preferred approach. Further, on-site evaluation is a flexible method that can be used as a part of a wide variety of evaluation approaches, in either single- or multiple-site programs (although we will focus particularly on the latter in this section). We discussed on-site evaluation briefly as a method in Chapter 15, for it can be used to collect data *within* either MSEs or cluster evaluations, its two companions in this chapter. However, it also qualifies as a form of multisite evaluation in its own right and is, therefore, treated more fully in this chapter.

There are two related reasons why on-site evaluation visits are made: (1) they are often required by legislation or by some funding or regulatory agency, and (2) on-site evaluation is viewed as a valuable technique in assisting programs to reach their full potential. Consequently, on-site evaluation can be used either for formative or summative purposes, although the latter is more common.

On-site evaluation is often used to judge the effectiveness or value of large-scale programs when (1) it is not feasible or desirable to use experimental or quasi-experimental designs for the evaluation; (2) there are no readily available objective, quantitative indices that can be used as a basis for determining program effects (e.g., test scores, hours of volunteer service, pregnancy rates among specified populations); and (3) program sponsors/funders want relevant evidence beyond the usual rhetoric or unsupported opinions offered by program directors and staff as the basis for judgments about the worth of the programs they operate. For educational programs that are not intended to raise student scores on standardized tests, on-site evaluation is perhaps the most common form of evaluation. In secondary and higher education institutions, accreditation site visits are familiar examples of on-site evaluation, but accrediting agencies' requirements and procedures are tailored to the particular needs and programs they serve and are seldom adaptable for efforts to develop an on-site evaluation procedure appropriate for use with other multiple-site programs. Thus, we will not discuss the philosophy or conduct of accreditation site visits in this chapter. (See Chapter 7, where accreditation is discussed.)

Except for accreditation site visits, on-site evaluation is frequently conducted in such a haphazard fashion that it is often discounted as a useful evaluation method. Critics—including staff in programs evaluated by site-visit teams—have complained that site visitors have wandered randomly through their programs, asked apparently aimless questions, and ended up making subjective judgments based on unarticulated criteria. While this may be a caricature of some on-site evaluations, it is such an uncomfortably accurate description of so many that one could almost conclude that the bad reputation of on-site evaluation is deserved. Our view is that it is not. Like any other form of evaluation, on-site evaluation can be done well or poorly. Our focus here is on the development and use of high-quality on-site evaluation procedures, processes, and systems to evaluate the effectiveness of multiple-site programs. Based on our experience with designing, implementing, and monitoring evaluation site visits to various funded programs in multiple sites, we are convinced that well-developed on-site evaluation can be a very effective and very flexible evaluation technique. For example, we believe on-site evaluation can be used to serve the following purposes in multisite evaluations:

- To monitor program compliance with funding agency regulations or guidelines;

- To interview program staff and other program participants (through individual or focus-group interviews) to understand how the program operates and how they feel about it;

- To collect data with on-site instruments, such as classroom tests or attitude scales, "on-the-spot" handout questionnaires for clinic patients, or observation checklists for use in recording prospective pilots' behavior and performance in commercial pilot training programs;

- To probe to understand anomalies or contradictions in data provided previously by sites;

- To provide funding agencies with qualitative descriptions of how well each site is accomplishing the agency's program goals and how successful the overall program is when viewed across sites;

- To rate each site on specific criteria and provide the funding agency with a summative "score" that might be used in decisions about continuing or discontinuing funding.

Obviously, several of these purposes might be accomplished simultaneously, depending on how the on-site evaluation system was set up. There are doubtless many more purposes we have not thought to list.

The Issue of Control in Multiple-Site On-Site Evaluation

An ideal on-site evaluation of a multiple-site program should, in our judgment, be a Controlled Prospective evaluation (cell 1 in Figure 19.1), when (1) the decision to use multiple evaluation sites is made before the evaluation begins, and (2) program implementation is uniform across sites, allowing site-visit teams to develop and use common measures at all program sites. When implementation of a program is intended to be the same, this would qualify as a "controlled implementation" approach.

In many multisite programs, however, considerable latitude is given to sites regarding how they implement the program. In such cases, the Uncontrolled Prospective evaluation (cell 2 in Figure 19.1) could allow evaluation to proceed so that evaluation procedures at each site are different and each site-visit team develops its own approach to match the form of the program it encounters at the particular site. Far too often this is the form that multiple-site on-site evaluation takes. While there will be cases where programs are so dissimilar across sites that a series of case studies is the only sensible evaluation approach, in most structured, multisite programs there are essential ingredients that should be present and specific criteria that should be met, *without which the program is not fulfilling, at that site, the intent of those who funded it.* In such cases we believe it is important for the on-site evaluation procedures to be standardized across sites so that they will provide program sponsors with critical data on how each site is performing, at least on those key dimensions. (This would shift the evaluation back to cell 1 in Figure 19.1.).

We recognize that it is not as easy to standardize on-site evaluation procedures across program sites as is the case with the more structured MSE approach we discussed earlier, but we believe that much more can and should be done to move as far as possible in that direction. We recommend the following as essential steps to facilitate standardization:

- Develop the evaluative questions that will be used at all sites;
- Develop on-site instruments, including rating scales to be used by site-visit teams;
- Make all necessary arrangements for site visits in ways that will reduce or eliminate site-visitor biases;
- Train team members in use of the instruments to standardize data collection and ratings through use of rating-scale anchor points;
- Summarize and report site-visit results so that both cross-site commonalities and specific site idiosyncracies can be understood.

Other Issues in Using Multiple-Site On-Site Evaluation

Several issues need to be considered as one determines how to make the best use of on-site evaluations. The way in which each of the following issues is resolved will determine how the specific on-site evaluation system is designed. In a multiple-site program, general on-site evaluation procedures and instruments should be designed for use in each of the separate on-site evaluations. These will include a general set of questions, criteria, and instruments developed at the outset so evaluators can be trained to use them thereafter at each site. Essential activities include the following:

1. Selecting the On-Site Evaluation Sample. If resources are limited, it will be necessary to conduct on-site evaluations of only a sample of the sites at which the program has been implemented. This sample might be selected systematically to include particular sites important for reasons peculiar to that program or to assure as much variability as possible along dimensions such as (1) funding level, (2) geographical location, (3) number of clients served, and so on. Usually a preferable strategy would be to stratify on such variables thought to be important and draw a stratified random sample. This also has the advantage of all sites' knowing they may be included, thus allowing the evaluation to provide some sense of accountability for all sites.

2. Collecting Data before the On-Site Visit. It is not necessary for site-visit teams to go into a site uninformed about how the program is being used in that site. Mailed questionnaire surveys can be used effectively to elicit key information about program parameters and details at that site before the site team arrives. The information produced by the questionnaire (or previsit telephone calls, examination of site documents, reports, etc.) also often provides clues of possible problems or issues that should be probed in greater depth during on-site visits.

3. Determining the Duration of the Site Visit. On-site evaluation visits can vary in duration and intensity from a brief, informal stroll through a program site to an intensive and extensive week-long observation and examination of virtually every facet of the program's operation and activities at that site. Theoretically, site visits could last indefinitely, or at least until the evaluation budget runs out. Practically, however, the cost of maintaining evaluators on site (e.g., lodging and food) usually prohibits use of ethnography and other methods that are time-extensive. In fact, in most program evaluations, a site visit of one to three days in duration may be adequate.

4. Deciding on the Number of Team Members. On-site teams can obviously vary in size from a single evaluator to a large team presided over by a team leader or coordinator. It seems obvious that, all things being equal, larger, more complex programs require larger numbers of team members to provide adequate coverage. It is also apparent that greater diversity of expertise can be represented in on-site teams with more team members. Typically, most on-site guidelines and procedures assume a two- or three-person team and, with some minor adjustments, can be used with larger on-site teams.

5. Assigning Responsibility for Managing a Multiple-Site System of On-Site Evaluation. On-site evaluation systems can be managed directly by the funding agency or they can be managed by an agency contracted to coordinate the overall on-site evaluation system. Management of on-site evaluations by either the funding agency or a contracted agency is greatly preferable (unless the evaluation is formative) to having the site arrange for their own site-visit team to conduct the evaluation. This latter arrangement seems too similar to the dubious practice of allowing a bank to audit its own books. A list of specific site-visit activities that must be planned and conducted appears in Chapter 15.

Before leaving this section, however, we should note that some multiple-site evaluations are hybrids of the type of on-site evaluation outlined here and the MSE approach discussed earlier in this chapter. For example, in a national, twelve-site evaluation of a major technology vendor's computerized curriculum for elementary school students (Worthen & Van Dusen, 1992), carefully standardized program implementation and student testing followed the MSE strategy, with site coordinators, a quasi-experimental design, and data aggregation across all sites. Additional data were collected by a series of intensive on-site visits to each of the twelve sites, not only collecting still more data on common dimensions and using standardized procedures but also having the on-site team collect some data on unique attributes of each site.

Another type of hybrid between these two multiple-site evaluation strategies is the "multisite/multimethod" variation (Louis, 1982), in which less structured, qualitative data are viewed as coequal in the evaluation with more structured data collected by familiar MSE procedures.

Cluster Evaluation

A third form of multiple-site program evaluation that originated in the W. K. Kellogg Foundation (WKKF) is a two-level approach that its developers termed

cluster evaluation.[2] Compared to the two more venerable approaches discussed previously, cluster evaluation is an emerging approach still in its adolescence, if not its childhood. Prior to 1992, cluster evaluation was almost unknown among professional evaluators, and the still-sparse literature on cluster evaluation has all been produced since then. Yet it appears as if cluster evaluation may well be here to stay. In their book *Evaluation for Foundations,* the Council on Foundations (1993) described the Kellogg approach to evaluating clusters of grants as "A Model for Foundation Programs" (p. 232). The American Evaluation Association (AEA) officially established a Topical Interest Group on Cluster Evaluation in 1994. In a recent book on educating health professionals for the communities they serve (Richards, 1995), cluster evaluation is portrayed as a key element in building essential partnerships to foster such advances in community health. WKKF's Director of Evaluation Ricardo Millett is chair of the AEA Cluster Evaluation Group and is using both that role and his Foundation position to create a continuing dialogue among evaluation experts aimed at refining and improving the concept, design, and conduct of cluster evaluation. It appears that the energy and openness exist that are needed to shape a new approach to the point where it can become broadly useful in conducting evaluations.

A Description of Cluster Evaluation and Its Rationale

Cluster evaluation's purposes and philosophical assumptions are quite different from those of the two approaches discussed so far in this chapter. These differences will be obvious as we define and describe cluster evaluation more specifically.

First, cluster evaluation should not be confused with cluster sampling. Rather, WKKF officers use the term in situations where several of their individual, local projects (usually funded under one broad program initiative) are collectively considered to constitute a "cluster" of projects that are similar in either sharing a common mission, a common strategy, or a common population. Although the projects are bound together by that common thread, each project has its unique context and is relatively autonomous in how it proposes to accomplish the broad program mission or goals for which the Foundation holds it responsible. These projects are each expected to have a local project evaluation to provide information specific to that project. In addition, WKKF commissions a cluster evaluation intended to examine broader knowledge by looking across all the projects in the cluster.

Just how this is done varies widely across clusters. As O'Sullivan and O'Sullivan (1994) have noted, "Kellogg has defined the cluster evaluation components but has not prescribed the cluster evaluation process." Nonetheless, a cluster evaluation plan is expected by Kellogg (1) to be driven by evaluation questions that deal with priority issues of Foundation officials, (2) to identify common information needed on all projects in order to provide a composite overview of

---

[2]The term *cluster evaluation* was first coined in 1988 by WKKF's director of evaluation, Ron Richards, in an evaluation of a Foundation-funded health initiative; the concept was further developed by him and his successors in that position, Jim Sanders and Ricardo Millett.

the overall success or failure of the cluster, and (3) to outline methods to collect such data. Further, the WKKF (1991) has identified four key characteristics of the cluster approach:

1. It looks across a group of projects to identify *common threads and themes* that, having cross-confirmation, take on greater significance;

2. It seeks not only to learn *what happened* with respect to a group of projects but *why* those things happened;

3. It happens in a *collaborative* way that allows all players—projects, foundation, and external evaluators—to contribute to and participate in the process so that what is learned is of value to everyone; and

4. The relationship between the projects and the external evaluators conducting the cluster evaluation is *confidential.* Evaluation findings of the cluster evaluation are reported back to the Foundation only in aggregate for the entire cluster and never for the individual projects. This ensures an environment in which projects can be comfortable in sharing with the cluster evaluators the realities of the work they have undertaken, problems and frustrations as well as triumphs. It greatly increases the usefulness of evaluation findings.

Thus, WKKF's overall strategy for cluster evaluation involves multiple responsibilities for both the Foundation staff and for the cluster evaluators. For the former, it is their responsibility to form the cluster of projects and to manage that cluster across the multiple years of funding. Meanwhile, it is the cluster evaluator's responsibility to evaluate the cluster by developing the methodology for the cluster evaluation, managing it for its duration, and negotiating and maintaining the respective roles, responsibilities, and relationships of cluster and project evaluators.

Various purposes for cluster evaluation have been articulated in WKKF documents and meetings of cluster evaluators the Foundation has sponsored. Each of the following statements is drawn from one or more of the handouts, overheads, brochures, handbooks, or conference proceedings produced and used by WKKF staff that describe the purpose of cluster evaluation:

- Answer the questions *What happened?* and *Why?* for the cluster of projects as a whole;
- Strengthen projects in the cluster through the cluster evaluators' providing technical assistance in evaluation to project evaluators;
- Strengthen projects through the cluster evaluators' facilitating or creating evaluation networking among the projects;
- Strengthen Foundation programs and policy making through collection of information about the context, implementation, and outcomes of the cluster;
- Identify common themes and threads that, having cross-project confirmation, take on greater significance;
- Identify pertinent "lessons learned" by one project that may allow other projects to avoid problems or enhance their success;

- Summarize or synthesize the project evaluations;
- Determine how well the collective cluster of projects has succeeded in achieving the funding objectives;
- Translate individual project findings into broad recommendations about the program/area under which the cluster is funded.

The WKKF evaluation staff have also stated unequivocally that it is not the purpose of cluster evaluation to do the following:

- Evaluate the success or failure of individual projects;
- Serve as a means for the Foundation to identify weak projects that should be terminated;
- Direct or oversee the project evaluations;
- Engage in metaevaluations of the project evaluations;
- Be intrusive to projects;
- Report information about any specific project(s) in the cluster to WKKF staff; only data aggregated across the cluster or lessons learned from *unidentified* projects would be shared with the Foundation.

Understanding Cluster Evaluation's Context

These statements about cluster evaluation may be better understood when viewed against the philosophy and value orientation WKKF holds for program evaluation. Stated most simply, the Foundation (WKKF, 1994) believes that "evaluation functions 'to improve, not to prove' " (p. 4). In operationalizing these values, WKKF asks cluster evaluators to assemble evidence that its program strategies contribute to their desired ends but cautions that it is unlikely that the Foundation will fund costly experimental studies that will "answer questions of attribution" or that "can provide rigorous (reliable/valid in methodological terms) causal effect estimates" (p. 4). Thus, cluster evaluators are asked to provide *compelling conclusions* to enable two of cluster evaluation's key audiences (WKKF's Board of Trustees and program staff) to answer the central question of whether the strategy that led to funding the cluster of projects was a wise investment of Foundation resources, without traditional methods for determining causation. No small challenge.

An additional part of the context that complicates efforts to gain wisdom by looking across cluster evaluations is the fact that WKKF officers have not standardized cluster evaluation procedures. Thus, those procedures have evolved in quite different directions, depending on the evaluation philosophy and methodological preferences of the various cluster evaluators and the conception of cluster evaluation held by the Foundation's various program directors. Tolerance for such diversity is an inevitable by-product of the value WKKF officers place on autonomy, flexibility, empowerment, and change, values held so deeply that some Foundation staff would likely resist any significant degree of standardization of cluster evaluation designs or procedures. Yet if cluster evaluation is allowed to be whatever circumstances and personalities dictate it should be, then it may never become more than an evaluation "shape-shifter," appearing and reappearing in various forms, depending on who within the Foundation is responsible at the moment for interpreting what cluster evaluation should be and do.

The challenges confronting cluster evaluation are in part a product of the culture and personality of its parent organization (WKKF) and the dynamic, open, and empowering nature of the Foundation's modus operandi. The lack of uniformity in the conception and definition of what cluster evaluation is, what its purposes are, or how it should be conducted reflects WKKF's valuation of high autonomy for grantees and the Foundation's willingness to sacrifice central control—and any form of coerced cohesiveness—in the interests of empowerment and trust of grantees. One can applaud such guiding principles and premises, even while fretting that they make it difficult to describe with any precision just what cluster evaluation is or how it should be conducted. The WKKF (1994) recognizes this difficulty, noting that its

> cluster evaluation model is a relatively new concept in Foundation program evaluation. The concept and practice is evolving. Its operational definition, purposes, and assumptions have varied in practice across W. K. Kellogg Foundation program areas (p. 4).

All of which suggests that (1) relationships of some cluster evaluations to existing types of evaluation may not hold for all other cluster evaluations, and (2) relationships that exist today may not hold tomorrow if cluster evaluation is significantly changed during its further evolution. These difficulties notwithstanding, there are some characteristics of cluster evaluation that seem to be at its core. We can depend on these in attempting to examine how cluster evaluation fits with our earlier "typology" of multiple-site evaluation strategies.

Comparing Cluster Evaluation and MSE

Returning to Figure 19.1, careful examination reveals that most cluster evaluations, as currently conducted, would fit best—if not exclusively—in cell 3, Uncontrolled Prospective multiple-site evaluations. Conversely, cell 1 is the preferred cell for MSE, where control of program implementation is emphasized. When program implementation is allowed to vary across sites (a hallmark of most cluster evaluations), MSE is viewed by many authors as seriously weakened because increased site autonomy has resulted in program-by-site interactions that confound outcomes. As Sinacore and Turpin (1991) put it:

> it is not clear whether those differences [observed differences in outcomes among the sites] are caused by the various program formats or by the unique features of the sites in which the program are provided (p. 7).

Yet this is exactly the type of variation that typically exists in cluster evaluations, in which efforts to control variance are replaced with attempts to capitalize on it by studying the relative impact of naturally varying implementation across projects to identify successes and failures calculated to help projects learn from one another. Moreover, a key difference between cluster evaluation and most other forms of MSE lies in the absence of control, except by persuasion, that cluster evaluators have over the site-specific evaluations. (See Hedrick et al. [1991] for a discussion of the issue of centralized control over site evaluations in MSE.)

In short, while cluster evaluation can be categorized as a subtype of MSE, its similarities are mostly superficial, and the contrasting perspectives and purposes of cluster evaluation and MSE suggest that they are actually rather distant conceptual relatives, not the close conceptual cousins they may appear to be on casual inspection. This fact has been recognized by Schmitz (1994), who contrasted the cluster evaluation she is directing for the WKKF with traditional conceptions of MSE, on several dimensions, as follows:[3]

Multisite Evaluation *"Evaluation for Confirmation"*	*Cluster Evaluation* *"Evaluation for Learning"*
• Single model, centrally designed, implemented at different sites	• Multiple models, designed by different sites, according to local needs, resources, and constraints
• Specifics of model known, pretested, fixed	• Specifics unknown; "cutting edge" and evolving models
• Limited number of narrowly defined goals that lead to dependent variables, common across sites	• Multiple possible goals, broadly defined, somewhat site-specific; not all goals or benefits known in advance
• Good framework for testing hypotheses, causal linkages, and generalizability	• Good framework for strengthening programs trying to operationalize guiding philosophy or set of principles at local level
• Top-down project management and evaluation	• Autonomous, locally driven project management; dual levels of evaluation
• Assumes controls can be established to maintain reliability and validity; believes in value of "generic model"	• Assumes some common goals, questions, experiences; believes that sharing information increases knowledge about "what" and "how"; values practical knowledge

Cluster Evaluation's Contribution to the Field of Evaluation

As one could infer from our earlier comments, we see cluster evaluation as still in its early developmental stages. Perhaps it is being in the throes of adolescence's

[3]We have altered slightly C. Schmitz's (1994) presentation and format and take responsibility if so doing has misunderstood or misrepresented her intent.

awkwardness that raises so many issues that still need to be resolved.[4] Yet adolescence has its positive aspects as well (after all, adolescents are energetic, idealistic, and creative), and the same is true of cluster evaluation. If the issues confronting it are resolved, there is great potential for cluster evaluation to make a broader contribution, for many philanthropic, state, and federal agencies fund programs with multiple projects that could use such a strategy, if cluster evaluation can be captured conceptually in ways that allow its use to be clearly understood by potential users in various contexts where a noncausal form of multiple-site evaluation is deemed appropriate. There is reason to believe that this might occur. For example, Sanders (1997) has laid out steps that cluster evaluations might follow and proposed common elements for inclusion in all cluster evaluations. Only future experience can assess the impact of these suggestions. In the meantime, Sanders contends that cluster evaluation is built on some of the same philosophical and methodological underpinnings as are other, more venerable ways of determining merit or fact.

> The stages of inquiry reflected in cluster evaluation design are not unique to cluster evaluation. Starting with the classic work of Glaser and Strauss . . . , there is a strong and well-documented tradition of the methodology used in cluster evaluation found in the literature under such labels as qualitative methods, case study methods, and naturalistic methods. What is unique about cluster evaluation is the combination of four characteristics . . . : (1) it is holistic, (2) it is outcome oriented, (3) it seeks generalizable learning, and (4) it involves frequent communications and collaborations among the partners. It is an approach to evaluation that is intrusive and affects the thinking and practices of project staff, the parent or funding organization, and the cluster evaluator along the way. It does not seek to establish causation through controlled comparative designs, but instead depends on naturalistic observations of many people to infer and test logical connections. The underlying paradigm is one of argumentation and rules of evidence such as those found in our legal system. It strives for documentation and logical conclusions that have been tested as fully as possible given resources, time, and methodological constraints of the evaluation. In terms of *The Program Evaluation Standards* (Joint Committee, 1994) it places a premium on all four attributes of sound program evaluation: utility, feasibility, propriety and accuracy (Sanders, 1997, pp. 400–402).

Other Approaches to Multiple-Site Evaluation

Earlier in this chapter we gave an example of how an evaluation of a multiple-site program could combine aspects of MSE with on-site visits to the multiple program sites. One could easily envision how combinations of cluster evaluation and multiple-site on-site evaluation could be used very effectively. (It is less clear how MSE and cluster evaluation could be combined, based as they are on strikingly different priorities and premises.)

---

[4]A discussion of the challenges confronting cluster evaluation has been provided by Worthen and Matsumoto (1994).

We make no pretense that the three types of multiple-site evaluations we have presented are all-encompassing. For example, descriptions of nine illustrative case studies of multiple-site evaluations conducted within foundations (Council on Foundations, 1993) reveal that five do not fit precisely into any one of the three types of multiple-site evaluations we have discussed. Yet we believe the three types we have covered are not only the most common and most useful but are also illustrative of the range of approaches that can be used to enhance evaluation of multiple-site programs.

Major Concepts and Theories

1. Evaluation conducted across multiple sites of a program, either nationally or locally, are termed *multiple-site evaluations*. The three most common types are multisite evaluations, on-site evaluations at multiple sites, and cluster evaluations.

2. In a prospective multiple-site evaluation, the intent before the evaluation is to use multiple sites, whereas in a retrospective multiple-site evaluation, the use of data from different evaluations on similar topics is an afterthought.

3. In some multiple-site evaluations, the way programs are implemented is the same across all locations (controlled), but other multiple-site evaluations include sites in which the program was not implemented the same across all locations (uncontrolled).

4. Multisite evaluations of large-scale social programs can take the form of large-scale experimental or quasi-experimental studies and use randomization as well as statistical analysis of data. These evaluations are most often controlled prospective multiple-site evaluations and are often conducted in response to political and social demands and to increase the generalizability and statistical power of the evaluation.

5. When multisite evaluations are conducted, several considerations must be attended to including, but not limited to, staff training across sites, the evaluators' knowledge of the system within which the program operates, and the difficulty of maintaining quality control in data collection, organization, and verification across sites.

6. As one of the most frequently used evaluation strategies, on-site evaluations involve evaluation teams visiting either all or a sample of sites implementing the program. These visits enable the evaluation team to collect site-specific as well as overall program effectiveness data when it is not feasible to conduct experimental or quasi-experimental studies, when there are no existing data that can be used to judge program quality, or when the program sponsor wants additional evidence to support or to counter unsubstantiated judgments about program effectiveness.

7. Program implementation that follows the controlled prospective approach yields the most ideal conditions in which one might conduct an on-site evaluation.

8. The newest form of multiple-site evaluations is cluster evaluation in which clusters of projects across sites and levels that deal with the same theme or topic are evaluated together. Note that each of these projects has its own unique context and level of autonomy to attain the goals set by its sponsoring foundations.

9. Cluster evaluations look at common themes across projects to explain not only what happened but why something happened. This approach demands collaboration across project evaluations, the funder, and external cluster evaluators; and the relationships and communication between external evaluators and the projects remain strictly confidential.

10. The main purpose for conducting a cluster evaluation is to improve programs. Most cluster evaluations can be categorized as uncontrolled prospective multiple-site evaluations.

Discussion Questions

1. What are some of the major reasons that multiple-site evaluations are conducted? How do these reasons differ from the reasons for conducting single-site evaluations?

2. What types of evaluation approaches can be applied to multiple-site evaluations? How do these differ from the approaches that can be used in single-site evaluations?

Application Exercises

1. Identify and explain the similarities and differences between multisite evaluation (MSE) and cluster evaluation, and between MSE and multiple-site on-site evaluation.

2. Select a multiple-site program with which you are familiar. Analyze how each of the three major types of multiple-site evaluations described in this chapter might be applied to it, and decide which approach you think would be best. Explain why.

3. Discuss which of the cells in Figure 19.1 you think would yield the best evaluation. The worst. Justify your judgments.

4. Consider a multisite evaluation of a national program designed to increase the positive attitudes of children toward exercise and health. In this evaluation, it was found that children at four of the ten sites experienced a decrease in positive attitudes and an increase in unhealthy behaviors. Given what you know about multisite evaluations, what are some of the issues that may be raised with these findings? How would you interpret these results?

5. You have been asked to conduct an on-site evaluation study of the effectiveness of evaluation internships for graduate students in ten national evaluation centers. The budget for this evaluation is $150,000 and the sponsors would like you to visit either all the sites or a sample of the ten sites. Describe in full detail the course of action you would take in planning this evaluation study, including all the issues you would need to consider and how you will address those issues.

Suggested Readings _____

Council on Foundations. (1993). *Evaluation for foundations: Concepts, cases, guidelines, and resources.* Chapter 11: The Kellogg approach to evaluating clusters of grants (pp. 232–251). San Francisco: Jossey-Bass.

Sanders, J. R. (1997). Cluster evaluation. In E. Chelimsky and W. R. Shadish (Eds.), *Evaluation for the 21st century,* (pp. 396–404). Thousand Oaks, CA: Sage.

Sinacore, J. M., & Turpin, R. S. (1991). Multiple sites in evaluation research: A survey of organizational and methodological issues. In R. S. Turpin & J. M. Sinacore (Eds.), *Multisite evaluations.* New Directions for Program Evaluation, No. 50 (pp. 5–18). San Francisco: Jossey-Bass.

Worthen, B. R., & White, K. R. (1987). *Evaluating educational and social programs: Guidelines for proposal reviews, onsite evaluations, evaluation contracts and technical assistance.* Hingham, MA: Kluwer-Nijhoff,.

Worthen, B. R., & Schmitz, C. C. (1997). Conceptual challenges confronting cluster evaluation. *Evaluation: The International Journal of Theory, Research, and Practice,* 3(3), 300–319.

20

Conducting Evaluation of Organizations' Renewal and Training in Corporate and Nonprofit Settings

Orienting Questions

1. How does evaluation in nonprofit organizations differ from evaluation in public agencies?
2. What typical questions are asked in the evaluation of training? What should be the focus of new questions?
3. How have trends in personnel evaluation mirrored those in program evaluation?
4. Is Total Quality Management (TQM) a mode of empowerment evaluation?
5. What can evaluators learn from strategic planning? How do quality control (QC) and quality assurance (QA) differ from program evaluation?

While much of program evaluation takes place in the public sector, the tools of evaluation are now used in many different settings. The *independent sector,* or non-profit organizations, now delivers many services that were previously delivered by state or local governments, school districts, and other public institutions. Yet, these services and the stakeholders of these services still need evaluation information to make decisions and learn about these new approaches to service delivery. *Training* has become a major focus of organizations as the global economy and technological change require that workers are constantly retrained to meet the demands of the competitive corporate world. With this training, keyed more than ever to organizational performance, come new demands for training in evaluation. *Personnel evaluation,* performance appraisal, and its incumbent tools, have become an integral part of the career of some evaluators. Finally, the corporate world, followed by the public and nonprofit sectors, has adopted new methods for organizational assessment that, though called by other names, are related to evaluation and have implications for the evaluator's work. These methods include strategic planning, Total Quality Management, quality control, and quality assurance. They are similar to evaluation in that they are designed to determine or document a thing's value (a process, a goal, a strategy) and they call for the systematic collection of information to make these determinations. This chapter will discuss some of these new settings and methods and their implications for evaluation.

Though these methods are new to some in program evaluation, others have noted that evaluation encompasses more than simply program evaluation. Scriven (1993) writes that "the term *program evaluation* has become a label for a limited approach, covering only part of what is required in order to do adequate program evaluation. . . . A widening of one's perspective on program evaluation helps one to avoid reinvention of the wheel and omission of relevant aspects of what one is supposed to be evaluating" (p. 3). The Joint Committee on Standards for Educational Evaluation (1988) expanded their focus to personnel evaluation in 1988 with the publication of standards in that field. Chelimsky (1985), though narrower in her focus, describes how the definition of evaluation has broadened over the years to entail more than program results or effectiveness.

The methods to be reviewed in this chapter, then, can be viewed broadly as part of the total purview of evaluation. As evaluation expands its scope, evaluators find themselves being employed in increasingly diverse settings. Even as early as the mid-1980s, one in three recent graduates of doctoral evaluation programs were taking jobs outside the public sector (May, Fleischer, Scheirer, and Cox, 1986). Evaluators need to be ready and able to adapt their knowledge and skills to new approaches and contexts. This chapter is designed to introduce readers to some of these applications.

Evaluation in the Nonprofit Sector

One of the legacies of the early 1980s has been **privatization**—the move by various government agencies to contract out services that they previously delivered. Typically, these services are contracted to organizations in the nonprofit, or independent, sector though contracting to for-profit corporations has also occurred. (Providing school lunches and maintaining school buildings are among the functions that have been contracted out to private corporations. Some school districts are contracting with the Edison Project and similar organizations to manage and deliver instruction for entire schools. Charter schools represent another new kind of "semi-public" entity whose specific characteristics vary from state to state.)

Privatization has been accompanied by devolution, the delegation of federal programs to states and localities for adaptation and delivery. The federal government may be the supplier of funds, but it is state and local governments, and often, through their delegation, nonprofit organizations, who are making the decisions about which programs to deliver and how to implement them. Don Kettl (2000) writes:

> Over the last generation, American government has undergone a steady, but often unnoticed transformation. Its traditional processes and institutions have become more marginal to the fundamental debates. Meanwhile, new processes and institutions—often nongovernmental ones—have become more central to public policy. In doing the peoples' work to a large and growing degree, American governments share responsibility with other levels of government, with private companies, and with nonprofit organizations (p. 488).

The **nonprofit sector** has been defined as "a set of organizations that is privately incorporated but serving some public purpose, such as the advancement of health, education, scientific progress, social welfare, or pluralism" (Salamon, 1992, p. 5). In the United States, these nonprofit organizations have a special tax status. Though nonprofit organizations have existed in the United States since the 1700s, their role is changing dramatically with the massive move to privatization of public services (O'Neill, 1989).

The independent sector is growing. The number of nonprofit organizations has increased from approximately 12,000 in 1940 to 1.5 million today (Boris, 1999). The number of people employed by nonprofit organizations is three times the size of the federal civilian workforce (Zimmermann, 1994). The largest proportion of nonprofit organizations are focused on the health arena; education is the second largest sector (Clotfelder, 1992). Other major areas of nonprofit service delivery include social services, mental health, youth programs, employment and training, and child care. Many of the programs typically studied by program evaluators are being contracted out to this sector. Most of those who work in the nonprofit arena expect the current trends to continue well into the future (Milward, 1994).

Those who work in these settings have concerns about the impact of privatization. Health care professionals worry about less access for the poor as nonprofit and for-profit hospitals compete for resources (Salkever & Frank, 1992). Education professionals worry that the needs of low-income students will be ignored or that the public schools will be left with students whose needs are increasingly difficult and costly to meet (Schwartz & Baum, 1992). Those working in the independent sector worry about their increasing dependence on government resources (Smith & Lipsky, 1993). The term *independent sector* could well become an oxymoron for nonprofits.

The Impact of Privatization on Evaluation

While these questions illustrate some of the concerns of managers and policy makers, there are also concerns for evaluation. How will privatization affect evaluation? What will be the role of the evaluator in the contracting organization? In the nonprofit organization?

In many ways, evaluation will take on a much more primary role for government agencies as they contract out services. Once a public agency rids itself of the direct responsibility of delivering the service, its role then becomes *primarily* one of monitoring the contract. Haque (2001) has reviewed some of the challenges to accountability presented by the trend toward privatization in both the United States and around the world. He notes that some countries have established governmental organizations with the specific purpose of reviewing these contracts. For example, Canada has created the Office of Privatization and Regulatory Affairs; France established the Committee for the Renewal of the Public Service to monitor government contracts with nonprofit and for-profit organizations.

The public expects the government to make sure that services are delivered efficiently and effectively, that fraud does not occur, and that legislative intents are met. The demand for privatization has centered around the belief that other sectors can deliver services in better ways than have government agencies. Someone will need to determine whether this is so. In its role as contractor, the public agency will have many information needs. With privatization, the agency is further removed from the delivery of services and, thus, will have even less knowledge of which clients are being served and the nature of the services being delivered. Questions addressed might include these:

- To what extent is the target audience reached?
- Are services delivered as planned, with the desired expertise and the proper intensity? Are the services congruent with the program model?
- Are desired outcomes achieved?
- What is the impact of service delivery on the community as a whole? What side effects exist?

With privatization, evaluation will address many of the usual questions of program evaluation as well as new ones associated with privatization itself, such as:

- Is the delivery of services by other sectors more efficient than delivery of the services through government agencies?
- Is it more effective?
- If it is more efficient or more effective, what are the costs?

As public agencies struggle to define their role as contractor and evaluator, others question whether government agencies will be capable of fulfilling the role. Milward, Provan, and Smith (1994) note that government's lack of ability to manage contracts with nonprofits is a major problem. Milward (1994) writes:

> Policy design, control of the implementation process, and evaluation of the quality of the contracted services can, and often do remain, the job of the public agency. However, the capacity limitations that led to contracting out in the first place may extend to the guidance and evaluation functions of government (p. 76).

While some express concerns about the ability of the public agency to monitor and evaluate nonprofit contracts, others, especially those in the nonprofit sector, express concerns with the overbearing role of the funding agency in controlling and mandating the specifics of evaluation. One of the present authors worked with a training organization whose state funding source wanted a comprehensive evaluation of each of the over 250 training programs delivered by the organization to county social services agencies each year, without regard to the status of the program or the information needs of any stakeholders. The policy was simply that all training programs, regardless of length, longevity, or past evaluations, should be evaluated comprehensively each year. If carried out, the evaluations would have cost more than the training! Ignorance of the use and methods of evaluation and fear of not monitoring adequately can lead to excesses. Thus, a major challenge to evaluators and managers in contracting agencies will be defining their role. This role will include determining the nature of questions that must be answered to monitor government resources adequately and those questions that should be adapted or developed by the agency delivering the services to help them to improve delivery.

We think the solution in regard to evaluation roles will eventually be a delineation of (1) evaluation questions typically answered by all contractors, to serve summative decisions regarding future contracts, and (2) evaluation questions that may be selected (perhaps from a list provided by contractors) or developed by the nonprofit agency itself (with sign-off by the contractor). This second category of questions would be studied primarily for formative purposes to improve service delivery. Both sets of questions would be developed with each new contracting initiative or, perhaps, with each new contractor. While the mandated questions to be answered would be somewhat similar across contracts, there is no magic set of questions that *all* contractors should answer in *all* circumstances. The optional, or formative, questions would, of course, need to be rather specific to the contract(s) at hand. We recommend that a sample of such questions be developed by the public agency, because often nonprofit organizations, particularly small ones, are new to evaluation and may not know the types of helpful questions that evaluation could address. Nonprofit organizations that have experience with evaluation should, of course, be permitted to develop their own questions.

We have found through our work with nonprofit organizations that they often see evaluation as solely for the funding agency to meet accountability concerns. In the course of defining roles, it will be critical for the public funding agency to demonstrate to nonprofit deliverers that evaluation can be used to meet *their own* information needs. This will be a difficult balancing act, because the public funding agency will need data for itself to make summative decisions and meet the public demand for accountability. However, if evaluation is to be used to improve the delivery of services, we have learned it must be close to those delivering the product. Funding agencies can demonstrate their commitment to the use of evaluation for formative purposes by deliverers by recognizing that some evaluation information is *not* for the funding source but solely for the provider's information needs. Sanders (2002) has proposed that organizations, including nonprofit organizations, move toward mainstreaming evaluation within their organization so that evaluation becomes a natural part of the organization's culture. Some excellent guides for internal evaluation by nonprofit organizations are available to help nonprofit organizations develop their effectiveness on a continuing basis (Gray, 1993; Gray & Stockdill, 1995).

The Role of Evaluation within the Nonprofit Agency

We have discussed how privatization or contracting out will change the role of evaluation in the funding agencies. What about the role of evaluation in the independent sector itself? Nonprofit organizations increasingly require the expertise of evaluators to help them meet the demands of government contracts even as they work to improve their capacity to do their own evaluation. Larger nonprofit organizations have and will develop internal capacities for evaluations. The high demand for evaluators in the nonprofit sector is evidenced by a study of job postings to the American Evaluation Association Job Bank from 2000 to 2002 (Camacho & Vicinanza, 2002). Postings for positions in the nonprofit sector exceeded all other sectors, including government, public schools, colleges and universities, and for-profit organizations in both 2001 and 2002. Brett, Hill-Mead, and Wu (2000) provide a useful case study of evaluation practice in a national multi-site community service program and how it has been organized to facilitate use. Although job growth in evaluation is strong in the nonprofit sector, many small nonprofit organizations will continue to rely on external evaluators for special projects.

The challenge to the evaluator working in nonprofit settings will be negotiating the evaluation responsibilities of the organization with the funding agency and helping the organization view evaluation as something that can help it in managing and delivering services. In many organizations, bringing about this attitude change among potential internal users and stakeholders will be the greatest challenge facing the evaluator. If the funding agency is uncooperative, the job will be made doubly difficult.

Another facet of the nonprofit sector that is pertinent for the evaluator is the structure and financing of the organization itself. Directors of nonprofit organizations are responsible to a board of directors. The board is typically composed of individuals with varying backgrounds who have volunteered to serve in this capacity. Board members are often selected for their personal fund-raising capabilities in the community. Relations with the board can be a major concern of managers. Individual board members' interests and attitudes can have a major influence on the operation of the organization. These relationships are new to evaluators who have worked only in public settings, but the evaluator new to nonprofits would do well to spend some time getting to know the board and considering its influence on the organization.

Similarly, fund-raising and community relations are a major focus of nonprofit organizations, and recruiting and training of volunteers can be an important activity. These and other characteristics of the independent sector distinguish it from the public agency. These differences can change the nature of evaluation as they create new evaluation questions and arenas of investigation and new configurations of stakeholders.[1]

Evaluating Corporate Training Programs

Corporations today are struggling to compete in the global economy. New technologies in the work world demand an adaptable workforce with the knowledge and skills required for work that is constantly changing. Business today requires continuous training and retraining of the workforce to remain competitive. As a result, there has been enormous growth in the training field. Carnevale, Gainer, and Villet (1990) estimate that employers in the United States spend approximately $30 billion annually on formal training programs. Brinkerhoff (1989) writes: "The investment of private industry in education and training rivals, in scope and resources, the total public education enterprise" (p. 1).

At the same time the nature of the training industry is changing dramatically. In 1989, Brinkerhoff predicted that "the days of the richly endowed training department with its fat program catalogs are numbered" (p. 1). In 1994, Galagan showed his prediction to be correct. Cost-cutting, downsizing, and reorganizing have led to the "restructuring" of training. A survey by *Training and Development* journal found that 55 percent of trainers reported working in companies that reorganized or restructured training in the past year, while 18 percent reported changing jobs (Galagan, 1994).

What is happening? Those in the training field note that, in today's competitive environment, organizations are more concerned with performance and the impact of training on the organization. Swanson (1989) has described two models of training: the psychology model and the economics model. The *psychology model* focuses on the individual. The goal of training is to add to trainees' expertise and/or reduce their anxiety. Much of training in the 1980s focused on this model. Trainers' knowledge and skills were in the areas of instructional development and design, the adult learning model, and training techniques and methods. The *economic model* focuses on training to reduce or contain costs to the organization. Swanson sees this model as more compatible with the goals of profit-minded organizations.

In fact, organizations are restructuring training for high performance. Galagan (1994) observes "a seismic shift in the role of training in organizations that are in search of better performance" (p. 22). In a survey of human resource development managers, Carnevale and Carnevale (1994) found the biggest current trend was the creation of the high-performance work organization. Work is reorganized, redesigned, and reengineered to improve performance. They urge trainers to "think performance."

---

[1]The Greater Kalamazoo (Michigan) Evaluation Project has developed an evaluation guide for non-profits, "Evaluation for Learning." It is available from the Greater Kalamazoo United Way.

In predicting this trend in training, Brinkerhoff argued that evaluation could be "the key to the success of training in the future" (1989, p. 1). This success can occur by trainers' expanding their roles or through evaluators' becoming more involved in training or, more likely, some of both. Currently, the most common evaluator of training is the trainer herself (Brandenburg, 1989). Trainers must expand their role to be less involved in instructional design and more involved in planning and evaluation for the organization. In this role, the trainer helps identify problems in the organization that hinder productivity and recommends solutions. Training is, thus, one of a number of possible solutions the "trainer" might recommend. In this manner, the trainer becomes more of a specialized program evaluator or an industrial psychologist. Given many trainers' limited skills in evaluation, evaluators may need to be partners in this process. (Or trainers will need to get more training!)

Models for Evaluating Training

What has been the role of evaluation in training? Probably the best-known model for evaluating training was proposed by Kirkpatrick (1977, 1983). Kirkpatrick indicates that training can be evaluated at four levels, as shown in Figure 20.1.

This model has been predominant in the field of training evaluation for some time. However, a competing model for evaluating training is one that has already been presented in this book: the CIPP model, with its four levels of evaluation, namely, context, input, process, and product. A study of members of the American Society of Training and Development (ASTD) revealed that users of the CIPP model outnumbered users of the Kirkpatrick model (Galvin, 1983). We find the Kirkpatrick model useful here, however, to illustrate the different questions the evaluator might address in a training setting.

With the current emphasis on the high-performance organization, training evaluation will need to focus more on the fourth level of the Kirkpatrick model. That is, the evaluation of training must show the impact of that training, not only on the individual but on the organization as well. However, traditionally the most common means of evaluating training have been in-class questionnaires (satis-

FIGURE 20.1   *Kirkpatrick's Model of Evaluation Training*

Level	Questions
1. Reaction	Were the participants pleased with the program?
2. Learning	What did the participants learn in the program?
3. Behavior	Did the participants change their behavior based on what was learned?
4. Results	Did the change in behavior positively affect the organization?

Source: From *Handbook of Training Evaluation and Measurement Methods* (2nd ed.), p. 44, by Jack J. Phillips. Copyright © 1991 by Gulf Publishing Company, Houston, Texas. Used with permission. All rights reserved.

faction) and pre-post testing of learners' performance (LDP Associates, 1986). These methods address only levels 1 and 2 in Kirkpatrick's model.

Brinkerhoff (2003) has proposed a new approach called the Success Case Method (SCM) to evaluate training and organizational change. The goal of SCM is to help managers, trainers, and evaluators identify potential changes or actions that have a high probability of success. SCM is used to gather information about four key questions:

1. What is happening: Who is having success and who is not?
2. What results are being achieved: What goals are met and what goals are not being met? What unintended results are happening?
3. What is the value of the results: What is the return on the investment? How much more value could it produce if it were working better?
4. How can it be improved: What could be done to get more people to use it? How can others be more like those who are most successful?

While Kirkpatrick's model is an outcome- or results-oriented model, Brinkerhoff collapses all results into the second question and then develops questions to focus evaluation on other issues: description (question one), value (question three), and formative issues (question four). The evaluator of corporate training can use the Kirkpatrick model to identify the levels of results that should be examined, then Brinkerhoff's approach to raise awareness of other issues that should be addressed by the evaluation.

Other Considerations in Evaluating Training

In addition to needing to focus more on results and organizational impact, trainers and evaluators need to be involved more in needs assessment. One type of needs assessment for training is **front-end analysis** (Robinson & Robinson, 1989), which involves collecting data to assist in examining solutions for performance problems. To maximize the likelihood that training will have an impact, trainers need to examine the nature of the performance problem. What is going wrong? What is decreasing productivity? How can productivity be increased? Will improved knowledge and skills solve the problem? Will increased motivation? Retraining of supervisors? Training for better teamwork or creative problem solving? New tools or technology? Who will it be most productive to train? Or is re-engineering or job design the solution?

The trainer/evaluator should spend much time exploring the nature of the problem in front-end analysis. The results of such analysis can then provide useful information for targeting the training to the right audience, with the right methods and follow-up on the job. Further, if the solution is to be found in alternatives other than training, the evaluator/trainer can recommend these alternatives.

Brinkerhoff (1989) describes three zones for the evaluation of training: before, during, and after training. He argues that the greatest returns are in studying zones 1 and 3. Questions that would be addressed by each zone include the following:

Zone 1: What is the problem? Who would benefit most from training? What is the payoff of training likely to be? Whose support is needed to make the training work? What organization and individual performance barriers will impede training results? What kind of training works best?

Zone 2: How well do trainees learn? How much do trainees like the training? What learning activities are working best? How is the training going? What about the training should be changed? How well is the instructor doing?

Zone 3: How much of the training is being used? Who is using the training best? Why is the training not being used? What is happening that is undermining the training? How is the training being supported? What kind of benefits result from the training? (p. 13).

These questions require that the traditional program evaluator use her evaluation skills to address new questions, to apply them to a different entity (training), and in a new setting (corporations). Are these different questions the only differences in evaluating training in the corporate setting and program evaluation? No. Just as the evaluator working in the nonprofit sector must be cognizant of the different environment and context for her evaluation, the evaluator in the corporate sector must learn the customs of this environment. What is different? Experts in public and business administration argue this issue. While some differences are oversimplified, there are important distinctions. Corporate sector managers are accountable only to those within their organization. Information is proprietary and not subject to the scrutiny public sector evaluators are accustomed to. Finally, profitability is the bottom line though the rationality this bottom line brings to decision making is often inflated. Fads and mismanagement occur in the corporate sector just as often as in the public sector, as we have become aware in the early part of the twenty-first century.

In contrast, decision makers in the public sector report to many audiences: federal, state, and local legislative and executive officials; interest groups; clients; the public in general; and so on. By its very nature, evaluation in the public sector is more public. Evaluation in corporations is not public information.

Swanson (1989) appears skeptical about the ability of evaluators, whom he sees as having a primarily public-sector orientation, to adapt to corporate environments. He characterizes decisions made in the corporate world as those made by the venture capitalist who must make big decisions quickly based on limited information. In contrast, he sees the public sector-oriented evaluator as more like an accountant who "tediously adds up pennies . . . waiting for all the data before filing an accurate report" (p. 72). While we think that Swanson may have confused evaluators too much with accountants and may not be sufficiently aware of the changing environments in which public-sector evaluators work, his description helps illustrate what many see as major contextual differences. Ultimately, in corporate settings, the stakeholder is the organization and the bottom line is profit. The evaluator of training in the corporate setting must be prepared to work proactively to develop programs that will improve productivity and to measure the impact of such programs on the organization's productivity.

Personnel Evaluation

As in the training field, the roles of program evaluators and industrial psychologists may overlap when it comes to personnel evaluation. However, the skills of program evaluators are particularly useful in this area for both methodological and political reasons. Methodologically, program evaluators can bring new approaches to personnel evaluation even though it has been a highly specialized and technical field.

Traditionally, most personnel evaluation has been supervisory-based. Industrial psychologists have used other sources, such as peers, teams, subordinates, and customers or clients, to provide input (Cascio, 1991; Halachimi, 1995). But such sources often fail to be credible within the organization in spite of studies in industrial psychology that show the validity of some of these sources. Program evaluators who frequently combine quantitative and qualitative methods from several different sources to assess the same construct bring new skills to the evaluation of personnel or, as the term is more traditionally known, **performance appraisal.** Politically, program evaluators have been working in environments fraught with many political concerns. Their training and experience dealing with the concerns of various stakeholders can help them enter this sensitive arena.

What is performance appraisal or personnel evaluation? It is the assessment of an individual employee's abilities and performance. Performance appraisal can occur for many reasons. Two quite different reasons are employee development (training, future promotion) and compensation. Those in the field of performance appraisal urge that these two purposes be addressed separately (Sylvia, 1994). Let's briefly review the two types:

- *Employee development:* This type of performance appraisal is future-oriented and works best when the employee works collaboratively with the supervisor to identify areas for further training and development. Such areas might be to remedy deficiencies or to permit the employee to progress toward personal career goals or acquire new knowledge and skills needed by the organization. Performance appraisal for employee development is primarily an individualized activity. Comparisons with others are *not* integral to the process.

- *Compensation and rewards:* In contrast, performance appraisals for purposes of compensation in merit pay situations *must* involve comparisons across employees and, as such, the collection of information must be more uniform. While some argue that individual performance appraisals and merit pay are not an effective means of increasing productivity in today's team-centered environments, performance appraisal continues in most organizations (Bowman, 1994).

It is important that the person developing the performance appraisal distinguish between these two purposes, as the nature of the information collected for the performance appraisal will differ.

Performance Appraisal Methods

To develop a performance appraisal system, the personnel specialist must first identify the *critical components* of the job to be evaluated. These tasks, or the knowledge, skills, behaviors, or traits necessary to perform the tasks, might be identified from job-analysis studies or other methods specific to performance appraisal. Forms are developed and completed, typically by the supervisor, to collect information on the respondent's (supervisor's) perceptions of the employee's job performance. Forms vary from those that measure rather general traits (e.g., punctuality, loyalty, or ability to work with others) to behaviorally anchored rating scales (BARS), which list critical behaviors and examples of various levels of behavior. BARS probably represent the most sophisticated of the relatively well-known procedures for performance appraisal and involve (1) collecting data from job incumbents and supervisors regarding critical components of the job, and (2) brief narrative examples of work at various levels (poor to outstanding) for each component (Smith & Kendall, 1963). These examples are called "critical incidents" (Flanagan, 1954). Other tasks for the personnel specialist in performance appraisal include training supervisors in the use of the forms and means for providing feedback to employees.

An important new set of guides for the evaluation of teachers, school administrators, and educational specialists has been developed by CREATE, the Center for Research on Educational Accountability and Teacher Evaluation (Farland & Gullickson, 1995). These guides provide models and procedures for conducting personnel evaluations of teachers. The CREATE materials were designed to meet the Personnel Evaluation Standards (Joint Committee, 1988).

Performance appraisal comes out of the scientific school of management and has been highly quantitative in focus, though narrative feedback forms and Management by Objective (MBO) methods have been used when the purpose of the appraisal is employee development. The original goal of performance appraisal was to find a valid, reliable, and completely unbiased way of measuring employees' work behavior. While such goals seem naive, they reflect the strong beliefs in the United States that pay should be "fair"—that is, based on performance, not politics—and that good employees should be rewarded with greater compensation.

In the 1980s, dissatisfaction with the measurement focus arose primarily because managers and supervisors felt left out of the picture and organizations often saw little link between performance appraisals and organizational goals and productivity. Nigro and Nigro (2000) note that performance appraisals had not been linked to solving organizational problems and, thus, were seen as irrelevant by many managers. Today, the focus is on using performance appraisals to communicate with employees about organizational goals and standards and to work with them to achieve those. They cite the Georgia Performance Management Process

(PMP) as exemplary in this regard (Georgia Merit System, 1997). This plan is designed to help employees and managers collaborate in achieving goals and to facilitate the communication process. These processes mirror the move in evaluation toward greater participation from many stakeholder groups. In addition, the link of performance evaluation to organizational goals brings performance appraisal further into the domain of evaluation, particularly formative evaluations designed to improve performance.

Lovich (1990) has characterized some of the difficulties in performance appraisal as being caused by an undue focus on measurement and a failure to consider the importance of communication and process. Those interested in the techniques of appraisal have a primary concern with "the perfection of the test; that is, the focus of attention is the identification of problems associated with the measurement of performance (e.g., halo effect in ratings, or response bias in rating categories)" (pp. 91–92). For those concerned with process, "The problem of appropriate measurement of past performance is less important than attention to future performance" (p. 92). From this school comes a concern with the *process* of communications between supervisors and employees and the development of means to improve performance through improving the dialogue between supervisors and employees about individual performance.

These current trends in performance appraisal are highlighted to illustrate some of the debates in personnel evaluation that are similar to those occurring in program evaluation. Thus, at about the same time personnel specialists were hearing of the need to abandon their focus on measurement validity and focus on the manager's and the organization's needs, program evaluators were hearing Cronbach (1982) declare that internal and external validity should not be as important in evaluation as the user's own judgment of the validity of the study. Campbell (1969) depicted knowledge in disciplines as overlapping like the scales of a fish. He argued that we need to examine more assiduously the scales overlapping our own, and those scales overlapping them, to learn. Through examining performance appraisal and its history, we learn more about evaluation.

Other Methods of Organizational Assessment

Total Quality Management

Total Quality Management (TQM) has been used by many public-, private-, and nonprofit-sector organizations to improve organizational productivity. It has had a major influence on management in the public sector for the past twenty years (Berman, 1997). By 1991, TQM had been adopted by over 3,000 corporations and 40 governments in the United States (Milakovich, 1991). By 1992, 80 percent of the Fortune 1000 companies had quality improvement programs (Lawler, Mohrman, & Ledford, 1992). The U.S. General Accounting Office reported in 1992 that over two-thirds of federal agencies were using some form of TQM. TQM has also influenced the public sector through Osborne and Gaebler's

(1992) popular book, *Reinventing Government: How the Entrepreneurial Spirit Is Transforming the Public Sector,* which adopted many TQM principles. Vice President Al Gore's (1993) report of the National Performance Review has now applied these methods to many ventures in the public sector.

What is TQM? Ironically, the developer of Total Quality Management published an article on evaluation in the first volume of the *Handbook of Evaluation Research* (Deming, 1975). W. Edwards Deming, the unlikely guru of TQM, is a statistician who worked on organizational efficiency issues in the corporate world. Becoming dissatisfied with the failure of American companies to adopt his techniques, he went to Japan after World War II to help in efforts to reestablish their economy. His methods for improving organizational processes became quite successful in that country, while he remained relatively unknown here. In 1980, Americans watched *NBC White Paper: If Japan Can Do It, Why Can't We?,* which introduced many to Deming's methods (Fellers, 1992). TQM has spread through the corporate world and, as noted, is now being adopted widely in the public and nonprofit sectors.

The Methods of TQM.   Total Quality Management involves several components. First, it is designed to improve organizational efficiency and productivity through examining suppliers, the work process itself, and customer satisfaction. Taking a systems perspective, these might be viewed as elements of the input, process, and output functions. *Suppliers* are defined broadly as anyone or anything that provides information or materials necessary to perform the task at hand. Suppliers could be companies delivering hard products, other units or people in the organization providing information, or other agencies supplying resources, technical assistance, or even clients. Similarly, customers might be internal or external to the corporation or organization. To improve efficiency, the organization uses TQM to examine how interactions with the suppliers can improve organizational efficiency. In other words, how can the right supplies be received more quickly at the right place and in the right amount?

The *work process* itself is then examined and broken into steps to determine how it might be made more efficient or effective. Are any of the present steps unnecessary or duplicative? Why is each step performed? What is its purpose, goal, or objective? Are these purposes and objectives necessary to achieve the desired end product? Can any step be eliminated? (Deming, 1986).

Finally, though not necessarily last, TQM examines *customer satisfaction* as the ultimate outcome. If customers are not satisfied, the process is reexamined. The *ultimate* goal in all TQM work is meeting customer needs and satisfying customers. In the corporate world, the ultimate customer is obviously the person who buys the product, though even in the corporate world there are other customers. Customers for training programs can include trainees, supervisors, managers, and the organization. Customers for the purchasing department are those employees within the organization ordering the product. Defining customers in the public setting becomes a little more difficult, and some question the utility of TQM in the government setting for precisely this reason (Swiss, 1992). Who is the customer for a welfare department? The welfare client? Employers? The general public? Who is the customer for the U.S. Department of Commerce? Large or small businesses? Employees? All citizens? Obviously, those in government must work harder to define their customer(s), but it can be done, as demonstrated in case studies by Rago (1994) in a state mental health agency and Cohen and Eimicke (1994) in a metropolitan parks and recreation department. While TQM began in manufacturing settings, it is now used widely in both public and private organizations whose focus is on service rather than production. As these case studies demonstrate, like manufacturing tasks, service tasks can be broken into steps and studied for quality and improvement.

These are the components TQM examines or studies, but TQM has two critical characteristics that link it to evaluation today. First, being a statistician, Deming (1986) urged that these components be studied through *systematic collection of data*. Data, through interviews, monitoring, or existing information, are collected to examine current operations or problem areas. Results of this data-collection process are reviewed and new systems are proposed. These systems are then pilot-tested and new information is collected. Processes are revised or replaced, based on these pilot tests. TQM envisions the organization in a constant process of testing and examination. Employees are asked to question standard operating procedures (SOPs) and to change continually to achieve quality. (Perhaps Deming read Campbell's "Reforms As Experiments," published in the same edition of the *Handbook of Evaluation*?)

Second, TQM is not conducted by methodological experts, though they can serve as facilitators, but by *worker teams*. This attribute is critical to the success of TQM. Deming (1986) believed the workers closest to the job knew the most about the work process and, hence, were in the best place to identify problems and recommend improvements. TQM gives those workers the opportunity to question processes and make changes while encouraging them to define their goals in relation to quality products and customer needs.

This element of TQM is not so akin to the traditional, social science experimental views of evaluation as to those of the new "empowerment evaluation" (Fetterman, 1994, 2001). Just as Fetterman argues that stakeholders can do the evaluation and become empowered, Deming and other TQM advocates argue that worker teams can be trained to collect data on work and make recommendations for improvement. And, as in Fetterman's empowerment approach, worker participation leads to better questions, better solutions, and, most important, better adoption of those solutions by the workers themselves. TQM empowers the worker to question, study, and change the workplace to better meet customer needs.

How does TQM differ from evaluation? One major difference is that its scope is often narrower. TQM rarely evaluates "programs." Instead, TQM focuses on "production line operations." Its primary focus of study is SOPs, or standard operating procedures. As such, TQM is often concerned with monitoring processes, although causes of problems in standard operating procedures are sought. Hackman and Wageman (1995) note that "the single most commonly used [TQM] technique is formation of short-term problem-solving teams with the overall objective of simplifying and streamlining work practices" (p. 315). The principal outcomes examined are length of time to complete certain tasks and customer satisfaction. Like evaluation, TQM collects data from many sources, and data collection can make use of both qualitative and quantitative methods. Extensive use is made of interviews, customer-satisfaction surveys, and checklists for monitoring purposes, as well as specialized TQM measures, but any method appropriate to the purpose can be used.

Implications of TQM.   What can evaluators learn from TQM? TQM, like Fetterman's (2001) empowerment approach, brings evaluation to the layperson. If successful, TQM can encourage organizations and employees to question and assess new ventures. TQM changes the organizational culture from blind advocacy to healthy skepticism. As such, TQM was one of the predecessors to the organizational learning strategies proposed by Preskill and Torres (1999).

One of the major problems evaluators face in many organizations is the fear of evaluation and a high degree of loyalty to the present mode of delivery. Scriven (1993) writes: "The roots of resistance to evaluation go very deep indeed, and it is wise not to underestimate their strength. For many people, to concede that their work needs evaluation is to concede that they lack competence. It is part of the ego's survival repertoire to be self-sufficient" (p. 88). Years ago, Campbell (1975) advised managers that they should act as advocates for the problem they are trying to solve, not the solution. In such a manner, they can feel more comfortable in testing new modes of delivery without fear that failure of this mode will jeopardize their future. Instead, by advocating for the problem and testing the solution, they have shown the wise ability to recognize that solutions are tough and must be constantly evaluated. Managers have not responded to Campbell's suggestion enthusiastically, and evaluators have continued to struggle with managers' allegiance to programs and resistance to evaluation. TQM and other organizational learning strategies could bring about this long-desired change. That is, it could make questioning and open discussion of failure acceptable in the organizational culture, and that would ease the work of program evaluators enormously.

Some wonder if TQM may be another passing fad, like MBO, Quality Circles, or Planning, Programming, and Budgeting System (PPBS). Perhaps. As with any method, its advocates often promise too much. Hackman & Wageman (1995) note: "TQM, in our view, is far more likely gradually to lose the prominence and popularity it now enjoys than it is to revolutionize organizational practice" (p. 338). They note further, with regret, that recent implementations of TQM tend to ignore the empirical elements of TQM (monitoring, data collection and analysis, pilot-testing) and focus instead on the interpersonal skills and group process techniques of TQM: "Science is fading, the slogans are staying, and the implications are worrisome" (p. 338).

Nevertheless, each of these "fads" leaves something behind. That is, each method has some lasting influence on the organizational culture. MBO led organizations to think more about goals and objectives. Quality Circles left an impact on participatory management. TQM's legacy may be to begin to change the organizational culture to a questioning environment, to use the systematic collection of information to improve organizational processes, or to involve employees at the line level to identify problems and solutions. Each of these legacies will be beneficial to program evaluation.

Strategic Planning

Strategic planning has been around longer than TQM. It became popular in the 1970s in corporate settings and began to be adopted by many public-sector organizations in the early 1980s. **Strategic planning** has been defined as

> a management process that combines four basic features: (1) a clear statement of the organization's mission; (2) the identification of the agency's external constituencies or stakeholders, and the determination of their assessment of the agency's purposes and operations; (3) the delineation of the agency's strategic goals and objectives, typically in a 3- to 5-year plan; and (4) the development of strategies to achieve them (Berry, 1994, p. 323).

Some research has shown that strategic planning has not been successful in the corporate sector (Mintzberg, 1994). However, strategic planning continues to be used widely in public agencies. Between 1980 and 1991, more than 264 state agencies, from almost every state, initiated strategic planning (Berry, 1994). Research has shown that strategic planning is used in 60 percent of state agencies. Further, directors of these agencies view strategic planning positively and see it as helpful for decision making (Berry & Wechsler, 1995).

Strategic planning provides important input for program evaluation. It highlights the major goals and directions of the organization. If the planning is longitudinal, it can show changes or shifts in the focus of the organization. The goals and objectives defined through strategic planning can provide early information for planning an evaluation. Through interviews, the evaluator can determine whether these goals and objectives are still being pursued and, if so, what progress is being made toward achieving them. In cases when a goal or objective has been neglected or purposely put on the back burner, learning more about the history of this goal and reasons for its neglect can tell the evaluator much about the environmental context of the evaluation and the influence of various stakeholders. If a goal or objective is linked to the question to be answered in the evaluation, the strategies developed during strategic planning to achieve these related goals and objectives can provide milestones for process evaluation or, at minimum, provide foundation for discussion of progress with stakeholders. Were the strategies followed? If so, what progress was made? Did the stakeholder view the strategy as the appropriate one to take? What problems were encountered in implementing the strategy? What changes were made? Why? In other words, the strategic plan can provide the evaluator with crucial information about both the context of the evaluation and, possibly, the evaluation object itself.

Evaluators have not often been heavily involved in strategic planning. Few references to strategic planning are noted in the evaluation literature. However, evaluators should not shy away from this area. Like needs assessment, strategic planning provides information for decision making about future directions. Strategic planning differs from needs assessment in that it does not focus on a particular program or population but on the future of the organization as a whole. Thus, it is higher-level planning. But, if evaluators are to have real impact on organizations, both public and private, they must be involved in decisions at many different levels.

In the context of corporate training, Brinkerhoff (1989) has suggested that evaluators have been most successful not when they have tried to win support for evaluation as a separate activity but rather when they "have sought ways to weave evaluation thinking and activities into already existing and valued operations" (p. 2). This is consistent with Sanders' (2002) concept of mainstreaming evaluation. Strategic planning provides an opportunity for evaluators to do just that. More than a few evaluators have argued that we need to become more involved in planning (Fitzpatrick & Bickman, 2002; Patton, 1994; Reichardt, 1994). While these authors refer primarily to program planning, strategic planning provides the opportunity for the inclusion of evaluation thinking at the highest levels.

Quality Control/Quality Assurance

Quality control and **quality assurance** are terms used in corporations and some public-sector settings (e.g., hospitals), to refer to processes akin to monitoring evaluation. As such, evaluators should be familiar with these terms and their application.

To illustrate the relationship of quality control and quality assurance to evaluation, Brandenburg (1989) describes them under the heading "New Terms for Familiar Functions" (p. 85). Brandenburg views quality control as the monitoring of inputs and processes; he defines quality assurance as the monitoring of products. *Quality control* mechanisms are designed to provide managers with feedback about whether things are going smoothly at the beginning and middle of the process. The term *quality assurance* begins to be used more when the object to be monitored is closer to the end of the process. However, it would be misleading to imply that quality assurance always measures final outcomes. Instead, it simply measures things that are closer to the end product than quality control does. Because of this ambiguity (when is the thing measured *close enough* to the end product to be considered quality assurance rather than quality control?), the terms are often used interchangeably and what might be labeled "quality control" at one organization is "quality assurance" at another.

Both quality control and quality assurance mechanisms are monitoring devices for collecting routine information on program processes. Both activities serve primarily formative decisions because the audience is typically workers and line managers who are responsible for decisions about improving programs, not policy makers, who typically make the more summative decisions.

Quality assurance and quality control systems are often designed by managers or worker teams who work with the process. They are the primary audience. Sometimes, management information systems (MIS) specialists are involved if the information is to be collected or analyzed by computer. Most MIS products serve a quality control or quality assurance function. Evaluators are rarely involved because the information to be collected is relatively straightforward, (e.g., inventories, supplies, treatment plans, lesson plans, or attendance).

In the public sector, quality assurance is used heavily in hospital and mental health settings and refers to the review of medical or clinical care records. The Joint Commission on Accreditation of Hospital Organizations (JCAHO) uses quality assurance methods for its reviews of institutions. The emphasis is on compliance. The question they are trying to answer is, Do the hospital records comply with JCAHO standards for accountability? Data collection is primarily devoted to sampling records and using checklists to determine the degree of compliance on each standard. Client outcomes are not examined. The assumption is that if the records show appropriate and adequate care, desired outcomes will be achieved. A mental health administrator observed to one of the present authors that a good mental health center should strive for a C from JCAHO; receiving an A probably means you are spending too much time on records and too little time on patient care! Of course, the examination of existing documents is cheaper than validly assessing client outcomes, but the comment does help to illustrate the distinction between program evaluation and quality assurance.

Other differences between evaluation and quality control mechanisms include the nature of use. Quality assurance information can be used with routine frequency (daily, weekly) and is often used to improve the performance of individual workers (e.g., clinicians whose treatment plans are not in compliance are asked to improve). Evaluation results, even with our moving toward sharing results with stakeholders as they emerge, are generally available less frequently and typically do not identify individual workers at fault but rather processes that could be improved.

As with program evaluation, some quality assurance efforts have emerged due to legislative mandates. The 1972 amendments to the Social Security Act (PL 92-603) established Professional Standards Review Organizations to use quality assurance to make sure that funds for Medicare, Medicaid, and the Maternal and Child Health Programs were spent on "medically necessary and high quality care" (Tash & Stahler, 1984). And, like program evaluation, quality assurance and quality control mechanisms aim to provide feedback to improve programs. Coulton (1987) writes: "A successful organization continually looks for, finds, and solves problems. In this context, quality assurance—with its cycle of monitoring, in-depth problem analysis, and corrective action—serves as a self-correcting function within an organization" (p. 443).

Some (Royse, 1992) see the boundaries between quality assurance and program evaluation becoming blurred. As with the other strategies reviewed in this chapter, quality control and quality assurance mechanisms provide opportunities for evaluators to use their skills in the defining of information needs and the collection of information to meet those needs. These actions address Brinkerhoff's (1989) suggestion of using other methods for instilling evaluation thinking into the organization and, in so doing, helping it deliver a better product. As with TQM, quality control and quality assurance focus mostly on process. Unlike TQM, the data collection in quality control and quality assurance systems tends to focus on more stable, or less transitory, information needs.

Through work in each of these arenas—evaluation in the nonprofit sector, corporate training evaluation, personnel evaluation, and the organizational assessment strategies reviewed here (TQM, strategic planning, quality control, and quality assurance)—the evaluator broadens her own skills and experience. Just as visiting other countries helps the traveler learn more about her own culture, working in different settings can help evaluators recognize new characteristics of their own traditional evaluation context. Similarly, evaluating new things or working with other methods of organizational appraisal can expand the evaluator's view of potential evaluation questions and data collection methods and strategies.

Major Concepts and Theories

1. This chapter concerns the role of evaluation in improving organizations. It reviews the expanding role of evaluation in nonprofit organizations and the changing roles of evaluation in training. Finally, the chapter covers organizational activities that overlap with evaluation. These are areas in which evaluators can become involved and use their evaluation skills to improve organizational productivity.

2. Privatization of government services is increasing and, with it, the growth of the nonprofit sector. Government evaluators will monitor the work of nonprofits for accountability purposes and summative decisions. Evaluators within nonprofits will need to adapt to a new and different environment.

3. The most common models for evaluating training are the Kirkpatrick model and Stufflebeam's CIPP model. Evaluations of training are moving toward a focus on changes in performance.

4. Performance appraisals, or personnel evaluation, are used for compensation, promotion, retention, and feedback for performance improvement. Evaluation methods can be applied to this technique by considering new sources and methods for collecting information.

5. Total Quality Management (TQM), strategic planning, quality control, and quality assurance are all methods used by organizations to improve performance. Each makes use of evaluation-related methods and ways of thinking. By becoming involved in these methods, the evaluator can better contribute to overall organizational productivity.

Discussion Questions

1. Why are evaluations conducted in corporate and nonprofit settings? How would an evaluation in these settings differ from one in the public arena?

2. Compare and contrast Kirkpatrick's four levels of training evaluation with the CIPP evaluation model as applied to a training effort. What differences might emerge in evaluating the effort? What similarities exist? Which would you prefer to employ when evaluating training programs?

3. What skills do traditional program evaluators bring to the consideration of performance appraisals in organizations?

4. Why do you think TQM makes use of worker teams? How does this approach compare to Fetterman's Empowerment Evaluation?

5. Compare and contrast evaluation and TQM. What differences exist between the two? Similarities?

Application Exercises

1. Interview a manager in the nonprofit sector. How does her organization conduct evaluation? How does it differ from the approaches you have read about in this text? How is it like the approaches you have learned? Compare what you learn with others in your class.

2. You have been hired to conduct an evaluation of a program for training new supervisors in how to conduct performance appraisals. What would you do first to plan the evaluation? What types of questions might you suggest the evaluation address? What kinds of measures would you use to address process? What outcomes?

3. Find an article in the library that makes use of quality control or quality assurance measures. How do these measures differ from those typically used in evaluation? How are they like typical evaluation measures? How does the context differ from evaluation? How is it like evaluation?

4. Read one of the case studies on TQM referenced in this chapter. How does its application differ from evaluation? How does it differ from Fetterman's (2001) empowerment approach? (Read the Fetterman reference.)

5. Which do you think should be more important in performance appraisal, the accuracy of the assessment of the individual's performance or the ability of the feedback process to lead to improvement in performance? Why? Does your priority on these two issues mirror your priorities in evaluation? Why or why not?

Suggested Readings

Boris, E. T., & Steuerle, E. (Eds.). (1999). *Nonprofit and government.* Washington, DC: Urban Institute Press.

Brinkerhoff, R. O. (Ed.). (1989). *Evaluating training programs in business and industry.* New Directions for Program Evaluation, No 44. San Francisco: Jossey-Bass.

Deming, W. E. (1986). *Out of the crisis.* Cambridge: Massachusetts Institute of Technology, Center for Advanced Engineering Study.

Firstenberg, P. (1996). *The 21st century nonprofit: Remaking the organization in the post-government era.* New York: Foundation Center.

Gray, S. T., & Stockdill, S. H. (1995). *Evaluation with power.* San Francisco: Jossey-Bass.

Hackman, R., & Wageman, R. (1995). Total Quality Management: Empirical, conceptual, and practical issues. *Administrative Science Quarterly, 40,* 309–342.

Osborne, D., & Gaebler, T. (1992). *Reinventing government: How the entrepreneurial spirit is transforming the public sector.* Reading, MA: Addison-Wesley.

Russ-Eft, D., & Preskill, H. (2001). *Evaluation in organizations.* Cambridge, MA: Perseus.

Sanders, J. R. (2002). Presidential address: On mainstreaming evaluation. *American Journal of Evaluation, 23,* 253–259.

21

The Future of Evaluation

Orienting Questions _____

1. How are future program evaluations likely to be different from current evaluations in
   • the way in which political considerations are handled?
   • the methods that will be used?
   • the involvement of stakeholders?
   • how they are reported?
2. What is the likely future of programs for training evaluators (both for graduate degrees and for in-service training)?
3. What will be important developments for evaluation in the future?

We have reached the last chapter of this book, but we have only begun to share what is known about program evaluation. The references we have made to other writings reflect only a fraction of the existing literature in this growing field. In choosing to focus attention on (1) alternative approaches to program evaluation, and (2) practical guidelines for planning, conducting, reporting, and using evaluation studies, we have tried to emphasize what we believe is most important to include in any single volume that aspires to give a broad overview of such a complex and multifaceted field. We hope we have selected well, but we encourage students and evaluation practitioners to go beyond this text to explore the richness and depth of other evaluation literature. In this final chapter, we share our perceptions and those of a few of our evaluation colleagues about evaluation's future.

The Future of Evaluation

Hindsight is inevitably better than foresight, and ours is no exception. Yet present circumstances permit us to hazard a few predictions that we believe will hold true for program evaluation in the next few decades. History will prove whether or not our predictions are sufficiently accurate to allow prophecy to be added to the repertoire of techniques useful to evaluators.

We believe that evaluation will continue to spread rapidly around the globe, until there are few countries, territories, provinces, states, and locales in which program evaluations are not at least an occasional occurrence. As we have noted, the spreading interest in program evaluation has been evident for some years in the development of evaluation associations and activities around the world. We also believe that evaluation will become an increasingly useful force in the following ways:

- Improving programs, thus improving the lot of those intended to benefit from those programs;
- Improving policy making by governing boards, legislators, and congressional and parliamentary bodies;
- Aiding in corporate or public "quality improvement" efforts;
- Improving societies through improving the social conditions programs address;
- Improving even itself.

If these predictions seem overly optimistic, it may underscore our earlier point that evaluators may not always be completely unbiased. Yet these forecasts do not strike us as unrealistic or overdrawn; we are willing to submit them to the test of time.

Now let us move to more specific predictions concerning the profession of evaluation and its practice.[1]

Predictions concerning the Profession of Evaluation

1. Evaluation will become an increasingly useful force in our society, in improving programs and policies in public, nonprofit, and the private sector. Many of the movements we have discussed in this text, performance monitoring, organizational renewal, and others, illustrate the increasing interest in and impact of evaluation in different sectors.

2. Evaluation will expand into other fields or disciplines, beyond its now venerable role in education and psychology to expanded roles in housing, social welfare, environmental programs, city planning, transportation, health, criminal justice, biotechnology, recreation, and management programs in many

---

[1]These predictions draw heavily from Worthen (2001).

organizations (Love, 2001; Rogers, 2001; Worthen, 2001). Working in these new areas will prompt evaluators to expand their repertoire of approaches and methods to adapt to these new contexts, new political dynamics, and new issues to explore and investigate.

3. Evaluation will become increasingly institutionalized in the United States and in other developed countries as the pressure for accountability weighs heavily on governments and nonprofit organizations that deliver vital services. Virtually every trend points to more, not less, evaluation in the public, private, and nonprofit sectors in the future. In some organizations, the focus is on documenting outcomes in response to external political pressures. In other organizations, evaluation is being used for organizational growth and development (which should, ultimately, improve the achievement of those outcomes). In each context, however, evaluation is in demand.

4. Evaluation will continue to spread rapidly around the globe until there are few countries where program evaluations are not at least an occasional occurrence, and the number of national and multinational professional societies for evaluation will burgeon.

5. The opportunity for careers in evaluation will gradually increase as the demands for evaluation and related skills grow. Graduate programs in evaluation are unlikely to expand significantly, however, despite increasing demand for evaluators. There may be some growth in existing programs, where institutions have already invested in training of evaluators, but the demand will not be well enough understood by university administrators to result in significant numbers of universities and colleges initiating programs for training evaluators. Rather, many evaluators will continue to receive their basic training in more traditional disciplines' training programs. The need for in-service education in evaluation will expand dramatically as educators, public and nonprofit administrators, corporate officers, and those in a variety of other roles are asked to assume some responsibility for carrying out evaluation studies alongside their other professional duties. We also expect that evaluation training will become more applied, in coming years, with much of it coming through internships on ongoing evaluation studies or in evaluation organizations where such internships might span several program evaluations. Finally, we expect to see more interdisciplinary Ph.D. programs concentrating in evaluation (Stufflebeam, 2001b).

6. Internal evaluation will, despite its risks, become more important because of its benefits. Internal evaluators know the organizational environment and can provide an important ongoing influence to encourage organizational learning and to use evaluation skills across the organization in many different endeavors, from using new information technology to human resource management to traditional evaluation of programs. We predict there will be increased cooperation between internal and external evaluators for high-profile outcome evaluations as well as for organizational development (OD) activities when the external "evaluator" may be an OD specialist.

7. Professional associations and activities in evaluation will grow slowly but steadily. The American Evaluation Association (AEA) and other societies of practicing evaluators and/or evaluation theoreticians will continue to contribute to evaluation's maturation. The interest in credentialing or licensing evaluators has diminished due to the difficulties in defining an ever-expanding and changing field. Instead, professional associations are moving to educate elected officials, policy makers, and the public about evaluation-related issues. Like other professional associations, the American Evaluation Association recently took its first public position as an association with its Statement on High-Stakes Testing (American Evaluation Association, 2002). Through these efforts, and lobbying and continuing education efforts regarding evaluation practice and standards, associations will work to educate stakeholders about the potential that evaluation offers and the risks entailed in using it inappropriately.

8. Evaluation literature will increase in both quantity and quality, but relatively little of it will be based on research into the process of evaluation itself. Current funding agencies do not seem interested in supporting research on the evaluation process. Thus, the empirical knowledge base in evaluation will increase very slowly. As evaluation expands, there is a critical need for more research on what occurs in evaluations, what works and what doesn't, in reference to politics, practice, participation, and use.

Predictions concerning the Practice of Evaluation

As the profession grows and expands, practice will change even more dramatically.

1. There will be fewer large-scale studies. Instead, evaluation practice will include a combination of outcome focus for performance measurement and accountability, formative studies for organizational improvement and learning, small qualitative studies to inform particular needs of local stakeholders about program practices that work, and development of program theory to assist in program development and management (House, 2001; Newcomer, 2001).

2. Approaches to evaluation will become more eclectic and adaptive to contextual circumstances. Program evaluation will continue to be pluralistic, and fundamental differences will continue to separate some on philosophical grounds. However, the stridency over alternative paradigms and methods has largely subsided as pragmatic evaluators have found it both possible and productive to draw on both the objectivist and subjectivist traditions in developing multiple approaches to describing the programs they evaluate. Single-method evaluations will be increasingly seen, by professional evaluators if not by the public and some elected officials, as simplistic and inadequate for evaluation of complex programs or those serving diverse populations. Triangulation, cross-validation, and iterative, expansive designs will be used more routinely to allow the complementarity of qualitative and quantitative approaches to enrich evaluation work.

The usefulness of the different approaches will lie less in having any one of them serve as a model to be followed slavishly but rather, as House (1994) has suggested, as collectively comprising the "grammar of evaluation" that evaluators must understand and be skilled in using:

> [One] might see the evaluation models as something like model sentences in a grammar of evaluation. . . . As one progresses, . . . one does not need to think about the models consciously, except to correct particular errors or study the grammar itself.
>
> Similarly, . . . experienced evaluators can construct evaluation designs which do not depend explicitly on particular models. Actual evaluation designs can be combinations of elements from different models, . . . just as speakers can produce novel grammatical sentences once they have learned the basic grammar of a language (pp. 241–242).

3. Evaluation (and evaluators) will become more politically sophisticated as evaluators increasingly recognize that their studies are both technical and political endeavors, requiring them to struggle with new conceptualizations of how evaluations can serve their political role well without being discounted by skeptics as merely another political (and, thus, to many a noncredible) activity. Evaluators will need increasingly sophisticated political skills to work with different groups, to educate others about evaluation, to facilitate the selection of evaluation questions and appropriate measures, to ensure accurate interpretations, and to encourage use or influence of results. Performance measurement and the multiple stakeholders involved in participatory evaluation are examples of circumstances fraught with politics.

4. Attention to ethical issues will increase as evaluators become more involved in political issues. The present evaluation *Standards* and *Guiding Principles*—and their descendants—provide a means for maintaining the credibility of evaluation and educating others about expectations for evaluation in an increasingly politicized environment. Professional accountants have strengthened their ethical codes and training of practitioners in the face of public disillusionment concerning the "independent" role of accountants in reviewing the financial practices of corporations (Fitzpatrick, 1999). Evaluators can avoid the debacle that the Arthur Anderson Accounting firm faced in its auditing of Enron by strengthening the ethical education of current and future evaluators.

5. Electronic and other technological advances will alter the way evaluators report, enabling broader use of "storytelling" (case studies, scenarios, and typical profiles) in electronic, audio, and video forms that supplement written reports, which will continue to be used but will increasingly be disseminated electronically.

6. Advances in electronic and other technological media will also alter dramatically our techniques of data collection and analysis. With new hardware and software developments that allow much more efficient and accurate collection of data, new ways to relate extant databases, and other advances opening new vistas, evaluators' many traditional techniques, such as mailed questions and paper-and-pencil tests, will, however, continue in use throughout the next decade and, possibly, well into the next.

7. Efforts will increase to democratize evaluation not only by broadening participation in evaluation to many different stakeholders, but also by using evaluation as an instrument to identify inequality and injustice in society and its various institutions. Participative and constructivist evaluation approaches have become more dominant in the recent past. Evaluators have worked to involve many different stakeholder groups, especially those who are often disenfranchised. These efforts will continue. But, as we have recognized the need for increasing the numbers and types of stakeholders involved in evaluation, we have also realized the complexities of that task. Mark (2001) observes that we have acted as if there is only one approach to stakeholder involvement and that approach, typically, is simply more involvement. He argues: "Our debate, based on experience and evidence, might be about the proper range of stakeholder involvement in different circumstances. Our discussion would become more nuanced, equally emphasizing the costs (e.g., workload, capacity) as well as the benefits (e.g., ownership, likelihood of use) of stakeholder involvement" (pp. 463–464).

In regard to the purpose of evaluation, we believe that efforts to redefine evaluation as primarily an instrument to achieve social betterment rather than a means of determining merit or worth will be gradually replaced with a vision that the two are not incompatible. Evaluation of any social policy or program can examine its merit on egalitarian or other worthy grounds, thus contributing to social betterment.

8. The performance measurement movement will grow in response to persistent demands for accountability. Performance measurement, in some form or fashion, is now mandated in most local, state, and federal government agencies and nonprofit organizations led by initiatives from United Way and the World Bank. Expectations from the public and from policy makers who mandated performance measurement are high. Yet, most managers lack the expertise to collect meaningful measures of outcomes. Newcomer (2001) notes that professional evaluators will play an important role in making this process more than simply a reporting exercise. Evaluators can help build program theory to link outcomes to program activities and, hence, make the outcome information useful for formative purposes. Further, evaluators' methodological expertise will be necessary to measure outcomes.

Performance measurement, however, also presents potential hazards for the evaluation field. Just as states' testing of students on educational standards has grossly simplified learning goals and focused educational evaluation activities on just this issue, so, too, can performance measurement simplify and narrow evaluation activities. Many policy makers and managers underestimate the challenge of measuring program outcomes and, because of the mandated nature of performance measurement, tend to see performance measurement as all that evaluation does. Evaluators need to be active in this area to bring their expertise to bear.

A Vision for Evaluation

The above represent our predictions for the profession and practice of evaluation. We also have some visions, or goals, for evaluation. These differ from predictions in that the evidence is not so clear as to whether these visions will be realized. Nevertheless, we would be remiss if we ended this book without describing that vision. It includes:

1. A global valuing of evaluation that cuts across boundaries of professional fields, job categories, sectors of society, geopolitical lines, cultures—that is, formal disciplined evaluation as a pervasive value. How will we bring about this valuing? By making others aware of evaluation and its importance. By helping those who are mandated to do evaluations to see its worth even when it is not mandated. By instilling evaluation institutions, policies and procedures, and evaluative ways of thinking in organizations (Sanders, 2001).

2. To continue a constructive use of multiple methods and eclectic approaches to achieve the many different purposes of evaluation. The debates over qualitative and quantitative methods have subsided and many have moved on to the practical issues of applying their now increased methodological tools in a variety of settings. To avoid future divisive debates we should recognize the plurality of evaluation purposes, questions, and settings. An evaluator working with the U.S. government on performance monitoring issues is facing different methodological and political challenges from the evaluator designing a special, formative study for a nonprofit agency on their work with a new group of clients. Rather than debate the different choices these evaluators make, we should study their choices and learn more about what approaches work best in different settings. As evaluators, we should be the first to learn not to judge decisions made in other evaluations without sufficient information. We need to work harder to defer that judgment and explore and collect information on those choices. Let's develop thick descriptions about evaluations!

3. Increase the use of metaevaluation to improve evaluation practice. One type of publication that is regrettably rare in the evaluation journals are critiques of prior evaluation reports, metaevaluations. Despite the acceptance and availability of the Joint Committee's *Standards,* few evaluations appear to be subjected to any closer scrutiny now than before their publication. To learn from our own work, we must be open to its review and evaluation. As others learn from our evaluations, evaluators can learn from evaluations of their own work.

Conclusion

We leave the reader with two final thoughts.

First, all that experience and research can teach convinces us that evaluation, properly conducted, has great potential for improving programs and practices in education, human services, business—in virtually every area of society. Managers, policy makers, and other stakeholders have become aware that some evaluation studies are misused or ignored, with the result that some individuals have argued for decreased emphasis on the evaluative process. But that seems no more sensible than abandoning medical diagnosis because science has not yet successfully eliminated all disease. Knowledge about evaluation has grown impressively in the near quarter century since our first book was published, but its conclusion still rings true:

> Most systems have most of the earmarks of classical bureaucracies and, historically, have been reasonably successful in resisting change in practices and policies. Recently, strong social forces have coalesced to push many systems out from behind their barriers; change has become a much more frequent reality. However, without a tradition of planned change or systematic inquiry into the effectiveness of potential new programs, the changes which are occurring can be often little more than random adoption of faddish innovations. Perhaps the most important deficiency which fosters such a situation is the lack of dependable information on the performance of available products, practices, and programs. Without such information, practitioners cannot readily correct deficiencies or malfunctions in present practices or intelligently select new products or practices for adoption.
>
> Evaluation . . . holds great promise in providing field workers with badly needed information which can be used to improve the processes of human service. While obviously not a panacea, evaluation can have a profound impact on the human services professions (Worthen & Sanders, 1973, pp. 348–349).

The second thought we wish to leave with readers is this: Despite great strides, it is increasingly apparent how little we really do know about evaluation, compared to what we need to know. It is our earnest hope that this book has added to that knowledge and, thus, helped to illuminate the thousand points of darkness that still constitute current processes for creating and implementing the policies and programs intended to improve the lot of humankind.

Application Exercise

Relax. We think you've done enough. Besides, we have no idea how to have you meaningfully apply our predictions about evaluation's future. If you do, we will welcome your suggestions for future editions.

Suggested Readings

Mark, M. M. (2001). Evaluation's future: Furor, futile, or fertile? *American Journal of Evaluation, 22,* 457–480.

Smith, M. F. (2001). Evaluation: Preview of the future #2. *American Journal of Evaluation, 22,* 281–300.

See the entire issues of *American Journal of Evaluation* (2002), *22,* and *Evaluation Practice* (1994), *15.* Each of these issues focuses on reflections concerning evaluation theories, practice, and status as a profession and predictions concerning the future.

Appendix

Evaluation-Related Web Sites

Evaluation Organizations

www.eval.org The Web site for the American Evaluation Association describes activities, conferences, programs of the organization, lists local affiliates and topical interest groups, presents the *Guiding Principles of Evaluation* as well as the Joint Committee *Standards,* and provides links to collections of evaluation resources, foundations that fund evaluation activities, governmental organizations and NGOs that conduct evaluation activities. It also provides links to seventeen evaluation associations in other countries.

www.eval.org/hstlinks.htm This address links the user to the American Evaluation Association statement on high-stakes testing currently being used in forty-nine states across the United States. It includes a link to references in this area.

www.bama.ua.edu/archives/evaltalk.html This site will instruct you in how to register for participation in EvalTalk, the American Evaluation Association list-serv, which conducts an active on-line discussion of evaluation issues. For other questions on EvalTalk, contact Kathy Bolland at kbolland@sw.ua.edu. She is the administrator of the listserv.

http://home.wmis.net/~russon/icce/ This is the site for the International and Cross-Cultural Evaluation Topical Interest Group of the American Evaluation Association. It offers paper sessions, symposiums, and professional development for those interested in cross-cultural issues.

www.evaluationcanada.ca This is the home page for the Canadian Evaluation Society.

www.parklane.com.au/aes/ This is the home page for the Australasian Evaluation Society. Their mission is to improve public sector effectiveness through better evaluation. Visitors to this Web site can access libraries of information on research abstracts and evaluation research. References are available on benchmarking, budget analysis, ethics, evaluation methodology, evaluation theory, program management, qualitative methods, and quantitative methods.

Sites with Publications and Reports

www.wmich.edu/evalctr The Web site for the Center for Evaluation at Western Michigan University contains evaluation checklists, papers, and reports, a glossary of evaluation terms, bibliographies, information on the Joint Committee and the *Standards* it developed for program evaluation, personnel evaluation, and student evaluation, and a directory of evaluators.

http://citnews.unl.edu/TOP This Web site was developed by Kay Rockwell of the University of Nebraska-Lincoln and Claude Bennett of the U.S. Department of Agriculture. It describes their seven-level hierarchy for targeting program outcomes (TOP) and ways to integrate program evaluation with program development.

www.eval.org/EvaluationLinks/QDA.htm This Web site provides brief descriptions of software to analyze qualitative data and links to the site for each data package. Some software samples are available for download. Some of the links provide information on qualitative methods.

http://.ericae.net/ This Web site is sponsored by the ERIC Clearinghouse on Assessment and Evaluation. It provides a comprehensive list of educational assessment resources including a searchable test review and test/instrument locator. This site also includes resources on evaluation and research methodology. The Web site offers online access to 550 publications concerning evaluation and assessment.

http://members.home.net/gpic/evalwebindex.htm The Evaluation Clearinghouse Web site is sponsored by Government Performance Information Consultants (Canada). This site provides an extensive list of evaluation resources, including many in Canada.

http://oerl.sri.com The Online Evaluation Research Library is funded by the National Science Foundation and provides a catalogue of plans, instruments, and reports from past and current project evaluations as well as guidelines for improving evaluation.

http://gsociology.icaap.org/methods/ Resources for Methods in Evaluation and Social Research is a site that gives a "how to" approach to guidelines of methodology and evaluation. It also provides links to Web pages designed to provide links to information about human research practices, research guidelines, and professional standards and ethics.

http://www.policy-evaluation.org/ This is a site designed to provide many of the same resources as the other compilation sites, but gives more in-depth coverage of international sites and resources. Included in their resources are journals, databases, research centers, and links to international organizations' Web sites.

http://trochim.human.cornell.edu/ Bill Trochim's Web site provides an on-line textbook and handbook. This resource provides tutorials, simulations, and pointers for conducting research and evaluation.

http://www.ariassociates.haverford.edu/ The Action Evaluation Research Institute offers a new approach to evaluation. The keys to Action Evaluation are participation by all stakeholders from the beginning, and reflexivity, meaning that the stakeholders reflect and examine the goals and outcomes of their organizations as a group. This Web site gives the details of this unique approach to evaluation.

http://www.vanderbilt.edu/CERM/ Vanderbilt University's Institute for Policy Studies hosts this Web site. There are links to recent publications on evaluation and research methods as well as information on recent Vanderbilt evaluation projects.

http://www.usu.edu/eval/ The Center for Policy and Program Evaluation at Utah State University provides access to current research and evaluations conducted by the University staff. Links to current evaluation reports are also provided on this Web site.

http://www.appliedsurveyresearch.org/evaluations.htm Applied Survey Research is an evaluation firm that works with organizations to gather information and survey research in order to evaluate programs. This Web site includes examples of their past information collection as well as their past evaluations and assessments of programs.

Sites with a Focus on Special Types of Programs

www.unl.edu/buros/ The Oscar and Luella Buros Center for Testing provides resources for assessment, consultation, and outreach. It gives advice on test development, evaluation, and oversight. This organization conducts audit, accreditation, research, and consultation services to organizations wanting to improve their evaluation and testing practices.

www.icma.org/go.cfm This Web site was developed by the Center for Performance Measurement at the International City Managers Association (ICMA). They assist 120 cities in the U.S. and Canada on performance measurement. It contains information on how to measure, compare, and improve municipal service delivery programs.

http://unitedway.org/outcomes This site, Outcome Measurement Resource Network, describes United Way's approach to outcome measurement. It contains downloadable documents to assist in identifying and measuring program and community outcomes.

www.cdc.gov/eval/framework.htm This site presents the evaluation framework used by the U.S. Centers for Disease Control, its approach to evaluation, and representative reports.

www.worldbank.org/poverty/library/impact.pdf A site developed by the World Bank that presents case studies and discussions of impact evaluations in developing countries.

www.vserp.org A site established by the Voluntary Sector Evaluation Research Project with the Center for Voluntary Sector Research and Development at the University of Ottawa, Canada. Presents downloadable manuals and bibliographies for evaluation in voluntary organizations.

www.ed.gov/pubs/EdTechGuide/ Presents information and documents for educators on evaluating programs using technology in schools.

www.gao.gov Presents reports developed by the prestigious Governmental Accounting Organization in the United States and a discussion of their approach to large-scale evaluations of federal programs.

www.cse.ucla.edu/ The site for the Center for Research on Evaluation, Standards, and Student Testing includes reports, policy briefs, newsletters, a test locator, and school portfolios.

www.ets.org The Web site for the Educational Testing Service, this Web site provides information on assessment in higher education.

www.gse.harvard.edu/hfrp/eval.html The site for the Harvard Family Research Project describes innovative methods and emerging trends in evaluation and publishes the periodical *The Evaluation Exchange.*

www.stanford.edu/~davidf/empowermentevaluation.html David Fetterman's site on empowerment evaluation provides guides for conducting empowerment evaluation, software, and virtual conferencing.

Other Relevant Web Sites

http://www.eval.org/Insurance.htm This link from the American Evaluation Association provides evaluators with information on obtaining insurance. Two options are provided and links to more information are given. Insurance options include liability and equipment insurance.

References

Abma, T. A., & Stake, R. E. (2001). Stake's responsive evaluation: Core ideas and evolution. In J. C. Greene & T. A. Abma (Eds.), *Responsive evaluation*. New Directions for Program Evaluation, No. 92, 7–22. San Francisco: Jossey-Bass.

Adams, K. A. (1983, April). *When to "hold em" and when to "fold em": Ethical problems of internal evaluators*. Paper presented at the annual meeting of the American Educational Research Association, Montreal, Canada.

Aday, L. A. (1989). *Designing and conducting health surveys: A comprehensive guide*. San Francisco: Jossey-Bass.

Adler, P. A., & Adler, P. (1994). Observational techniques. In N. K. Denzin & Y. S. Lincoln (Eds.), *Handbook of qualitative research*. Thousand Oaks, CA: Sage.

Affholter, D. P. (1994). Outcome monitoring. In J. S. Wholey, H. P. Hatry, & K. E. Newcomer (Eds.), *Handbook of practical program evaluation*. San Francisco: Jossey-Bass.

Agar, M. (2000). Border lessons: Linguistic "rich points" and evaluative understanding. In R. K. Hopson (Ed.), *How and why language matters in evaluation*. New Directions for Evaluation, No. 86, 93–109. San Francisco: Jossey-Bass.

Alexander, R. R. (1977). Educational criticism of three art history classes. Unpublished doctoral dissertation, Stanford University. (University Microfilms no. 78–2125)

Alkin, M. C. (1969). Evaluation theory development. *Evaluation Comment, 2*, 2–7.

Alkin, M. C. (1991). Evaluation theory development: II. In M. W. McLaughlin & D. C. Phillips (Eds.), *Evaluation and education: At quarter century*. Ninetieth Yearbook of the National Society for the Study of Education, Part II. Chicago: University of Chicago Press.

Alkin, M. C., & Solmon, L. C. (Eds.). (1983). *The costs of evaluation*. Beverly Hills, CA: Sage.

Alkin, M. C., Stecher, B. M., & Geiger, F. L. (1982). *Title I evaluation: Utility and factors influencing use*. Nothridge, CA: Educational Evaluation Associates.

Altschuld, J. W. (1999). The certification of evaluators: Highlights from a report submitted to the Board of Directors of the American Evaluation Association. *American Journal of Evaluation, 20*, 481–494.

Altschuld, J. W., Engle, M., Cullen, C., Kim, I., & Macce, B. R. (1994). The 1994 directory of evaluation training programs. In J. W. Altschuld & M. Engle (Eds.), *The preparation of professional evaluators: Issues, perspectives, and programs*. New Directions for Program Evaluation, No. 62, 71–94. San Francisco: Jossey-Bass.

American Anthropological Association. (1990). *Statements on ethics: Principles of professional responsibility*. Arlington, VA: Author.

American Educational Research Association. (1992). Ethical standards. *Educational Researcher, 21*, 23–26.

American Evaluation Association. (1995). Guiding principles for evaluators. In W. R. Shadish, D. L. Newman, M. A. Scheirer, & C. Wye (Eds.), *Guiding principles for evaluators*. New Directions for Program Evaluation, No. 34, 19–26.

American Evaluation Association. (2002). *Position statement on high stakes testing in Pre K–12 Education*. Fairhaven, MA: American Evaluation Association.

Amie, M. (1995). The Australasian Evaluation Society. *Evaluation, 1*, 124–125.

Anderson, R. C. (1983). Reflections on the role of peer review in competitions for federal research. *Educational Researcher, 12*, 3–5.

Anderson, R. S., & Speck, B. W. (Eds.). (1998). *Changing the way we grade student performance: Classroom assessment and the new learning paradigm*. New Directions for Teaching and Learning, No. 74. San Francisco: Jossey-Bass.

Anderson, S. B., & Ball, S. (1978). *The profession and practice of program evaluation*. San Francisco: Jossey-Bass.

Angrosino, M. V., & Mays de Perez, K.A. (2000). Rethinking observation: From method to context. In N. K. Denzin & Y. S. Lincoln (Eds.), *Handbook of qualitative research,* 2nd ed. Thousand Oaks, CA: Sage.

Auerbach, C., Garrison, L. K., Hurst, W., & Mermin, S. (1961). The adversary system. In C. Auerbach & S. Mermin (Eds.), *The legal process.* San Francisco: Chandler.

Babbie, E. (1992). *The practice of social research* (6th ed.). Belmont, CA: Wadsworth.

Bailey, M. T. (1992). Do physicists use case studies? Thoughts on public administration research. *Public Administration Review,* 52, 47–54.

Baker, E. L., & Niemi, D. (1996). School and program evaluation. In D. C. Berliner & R. C. Calfee (Eds.), *Handbook of educational psychology.* New York: Macmillan.

Barrios, N. B., & Foster, G. R. (1987, April). *Utilization of evaluation information: A case study approach investigating factors related to evaluation utilization in a large state agency.* Paper presented at the annual meeting of the American Evaluation Association, Boston. (ED 292 814)

Basch, C. E. (1987). Focus group interviews: An underutilized technique for improving theory and practice in health education. *Health Education Quarterly,* 14, 411–448.

Bell, J. B. (1994). Managing evaluation projects step by step. In J. S. Wholey, H. P. Hatry, & K. E. Newcomer (Eds.), *Handbook of practical program evaluation.* San Francisco: Jossey-Bass.

Bell, W. (1983). *Contemporary social welfare.* New York: Macmillan.

Benkofske, M. (1994a). Personal communication. Reprinted with permission.

Benkofske, M. (1994b, November). *When the qualitative findings are negative.* Paper presented at the annual meeting of the American Evaluation Association, Boston.

Berk, R. A. (1986). Minimum competency testing: Status and potential. In B. S. Plake & J. C. Witt (Eds.), *The future of testing* (pp. 84–144). Hillsdale, NJ: Lawrence Erlbaum.

Berk, R. A. (1994). Three trends in evaluation research. *Evaluation Practice,* 15, 261–264.

Berman, E. (1997). The challenge of Total Quality Management. In C. Ban & N. M. Riccucci (Eds.), *Public personnel management: Current concerns—future challenges.* New York: Longman.

Bernard, H. R. (2000). *Social research methods: Qualitative and quantitative approaches.* Thousand Oaks, CA: Sage.

Bernhardt, V. L. (1984, October). *Evaluation processes of regional and national education accrediting agencies: Implications for redesigning an evaluation process in California.* Paper presented at the annual meeting of the American Educational Research Association, New Orleans.

Bernstein, D. J. (1999). Comments on Perrin's "Effective use and misuse of performance measurement." *American Journal of Evaluation,* 20, 85–94.

Berry, F. S. (1994). Innovation in public management: The adoption of strategic planning. *Public Administration Review,* 54, 322–329.

Berry, F. S., & Wechsler, B. (1995). State agencies' experience with strategic planning: Findings from a national survey. *Public Administration Review,* 55, 159–168.

Bickman, L. (Ed.). (1987). *Using program theory in evaluation.* New Directions for Program Evaluation, No. 33. San Francisco: Jossey-Bass.

Bickman, L. (Ed.) (1990). *Advances in program theory.* New Directions in Program Evaluation, No. 47. San Francisco: Jossey-Bass.

Bickman, L. (1994). An optimistic view of evaluation. *Evaluation Practice,* 15, 255–259.

Bickman, L. (2002). The death of treatment as usual: An excellent first step on a long road. *Clinical Psychology,* in press.

Bickman, L., Noser, K., & Summerfelt, W. T. (1999). Long-term effects of a system of care on children and adolescents. *Journal of Behavioral Health Services & Research,* 26, 185–202.

Bloom, B. S., Engelhart, M. D., Furst, E. J., Hill, W. H., & Krathwohl, D. R. (1956). *Taxonomy of educational objectives: Handbook I. Cognitive domain.* New York: David McKay.

Bloom, B. S., Hastings, J. T., & Madaus, G. F. (1971). *Handbook of formative and summative evaluation of student learning.* New York: McGraw-Hill.

Bonnet, D. G. (1998). Commentary: Achieving the untroubled slumber. *American Journal of Evaluation,* 19, 230–232.

Boris, E. T. (1999). Nonprofit organizations in a democracy: Varied roles and responsibilities. In E. T. Boris & E. Steuerle (Eds.), *Nonprofit and government.* Washington, DC: Urban Institute Press.

Boruch, R. F., & Cordray, D. S. (Eds.). (1980). *An appraisal of educational program evaluation: Federal, state, and local agencies.* Washington, DC: U.S. Department of Education.

Bowman, J. S. (1994). At last an alternative to performance appraisal: Total Quality Management. *Public Administration Review,* 54, 129–136.

Brager, G. L., & Mazza, P. (1979). The level of analysis and the level of presentation are not the same. *Educational Evaluation and Policy Analysis, 3,* 105–106.

Brandenburg, D. C. (1989). Evaluation and business issues: Tools for management decision making. In R. O. Brinkerhoff (Ed.), *Evaluating training programs in business and industry.* New Directions for Program Evaluation, No. 44, 83–100. San Francisco: Jossey-Bass.

Brandon, P. R. (1998). Stakeholder participation for the purpose of helping ensure evaluation validity: Bridging the gap between collaborative and non-collaborative evaluations. *American Journal of Evaluation, 19,* 325–337.

Brandon, P. R., Lindberg, M. A., & Wang, Z. (1993). Involving program beneficiaries in the early stages of evaluation: Issues of consequential validity and influence. *Educational Evaluation and Policy Analysis, 15,* 420–428.

Brandt, R. S. (Ed.). (1981). *Applied strategies for curriculum evaluation.* Alexandria, VA: Association for Supervision and Curriculum Development.

Braverman, M. T. (1996). Sources of survey error: Implications for evaluation studies. In M. T. Braverman & J. K. Slater (Eds.), *Advances in survey research.* New Directions for Evaluation, No. 70, 17–28. San Francisco: Jossey-Bass.

Braverman, M. T., & Slater, J. K. (Eds.). (1996). *Advances in survey research.* New Directions for Evaluation, No. 70. San Francisco: Jossey-Bass.

Braybrooke, D., & Lindblom, C. E. (1963). *A strategy of decision.* New York: Free Press.

Brett, B., Hill-Mead, L., & Wu, S. (2000). Perspectives on evaluation use and demand by users: The case of City Year. In V. J. Caracelli & H. Preskilll (Eds.), *The expanding scope of evaluation use.* New Directions for Evaluation, No. 88. San Francisco: Jossey-Bass.

Brickell, H. M. (1978). The influence of external political factors on the role and methodology of evaluation. In T. D. Cook, M. L. Del Rosario, K. M. Hennigan, M. M. Mark, & W. M. K. Trochim (Eds.), *Evaluation studies review annual* (Vol. 3). Beverly Hills, CA: Sage.

Brinkerhoff, R. O. (1989). Using evaluation to transform training. In R. O. Brinkerhoff (Ed.), *Evaluating training programs in business and industry.* New Directions for Program Evaluation, No. 44, 5–20. San Francisco: Jossey-Bass.

Brinkerhoff, R. O. (2003). *The success case method: How to quickly find out what's working and what's not.* San Francisco: Berrett Kohler.

Brinkerhoff, R. O., Brethower, D. M., Hluchyj, T., & Nowakowski, J. R. (1983). *Program evaluation: A practitioner's guide for trainers and educators.* Boston: Kluwer-Nijhoff.

Brodsky, S. L., & Smitherman, H. O. (1983). *Handbook of scales for research in crime and delinquency.* New York: Plenum.

Brown, C. L. (2000). Sociolinguistic dynamics of gender in focus groups. In R. K. Hopson (Ed.), *How and why language matters in evaluation.* New Directions for Evaluation, No. 86, 55–68. San Francisco: Jossey-Bass.

Brown, R. D., & Newman, D. L. (1992). Ethical principles and evaluation standards: Do they match? *Evaluation Review, 16,* 650–663.

Brunner, I., & Guzman, A. (1989). Participatory evaluation: A tool to assess projects and empower people. In R. F. Conner and M. Hendricks (Eds.), *International innovations in evaluation methodology.* New Directions for Evaluation, No. 42. San Francisco: Jossey-Bass.

Bryk, A. S. (Ed.). (1983). *Stakeholder-based evaluation.* New Directions for Program Evaluation, No. 17, San Francisco: Jossey-Bass, 1983.

Buchanan, G. N., & Wholey, J. S. (1972). Federal level evaluation. *Evaluation, 1,* 17–22.

Burke, B. (1998). Evaluating for a change: Reflections on participatory methodology. In E. Whitmore (Ed.), *Understanding and practicing participatory evaluation.* New Directions for Evaluation, No. 80, 43–56. San Francisco: Jossey-Bass.

Camacho, J., & Vicinanza, N. (2002). *The AEA job bank: Growing opportunities in 2002.* Paper presented at the annual conference of the American Evaluation Association, Washington, DC.

Campbell, D. (1969a). Ethnocentrism of disciplines and the fish-scale model of omniscience. In M. Sheriff & C. Sherif (Eds.), *Inter-disciplinary relationships in the social sciences.* Chicago: Aldine.

Campbell, D. T. (1969b). Reforms as experiments. *American Psychologist, 24,* 409–429.

Campbell, D. (1975). Reforms as experiments. In E. Struening & M. Guttentag (Eds.), *Handbook of evaluation research* (Vol. 1). Beverly Hills, CA: Sage.

Campbell, D. T. (1984). Can we be scientific in applied social science? In R. F. Conner, D. G. Altman, & C. Jackson (Eds.), *Evaluation studies review annual* (Vol. 9). Beverly Hills, CA: Sage.

Campbell, D. T., & Stanley, J. C. (1966). *Experimental and quasi-experimental designs for research.* Chicago: Rand McNally.

Canadian Evaluation Society. (1992). Standards for program evaluation in Canada: A discussion paper. *Canadian Journal of Program Evaluation, 7,* 157–170.

Caracelli, V. J., & Greene, J. C. (1997). Crafting mixed-method evaluation designs. In J. C. Greene & V. J. Caracelli (Eds.), *Advances in mixed-method evaluation: The challenges and benefits of integrating diverse paradigms.* New Directions for Program Evaluation, No. 74. San Francisco: Jossey-Bass.

Carnevale, A. P., & Carnevale, E. S. (1994). Growth patterns in workplace training. *Training and Development, 48,* 22–28.

Carnevale, A. P., Gainer, L. J., & Villet, J. (1990). *Training in America.* San Franscisco: Jossey-Bass.

Caro, F. G. (Ed.). (1971). *Readings in evaluation research.* New York: Russell Sage.

Cascio, W. F. (1991). *Applied psychology in personnel management.* Reston, VA: Reston.

Chelimsky, E. (1997). The coming transformations in evaluation. In E. Chelimsky & W. R. Shadish (eds), *Evaluation for the 21st Century: A handbook.* Thousand Oaks, CA: Sage.

Chelimsky, E. (1998). The role of experience in formulating theories of evaluation practice. *American Journal of Evaluation, 20,* 35–56.

Chelimsky, E. (1985). Old patterns and new directions in program evaluation. In E. Chelimsky (Ed.), *Program evaluation: Patterns and directions.* Washington, DC: American Society for Public Administration.

Chelimsky, E. (1987). The politics of program evaluation. In D. S. Cordray, H. S. Bloom, & R. J. Light (Eds.), *Evaluation practice in review.* New Directions for Program Evaluation, No. 34, 5–21. San Francisco: Jossey-Bass.

Chelimsky, E. (1992). "Views of Eleanor Chelimsky." Quoted in C. Wye & R. Sonnichsen, Another look at the future of program evaluation in the federal government: Five views. *Evaluation Practice, 13,* 185–195.

Chelimsky, E. (1994). Evaluation: Where are we? *Evaluation Practice, 15,* 339–345.

Chelimsky, E. (1995). Comments on the Guiding Principles. In W. R. Shadish, D. L. Newman, M. A. Scheirer, & C. Wye (Eds.), *Guiding Principles for Evaluators.* New Directions for Program Evaluation, No. 66, 53–54. San Francisco: Jossey-Bass.

Chelimsky, E., & Shadish, W. R. (1997). *Evaluation for the 21st century: A handbook.* Thousand Oaks, CA: Sage.

Chen, H. (1990). *Theory-driven evaluations.* Newbury Park, CA: Sage.

Chen, H. (1994). Current trends and future directions in program evaluation. *Evaluation Practice, 15,* 229–238.

Chen, H. (1996). A comprehensive typology for program evaluation. *Evaluation Practice, 17,* 121–130.

Chen, H., & Rossi, P. H. (1983). Evaluating with sense: The theory-driven approach. *Evaluation Review, 7,* 283–302.

Clark, N. (1952). *The Gantt chart.* London: Pitman & Sons.

Clotfelder, C. T. (Ed.). (1992). *Who benefits from the nonprofit sector?* Chicago: University of Chicago Press.

Clyne, S. F. (1982). The judicial evaluation model: A case study. Unpublished doctoral dissertation, Boston College, Boston.

Cohen, S. (1978). Science and the tabloid press. *APA Monitor, 9*(3), 1.

Cohen, S., & Eimicke, W. (1994). Project-focused Total Quality Management in the New York City Department of Parks and Recreation. *Public Administration Review, 54,* 450–456.

Comptroller General of the United States. (1988). *Government auditing standards.* Washington, DC: U.S. General Accounting Office.

Conner, R. F., Altman, D. G., & Jackson C. (Eds.). (1984). *Evaluation studies review annual* (Vol. 9). Beverly Hills, CA: Sage.

Conoley, J. C., & Impara, J. C. (1995). *The twelfth mental measurements yearbook.* Lincoln, NE: University of Nebraska Press.

Conrad, K. J. (Ed.). (1994). *Critically evaluating the role of experiments.* New Directions for Program Evaluation, No. 63. San Francisco: Jossey-Bass.

Cook, D. L. (1966). *Program evaluation and review technique: Applications in education* (Monograph no. 17). Washington, DC: U.S. Office of Education Cooperative Research.

Cook, T. D. (1985). Postpositivist critical multiplism. In R. L. Shotland & M. M. Mark (Eds.), *Social science and social policy.* Beverly Hills, CA: Sage.

Cook, T. D. (1997). Lessons learned in evaluation over the past 25 years. In E. Chelimsky & W. R. Shadish (Eds.), *Evaluation for the 21st century: A handbook.* Thousand Oaks, CA: Sage.

Corcoran, K., & Fisher, J. (1987). *Measures for clinical practice: A sourcebook.* New York: Free Press.

Cordray, D. S., & Lipsey, M. W. (1987). Evaluation studies for 1986: Program evaluation and program research. In D. S. Cordray & M. W. Lipsey (Eds.), *Evaluation studies review annual* (Vol. 5, pp. 17–44). Beverly Hills, CA: Sage.

Cottingham, P. H. (1991). Unexpected lessons: Evaluation of job-training programs for single mothers. In R. S. Turpin & J. M. Sinacore (Eds.), *Multisite evaluations.* New Directions for Program Evaluation, No. 50, 59–70. San Francisco: Jossey-Bass.

Coulton, C. J. (1987). Quality assurance. In S. M. Rosen, D. Fanshel, & M. E. Lutz (Eds.), *Encyclopedia of social work.* Silver Spring, MD: National Association of Social Workers.

Council on Foundations. (1993). *Evaluation for foundations: Concepts, cases, guidelines, and resources.* San Francisco: Jossey-Bass.

Coupal, F. P., & Simoneau, M. (1998). A case study of participatory evaluation in Haiti. In E. Whitmore (Ed.), *Understanding and practicing participatory evaluation.* New Directions for Evaluation, No. 74. San Francisco: Jossey-Bass.

Cousins, J. B., & Earl, L. M. (1992). The case for participatory evaluation. *Educational Evaluation and Policy Analysis, 14*(4), 397–418.

Cousins, J. B., & Earl, L. M. (1995). *Participatory evaluation in education: Studies in evaluation use and organizational learning.* London: Falmer.

Cousins, J. B., & Leithwood, K. A. (1985). *The state of the art of empirical research on evaluation utilization.* Toronto: Ontario Institute for Studies in Education.

Cousins, J. B., & Leithwood, K. A. (1986). Current empirical research on evaluation utilization. *Review of Educational Research, 56*, 331–364.

Cousins, J. B., & Whitmore, E. (1998). *Framing participatory evaluation.* New Directions for Evaluation, No. 80, 5–23.

Covert, R. W. (1988). Ethics in evaluation: Beyond the standards. *Evaluation Practice, 9*, 32–37.

Covert, R. W. (1992, November). *Successful competencies in preparing professional evaluators.* Paper presented at the annual meeting of the American Evaluation Association, Seattle.

Covert, R. W. (1995). A twenty-year veteran's reflections on the Guiding Principles for Evaluators. In W. R. Shadish, D. L. Newman, M. A. Scheirer, & C. Wye (Eds.), *Guiding Principles for Evaluators.* New Directions for Program Evaluation, No. 66, 35–45. San Francisco: Jossey-Bass.

Cronbach, L. J. (1963). Course improvement through evaluation. *Teachers College Record, 64*, 672–683.

Cronbach, L. J. (1982). *Designing evaluations of educational and social programs.* San Francisco: Jossey-Bass.

Cronbach, L. J., Ambron, S. R., Dornbusch, S. M., Hess, R. D., Hornik, R. C., Phillips, D. C., Walker, D. F., & Weiner, S. S. (1980). *Toward reform of program evaluation.* San Francisco: Jossey-Bass.

Datta, L. (1995). *Multimedia evaluations: A landscape with case studies.* Paper presented at the International Evaluation Conference, Vancouver, Canada.

Datta, L. (1999). The ethics of evaluation neutrality and advocacy. In J. L. Fitzpatrick & M. Morris (Eds.), *Current and emerging ethical challenges in evaluations.* New Directions for Evaluation, No. 82, 77–88. San Francisco: Jossey-Bass.

Deming, W. E. (1975). The logic of evaluation. In E. Struening & M. Guttentag (Eds.), *Handbook of evaluation research* (Vol. 1). Beverly Hills, CA: Sage.

Deming, W. E. (1986). *Out of crisis.* Cambridge, MA: Massachusetts Institute of Technology, Center for Advanced Engineering Study.

Dennis, M. L., & Boruch, R. F. (1989). Randomized experiments for planning and testing projects in developing countries: Threshold conditions. *Evaluation Review, 13*, 292–309.

Denzin, N. K. (1978). *The research act.* Chicago: Aldine.

Denzin, N. K., & Lincoln, Y. S. (Eds.). (2000). *Handbook of qualitative research.* (2nd ed.). Thousand Oaks, CA: Sage.

Dickey, F. G., & Miller, J. W. (1972). *A current perspective on accreditation.* Washington, DC: American Association for Higher Education.

Dillman, D. A. (1978). *Mail and telephone surveys: The Total Design Method.* New York: Wiley.

Dillman, D. A. (1983). Mail and other self-administered questionnaires. In P. H. Rossi, J. D. Wright, and A. B. Anderson (Eds.), *Handbook of survey research.* New York: Academic.

Dillman, D. A., & Sangster, R. (1991). *Mail surveys: A comprehensive bibliography, 1974–1989.* Chicago: Council of Planning Librarians.

Dillman, D. A., Sangster, R. L., Tarnai, J., & Rockwood, T. H. (1996). Understanding differences in people's answers to telephone and mail surveys. In M. T. Braverman & J. K. Slater (Eds.), *Advances in survey research.* New Directions for Evaluation, No. 70, 45–62. San Francisco: Jossey-Bass.

Dillman, D. A., & Tarnai, J. (1991). Mode effects of cognitively-designed recall questions: A comparison of answers to telephone and mail surveys. In P. P. Biemer, R. M. Brover, L. E. Lyberg, N. A. Mathiowetz, & S. Sudman (Eds.), *Measurement errors in surveys.* New York: Wiley.

Dodson, S. C. (1994). Interim summative evaluation: Assessing the value of a long term or ongoing program, during its operation. Unpublished doctoral dissertation, Western Michigan University, Kalamazoo.

Donaldson, S. I. (2002). Theory-driven program evaluation in the new millennium. In S. I.

Donaldson & M. Scriven (Eds.), *Evaluating social programs and problems: Visions for the new millennium.* Hillsdale, NJ: Erlbaum.

Douglas, J. D. (1976). *Investigative social research.* Beverly Hills, CA: Sage.

Duffy, B. P. (1994). Use and abuse of internal evaluation. In C. J. Stevens & M. Dial (Eds.), *Preventing the misuse of evaluation.* New Directions for Program Evaluation, No. 64, 25–32. San Francisco: Jossey-Bass.

Durlak, J. A., & Lipsey, M. W. (1991). A practitioner's guide to meta-analysis. *American Journal of Community Psychology, 19,* 291–332.

Eash, M. J. (1970, April). *Developing an instrument for the assessment of instructional materials.* Paper presented at the annual meeting of the American Educational Research Association, Minneapolis.

Eisner, E. W. (1975, April). *The perceptive eye: Toward the reformation of educational evaluation.* Invited address at the American Educational Research Association, Washington, DC.

Eisner, E. W. (1979a). *The educational imagination: On the design and evaluation of school programs.* New York: Macmillan.

Eisner, E. W. (1979b). The use of qualitative forms of evaluation for improving educational practice. *Educational Evaluation and Policy Analysis, 1,* 11–19.

Eisner, E. W. (1991). Taking a second look: Educational connoisseurship revisited. In M. W. McLaughlin & D. C. Phillips (Eds.), *Evaluation and education: At quarter century. Ninetieth Yearbook of the National Society for the Study of Education, Part II.* Chicago: University of Chicago Press.

Elder, G. H., Jr., Pavalko, E. K., Clipp, C. (1993). *Working with archival data: Studying lives.* Newbury Park, CA: Sage.

ETS Test Collection Catalogue. (1991). Phoenix, AZ: Oryx.

Evaluation Research Society Standards Committee. (1982). Evaluation Research Society standards for program evaluation. In P. H. Rossi (Ed.), *Standards for evaluation practice.* New Directions for Program Evaluation, No. 15, 7–19. San Francisco: Jossey-Bass.

Farland, D. S., & Gullickson, A. R. (1995). *Handbook for developing a teacher performance evaluation manual: A metamanual.* Kalamazoo, MI: Center for Research on Educational Accountability and Teacher Evaluation.

Fellers, G. (1992). *The Deming vision.* Milwaukee, WI: ASQC Quality Press.

Fetterman, D. M. (1984). *Ethnography in educational evaluation.* Beverly Hills, CA: Sage.

Fetterman, D. M. (1992). In response to Lee Sechrest's 1991 AEA presidential address: Roots: Back to our first generation. *Evaluation Practice, 13,* 171–172.

Fetterman, D. M. (1994). Empowerment evaluation. *Evaluation Practice, 15,* 1–15.

Fetterman, D. M. (1995). In response to Dr. Daniel Stufflebeam's empowerment evaluation, objectivist evaluation, and evaluation standards: Where the future of evaluation should not go and where it needs to go, October 1994, 321–338. *Evaluation Practice, 16*(2), 179–199.

Fetterman, D. M. (1996). Empowerment evaluation: An introduction to theory and practice. In D. M. Fetterman, S. Kaftarian, & A. Wandersman (Eds.), *Empowerment evaluation: Knowledge and tools for self-assessment and accountability.* Thousand Oaks, CA: Sage.

Fetterman, D. M. (1997). Empowerment evaluation: A response to Patton and Scriven. *Evaluation Practice, 18*(3), 253–266.

Fetterman, D. M. (1998). *Ethnography, step by step.* (2nd ed.). Thousand Oaks, CA: Sage.

Fetterman, D. M. (2000). *Foundations of empowerment evaluation.* Thousand Oaks, CA: Sage.

Fetterman, D. M. (2001). Empowerment evaluation. *Evaluation Practice, 15,* 1–15.

Fetterman, D. M., Kaftarian, S., and Wandersman, A. (Eds.). (1996). *Empowerment evaluation: Knowledge and tools for self-assessment and accountability.* Thousand Oaks, CA: Sage.

Fielding, N. G., (2000). The shared fate of two innovations in qualitative methodology: The relationship of qualitative software and secondary analysis of archived qualitative data. *Qualitative Social Research* [online], 1, Available from http://caqdas.sos.surrey.ac.uk/news.

Fielding, N. G., & Lee, R. M. (1998). *Computer analysis and qualitative research.* Thousand Oaks, CA: Sage.

Fink, A. (1995). *How to design surveys.* Thousand Oaks, CA: Sage.

Finnan, C., & Davis, S. C. (1995, April). *Linking project evaluation and goals-based teaching evaluation: Evaluating the accelerated schools.* Paper presented at the annual meeting of the American Educational Research Association, San Francisco.

Fischer, C. T., & Wertz, F. J. (2002). Empirical phenomenological analyses of being criminally victimized. In A. M. Huberman & M. B. Miles (Eds.), *The qualitative researcher's companion.* Thousand Oaks, CA: Sage.

Fitzgibbon, C. T., & Morris L. L. (1975). Theory-based evaluation. *Evaluation Comment, 5*(1), 1–4.

Fitzpatrick, J. L. (1988). *Alcohol education programs for drunk drivers.* Colorado Springs: Center for Community Development and Design.

Fitzpatrick, J. L. (1989). The politics of evaluation with privatized programs: Who is the audience? *Evaluation Review, 13,* 563–578.

Fitzpatrick, J. L. (1992). Problems in the evaluation of treatment programs for drunk drivers: Goals and outcomes. *Journal of Drug Issues, 22,* 155–167.

Fitzpatrick, J. L. (1994). Alternative models for the structuring of professional preparation programs. In J. W. Altschuld & M. Engle (Eds.), *The preparation of professional evaluators: Issues, pespectives, and programs.* New Directions for Program Evaluation, No. 62, 41–50. San Francisco: Jossey-Bass.

Fitzpatrick, J. L. (1999). Ethics in disciplines and professions related to evaluation. In J. L. Fitzpatrick & M. Morris (Eds.), *Current and emerging ethical challenges in evaluation.* New Directions for Evaluation, No. 82. San Francisco: Jossey-Bass.

Fitzpatrick, J. L., & Bickman, L. (2002). Evaluation of the Ft. Bragg and Stark County systems of care for children and adolescents: A dialogue with Len Bickman. *American Journal of Evaluation, 23,* 67–80.

Fitzpatrick, J. L., & Fetterman, D. (2000). The evaluation of the Stanford Teacher Education Program (STEP): A dialogue with David Fetterman. *American Journal of Evaluation, 20,* 240–259.

Fitzpatrick, J. L., & Greene, J. (2001). Evaluation of the Natural Resources Leadership Program: A dialogue with Jennifer Greene. *American Journal of Evaluation, 22,* 81–96.

Fitzpatrick, J. L., & Henry, G. (2000). The Georgia Council for School Performance and its performance monitoring system: A dialogue with Gary Henry. *American Journal of Evaluation, 21,* 105–117.

Flanagan, J. C. (1954). The critical incident technique. *Psychological Bulletin, 51,* 327–358.

Flexner, A. (1910). *Medical education in the United States and Canada* (Bulletin no. 4). New York: Carnegie Foundation for the Advancement of Teaching.

Flexner, A. (1960). *Abraham Flexner: An autobiography.* New York: Simon & Schuster.

Floden, R. E. (1983). Flexner, accreditation, and evaluation. In G. F. Madaus, M. Scriven, & D. L. Stufflebeam (Eds.), *Evaluation models: Viewpoints on educational and human services evaluation.* Boston: Kluwer-Nijhoff.

Flores, J. G., & Alonso, C. G. (1995). Using focus groups in educational research. *Evaluation Review, 19,* 84–101.

Folz, D. H., & Hazlett, J. M. (1991). Public participation and recycling performance: Explaining program success. *Public Administration Review, 51,* 526–535.

Fontana, A., & Frey, J. H. (2000). Interviewing: From structured questions to negotiated text. In N. K. Denzin & Y. S. Lincoln (Eds.), *Handbook of qualitative research.* Thousand Oaks, CA: Sage.

Fowler, F. J., Jr. (1988). *Survey research methods.* Newbury Park, CA: Sage.

Frank, J. N. (1949). *Courts on trial.* Princeton, NJ: Princeton University Press.

Freeman, H. E., Klein, R. E., Townsend, J. W., & Lechtig, A. (1980). Nutrition and cognitive development among rural Guatemalan children. *American Journal of Public Health, 70,* 1277–1285.

Galagan, P. (1994). Reinventing the profession. *Training and Development, 48,* 20–27.

Galvin, J. G. (1983). What can trainers learn from educators about evaluating management training? *Training and Development Journal, 37,* 52, 54–57.

Georgia Merit System. (1997). *Manager's guide: Georgia Performance Management Process.* Atlanta: Training & Organization Development Division.

Gephart, W. J. (1978). The facets of the evaluation process: A starter set. Unpublished manuscript. Bloomington, IN: Phi Delta Kappan.

General Accounting Office. (1992). *Quality management: A survey of federal organizations.* Washington, DC: U.S. General Accounting Office.

Giventer, L. L. (1996). *Statistical analysis for public administration.* Belmont, CA: Wadsworth.

Glass, G. V., McGraw, B., & Smith, M. L. (1981). *Meta-analysis in social research.* Newbury Park, CA: Sage.

Goodlad, J. (1979). *What schools are for.* Bloomington, IN: Phi Delta Kappa Educational Foundation.

Gore, A. (1993). *From red tape to results: Creating a government that works better and costs less: The report of the National Performance Review.* New York: Plume.

Grasso, P. G. (1996). The end of an era: Closing the U.S. General Accounting Office's Program Evaluation and Methodology Division. *Evaluation Practice, 17,* 115–117.

Gray, S. T. (Ed.). (1993). *A vision of evaluation.* Washington, DC: Independent Sector.

Gray, S. T., & Stockdill, S. H. (1995). *Evaluation with power.* Washington, DC: Independent Sector.

Greenberg, D., Meyer, R. H., & Wiseman, M. (1994). Multisite employment and training program evaluations: A tale of three studies. *Industrial and Labor Relations Review, 47,* 679–691.

Greene, J. C. (1987). Stakeholder participation in evaluation design: Is it worth the effort? *Evaluation and Program Planning, 10,* 379–394.

Greene, J. C. (1988). Stakeholder participation and utilization in program evaluation. *Evaluation Review, 12,* 91–116.

Greene, J. C. (1997). Evaluation as advocacy. *Evaluation Practice, 18,* 25–35.

Greene, J. C., and Abma, T. (Eds.). (2001). *Responsive evaluation.* New Directions for Evaluation, No. 92. San Francisco: Jossey-Bass.

Greene, J. C., & Caracelli, V. J. (Eds.) (1997). *Advances in mixed-method evaluation: The challenges and benefits of integrating diverse paradigms.* New Directions for Program Evaluation, No. 74. San Francisco: Jossey-Bass.

Greene, J. C., Caracelli, V. J., & Graham, W. F. (1989). Toward a conceptual framework for mixed-method evaluation designs. *Educational Evaluation and Policy Analysis, 11,* 255–274.

Greiner, J. M. (1994). Use of ratings by trained observers. In J. S. Wholey, H. P. Hatry, & K. E. Newcomer (Eds.), *Handbook of practical program evaluation.* San Francisco: Jossey-Bass.

Guastello, S. J., & Guastello, D. D. (1991). How organizations differ: Implications for multisite program evaluation. In R. S. Turpin & J. M. Sinacore (Eds.), *Multisite evaluations.* New Directions for Program Evaluation, No. 50, 71–81. San Francisco: Jossey-Bass.

Guba, E. G. (1969). The failure of educational evaluation. *Educational Technology, 9,* 29–38.

Guba, E. G. (1978). *Toward a methodology of naturalistic inquiry in educational evaluation.* (Monograph Series no. 8). Los Angeles: University of California, Center for the Study of Evaluation.

Guba, E. G. (1981). Investigative reporting. In N. L. Smith (Ed.), *Metaphors for evaluation: Sources of new methods.* New Perspectives in Evaluation (Vol. 1). Beverly Hills, CA: Sage.

Guba, E. G., & Lincoln, Y. S. (1981). *Effective evaluation.* San Francisco: Jossey-Bass.

Guba, E. G., & Lincoln, Y. S. (1989). *Fourth generation evaluation.* Thousand Oaks, CA: Sage.

Guba, E., & Lincoln, Y. S. (1994). Competing paradigms in qualitative research. In N. K. Denzin & Y. S. Lincoln (Eds.), *Handbook of qualitative research.* Thousand Oaks, CA: Sage.

Hackman, R., & Wageman, R. (1995). Total Quality Management: Empirical, conceptual, and practical issues. *Administrative Science Quarterly, 40,* 309–342.

Haque, M. S. (2001). The diminishing publicness of public service under the current mode of governance. *Public Administration Review, 61,* 65–82.

Halachimi, A. (1995). The practice of performance appraisal. In J. Rabin, T. Vocino, W. B. Hildreth, & G. J. Miller (Eds.), *Handbook of public personnel administration.* New York: Marcel Dekker.

Haladyna, T. M., Nolen, S. B., & Haas, N. S. (1991). Raising standardized achievement test scores and the origins of test score pollution. *Educational Researcher, 20*(5), 2–7.

Halpern, E. S. (1983, April). *Auditing naturalistic inquiries: Some preliminary applications. Part I. Development of the process. Part 2. Case study application.* Paper presented at the annual meeting of the American Educational Research Association, Montreal.

Hamilton, D. (1977). Making sense of curriculum evaluation: Continuities and discontinuities in an educational idea. In L. Shulman (Ed.), *Review of research in education* (Vol. 5). Itasca, IL: Peacock.

Hamilton, D., Jenkins, D., King, C., MacDonald, B., & Parlett, M. (Eds.). (1977). *Beyond the numbers game: A reader in educational evaluation.* Berkeley, CA: McCutchan.

Hammond, R. L. (1973). Evaluation at the local level. In B. R. Worthen & J. R. Sanders, *Educational evaluation: Theory and practice.* Belmont, CA: Wadsworth.

Harmon, M. (1995). The changing role of assessment in evaluating science education reform. In R. G. O'Sullivan (Ed.), *Emerging roles of evaluation in science education reform.* New Directions for Program Evaluation, No. 65, 31–51. San Francisco: Jossey-Bass.

Hebert, Y. M. (1986). Naturalistic evaluation in practice: A case study. In D. D. Williams (Ed.), *Naturalistic evaluation.* New Directions for Program Evaluation, No. 30, 3–21. San Francisco: Jossey-Bass.

Hedrick, S. C., Sullivan, J. H., Ehreth, J. L., Rothman, M. L., Connis, R. T., & Erdly, W. W. (1991). Centralized versus decentralized coordination in the adult day health care evaluation study. In R. S. Turpin & J. M. Sinacore (Eds.), *Multisite evaluations.* New Directions for Program Evaluation, No. 50, 19–31. San Francisco: Jossey-Bass.

Hedrick, T. E. (1994). The quantitative-qualitative debate: Possibilities for integration. In C. S. Reichardt & S. F. Rallis (Eds.), *The qualitative-quantitative debate: New perspectives.* New Directions for Program Evaluation, No. 61, 45–52. San Francisco: Jossey-Bass.

Hendricks, M., & Conner, R. F. (1995). International perspectives on the Guiding Principles. In W. R. Shadish, D. L. Newman, M. A. Scheirer, & C. Wye (Eds.), *Guiding principles for evaluators.* New Directions for Program Evaluation, No. 66, 77–90. San Francisco: Jossey-Bass.

Henry, G. T. (1990). *Practical sampling.* Newbury Park, CA: Sage.

Henry, G. T. (1996). Does the public have a role in evaluation: Surveys and democratic discourse. In M. T. Braverman & J. K. Slater (Eds.), *Advances in survey research.* New Directions for Evaluation, No. 70, 3–16. San Francisco: Jossey-Bass.

Henry, G. T. (Ed.). (1997). *Creating effective graphs: Solutions for a variety of evaluation data.* New Directions for Evaluation, No. 73. San Francisco: Jossey-Bass.

Henry, G. T. (2000). Why not use? In V. J. Caracelli & H. Preskill (Eds.), *The expanding scope of evaluation use.* New Directions for Evaluation, No. 88, 85–98. San Francisco: Jossey-Bass.

Henry, G. T., & Mark, M. M. (in press). Beyond use: Understanding evaluation's influence on attitudes and actions. *American Journal of Evaluation.*

Herman, J. L., Aschbacher, P. R., & Winters, L. (1992). *A practical guide to alternative assessments.* Alexandria, VA: Association for Supervision and Curriculum Development.

Herrell, J., & Straw, R. (Eds.). (2002). *Conducting multiple site evaluations in real-world settings.* New Directions for Evaluation, No. 94. San Francisco: Jossey-Bass.

Hodgkinson, H., Hurst, J., & Levine, H. (1975). *Improving and assessing performance: Evaluation in higher education.* Berkeley, CA: University of California Center for Research and Development in Higher Education.

Holsti, O. (1969). *Content analysis for the social sciences and humanities.* Reading, MA: Addison-Wesley.

Honea, G. E. (1992). Ethics and public sector evaluators: Nine case studies. Unpublished doctoral dissertation, University of Virginia, Department of Educational Studies.

Hood, S. (2000). Commentary on deliberative democratic evaluation. In K. E. Ryan & L. Destefano (Eds.), *Evaluation as a democratic process: Promoting inclusion, dialogue, and deliberation.* New Directions in Program Evaluation, No. 83. San Francisco: Jossey-Bass.

Hoppe, M. J., Wells, E. A., Morrison, D. M., Gillmore, M. R., & Wildson, A. (1995). Using focus groups to discuss sensitive topics with children. *Evaluation Review, 19,* 102–114.

Horst, P., Nay, J. N., Scanlon, J. W., & Wholey, J. S. (1974). Program management and the federal evaluator. *Public Administration Review, 34,* 300–308.

House, E. R. (1976). Justice in evaluation. In G. V. Glass (Ed.), *Evaluation studies review annual* (Vol. 1). Beverly Hills, CA: Sage.

House, E. R. (1980). *Evaluating with validity.* Beverly Hills, CA: Sage.

House, E. R. (1983a). Assumptions underlying evaluation models. In G. F. Madaus, M. Scriven, & D. L. Stufflebeam (Eds.), *Evaluation models: Viewpoints on educational and human services evaluation.* Boston: Kluwer-Nijhoff.

House, E. R. (Ed.). (1983b). *Philosophy of evaluation.* New Directions for Program Evaluation, No. 19. San Francisco: Jossey-Bass.

House, E. R. (1988). *Jesse Jackson and the politics of charisma: The rise and fall of the PUSH/Excel program.* Boulder, CO: Westview.

House, E. R. (1990). Methodology and justice. In K. A. Sirotnik (Ed.), *Evaluation and social justice: Issues in public education.* New Directions for Program Evaluation, No. 45, 23–36. San Francisco: Jossey-Bass.

House, E. R. (1993). *Professional evaluation.* Newbury Park, CA: Sage.

House, E. R. (1994a). The future perfect of evaluation. *Evaluation Practice, 15,* 239–247.

House, E. R. (1994b). Integrating the quantitative and qualitative. In C. S. Reichardt & S. F. Rallis (Eds.), *The qualitative-quantitative debate: New perspectives.* New Directions for Program Evaluation, No. 61, 13–22. San Francisco: Jossey-Bass.

House, E. R. (1995). Principled evaluation: A critique of the AEA Guiding Principles. In W. R. Shadish, D. L. Newman, M. A. Scheirer, & C. Wye (Eds.), *Guiding principles for evaluators.* New Directions for Program Evaluation, No. 66, 27–34. San Francisco: Jossey-Bass.

House, E. R. (2001). Unfinished business: Causes and values. *American Journal of Evaluation, 22,* 309–316.

House, E. R., & Howe, K. R. (1999). *Values in evaluation and social research.* Thousand Oaks, CA: Sage.

Huberman, A. M., & Miles, M. B. (1994). Data management and analysis methods. In N. K. Denzin & Y. S. Lincoln (Eds.), *Handbook of qualitative research.* Thousand Oaks, CA: Sage.

Hudson, W. W. (1982). *The clinical measurement package: A field manual.* Homewood, IL: Dorsey.

Huxley, E. (1982). *The flame trees of Thika: Memories of an African childhood.* London: Chatto & Windus.

Independent Sector. (1995). *Evaluation with power.* Washington, DC: Author.

Jaeger, R. M. (1989). Certification of student competence. In R. L. Linn (Ed.), *Educational measurement.* London: Collier Macmillan.

Jaeger, R. M. (1990). *Statistics: A spectator sport.* (2nd ed.). Newbury Park, CA: Sage.

Johnston, P., & Swift, P. (1994). Effects of randomization on a homeless services initiative: A comment. In K. J. Conrad (Ed.), *Critically evaluating the role of experiments*. New Directions for Program Evaluation, No. 3. San Francisco: Jossey-Bass.

Joint Committee on Standards for Educational Evaluation. (1981). *Standards for evaluations of educational programs, projects, and materials*. New York: McGraw-Hill.

Joint Committee on Standards for Educational Evaluation. (1988). *Personnel evaluation standards*. Newbury Park, CA: Corwin.

Joint Committee on Standards for Educational Evaluation. (1994). *The program evaluation standards* (2nd ed.). Thousand Oaks, CA: Sage.

Joint Committee on Standards for Educational Evaluation. (2003). *The student evaluation standards*. Thousand Oaks, CA: Corwin.

Jones, S. C., & Worthen, B. R. (1999). AEA members' opinions concerning evaluator certification. *American Journal of Evaluation, 20,* 495–506.

Jorgensen, D. L. (1989). *Participant observation: A methodology for human studies*. Newbury Park, CA: Sage.

Justiz, M. J., & Moorman, H. N. (1985). New NIE peer review procedures. *Educational Researcher, 14*(1), 5–11.

Kaplan, A. (1964). *The conduct of inquiry*. San Francisco: Chandler.

W. K. Kellogg Foundation (WKKF). (1991). *Information on cluster evaluation*. Battle Creek, MI: Author.

W. K. Kellogg Foundation (WKKF). (1994). *Improving cluster evaluation: Some areas for consideration*. Battle Creek, MI: Author.

Kellow, J. T. (1998). Beyond statistical significance tests: The importance of using other estimates of treatment effects to interpret evaluation results. *American Journal of Evaluation, 19,* 123–134.

Kelly, E. F. (1978). Curriculum criticism and literary criticism: Comments on the anthology. In G. Willis (Ed.), *Qualitative evaluation*. Berkeley, CA: McCutchan.

Kennedy, M., Apling, R., & Neumann, W. (1980). *The role of evaluation and test information in public schools*. Cambridge, MA: Huron Institute.

Kettl, D. F. (2000). The transformation of governance: Globalization, devolution, and the role of government. *Public Administration Review, 60,* 488–497.

King, J. A. (1988). Research on evaluation use and its implications for evaluation research and practice. *Studies in Educational Evaluation, 14,* 285–299.

King, J. A. (1998). Making sense of participatory evaluation practice. In E. Whitmore (Ed.), *Understanding and practicing participatory evaluation*. New Directions for Evaluation, No. 80, 57–68. San Francisco: Jossey-Bass.

King, J. A., Stevahn, L., Ghere, G., & Minnema, J. (2001). Toward a taxonomy of essential evaluator competencies. *American Journal of Evaluation, 22,* 229–247.

King, J. A., Thompson, B., & Pechman, E. M. (1981). *Evaluating utilization: A bibliography*. New Orleans: New Orleans Public Schools.

King, J. A., Thompson, B., & Pechman, E. M. (1982). *Improving evaluation use in local schools*. (Final Report for NIE-G-80–0082). New Orleans: New Orleans Public Schools.

Kiresuk, T. J., Smith, A., & Cardillo, J. E. (Eds.). (1994). *Goal attainment scaling: Applications, theory, and measurement*. Hillsdale, NJ: Lawrence Erlbaum.

Kirkhart, K. E. (2000). Reconceptualizing evaluation use: An integrated theory of influence. In V. J. Caracelli & H. Preskill (Eds.), *The expanding scope of evaluation use*. New Directions for Evaluation, No. 88. San Francisco: Jossey-Bass.

Kirkpatrick, D. L. (1977). Evaluating training programs: Evidence vs. proof. *Training and Development Journal, 31,* 9–12.

Kirkpatrick, D. L. (1983). Four steps to measuring training effectiveness. *Personnel Administrator, 28,* 19–25.

Kirkwood, R. (1982). Accreditation. In H. E. Mitzel (Ed.), *Encyclopedia of educational research* (Vol. 1, 5th ed.). New York: Free Press.

Kitchener, K. S. (1984). Intuition, critical thinking, and ethical principles: The foundation of ethical decisions in counseling psychology. *Counseling Psychologist, 12,* 43–55.

Kourilsky, M., & Baker, E. (1976). An experimental comparison of interaction, advocacy, and adversary evaluation. *Center on Evaluation, Development, and Research (CEDR) Quarterly, 9,* 4–8.

Krathwohl, D. R., Bloom, B. S., & Masia, B. B. (1964). *Taxonomy of educational objectives: Handbook II. Affective domain*. New York: David McKay.

Krueger, R. A., & Casey, M. (2000). *Focus groups: A practical guide for applied research* (3rd ed.). Thousand Oaks, CA: Sage.

Kvale, S. (1996). *InterViews: An introduction to qualitative research interviewing*. Thousand Oaks, CA: Sage.

Lackey, J. F., Moberg, D. P., & Balistrieri, M. (1997). By whose standards? Reflections on empowerment evaluation and grassroots groups. *Evaluation Practice, 18*(2), 137–146.

Lavrakas, P. J. (1987). *Telephone survey methods: Sampling, selection, and supervision.* Newbury Park, CA: Sage.

Lawler, E. E., III, Mohrman, S. A., & Ledford, G. E., Jr. (1992). *Employee involvement and Total Quality Management: Practices and results in Fortune 1000 companies.* San Francisco: Jossey-Bass.

Layard, R., & Glaister, S. (Eds.). (1994). *Cost–benefit analysis.* New York: Cambridge University Press.

LDP Associates, Inc. (1986). *What companies do to evaluate the effectiveness of training programs.* Gardner, MA: Author.

Lee, A. M., & Holly, F. R. (1978, April). *Communicating evaluation information: Some practical tips that work.* Paper presented at the annual meeting of the American Educational Research Association, Toronto.

Lessinger, L. M., & Tyler, R. W. (Eds.). (1971). *Accountability in education.* Worthington, OH: Charles A. Jones.

Lester, P. E., & Bishop, L. K. (2000). *Handbook of tests and measurement in education and the social sciences* (2nd ed.). Lanham, MD: Scarecrow.

Levin, H. M, & McEwan, P. J. (2001). *Cost-effectiveness analysis: Methods and applications.* Thousand Oaks, CA: Sage.

Levin, H. M., Glass, G. V., & Meister, G. R. (1987). Cost-effectiveness of computer-assisted instruction. *Evaluation Review, 11,* 50–72.

Levine, M., Brown, E., Fitzgerald, C., Goplerud, E., Gordon, M. E., Jayne-Lararus, C., Rosenberg, N., & Slater, J. (1978). Adapting the jury trial for program evaluation: A report of an experience. *Evaluation and Program Planning, 1,* 177–186.

Levitan, S. A. (1992). *Evaluation of federal social programs: An uncertain impact.* Washington, DC: George Washington University Center for Social Policy Studies.

Leviton, L. C., & Hughes, E. F. X. (1981). Research on the utilization of evaluations: A review and synthesis. *Evaluation Review, 5,* 524–548.

Light, R. J. (Ed.). (1983). *Evaluation studies review annual* (Vol. 8). Beverly Hills, CA: Sage.

Light, R. J., & Smith, P. V. (1970). Choosing a future: Strategies for designing and evaluating new programs. *Harvard Educational Review, 40,* 1–28.

Lincoln, Y. S. (1991). The arts and sciences of program evaluation. *Evaluation Practice, 12,* 1–8.

Lincoln, Y. S., & Guba, E. (1981, October). *Do evaluators wear grass skirts? "Going native" and ethnocentrism as problems in utilization.* Paper presented at the annual meeting of the Evaluation Research Society, Austin, TX.

Lincoln, Y. S., & Guba, E. G. (1985). *Naturalistic inquiry.* Beverly Hills, CA: Sage.

Lincoln, Y. S., & Guba, E. G. (1992). In response to Lee Sechrest's 1991 AEA presidential address: Roots: Back to our first generation. *Evaluation Practice, 13,* 165–170.

Lincoln, Y. S., & Guba, E. G. (1994). RSVP: We are pleased to accept your invitation. *Evaluation Practice, 13,* 179–192.

Lipsey, M. W. (1990). *Design sensitivity: Statistical power for experimental research.* Newbury Park, CA: Sage.

Lipsey, M. W. (2000). Method and rationality are not social diseases. *American Journal of Evaluation, 21,* 221–224.

Louis, K. S. (1982). Multisite/multimethod studies: An introduction. *American Behavorial Scientist, 26,* 6–22.

Love, A. J. (1991). *Internal evaluation: Building organizations from within.* Newbury Park, CA: Sage.

Love, A. J. (2001). The future of evaluation: Catching rocks with cauldrons. *American Journal of Evaluation, 22,* 437–444.

Lovich, N. P. (1990). Performance appraisal. In S. W. Hays & R. C. Kearney (Eds.), *Public personnel administration: Problems and prospects.* Englewood Cliffs, NJ: Prentice-Hall.

Lyman, D. R., Milich, R., Zimmerman, R., Novak, S. P., Logan, T. K., Martin, C. (1999). Project DARE: No effects at 10-year follow-up. *Journal of Consulting and Clinical Psychology, 67,* 590–593.

Mabry, L. (1999). Circumstantial ethics. *American Journal of Evaluation, 20,* 199–212.

MacDonald, G., Starr, G., Schooley, M., Yee, S. L., Klimowski, K. Turner, K. (2001). *Introduction to program evaluation for comprehensive tobacco control programs.* Atlanta: Centers for Disease Control and Prevention.

MacDonald, J. B. (1974). An evaluation of evaluation. *Urban Review, 7,* 3–14.

MacDonald, J. B. (1976). Evaluation and the control of education. In D. Tawney (Ed.), *Curriculum evaluation today: Trends and implications.* Schools Council Research Studies Series. London: Macmillan.

Madaus, G. F. (1982). The clarification hearing: A personal view of the process. *Educational Researcher, 11*(1), 4, 6–11.

Madaus, G. F. (1983). *The courts, validity, and minimum competency testing.* Boston: Kluwer-Nijhoff.

Madaus, G. F., Scriven, M., & Stufflebeam, D. L. (Eds.). (1983). *Evaluation models: Viewpoints on educational and human services evaluation.* Boston: Kluwer-Nijhoff.

Madaus, G. F., & Stufflebeam, D. L. (Eds.). (1989). *Educational evaluation: Classic works of Ralph W. Tyler.* Boston: Kluwer Academic.

Mager, R. F. (1962). *Preparing instructional objectives.* Palo Alto, CA: Fearon.

Malcolm, C., & Welch, W. (1981). *Case study evaluations: A case in point. An illustrative report and methodological analysis of case study evaluations.* Minneapolis: University of Minnesota, Minnesota Research and Evaluation Center.

Manning, P. K., & Cullum-Swan, B. (1994). Narrative, content, and semiotic analysis. In N. K. Denzin & Y. S. Lincoln (Eds.), *Handbook of qualitative research.* Thousand Oaks, CA: Sage.

Mark, M. M. (2001). Evaluation's future: Furor, futile, or fertile? *American Journal of Evaluation, 22,* 457–480.

Mark, M. M., Henry, G. T., & Julnes, G. (1999). Toward an integrative framework for evaluation practice. *American Journal of Evaluation, 20,* 177–198.

Mark, M. M., & Shotland, R. L. (1985a). *Multiple methods in program evaluation.* New Directions for Program Evaluation, No. 35. San Francisco: Jossey-Bass.

Mark, M. M., & Shotland, R. L. (1985b). Stakeholder-based evaluation and value judgements: The role of perceived power and legitimacy in the selection of stakeholder groups. *Evaluation Review, 9,* 605–626.

Markham, A. N. (1998). *Life online: Researching real experience in virtual space.* Walnut Creek, CA: AltaMira.

Marsden, L. R. (1991, May). *Program evaluations and politicians.* Paper presented at the annual meeting of the Canadian Evaluation Society, Vancouver.

Mathison, S. (1991). Role conflicts for internal evaluators. *Evaluation and Program Planning, 14,* 173–179.

Mathison, S. (1999). Rights, responsibilities, and duties: A comparison of ethics for internal and external evaluators. In J. L. Fitzpatrick & M. Morris (Eds.), *Current and emerging challenges in evaluation.* New Directions for Evaluation, No. 82. San Francisco: Jossey-Bass.

Mathison, S. (2001). What's it like when the participatory evaluator is a "genuine" stakeholder? *American Journal of Evaluation, 22*(1), 29–35.

Maxwell, G. S. (1984). A rating scale for assessing the quality of responsive/illuminative evaluations. *Educational Evaluation and Policy Analysis, 6,* 131–138.

Maxwell, J. A., Bashook, G., & Sandlow, C. J. (1986). Combining ethnographic and experimental methods in educational evaluation. In D. M. Fetterman & M. A. Pitman (Eds.), *Educational evaluation: Ethnography in theory, practice, and politics.* Beverly Hills, CA: Sage.

May, R. M., Fleischer, M., Scheirer, C. J., & Cox, G. B. (1986). Directory of evaluation training programs. In B. G. Davis (Ed.), *Teaching of evaluation across the disciplines.* New Directions for Program Evaluation, No. 29, 71–98. San Francisco: Jossey-Bass.

Mayeske, G. W. (1995). Letter to the editor. *Evaluation Practice, 16,* 211–212.

McBride, M. E., Bertrand, J. T., Santiso, R., & Fernandez, V. H. (1987). Cost-effectiveness of the APTOGSM program for voluntary surgical contraception in Guatemala. *Evaluation Review, 11,* 300–326.

McCall, R. B., Ryan, C. S., & Green, B. L. (1999). Some non-randomized constructed comparison groups for evaluating age-related outcomes of intervention programs. *American Journal of Evaluation, 2,* 213–226.

McClintock, C. (1987). Conceptual and action heuristics: Tools for the evaluator. In L. Bickman (Ed.), *Using program theory in evaluation.* New Directions for Program Evaluation, No. 33, 43–57. San Francisco: Jossey-Bass.

McCracken, G. (1988). *The long interview.* Qualitative Research Methods Series, no. 13. Newbury Park, CA: Sage.

McCutcheon, G. (1978). Of solar systems, responsibility, and basics: An educational criticism of Mr. Clement's fourth grade. In G. Willis (Ed.), *Qualitative evaluation.* Berkeley, CA: McCutchan.

McDowell, I., & Newell, C. (1987). *Measuring health: A guide to rating scales and questionnaires.* New York: Oxford University Press.

McGee, D., & Starnes, C. (1988). *Evaluation as empowerment: Holistic evaluation across the curriculum.* Quebec, Canada: Research and Development, John Abbott College. (ERIC Document Reproduction Service No. ED 319-425).

McKillip, J. (1987). *Need analysis: Tools for the human services and education.* Newbury Park, CA: Sage.

McKinley, W. (1998). Commentary: Mitroff's ethical management: The colonization of truth. *Journal of Management Inquiry, 7,* (1), 80–85.

Merriam-Webster's Collegiate Dictionary (7th ed.). (1967). Springfield, MA: Merriam-Webster.

Merrow, J. (2001). Undermining standards. *Phi Delta Kappan, 82* (9), 652.

Mertens, D. M. (1994). Training evaluators: Unique skills and knowledge. In J. W. Altschuld & M. Engle (Eds.), *The preparation of professional evaluators: Issues, perspectives, and programs.* New Directions for Program Evaluation, No. 62, 17–27. San Francisco: Jossey-Bass.

Mertens, D. M. (1995). Identifying and respecting differences among participants in evaluation studies. In W. R. Shadish, D. L. Newman, M. A. Scheirer, & C. Wye (Eds.), *Guiding principles for evaluators.* New Directions for Program Evaluation, No. 66, 91–97. San Francisco: Jossey-Bass.

Mertens, D. M. (1999). Inclusive evaluation: Implications of transformative theory for evaluation. *American Journal of Evaluation, 20,* 1–14.

Mertens, D. M. (2001). Inclusivity and transformation: Evaluation in 2010. *American Journal of Evaluation, 22,* 367–374.

Mertens, D. M. & Russon, C. (2000). A proposal for the International Organization for Cooperation in Evaluation. *American Journal of Evaluation, 21,* 275–283.

Metfessel, N. S., & Michael, W. B. (1967). A paradigm involving multiple criterion measures for the evaluation of the effectiveness of school programs. *Educational and Psychological Measurement, 27,* 931–943.

Michalski, G. V., & Cousins, J. B. (2001). Multiple perspectives on training evaluation: Probing stakeholder perceptions in a global network development firm. *American Journal of Evaluation, 22,* 37–53.

Milakovich, M. E. (1991). Total Quality Management in the public sector. *National Productivity Review, 10,* 195–213.

Miles, M. B., & Huberman, A. M. (1984). *Qualitative data analysis: A sourcebook of new methods.* Newbury Park, CA: Sage.

Miles, M. B., & Huberman, A. M. (1994). *Qualitative data analysis* (2nd ed.). Thousand Oaks, CA: Sage.

Mills, A. S., Massey, J. G., & Gregersen, H. M. (1980). Benefit-cost analysis of Voyageurs National Park. *Evaluation Review, 4,* 715–738.

Milward, H. B. (1994). Nonprofit contracting and the hollow state. *Public Administration Review, 54,* 73–77.

Milward, H. B., Provan, K. G., & Smith, L. J. (1994). Human service contracting and coordination: The market for mental health services. In J. L. Perry (Ed.), *Research in public administration* (Vol. 3). Greenwich, CT: JAI.

Mintzberg, H. (1994). *The rise and fall of strategic planning.* New York: Free Press.

Mitchell, R. (1992). *Testing for learning.* New York: Free Press.

Mitroff, I. I. (1998). On the fundamental importance of ethical management: Why management is the most important of all human activities. *Journal of Management Inquiry, 7*(1), 68–79.

Morgan, D. L. (1997). *Focus groups as qualitative research.* Thousand Oaks, CA: Sage.

Morrell, J. A. (2000). Internal evaluation: A synthesis of traditional methods and industrial engineering. *American Journal of Evaluation, 21,* 41–52.

Morris, L. L., & Fitzgibbon, C. T. (1978). *How to deal with goals and objectives.* Beverly Hills, CA: Sage.

Morris, M., & Cohn, R. (1993). Program evaluators and ethical challenges: A national survey. *Evaluation Review, 17,* 621–642.

Morrisett, I., & Stevens, W. W. (1967). *Steps in curriculum analysis outline.* Boulder: University of Colorado, Social Science Education Consortium.

Moss V. D., & Worthen, B. R. (1991). Do personalization and postage make a difference in response rates to surveys of professional populations? *Psychological Reports, 68,* 692–694.

Mowbray, C. T., & Herman, S. E. (1991). Using multiple sites in mental health evaluations: Focus on program theory and implementation issues. In R. S. Turpin & J. M. Sinacore (Eds.), *Multisite evaluations.* New Directions for Program Evaluation, No. 50, 45–57. San Francisco: Jossey-Bass.

Mueller, M. R. (1998). The evaluation of Minnesota's Early Childhood Family Education Program: A dialogue. *American Journal of Evaluation, 19,* 80–99.

National Performance Review. (1993). *Reaching public goals: Managing government for results.* Washington, DC: Government Printing Office.

Nay, J., & Kay, P. (1982). *Government oversight and evaluability assessment.* Lexington, MA: Heath.

Neurath, O., Cernap, R., & Morris, C. (Eds.). (1955). *Fundamentals of the unity of science: Toward an encyclopedia of unified science.* Foundations of the Unity of Science series (Vols. 1–2). Chicago: University of Chicago Press.

Newcomer, K. E. (2001). Tracking and probing program performance: Fruitful path or blind alley for evaluation professionals? *American Journal of Evaluation, 22,* 337–342.

Newman, D. L. (1988, April). *Teachers' willingness to participate in evaluation: The effect of past participation and perceptions of usefulness.* Paper presented at the annual meeting of the American Educational Research Association, New Orleans.

Newman, D. L. (1995). The future of ethics in evaluation: Developing the dialogue. In W. R. Shadish, D. L. Newman, M. A. Scheirer, & C. Wye (Eds.), *Guiding principles for evaluators.* New Directions for Program Evaluation. No. 66, 99–111. San Francisco: Jossey-Bass.

Newman, D. L., & Brown, R. D. (1996). *Applied ethics for program evaluation.* Beverly Hills, CA: Sage.

Nigro, L. G., & Nigro, F. A. (2000). *The new public personnel administration.* Itasca, IL: Peacock.

Nilsson, N., & Hogben, D. (1983). Metaevaluation. In E. R. House (Ed.), *Philosophy of evaluation.* New Directions for Program Evaluation, No. 19, 83–97. San Francisco: Jossey-Bass.

Nowakowski, J., Bunda, M. A., Working, R., Bernacki, G., & Harrington, P. (1985). *A handbook of educational variables.* Boston: KluwerNijhoff.

O'Neill, M. (1989). *The third America: The emergence of the nonprofit sector in the United States.* San Francisco: Jossey-Bass.

Osborne, D., & Gaebler, T. (1992). *Reinventing government: How the entrepreneurial spirit is transforming the public sector.* Reading, MA: Addison-Wesley.

O'Sullivan, E., & Rassel, G. R. (1995). *Research methods for public administrators* (2nd ed.). White Plains, NY: Longman.

O'Sullivan, R. G., & O'Sullivan, J. M. (1994, May). *Evaluation voices: Promoting cluster evaluation from within programs.* Paper presented at the annual meeting of the Canadian Evaluation Society, Montreal, Canada.

O'Sullivan, R. G., & Tennant, C. V. (1993). *Programs for at-risk students: A guide to evaluation.* Newbury Park, CA: Sage.

Owens, T. R. (1971, February). *Application of adversary proceedings for educational evaluation and decision making.* Paper presented at the annual meeting of the American Educational Research Association, New York.

Owens, T. R. (1973). Educational evaluation by adversary proceeding. In E. R. House (Ed.), *School evaluation: The politics and process.* Berkeley, CA: McCutchan.

Palumbo, D. J. (1987). *The politics of program evaluation.* Newbury Park, CA: Sage.

Parlett, M., & Dearden, G. (Eds.). (1977). *Introduction to illumination evaluation: Studies in higher education.* Cardiff-by-the-Sea, CA: Pacific Soundings.

Parlett, M., & Hamilton, D. (1976). Evaluation as illumination: A new approach to the study of in-

novative programs. In G. V. Glass (Ed.), *Evaluation studies review annual* (Vol. 1). Beverly Hills, CA: Sage.

Passamani, E. (1991). Clinical trials: Are they ethical? *New England Journal of Medicine, 324,* 1589–1592.

Patterson, M. (n.d.). *Instructional materials review form.* Tallahassee: Florida State University, Center for Instructional Development and Services.

Patton, M. Q. (1975). *Alternative evaluation research paradigm.* Grand Forks: North Dakota Study Group on Evaluation.

Patton, M. Q. (1986). *Utilization-focused evaluation* (2nd ed.). Beverly Hills, CA: Sage.

Patton, M. Q. (1987a). The evaluator's responsibility for utilization. *Evaluation Practice, 9,* 5–24.

Patton, M. Q. (1987b). *How to use qualitative methods in evaluation.* Newbury Park, CA: Sage.

Patton, M. Q. (1988). Politics and evaluation. *Evaluation Practice, 9,* 89–94.

Patton, M. Q. (1990). The challenge of being a profession. *Evaluation Practice, 11,* 45–51.

Patton, M. Q. (1991). Towards utility in reviews of multivocal literatures. *Review of Educational Research, 61*(3), 287–292.

Patton, M. Q. (1994). Developmental evaluation. *Evaluation Practice, 15*(3), 311–319.

Patton, M. Q. (1996). *Utilization-focused evaluation* (3rd ed.). Thousand Oaks, CA: Sage.

Patton, M. Q. (1997a). Of vacuum cleaners and toolboxes: A response to Fetterman's response. *Evaluation Practice, 18*(3), 267–270.

Patton, M. Q. (1997b). Toward distinguishing empowerment evaluation and placing it in a larger context. *Evaluation Practice, 18*(2), 147–163.

Patton, M. Q. (2000). Overview: Language matters. In R. K. Hopson (Ed.), *How and why language matters in evaluation.* New Directions for Evaluation, No. 86, 5–16. San Francisco: Jossey-Bass.

Patton, M. Q. (2002). *Qualitative evaluation and research methods* (3rd ed.). Thousand Oaks, CA: Sage.

Paulson, S. F. (1964, November). The effects of the prestige of the speaker and acknowledgment of opposing arguments on audience retention and shift of opinion. *Speech Monographs,* pp. 267–271.

Pawson, R., & Tilley, N. (1997). *Realistic evaluation.* Thousand Oaks, CA: Sage.

Perloff, R. E., & Perloff, E. (Eds.). (1980). *Values, ethics, and standards in evaluation.* New Directions for Program Evaluation, No. 7. San Francisco: Jossey-Bass.

Perloff, R. M., Padgett, V. R., & Brock, T. C. (1980). Sociocognitive biases in the evaluation process.

In R. E. Porloff & E. Porloff (Eds.), *Values, ethics, and standards in evaluation.* New Directions for Program Evaluation, No. 7, 11–26. San Francisco: Jossey-Bass.

Perrin, B. (1998). Effective use and misuse of performance measurement. *American Journal of Evaluation, 19,* 367–379.

Perrone, V. (1991). *Expanding student assessment.* Alexandria, VA: Association for Supervision and Curriculm Development.

Peshkin, A. (1993). The goodness of qualitative research. *Educational Researcher, 22,* 23–29.

Peterson, R. A. (2000). *Constructing effective questionnaires.* Thousand Oaks, CA: Sage.

Plake, B. S., & Impara, J. C. (Eds.) (2001). *The fourteenth mental measurements yearbook.* Lincoln, NB: University of Nebraska Press.

Popham, W. J. (1975). *Educational evaluation.* Englewood Cliffs, NJ: Prentice-Hall.

Popham, W. J., & Carlson, D. (1977). Deep dark deficits of the adversary evaluation model. *Educational Researcher, 6*(6), 3–6.

Popham, W. J., Eisner, E. W., Sullivan, H. J., & Tyler, L. L. (1969). *Instructional objectives* (American Educational Research Association Monograph Series on Curriculum Evaluation no. 3). Chicago: Rand McNally.

Posavac, E. J. (1994). Misusing program evaluation by asking the wrong question. In C. J. Stevens & M. Dial (Eds.), *Preventing the misuse of evaluation.* New Directions for Program Evaluation, No. 64, 69–78. San Francisco: Jossey-Bass.

Posavac, E. J., & Carey, R. (1991). *Program evaluation: Methods and case studies.* Englewood Cliffs, NJ: Prentice-Hall.

Preskill, H. & Torres, R. T. (1999). *Evaluative inquiry for learning in organizations.* Thousand Oaks, CA: Sage.

Preskill, H., & Torres, R. T. (2000). The learning dimension of evaluation use. In V. J. Caracelli & H. Preskilll (Eds.), *The expanding scope of evaluation use.* New Directions for Evaluation, No. 88. San Francisco: Jossey-Bass.

Provus, M. M. (1971). *Discrepancy evaluation.* Berkeley, CA: McCutchan.

Provus, M. M. (1973). Evaluation of ongoing programs in the public school system. In B. R. Worthen & J. R. Sanders (Eds.), *Educational evaluation: Theory and practice.* Belmont, CA: Wadsworth.

Rago, W. V. (1994). Adapting Total Quality Management (TQM) to government: Another point of view. *Public Administration Review, 54,* 61–64.

Raizen, S. A., & Rossi, P. H. (1981). *Program evaluation in education: When? How? To what ends?* Washington, DC: National Academy Press.

Rallis, S. F., & Rossman, G. B. (2000). Dialogue for learning: Evaluator as critical friend. In R. K. Hopson (Ed.), *How and why language matters in evaluation.* New Directions for Evaluation, No. 86, 81–92. San Francisco: Jossey-Bass.

Rappaport, J. (1987). Terms of empowerment/exemplars of prevention: Toward a theory for community psychology. *American Journal of Community Psychology, 15*(2), 121–148.

Reichardt, C. S. (1994). Summative evaluation, formative evaluation, and tactical research. *Evaluation Practice, 15,* 275–281.

Reichardt, C. S., & Rallis, S. F. (1994). Qualitative and quantitative inquiries are not incompatible: A call for a new partnership. In C. S. Reichardt & S. F. Rallis (Eds.), *The qualitative-quantitative debate: New perspectives.* New Directions for Program Evaluation, No. 61, 85–91. San Francisco: Jossey-Bass.

Reichardt, C. S., Trochim, W. K., & Cappelleri, J. C. (1995). Reports of the death of regression-discontinuity analysis are greatly exaggerated. *Evaluation Review, 19,* 39–63.

Reineke, R. A. (1991). Stakeholder involvement in evaluation: Suggestions for practice. *Evaluation Practice, 12,* 39–44.

Reinhard, D. (1972). Methodology for input evaluation utilizing advocate and design teams. Unpublished doctoral dissertation, Ohio State University, Columbus.

Richards, R. V. (Ed.). (1995). *Building partnerships: Educating health professionals for the communities they serve.* San Francisco: Jossey-Bass.

Riccio, J. A., & Orenstein, A. (1996). Understanding best practices for operating welfare-to-work programs. *Evaluation Review, 20,* 3–28.

Rice, J. M. (1915). *The people's government: Efficient, bossless, graftless.* Philadelphia: John C. Winston.

Ridings, J. M., & Stufflebeam, D. L. (1981). Evaluation reflections: The project to develop standards for educational evaluation: Its past and future. *Studies in Educational Evaluation, 7,* 3–16.

Ripley, W. K. (1985). Medium of presentation: Does it make a difference in the reception of evaluation information? *Educational Evaluation and Policy Analysis, 7,* 417–425.

Rippey, R. M. (Ed.). (1973). *Studies in transactional evaluation.* Berkeley, CA: McCutchan.

Robinson, D. G., & Robinson, J. C. (1989). *Training for impact: How to link training to business needs and measure the results.* San Francisco: Jossey-Bass.

Rogers, P. J. (2000). Program theory: Not whether programs work but how they work. In D.

Stufflebeam, G. Madaus, and T. Kellaghan (Eds.), *Evaluation models*. Boston: Kluwer Academic.

Rogers, P. J. (2001). The whole world is evaluating half-full glasses. *American Journal of Evaluation, 22,* 431–436.

Rogers, P. J., Hacsi, T., Petrosino, A., & Huebner, T. (Eds.). (2000). *Program theory in evaluation: Challenges and opportunities*. New Directions for Evaluation, No. 87. San Francisco: Jossey-Bass.

Rodgers, P. J., & Worthen, B. R. (April, 1995). *A meta-analysis of factors that influence the response rate of mailed questionnaires*. Presented at the annual meeting of the American Educational Research Association. San Francisco, California.

Rosenbaum, D. (1998). Assessing the effects of school-based drug education: A six-year multilevel analysis of project D.A.R.E. *Journal of Crime and Delinquency, 35,* 381–412.

Rossi, P. H. (1971). Boobytraps and pitfalls in the evaluation of social action programs. In F. G. Caro (Ed.), *Readings in evaluation research*. New York: Sage.

Rossi, P. H., & Freeman, H. E. (1985). *Evaluation: A systematic approach* (3rd ed.). Beverly Hills, CA: Sage.

Rossi, P. H., & Freeman, H. E. (1993). *Evaluation: A systematic approach* (5th ed.). Newbury Park, CA: Sage.

Rossi, P. H., Freeman, H. E., & Lipsey, M. E. (1998). *Evaluation: A systematic approach* (6th ed.). Newbury Park, CA: Sage.

Rossi, P. H., & Wright, J. D. (1985). Social science research and the politics of gun control. In R. L. Shotland & M. M. Mark (Eds.), *Social science and social policy*. Beverly Hills, CA: Sage.

Royse, D. (1992). *Program evaluation*. Chicago: Nelson-Hall.

Rubin, H. J., & Rubin, I. S. (1995). *Qualitative interviewing*. Thousand Oaks, CA: Sage.

Sadler, D. R. (1981). Intuitive data processing as a potential source of bias in naturalistic evaluations. *Educational Evaluation and Policy Analysis, 3,* 25–31.

Salamon, L. M. (1992). *America's nonprofit sector: A primer*. New York: Foundation Center.

Salant, P., & Dillman, D. (1994). *How to conduct your own survey*. New York: John Wiley.

Salkever, D. S., & Frank, R. G. (1992). Health services. In C. T. Clotfelder (Ed.), *Who benefits from the nonprofit sector?* Chicago: University of Chicago Press.

Sanders, J. R. (1979). The technology and art of evaluation. A review of seven evaluation primers. *Evaluation News, 12,* 2–7.

Sanders, J. R. (1982). *A design for improving level 2 and low achieving student performance in the Shaker Heights City School District*. Kalamazoo: Western Michigan University, Evaluation Center.

Sanders, J. R. (1983). Cost implications of the standards. In M. C. Alkin & L. C. Solman (Eds.), *The cost of evaluation*. Beverly Hills, CA: Sage.

Sanders, J. R. (1995). Standards and principles. In W. R. Shadish, D. L. Newman, M. A. Scheirer, & C. Wye (Eds.) *Guiding principles for evaluators*. New Directions for Program Evaluation, No. 66, 47–52. San Francisco: Jossey-Bass.

Sanders, J. R. (1997). Cluster evaluation. In E. Chelimsky & W. R. Shadish (Eds.), *Evaluation for the 21st century: A resource book*. Thousand Oaks, CA: Sage.

Sanders, J. (2000). *Evaluating school programs*. (2nd ed.) Thousand Oaks, CA: Corwin.

Sanders, J. R. (2002). A vision for evaluation. *American Journal of Evaluation, 22,* 363–366.

Sanders, J. (2002). Presidential address: On mainstreaming evaluation. *American Journal of Evaluation, 25*(3), 253–259.

Sanders, J. R., & Cunningham, D. J. (1973). A structure for formative evaluation in product development. *Review of Educational Research, 43,* 217–236.

Sanders, J. R., & Cunningham, D. J. (1974). Techniques and procedures for formative evaluation. In G. D. Borich (Ed.), *Evaluating educational programs and products*. Englewood Cliffs, NJ: Educational Technology.

Sanders, J. R., & Nafziger, D. (1976). *A basis for determining the adequacy of evaluation designs*. Occasional Paper Series, Paper No. 6. Kalamazoo, MI: Western Michigan University Evaluation Center.

Sanders, J. R., & Sachse, T. P. (1977). Applied performance testing in the classroom. *Journal of Research and Development in Education, 10,* 92–104.

Schaefer, D. R., & Dillman, D. A. (1998). Development of a standard E-mail methodology. *Public Opinion Quarterly, 62,* 3787–397.

Schmitz, C. C. (1994). What kind of evaluation is the CBPH cluster evaluation? (Mimeo, 3 pp.)

Schmoker, M., & Marzano, R. J. (1999). Realizing the promise of standards-based education. *Educational Leadership, 56,* 17–21.

Schnoes, C. J., Murphy-Berman, V., & Chambers, J. M. (2000). Empowerment evaluation applied: Experiences, analysis and recommendations from a case study. *American Journal of Evaluation, 21,* 53–64.

Schofield, J. W., & Anderson, K. M. (1984). *Combining quantitative and qualitative methods in research on ethnic identity and intergroup relations.* Paper presented at the Society for Research on Child Development, Study Group on Ethnic Socialization, Los Angeles.

Schwandt, T. A. (1998). Commentary: Moral demands and strong evaluation. *American Journal of Evaluation, 19*, 227–229.

Schwandt, T. A. (2000). What ails evaluation practice. *American Journal of Evaluation, 21*, 225–229.

Schwandt, T. A. (2001). Responsiveness and everyday life. In J. C. Greene & T. A. Abma (Eds.), *Responsive evaluation.* New Directions for Evaluation, No. 92, 73–88. San Francisco: Jossey-Bass.

Schwartz, S., & Baum, S. (1992). Education. In C. T. Clotfelder (Ed.), *Who benefits from the nonprofit sector?* Chicago: University of Chicago Press.

Scott, A., & Sechrest, L. (1992). Theory-driven approaches to benefit cost analysis: Implications of program theory. In H. Chen & P. H. Rossi (Eds.), *Using theory to improve program and policy evaluations.* New York: Greenwood.

Scottish Council for Research in Education. (1990). The evaluation of educational programmes: Methods, uses, and benefits: Part A, Volume 24. *Report of the Educational Research Workshop.* North Berwick, Scotland, November 22–25, 1988. Bristol, PA: Taylor & Francis.

Scriven, M. (1967). The methodology of evaluation. In R. E. Stake (Ed.), *Curriculum evaluation.* (American Educational Research Association Monograph Series on Evaluation, No. 1, pp. 39–83). Chicago: Rand McNally.

Scriven, M. (1972). Pros and cons about goal-free evaluation. *Evaluation Comment, 3*, 1–7.

Scriven, M. (1973). The methodology of evaluation. In B. R. Worthen & J. R. Sanders (Eds.), *Educational evaluation: Theory and practice.* Belmont, CA: Wadsworth.

Scriven, M. (1974a). Evaluation perspectives and procedures. In W. J. Popham (Ed.), *Evaluation in education.* Berkeley, CA: McCutchan.

Scriven, M. (1974b). Standards for the evaluation of educational programs and products. In G. D. Borich (Ed.), *Evaluating educational programs and products.* Englewood Cliffs, NJ: Educational Technology.

Scriven, M. (1976). *The intellectual dimensions of evaluation research.* Paper presented at the fourth annual Pacific Northwest Evaluation Conference, Seattle, WA.

Scriven, M. (1980). *The logic of evaluation.* Interness, CA: Edgepress.

Scriven, M. (1984). Evaluation ideologies. In R. F. Connor, D. G. Altman, & C. Jackson (Eds.), *Evaluation studies review annual* (Vol. 9). Beverly Hills, CA: Sage.

Scriven, M. (1986). New frontiers of evaluation. *Evaluation Practice, 7*, 7–44.

Scriven, M. (1991a). Beyond formative and summative evaluation. In M. W. McLaughlin & D. C. Phillips (Eds.), *Evaluation and education: At quarter century* (pp. 19–64). Ninetieth Yearbook of the National Society for the Study of Education. Chicago: University of Chicago Press.

Scriven, M. (1991b). Key evaluation checklist. In M. Scriven (Ed.), *Evaluation thesaurus.* Thousand Oaks, CA: Sage.

Scriven, M. (1991c). *Evaluation thesaurus* (4th ed.). Newbury Park, CA: Sage.

Scriven, M. (1993). *Hard-won lessons in program evaluation.* New Directions for Program Evaluation, No. 58, 1–107. San Francisco: Jossey-Bass.

Scriven, M. (1994). The final synthesis. *Evaluation Practice, 15*, 367–382.

Scriven, M. (1996). Types of evaluation and types of evaluator. *Evaluation Practice, 17*, 151–162.

Scriven, M. (1997a). Comments on Fetterman's response. *Evaluation Practice, 18*(3), 271–272.

Scriven, M. (1997b). Empowerment evaluation examined. *Evaluation Practice, 18*(2), 165–175.

Scriven, M. (2002). Key evaluation checklist. [On-line.] Available: www.wmich.edu/evalctr/checklists.

Sechrest, L. (Ed.). (1980). *Training program evaluators.* New Directions for Program Evaluation, No. 8, San Francisco: Jossey-Bass.

Sechrest, L. (1985). Observer studies: Data collection by remote control. In L. Burstein, H. E. Freeman, & P. H. Rossi (Eds.), *Collecting evaluation data.* Beverly Hills, CA: Sage.

Sechrest, L. (1992). Roots: Back to our first generation. *Evaluation Practice, 13*, 1–7.

Sechrest, L., & Figueredo, A. J. (1993). Program evaluation. *Annual Review of Psychology, 44*, 645–674.

Shadish, W. R. (1993). Critical multiplism: A research strategy and its attendant tactics. In L. Sechrest (Ed.), *Program evaluation: A pluralistic enterprise.* New Directions for Program Evaluation, No. 60, 13–57. San Francisco: Jossey-Bass.

Shadish, W. R. (1994). Need-based evaluation theory: What do you need to know to do good evaluation? *Evaluation Practice, 15*, 347–358.

Shadish, W. R., Cook, T. D., & Campbell, D. T. (2002). *Experimental and quasi-experimental designs for generalized causal inference.* Boston, MA: Houghton Mifflin.

Shadish, W. R., Cook, T. D., & Leviton, L. C. (1991). *Foundations of program evaluation.* Newbury Park, CA: Sage.

Shadish, W. R., Newman, D. L., Scheirer, M. A., & Wye, C. (Eds.). (1995). *Guiding principles for evaluators.* New Directions for Program Evaluation, No. 66. San Francisco: Jossey-Bass.

Shotland, R. L., & Mark, M. M. (1987). Improving inferences from multiple methods. In M. M. Mark & R. L. Shotland (Eds.), *Multiple methods in program evaluation.* New Directions for Program Evaluation, No. 35. San Francisco: Jossey-Bass.

Shulman, L. S. (1985). Peer reviews: The many sides of virtue. *Educational Researcher, 14,* 12–13.

Sieber, J. E. (1980). Being ethical: Professional and personal decisions in program evaluation. In R. E. Perloff & E. Perloff (Eds.), *Values, ethics, and standards in evaluation.* New Directions for Program Evaluation, No. 7, 51–61. San Francisco: Jossey-Bass.

Simon, A., & Boyer, E. G. (1974). *Mirrors for behavior III: An anthology of observation instruments.* Philadelphia: Research for Better Schools.

Sinacore, J. M., & Turpin, R. S. (1991). Multiple sites in evaluation research: A survey of organizational and methodological issues. In R. S. Turpin & J. M. Sinacore (Eds.), *Multisite evaluations.* New Directions for Program Evaluation, No. 50, 5–18. San Francisco: Jossey-Bass.

Sjoberg, G. (1975). Politics, ethics, and evaluation research. In M. Guttentag & E. L. Struening (Eds.), *Handbook of evaluation research* (Vol. 2). Beverly Hills, CA: Sage.

Skaburskis, A. (1987). Cost-benefit analysis: Ethics and problem boundaries. *Evaluation Review, 11,* 591–611.

Smith, E. R., & Tyler, R. W. (1942). *Appraising and recording student progress.* New York: Harper & Row.

Smith, M. F. (1989). *Evaluability assessment: A practical approach.* Boston: Kluwer Academic.

Smith, M. F. (1994). Evaluation: Review of the past, preview of the future. *Evaluation Practice, 15,* 215–227.

Smith, M. F. (1999). Participatory evaluation: Not working or not tested? *American Journal of Evaluation, 20*(2), 295–308.

Smith, M. F. (2001). Evaluation: Preview of the future #2. *American Journal of Evaluation, 22,* 281–300.

Smith, N. L. (Ed.). (1981). *Metaphors for evaluation: Sources of new methods: New perspectives in evaluation* (Vol. 1). Beverly Hills, CA: Sage.

Smith, N. L. (1983). *Dimensions of moral and ethical problems in evaluation* (Paper and Report Series No. 92). Portland, OR: Northwest Regional Educational Laboratory, Research on Evaluation Program.

Smith, N. L. (1985). *Adversary and committee hearings as evaluation methods* (Paper and Report Series No. 110). Portland, OR: Northwest Regional Educational Laboratory, Research on Evaluation Program.

Smith, N. L. (1997, November). *An investigative framework for characterizing evaluation practice.* In N. L. Smith (Chair), Examining evaluation practice. Symposium conducted at the meeting of the American Evaluation Association, San Diego, CA.

Smith, N. L. (1998). Professional reasons for declining an evaluation contract. *American Journal of Evaluation, 19,* 177–190.

Smith, P. C., & Kendall, L. M. (1963). Retranslation of expectations: An approach to the construction of unambiguous anchors for rating scales. *Journal of Applied Psychology, 47,* 149–155.

Smith, R. (1984). *The new aesthetic curriculum theorists and their astonishing ideas: Some actual observations.* (The Monograph Series). Vancouver, Canada: University of British Columbia, Center for the Study of Curriculum and Instruction.

Smith, S. R., & Lipsky, M. (1993). *Non-profits for hire: The welfare state in the age of contracting.* Cambridge: Harvard University Press.

Sonnichsen, R. C. (2000). *High impact internal evaluation.* Thousand Oaks, CA: Sage.

Spiegel, A. N., Bruning, R. H., & Giddings, L. (1999). Using responsive evaluation to evaluate a professional conference. *American Journal of Evaluation, 20,* 57–67.

Spindler, G. (Ed.). (1982). *Doing the ethnography of schooling.* New York: Holt, Rinehart, & Winston.

Stake, R. E. (1967). The countenance of educational evaluation. *Teachers College Record, 68,* 523–540.

Stake, R. E. (1969). Evaluation design, instrumentation, data collection, and analysis of data. In J. L. Davis (Ed.), *Educational evaluation.* Columbus, OH: State Superintendent of Public Instruction.

Stake, R. E. (1970). Objectives, priorities, and other judgment data. *Review of Educational Research, 40,* 181–212.

Stake, R. E. (1972). Responsive evaluation. Unpublished manuscript.

Stake, R. E. (1975a). *Evaluating the arts in education: A responsive approach.* Columbus, OH: Merrill.

Stake, R. E. (1975b). *Program evaluation, particularly responsive evaluation* (Occasional Paper No. 5).

Kalamazoo: Western Michigan University Evaluation Center.

Stake, R. E. (1978). The case study method in social inquiry. *Educational Researcher, 7,* 5–8.

Stake, R. E. (1980). Program evaluation, particularly responsive evaluation. In W. B. Dockrell & D. Hamilton (Eds.), *Rethinking educational research.* London: Hodeder & Stoughton.

Stake, R. E. (1981). Case study methodology: An epistemological advocacy. In W. Welch (Ed.), *Case study methodology in educational evaluation.* Minneapolis: Minnesota Research and Evaluation Center.

Stake, R. E. (1988). Case study methods in educational research: Seeking sweet water. In R. M. Jaeger (Ed.), *Complementary methods for research in education.* Washington, DC: American Educational Research Association.

Stake, R. E. (1991). Retrospective on "The countenance of educational evaluation." In M. W. McLaughlin & D. C. Phillips (Eds.), *Evaluation and education: At quarter century.* Ninetieth Yearbook of the National Society for the Study of Education, Part II. Chicago: University of Chicago Press.

Stake, R. E. (1992). A housing project school. In J. Nowakowski, M. Stewart, & W. Quinn (Eds.), *Monitoring implementation of the Chicago Public Schools' systemwide school reform goals and objectives plan.* Oakbrook, IL: North Central Regional Educational Laboratory.

Stake, R. E. (1994). Case studies. In N. K. Denzin & Y. S. Lincoln (Eds.), *Handbook of qualitative research.* Thousand Oaks, CA: Sage.

Stake, R. E. (1995). *The art of case study research.* Thousand Oaks, CA: Sage.

Stake, R. E. (2000a). Case studies. In N. K. Denzin & Y. S. Lincoln (Eds.), *Handbook of qualitative research* (2nd edition). Thousand Oaks, CA: Sage.

Stake, R. E. (2000b). A modest commitment to the promotion of democracy. In K. E. Ryan & L. DeStefano (Eds.), *Evaluation as a democratic process: Promoting inclusion, dialogue, and deliberation.* New Directions for Evaluation, No. 85, 97–106. San Francisco: Jossey-Bass.

Stake, R. E., & Gjerde, C. (1974). An evaluation of T-CITY, The Twin City Institute for Talented Youth. In R. H. P. Kraft, L. M. Smith, R. A. Pohland, C. J. Brauner, & C. Gjerde (Eds.), *Four evaluation examples: Anthropological, economic, narrative, and portrayal* (AERA Monograph Series on Curriculum Evaluation No. 7). Chicago: Rand McNally.

Stenzel, N. (1976). *Adversary processes and their potential use in evaluation for the Illinois Office of Education.* Springfield, IL: Illinois Department of Education.

Stenzel, N. (1982). Committee hearings as an evaluation format. In N. L. Smith (Ed.), *Field assessments of innovative evaluation methods.* New Directions for Program Evaluation, No. 13, 83–100. San Francisco: Jossey-Bass.

Stephan, A. S. (1935). *Prospects and possibilities: The New Deal and the new social research.* Chapel Hill: University of North Carolina Press.

Strauss, A., & Corbin, J. M. (1998). *Basics of qualitative research: Techniques and procedures for developing grounded theory.* Thousand Oaks, CA: Sage.

Stufflebeam, D. L. (1968). *Evaluation as enlightenment for decision making.* Columbus: Ohio State University Evaluation Center.

Stufflebeam, D. L. (1971). The relevance of the CIPP evaluation model for educational accountability. *Journal of Research and Development in Education, 5,* 19–25.

Stufflebeam, D. L. (1973a). Excerpts from "Evaluation as enlightenment for decision making." In B. R. Worthen & J. R. Sanders (Eds.), *Educational evaluation: Theory and practice.* Belmont, CA: Wadsworth.

Stufflebeam, D. L. (1973b). An introduction to the PDK book: Educational evaluation and decision-making. In B. R. Worthen & J. R. Sanders (Eds.), *Educational evaluation: Theory and practice.* Belmont, CA: Wadsworth.

Stufflebeam, D. L. (1974). *Metaevaluation* (Occasional Paper No. 3). Kalamazoo: Western Michigan University Evaluation Center.

Stufflebeam, D. L. (1977, April). Working paper on needs assessment in evaluation. Paper presented at the American Educational Research Association Evaluation Conference, San Francisco.

Stufflebeam, D. L. (1981). A review of progress in educational evaluation. Paper presented at the annual meeting of the Evaluation Network, Austin, TX.

Stufflebeam, D. L. (1991). Professional standards and ethics for evaluators. In M. W. McLaughlin & D. C. Phillips (Eds.), *Evaluation and education: At quarter century.* Ninetieth Yearbook of the National Society for the Study of Education, Part II. Chicago: University of Chicago Press.

Stufflebeam, D. L. (1994). Empowerment evaluation, objectivist evaluation, and evaluation standards: Where the future of evaluation should not go and where it needs to go. *Evaluation Practice, 15,* 321–338.

Stufflebeam, D. L. (2000). Lessons in contracting for evaluations. *American Journal of Evaluation, 21,* 293–314.

Stufflebeam, D. L. (2001a). Evaluation checklists: Practical tools for guiding and judging evaluations. *American Journal of Evaluation, 22,* 71–79.

Stufflebeam, D. L. (2001b). *Evaluation models.* New Directions for Evaluation, No. 89. San Francisco: Jossey-Bass.

Stufflebeam, D. L., Foley, W. J., Gephart, W. J., Guba, E. G., Hammond, R. L., Merriman, H. O., & Provus, M. M. (1971). *Educational evaluation and decision making.* Itasca, IL: Peacock.

Stufflebeam, D. L., Madaus, G., and Kellaghan, T. (Eds.). (2000). *Evaluation models.* Boston: Kluwer Academic.

Stufflebeam, D. L., & Shinkfield, A. J. (1985). *Systematic evaluation.* Boston: Kluwer-Nijhoff.

Suarez, T. (1981). A planning guide for the evaluation of educational programs. Unpublished manuscript, Chapel Hill, University of North Carolina.

Suarez, T. (1990, November). *Living with the mixed message: The effect of government-sponsored evaluation requirements on the practice of evaluation.* Paper presented at the annual meeting of the American Evaluation Association, Washington, DC.

Suchman, E. (1967). *Evaluative research.* New York: Sage.

Sudman, S., & Bradburn, N. M. (1982). *Asking questions: A practical guide to questionnaire design.* San Francisco: Jossey-Bass.

Sullivan, P. (2000). Futile resistance. *Reason, 31* (8), 12.

Swanson, R. A. (1987). Training technology system: A method for identifying and solving training problems in industry and business. *Journal of Industrial Teacher Education, 24,* 7–17.

Swanson, R. A. (1989). Everything important in business and industry is evaluated. In R. O. Brinkerhoff (Ed.), *Evaluating training programs in business and industry.* New Directions for Program Evaluation, No. 44, 71–82. San Francisco: Jossey-Bass.

Sweetland, R. C., & Keyser, D. J. (1986). *Tests: A comprehensive reference for assessments in psychology, education, and business.* Kansas City, MO: Test Corporation of America.

Swiss, J. (1992). Adapting Total Quality Management to government. *Public Administration Review, 52,* 356–362.

Sylvia, R. D. (1994). *Public personnel administration.* Belmont, CA: Wadsworth.

Sylvia, R. D., Meier, K. J., & Gunn, E. M. (1985). *Program planning and evaluation for the public manager.* Monterey, CA: Brooks/Cole.

Tallmadge, G. K. (1977). *Ideabook: JDRP* (ERIC DL 48329). Washington, DC: U.S. Government Printing Office.

Tallmadge, G. K., & Wood, C. T. (1976). *Users guide: ESEA Title I evaluation and reporting system.* Mountain View, CA: RMC Research Corporation.

Talmage, H. (1982). Evaluation of programs. In H. E. Mitzel (Ed.), *Encyclopedia of educational research* (5th ed.). New York: Free Press.

Tandon, R. (1981). Participatory research in the empowerment of people. *Convergence, 14*(3), 20–29.

Tash, W. R., & Stahler, G. J. (1984). Current status of quality assurance in mental health. *American Behavioral Scientist, 27,* 608–630.

Tessmer, M., & Wedman, J. (1992, April). *The practice of instructional design: A survey of what designers do, don't do, and why they don't do it.* Paper presented at the annual meeting of the American Educational Research Association, San Francisco.

Tharp, R. G., & Gallimore, R. (1979). The ecology of program research and evaluation: A model of evaluation succession. In L. Sechrest, S. G. West, M. A. Phillips, R. Rechner, & W. Yeaton (Eds.), *Evaluation Studies Review Annual, 4,* 39–60.

Thompson, B. (1994, April). *The revised Program Evaluation Standards and their correlation with the evaluation use literature.* Paper presented at the annual meeting of the American Educational Research Association, New Orleans.

Thompson, M. S. (1980). *Benefit-cost analysis for program evaluation.* Beverly Hills, CA: Sage.

Thompson, S. (2001). The authentic standards movement and its evil twin. *Phi Delta Kappan, 82*(5), 358–362.

Tittle, C. K. (1984, April). *Professional standards and equity: The role of evaluators and researchers.* Paper presented at the annual meeting of the American Educational Research Association, New Orleans.

Travers, R. M. W. (1983). *How research has changed American schools.* Kalamazoo, MI: Mythos Press.

Trochim, W. M. K. (1984). *Research design for program evaluation: The regression–discontinuity approach.* Newbury Park, CA: Sage.

Trochim, W. M. K., & Linton, R. (1986). Conceptualization for planning and evaluation. *Evaluation and Program Planning, 9,* 289–308.

Turner, S. D., Hartman, J., Nielsen, L. A., & Lombana, J. (1988). Fostering utilization through multiple data-gathering methods. *Studies in Educational Evaluation, 14,* 113–133.

Turpin, R. S., & Sinacore, J. M. (Eds.). (1991). *Multisite evaluations.* New Directions for Program Evaluation, No. 50. San Francisco: Jossey-Bass.

Tushnet, N. C. (1995, April). *Toward a general approach to multisite program evaluation.* Paper presented at the annual meeting of the American Educational Research Association, San Francisco. (ERIC no. 383 733)

Tyler, R. W. (1942). General statement on evaluation. *Journal of Educational Research, 35,* 492–501.

Tyler, R. W. (1950). *Basic principles of curriculum and instruction.* Chicago: University of Chicago Press.

Tyler, R. W. (1991). General statement on program evaluation. In M. W. McLaughlin & D. C. Phillips (Eds.), *Evaluation and education: At quarter century.* Ninetieth Yearbook of the National Society for the Study of Education, Part II. Chicago: University of Chicago Press.

United Way of America. (1996). *Measuring program outcomes.* Alexandria, VA: United Way of America.

U.S. Department of Health and Human Services, Office for Substance Abuse Prevention. (1991). *Prevention plus III.* Rockville, MD: Author.

U.S. General Accounting Office. (1992). *Quality management: A survey of federal organizations.* Washington, DC: Author.

Vallance, E. (1978). Scanning horizons and looking at weeks: A critical description of "The Great Plains Experience." In G. Willis (Ed.), *Qualitative evaluation.* Berkeley, CA: McCutchan.

Van Mondfrans, A. (1985). Guidelines for reporting evaluation findings. Unpublished manuscript, Brigham Young University, College of Education, Provo, UT.

Vaughn, S., Schumm, J. S., & Sinagub, J. M. (1996). *Focus group interviews in education and psychology.* Thousand Oaks, CA: Sage.

Vroom, P. E., Colombo, M., & Nahan, N. (1994). Confronting ideology and self-interest: Avoiding misuse of evaluation. In C. J. Stevens & M. Dial (Eds.), *Preventing the misuse of evaluation.* New Directions for Program Evaluation, No. 64, 49–59. San Francisco: Jossey-Bass.

Wachtman, E. L. (1978, March). *Evaluation as a story: The narrative quality of educational evaluation.* Paper presented at the annual meeting of the American Educational Research Association, Toronto, Canada.

Wadsworth, Y. (2001). Becoming responsive—and some consequences for evaluation as dialogue across distance. In J. C. Greene & T. A. Abma (Eds.), *Responsive evaluation.* New Directions for

Program Evaluation, No. 92, 45–58. San Francisco: Jossey-Bass.

Walberg, H. J., & Haertel, G. D. (Eds.). (1990). *The international encyclopedia of educational evaluation.* New York: Pergamon.

Waples, D., & Tyler, R. W. (1930). *Research methods and teacher problems.* New York: Macmillan.

Webb, E. J., Campbell, D. T., Schwartz, R. D., & Sechrest, L. (1966). *Unobtrusive measures: Nonreactive research in the social sciences.* Chicago: Rand McNally.

Weiss, C. H. (1972). *Evaluation research: Methods for assessing program effectiveness.* Englewood Cliffs, NJ: Prentice-Hall.

Weiss, C. H. (1973). Where politics and evaluation research meet. *Evaluation, 1,* 37–45.

Weiss, C. H. (1977). *Using social research in public policy making.* Lexington, MA: Lexington Books.

Weiss, C. H. (1980). Knowledge creep and decision accretion. *Knowledge: Creation, Utilization, Diffusion, 1,* 381–404.

Weiss, C. H. (1984). Toward the future of stakeholder approaches in evaluation. In R. F. Conner, D. G. Altman, & C. Jackson (Eds.), *Evaluation studies review annual* (Vol. 9). Beverly Hills, CA: Sage.

Weiss, C. H. (1987). Evaluating social programs: What have we learned? *Society, 25,* 40–45.

Weiss, C. H. (1991). Evaluation research in the political context: Sixteen years and four administrations later. In M. W. McLaughlin & D. C. Philips (Eds.), *Evaluation and education: At quarter century.* Chicago: University of Chicago Press.

Weiss, C. H. (1993). Politics and evaluation: A reprise in mellower overtones. *Evaluation Practice, 14,* 107–109.

Weiss, C. H. (1997). Theory-based evaluation: Past, present, and future. In D. Rog and D. Fournier (Eds.), *Progress and future directions in Evaluation: Perspectives on theory, practice, and methods.* New Directions for Evaluation, No. 76. San Francisco: Jossey-Bass.

Weiss, C. H. (1998a). *Evaluation.* Upper Saddle River, NJ: Prentice-Hall.

Weiss, C. H. (1998b). Have we learned anything new about the use of evaluation? *American Journal of Evaluation, 19,* 21–33.

Weiss, C. H., & Bucuvalas, M. J. (1980). Truth tests and utility tests: Decision-makers' frames of reference for social science research. *American Sociological Review, 45,* 302–313.

Weitzman, E. A., & Miles, M. B. (1994). *Computer programs for qualitative data analysis.* Thousand Oaks, CA: Sage.

Whitmore, E. (Ed.). (1998). *Understanding and practicing participatory evaluation.* New Directions for Evaluation, No. 80. San Francisco: Jossey-Bass.

Wholey, J. S. (1983). *Evaluation and effective public management.* Boston: Little, Brown.

Wholey, J. S. (1986). Using evaluation to improve government performance. *Evaluation Practice, 7,* 5–13.

Wholey, J. S. (1987). Evaluability assessment: Developing program theory. In L. Bickman (Ed.), *Using program theory in evaluation.* New Directions for Program Evaluation, No. 33, 77–92. San Francisco: Jossey-Bass.

Wholey, J. S. (1994). Assessing the feasibility and likely usefulness of evaluation. In J. S. Wholey, H. P. Hatry, & K. E. Newcomer (Eds.), *Handbook of practical program evaluation.* San Francisco: Jossey-Bass.

Wholey, J. S. (1996). Formative and summative evaluation: Related issues in performance measurement. *Evaluation Practice, 17,* 145–149.

Wholey, J. S., Hatry, H. P., & Newcomer, K. E. (Eds.). (1994). *Handbook of practical program evaluation.* San Francisco: Jossey-Bass.

Wholey, J. S., & White, B. F. (1973). Evaluation's impact on Title I elementary and secondary education program management. *Evaluation, 1,* 73–76.

Whyte, W. F. (Ed.). (1991). *Participatory action research.* Thousand Oaks, CA: Sage.

Williams, A., & Giardina, E. (Eds.). (1993). *The theory and practice of cost-benefit analysis.* Brookfield, VT: Edward Elgar.

Winston, J. (1999). Understanding performance measurement: A response to Perrin. *American Journal of Evaluation, 20,* 95–100.

Winston, J. A. (1995). Defining program. An E-mail message sent by Jerome Winston (Director of Program for Public Sector Evaluation, Royal Melbourne Institute of Technology, Victoria, Australia) to multiple recipients of the American Evaluation Association Discussion List, EvalTalk, July 25, 1995.

Witkin, B. R., & Altschuld, J. W. (1995). *Planning and conducting needs assessments.* Thousand Oaks, CA: Sage.

Wolcott, H. (1976). Criteria for an ethnographic approach to research in schools. In J. T. Roberts & S. K. Akinsanga (Eds.), *Schooling in the cultural context.* New York: David McKay.

Wolf, R. L. (1975). Trial by jury: A new evaluation method. *Phi Delta Kappan, 57,* 185–187.

Wolf, R. L. (1979). The use of judicial evaluation methods in the formulation of educational policy. *Educational Evaluation and Policy Analysis, 1,* 19–28.

Wolf, R. L., & Tymitz, B. (1977). Toward more natural inquiry in education. *Center on Evaluation, Development, and Research (CEDR) Quarterly, 10,* 7–9.

Worthen, B. R. (1972, April). *Impediments to the practice of educational evaluation.* Paper presented at the annual meeting of the American Educational Research Association, Chicago.

Worthen, B. R. (1975). Competencies for educational research and evaluation. *Educational Researcher, 4,* 13–16.

Worthen, B. R. (1977, April). *Eclecticism and evaluation models: Snapshots of an elephant's anatomy?* Paper presented at the annual meeting of the American Educational Research Association, New York.

Worthen, B. R. (1978, April). *Metaphors and methodologies for evaluation.* Paper presented at the annual meeting of the American Educational Research Association, Toronto, Canada.

Worthen, B. R. (1981). Journal entries of an eclectic evaluator. In R. S. Brandt (Ed.), *Applied strategies for curriculum evaluation.* Alexandria, VA: Association for Supervision and Curriculum Development.

Worthen, B. R. (1994). Is evaluation a mature profession that warrants the preparation of evaluation professionals? In J. W. Altschuld & M. Engle (Eds.), *The preparation of professional evaluators: Issues, perspectives, and programs.* New Directions for Program Evaluation, No. 62, 3–15. San Francisco: Jossey-Bass.

Worthen, B. R. (1995). Some observations about the institutionalization of evaluation. *Evaluation Practice, 16,* 29–36.

Worthen, B. R. (1996). A survey of *Evaluation Practice* readers. *Evaluation Practice, 17,* 85–90.

Worthen, B. R. (1999). Critical challenges confronting certification of evaluators. *American Journal of Evaluation, 20,* 533–555.

Worthen, B. R. (2001). Whither evaluation? That all depends. *American Journal of Evaluation, 22,* 409–498.

Worthen, B. R., Borg, W. R., & White, K. R. (1993). *Measurement and evaluation in the schools.* White Plains, NY: Longman.

Worthen, B. R., & Matsumoto, A. (1994, November). *Conceptual challenges confronting cluster evaluation.* Paper presented at the annual meeting of the American Evaluation Association, Boston.

Worthen, B. R., & Sanders, J. R. (1973). *Educational evaluation: Theory and practice.* Belmont, CA: Wadsworth.

Worthen, B. R., & Sanders, J. R. (1984). *Content specialization and educational evaluation: A necessary marriage?* (Occasional Paper No. 14). Kalamazoo: Western Michigan University, Evaluation Center.

Worthen, B. R., & Sanders, J. R. (1987). *Educational evaluation: Alternative approaches and practical guidelines.* New York: Longman.

Worthen, B. R., Sanders, J. R., & Fitzpatrick, J. L. (1997). *Program evaluation: Alternative approaches and practical guidelines* (2nd ed.). New York: Longman.

Worthen, B. R., & Schmitz, C. C. (1997). Conceptual challenges confronting cluster evaluation. *Evaluation: The International Journal of Evaluation, 3,* 300–319.

Worthen, B. R., & Valcarce, R. W. (1985). Relative effectiveness of personalized and form covering letters in initial and follow-up mail surveys. *Psychological Reports, 57,* 735–744.

Worthen, B. R., & Van Dusen, L. M. (1992). *Executive summary to a two-year comprehensive assessment of Basic Learning System implementation models.* Logan, UT: Western Institute for Research and Evaluation/Utah State University Department of Psychology.

Worthen, B. R., & White, K. R. (1987). *Evaluating educational and social programs: Guidelines for proposal reviews, on-site evaluation, evaluation contracts, and technical assistance.* Boston: Kluwer-Nijhoff.

Worthen, B. R., White, K. R., Fan, X., & Sudweeks, R. R. (1999). *Measurement and assessment in schools* (2nd ed.). New York: Addison Wesley Longman.

Wright, W. J., & Sachse, T. (1977, April). *Payoffs of adversary evaluation.* Paper presented at the annual meeting of the American Educational Research Association, New York.

Yates, B. T. (1996). *Analyzing costs, procedures, processes, and outcomes in human services.* Thousand Oaks, CA: Sage.

Yin, R. K. (1989). *Case study research: Design and methods.* Thousand Oaks, CA: Sage.

Yin, R. K. (1994). *Case study research: Design and methods.* Applied Social Research Methods, Vol. 5. Thousand Oaks, CA: Sage.

Zemke, R. (1985). The systems approach, a nice theory but . . . *Training, 10,* 103–108.

Zimmermann, U. (1994). Exploring the nonprofit motive (or: What's in it for you?). *Public Administration Review, 54,* 398–402.

Author Index

Subject Index